AF119789

Special Topics in Differential Equations with Applications

Special Topics in Differential Equations with Applications

Editors

Hatıra Günerhan
Francisco Martínez González
Mohammed K. A. Kaabar

MDPI

Basel • Beijing • Wuhan • Barcelona • Belgrade • Novi Sad • Cluj • Manchester

Editors
Hatıra Günerhan
Department of Mathematics
Kafkas University
Kars
Turkey

Francisco Martínez González
Departamento de Matemática
Aplicada y Estadística
Universidad Politécnica de
Cartagena
Cartagena
Spain

Mohammed K. A. Kaabar
Chinese Institute of Electric
Power
Samarkand International
University of Technology
Samarkand
Uzbekistan

Editorial Office
MDPI AG
Grosspeteranlage 5
4052 Basel, Switzerland

This is a reprint of articles from the Special Issue published online in the open access journal *Axioms* (ISSN 2075-1680) (available at: www.mdpi.com/journal/axioms/special_issues/IL225829S0).

For citation purposes, cite each article independently as indicated on the article page online and as indicated below:

Lastname, A.A.; Lastname, B.B. Article Title. *Journal Name* **Year**, *Volume Number*, Page Range.

ISBN 978-3-7258-1648-4 (Hbk)
ISBN 978-3-7258-1647-7 (PDF)
doi.org/10.3390/books978-3-7258-1647-7

© 2024 by the authors. Articles in this book are Open Access and distributed under the Creative Commons Attribution (CC BY) license. The book as a whole is distributed by MDPI under the terms and conditions of the Creative Commons Attribution-NonCommercial-NoDerivs (CC BY-NC-ND) license.

Contents

About the Editors . . . . **vii**

Preface . . . . **ix**

Ravi Agarwal, Snezhana Hristova and Donal O'Regan
Mittag-Leffler-Type Stability of BAM Neural Networks Modeled by the Generalized Proportional Riemann–Liouville Fractional Derivative
Reprinted from: *Axioms* **2023**, *12*, 588, doi:10.3390/axioms12060588 . . . . **1**

Rodica Cimpoiasu and Radu Constantinescu
New Wave Solutions for the Two-Mode Caudrey–Dodd– Gibbon Equation
Reprinted from: *Axioms* **2023**, *12*, 619, doi:10.3390/axioms12070619 . . . . **18**

Corrado Mascia
Periodic Solutions of Quasi-Monotone Semilinear Multidimensional Hyperbolic Systems
Reprinted from: *Axioms* **2023**, *12*, 208, doi:10.3390/axioms12020208 . . . . **28**

Tatyana V. Redkina, Arthur R. Zakinyan, Robert G. Zakinyan and Olesya B. Surneva
Hierarchies of the Korteweg–de Vries Equation Related to Complex Expansion and Perturbation
Reprinted from: *Axioms* **2023**, *12*, 371, doi:10.3390/axioms12040371 . . . . **39**

Hristo Kiskinov, Ekaterina Madamlieva and Andrey Zahariev
Hyers–Ulam and Hyers–Ulam–Rassias Stability for Linear Fractional Systems with Riemann–Liouville Derivatives and Distributed Delays
Reprinted from: *Axioms* **2023**, *12*, 637, doi:10.3390/axioms12070637 . . . . **59**

Xiaoming Wang, Jehad Alzabut, Mahammad Khuddush and M. Fečkan
Solvability of Iterative Classes of Nonlinear Elliptic Equations on an Exterior Domain
Reprinted from: *Axioms* **2023**, *12*, 474, doi:10.3390/axioms12050474 . . . . **78**

Evangelos Melas, Costas Poulios, Elias Camouzis, John Leventides and Nick Poulios
Study of the Hypergeometric Equation via Data Driven Koopman-EDMD Theory
Reprinted from: *Axioms* **2023**, *12*, 134, doi:10.3390/axioms12020134 . . . . **95**

Armando Ciancio, Vincenzo Ciancio and Bruno Felice Filippo Flora
A Fractional Rheological Model of Viscoanelastic Media
Reprinted from: *Axioms* **2023**, *12*, 243, doi:10.3390/axioms12030243 . . . . **106**

Kamel Al-Khaled and Haneen Jafer
Two Reliable Computational Techniques for Solving the MRLW Equation
Reprinted from: *Axioms* **2023**, *12*, 174, doi:10.3390/axioms12020174 . . . . **119**

Musa Rahamh Gadallah and Hassan Eltayeb
Solutions of Time Fractional(1 + 3)-Dimensional Partial Differential Equations by the Natural TransformDecomposition Method (NTDM)
Reprinted from: *Axioms* **2023**, *12*, 958, doi:10.3390/axioms12100958 . . . . **134**

Fahd Masood, Osama Moaaz, Ghada AlNemer and Hamdy El-Metwally
More Effective Criteria for Testing the Asymptotic and Oscillatory Behavior of Solutions of a Class of Third-Order Functional Differential Equations
Reprinted from: *Axioms* **2023**, *12*, 1112, doi:10.3390/axioms12121112 . . . . **151**

Fahd Masood, Osama Moaaz, Sameh S. Askar and Ahmad Alshamrani
New Conditions for Testing the Asymptotic Behavior of Solutions of Odd-Order Neutral Differential Equations with Multiple Delays
Reprinted from: *Axioms* **2023**, *12*, 658, doi:10.3390/axioms12070658 . . . . **173**

Liben Wang, Xingyong Zhang and Cuiling Liu
Ground State Solutions for a Non-Local Type Problem in Fractional Orlicz Sobolev Spaces
Reprinted from: *Axioms* **2024**, *13*, 294, doi:10.3390/axioms13050294 . . . . **188**

Hail S. Alrashdi, Osama Moaaz, Sameh S. Askar, Ahmad M. Alshamrani and Elmetwally M. Elabbasy
More Effective Conditions for Testing the Oscillatory Behavior of Solutions to a Class of Fourth-Order Functional Differential Equations
Reprinted from: *Axioms* **2023**, *12*, 1005, doi:10.3390/axioms12111005 . . . . **210**

Abu Bakr Elbukhari, Zhenbin Fan and Gang Li
The Regional Enlarged Observability for Hilfer Fractional Differential Equations
Reprinted from: *Axioms* **2023**, *12*, 648, doi:10.3390/axioms12070648 . . . . **223**

Xiaoming Wang, Rimsha Ansar, Muhammad Abbas, Farah Aini Abdullah and Khadijah M. Abualnaja
The Investigation of Dynamical Behavior of Benjamin–Bona–Mahony–Burger Equation with Different Differential Operators Using Two Analytical Approaches
Reprinted from: *Axioms* **2023**, *12*, 599, doi:10.3390/axioms12060599 . . . . **242**

Rebiai Ghania, Lassaad Mchiri, Mohamed Rhaima, Mohamed Hannabou and Abdellatif Ben Makhlouf
Stability Results for the Darboux Problem of Conformable Partial Differential Equations
Reprinted from: *Axioms* **2023**, *12*, 640, doi:10.3390/axioms12070640 . . . . **265**

Farah M. Al-Askar, Clemente Cesarano and Wael W. Mohammed
The Influence of White Noise and the Beta Derivative on the Solutions of the BBM Equation
Reprinted from: *Axioms* **2023**, *12*, 447, doi:10.3390/axioms12050447 . . . . **274**

Peng Xu, Bing-Qi Zhang, Huan Huang and Kang-Jia Wang
Study on the Nonlinear Dynamics of the (3+1)-Dimensional Jimbo-Miwa Equation in Plasma Physics
Reprinted from: *Axioms* **2023**, *12*, 592, doi:10.3390/axioms12060592 . . . . **286**

About the Editors

Hatıra Günerhan

Dr. Hatira Günerhan is an Associate Professor in the Department of Mathematics, Kafkas University, Kars, Turkey. She received her Ph.D. degree in Applied Mathematics from Atatürk University in 2013. Her research interests include applied mathematics, fractional differential equations, and nonlinear partial differential equations.

Francisco Martínez González

Dr. Francisco Martínez González is a Tenured Associate Professor at the Universidad Politécnica de Cartagena, Spain. He received his Ph.D. degree in Physics from Universidad de Murcia in 1992. His research interests include nonlinear dynamics methods and their applications, fractional calculus, fractional differential equations, multivariate calculus or special functions, and the divulgation of mathematics.

Mohammed K. A. Kaabar

Prof. Dr. Mohammed K. A. Kaabar is a Full Professor of Mathematics at the Samarkand International University of Technology,, was listed as one of the World's Top 2% Scientists by Stanford University, and he received his BSc, MSc, and PhD degrees in Mathematics from Washington State University, Pullman, Washington, USA, and Universiti Malaya, Kuala Lumpur, Malaysia, respectively. He has global and diverse experience in teaching/research. He has worked as a Professor of Mathematics, a Math Lab Instructor, and a Lecturer at various US institutions, such as Moreno Valley College, California, USA, Washington State University, Washington, USA, and Colorado Early Colleges, Colorado, USA. He is an aspiring educator, a researcher, a keynote speaker at conferences held in various countries, and a Director of KAABAR-WANG TECH INSTITUTE in Samarkand, Uzbekistan. His research interests include applied mathematics, fractional calculus, nonlinear partial differential equations, fractal calculus, and mathematical physics. He is a Foreign Member at the Science and Democracy Network, Harvard Kennedy School at Harvard University, USA, Elected Foreign Member of the Academy of Engineering Sciences of Ukraine, Scientist and Researcher at the Palestine Academy for Science and Technology, Emeritus Editor of AMS Blogs at the American Mathematical Society, RI, USA, and Editor for 25 high-quality journals.

Preface

In science and engineering, differential equations play an important role in all models and systems. This topic is very special due to the variety of classes for differential equations, and the fact that each class is essential while studying applied sciences and engineering. Some examples of the most interesting Special Issues in differential equations include fractional differential equations, nonlinear partial differential equations, fractal fractional differential equations, sequential fractional pantograph q-differential equations, and stochastic differential equations. Each of these topics arise in various subjects such as control theory, signal processing, fluid dynamics, plasma physics, quantum field theory, electric circuits, and nonlinear fiber optics. All these topics can be investigated theoretically and numerically with the help of many new or generalized mathematical tools and numerical techniques. The main aim of this Special Issue is to create a collection of state-of-the-art research studies on Special Issues in differential equations with applications in science and engineering to provide researchers with the most recent advances in these topics, which are very important in modeling various scientific phenomena. This Special Issue, entitled "Special Topics in Differential Equations with Applications," has published important research articles in the field of differential equations, authored by several well-known mathematicians and scientists from diverse countries worldwide, such as the USA, Ireland, Italy, France, Slovakia, Greece, Austria, Romania, Bulgaria, Malaysia, Türkiye, Tunisia, Pakistan, India, China, Jordan, Sudan, Morocco, Egypt, Algeria, China, Russia, and Saudi Arabia.

Hatıra Günerhan, Francisco Martínez González, and Mohammed K. A. Kaabar
Editors

axioms

Article

Mittag-Leffler-Type Stability of BAM Neural Networks Modeled by the Generalized Proportional Riemann–Liouville Fractional Derivative

Ravi P. Agarwal [1], Snezhana Hristova [2,*] and Donal O'Regan [3]

1 Department of Mathematics, Texas A&M University-Kingsville, Kingsville, TX 78363, USA; ravi.agarwal@tamuk.edu
2 Faculty of Mathematics and Informatics, Plovdiv University, Tzar Asen 24, 4000 Plovdiv, Bulgaria
3 School of Mathematical and Statistical Sciences, University of Galway, H91 TK33 Galway, Ireland; donal.oregan@nuigalway.ie
* Correspondence: snehri@uni-plovdiv.bg

Abstract: The main goal of the paper is to use a generalized proportional Riemann–Liouville fractional derivative (GPRLFD) to model BAM neural networks and to study some stability properties of the equilibrium. Initially, several properties of the GPRLFD are proved, such as the fractional derivative of a squared function. Additionally, some comparison results for GPRLFD are provided. Two types of equilibrium of the BAM model with GPRLFD are defined. In connection with the applied fractional derivative and its singularity at the initial time, the Mittag-Leffler exponential stability in time of the equilibrium is introduced and studied. An example is given, illustrating the meaning of the equilibrium as well as its stability properties.

Keywords: BAM neural networks; Mittag-Leffler-type stability; fractional differential equations; generalized proportional Riemann–Liouville fractional derivative

MSC: 34A34; 34A08; 34D20

Citation: Agarwal, R.P.; Hristova, S.; O'Regan, D. Mittag-Leffler-Type Stability of BAM Neural Networks Modeled by the Generalized Proportional Riemann–Liouville Fractional Derivative. *Axioms* **2023**, *12*, 588. https://doi.org/10.3390/axioms12060588

Academic Editor: Hatıra Günerhan

Received: 20 May 2023
Revised: 12 June 2023
Accepted: 13 June 2023
Published: 14 June 2023

Copyright: © 2023 by the authors. Licensee MDPI, Basel, Switzerland. This article is an open access article distributed under the terms and conditions of the Creative Commons Attribution (CC BY) license (https://creativecommons.org/licenses/by/4.0/).

1. Introduction

One of the main qualitative properties of the solutions of differential equations is stability. There are various types of stability defined, studied and applied to different types of differential equations, especially to fractional differential equations. The stability of Hadamard fractional differential equations is studied in [1]. The stability of Caputo-type fractional derivatives are studied by many authors, and many sufficient conditions are obtained (for example, see Mittag-Leffler stability in [2], and the application of Lyapunov functions in [3]). Concerning fractional differential equations with Riemann–Liouville fractional derivatives, the stability of linear systems is studied in [4], nonlinear systems in [5,6], Lyapunov functions are applied and comparison results are established in [7], practical stability is studied in [8], and existence and Ulam stability in [9]. Note that the initial condition for fractional differential equations with the Riemann–Liouville-type fractional derivative is totally different from the initial condition for ordinary differential equations or for fractional differential equations with Caputo-type derivatives. Some authors did not take this into account, and consequently, a gap exists in the study of stability. Concerning the basic concepts of the stability for Riemann–Liouville fractional differential equations, we note [10], in which several up-to-date types of fractional derivatives are defined, studied and applied to differential equations. Recently, the so-called generalized proportional fractional integrals and derivatives were defined (see [11,12]). Similar to classical fractional derivatives, there are two main types of generalized proportional fractional derivatives: Caputo-type and Riemann–Liouville-type. Several results concerning the existence (see, for example, [13,14]), integral presentation of the solutions (see, for example, [15]), stability properties (see, for example, [16,17]) and applications to some models (see, for example, [16]) are considered with the Caputo type of generalized proportional fractional derivatives. Additionally, there are some results concerning the Riemann–Liouville type. Some existence results are obtained in [18]. In [19,20], the oscillation properties of fractional differential equations with a generalized proportional Riemann–Liouville fractional derivative are studied. The existence and uniqueness of a coupled system is studied in [21] in the case of three-point generalized fractional integral boundary conditions. In this paper, initially, we prove some comparison results for generalized proportional Riemann–Liouville fractional derivatives. Additionally, we discuss the behavior of the solutions on small enough intervals about the initial time. Some examples are given, illustrating the necessity of excluding the initial time when the stability is studied. The obtained results are a basis for studying a stability property of the equilibrium of a model of neural networks. The models of neural networks are important issues due to their successful application in pattern recognition, artificial intelligence, automatic control, signal processing, optimization, etc. In the past decades, several types of fractional derivatives were applied to the models of neural networks to describe the dynamics of the neurons more adequately. Many qualitative properties of their equilibrium have been studied. In this paper, we apply the generalized proportional Riemann–Liouville fractional derivative to the BAM model of neutral networks. Recently, bi-directional associative memory (BAM) neural networks were extensively investigated and successfully applied to signal processing, pattern recognition, associative memory and optimization problems. For more adequate modeling of the dynamics of the state of neurons, several types of derivatives are applied, including various types of fractional derivatives. We refer the reader, for example, to the study of existence and stability for models with ordinary derivatives and discontinuous neuron activations [22], the delay model [23], and the study of stability for a model with the Caputo fractional derivative [24]. Reviews of the application of fractional derivatives to the neural networks are given in [25,26].

One of the main properties of the applied fractional derivative is its singularity at the initial time. In connection with this, we define in an appropriate way an exponential Mittag-Leffler stability in time, excluding the initial time. Additionally, two types of equilibrium, deeply connected with the applied fractional derivative, are defined. Sufficient conditions based on the new comparison results are obtained and illustrated with examples. The rest of this paper is organized as follows. In Section 2, some notes on fractional calculus are provided; the basic definitions of the generalized proportional fractional integrals and derivatives are given in the case when the order of fractional derivative is in the interval $(0,1)$ and the parameter is in $(0,1]$. The connection with the tempered fractional integrals and the derivatives is discussed. In Section 3, we prove some comparison results for generalized Riemann–Liouville fractional derivatives. In Section 4, the model of BAM neural networks with GPRLFD is set up and studied. Two types of equilibriums are defined. These definitions are deeply connected with the applied GPRLFD and its properties, which are totally different from those of ordinary derivatives and Caputo-type fractional derivatives. The Mittag-Leffler exponential stability in time of both types of equilibriums is defined and studied. Finally, an example is given to illustrate the theoretical results and statements.

2. Some Notes on Fractional Calculus

The main goal in this paper is to apply a partial case of fractional derivatives to a model and to investigate the stability behavior of the model. In connection with this, we will give a brief discussion about fractional derivatives known in the literature. The main idea of fractional calculus is the generalization of the differential operator to an operator with any real or complex number order. The most standard of these operators are the Riemann–Liouville fractional integral and derivatives (for basic definitions and properties, see, for example, the classical books [27–30]). In the last few decades, many different definitions have been proposed. As a comprehensive definition appealing to general principles of mathematics, the fractional derivative is a fractional power of the infinitesimal generator of a strictly continuous semigroup of contractions. We mention the Marchaud operator, generated by a semigroup, which is well described and compared with the existing ones in the paper [31], and its detailed presentation, together with the constructions with the exponential multiplier, is given in the classical book [29]. Additionally, a differential operator with a fractional integro-differential operator composition in final terms is presented and studied in [32]. Another way to generalize the classical definitions is the approach whereby some multipliers can be added to make a new construction with some similar properties. For more information about the definitions of fractional integrals and derivatives with exponential kernel, called tempered fractional integrals and derivatives, and some applications to stochastic process, Brownian motion, etc., we refer the reader to [33]. Recently, refs. [11,12] generalized fractional integrals and derivatives by considering exponential functions with a fraction in the power, and these were called generalized proportional fractional ones. The used parameter in the exponential kernel gives us more detailed information.

We recall some basic definitions and properties relevant to the generalized proportional fractional derivative and integral. The terms and notations are adopted from [11,12].

Definition 1. *Ref. [11] (The generalized proportional fractional integral) (GPFI) Let $v : [a,b] \to \mathbb{R}$, $b \leq \infty$, and $\rho \in (0,1]$, $q \geq 0$. We define the GPFI of the function v by $({}_a\mathcal{I}^{0,\rho}v)(t) = v(t)$ and*

$$({}_a\mathcal{I}^{q,\rho}v)(t) = \frac{1}{\rho^q\Gamma(q)}\int_a^t e^{\frac{\rho-1}{\rho}(t-s)}(t-s)^{q-1}v(s)\,ds, \quad t \in (a,b]. \tag{1}$$

Definition 2. *Ref. [11] (The generalized proportional Riemann–Liouville fractional derivative) (GPRLFD) Let $v : [a,b] \to \mathbb{R}$, $b \leq \infty$, and $\rho \in (0,1]$, $q \in (0,1)$. Define the GPRLFD of the function v by*

$$\begin{aligned}({}_a^R\mathcal{D}^{q,\rho}v)(t) = &\frac{1}{\rho^{1-q}\Gamma(1-q)}\Big((1-\rho)\int_a^t e^{\frac{\rho-1}{\rho}(t-s)}(t-s)^{-q}v(s)\,ds \\ &+\rho\frac{d}{dt}\int_a^t e^{\frac{\rho-1}{\rho}(t-s)}(t-s)^{-q}v(s)\,ds\Big), \quad t \in (a,b].\end{aligned} \tag{2}$$

Remark 1. *The constructions with the exponential multiplier were considered also in the monograph [29].*

Remark 2. *The parameter q in Definitions 1 and 2 is interpreted as an order of integration and differentiation, respectively. The parameter ρ is connected with the power of the exponential function. In the case $\rho = 1$, the given fractional integral and derivative reduce to the classical Riemann–Liouville fractional integral*

$${}_aI_t^q v(t) = \frac{1}{\Gamma(q)}\int_a^t (t-s)^{q-1}v(s)\,ds, \tag{3}$$

and the Riemann–Liouville fractional derivative

$${}_a^{RL}D_t^q v(t) = \frac{1}{\Gamma(1-q)}\frac{d}{dt}\int_a^t (t-s)^{-q}v(s)\,ds, \tag{4}$$

The relation between the GPRLFD and the Riemann–Liouville fractional derivative is given in the following Lemma.

Lemma 1. *Let $\rho \in (0,1]$, $q \in (0,1)$, and $v \in C([a,b])$, $b \leq \infty$. Then,*

$$({}_a\mathcal{D}^{q,\rho}v)(t) = \rho^q e^{\frac{\rho-1}{\rho}t}\left({}_a^{RL}D_t^q\left(e^{\frac{1-\rho}{\rho}t}v(t)\right)\right), \quad t \in (a,b]. \tag{5}$$

Proof. From Equations (2) and (4), we have

$$\begin{aligned}
({}_a^R\mathcal{D}^{q,\rho}v)(t) &= \frac{1}{\rho^{1-q}\Gamma(1-q)}\Big((1-\rho)\int_a^t e^{\frac{\rho-1}{\rho}(t-s)}(t-s)^{-q}v(s)\,ds \\
&\quad +\rho\frac{d}{dt}e^{\frac{\rho-1}{\rho}t}\int_a^t e^{\frac{1-\rho}{\rho}s}(t-s)^{-q}v(s)\,ds\Big) \\
&= \frac{1}{\rho^{-q}\Gamma(1-q)}e^{\frac{\rho-1}{\rho}t}\frac{d}{dt}\int_a^t e^{\frac{1-\rho}{\rho}s}(t-s)^{-q}v(s)\,ds \\
&= \rho^q e^{\frac{\rho-1}{\rho}t}({}_a^{RL}D_t^q e^{\frac{1-\rho}{\rho}t}v(t)).
\end{aligned}$$

□

Remark 3. *The equality (5) gives us an opportunity to apply some of the properties known in the literature for Riemann–Liouville fractional derivatives to GPRLFD. However, it does not allow us to directly apply properties of the solutions of fractional differential equations with Riemann–Liouville fractional derivatives to those with GPRLFD. That is why it is absolutely necessary to study independently differential equations with GPRLFD and to obtain sufficient conditions for some qualitative properties of their solutions, such as various types of stability.*

Define the set

$$C_{q,\rho}([a,b],\mathbb{R}^n) = \{v : [a,b] \to \mathbb{R}^n : \text{ for any } t \in (a,b] \text{ there exists } ({}_a^{RL}\mathcal{D}^{q,\rho}v)(t) < \infty\}.$$

We will provide some results which are partial cases of the obtained ones in [12] and which will be used in our further considerations.

Lemma 2. (semigroup property) *(Theorem 3.8, Corollary 3.10, Theorem 3.11, Lemma 3.12 [12]) If $\rho \in (0,1]$, $Re(q) > 0$, $Re(\beta) > 0$, and $v \in C([a,b])$, $b \le \infty$, we have the following:*

$$\begin{aligned}
&{}_a\mathcal{I}^{q,\rho}\left({}_a\mathcal{I}^{\beta,\rho}v\right)(t) = {}_a\mathcal{I}^{\beta,\rho}({}_a\mathcal{I}^{q,\rho}v)(t) = \left({}_a\mathcal{I}^{q+\beta,\rho}v\right)(t) \\
&({}_a^R\mathcal{D}^{\beta,\rho}\,{}_a\mathcal{I}^{q,\rho}v)(t) = {}_a\mathcal{I}^{q-\beta,\rho}v)(t), \qquad 0 < \beta < q, \\
&({}_a^R\mathcal{D}^{q,\rho}\,{}_a\mathcal{I}^{q,\rho}v)(t) = v(t) \\
&{}_a\mathcal{I}^{q,\rho}({}_a^R\mathcal{D}^{q,\rho}v)(t) = v(t) - \frac{({}_a\mathcal{I}^{1-q,\rho}v)(a)}{\rho^{q-1}\Gamma(q)}e^{\frac{\rho-1}{\rho}(t-a)}(t-a)^{q-1}.
\end{aligned} \tag{6}$$

Lemma 3. *(Lemma 2 [15]) Let $\rho \in (0,1]$, $q \in (0,1)$, and $y \in C([a,b],\mathbb{R})$.*

(i) Let there exist a limit $\lim_{t\to a+}\left(e^{\frac{1-\rho}{\rho}t}(t-a)^{1-q}y(t)\right) = c < \infty$. Then, $({}_a\mathcal{I}^{1-q,\rho}y)(a) = c\frac{\Gamma(q)}{\rho^{1-q}}e^{\frac{\rho-1}{\rho}a}$.

(ii) Let $({}_a\mathcal{I}^{1-q,\rho}y)(a+) = b < \infty$. If there exists the limit $\lim_{t\to a+}\left(e^{\frac{1-\rho}{\rho}t}(t-a)^{1-q}y(t)\right)$, then $\lim_{t\to a+}\left(e^{\frac{1-\rho}{\rho}t}(t-a)^{1-q}y(t)\right) = \frac{b\rho^{1-q}e^{\frac{1-\rho}{\rho}a}}{\Gamma(q)}$.

Lemma 4. *Example 4.4 in [11] The solution of the initial value problem (IVP) for the scalar linear GPRLFDE*

$$({}_a^{RL}\mathcal{D}^{q,\rho}u)(t) = \rho^q\lambda u(t) + f(t), \ ({}_a\mathcal{I}^{1-q,\rho}u)(a+) = u_0, \ q \in (0,1), \ \rho \in (0,1]$$

has a solution $v \in C_{q,\rho}([a,\infty))$ *given by*

$$u(t) = u_0\rho^{1-q}e^{\frac{\rho-1}{\rho}(t-a)}(t-a)^{q-1}E_{q,q}(\lambda(t-a)^q) + \rho^{-q}\int_a^t E_{q,q}(\lambda(t-s)^q)e^{\frac{\rho-1}{\rho}(t-s)}(t-s)^{q-1}f(s)ds,$$

where $E_{q,q}(t)$ *is the Mittag-Leffler function of two parameters,* $\lambda \in \mathbb{R}$.

Corollary 1. ${}_a^{RL}\mathcal{D}^{q,\rho}(e^{\frac{\rho-1}{\rho}(t-a)}(t-a)^{q-1}) = 0, \ t > a.$

The proof of Corollary 1 follows from Lemma 4 with $\lambda = 0, f(t) \equiv 0$ and the equality $E_{q,q}(0) = \frac{1}{\Gamma(q)}$.

Proposition 1. *(Proposition 3.7 in [11]).* ${}_a^{RL}\mathcal{D}^{q,\rho}(e^{\frac{\rho-1}{\rho}(t-a)}) = \frac{1}{\rho^q\Gamma(1-q)}e^{\frac{\rho-1}{\rho}(t-a)}(t-a)^{-q}$, $t > a$.

Remark 4. *In Theorem 2.1 [34], it is proved that tempered fractional integrals and derivatives could be theoretically expressed as an infinite series of classical Riemann–Liouville fractional integrals and derivatives. The same is true for GPFI and GPRLFD. However, the practical application of infinite series is very difficult. It requires independent study of differential equations with GPRLFD and finding applicable sufficient conditions for the properties of their solutions.*

3. Comparison Results for GPRLFD

Lemma 5. *Let* $v \in C([a,b],\mathbb{R})$, $a < b < \infty$ *be Lipschitz, and let there exist a point* $T \in (a,b]$ *such that* $v(T) = 0$, *and* $v(t) < 0$, *for* $a \le t < T$. *Then, if the GPRLFD of* v *exists for* $t = T$ *with* $q \in (0,1)$, $\rho \in (0,1]$, *then the inequality* $({}_a^{RL}\mathcal{D}^{q,\rho}v)(t)|_{t=T} \ge 0$ *holds.*

Proof. Let $H(t) = \int_a^t e^{\frac{\rho-1}{\rho}(t-s)}(t-s)^{-q}v(s)\,ds$ for $t \in [a,b]$. According to (2), we have

$$\begin{aligned}({}_a^{R}\mathcal{D}^{q,\rho}v)(T) &= \frac{1}{\rho^{1-q}\Gamma(1-q)}\Big((1-\rho)H(T) + \rho\lim_{h\to0+}\frac{H(T-h)-H(T)}{h}\Big)\\ &= \frac{1}{\rho^{1-q}\Gamma(1-q)}\lim_{h\to0+}\Big((1-\rho)H(T) + \rho\frac{H(T-h)-H(T)}{h}\Big).\end{aligned} \tag{7}$$

There exists a constant $K > 0$ such that $0 > v(s) = v(s) - v(T) \ge K(s-T)$ for $s \in [T-h,T), h > 0$, and

$$\begin{aligned}\int_{T-h}^T e^{\frac{1-\rho}{\rho}s}(T-s)^{-q}v(s)\,ds &> -K\int_{T-h}^T e^{\frac{1-\rho}{\rho}s}(T-s)^{1-q}\,ds\\ &= \frac{Ke^{\frac{1-\rho}{\rho}T}}{(\frac{1-\rho}{\rho})^{2-q}}\Big(\Gamma(2-q,h\frac{1-\rho}{\rho}) - \Gamma(2-q)\Big) \equiv M(h),\end{aligned} \tag{8}$$

where $\Gamma(.,.)$ is the incomplete Gamma function and

$$\lim_{h\to0+}\frac{\Gamma(2-q,h\frac{1-\rho}{\rho}) - \Gamma(2-q)}{h} = 0. \tag{9}$$

Thus, using $e^{\frac{\rho-1}{\rho}h}(T-h-s)^q < (T-s)^q$ for $s \in [T-h,T), h > 0, \rho \in (0,1]$, and $v(s) < 0$ on $[a,T)$ we get

$$\begin{aligned}
&H(T-h) - H(T) = \int_a^T \Big(e^{\frac{\rho-1}{\rho}(T-h-s)}(T-h-s)^{-q} - e^{\frac{\rho-1}{\rho}(T-s)}(T-s)^{-q}\Big)v(s)\,ds \\
&-\int_{T-h}^T e^{\frac{\rho-1}{\rho}(T-s)}\Big(e^{\frac{1-\rho}{\rho}h}(T-h-s)^{-q} - (T-s)^{-q}\Big)v(s)\,ds \\
&+\int_{T-h}^T e^{\frac{\rho-1}{\rho}(T-s)}(T-s)^{-q}v(s)\,ds \\
&\geq \int_a^T \Big(e^{\frac{\rho-1}{\rho}(T-h-s)}(T-h-s)^{-q} - e^{\frac{\rho-1}{\rho}(T-s)}(t-s)^{-q}\Big)v(s)\,ds + M(h)e^{\frac{\rho-1}{\rho}T}.
\end{aligned} \tag{10}$$

Using (8)–(10), we obtain

$$\begin{aligned}
&\lim_{h\to 0+}\Big((1-\rho)H(T) + \frac{\rho}{h}(H(t) - H(T-h))\Big) \\
&\geq (1-\rho)\int_a^T e^{\frac{\rho-1}{\rho}(T-s)}(t-s)^{-q}v(s)\,ds \\
&+\rho\int_a^T \lim_{h\to 0+}\frac{e^{\frac{\rho-1}{\rho}(T-h-s)}(T-h-s)^{-q} - e^{\frac{\rho-1}{\rho}(T-s)}(T-s)^{-q}}{h}v(s)\,ds \\
&+\lim_{h\to 0+}\frac{M(h)}{h}\rho e^{\frac{\rho-1}{\rho}T} \\
&= (1-\rho)\int_a^T e^{\frac{\rho-1}{\rho}(T-s)}(T-s)^{-q}v(s)\,ds + \rho\int_a^T \frac{d}{dT}\Big(e^{\frac{\rho-1}{\rho}(T-s)}(T-s)^{-q}\Big)v(s)\,ds \\
&= (1-\rho)\int_a^T e^{\frac{\rho-1}{\rho}(T-s)}(T-s)^{-q}v(s)\,ds \\
&+\int_a^T \Big((\rho-1)e^{\frac{\rho-1}{\rho}(T-s)}(T-s)^{-q} - q\rho e^{\frac{\rho-1}{\rho}(T-s)}(t-s)^{-1-q}\Big)v(s)\,ds \\
&= -q\rho\int_a^T e^{\frac{\rho-1}{\rho}(T-s)}(T-s)^{-1-q}v(s)\,ds > 0.
\end{aligned} \tag{11}$$

□

Example 1. *Consider* $v(t) = e^{\frac{\rho-1}{\rho}t}(t-2)$ *for* $t \in [0,2], \rho = 0.5$. *Note that* $v(t) < 0$ *for* $t \in [0,2)$, $v(2) = 0$ *and for any* $q \in (0,1)$ *we have*

$$\begin{aligned}
({}_0^R\mathcal{D}^{q,\rho}v)(t)|_{t=2} &= \frac{1}{0.5^{1-q}\Gamma(1-q)}\Big(0.5\int_0^2 e^{-(2-s)}(s-2)^{-q}e^{-s}(2-s)\,ds \\
&+0.5\frac{d}{dt}\int_0^t e^{-(t-s)}(t-s)^{-q}e^{-s}(s-2)\,ds|_{t=2}\Big) \\
&= \frac{1}{0.5^{-q}\Gamma(1-q)}\Big(-e^{-2}\int_0^2 (2-s)^{1-q}\,ds + \frac{d}{dt}e^{-t}\int_0^t (t-s)^{-q}(s-2)\,ds|_{t=2}\Big) \\
&= \frac{1}{0.5^{-q}\Gamma(1-q)}\Big(-\frac{2^{2-q}}{(2-q)e^2} + \frac{d}{dt}\big(\frac{e^{-t}t^{1-q}(t+2q-4)}{2-3q+q^2}\big)|_{t=2}\Big) \\
&= \frac{1}{0.5^{-q}\Gamma(1-q)}\Big(-\frac{2^{2-q}}{(2-q)e^2} + 2^{-q}\frac{4-2q^2}{(2-3q+q^2)e^2}\Big) > 0.
\end{aligned} \tag{12}$$

Remark 5. *A similar claim to Lemma 5, but for the Riemann–Liouville fractional derivatives, is proved in [7].*

Lemma 6. *Let $g \in C([t_0, b] \times \mathbb{R}, \mathbb{R})$, the functions $\mu, \nu \in C_{q,\rho}([t_0, b], \mathbb{R})$ be Lipschitz and satisfy the inequalities*

$$({}_{t_0}^{RL}\mathcal{D}^{q,\rho}\mu)(t) < g(t, \mu(t)), \ t \in (t_0, b], \quad \lim_{t \to t_0+} \left(e^{\frac{1-\rho}{\rho}(t-t_0)}(t-t_0)^{1-q}\mu(t) \right) = \mu_0 \frac{\rho^{q-1}}{\Gamma(q)}, \tag{13}$$

and

$$({}_{t_0}^{RL}\mathcal{D}^{q,\rho}\nu)(t) \geq g(t, \nu(t)), \ t \in (t_0, b], \quad \lim_{t \to t_0+} \left(e^{\frac{1-\rho}{\rho}(t-t_0)}(t-t_0)^{1-q}\nu(t) \right) = \nu_0 \frac{\rho^{q-1}}{\Gamma(q)}. \tag{14}$$

Then, if $\mu_0 < \nu_0$, the inequality $\mu(t) < \nu(t)$, $t \in (t_0, b]$ holds.

Proof. Suppose the contrary. Because $\mu_0 < \nu_0$, and the functions $e^{\frac{1-\rho}{\rho}(t-t_0)}(t-t_0)^{1-q}\mu(t)$ and $e^{\frac{1-\rho}{\rho}(t-t_0)}(t-t_0)^{1-q}\nu(t)$ are continuous, there exists a point $\tau \in (t_0, b]$ such that $\mu(t) < \nu(t)$, $t \in [t_0, \tau)$ and $\mu(\tau) = \nu(\tau)$. According to Lemma 5, for $v = \mu - \nu$, $a = t_0$ we obtain $0 = g(\tau, \mu(\tau)) - g(\tau, \nu(\tau)) > ({}_{t_0}^{RL}\mathcal{D}^{q,\rho}\mu)(t)|_{t=\tau} - ({}_{t_0}^{RL}\mathcal{D}^{q,\rho}\nu)(t)|_{t=\tau} = ({}_{t_0}^{RL}\mathcal{D}^{q,\rho}\mu - \nu)(t)|_{t=\tau} \geq 0$.

The obtained contradiction proves the claim. □

In the case when the initial condition contains the generalized proportional fractional integral, we obtain the following result.

Corollary 2. *Let $g \in C([t_0, b] \times \mathbb{R}, \mathbb{R})$, the functions $\mu, \nu \in C_{q,\rho}([t_0, b], \mathbb{R})$ be Lipschitz and satisfy the inequalities*

$$({}_{t_0}^{RL}\mathcal{D}^{q,\rho}\mu)(t) < g(t, \mu(t)), \ t \in (t_0, b], \quad ({}_{t_0}\mathcal{I}^{1-q,\rho}\mu)(t)|_{t=t_0} = \mu_0, \tag{15}$$

and

$$({}_{t_0}^{RL}\mathcal{D}^{q,\rho}\nu)(t) \geq g(t, \nu(t)), \ t \in (t_0, b], \quad ({}_{t_0}\mathcal{I}^{1-q,\rho}\nu)(t)|_{t=t_0} = \nu_0. \tag{16}$$

Then, if $\mu_0 < \nu_0$, the inequality $\mu(t) < \nu(t)$, $t \in (t_0, b]$ holds.

Corollary 3. *Let the functions $\mu, \nu \in C_{q,\rho}([t_0, b], \mathbb{R})$ be Lipschitz and satisfy the inequalities*

$$\begin{aligned} &({}_{t_0}^{RL}\mathcal{D}^{q,\rho}\mu)(t) < ({}_{t_0}^{RL}\mathcal{D}^{q,\rho}\nu)(t), \ t \in (t_0, b], \\ &\lim_{t \to t_0+} \left(e^{\frac{1-\rho}{\rho}(t-t_0)}(t-t_0)^{1-q}\mu(t) \right) < \lim_{t \to t_0+} \left(e^{\frac{1-\rho}{\rho}(t-t_0)}(t-t_0)^{1-q}\nu(t) \right). \end{aligned} \tag{17}$$

Then, the inequality $\mu(t) < \nu(t)$, $t \in (t_0, b]$ holds.

Lemma 7. *Let the function $\nu \in C_{q,\rho}([t_0, b], \mathbb{R})$ and $\nu^2 \in C_{q,\rho}([t_0, b], \mathbb{R})$. Then, the inequality*

$$({}_{t_0}^{RL}\mathcal{D}^{q,\rho}\nu^2)(t) \leq 2\nu(t)({}_{t_0}^{RL}\mathcal{D}^{q,\rho}\nu)(t), \ t \in (t_0, b] \tag{18}$$

holds.

Proof. Fix a point $T \in (t_0, b]$ and define the function $\mu(s) = (\nu(T) - \nu(s))^2$ for all $s \in [t_0, T]$. The function $(-\mu(s))$ satisfies all the conditions of Lemma 5 for $v = -\nu$, $a = t_0$, and we obtain $({}_{t_0}^{RL}\mathcal{D}^{q,\rho}(-\mu)(t)|_{t=T} \geq 0$, i.e., applying Definition 2, we get

$$({}_{t_0}^{RL}\mathcal{D}^{q,\rho}(\mu)(t)|_{t=T} = \frac{1}{\rho^{1-q}\Gamma(1-q)} \lim_{h \to 0+} \left((1-\rho)H(T) + \rho \frac{H(T-h) - H(T)}{h} \right) \leq 0, \tag{19}$$

where $H(t) = \int_{t_0}^{t} e^{\frac{\rho-1}{\rho}(t-s)}(t-s)^{-q}\mu(\sigma)\, d\sigma$, $t \in [t_0, b]$.

Define the functions

$$P(t) = \int_{t_0}^{t} e^{\frac{\rho-1}{\rho}(t-s)}(t-s)^{-q}v(s)\,ds,\ t \in [t_0, b]$$

and

$$W(t) = \int_{t_0}^{t} e^{\frac{\rho-1}{\rho}(t-s)}(t-s)^{-q}v^2(s)\,ds,\ \ t \in [t_0, b].$$

According to Definition 2, we have

$$\begin{aligned}({}_{t_0}^{RL}\mathcal{D}^{q,\rho}v)(t) &= \frac{1}{\rho^{1-q}\Gamma(1-q)}\Big((1-\rho)P(t) + \rho \lim_{h\to 0+}\frac{P(t-h)-P(t)}{h}\Big)\\ &= \frac{1}{\rho^{1-q}\Gamma(1-q)}\lim_{h\to 0+}\Big((1-\rho)P(t) + \rho\frac{P(t-h)-P(t)}{h}\Big)\end{aligned} \tag{20}$$

and

$$({}_{t_0}^{RL}\mathcal{D}^{q,\rho}v^2)(t) = \frac{1}{\rho^{1-q}\Gamma(1-q)}\lim_{h\to 0+}\Big((1-\rho)W(t) + \rho\frac{W(t-h)-W(t)}{h}\Big). \tag{21}$$

Note

$$v^2(s) - 2v(T)v(s) = (v(T)-v(s))^2 - v^2(s) = \mu(s) - v^2(s) \le \mu(s),\ s \in [t_0, T], \tag{22}$$

and

$$\begin{aligned}&W(T) - 2v(T)P(T) = \int_{t_0}^{T} e^{\frac{\rho-1}{\rho}(T-s)}(T-s)^{-q}\big(v^2(\sigma) - 2v(T)v(\sigma)\big)\,d\sigma\\ &\le \int_{t_0}^{T} e^{\frac{\rho-1}{\rho}(T-s)}(T-s)^{-q}\mu(\sigma)\,d\sigma = H(T),\\ &W(T-h) - 2v(T)P(T-h) = \int_{t_0}^{T-h} e^{\frac{\rho-1}{\rho}(T-h-s)}(T-h-s)^{-q}\big(v^2(\sigma) - 2v(T)v(\sigma)\big)\,d\sigma\\ &\le \int_{t_0}^{T-h} e^{\frac{\rho-1}{\rho}(T-h-s)}(T-h-s)^{-q}\mu(\sigma)\,d\sigma = H(T-h).\end{aligned} \tag{23}$$

Then,

$$\begin{aligned}&({}_{t_0}^{RL}\mathcal{D}^{q,\rho}v^2)(T) - 2v(T)({}_{t_0}^{RL}\mathcal{D}^{q,\rho}v)(T)\\ &= \frac{1}{\rho^{1-q}\Gamma(1-q)}\lim_{h\to 0+}\Big((1-\rho)(W(T) - 2v(T)P(T))\\ &+\rho\frac{(W(T-h) - v(T)P(T-h) - (W(T) - v(T)P(T))}{h}\Big)\\ &= \frac{1}{\rho^{1-q}\Gamma(1-q)}\lim_{h\to 0+}\Big((1-\rho)(W(T) - 2v(T)P(T))\\ &+\rho\frac{(W(T-h) - v(T)P(T-h)) - (W(T) - v(T)P(T))}{h}\Big)\\ &\le \frac{1}{\rho^{1-q}\Gamma(1-q)}\lim_{h\to 0+}\Big((1-\rho)H(T) + \rho\frac{H(T-h)-H(T)}{h}\Big)\\ &= ({}_{t_0}^{RL}\mathcal{D}^{q,\rho}\mu)(T) \le 0.\end{aligned} \tag{24}$$

Because $T \in (t_0, b]$ is an arbitrary point, the claim is proved. □

Corollary 4. *Let the functions* $v_i \in C_{q,\rho}([t_0,b],\mathbb{R})$ *and* $v_i^2 \in C_{q,\rho}([t_0,b],\mathbb{R})$, $i = 1,2,\ldots,n$. *Then, the inequality*

$$({}_{t_0}^{RL}\mathcal{D}^{q,\rho}\sum_{i=1}^{n} v_i^2(\cdot))(t) \leq 2\sum_{i=1}^{n} v_i(t)({}_{t_0}^{RL}\mathcal{D}^{q,\rho}v_i(\cdot))(t), \quad t \in (t_0,b] \tag{25}$$

holds.

Remark 6. *Note that several authors ([35]) used the inequality* (25) *for the Riemann–Liouville fractional derivative to prove the main results, citing the results from [3,36], which concern the Caputo fractional derivative.*

Remark 7. *Fractional differential operators in a variety of settings under general assumptions regarding the weighted factor were considered by Kukushkin [37], and we refer the reader to that paper for a nice overview.*

4. BAM Neural Networks Modeled by GPRLFD

The general model of the fractional-order BAM neural networks with the GPRLFD is described by the following state equations:

$$\begin{aligned}
({}_0^{RL}\mathcal{D}^{q,\rho}x_i)(t) &= -a_i(t)x_i(t)) + \sum_{k=1}^{m} b_{i,k}(t)f_k(y_k(t)) + I_i(t), \quad t > 0,\ i = 1,2,\ldots,n, \\
({}_0^{RL}\mathcal{D}^{q,\rho}y_j)(t) &= -c_j(t)y_j(t)) + \sum_{k=1}^{n} d_{j,k}(t)g_k(y_k(t)) + J_j(t), \quad t > 0,\ j = 1,2,\ldots,m,
\end{aligned} \tag{26}$$

where $x_i(t)$ and $y_j(t)$ are the state variables of the i-th neuron in the first layer at time t and the state variables of the j-th neuron in the second layer at time t, respectively, n and m are the numbers of units in the first and second layers in the neural network, ${}_0^{RL}\mathcal{D}^{q,\rho}$ denotes the GPRLFD of order $q \in (0,1)$, $\rho \in (0,1]$, $f_i(u)$ and $g_j(u)$ denote the activation functions, $b_{i,k}(t), d_{i,k}(t) : [0,\infty) \to \mathbb{R}$ denote the connection weight coefficients of the neurons, $a_i(t), c_j(t) : [0,\infty) \to (0,\infty)$ represent the decay coefficients of signals at time t, and $I_i(t), J_j(t)$ denotes the external inputs of the first and second layers, respectively, at time t.

The initial conditions associated with the model (26) can be written in the form

$$({}_0\mathcal{I}^{1-q,\rho}x_i)(t)|_{t=0} = x_i^0, \quad ({}_0\mathcal{I}^{1-q,\rho}y_j)(t)|_{t=0} = y_j^0, \quad i = 1,2\ldots,n,\ j = 1,2,\ldots,m. \tag{27}$$

Remark 8. *According to Lemma 3, the initial conditions* (27) *could be replaced by initial conditions of the type*

$$\lim_{t\to 0+}\left(e^{\frac{1-\rho}{\rho}t}t^{1-q}x_i(t)\right) = x_i^0\frac{\rho^{q-1}}{\Gamma(q)}, \quad \lim_{t\to 0+}\left(e^{\frac{1-\rho}{\rho}t}t^{1-q}y_i(t)\right) = y_i^0\frac{\rho^{q-1}}{\Gamma(p)}. \tag{28}$$

The goal of this paper is to study a special type of stability of the model (26) with initial conditions (27) or their equivalent (28).

Initially, we will consider an example to discuss some properties of the solutions of equations with the generalized proportional Riemann–Liouville fractional derivative.

Example 2. *Consider the initial value problem for the scalar differential equation with GPRLFD*

$$({}_0^{RL}\mathcal{D}^{q,\rho}u)(t) = -u(t), \quad ({}_0\mathcal{I}^{1-q,\rho}u)(0+) = u_0,$$

where $q \in (0,1)$, $\rho \in (0,1]$. According to Lemma 4 with $\lambda = -\frac{1}{\rho^q}$, $f(t,u) \equiv 0$, the solution is given by

$$u(t;u_0) = u_0 \rho^{1-q} e^{\frac{\rho-1}{\rho}t} t^{q-1} E_{q,q}(-(\frac{t}{\rho})^q).$$

For any nonzero initial value, we have $\lim_{t\to 0+} u(t;u_0) = \infty$ and $\lim_{t\to\infty} u(t;u_0) = 0$. Then, for any $\epsilon > 0$ there exists $T = T(\epsilon, u_0)$ such that $|u(t;u_0)| < \epsilon$ for $t > T$, but we could not find a nonzero initial value u_0 such that $|u(t;u_0)| < \epsilon$ for $t \geq 0$.

The above example illustrates that any type of stability for differential equations with GPRLFD has to be defined in a different way than those for ordinary differential equations or differential equations with the Caputo-type fractional derivative. The initial time has to be excluded. Some authors do not exclude the initial time (it is usually 0), and they do not note that order $q \in (0,1)$ of the Riemann–Liouville fractional derivative of a constant depends on the expressions t^{-q} and t^{q-1},which are not bounded for points close enough to the initial time 0 (see, for example, [38–40]). Note that the main concepts of stability of the Riemann–Liouville fractional derivative are discussed and studied in [10].

We now introduce the class Λ of Lyapunov-like functions, which will be used to investigate the stability of the model (26).

Definition 3. *Let $\Delta \subset \mathbb{R}^n$, $0 \in \Delta$. We will say that the function $V(x) : \Delta \to \mathbb{R}_+$ belongs to the class $\Lambda(\Delta)$ if $V(x) \in C(\Delta)$ and it is locally Lipschitzian.*

Remark 9. *Lyapunov functions could be applied with the quadratic function $V(x) = \sum_{i=1}^n x_i^2$, $x = (x_1, x_2, \ldots, x_n)$ for which Corollary 4 could be applied.*

Note that some authors, when applying Lyapunov functions to fractional differential equations, use the equality $({}_{t_0}^{RL}D^q|v|)(t) = sign(v(t))({}_{t_0}^{RL}D^q v)(t)$ (see, for example, (31)). However, this equality is not true for all continuous functions v.

Example 3. *Let $v(t) = t-1$, $t \in [0,2]$, $q = 0.3$, $t_0 = 0$. Then, for $t \in (1,2)$, we get*

$$\begin{aligned}
{}_0^{RL}D_t^{0.3}|t-1| &= \frac{1}{\Gamma(0.7)}\frac{d}{dt}\int_0^t (t-s)^{-0.3}|s-1|ds \\
&= \frac{1}{\Gamma(0.7)}\frac{d}{dt}\int_0^t (t-s)^{-0.3} sign(s-1)\,(s-1)ds \\
&= \frac{1}{\Gamma(0.7)}\frac{d}{dt}\Big(-\int_0^1 (t-s)^{-0.3}\,(s-1)ds + \int_1^t (t-s)^{-0.3}\,(s-1)ds\Big) \\
&\neq \frac{1}{\Gamma(0.7)}\frac{d}{dt}\int_0^t (t-s)^{-0.3}(s-1)ds = sign(t-1)\Big({}_0^{RL}D_t^{0.3}(t-1)\Big).
\end{aligned} \tag{29}$$

In connection with the above remark and example, we will use the quadratic function as a Lyapunov function.

We will define the equilibrium of the neural networks (26) and (27). Usually, the equilibrium is a point whose derivative is zero, and satisfies an appropriate algebraic equation. In the case where the generalized proportional derivative (Caputo or Riemann–Liouville type) is taken for a nonzero constant, then the result is not equal to zero (which is true for the ordinary derivative and the Caputo derivative). For the generalized proportional Caputo fractional derivative, the equilibrium is defined by $Ce^{\frac{\rho-1}{\rho}t}$ and studied for some types of stability in [16]. In the case of the Riemann–Liouville fractional derivative, the equilibrium is defined as a constant in [39], but because ${}_0^{RL}D_t^q 1 = \frac{t^{-q}}{\Gamma(1-q)}$, the algebraic system (12) [39] could not be satisfied for all $t \geq 0$ because the right-hand side part does not depend on t but the left-hand side part depends on the variable t^{-q}, which has no bound as $t \to 0+$.

A similar situation occurs with the GPRLFD. We will study the stability behavior of the model (26) in several cases.

4.1. General Case of the Model

Consider the model (26) in the general case, when at least one of the coefficients and the external inputs in both layers are variable in time.

4.1.1. Variable in Time Equilibrium

Applying Corollary 1 with $a = 0$, we will define the equilibrium of (26):

Definition 4. *The function $U^*(t) = (x^*(t), y^*(t)) : (0, \infty) \to \mathbb{R}^{n+m}$, where $x^*(t) = Ce^{\frac{\rho-1}{\rho}t}t^{q-1}$ and $y^*(t) = Ke^{\frac{\rho-1}{\rho}t}t^{q-1}$ with $C = (C_1, C_2, \dots, C_n)$, $K = (K_1, K_2, \dots, K_m)$, $C_i = const, i = 1,2,\dots,n$, $K_j = const, j = 1,2,\dots,m$, is called an equilibrium of the model of fractional order BAM neural networks (26) if the equalities*

$$\begin{aligned} a_i(t)C_i e^{\frac{\rho-1}{\rho}t}t^{q-1} &= \sum_{k=1}^{m} b_{i,k}(t) f_k(K_k e^{\frac{\rho-1}{\rho}t}t^{q-1}) + I_i(t),\ t \geq 0,\ \ i = 1,2\dots,n \\ b_j(t)K_j e^{\frac{\rho-1}{\rho}t}t^{q-1} &= \sum_{k=1}^{n} d_{j,k}(t) g_k(C_k e^{\frac{\rho-1}{\rho}t}t^{q-1}) + J_j(t),\ t \geq 0,\ \ j = 1,2\dots,m \end{aligned} \tag{30}$$

hold.

Note that $\lim_{t\to 0+}\left(e^{\frac{1-\rho}{\rho}t}t^{1-q}U^*(t)\right) = U^0$ where $U^0 = (C, K)$, and therefore, the equilibrium $U^*(t)$ is a solution of the model (26) and (27) with $x_0 = C\frac{\Gamma(q)}{\rho^{1-q}}$ and $y_0 = K\frac{\Gamma(q)}{\rho^{1-q}}$.

Let $U^*(t)$ be an equilibrium of (26) defined by Definition 4. Consider the change of variables $u(t) = x(t) - x^*(t), v(t) = y(t) - y^*(t),\ t \geq 0$, in system (26). Then, we obtain

$$\begin{aligned} ({}_0^{RL}\mathcal{D}^{q,\rho}u_i)(t) &= -a_i(t)u_i(t) + \sum_{k=1}^{m} b_{i,k}(t)F_k(t, v_k(t)),\ \ t > 0,\ i = 1,2,\dots,n, \\ ({}_0^{RL}\mathcal{D}^{q,\rho}v_j)(t) &= -b_j(t)v_j(t) + \sum_{k=1}^{n} d_{j,k}(t)G_k(t, u_k(t)),\ \ t > 0,\ j = 1,2,\dots,m, \end{aligned} \tag{31}$$

where $F_j(t,u) = f_j(u + y_j^*(t)) - f_j(y_j^*(t))$, $G_i(t,u) = g_i(u + x_i^*(t)) - g_i(x_i^*(t))$, $i = 1,2,\dots,n, j = 1,2,\dots,m$ for $t > 0,\ u \in \mathbb{R}$.

The initial conditions associated with the revised model (31) can be written in the form

$$\begin{aligned} ({}_0\mathcal{I}^{1-q,\rho}u_i)(t)|_{t=0} &= x_i^0 - C_i\frac{\Gamma(q)}{\rho^{1-q}},\ \ i = 1,2\dots,n, \\ ({}_0\mathcal{I}^{1-q,\rho}v_j)(t)|_{t=0} &= y_j^0 - K_j\frac{\Gamma(q)}{\rho^{1-q}},\ j = 1,2,\dots,m. \end{aligned} \tag{32}$$

Note that the system (31) has a zero solution (with zero initial values).

Definition 5. *Let $\alpha \in (0,1)$ and $\rho \in (0,1]$. The equilibrium $U^*(t)$ of (26) is called* Mittag-Leffler exponentially stable in time *if there exists $T > 0$ such that, for any solution $U(t) = (x(t), y(t))$ of (26) and (27), the inequality*

$$\|U(t) - U^*(t)\| \leq \Xi\left(\left\|v^0 - U^0\frac{\Gamma(q)}{\rho^{1-q}}\right\|\right)e^{\lambda\frac{\rho-1}{\rho}t}E_{q,q}(-\lambda t^q),\ t \geq T,$$

holds, where $v^0 = (x^0, y^0)$, $\lambda > 0$ is a constant, and $\Xi \in C([0,\infty),[0,\infty))$, $\Xi(0) = 0$, is a given locally Lipschitz function.

Remark 10. *The Mittag-Leffler exponential stability in time of the equilibrium* $(x^*(t), y^*(t))$ *of* (26) *implies that every solution* $(x(t), y(t))$ *of the model* (26) *satisfies* $\lim_{t\to\infty} \|x(t) - x^*(t)\| = 0$, $\lim_{t\to\infty} \|y(t) - y^*(t)\| = 0$ *for any initial values.*

Theorem 1. *Let the following assumptions hold:*

1. $q \in (0,1)$ *and* $\rho \in (0,1]$.
2. *The functions* $a_i, c_j \in C(\mathbb{R}_+, (0,\infty)), b_{i,j}, d_{j,i}, I_i, J_j \in C(\mathbb{R}_+, \mathbb{R})$, $i = 1,2,\ldots,n$, $j = 1,2,\ldots,m$.
3. *The activation functions* $f_i, g_j \in C(\mathbb{R}, \mathbb{R})$, *and there exist positive constants* μ_i, η_j $i = 1,2,\ldots,n$, *such that* $|f_i(v) - f_i(w)| \le \mu_i|v - w|$ *and* $|g_j(v) - g_j(w)| \le \eta_j|v - w|$ *for* $v, w \in \mathbb{R}, i = 1,2,\ldots,n$, $j = 1,2,\ldots,m$.
4. *There exist constants* $C_i, K_j, i = 1,2,\ldots,n$, $j = 1,2,\ldots,m$, *such that the algebraic system* (30) *is satisfied for all* $t \ge 0$.
5. *There exist constants* $\lambda_i, \mu_j > 0$, $i = 1,2,\ldots,n$, $j = 1,2,\ldots,m$, *such that the inequalities*

$$2a_i(t) - \sum_{k=1}^{m} |b_{i,k}(t)| - \eta_i^2 \sum_{j=1}^{m} |d_{j,i}(t)| \ge \lambda_i, \quad t \ge 0, \quad i = 1,2,\ldots,n$$

$$2c_j(t) - \sum_{k=1}^{n} |d_{j,k}(t)| - \mu_j^2 \sum_{i=1}^{n} |b_{i,j}(t)| \ge \mu_j, \quad t \ge 0, \quad j = 1,2,\ldots,m.$$

hold.

Then, the equilibrium $U^*(t) = (C_1, C_2, \ldots, C_n, K_1, K_2, \ldots, K_m)e^{\frac{\rho-1}{\rho}t}t^{q-1}$ *of model* (26) *is Mittag-Leffler exponentially stable.*

Remark 11. *Condition 4 of Theorem 1 guarantees the existence of the equilibrium* $U^*(t)$ *of* (26).

Proof. Consider the Lyapunov function $V(x,y) = 0.5\sum_{i=1}^{n} x_i^2 + 0.5\sum_{j=1}^{m} y_j^2$, $x \in \mathbb{R}^n$, $y \in \mathbb{R}^m$.

Let $U(\cdot) = (x(\cdot), y(\cdot)) \in \mathbb{R}^{n+m}$ be a solution of (26) and (27), and let $X(t) = x(t) - x^*(t), Y(t) = y(t) - y^*(t)$, $t \ge 0$ where $U^*(\cdot) = (x^*(\cdot), y^*(\cdot))$.

Then, according to Corollary 4, we get

$$\begin{aligned}
&({}_0^{RL}\mathcal{D}^{q,\rho}V(X(\cdot),Y(\cdot)))(t) = 0.5\sum_{i=1}^{n}({}_0^{RL}\mathcal{D}^{q,\rho}X_i^2(\cdot))(t) + 0.5\sum_{j=1}^{m}({}_0^{RL}\mathcal{D}^{q,\rho}Y_j^2(\cdot))(t) \\
&\le \sum_{i=1}^{n} X_i(t)({}_0^{RL}\mathcal{D}^{q,\rho}X_i(\cdot))(t) + \sum_{j=1}^{m} Y_j(t)({}_0^{RL}\mathcal{D}^{q,\rho}Y_j(\cdot))(t) \\
&= \sum_{i=1}^{n}\left(-a_i(t)X_i^2(t) + \sum_{k=1}^{m} b_{i,k}(t)X_i(t)F_k(t,Y_k(t))\right) \\
&\quad + \sum_{j=1}^{n}\left(-c_j(t)Y_j^2(t) + \sum_{k=1}^{n} dj,k(t)Y_j(t)G_k(t,X_k(t))\right) \\
&\le \sum_{i=1}^{n}\left(-a_i(t)X_i^2(t) + \sum_{k=1}^{m} |b_{i,k}(t)|0.5(X_i^2(t) + F_k^2(t,Y_k(t))\right) \\
&\quad + \sum_{j=1}^{m}\left(-c_i(t)Y_j^2(t) + \sum_{k=1}^{n} |d_{j,k}(t)|0.5(Y_j^2(t) + G_k^2(t,X_k(t))\right) \\
&\le \sum_{i=1}^{n}\left(-a_i(t) + 0.5\sum_{k=1}^{m} |b_{i,k}(t)| + 0.5\eta_i^2\sum_{j=1}^{m} |d_{j,i}(t)|\right)X_i^2(t) \\
&\quad + \sum_{j=1}^{m}\left(-c_j(t) + 0.5\sum_{k=1}^{n} |d_{j,k}(t)| + 0.5\mu_j^2\sum_{i=1}^{n} |b_{i,j}(t)|\right)Y_j^2(t) \\
&\le -\gamma V(X(t),Y(t)),
\end{aligned} \tag{33}$$

where $\gamma = \min_{i=1,2,\ldots,n,\ j=1,2,\ldots,m}\{\lambda_i, \mu_j\}$.

Additionally, we have

$$\begin{aligned}
\lim_{t\to 0+}\left(e^{\frac{1-\rho}{\rho}t}t^{1-q}V(X(t),Y(t))\right) &= 0.5\lim_{t\to 0+}\left(e^{\frac{1-\rho}{\rho}t}t^{1-q}\left(\sum_{i=1}^{n}X_i^2+\sum_{j=1}^{m}Y_j^2\right)\right)\\
&= 0.5\sum_{i=1}^{n}\left(x_i^0\frac{\rho^{1-q}}{\Gamma(q)}-C_i\right)^2+0.5\sum_{j=1}^{m}\left(y_j^0\frac{\rho^{1-q}}{\Gamma(q)}-K_j\right)^2 \\
&= 0.5\left(\frac{\rho^{1-q}}{\Gamma(q)}\right)^2\left(\left\|v^0-U^0\frac{\Gamma(q)}{\rho^{1-q}}\right\|\right)^2 < u_0\frac{\rho^{1-q}}{\Gamma(q)},
\end{aligned} \tag{34}$$

where $u_0 = \frac{\rho^{1-q}}{\Gamma(q)}\left(\left\|v^0-U^0\frac{\Gamma(q)}{\rho^{1-q}}\right\|\right)^2$, $v^0=(x^0,y^0)$, $U^0=(C,K)$.

Consider the scalar equation $({}_0^{RL}\mathcal{D}^{q,\rho}u(\cdot))(t) = -\gamma u(t)$ with the initial condition $({}_0\mathcal{I}^{1-q,\rho}u)(t)|_{t=0} = u_0$. According to Lemma 4, it has a solution

$$u(t) = u_0\rho^{1-q}e^{\frac{1-\rho}{\rho}t}t^{q-1}E_{q,q}(-\gamma(\frac{t}{\rho})^q).$$

Because $\lim_{t\to\infty}t^{q-1}=0$, there exists $T=T(q)>0$ such that $t^{q-1}\le 1$ for $t\ge T$. According to Corollary 3, we obtain for $t\ge T$

$$V(X(t),Y(t)) < u(t) \le \frac{\rho^{2-2q}}{\Gamma(q)}\left(\left\|v^0-U^0\frac{\Gamma(q)}{\rho^{1-q}}\right\|\right)^2 e^{\frac{1-\rho}{\rho}t}E_{q,q}(-\gamma(\frac{t}{\rho})^q).$$

Thus, the equilibrium $U^*(\cdot)$ is Mittag-Leffler exponentially stable with $\Xi(u)=\frac{\rho^{2-2q}}{\Gamma(q)}u^2$. □

4.1.2. Constant Equilibrium

We define the equilibrium of the model (26) as a constant vector in the form $V^* = (C_1, C_2, \ldots, C_{n+m})$.

From Equation (5), using CAS Wolfram Mathematica, we obtain

$$({}_a\mathcal{D}^{q,\rho}1)(t) = \rho^q e^{\frac{\rho-1}{\rho}t}\left({}_a^{RL}D_t^q\left(e^{\frac{1-\rho}{\rho}t}\right)\right) = (1-\rho)^q\left(1-\frac{\Gamma(-q,\frac{1-\rho}{\rho}t)}{\Gamma(-q)}\right) \tag{35}$$

where $\Gamma(a,x) = \int_x^\infty t^{a-1}e^{-t}dt$ is the upper incomplete gamma function. It is clear that $\lim_{t\to 0}\frac{\Gamma(-q,\frac{1-\rho}{\rho}t)}{\Gamma(-q)}=\infty$ and $\lim_{t\to\infty}\frac{\Gamma(-q,\frac{1-\rho}{\rho}t)}{\Gamma(-q)}=0$ for $q\in(0,1)$ and $\rho\in(0,1]$.

Based on (35), we will define the constant equilibrium of (26).

Definition 6. *The constant vector $V^* = (C_1, C_2, \ldots, C_{n+m})$ is called a constant equilibrium of the model of fractional order BAM neural networks (26) if the equalities*

$$\begin{aligned}
C_i\left((1-\rho)^q\left(1-\frac{\Gamma(-q,\frac{1-\rho}{\rho}t)}{\Gamma(-q)}\right)+a_i(t)\right) &= \sum_{k=1}^{m}b_{i,k}(t)f_k(C_{n+k})+I_i(t),\ t\ge 0,\ i=1,2\ldots,n\\
C_{n+j}\left((1-\rho)^q\left(1-\frac{\Gamma(-q,\frac{1-\rho}{\rho}t)}{\Gamma(-q)}\right)+b_j(t)\right) &= \sum_{k=1}^{n}d_{j,k}(t)g_k(C_k)+J_j(t),\ t\ge 0,\ j=1,2\ldots,m
\end{aligned} \tag{36}$$

hold.

Note that $\lim_{t\to 0+}\left(e^{\frac{1-\rho}{\rho}t}t^{1-q}V^*\right)=0$, and therefore, the equilibrium V^* is a solution of the model (26) and (27) with $x_0=y_0=0$.

Let V^* be a constant equilibrium of (26) defined by Definition 6. Consider the change of variables $u_i(t)=x_i(t)-C_i, v_j(t)=y_j(t)-C_{n+j},\ t\geq 0$, in system (26). Then, applying (35) and (36), we obtain

$$\begin{aligned}({}_0^{RL}\mathcal{D}^{q,\rho}u_i)(t)&=-a_i(t)u_i(t)+\sum_{k=1}^m b_{i,k}(t)F_k(v_k(t)),\ \ t>0,\ i=1,2,\dots,n,\\({}_0^{RL}\mathcal{D}^{q,\rho}v_j)(t)&=-b_j(t)v_j(t)+\sum_{k=1}^n d_{j,k}(t)G_k(u_k(t)),\ \ t>0,\ j=1,2,\dots,m,\end{aligned}\tag{37}$$

where $F_j(u)=f_j(u+C_{n+j})-f_j(C_{n+j}), G_i(u)=g_i(u+C_i)-g_i(C_i), u\in\mathbb{R}, i=1,2,\dots,n$, $j=1,2,\dots,m, u\in\mathbb{R}$.

Note that the system (31) has a zero solution (with zero initial values).

Definition 7. *Let $\alpha\in(0,1)$ and $\rho\in(0,1]$. The constant equilibrium V^* of (26) is called* Mittag-Leffler exponentially stable in time *if there exists $T>0$ such that, for any solution $U(t)=(x(t),y(t))$ of (26) and (27), the inequality*

$$\|U(t)-V^*\|\leq\Xi\left(\left\|v^0\right\|\right)e^{\lambda\frac{\rho-1}{\rho}t}E_{q,q}(-\lambda t^q),\ t\geq T,$$

holds, where $v^0=(x^0,y^0)$, $\lambda>0$ is a constant, and $\Xi\in C([0,\infty),[0,\infty))$, $\Xi(0)=0$, is a given locally Lipschitz function.

Theorem 2. *Let the conditions of Theorem 1 be satisfied. Then, the constant equilibrium $V^*=(C_1,C_2,\dots,C_{n+m})$ of model (26) is Mittag-Leffler exponentially stable.*

The proof is similar to the one in Theorem 1, so we omit it.

4.2. Partial Case—Constant Coefficient and Constant Inputs in the Model

Let all coefficients in both layers, as well as the external inputs, be constants, i.e., $a_i(t)\equiv a_i, c_j(t)\equiv c_j, b_{i,k}(t)\equiv b_{i,k}, d_{j,k}(t)\equiv d_{j,k}, I_i(t)\equiv I_i,\ J_j(t)\equiv J_j,\ i=1,2,\dots,n$, $j=1,2,\dots,m$.

Then, for a variable in time equilibrium, the algebraic system (30) reduces to

$$\begin{aligned}a_iC_ie^{\frac{\rho-1}{\rho}t}t^{q-1}&=\sum_{k=1}^m b_{i,k}f_k(K_ke^{\frac{\rho-1}{\rho}t}t^{q-1})+I_i,\ t\geq 0,\ \ i=1,2\dots,n,\\b_jK_je^{\frac{\rho-1}{\rho}t}t^{q-1}&=\sum_{k=1}^n d_{j,k}g_k(C_ke^{\frac{\rho-1}{\rho}t}t^{q-1})+J_j,\ t\geq 0,\ \ j=1,2\dots,m.\end{aligned}\tag{38}$$

The system (38) could have a solution $(C_1,C_2,\dots,C_n,K_1,\dots,K_m)$, i.e., the model (26) could have a variable in time equilibrium.

For a constant equilibrium, the algebraic system (36) reduces to

$$\begin{aligned}C_i(1-\rho)^q\left(1-\frac{\Gamma(-q,\frac{1-\rho}{\rho}t)}{\Gamma((-q)}\right)&=-a_iC_i+\sum_{k=1}^m b_{i,k}f_k(C_{n+k})+I_i,\ t\geq 0,\ \ i=1,2\dots,n\\C_{n+j}(1-\rho)^q\left(1-\frac{\Gamma(-q,\frac{1-\rho}{\rho}t)}{\Gamma(-q)}\right)&=-b_jC_{n+j}+\sum_{k=1}^n d_{j,k}g_k(C_k)+J_j,\ t\geq 0,\ \ j=1,2\dots,m\end{aligned}\tag{39}$$

If there is no external input, i.e., $I_i = 0$, $J_j = 0$ and $f_i(0) = 0, g_j(0) = 0$, $i - 1,2,\dots,n$, $j = 1,2,\dots,m$, then the system (39) has a zero solution $C_k = 0$, $k = 1,2,\dots,n+m$, i.e., the model (26) has a zero equilibrium.

If there is external input, i.e., at least one of I_i, J_j are nonzero, then the system (39) has no solution; thus, the model has no constant equilibrium.

5. Examples

Example 4. *Consider the following BAM neural networks of two layers with two neurons with the GPRLFD:*

$$
\begin{aligned}
({}_0^{RL}\mathcal{D}^{\alpha,\rho}x_1)(t) &= -x_1(t) + \frac{0.1}{1+e^{-y_1(t)}} - 0.05,\\
({}_0^{RL}\mathcal{D}^{\alpha,\rho}x_2)(t) &= -\left(1+e^{\frac{\rho-1}{\rho}t}\right)x_2(t) - e^{\frac{\rho-1}{\rho}t}\frac{1}{1+e^{-y_2(t)}} + e^{\frac{\rho-1}{\rho}t},\\
({}_0^{RL}\mathcal{D}^{\alpha,\rho}y_1)(t) &= -\left(1+0.5e^{\frac{\rho-1}{\rho}t}\right)y_1(t) - e^{\frac{\rho-1}{\rho}t}\frac{1}{1+e^{-x_1(t)}} + \frac{1}{1+e^{-x_2(t)}} + 0.5(e^{\frac{\rho-1}{\rho}t}-1)\\
({}_0^{RL}\mathcal{D}^{\alpha,\rho}y_2)(t) &= -\left(1.5+e^{\frac{\rho-1}{\rho}t}\right)y_2(t) - \frac{1}{1+e^{-y_2(t)}} + 0.5,
\end{aligned}
\tag{40}
$$

with coefficients $a_1(t) = 1$, $a_2(t) = 1+e^{\frac{\rho-1}{\rho}t}$, $c_1(t) = 1+0.5e^{\frac{\rho-1}{\rho}t}$, $c_2(t) = 1.5+e^{\frac{\rho-1}{\rho}t}$, *the activation functions* $f_k(u), g_k(u) = \frac{1}{1+e^{-u}} > 0$, $k = 1,2, u \in \mathbb{R}$, *are equal to the sigmoid function with* $\mu_k = \eta_k = 0.25$, *the external inputs are given by*

$$
I_1(t) = -0.05,\ I_2(t) = e^{\frac{\rho-1}{\rho}t},\ J_1(t) = 0.5(e^{\frac{\rho-1}{\rho}t}-1),\ J_2(t) = 0.5,
$$

and

$$
B = \{b_{i,k}(t)\} = \begin{bmatrix} 0.1 & 0 \\ 0 & -e^{\frac{\rho-1}{\rho}t} \end{bmatrix}, \quad D = \{d_{i,k}(t)\} = \begin{bmatrix} -e^{\frac{\rho-1}{\rho}t} & 1 \\ 0 & -1 \end{bmatrix}.
$$

Then, the algebraic system (30) *reduces to*

$$
\begin{aligned}
a_1(t)C_1e^{\frac{\rho-1}{\rho}t}t^{q-1} &= \frac{b_{1,1}}{1+e^{-K_1e^{\frac{\rho-1}{\rho}t}t^{q-1}}} + I_1(t),\ t \geq 0,\\
a_2(t)C_2e^{\frac{\rho-1}{\rho}t}t^{q-1} &= \frac{b_{2,2}}{1+e^{-K_2e^{\frac{\rho-1}{\rho}t}t^{q-1}}} + I_2(t),\ t \geq 0,\\
c_1(t)K_1e^{\frac{\rho-1}{\rho}t}t^{q-1} &= d_{1,1}(t)\frac{1}{1+e^{-C_1e^{\frac{\rho-1}{\rho}t}t^{q-1}}} + d_{1,2}(t)\frac{1}{1+e^{-C_2e^{\frac{\rho-1}{\rho}t}t^{q-1}}} + J_1(t),\\
c_2(t)K_2e^{\frac{\rho-1}{\rho}t}t^{q-1} &= d_{2,1}(t)\frac{1}{1+e^{-C_1e^{\frac{\rho-1}{\rho}t}t^{q-1}}} + d_{2,2}(t)\frac{1}{1+e^{-C_2e^{\frac{\rho-1}{\rho}t}t^{q-1}}} + J_2(t),\ t \geq 0.
\end{aligned}
\tag{41}
$$

The system (41) *has a zero solution* $C_1 = C_2 = K_1 = K_2 = 0$.

Then, for $\rho \in (0,1]$, $q \in (0,1)$, *system* (40) *has the equilibrium* $U^*(t) = (0,0,0,0)$. *Additionally, Condition 5 of Theorem 1 is satisfied because of the inequalities*

$$
\begin{aligned}
2a_1(t) - |b_{1,1}(t)| - |b_{1,2}(t)| - \eta_1^2|d_{1,1}(t)| - \eta_2^2|d_{2,1}(t)| &\geq \lambda_1 = 1.8375, \quad t \geq 0,\\
2a_2(t) - |b_{2,1}(t)| - |b_{2,2}(t)| - \eta_1^2|d_{1,2}(t)| - \eta_2^2|d_{2,2}(t)| &\geq \lambda_2 = 1.875, \quad t \geq 0,\\
2c_1(t) - |d_{1,1}(t)| - |d_{1,2}(t)| - \mu_1^2|b_{1,1}(t)| + \mu_2^2|b_{2,1}(t)| &\geq \mu_1 = 0.99375, \quad t \geq 0,\\
2c_2(t) - |d_{2,1}(t)| - |d_{2,2}(t)| - \mu_2^2|b_{1,2}(t)| + \mu_2^2|b_{2,2}(t)| &\geq \mu_2 = 1, \quad t \geq 0,
\end{aligned}
$$

According to Theorem 2, the zero equilibrium of (40) *is Mittag-Leffler exponentially stable, i.e., every solution* $(x_1(\cdot), y_2(\cdot), y_1(\cdot), y_2(\cdot))$ *of* (40) *with the initial condition*

$$({}_0\mathcal{I}^{1-q,\rho} x_i)(t)|_{t=0} = x_i^0, \quad ({}_0\mathcal{I}^{1-q,\rho} y_j)(t)|_{t=0} = y_j^0, \quad i, j = 1, 2,$$

satisfies the inequality

$$\sqrt{x_1^2(t) + x_2^2(t) + y_1^2(t) + y_2^2(t)} \leq \frac{\rho^{2-2q}}{\Gamma(q)} \Big((x_1^0)^2 + (x_2^0)^2 + (y_1^0)^2 + (y_2^0)^2 \Big) E_{q,q}(-\frac{0.99375}{\rho^q} t^q)$$

with $\gamma = min(1.8375, 1.875, 0.99375, 1)$.

Author Contributions: Conceptualization, R.P.A., S.H. and D.O.; methodology, R.P.A., S.H. and D.O.; formal analysis, R.P.A., S.H. and D.O.; investigation, R.P.A., S.H. and D.O.; writing—original draft preparation, R.P.A., S.H. and D.O.; writing—review and editing, R.P.A., S.H. and D.O. All authors have read and agreed to the published version of the manuscript.

Funding: S.H. is supported by the Bulgarian National Science Fund under Project KP-06-PN62/1.

Institutional Review Board Statement: Not applicable.

Informed Consent Statement: Not applicable.

Data Availability Statement: Not applicable.

Conflicts of Interest: The authors declare no conflict of interest.

References

1. Wang, G.; Pei, K.; Chen, Y.Q. Stability analysis of nonlinear Hadamard fractional differential system. *J. Franklin Inst.* **2019**, *356*, 6538–6654. [CrossRef]
2. Li, Y.; Chen, Y. Podlubny I. Stability of fractional-order nonlinear dynamic systems: Lyapunov direct method and generalized Mittag Leffler stability. *Comput. Math. Appl.* **2010**, *59*, 1810–1821. [CrossRef]
3. Aguila-Camacho, N.; Duarte-Mermoud, M.A.; Gallegos, J.A. Lyapunov functions for fractional order systems. *Comm. Nonlinear Sci. Numer. Simul.* **2014**, 19, 2951–2957. [CrossRef]
4. Qian, D.; Li, C.; Agarwal, R.P.; Wong, P.J.Y. Stability analysis of fractional differential system with Riemann–Liouville derivative. *Math. Comput. Modell.* **2010**, *52*, 862–874. [CrossRef]
5. Hristova, S.; Tersian, S.; Terzieva, R. Lipschitz Stability in Time for Riemann–Liouville Fractional Differential Equations. *Fractal Fract.* **2021**, *5*, 37. .fractalfract5020037 [CrossRef]
6. Liu, S.; Wu, X.; Zhou, X.F.; Jiang, W. Asymptotical stability of Riemann-Liouville fractional nonlinear systems. *Nonlinear Dyn.* **2016**, *86*, 65–71. [CrossRef]
7. Devi, J.V.; Rae, F.A.M.; Drici, Z. Variational Lyapunov method for fractional differential equations. *Comput. Math. Appl.* **2012**, *64*, 2982–2989. [CrossRef]
8. Agarwal, R.; Hristova, S.; O'Regan, D. Practical stability for Riemann–Liouville delay fractional differential equations. *Arab. J. Math.* **2021**, *10*, 271–283. [CrossRef]
9. Benchohra, M.; Bouriah, S.; Nieto, J.J. Existence and Ulam stability for nonlinear implicit differential equations with Riemann-Liouville fractional derivative. *Demonstr. Math.* **2019**, *52*, 437–450. [CrossRef]
10. Agarwal, R.; Hristova, S.; O'Regan, D. Stability Concepts of Riemann-Liouville Fractional-Order Delay Nonlinear Systems. *Mathematics* **2021**, *9*, 435. [CrossRef]
11. Jarad, F.; Abdeljawad, T.; Alzabut, J. Generalized fractional derivatives generated by a class of local proportional derivatives. *Eur. Phys. J. Spec. Top.* **2017**, *226*, 3457–3471. [CrossRef]
12. Jarad, F.; Abdeljawad, T. Generalized fractional derivatives and Laplace transform. *Discret. Contin. Dyn. Syst. Ser. S* **2020**, *13*, 709–722. [CrossRef]
13. Abbas, M.I.; Hristova, S. On the Initial Value Problems for Caputo-Type Generalized Proportional Vector-Order Fractional Differential Equations. *Mathematics* **2021**, *9*, 2720. [CrossRef]
14. Boucenna, D.; Baleanu, D.; Makhlouf, A.B.; Nagy, A.M. Analysis and numerical solution of the generalized proportional fractional Cauchy problem. *Appl. Numer. Math.* **2021**, *167*, 173–186. [CrossRef]
15. Hristova, S.; Abbas, M.I. Explicit Solutions of Initial Value Problems for Fractional Generalized Proportional Differential Equations with and without Impulses. *Symmetry* **2021**, *13*, 996. [CrossRef]
16. Almeida, R.; Agarwal, R.P.; Hristova, S.; O'Regan, D. Quadratic Lyapunov Functions for Stability of the Generalized Proportional Fractional Differential Equations with Applications to Neural Networks. *Axioms* **2021**, *10*, 322. [CrossRef]

17. Abbas, M.I. Controllability and Hyers-Ulam stability results of initial value problems for fractional differential equations via generalized proportional-Caputo fractional derivative. *Miskolc Math. Notes* **2021** *22*, 491–502. [CrossRef]
18. Hristova, S.; Abbas, M.I. Fractional differential equations with anti-periodic fractional integral boundary conditions via the generalized proportional fractional derivatives. *AIP Conf. Proc.* **2022**, *2459*, 030014. [CrossRef]
19. Alzabut, J.; Viji, J.; Muthulakshmi, V.; Sudsutad, W. Oscillatory Behavior of a Type of Generalized Proportional Fractional Differential Equations with Forcing and Damping Terms. *Mathematics* **2020**, *8*, 1037. [CrossRef]
20. Sudsutad, W.; Alzabut, J.; Tearnbucha, C.; Thaiprayoon, C. On the oscillation of differential equations in frame of generalized proportional fractional derivatives. *AIMS Math.* **2020**, *5*, 856–871. [CrossRef]
21. Abbas, M.I.; Ghaderi, M.; Rezapour, S.; Thabet, S.T.M. On a coupled system of fractional differential equations via the generalized proportional fractional derivatives. *J. Funct. Spaces* **2022**, *2022*, 4779213. [CrossRef]
22. Wu, H.; Li, Y. Existence and stability of periodic solution for BAM neural networks with discontinuous neuron activations. *Comput. Math. Appl.* **2008**, *56*, 1981–1993. [CrossRef]
23. Liu, M.; Jiang, H.; Hu, C.; Lu, B.; Li, Z. Novel Global Asymptotic Stability and Dissipativity Criteria of BAM Neural Networks With Delays. *Front. Phys.* **2022**, *10*, 898589. [CrossRef]
24. Syed Ali, M.; Hymavathi, M.; Kauser, S.A.; Boonsatit, N.; Hammachukiattikul, P.; Rajchakit, G. Synchronization of Fractional Order Uncertain BAM Competitive Neural Networks. *Fractal Fract.* **2022**, *6*, 14. [CrossRef]
25. Viera-Martin, E.; Gomez-Aguilar, J.F.; Solıs-Perez, J.E.; Hernandez-Perez, J.A.; Escobar-Jimenez, R.F. Artificial neural networks: A practical review of applications involving fractional calculus. *Eur. Phys. J. Spec. Top.* **2022**, *231*, 2059–2095. [CrossRef]
26. Maiti, M.; Sunder, M.; Abishek, R.; Kishore, B. Nagoor Basha Shaikand Watit Benjapolaku, Recent Advances and Applications of Fractional-Order Neural Networks. *Eng. J.* **2022**, *26*, 7. [CrossRef]
27. Das, S. *Functional Fractional Calculus*; Springer: Berlin/Heidelberg, Germany, 2011.
28. Podlubny, I. *Fractional Differential Equations*; Academic Press: San Diego, CA, USA, 1999.
29. Samko, S.G.; Kilbas, A.A.; Marichev, O.I. *Fractional Integrals and Derivatives: Theory and Applications*; Gordon and Breach Science Publ.: Philadelphia, PA, USA, 1993.
30. Kilbas, A.A.; Srivastava, H.M.; Trujillo, J.J. *Theory and Applications of Fractional Differential Equations*; Elsevier: Amsterdam, The Netherlands, 2006.
31. Ferrari, F. Weyl and Marchaud Derivatives: A Forgotten History. *Mathematics* **2018**, *6*, 6. [CrossRef]
32. Kukushkin, M.V. Abstract fractional calculus for m-accretive operators. *Intern. J. Appl. Math.* **2021**, *34*, 1–41. [CrossRef]
33. Sabzikar, F.; Meerschaert, M.M.; Chen, J. Tempered fractional calculus. *J. Comput. Phys.* **2015**, *293*, 14–28. [CrossRef]
34. Fernandez, A.; Ustaoglu, C. On some analytic properties of tempered fractional calculus. *J. Comput. Appl. Math.* **2020**, *366*, 112400. [CrossRef]
35. Liu, S.; Wu, X.; Zhang, Y.-J. Asymptotical stability of Riemann–Liouville fractional neutral systems. *Appl. Math. Lett.* **2017**, *69*, 168–173. [CrossRef]
36. Duarte-Mermoud, M.A.; Aguila-Camacho, N.; Gallegos, J.A.; Castro-Linares, R. Using general quadratic Lyapunov functions to prove Lyapunov uniform stability for fractional order systems. *Commun. Nonlinear Sci. Numer. Simulat.* **2015**, *22*, 650–659. [CrossRef]
37. Kukushkin, M.V. Spectral properties of fractional differential operators. *Elect. J. Diff. Eq.* **2018**, *29*, 1–24.
38. Qin, Z.; Wu, R.; Lu, Y. Stability analysis of fractionalorder systems with the Riemann–Liouville derivative. *Systems Sci. Control Eng. Open Access J.* **2014**, *2*, 727–731. [CrossRef]
39. Alidousti, J.; Ghaziani, R.K.; Eshkaftaki, A.B. Stability analysis of nonlinear fractional differential order systems with Caputo and Riemann–Liouville derivatives. *Turk. J. Math.* **2017**, *41*, 1260–1278. [CrossRef]
40. Zhang, R.; Yang, S.; Feng, S. Stability analysis of a class of nonlinear fractional differential systems with Riemann-Liouville derivative. *IEEE/CAA J. Autom. Sin.* **2016**, 1–7. [CrossRef]

Disclaimer/Publisher's Note: The statements, opinions and data contained in all publications are solely those of the individual author(s) and contributor(s) and not of MDPI and/or the editor(s). MDPI and/or the editor(s) disclaim responsibility for any injury to people or property resulting from any ideas, methods, instructions or products referred to in the content.

axioms

MDPI

Article

New Wave Solutions for the Two-Mode Caudrey–Dodd–Gibbon Equation

Rodica Cimpoiasu [1,†] and Radu Constantinescu [2,*,†]

[1] Applied Life Sciences and Biotechnologies Research Center, University of Craiova, 13 A. I. Cuza Street, 200585 Craiova, Romania; rodicimp@yahoo.com
[2] Department of Physics, University of Craiova, 13 A. I. Cuza Street, 200585 Craiova, Romania
* Correspondence: rconsta@yahoo.com; Tel.: +40-744345462
† These authors contributed equally to this work.

Abstract: In this paper, we present new dynamical properties of the two-mode Caudrey–Dodd–Gibbon (TMCDG) equation. This equation describes the propagation of dual waves in the same direction with different phase velocities, dispersion parameters, and nonlinearity. This study takes a full advantage of the Kudryashov method and of the exponential expansion method. For the first time, dual-wave solutions are obtained for arbitrary values of the nonlinearity and dispersive factors. Graphs of the novel solutions are included in order to show the waves' propagation, as well as the influence of the involved parameters.

Keywords: two-mode Caudrey–Dodd–Gibbon equation; Kudryashov method; exponential expansion method; dual-wave solutions

MSC: 35E05; 35G20; 74J35; 35C05

Citation: Cimpoiasu, R.; Constantinescu, R. New Wave Solutions for the Two-Mode Caudrey–Dodd–Gibbon Equation. *Axioms* **2023**, *12*, 619. https://doi.org/10.3390/axioms12070619

Academic Editors: Hatıra Günerhan, Francisco Martínez González, Mohammed K. A. Kaabar and Patricia J. Y. Wong

Received: 17 May 2023
Revised: 14 June 2023
Accepted: 20 June 2023
Published: 21 June 2023

Copyright: © 2023 by the authors. Licensee MDPI, Basel, Switzerland. This article is an open access article distributed under the terms and conditions of the Creative Commons Attribution (CC BY) license (https://creativecommons.org/licenses/by/4.0/).

1. Introduction

Two-mode nonlinear partial differential equations (NPDEs) represent extensions of the usual NPDEs. Both types of NPDEs, standard and two-mode, play a considerable role in explaining nonlinear phenomena appearing in nature [1]. Two-mode equations describe the interaction of solitons in gravitation, or the slow–fast propagation of waves in hydrodynamics. They can also model dynamical phenomena in variable magnetic fields appearing in plasma physics.

Standard evolutionary NPDEs involve a first-order partial derivative with respect to time, and describe the unidirectional motion of a single wave. Dual/two-mode equations are NPDEs of a second order in time, and govern the evolution of two-wave modes, propagating in the same direction and with the same dispersion relation, while the phase velocity and the linear and nonlinear parameters are different. The current investigations of the two-mode waves mainly use the method proposed by Korsunsky [2]. It shows that to derive the two-mode PDEs, it is necessary to collect, as two distinct components, the nonlinear terms $N(u, u_x u, \ldots)$ and the linear terms $L(u_{qx}, q \geq 2)$, other than u_t. in the last period of time, many authors considered topics related to two-mode PDEs [3–6]. The dynamics of the two-mode KdV equation associated with the standard-mode third -order KdV equation was studied by various analytical methods, including reductive perturbation [7], the Hamiltonian system [8], or Bell polynomials [9]. In [10], it was shown that the two modes are solitons that continue to propagate separately, without shape and velocity changes, and with the only effect of their collision consisting of some phase shifts. Rather similar methods to what we will apply in our paper, namely the Kudryashov and exponential expansion methods, were used in [11] for the two-mode Sawada–Kotera equation. Bright, dark, periodic, and singular-periodic dual-wave solutions were constructed using a slight different auxiliary equation, as we will consider here.

In [12] a dual-mode version of the nonlinear Schrödinger equation was studied, and its solution was expressed as a finite series of tanh-sech functions. More exactly, dual-mode dark and singular soliton solutions were obtained. The tanh expansion method and Kudryashov technique were used in [13] with the dual-mode Kadomtsev–Petviashvili equation to find the necessary constraint conditions that guarantee the existence of soliton solutions. Multiple kink solutions were pointed out in [14] for the two-mode Sharma–Tasso–Olver equation, as well as for the two-mode fourth-order Burgers equation by using the Cole–Hopf transformation combined with the simplified Hirota method. Three different techniques, including the Kudryashov expansion method that will be used here, were applied in [15] in order to study the dynamic behaviors for a dual-mode generalized Hirota–Satsuma coupled KdV system.

The contributions of this work are twofold. First, we find explicit dual-wave solutions for the dual/two-mode Caudrey–Dodd–Gibbon (TMCDG) equation for arbitrary nonlinearity and dispersion parameters, α and β. Previously, only the case $\alpha = \beta = \pm 1$ was considered in [16], using the Hirota method. The same method was applied in [17] on a more general form of TMCDG. Second, we study the influence of the mentioned parameters, as well as of s, which stands for phase velocity, on the wave propagations, showing how the dual-wave propagation depends on them.

The paper is organized as follows: After the Introduction, in Section 2, an overview on the general form of the TMCDG equation is provided. In Section 3 we present basic facts on the Kudryashov method [18,19] and the exponential expansion method [20]. The findings of our investigation, where the previous methods were applied to the TMCDG equation, are pointed out in Section 4. The analytical results were obtained using the Maple program. Some graphical representations of the solutions are included and discussed in Section 5. Section 6 is dedicated to some conclusions and final remarks.

2. Two-Mode Equations

2.1. Generic Two-Mode Equations

Korsunsky proposed in [2] a two-mode equation of the following form:

$$u_{2t} - s^2 u_{2x} + \left(\frac{\partial}{\partial t} - \alpha s \frac{\partial}{\partial x}\right) N(u,\, u_x u, \ldots) + \left(\frac{\partial}{\partial t} - \beta s \frac{\partial}{\partial x}\right) L(u_{qx},\, q \geq 2) = 0. \quad (1)$$

The starting point for obtaining Equation (1) is an evolutionary equation of the form $u_t + N(u, u_x u, \ldots) + L(u_{qx}, q \geq 2) = 0$. In Equation (1), $u(x,t)$ is the field function, $s > 0$ is the interaction phase velocity, and $|\alpha| \leq 1$, $|\beta| \leq 1$ represent parameters describing the nonlinearity and the dispersion, while $N(u, u_x u, \ldots)$ and $L(u_{qx}, q \geq 2)$ represent the nonlinear and linear parts, respectively. It is important to note that the existence of the dispersion is essential for finding soliton solutions [21,22]. The way of generating a two-mode equation used here for CDG could be also applied to other NPDs, for example, the Eckhaus–Kundu equation [23] or the Kundu–Mukherjee–Naskar equation [24].

2.2. Two-Mode Caudrey–Dodd–Gibbon (TMCDG) Equation

In this paper, we use a standard-mode equation such as [25–27]:

$$G_t + aG^2 G_x + bG_x G_{2x} + mGG_{3x} + G_{5x} = 0, \quad (2)$$

where a, b, m are positive parameters and G_{5x} is the linear term, while the nonlinear one is represented by $aG^2G_x + bG_xG_{2x} + mGG_{3x}$. It is used to describe various phenomena appearing in various fields, such as plasma physics, optics, hydrodynamics, and mathematical biology, as well as gauge field theory.

For $a = 180$, $b = m = 30$, Equation (2) becomes the Caudrey–Dodd–Gibbon (CDG) equation [28]:

$$G_t + 180G^2 G_x + 30G_x G_{2x} + 30GG_{3x} + G_{5x} = 0. \quad (3)$$

Based on the Korsunsky proposal scheme, the two-mode equation associated to Equation (3) is under the following form:

$$G_{2t} - s^2 G_{2x} + \left(\frac{\partial}{\partial t} - \alpha s \frac{\partial}{\partial x}\right)(180G^2 G_x + 30G_x G_{2x} + 30GG_{3x}) + \left(\frac{\partial}{\partial t} - \beta s \frac{\partial}{\partial x}\right) G_{5x} = 0. \tag{4}$$

A more general equation, starting from (2), was considered in [17]. In this paper, multisoliton solutions were generated using the Hirota method, the same method used in [16]. In our case, we chose a specific equation from the same class, but we pointed out other types of solutions, for example, the rational ones that were not reported in either of the mentioned papers.

For $s = 0$, the previous equation takes the form of an usual evolutionary equation of the type (2). By expanding the previous equation, we arrive at the equivalent expression:

$$\begin{aligned} &G_{2t} - s^2 G_{2x} + 30[12GG_x G_t + 6G^2 G_{xt} + G_{xt} G_{2x} + G_x G_{(2x)t} + G_t G_{3x} + GG_{(3x)t}] - \\ &30\alpha s\left[12G(G_x)^2 + 6G^2 G_{2x} + 30(G_{2x})^2 + 2G_x G_{3x} + GG_{4x}\right] + G_{(5x)t} - \beta s G_{6x} = 0. \end{aligned} \tag{5}$$

In order to solve (5), we use the wave variable $\xi = kx - ct$, and therefore, we transform it into the traveling wave equation of the following form:

$$\begin{aligned} &\left(c^2 - k^2 s^2\right) G'' - 30c[12kG(G')^2 + kG^2 G'' + k^3 (G'')^2 + 2k^3 G' G^{(3)} + k^3 GG^{(4)}] - \\ &30\alpha k^2 s[12G(G')^2 + G^2 G'' + k^2 (G'')^2 + 2k^2 G' G^{(3)} + k^2 GG^{(4)}] - k^5 (c + k\beta s) G^{(6)} = 0. \end{aligned} \tag{6}$$

In [16], a one-soliton solution was derived for (4) through the simplified Hirota method. It is obtained if—and only if—$\alpha = \beta$. In the next section, we will extend this result, showing how the equation can be solved for arbitrary nonlinearity and dispersion parameters, α and β. New dual-wave solutions of (4) will be reported for the first time, using two well-known solving methods: the Kudryashov and the exponential expansion methods. These are two of the methods for solving NPDEs based on the auxiliary equation techniques, but other alternative approaches, for example, attached flow [29], the symmetry method [30–33], or the BRST technique [34,35], could also be considered.

3. Brief Overview of The Applied Methods

In this section, we will take a brief review of the two methods applied later to the TMCDG equation. They are effective analytical methods for finding the traveling wave solutions of NPDEs with the generic form:

$$E(u,\ u_t,\ u_x,\ u_{tt},\ u_{xx},\ldots) = 0. \tag{7}$$

When the wave transformation is applied:

$$u(t,x) = u(\xi),\ \xi = kx - ct, \tag{8}$$

where k, c are constants, and Equation (7) becomes an ODE in $u = u(\xi)$ and its derivatives in respect to β:

$$F(u,\ u',\ u'',\ldots) = 0. \tag{9}$$

3.1. *The Kudryashov Method (KM)*

In this section, a brief overview of the KM method [36,37] is presented. Let us assume that the solution of Equation (9) can be expressed as follows:

$$u(\xi) = \sum_{j=0}^{N} a_j Q^j(\xi), \tag{10}$$

where the arbitrary constants $a_j, j = \overline{1,N}$, $a_N \neq 0$, are determined later, and $Q(\xi)$ is the solution of the equation [38]:

$$Q'(\xi) = Q^2(\xi) - Q(\xi). \tag{11}$$

The positive integer N can be determined by applying the homogeneous balance technique to Equation (9). The general solution of the auxiliary Equation (11) is:

$$Q(\xi) = \frac{1}{1 \pm de^{\xi}}, \forall d = const. \neq 0. \tag{12}$$

By substituting Equations (10) and (11) into Equation (9), we obtain a polynomial $R(Q(\xi))$, which can generate a set of algebraic equations allowing us to explicitly determine the parameters a_j, k, c. Then, using the solutions in Equation (10), we obtain wave solutions for the master Equation (7).

3.2. The Exponential Expansion Method (EEM)

Let us consider now the EEM [39]. In this case, the solution of (9) has to be assumed of the following form:

$$u(\xi) = \sum_{j=0}^{N} \rho_j e^{jf(\xi)}, \tag{13}$$

where $\rho_j, j = \overline{1,N}$ are arbitrary constants to be calculated, such that $\rho_N \neq 0$ and $f(\xi)$ are the solution of the following auxiliary equation:

$$f'(\xi) = pe^{-2f(\xi)} + re^{2f(\xi)}, \tag{14}$$

where the parameters p, r appear.

The value of N can be established by making the balance between the highest dispersion and nonlinearity in Equation (9). Inserting expansion (13) with the value of N along with the auxiliary Equation (14) into Equation (9) yields a polynomial $P(e^{f(\xi)})$.

Vanishing all the coefficients of $P(e^{f(\xi)})$, we obtain a system of equations that allows us to determine the parameters ρ_j, p, r, k, c, for which nontrivial wave solutions of Equation (7) exist.

4. Dual Wave Solutions of the TMCDG Equation

Let us apply now the two methods described above for finding wave solutions of the TMCDG Equation (4).

4.1. Application of the Kudryashov Method

By applying (10) and (11) and imposing the balance between the most nonlinear term G^2G'' and the higher-order derivative $G^{(6)}$, the generic solution of Equation (6) is expressed as:

$$G(\xi) = a_0 + a_1 Q(\xi) + a_2 [Q(\xi)]^2. \tag{15}$$

With (15) and (11), Equation (6) becomes an eight-degree polynomial in Q. If we solve the system generated when the various coefficients of the powers $Q^j, j = \overline{0,8}$ are set to zero, we obtain the following solutions:

Solution 1: $\forall k, \forall s > 0, \forall |\alpha| \leq 1$, and

$$\begin{gathered} a_0 = -\frac{k^2}{9}, \; a_1 = -a_2 = \frac{4k^2}{3}, \\ c_{1,2} = \pm ks, \; \beta = \frac{1 + 10\alpha}{9}, \; |\beta| \leq 1; \end{gathered} \tag{16}$$

Solution 2: $\forall k, \forall s > 0, \forall |\alpha| \leq 1, \forall a_2$ and

$$\begin{gathered} a_0 = \frac{a_2}{12}, \; a_1 = -a_2, \\ c_{3,4} = \frac{k\left[4k^2 a_2 + 3a_2^2 \pm \sqrt{16k^4 a_2^2 + 24k^2 a_2^3 + 9a_2^4 + 64k^2 a_2 s\alpha + 64s^2 + 48a_2^2 s\alpha}\right]}{8}, \\ \beta = \frac{\left\{\pm\sqrt{E}[a_2^2 + 3k^2 a_2 + 2k^4] - 3a_2^4 - 13k^2 a_2^3 - 2a_2^2[9k^4 + 4s\alpha] - 8k^2 a_2[k^4 + 3s\alpha]\right\}}{16sk^4}, \end{gathered} \tag{17}$$

with

$$E = 9a_2^4 + 24k^2a_2^3 + 16a_2^2(k^4 + 3s\alpha) + 64k^2a_2s\alpha + 64s^2, |\beta| \leq 1. \quad (18)$$

Plugging (16) and (17) into Equation (15) and considering the solution of (11), we obtain the following new dual-wave solutions:

$$G_{1,2}(x,t) = \frac{k^2}{3}\left[\frac{1}{3} + 4\left(\frac{1}{1+de^{(kx-c_{1,2}t)}} - \left(\frac{1}{1+de^{(kx-c_{1,2}t)}}\right)^2\right)\right], \forall d \quad (19)$$

$$G_{3,4}(x,t) = a_2\left[\frac{1}{12} - \frac{1}{1+de^{(kx-c_{3,4}t)}} + \left(\frac{1}{1+de^{(kx-c_{3,4}t)}}\right)^2\right], \forall d, \quad (20)$$

where the waves' velocities $c_{1,2}$ and $c_{3,4}$ are given by expressions (16) and (17).

4.2. Application of the Exponential Expansion Method (EEM)

To obtain the dual-wave solutions of the TMCDG equation through the EEM, the solution of Equation (6) is derived as follows:

$$G(\xi) = \rho_0 + \rho_1 e^{f(\xi)} + \rho_2 e^{2f(\xi)}. \quad (21)$$

By plugging Equation (21) along with the auxiliary Equation (14) into the traveling wave Equation (6), and equating the coefficients of various powers of exponential terms to zero, a set of algebraic equations involving $\rho_j, j = \overline{0,2}, p, r, c, k$ is derived. Its solution is obtained with the help of the Maple program, under the following form:

$$\forall\rho_0,\ \forall\rho_2,\ \forall s > 0,\ \forall k,\ \forall p, \forall r,\ |\alpha| = |\beta| = 1,\ \rho_1 = 0,\ c = \pm sk. \quad (22)$$

Substituting relations (22) into Equation (21), we should look for other TMCDG solutions in the following form:

$$G(\xi) = \rho_0 + \rho_2 e^{2f(\xi)}. \quad (23)$$

For example, taking into account the solution of the auxiliary Equation (14) and considering $pr > 0$, the dual-wave solution is derived as a periodic one:

$$G_{5,6}(x,t) = \rho_0 + \frac{\rho_2 p}{r}\tan[2\sqrt{pr}k(x \pm st) + q], \quad (24)$$

with $\rho_0, \rho_2, k, p, r, q, s > 0$ arbitrary constants.

5. Discussions on the Dual-Wave Solutions

Let us now analyze the dual-wave solutions obtained in the previous section. We will give here their graphical representations that will describe the dynamical behavior of the model.

Let us start with solutions (19). Their $3D$ and $2D$ graphics are presented in Figure 1 for the following values of the parameters $d = 3$, $k = 2$, and $\alpha = 0.8$, $\beta = 1$ for different s. Subgraphs (a_1–a_3) present the spatiotemporal variation of these solutions for $s = 1, 3, 10$, respectively. Subgraphs (b_1–b_3) depict the $2D$ plots of (a_1–a_3) when $x = 0$.

We observe that during their interaction, the two waves $G_1(x,t)$ and $G_2(x,t)$ keep their amplitudes unchanged, while their widths decrease when the phase velocity increases. These behaviors are shown in the $2D$ plots given by subgraphs (b_1–b_3). The influences of the wave number k and of the the interaction phase velocity s, on the motion of the waves (19) are shown, respectively, in subgraphs (a), (b) in Figure 2 . It can be seen from subgraph (a) that the profiles of G_1 and G_2 are stable for $k \in [0,1]$, while for k increasing from 1 to 5, they become different. This happens under particular values $x = 1, t = 1, s = 3, d = 3, \alpha = 0.8, \beta = 1$. On the other hand, the profile of G_2 is lower than that of G_1, and their profiles become stable for phase velocity $s > 6$, when $x = 1, t = 1$, $k = 1, d = 3, \alpha = 0.8, \beta = 1$ are considered.

Moreover, in order to analyze the dynamical behavior of the novel dual-mode solution (20), the $3D$ and $2D$ graphics are presented in Figure 3, considering the particular values of the free parameters as $a_2 = 0.1$, $d = 3$, $k = 2$, $\alpha = 0.2$, for various values of phase velocity s. Subgraphs (a_1–a_3) present the physical structure of the dual waves $G_3(x,t)$ and $G_4(x,t)$ upon increasing s ($s = 1, 3, 5$), which are, respectively, associated with the values of $\beta = 0.881, 0.971, 0.997$. The motion described by (20) looks like singular dual kink waves, as is clearly shown in subgraphs (b_1–b_3), representing the $2D$ plots of (a_1–a_3) for $x = 0$. The collision of the waves occurs for the phase velocity $s = 5$. The influence of parameters k, s, and α on the motion of dual waves (20) is illustrated in subgraphs (a–c) in Figure 4. When increasing both the wave number k within [1, 3] and the phase velocity s inside the interval of values s_{min} = 6.8 and $s_{max} = 12$, we observe that the profiles of $G_3(x,t)$ and $G_4(x,t)$ increase and remain fixed for any values $k > 3$, $s > 12$.

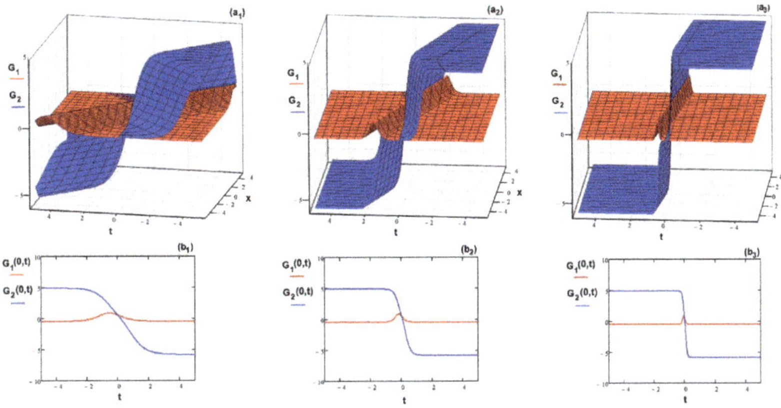

Figure 1. The $3D$ plots of the dual-wave solutions $G_1(x,t)$ (red color) and G_2 (blue color) given by (19), for $\alpha = 0.8$, $\beta = 1$, $d = 3$, $k = 2$, and (**a**$_1$) $s = 1$, (**a**$_2$) $s = 3$, (**a**$_3$) $s = 10$. The $2D$ cross-sections of (**a**$_1$–**a**$_3$) at $x = 0$ are plotted in (**b**$_1$–**b**$_3$).

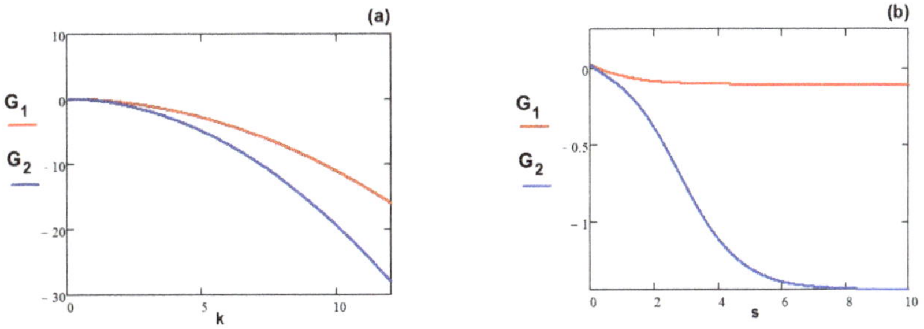

Figure 2. (**a**) The dependence on k when $s = 1$, $d = 3$, α = 0.8, $\beta = 1$, (**b**) the dependence on s when $k = 1$, $d = 3$, α = 0.8, $\beta = 1$ of the motion of the two-mode waves $G_1(x,t)$ (red color) and $G_2(x,t)$ (blue color) given by (19) for $x = 1$, $t = 1$.

Next, we will analyze the remainder of the obtained solutions. The $3D$ and $2D$ graphical configurations of the dual-mode solutions (24) are presented in Figure 5. Subgraphs (a_1), (a_2) show the physical structure of the two-mode waves $G_5(x,t)$ and $G_6(x,t)$ upon increasing s (s = 0.3 and $s = 1$, respectively), for $\rho_0 = 1$, $\rho_2 = 4$, k = 0.1, p = 0.5, $r = 2$, $q = 0$, $|\alpha| = |\beta| = 1$. Both waves have a periodic evolution, following *tan*-shapes that collide with each other. For a fixed-phase velocity parameter s, the periods of the dual waves are the same. As s increases, one can see from subgraphs (b_1) and (b_2) that the periodicity increases for $G_5(x,t)$ and $G_6(x,t)$. The impacts of the parameters k, s, on the motion of the two-mode waves (24), when $x = 3$, $t = 3$, $\rho_0 = 1$, $\rho_2 = 4$, p = 0.5, $r = 2$, $q = 0$, $|\alpha| = |\beta| = 1$, are presented in subgraphs (a)–(b) in Figure 6.

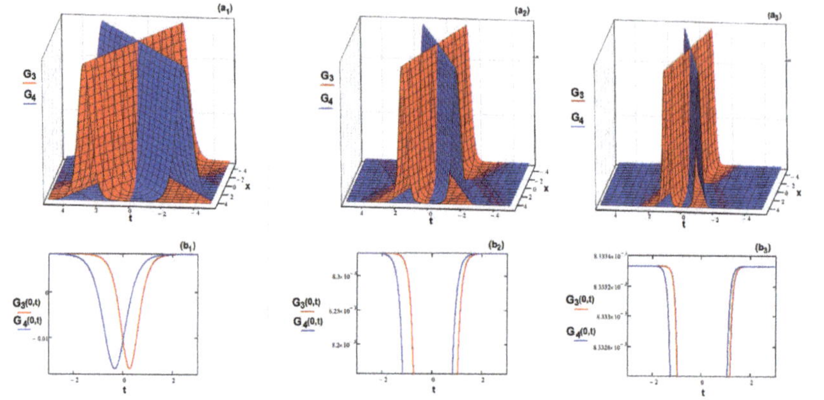

Figure 3. (**a**) The $3D$ plots of the dual-wave solutions $G_3(x,t)$ (red color) and $G_4(x,t)$ (blue color) given by (20) for a_2 = 0.1, $d = 3$, $k = 2$, α = 0.2 and variable s. Three phase velocities were considered: (**a**$_1$) $s = 1$, (**a**$_2$) $s = 3$, and (**a**$_3$) $s = 5$. The $2D$ cross-sections of (**a**$_1$–**a**$_3$) at $x = 0$ are plotted in (**b**$_1$–**b**$_3$).

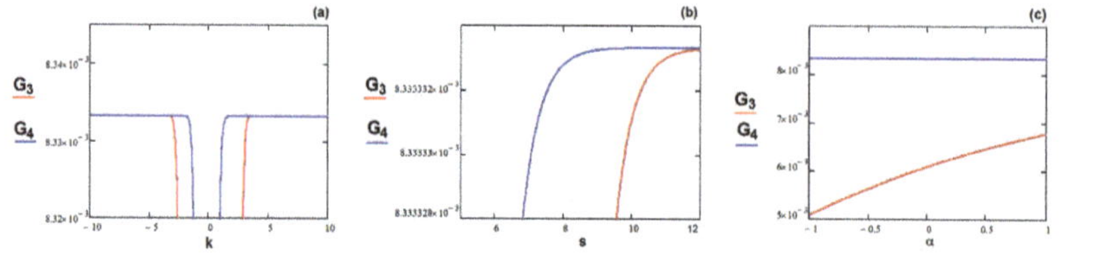

Figure 4. The effect on the motion of the two-mode waves $G_3(x,t)$ (red color) and $G_4(x,t)$ (blue color) given by (20), at $x = 3, t = 1$, of (**a**) wave number k when $s = 5$, α = 0.2, a_2 = 0.1, $d = 3$; (**b**) phase velocity s when $k = 2, \alpha = 0.2, a_2 = 0.1, d = 3$; and (**c**) the nonlinearity parameter α when $k = 2, s = 5$, a_2 = 0.1, $d = 3$.

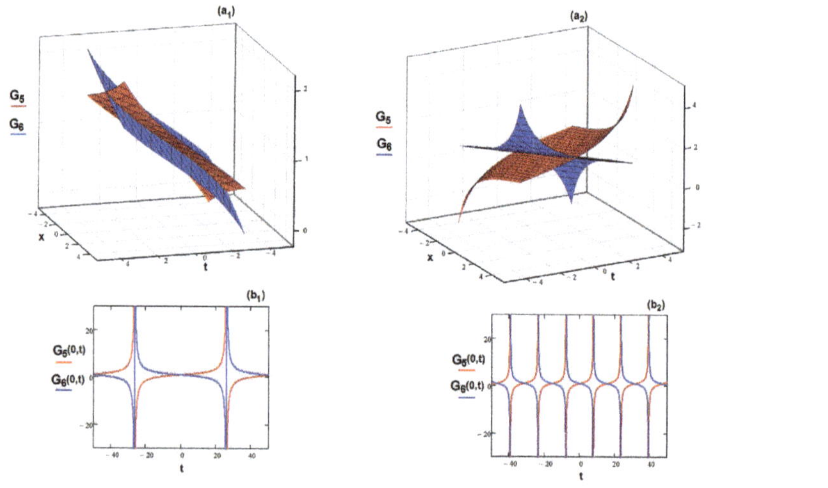

Figure 5. The $3D$ graphs of $G_5(x,t)$ (red color) and G_6 (blue color) given by (24), with $|\alpha| = |\beta| = 1$, $\rho_0 = 1, \rho_2 = 4, k = 0.1, p = 0.5, r = 2, q = 0$, and the phase velocities: (**a**$_1$) s = 0.3, (**a**$_2$) $s = 1$. The $2D$ graphs of (**a**$_1$,**a**$_2$) at $x = 0$ are plotted in (**b**$_1$,**b**$_2$).

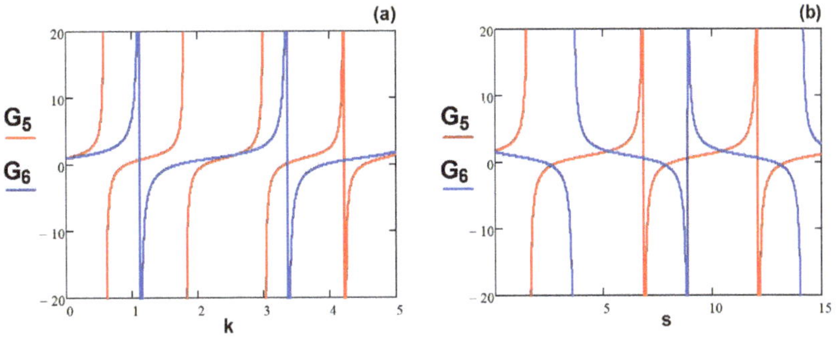

Figure 6. The effect on the motion of the two-mode waves $G_5(x,t)$ (red color) and $G_6(x,t)$ (blue color) given by (24) at $x = 3$, $t = 3$, of (**a**) the wave number k when $|\alpha| = |\beta| = 1$, $s = 0.3$, $\rho_0 = 1$, $\rho_2 = 4$, $p = 0.5$, $r = 2$, $q = 0$; (**b**) the phase velocity parameter s when $\rho_0 = 1$, $\rho_2 = 4$, $k = 0.1$, $p = 0.5$, $r = 2$, $q = 0$.

We discussed the TMCDG equation from the perspective of two solving methods: Kudryashov and exponential expansion. We illustrated the reach of the model in dual-mode wave solutions, and chose only a few of them. In the case of the Kudryashov method, we used the auxiliary equation in the form (11), accepting the rational solution (12). In these circumstances, the obtained dual waves (19) and (20) also had a rational form. When we applied the exponential expansion, we chose a periodic solution of the auxiliary Equation (14), and by consequence, we obtained the periodic dual wave (24).

6. Conclusions

In this work, we investigated the two-mode Caudrey–Dodd–Gibbon (TMCDG) equation, which reads:

$$G_{2t} - s^2 G_{2x} + 30\left(\frac{\partial}{\partial t} - \alpha s\frac{\partial}{\partial x}\right)(6G^2 G_x + G_x G_{2x} + G G_{3x}) + \left(\frac{\partial}{\partial t} - \beta s\frac{\partial}{\partial x}\right) G_{5x} = 0.$$

The Kudryashov expansion and the exponential expansion methods were implemented in order to construct new dual-wave solutions. Previously, in [16], soliton solutions for TMCDG were obtained only in the case of unitary parameters, $\alpha = \beta = \pm 1$.

In our article, novel dual-mode wave solutions given by (19), (20), and (24) are generated for arbitrary values of the nonlinearity and dispersion parameters, α and β. To the best of our knowledge, they are reported here for the first time. Some interesting properties of the dynamical behavior of the TMCDG model were pointed out using graphical representations of the new acquired solutions. They can be summarized as follows:

- The TMCDG equation admits all of the same classes of solutions—hyperbolic, harmonic, and rational—as the unimodal Equation (3). As examples, we show that, using the Kudryashov expansion method, the TMCDG waves move in dual-mode, bright, and kink-wave shapes, while using the exponential expansion method, the motion could appear as having a dual *tan*-periodic pattern. Of course, these are not the only solutions that can be generated; other solutions appear for different values of p and r.
- All solutions depend on the involved parameters, but the dependence is different. We note, for example, that the nonlinearity parameter β cannot take any value, but one depending on α. For $G_{1,2}(x,t)$, the dependence is linear, while for $G_{3,4}(x,t)$, a more complicated relation (17) appears. The periodic solution $G_{5,6}(x,t)$ asks for unitary values of the two parameters α and β, as the relation (22) shows.
- The influence of the main parameters (phase velocity s, wave number k and nonlinearity α) is explained using the graphic representation of the solutions. Depending on their values, the parameters can increase or decrease the velocity of the dual waves.

The approach used here can be applied to any evolutionary NPDE of interest in mathematical physics and engineering, in order to achieve new dual-wave equations and their associated solutions. We will investigate in future work the possibility of extending the two-mode procedure to other higher-dimensional NPDEs or to integrodifferential systems [40], as well as trying to implement alternative techniques [41,42].

Author Contributions: The authors made an equal contribution to this work, with special involvements as follows: conceptualization, R.C. (Rodica Cimpoiasu); methodology, R.C. (Rodica Cimpoiasu); formal analysis, R.C. (Radu Constantinescu); writing—review and editing, R.C. (Radu Constantinescu) and R.C. (Rodica Cimpoiasu). All authors have read and agreed to the published version of the manuscript.

Funding: This research received no external funding.

Acknowledgments: The authors acknowledge the support offered by ICTP through the NT-03 Grant and by the University of Craiova.

Conflicts of Interest: The authors declare no conflict of interest.

References

1. Zwillinger, D. *Handbook of Differential Equations*; Academic Press: New York, NY, USA, 1992.
2. Korsunsky, S.V. Soliton solutions for a second order KdV equation. *Phys. Lett. A* **1994**, *185*, 174–176. [CrossRef]
3. Wazwaz, A.M. A study on a two-wave mode Kadomtsev–Petviashvili equation: Conditions for multiple soliton solutions to exist. *Math. Method Appl. Sci.* **2017**, *40*, 4128–4133. [CrossRef]
4. Wazwaz, A.M. Two wave mode higher-order modified KdV equations: Essential conditions for multiple soliton solutions to exist. *Int. J. Numer. Method H.* **2017**, *27*, 2223–2230. [CrossRef]
5. Alquran, M.; Sulaiman, T.A.; Yusuf, A. Kink-soliton, singular-kink-soliton and singular-periodic solutions for a new two-mode version of the Burger-Huxley model: Applications in nerve fibers and liquid crystals. *Opt. Quant. Electron.* **2021**, *53*, 227. [CrossRef]
6. Jaradat, I.; Alquran, M. Geometric perspectives of the two-mode upgrade of a generalized Fisher–Burgers equation that governs the propagation of two simultaneously moving waves. *J. Comput. Appl. Math.* **2022**, *404*, 113908. [CrossRef]
7. Lee, C.T.; Liu, J.L. A Hamiltonian model and soliton phenomenon for a two-mode KdV equation. *Rocky Mt. J. Math.* **2011**, *41*, 1273–1289. [CrossRef]
8. Lee, C.T.; Lee, C.C. On wave solutions of a weakly nonlinear and weakly dispersive two-mode wave system. *Wave Random Complex* **2013**, *23*, 56–76. [CrossRef]
9. Wazwaz, A.M. Multiple soliton solutions and other exact solutions for a two-mode KdV equation. *Math. Method Appl. Sci.* **2017**, *40*, 2277–2283. [CrossRef]
10. Xiao, Z.J.; Tian, B.; Zhen, H.L; Chai, J.; Wu, X.Y. Multi-soliton solutions and Bcklund transformation for a two-mode KdV equation in a fluid. *Wave Random Complex* **2017**, *27*, 1–14. [CrossRef]
11. Kumar, D.; Park, C.; Tamanna, N.; Paul, G.C.; Osman, M.S. Dynamics of two-mode Sawada-Kotera equation: Mathematical and graphical analysis of its dual-wave solutions. *Results Phys.* **2020**, *19*, 103581. [CrossRef]
12. Jaradat, I.; Alquran, M.; Momani, S.; Biswas, A. Dark and singular optical solutions with dual-mode nonlinear Schrödinger's equation and Kerr-law nonlinearity. *Optik* **2018**, *172*, 822–825. [CrossRef]
13. Abu Irwaq, I.; Alquran, M.; Jaradat, I.; Baleanu, D. New dual-mode Kadomtsev–Petviashvili model with strong–weak surface tension: Analysis and application. *Adv. Differ. Equ.* **2018**, *2018*, 433. [CrossRef]
14. Wazwaz, A.M. Two-mode Sharma-Tasso-Olver equation and two-mode fourth-order Burgers equation: Multiple kink solutions. *Alex. Eng. J.* **2018**, *57*, 1971–1976. [CrossRef]
15. Alquran, M.; Jaradat, I.; Baleanu, D. Shapes and dynamics of dual-mode Hirota–Satsuma coupled KdV equations: Exact traveling wave solutions and analysis. *Chin. J. Phys.* **2019**, *58*, 49–56. [CrossRef]
16. Wazwaz, A.M. Two-mode fifth-order KdV equations: Necessary conditions for multiple-soliton solutions to exist. *Nonlinear Dynam.* **2017**, *87*, 1685–1691. [CrossRef]
17. Kumar, S.; Mohan, B.; Kumar, R. Lump, soliton, and interaction solutions to a generalized two-mode higher-order nonlinear evolution equation in plasma physics. *Nonlinear Dyn.* **2022**, *110*, 693–704. [CrossRef]
18. Alquran, M.; Alhami, R. Convex-periodic, kink-periodic, peakon-soliton and kink bidirectional wave-solutions to new established two-mode generalization of cahn-allen equation. *Results Phys.* **2022**, *34*, 105257. [CrossRef]
19. Cimpoiasu, R.; Pauna, A.S. Complementary wave solutions for the long-short wave resonance model via the extended trial equation method and the generalized Kudryashov method. *Open Phys.* **2018**, *16*, 419–426. [CrossRef]
20. Ferdous, F.; Hafez, M.G.; Akther, S. Oblique traveling wave closed-form solutions to space-time fractional coupled dispersive long wave equation through the generalized exponential expansion method. *Int. J. Comput. Math.* **2022**, *8*, 142. [CrossRef]
21. Babalic, C.N. Complete integrability and complex solitons for generalized Volterra system with branched dispersion. *Int. J. Mod. Phys. B* **2020**, *34*, 2050274. [CrossRef]
22. Babalic, C.N. Integrable discretization of coupled Ablowitz-Ladik equations with branched dispersion. *Rom. J. Phys.* **2018**, *63*, 114.

23. Cimpoiasu, R.; Constantinescu, R. Invariant solutions of the Eckhaus-Kundu model with nonlinear dispersion and non-Kerr nonlinearities. *Wave Random Complex* **2021**, *31*, 331–341. [CrossRef]
24. Cimpoiasu, R.; Rezazadeh, H.; Florian, D.A.; Ahmad, H.; Nonlaopon, K.; Altanji, M. Symmetry reductions and invariant-group solutions for a two-dimensional Kundu-Mukherjee-Naskar model. *Results Phys.* **2021**, *28*, 104583. [CrossRef]
25. Khater, M.M. Computational and numerical wave solutions of the Caudrey–Dodd–Gibbon equation. *Heliyon* **2023**, *9*, e13511. [CrossRef]
26. Polat, M.; Oruç, Ö. A combination of Lie group-based high order geometric integrator and delta-shaped basis functions for solving Korteweg-de Vries (KdV) equation. *Int. J. Geom. M.* **2021**, *18*, 2150216. [CrossRef]
27. Hu, X.B.; Li, Y. Some results on the Caudrey-Dodd-Gibbon-Kotera-Sawada equation. *J. Phys. A-Math. Gen.* **1991**, *24*, 3205. [CrossRef]
28. Majeed, A.M.; Rafiq, V.; Kamran, M.; Abbas, M.; Inc, M. Analytical solutions of the fifth-order time fractional nonlinear evolution equations by the unified method. *Mod. Phys. Lett. B* **2022**, *36*, 2150546. [CrossRef]
29. Ionescu, C. The sp(3) BRST Hamiltonian formalism for the Yang-Mills fields. *Mod. Phys. Lett. A* **2008**, *23*, 737–775. [CrossRef]
30. Adeyemo, O.D.; Khalique, C.M. Lie group theory, stability analysis with dispersion property, new soliton solutions and conserved quantities of 3D generalized nonlinear wave equation in liquid containing gas bubbles with applications in mechanics of fluids, biomedical sciences and cell biology. *Commun. Nonlinear Sci.* **2023**, *123*, 107261.
31. Márquez, A.P.; Bruzón, M.S. Lie point symmetries, traveling wave solutions and conservation laws of a non-linear viscoelastic wave equation. *Mathematics* **2021**, *9*, 2131. [CrossRef]
32. Cimpoiasu, R. Conservation Laws and associated Lie symmetries for 2D Ricci flow model. *Rom. J. Phys.* **2013**, *58*, 519–528.
33. Cimpoiasu, R. Multiple invariant solutions of the 3 D potential Yu–Toda–Fukuyama equation via symmetry technique. *Int. J. Mod. Phys. B* **2020**, *34*, 2050188. [CrossRef]
34. Ionescu, C.; Constantinescu, R. Solving Nonlinear Second-Order Differential Equations through the Attached Flow Method. *Mathematics* **2022**, *10*, 2811. [CrossRef]
35. Henneaux, M.; Teitelboim, C. *Quantization of Gauge Systems*; Princeton University Press: Princeton, NJ, USA, 1992.
36. Alquran, M. Optical bidirectional wave-solutions to new two-mode extension of the coupled KdV–Schrodinger equations. *Opt. Quant. Electron.* **2021**, *53*, 588. [CrossRef]
37. Jaradat, I.; Alquran, M. Construction of solitary two-wave solutions for a new two-mode version of the Zakharov-Kuznetsov equation. *Mathematics* **2020**, *8*, 1127. [CrossRef]
38. Akbar, M.A.; Akinyemi, L.; Yao, S.W.; Jhangeer, A.; Rezazadeh, H.; Khater, M.M.; Ahmad, H.; Inc, M. Soliton solutions to the Boussinesq equation through sine-Gordon method and Kudryashov method. *Results Phys.* **2021**, *25*, 104228. [CrossRef]
39. Akbar, M.A.; Ali, N.H.M.; Tanjim, T. Outset of multiple soliton solutions to the nonlinear Schrodinger equation and the coupled Burgers equation. *J. Phys. Commun.* **2019**, *3*, 095013. [CrossRef]
40. Vijayakumar, V.; Nisar, K.S.; Chalishajar, D.; Shukla, A.; Malik, M.; Alsaadi, A.; Aldosary, S.F. A note on approximate controllability of fractional semilinear integrodifferential control systems via resolvent operators. *Fractal Fract* **2022**, *6*, 73. [CrossRef]
41. Xu, G.Q.; Wazwaz, A.M. Bidirectional solitons and interaction solutions for a new integrable fifth-order nonlinear equation with temporal and spatial dispersion. *Nonlinear Dyn.* **2020**, *101*, 581–595. [CrossRef]
42. Cimpoiasu, R.; Cimpoiasu, V.; Constantinescu, R. Nonlinear dynamical systems in various space-time dimensions. *Rom. J. Phys.* **2010**, *55*, 25–35.

Disclaimer/Publisher's Note: The statements, opinions and data contained in all publications are solely those of the individual author(s) and contributor(s) and not of MDPI and/or the editor(s). MDPI and/or the editor(s) disclaim responsibility for any injury to people or property resulting from any ideas, methods, instructions or products referred to in the content.

axioms MDPI

Article

Periodic Solutions of Quasi-Monotone Semilinear Multidimensional Hyperbolic Systems

Corrado Mascia

Dipartimento di Matematica "G. Castelnuovo", Università degli Studi di Roma "La Sapienza", P.le Aldo Moro 5, I-00185 Rome, Italy; corrado.mascia@uniroma1.it

Abstract: This paper deals with the Cauchy problem for a class of first-order semilinear hyperbolic equations of the form $\partial_t f_i + \sum_{j=1}^{d} \lambda_{ij}\partial_{x_j} f_i = Q_i(f)$. where $f_i = f_i(x,t)$ $(i = 1,\dots,n)$ and $x = (x_1,\cdots,x_d) \in \mathbb{R}^d$ $(n \geq 2, d \geq 1)$. Under assumption of the existence of a conserved quantity $\sum_i \alpha_i f_i$ for some $\alpha_1,\dots,\alpha_n > 0$, of (strong) quasimonotonicity and an additional assumption on the speed vectors $\Lambda_i = (\lambda_{i1},\cdots,\lambda_{id}) \in \mathbb{R}^d$—namely, span $\{\Lambda_j - \Lambda_k : j = 1,\dots,n\} = \mathbb{R}^d$ for any k—it is proved that the set of constant steady state $\{\bar f \in \mathbb{R}^n : Q(\bar f) = 0\}$ is asymptotically stable with respect to periodic perturbations, i.e., any initial data given by an periodic L^1−perturbations of a constant steady state $\bar f$ leads to a solution converging to another constant steady state $\bar g$ (uniquely determined by the initial condition) as $t \to +\infty$.

Keywords: semilinear hyperbolic systems; stability analysis; quasi-monotonicity

MSC: 35L60; 35B35; 35B40

1. Introduction

In this paper, we deal with the following system of equations:

$$\partial_t f_i + \sum_{j=1}^{d} \lambda_{ij}\partial_{x_j} f_i = Q_i(f). \tag{1}$$

Here, $f = f(x,t)$, where $f = (f_1,\dots,f_n)$ and $x = (x_1,\cdots,x_d) \in \mathbb{R}^d$ $(n \geq 2, d \geq 1)$. The vectors $\Lambda_i = (\lambda_{i1},\cdots,\lambda_{id}) \in \mathbb{R}^d$ are called *speeds*, and the function $Q = (Q_1,\dots,Q_n)^\top \in C^1(\mathbb{R}^n,\mathbb{R}^n)$ is the *collision term*. In the following, we set $DQ = (q_{ij}) = (\partial Q_i/\partial f_j)$. We assume throughout the paper that the speeds Λ_i satisfy

$$\text{span}\,\{\Lambda_j - \Lambda_k : j = 1,\dots,n\} = \mathbb{R}^d \qquad \forall k \in \{1,\dots,n\} \tag{2}$$

This obviously implies that $n \geq d+1$ and that span $\{\Lambda_1,\cdots,\Lambda_n\} = \mathbb{R}^d$.

We consider the Cauchy problem for (1), given by the initial condition

$$f(x,0) = f^0(x) = (f_1^0(x),\cdots,f_n^0(x)), \tag{3}$$

where $f_0 : \mathbb{R}^d \to \mathbb{R}^n$. Precise assumptions on the initial datum f_0 will be given later.

On the collision term, we make the hypothesis:

$$\sum_{i=1}^{n} \alpha_i Q_i = 0 \qquad \text{for some } \alpha_i > 0 \qquad \text{(conservation of mass)}, \tag{4}$$

$$q_{ij} = \frac{\partial Q_i}{\partial f_j} > 0 \qquad \forall i \neq j \qquad \text{(strong quasi-monotonicity)}. \tag{5}$$

Citation: Mascia, C. Periodic Solutions of Quasi-Monotone Semilinear Multidimensional Hyperbolic Systems. *Axioms* **2023**, *12*, 208. https://doi.org/10.3390/axioms12020208

Academic Editors: Hatıra Günerhan, Francisco Martínez González and Mohammed K. A. Kaabar

Received: 28 December 2022
Revised: 8 February 2023
Accepted: 10 February 2023
Published: 16 February 2023

Copyright: © 2023 by the authors. Licensee MDPI, Basel, Switzerland. This article is an open access article distributed under the terms and conditions of the Creative Commons Attribution (CC BY) license (https://creativecommons.org/licenses/by/4.0/).

Condition (4) corresponds to asking for conservation of the quantity $\int_\Omega \sum \alpha_i f_i$ for any $\Omega \subset \mathbb{R}^d$ and that any growth or decrease of it is caused by flux through the boundary $\partial\Omega$. Indeed,

$$\frac{d}{dt}\int_\Omega \sum_{i=1}^n \alpha_i f_i \, dx = -\int_\Omega \operatorname{div}\left(\sum_{i=1}^n \alpha_i \Lambda_i f_i\right) + \int_\Omega \sum_{i=1}^n \alpha_i Q_i = -\int_{\partial\Omega} \left(\sum_{i=1}^n \alpha_i \Lambda_i f_i, \mathbf{n}\right) ds,$$

where $\mathbf{n}$ represents the outward normal vector of $\partial\Omega$.

Concerning condition (5), let us recall that for weakly coupled quasimonotone systems, it was proved in [1] that comparison results hold. In case of system (1) the weak quasi-monotonicity condition corresponds to asking a weaker version of (5)

$$\frac{\partial Q_i}{\partial f_j}(s) \geq 0 \qquad \forall i \neq j \quad \text{(weak quasi-monotonicity)}, \tag{6}$$

Hence, under this assumption, given f^0, g^0 initial data for the Cauchy problem (1)–(3) and denoted by f and g the corresponding solutions, there holds

$$f_i^0(x) \leq g_i^0(x) \quad \forall i \qquad \Rightarrow \qquad f_i(x,t) \leq g_i(x,t) \quad \forall i$$

for almost all $(x,t) \in \mathbb{R}^d \times (0,\infty)$. In order to prove asymptotic stability of the manifold of constant states, the stronger assumption (5) is needed. In the class of quasimonotone weakly coupled systems of the form (1), this assumption is sharp, as showed by the example contained in Section 3.

Let us introduce the following notation. Given $P = (P_1, \cdots, P_d) \in \mathbb{R}^d$, let

$$\Omega_P := [0, P_1] \times \cdots \times [0, P_d] \subset \mathbb{R}^d,$$

and, for $\phi = (\phi_1, \cdots, \phi_n) : \Omega_P \to \mathbb{R}^n$,

$$\|\phi\|_{1,\alpha} := \sum_{i=1}^n \alpha_i \int_{\Omega_P} |\phi_i(x)| \, dx.$$

Similar definitions can be given for the derivatives of ϕ. In what follows, the solutions of the problem are in spaces $L^1_\alpha(\Omega_P)$ or in $W^{1,1}_\alpha(\Omega_P)$ considered with the norms above defined. Finally, we will say that $\phi = (\phi_1, \cdots, \phi_n) : \mathbb{R}^d \to \mathbb{R}^n$ is a $P-$*periodic function* if $f(x+P) = f(x)$ for any $x \in \mathbb{R}^d$.

Theorem 1. *Assume (2), (4) and (5). Let $\bar{f} \in \mathbb{R}^n$ be such that $Q(\bar{f}) = 0$, $f_0(x) - \bar{f} \in L^1(\Omega_P, \mathbb{R}^n)$ and $P-$periodic for some $P \in \mathbb{R}^d$.*

Then, there is a unique global solution $f = f(x,t)$ of (1), (3) and $f \in C([0,\infty); \bar{f} + L^1_\alpha(\Omega_p, \mathbb{R}^n))$. Moreover, there exists (unique) $\bar{g} = (\bar{g}_1, \cdots, \bar{g}_n) \in \mathbb{R}^n$ with $Q(\bar{g}) = 0$ such that

$$\sum_{i=1}^n \alpha_i \int_{\Omega_P} (f_{0,i}(x) - \bar{g}_i) \, dx = 0 \quad \text{and} \quad \lim_{t\to+\infty} \|f(\cdot,t) - \bar{g}\|_{1,\alpha} = 0. \tag{7}$$

The above Theorem 1 gives sufficient condition for global orbital attractivity of the equilibrium manifold $\{\bar{f} : Q(\bar{f}) = 0\}$: any initial datum that is an L^1 perturbation of an equilibrium state gives raise to a solution asymptotically converging to a constant equilibrium state.

Since the comparison property holds, it is possible to prove a result of asymptotic stability of equilibrium states, i.e., a local result. Since the localization is guaranteed by comparison, the theorem is for L^∞ perturbations.

Theorem 2. *Assume (2), (4). Let $\bar{f} \in \mathbb{R}^n$ be such that*

$$Q(\bar{f}) = 0 \quad \text{and} \quad \frac{\partial Q_i}{\partial f_j}(\bar{f}) > 0 \quad (\forall i \neq j).$$

Consequently, there exists $\varepsilon > 0$ such that, for any $f_0 \in L^\infty(\Omega_P, \mathbb{R}^n)$ with $\|f_0 - \bar{f}\|_\infty < \varepsilon$, there exists a unique $\bar{g} \in \mathbb{R}^n$ with $Q(\bar{g}) = 0$ such that

$$\lim_{t \to +\infty} \|f(\cdot, t) - \bar{g}\|_{1,\alpha} = 0. \tag{8}$$

Before proving the result (see Section 2), we give some examples of semilinear hyperbolic systems fitting in our assumptions.

A first example fitting in the class (1) is the well-known discrete velocity Boltzmann model, introduced by Carleman,

$$\begin{cases} \partial_t f_1 - \partial_x f_1 = f_2^2 - f_1^2, \\ \partial_t f_2 + \partial_x f_2 = f_1^2 - f_2^2. \end{cases}$$

This system is clearly of the form (1) and hypothesis (4) holds for $\alpha_1 = \alpha_2 = 1$. Moreover, if we consider positive solutions, assumption (5) is satisfied and the conclusion of the theorem holds.

More results on large-time behavior of discrete velocity Boltzmann models are contained in [2]. There is considered a one-dimensional semilinear hyperbolic system with quadratic collision term. Moreover, conservation of mass, of momentum and entropy are assumed to be decreasing. On the contrary, under our assumptions, momentum cannot be conserved, and no hypothesis on entropy is made. The dissipation mechanism is encoded in the quasi-monotonicity condition (6).

Another significant class of systems of the form (1) enjoying the above assumptions is considered in [3]. The limit is studied as $\varepsilon \to 0$ of the solutions to

$$\partial_t f_i + \sum_{j=1}^{d} \lambda_{ij} \partial_{x_j} f_i = \frac{1}{\varepsilon}(M_i(u) - f_i), \tag{9}$$

where $u = \sum_i f_i$. The function $M = (M_1, \ldots, M_n)$ is assumed to be such that $\sum_i M_i(s) = s$ and $0 < M_i'(s) < 1$ for any s under consideration, so that assumptions (4) and (5) are satisfied. Moreover, additional conditions of consistency are assumed with the quasilinear equation

$$\partial_t u + \sum_{j=1}^{d} \partial_{x_j} A_j(u) = 0, \tag{10}$$

with $A_1, \ldots, A_d$ given flux functions. Such condition takes the form

$$\sum_{i=1}^{n} \lambda_{ij} M_i(s) = A_j(s) \qquad \forall j = 1, \ldots, d. \tag{11}$$

It is proved in [3] that the function $(f_1^\varepsilon, \ldots, f_n^\varepsilon)$ solution to the Cauchy problem for (9) converges in L^1 to some $(f_1^0, \ldots, f_n^0)$ such that $u^0 = \sum f_i^0$ is the entropy solution of the corresponding Cauchy problem for (10). See also [4] for the reduced version in the case $n = 2$.

In this context, there is an interesting connection between our result on asymptotic behavior and this singular limit result. Indeed, it is well known that the entropy solution for conservation law with initial periodic data converges to a constant as $t \to +\infty$. Since the entropy solution is approximated by solution of (9), it seems natural to ask if such asymptotic behavior is inherited by the same property of the semilinear system. This is exactly what this paper aims to achieve: to give a sufficient condition for asymptotic dissipation of periodic perturbations of constant steady states.

Let us stress that some general results on asymptotic behavior for conservation law with initial periodic data are considered in [5], proving dissipation of such perturbations of constant states. However, while in that case the dissipation is caused by the nonlinear transport effect, here, the main part of the dissipation is encoded in the structure of the zero-order term Q. Therefore, the dissipative mechanism seems rather different, at least from the point of view of differential equations. Let us stress that a discrepancy still remains: here, we also assume (2), while in [3], condition (11) is assumed.

2. Proof of Theorems 1 and 2

This section is devoted to the proof of Theorems 1 and 2. In the first part, we show the existence of the constant state $\bar{g} = (\bar{g}_1, \cdots, \bar{g}_n) \in \mathbb{R}^n$ such that

$$\sum_{i=1}^{n} \alpha_i \int\limits_{\Omega_P} (f_{0,i}(x) - \bar{g}_i)\, dx = 0.$$

In the second part, we consider the asymptotic behavior of the periodic perturbations of $\bar{g}$.

Lemma 1. *Let $Q = (Q_1, \ldots, Q_n)^\top = (q_{ij})_{i,j=1,\cdots,n}$ be a $n \times n$ matrix such that, for some $\alpha_i > 0$,*

$$\sum_{i=1}^{n} \alpha_i q_{ij} = 0 \quad j = 1, \cdots, n, \qquad \text{and} \qquad q_{ij} > 0 \quad \forall i \neq j.$$

Then, any square submatrix of order $n-1$ is nondegenerate. In particular,

$$\mathrm{rank}\, Q = n - 1.$$

Proof. Let $e_i := (q_{i1}, \cdots, q_{in}) \in \mathbb{R}^n$ for $i = 1, \cdots, n$. Since $\sum_i \alpha_i e_i = 0$, then let $Q = 0$.

The conclusion holds if there exist $n-1$ vectors in $\{e_1, \cdots, e_n\}$—linearly independent. Suppose by contradiction that this is not the case and assume (without restriction) that there is $(\beta_1, \cdots, \beta_{n-1}) \neq (0, \cdots, 0)$ such that $\sum\limits_{i=1}^{n-1} \beta_i e_i = 0$. Therefore,

$$\sum_{i=1}^{n-1} (k\beta_i - \alpha_i) q_{ij} = \alpha_n q_{nj} \qquad \forall j = 1, \cdots, n, \forall k \in \mathbb{R}. \tag{12}$$

If $\beta_i > 0$ for any i, then we can choose k such that $k\beta_i - \alpha_i > 0$ for any i. For $j = n$ in (2.01), we arrive at a contradiction:

$$0 > -\sum_{i=1}^{n-1} \alpha_j q_{nj} = \alpha_n q_{nn} = \sum_{i=1}^{n-1} (k\beta_i - \alpha_i) q_{in} > 0.$$

Hence, $\beta_h = \min\{\beta_1, \cdots, \beta_{n-1}\} < 0$. Let $k = \min\{\alpha_1, \cdots, \alpha_{n-1}\}/\beta_h < 0$ and $j = h$ in (2.01). Then

$$\sum_{i \neq h} (k\beta_i - \alpha_i) q_{ih} = q_{nh} > 0. \tag{13}$$

Since $\beta_h \leq \beta_i$ for any i and $k < 0$, it follows that

$$k\beta_i - \alpha_i \leq k\beta_h - \alpha_i = \min\{\alpha_1, \cdots, \alpha_n\} - \alpha_i \leq 0,$$

contradicting (13). $\square$

Proposition 1. *Let* $Q = (Q_i)_{i=1,\cdots,n}$ *and* $\bar{f} = (\bar{f}_i)_{i=1,\cdots,n}$ *be such that*

$$\sum_{i=1}^{n} \alpha_i Q_i = 0 \quad (\alpha_i > 0), \qquad rank\left(\frac{\partial Q_i}{\partial f_j}\right) = n-1 \quad and \quad Q(\bar{f}) = 0.$$

Then, for any $C \in \mathbb{R}$*, there exists a unique* $\bar{g} = (\bar{g}_1, \cdots, \bar{g}_n) \in \mathbb{R}^n$ *such that*

$$Q(\bar{g}) = 0 \qquad and \qquad \sum_{i=1}^{n} \alpha_i \bar{g}_i \, dx = C.$$

Proof. First of all, we prove uniqueness. Assume that there exists $f = (f_i)$ and $g = (g_i)$ such that $Q(f) = Q(g) = 0$ and $\sum_{i=1}^{n} \alpha_i f_i = \sum_{i=1}^{n} \alpha_i g_i$. Then, it holds that

$$\begin{cases} 0 = Q_i(f) - Q_i(g) = \sum_{j=1}^{n} \frac{\partial Q_i}{\partial f_j}(\xi)(f_j - g_j), & i = 1, \cdots, n, \\ 0 = \sum_{j=1}^{n} \alpha_j (f_j - g_j). \end{cases} \tag{14}$$

Let $e_0 := (\alpha_1, \cdots, \alpha_n)$ and $e_n := (q_{ij})_{i,j=1,\cdots,n}$ where $q_{ij} := \partial Q_i / \partial f_j$. We claim that there are $n-1$ vectors in $\{e_1, \cdots, e_n\}$, say, for simplicity, $e_1, \cdots, e_{n-1}$, such that $e_0, \cdots, e_{n-1}$ are linearly independent. □

By Lemma 1, there are $n-1$ linearly independent vectors in $\{e_1, \cdots, e_n\}$, say, $e_1, \cdots, e_{n-1}$. Assume by contradiction that there is $(\gamma_0, \cdots, \gamma_{n-1}) \neq (0, \cdots, 0)$ such that $\sum_{i=0}^{n-1} \gamma_i e_i = 0$. Moreover, $\gamma_0 \neq 0$. Thus, there are $(\beta_1, \cdots, \beta_{n-1}) \neq (0, \cdots, 0)$ such that $e_0 = \sum_{i=1}^{n-1} \beta_i e_i$. Hence, it holds that

$$\begin{cases} \sum_{i=1}^{n-1} \beta_i q_{ij} = \alpha_i & j = 1, \cdots, n, \\ \sum_{i=1}^{n-1} \alpha_i q_{ij} = -\alpha_n q_{nj} & j = 1, \cdots, n \end{cases}$$

Multiplying by k the first of the two equation and subtracting the other, we obtain

$$\sum_{i=1}^{n-1} (k\beta_i - \alpha_j) q_{ij} = k\alpha_i - \alpha_n q_{nj}, \qquad j = 1, \cdots, n \quad \forall k \in \mathbb{R}. \tag{15}$$

If $\beta_i \leq 0$ for any i, then $k\beta_i - \alpha_j < 0$ for any $k > 0$ and for any i. Choosing $j = n$ in (15), we obtain a contradiction.

Therefore, $\beta_h := \max\{\beta_1, \cdots, \beta_{n-1}\} > 0$. Choose $k = \max\{\alpha_1, \cdots, \alpha_{n-1}\}/\beta_h > 0$. Then,

$$k\beta_i - \alpha_j \leq k\beta_h - \alpha_j = \max\{\alpha_1, \cdots, \alpha_{n-1}\} - \alpha_j \leq 0$$

Putting $j = n$ in (15), we arrive at a contradiction. Thus, $e_0, \cdots, e_{n-1}$ are linearly independent and the conclusion follows from (14).

In order to prove existence, let us introduce the set

$$\mathcal{C} := \{C \in \mathbb{R} : \exists \bar{g} = (\bar{g}_1, \cdots, \bar{g}_n) \in \mathbb{R}^n \text{ s.t. } Q(\bar{g}) = 0 \text{ and } \sum_{i=1}^{n} \alpha_i \bar{g}_i \, dx = C\}.$$

By definition, $\mathcal{C}$ is closed and since $Q(\bar{f}) = 0$, $\mathcal{C} \neq \emptyset$. Moreover, since rank $\left(\frac{\partial Q_i}{\partial f_j}\right) = n-1$, we can apply Implicit Function Theorem and deduce that $\mathcal{C}$ is an open set. Therefore, $\mathcal{C} = \mathbb{R}$.

Proof of Theorem 1. Let f, g be solutions of (1). Then, it holds that

$$\partial_t(f_i - g_i) + \sum_{i=1}^{d} \lambda_{ij}\partial_{x_j}(f_i - g_i) = \big(Q_i(f) - Q_i(g)\big). \tag{16}$$

Multiplying (16) by $\alpha_i \mathrm{sgn}\,(f_i - g_i)$, integrating on Ω_P and summing on i, we obtain

$$\frac{d}{dt}\|f - g\|_{1,\alpha} = \int_{\Omega_P} I(x,t)\,\mathrm{dx}, \tag{17}$$

where

$$I(x,t) := \sum_{i=1}^{n} \alpha_i \mathrm{sgn}\,(f_i - g_i)(Q_i(f) - Q_i(g)).$$

Using Lagrange theorem on $Q_i(f) - Q_i(g)$, we obtain

$$\begin{aligned} I(x,t) &= \sum_{i,j=1}^{n} \alpha_i \mathrm{sgn}\,(f_i - g_i)\frac{\partial Q_i}{\partial f_j}(f_j - g_j) = \\ &= \sum_{i=1}^{n}\sum_{j\neq i} \alpha_i \mathrm{sgn}\,(f_i - g_i)\frac{\partial Q_i}{\partial f_j}(f_j - g_j) + \sum_{i=1}^{n} \alpha_i \frac{\partial Q_i}{\partial f_i}\,|f_i - g_i|. \end{aligned} \tag{18}$$

By hypothesis (4), we deduce

$$\alpha_i \frac{\partial Q_i}{\partial f_i} = -\sum_{j\neq i} \alpha_j \frac{\partial Q_j}{\partial f_i},$$

therefore (changing the order of summation in the first sum),

$$\begin{aligned} I &= \sum_{i,j=1}^{n} \alpha_i \mathrm{sgn}\,(f_i - g_i)\frac{\partial Q_i}{\partial f_j}(f_j - g_j) - \sum_{i,j=1}^{n} \alpha_j \frac{\partial Q_j}{\partial f_i}|f_i - g_i| = \\ &= \sum_{j=1}^{n}\Big(\sum_{i=1}^{n} \alpha_i \Big[\mathrm{sgn}\,(f_i - g_i)\mathrm{sgn}\,(f_j - g_j) - 1\Big]\frac{\partial Q_i}{\partial f_j}\Big)|f_j - g_j| \le 0. \end{aligned} \tag{19}$$

From this estimate, we immediately deduce global existence and L^1–continuous dependence on the initial data of solution of (1), (3) under the assumptions of the Theorem. By (19), we deduce the result for general initial data by density argument. □

In order to obtain compactness property, we restrict our attention to initial data f_0 such that

$$\|\partial_{x_h} f_0\|_{1,\alpha} < +\infty, \qquad \forall h.$$

From (1), deriving with respect to x_h, and setting $w_{ih} := \partial_{x_h} f_i$, we obtain

$$\partial_t w_{ih} + \sum_{i=1}^{d} \lambda_{ij}\partial_{x_j} w_{ih} = \sum_{i=1}^{n} \frac{\partial Q_i}{\partial f_j}(f) w_{jh}. \tag{20}$$

Multiplying by $\alpha_i \mathrm{sgn}\, w_{ih}$, integrating on Ω_P and summing on i, we obtain

$$\frac{d}{dt}\|w_h\|_{1,\alpha} = \int_{\Omega_P} \sum_{i,j} \alpha_i \mathrm{sgn}\, w_{ih} \frac{\partial Q_i}{\partial f_j}(f) w_{jh}\,\mathrm{dx},$$

where $w_h = (w_{1h}, \cdots, w_{nh})$. Proceeding as above, we obtain

$$\frac{d}{dt}\|w_h\|_{1,\alpha} = \int_{\Omega_p} J(x,t)\,\mathrm{dx} \tag{21}$$

where

$$J(x,t) := \sum_{j=1}^{n}\Big(\sum_{i=1}^{n}\alpha_i\Big[\text{sgn } w_{ih}\text{sgn } w_{jh}-1\Big]\frac{\partial Q_i}{\partial f_j}\Big)|w_{jh}| \leq 0.$$

Let $\bar{f} \in \mathbb{R}^n$ be such that $Q(\bar{f}) = 0$ and assume f_0 be a $P-$periodic function, such that $f_0(x) - \bar{f} \in L^1(\Omega_P, \mathbb{R}^n)$ and $\|\partial_{x_h} f_0\|_{1,\alpha} < +\infty$ for any $h = 1, \cdots, n$. Then, by the previous calculations, for any $t > 0$,

$$\|f - \bar{f}\|_{1,\alpha} + \|\partial_{x_h} f\|_{1,\alpha} \leq \|f_0 - \bar{f}\|_{1,\alpha} + \|\partial_{x_h} f_0\|_{1,\alpha}.$$

These estimates provide the required compactness.

Next, let us introduce the following definition:

$$\mathcal{F}_s := \{f(\cdot,t) : \Omega_P \to \mathbb{R}^n : t > s\}.$$

From (19) and (21), we deduce that $\mathcal{F}_s - \bar{f}$ is a compact set of L^1_α, for any s. Thus,

$$\emptyset \neq \mathcal{A} := \bigcap_{s>0} \mathcal{F}_s \subset \bar{f} + L^1_\alpha.$$

Let $a_0 \in \mathcal{A}$ and let $a = a(x,t)$ be the solution of (1) with initial condition $f(x,0) = a_0(x)$. Then,

$$\|a(\cdot,t) - \bar{f}\|_{1,\alpha} = \text{constant} \qquad \forall \bar{f} \in \mathbb{R}^n \text{ s.t. } Q(\bar{f}) = 0.$$

Therefore, we deduce from (19) with $f = a$ and $g = \bar{f} \in \mathbb{R}^n$ with $Q(\bar{f}) = 0$

$$\sum_{i,j=1}^{n}\alpha_i\Big[\text{sgn }(a_i - \bar{f}_i)\text{sgn }(a_j - \bar{f}_j) - 1\Big]\frac{\partial Q_i}{\partial f_j}|a_j - \bar{f}_j| = 0,$$

for any $t > 0$ and almost all $x \in \Omega_P$. Therefore, for any $i, j = 1, \ldots, n$,

$$\Big[\text{sgn }(a_i - \bar{f}_i)\text{sgn }(a_j - \bar{f}_j) - 1\Big]\frac{\partial Q_i}{\partial f_j}|a_j - \bar{f}_j| = 0, \quad \forall t > 0, \text{ a.e. in } \Omega_P. \tag{22}$$

From assumption (5), it follows that if $i \neq j$,

$$\Big[\text{sgn }(a_i - \bar{f}_i)\text{sgn }(a_j - \bar{f}_j) - 1\Big]|a_j - \bar{f}_j| = 0, \quad \forall t > 0, \text{ a.e. in } \Omega_P.$$

Hence, for any i and for any $t > 0$, a.e. in Ω_P

$$a_i(x,t) \leq \bar{f}_i \quad \forall i \qquad \text{or} \qquad \bar{f}_i \leq a_i(x,t) \quad \forall i. \tag{23}$$

Note that if $\sum k_i a_i = \sum k_i b_i$ for some a_i, b_i with $a_i \leq b_i$ for any i, then either $k_j \leq 0$ for some $j \in \{1, \ldots, n\}$ or $a_i = b_i$ for any i. Indeed, assuming by contradiction that $k_i > 0$ for any i, then $\sum_{i=1}^{n} k_i(a_i - b_i) = 0$ implies $a_i = b_i$ for any i. For any $t > 0$ and for almost any $x \in \Omega_p$, by Proposition 1, there exists a unique $\bar{g} = (\bar{g}_1, \ldots, \bar{g}_n)$ such that $Q(\bar{g}) = 0$ and $\sum \alpha_i \bar{g}_i = \sum \alpha_i a_i(x,t)$. Hence, by (23) and by the previous statement, we find that $a_i(x,t) = \bar{g}_i$ for any i. Therefore, we have proved that

$$Q(a(x,t)) = 0 \qquad \forall t > 0, \quad \text{a.e. in } \Omega_P.$$

Here, we stress that, since Q is Lipschitz-continuous and $a(\cdot,t) \to a_0(\cdot)$ as $t \to 0^+$ in L^p, we can deduce that any function $a_0 \in \mathcal{A}$ takes values in the equilibrium manifold of Q, i.e., $Q(a_0) = 0$ a.e. for any $a_0 \in \mathcal{A}$. Let us note that this conclusion is a consequence of assumptions (6) and $\text{rank}(\partial Q_i/\partial f_j) = n - 1$.

At this point, we have proved that $a = (a_1, \ldots, a_n)$ is a solution of

$$\partial_t a_i + \sum_{i=1}^{d} \lambda_{ij} \partial_{x_j} a_i = 0, \qquad a(x,0) = a_0(x).$$

Hence, we know that a is

$$a(x,t) = (a_1(x - \Lambda_1 t), \ldots, a_n(x - \Lambda_n t)),$$

where $\Lambda_i = (\lambda_{i1}, \ldots, \lambda_{id})$ are the speeds defined at the very beginning.

In order to conclude the proof, we have to show that a is indeed a constant function. This is achieved by the following

Proposition 2. *Assume the same hypothesis of Theorem 1. Let $\phi = (\phi_1, \ldots, \phi_n) \in L^1(\Omega_p, \mathbb{R}^n)$ be such that*

$$Q(\phi_1(x - \Lambda_1 t), \ldots, \phi_n(x - \Lambda_n t)) = 0 \qquad \textit{for almost any } (x,t) \in \Omega_P, \tag{24}$$

then there exists $c_i \in \mathbb{R}$ such that

$$\phi_i(x) = c_i \qquad \forall i = 1, \ldots, n, \quad \textit{for almost any } x \in \Omega_P.$$

Proof of Proposition 2. First of all, let us assume that $\phi \in C^1(\Omega_P, \mathbb{R}^n)$. Calculating $Q(\phi_1(x - \Lambda_1 t), \ldots, \phi_n(x - \Lambda_n t))$ at $x = \Lambda_j t$ and deriving with respect to t, we obtain

$$\sum_{h=1}^{n} \sum_{k=1}^{d} \frac{\partial Q_l}{\partial f_h} \frac{\partial \phi_h}{\partial x_k} (\lambda_{jk} - \lambda_{hk}) = 0 \qquad \forall l = 1, \ldots, n.$$

Setting $w_h = \sum_k \frac{\partial \phi_h}{\partial x_k} (\lambda_{jk} - \lambda_{hk}) = \nabla \phi_h \cdot (\Lambda_j - \Lambda_h)$, we arrive at the linear system

$$\sum_{h=1}^{n} q_{lh} w_h = 0.$$

Since $w_j = 0$ and any square submatrix of (q_{ij}) of order $n-1$ is on degenerate (Lemma 1), we deduce that $w_h = 0$ for any h. Rewriting

$$\nabla \phi_h \cdot (\Lambda_j - \Lambda_h) = 0 \qquad \forall h, j.$$

Since the set $\Lambda_1 - \Lambda_h, \ldots, \Lambda_n - \Lambda_h$ spans all $\mathbb{R}^d$, $\nabla \phi_h = 0$ and the conclusion follows.

The general case for ϕ can be proved by the density argument. Indeed, given $\phi \in L^1(\Omega_P, \mathbb{R}^n)$ with values in a regular subset of $\mathbb{R}^n$, say, Γ, then there exists a sequence $\phi_j \in C^1(\Omega_P, \mathbb{R}^n)$ such that

$$\phi_j(\Omega_P) \subset \Gamma \qquad \forall j, \qquad \lim_{j \to \infty} \|\phi_j - \phi\|_1 = 0.$$

Therefore, $Q(\phi(x)) = 0$ implies $Q(\phi_j(x)) = 0$. By the previous analysis, ϕ_j is constant for any j, and so, passing to the limit, ϕ is constant too. □

This concludes the proof of the Proposition and, consequently, of Theorem 1. Theorem 2 can be proved following the same approach by applying at the very beginning comparison results and regularity of Q in order to guarantees that condition (5) is satisfied for any value of f under consideration.

3. Some Examples and Counterexamples

3.1. A Counterexample about the Condition on Λ_i

Here, we want to show that if for some k it holds $\text{span}\{\Lambda_i - \Lambda_k\}_{i=1,\dots,n} \neq \mathbb{R}^d$, then system (1) has nonconstant periodic traveling waves, which precludes the asymptotic stability of the set $\{\bar{f} : Q(\bar{f}) = 0\}$.

Therefore, assume that $\text{span}\{\Lambda_i - \Lambda_n\}_{i=1,\dots,n} \neq \mathbb{R}^d$, then, by changing the x variable $x \to x - \Lambda_n t$, we obtain a system of the same form with speeds $\tilde{\Lambda}_1, \dots, \tilde{\Lambda}_n$ such that $\text{span}\{\tilde{\Lambda}_i\}_{i=1,\dots,n-1} \neq \mathbb{R}^d$ and $\tilde{\Lambda}_n = 0$.

Without restriction, assume $e_1 \equiv (1, 0, \cdots, 0) \in \text{span}\{\tilde{\Lambda}_1, \dots, \tilde{\Lambda}_{n-1}\}^\perp$. Then, we look for a solution to (1) in the form

$$f(x) \equiv (f_1, \dots, f_n)(x) = (c_1, \dots, c_n) g(x_1) \equiv c g(x_1), \tag{25}$$

with the vector $c \in \mathbb{R}^n$ and the function $g \in C^1(\mathbb{R})$ to be determined. By hypothesis on e_1, it follows $\tilde{\lambda}_{i1} = 0$ for any i, so that

$$\sum_{j=1}^{d} \tilde{\lambda}_{ij} \partial_{x_j} f_i = \sum_{j=1}^{d} \tilde{\lambda}_{ij} c_i \partial_{x_j} g(x_1) = \tilde{\lambda}_{i1} c_i g'(x_1) = 0.$$

Next, we impose that $Q(f) = 0$. In the case of linear collision term Q, that is, $Q_i(f) = \sum_{j=1}^{n} q_{ij} f_j$, we obtain

$$Q_i(f_i(x)) = \left(\sum_{j=1}^{n} q_{ij} c_j \right) g(x_1) = 0 \qquad \forall x \in \mathbb{R}^d.$$

Hence, by choosing $c \in \mathbb{R}^n$ so that $\sum_{j=1}^{n} q_{ij} c_j = 0$ (recall that $\text{rank}(q_{ij}) = n - 1$), we find that any function of the form (25) is solution of (1) for any function $g \in C^1(\mathbb{R})$. In the nonlinear case, we can conclude the same kind of result by applying the Implicit Function Theorem close to a constant steady state. Coming back to the original variable x, we obtain a nonconstant traveling wave solution with speed of propagation Λ_k.

3.2. The One-Dimensional 2 × 2 Linear Example

It is interesting to stress with a one-dimensional 2×2 linear example fitting in the form (1) that in the class of weakly coupled quasimonotone systems, the assumptions of Theorem 1 may not be weakened. Consider the system

$$\begin{cases} \partial_t f_1 - \lambda \partial_x f_1 = -a f_1 + b f_2, \\ \partial_t f_2 + \lambda \partial_x f_2 = +a f_1 - b f_2, \end{cases} \tag{26}$$

where $a, b \in \mathbb{R}$ and $\lambda \geq 0$ (the general one-dimensional 2×2 case can be reduced to this one by a simple change of variables). The assumption (5) corresponds to $a, b > 0$, while (6) reads in this case as $a, b \geq 0$. It is also interesting to stress that

$$\text{rank}\left(\frac{\partial Q_i}{\partial f_j} \right) = \text{rank}\begin{pmatrix} -a & +b \\ +a & -b \end{pmatrix} = 1 \qquad \Longleftrightarrow \qquad (a, b) \neq (0, 0),$$

(for the rôle of condition $\text{rank}(\partial Q_i / \partial f_j) = n - 1$, see Proposition 1).

Hence, if we choose $a > b = 0$, we have a weak quasimonotone system that is not a strong quasimonotone and that has Jacobian of the collision term Q of rank one.

Given the initial condition

$$(f_1, f_2)(x, 0) = (f_1^0, f_2^0)(x),$$

the solution is given by the explicit formula

$$\begin{cases} f_1(x,t) = f_1^0(x+\lambda t)e^{-at}, \\ f_2(x,t) = f_2^0(x-\lambda t) + a\int_0^t f_1^0(x-\lambda(t-\tau)+\lambda\tau)e^{-a\lambda\tau}\,d\tau. \end{cases}$$

Then, it is immediate to see that if $f_1^0 \equiv 0$, the solution is

$$(f_1, f_2)(x,t) = (0, f_2^0(x-\lambda t)),$$

that does not converge to any constant state.

The same class of system can be used to show the necessity of conditions on the speeds λ_{ij}, in this case $-\lambda, \lambda$. Indeed, assume $\lambda = 0$ (so that hypothesis of Theorems 1 and 2 do not hold). Then, the system (26) reduces to a system of ordinary differential equations of the form

$$f_1' = -af_1 + bf_2, \quad f_2' = +af_1 - bf_2. \tag{27}$$

The asymptotic behavior is determined by the eigenvalues and corresponding eigenvector of the matrix $A = \begin{pmatrix} -a & +b \\ +a & -b \end{pmatrix}$. A straightforward computation reveals that the eigenvalues are 0 and $-(a+b)$, so that if the system satisfies (5), i.e., $a, b > 0$, then the solution asymptotically belongs to the set $\{(f_1, f_2) : af_1 = bf_2\}$, with no convergence to constant states for general initial data.

Finally, we conclude with some heuristics again for system (26), showing from a different point of view where the asymptotic stability comes from. Applying the Fourier analysis, we obtain the following system of ordinary differential equations

$$\begin{cases} \hat{f}_1' = (-a + i\lambda k)\hat{f}_1 + b\hat{f}_2, \\ \hat{f}_2' = +a\hat{f}_1 + (-b - i\lambda k)\hat{f}_2. \end{cases} \tag{28}$$

Stability analysis corresponds to looking for the sign of the real part of any eigenvalue μ of the matrix of coefficients in the right-hand side of (28). Setting $\mu = X + iY$, we obtain the algebraic system

$$\begin{cases} X^2 - Y^2 + (a+b)X + \lambda^2 k^2 = 0, \\ 2XY + (a+b)Y - \lambda k(b-a) = 0, \end{cases}$$

from which we deduce (for $\lambda > 0$)

$$k^2 = F(X) := -\frac{X(X+a+b)\left(X + \frac{a+b}{2}\right)^2}{\lambda^2 (X+a)(X+b)}.$$

Imposing the necessary condition of stability $F(X) < 0$ for any $X > 0$, we deduce that $a, b \geq 0$, which corresponds to the weak quasimonotonicity assumption. For small X, we have for $a, b > 0$

$$k^2 = -F(X) = -\frac{(a+b)^3}{4\lambda^2 ab}X + o(X) \qquad \text{as } X \to 0,$$

so that the strong quasimonotonicity assumption corresponds to asking that the function F has finite negative slope at $X = 0$.

Funding: This research received no external funding.

Data Availability Statement: Data sharing not applicable.

Acknowledgments: The author thanks the referees for the careful reading of the manuscript.

Conflicts of Interest: The author declares no conflict of interest.

References

1. Hanouzet, B.; Natalini, R. Weakly coupled systems of quasilinear hyperbolic equations. *Differ. Integral Equ.* **1996**, *9*, 1279–1292. [CrossRef]
2. Beale, J.T. Large-time behavior of discrete velocity Boltzmann equations. *Commun. Math. Phys.* **1986**, *106*, 659–678. [CrossRef]
3. Natalini, R. A discrete kinetic approximation of entropy solutions to multidimensional scalar conservation laws. *J. Differ. Equ.* **1998**, *148*, 292–317. [CrossRef]
4. Natalini, R. Convergence to equilibrium for the relaxation approximations of conservation laws. *Comm. Pure Appl. Math.* **1996**, *49*, 795–823. [CrossRef]
5. Chen, G.-Q.; Frid, H. Decay of Entropy Solutions of Nonlinear Conservation Laws. *Arch. Ration. Mech. Anal.* **1999**, *146*, 95–127. [CrossRef]

Disclaimer/Publisher's Note: The statements, opinions and data contained in all publications are solely those of the individual author(s) and contributor(s) and not of MDPI and/or the editor(s). MDPI and/or the editor(s) disclaim responsibility for any injury to people or property resulting from any ideas, methods, instructions or products referred to in the content.

axioms

MDPI

Article

Hierarchies of the Korteweg–de Vries Equation Related to Complex Expansion and Perturbation

Tatyana V. Redkina [1], Arthur R. Zakinyan [1,2,*], Robert G. Zakinyan [1,2] and Olesya B. Surneva [1]

1 North-Caucasus Center for Mathematical Research, North-Caucasus Federal University, 1 Pushkin Street, 355017 Stavropol, Russia; tvr59@mail.ru (T.V.R.); zakinyan@mail.ru (R.G.Z.); surnevao@mail.ru (O.B.S.)
2 Physical-Technical Faculty, North-Caucasus Federal University, 1 Pushkin Street, 355017 Stavropol, Russia
* Correspondence: zakinyan.a.r@mail.ru

Abstract: We consider the possibility of constructing a hierarchy of the complex extension of the Korteweg–de Vries equation (cKdV), which under the assumption that the function is real passes into the KdV hierarchy. A hierarchy is understood here as a family of nonlinear partial differential equations with a Lax pair with a common scattering operator. The cKdV hierarchy is obtained by examining the equation on the eigenvalues of the fourth-order Hermitian self-conjugate operator on the invariant transformations of the eigenvector-functions. It is proved that for an operator $\hat{H}_n$ to transform a solution of the equation on eigenvalues $(\hat{M} - \lambda E)V = 0$ into a solution of the same equation, it is necessary and sufficient that the complex function $u(x,t)$ of the operator $\hat{M}$ satisfies special conditions that are the complexifications of the KdV hierarchy equations. The operators $\hat{H}_n$ are constructed as differential operators of order $2n + 1$. We also construct a hierarchy of perturbed KdV equations (pKdV) with a special perturbation function, the dynamics of which is described by a linear equation. It is based on the system of operator equations obtained by Bogoyavlensky. Since the elements of the hierarchies are united by a common scattering operator, it remains unchanged in the derivation of the equations. The second differential operator of the Lax pair has increasing odd derivatives while retaining a skew-symmetric form. It is shown that when perturbation tends to zero, all hierarchy equations are converted to higher KdV equations. It is proved that the pKdV hierarchy equations are a necessary and sufficient condition for the solutions of the equation on eigenvalues to have invariant transformations.

Keywords: Lax pairs; complexification of the Korteweg–de Vries equation; Korteweg–de Vries hierarchies; integrable partial differential equations; perturbations of the Korteweg–de Vries equation

MSC: 35Q53

Citation: Redkina, T.V.; Zakinyan, A.R.; Zakinyan, R.G.; Surneva, O.B. Hierarchies of the Korteweg–de Vries Equation Related to Complex Expansion and Perturbation. *Axioms* **2023**, *12*, 371. https://doi.org/10.3390/axioms12040371

Academic Editors: Hatıra Günerhan, Francisco Martínez González and Mohammed K. A. Kaabar

Received: 16 March 2023
Revised: 7 April 2023
Accepted: 11 April 2023
Published: 12 April 2023

Copyright: © 2023 by the authors. Licensee MDPI, Basel, Switzerland. This article is an open access article distributed under the terms and conditions of the Creative Commons Attribution (CC BY) license (https://creativecommons.org/licenses/by/4.0/).

1. Introduction

After the discovery by Gardner, Greene, Kruskal and Miura of the inverse scattering problem method in 1967 [1] and a number of fully integrable equations, the interest in solitons has been growing continuously. In wave dynamics problems, one often has to deal with nonlinear equations containing terms with high-order spatial derivatives characterizing nonlinearity, dispersion and dissipation [2,3]. Thus, in deformable media with microstructures, soliton solutions of the Korteweg–de Vries hierarchy equations arise [4]. Special polynomials related to rational solutions of the KdV hierarchy are presented in [5]. In [6], an algorithmic method for obtaining a Lax pair for the hierarchy of the modified KdV equation (mKdV) is given. The integration of the modified KdV hierarchy with an integral source type is proposed in [7]. In [8], the connection of the stationary KdV hierarchy with the second Painlevé hierarchy is traced, and periodic solutions of the hierarchy are constructed.

The Kadomtsev–Petviashvili (KP) equation is related to the KdV equation:

$$(u_t + 6uu_x + u_{xxx})_x + 3\lambda u_{yy} = 0$$

which is also called the two-dimensional KdV equation. The relationship of these equations is informal. The KP equation is used to describe acoustic waves of small amplitude and long wavelength in plasma that have been subjected to transverse perturbations in the y-axis direction. Without transverse perturbations, the dynamics are described by the KdV equation. The KP hierarchies investigated in [9] extended the KdV family. Furthermore, (2+1)-dimensional hierarchies of evolutionary equations with Hamiltonian structure are developed in [10].

In recent decades, nonlinear science has attracted a large number of researchers to create models with a higher number of dimensions ($n \geq 2$), as well as use fractional differentiation. Thus, in [11], a (3+1)-dimensional equation of the type of the second equation of the KdV hierarchy, which is a fifth-order equation, was obtained:

$$D_t^{\alpha} u + 6u_y u_x + u_{xxy} + u_{xxxxz} + 60u_x^2 u_z + 10u_z u_{xxx} + 20u_x u_{xxz} + 6u_z u_x + u_{xxz} = 0,$$

where D_t^{α} denotes a fractional differential operator of order $\alpha > 0$ on time t in the sense of the Riemann–Liouville fractional derivative. Using fractional Lie group methods, symmetries of the equation are obtained in [11]. Using a suitable conservation theorem, conservation laws are obtained, which lead to a deeper understanding of this dynamical model.

In [12], the dynamics of optical solitons are described using integrable hierarchies for two types of perturbations—in particular, hierarchies for the KdV equation, mKdV, KdV-sine-Gordon equation, and the nonlinear Schrödinger equation. The Clairin's method for the system of two third-order equations related to the integrable perturbation and complexification of the Korteweg–de Vries equation was developed in [13].

The purpose of this paper is to extend the ideas about the possibilities of constructing various hierarchies of the KdV equation, including their complex extension and perturbed systems.

In [14–16], the hierarchies of the complex extension of the Korteweg–de Vries equation (cKdV) and the system describing a hierarchy of perturbed KdV equations (pKdV), i.e., transformations for the first equation of the KdV hierarchy, were constructed. The cKdV and pKdV hierarchies constructed in this paper have a fourth-order scattering operator written in matrix form. The equations belonging to the same hierarchy are connected by a common scattering operator, so for the construction of the cKdV and pKdV hierarchies we used the available scattering operators taken from [14–16]. However, to derive the equations of the hierarchies themselves it was necessary to analyze the equation for eigenvalues and to determine whether there exist non-trivial differential operators transforming its solutions into themselves. It turned out that such operators exist if and only if the potential function of the scattering operator satisfies special partial differential equations, these equations being the families of cKdV and pKdV. The pKdVs we obtained are close in structure to the super-integrable physical models of [11]. These equations are discussed in more detail in Part 2 of the paper.

2. Construction of the Complexification Hierarchy of the Korteweg–de Vries Equation

The Lax method [17] uses the operator equation to obtain a family of integrable partial derivative equations of the general form $u_t = F(u, u_x, u_{xx}, \ldots)$:

$$\hat{M}_t = \left[\hat{M}, \hat{B}_n\right], \tag{1}$$

where $\hat{M}$ and $\hat{B}_n$ are differential operators of the matrix form parametrically dependent on t. The form of the operator $\hat{B}_n$ is chosen so that the commutator $\left[\hat{M}, \hat{B}_n\right] = \hat{M}\hat{B}_n - \hat{B}_n\hat{M}$ and the derivative $\frac{\partial \hat{M}}{\partial t}$ are multiplication operators on some functions.

It is well known that relation (1) underlies the applicability of the inverse scattering problem to the nonlinear evolution equations, so using the terminology adopted in soliton theory we will call $\hat{M}$ the scattering operator. The most important feature of the pair of Lax matrix operators $\hat{M}$, $\hat{B}_n$ is that the time derivative is not included in the operator $\hat{M}$. Thus, we can consider t as a parameter and investigate the spectral properties of this operator, i.e., investigate solutions of the equation on eigenvalues:

$$(\hat{M} - \lambda E)V = 0, \tag{2}$$

where E is a unit matrix, λ is a spectral parameter, $V(\lambda, x, t)$ is the vector eigenfunction. This equation on the vector function $V(\lambda, x, t)$ is a spectral problem for the matrix operator $\hat{M}$; sometimes it is also called an auxiliary linear problem for the nonlinear equation in question. Note that the Lax Equation (1) is equivalent to the pair of linear Equations (2) and (3):

$$V_t = -\hat{B}_n V. \tag{3}$$

Here, it is appropriate to emphasize that the consistency of Equations (2) and (3) means only the existence of their common solution, but not that each solution of one of them will also be a solution of the other. Therefore, the combination $V_t + \hat{B}_n V$ need not be zero, and under certain conditions it can also satisfy Equation (2).

In [11–13], the Hermitian-self-conjugate operator of the fourth order, written in matrix form, was used as the scattering matrix operator $\hat{M}$:

$$\hat{M} = \begin{pmatrix} 0 & \hat{L} \\ \bar{\hat{L}} & 0 \end{pmatrix}, \tag{4}$$

where "–" above the letter denotes the complex conjugation, and $\hat{L}$ is an operator that depends on the complex function $u(x, t)$ and has the form of the Sturm–Liouville operator:

$$\hat{L} = -\frac{\partial^2}{\partial x^2} + u(x, t). \tag{5}$$

Function $u(x, t)$ in the terminology of the inverse scattering problem method is called the potential energy (potential).

An odd-order matrix operator $\hat{B}_n$ with matrix coefficients of diagonal form 2×2:

$$\hat{B}_n = \begin{pmatrix} A_{1(2n+1)} & 0 \\ 0 & A_{2(2n+1)} \end{pmatrix} \frac{\partial^{2n+1}}{\partial x^{2n+1}} + \sum_{k=0}^{2n-1} \begin{pmatrix} A_{1k} & 0 \\ 0 & A_{2k} \end{pmatrix} \frac{\partial^k}{\partial x^k}, \tag{6}$$

where $n \geq 1$ is a fixed natural number ($n \in N$), $A_{ik}(\lambda, x, t)$, $i = 1, 2$ are arbitrary functions differentiable as many times as necessary by all variables, and λ is an arbitrary complex parameter. The matrix operator $\hat{B}_n$ form is refined by closing (1) to a single equation.

In the present paper we investigate the equation for eigenvalues (2) and search for invariant transformations of operator $\hat{H}_n$, which map the eigenfunctions of the operator $\hat{M}$ into themselves. The conditions that lead to the possibility of the existence of such transformations turn out to be nonlinear partial differential equations that are a hierarchy of the complex extension of the KdV equation (cKdV—KdV complexification). Obtaining proof of the existence of such a hierarchy is carried out by the method of mathematical induction, so we divide it into stages.

2.1. *Transformation Operators of a Special Kind for n = 1*

Let us write (6) at $n = 1$ as

$$\hat{B}_1 = A\frac{\partial^3}{\partial x^3} + N\frac{\partial}{\partial x} + P, \tag{7}$$

where

$$A = \begin{pmatrix} A_1(\lambda,x,t) & 0 \\ 0 & A_2(\lambda,x,t) \end{pmatrix},\ N = \begin{pmatrix} N_1(\lambda,x,t) & 0 \\ 0 & N_2(\lambda,x,t) \end{pmatrix}, P = \begin{pmatrix} P_1(\lambda,x,t) & 0 \\ 0 & P_2(\lambda,x,t) \end{pmatrix}$$

are the matrices of diagonal form 2×2 with functions $A_i(\lambda,x,t)$, $N_i(\lambda,x,t)$, $P_i(\lambda,x,t)$, $i = 1, 2$ differentiable the required number of times by all variables, λ is the arbitrary complex parameter.

Lemma 1. *For an operator $\hat{M}$ of the form (4) there exists a $\hat{B}_1$ operator of the form (7) such that $(\hat{M} - \lambda E)\hat{B}_1$ is a product operator, E is a unit matrix, and λ is an arbitrary complex parameter.*

Proof of Lemma 1. Let us establish that there exists an operator $\hat{B}_1$ of the form (7) that translates the vector-function $V = \begin{pmatrix} v_1(\lambda,x,t) \\ v_2(\lambda,x,t) \end{pmatrix}$, satisfying the equation on eigenvalues (2)

$$\hat{M}V = \lambda V, \text{ or the system } \begin{cases} -v_{1xx} + \bar{u}v_1 = \lambda v_2, \\ -v_{2xx} + uv_2 = \lambda v_1, \end{cases} \tag{8}$$

into functions $\hat{B}_1[V]$, satisfying the equation:

$$(\hat{M} - \lambda E)\hat{B}_1 V = F(x,t)V, \tag{9}$$

where $F(x,t)$ is a functional matrix 2×2 containing no differentiation operators and a λ parameter.

Let us write the left part of (9) in matrix form and substitute the value of the operator $\hat{L}$ from (5); then, we obtain

$$\begin{gathered} \begin{pmatrix} -A_{2xx}v_{2xxx} - 2A_{2x}v_{2xxxx} - A_2 v_{2xxxxx} + uA_2 v_{2xxx} \\ -A_{1xx}v_{1xxx} - 2A_{1x}v_{1xxxx} - A_1 v_{1xxxxx} + \bar{u}A_1 v_{1xxx} \end{pmatrix} - \lambda \begin{pmatrix} A_1 v_{1xxx} + N_1 v_{1x} + P_1 v_1 \\ A_2 v_{2xxx} + N_2 v_{2x} + P_2 v_2 \end{pmatrix} \\ + \begin{pmatrix} -N_{2xx}v_{2x} - 2N_{2x}v_{2xx} - N_2 v_{2xxx} + uN_2 v_{2x} - P_{2xx}v_2 - 2P_{2x}v_{2x} - P_2 v_{2xx} + uP_2 v_2 \\ -N_{1xx}v_{1x} - 2N_{1x}v_{1xx} - N_1 v_{1xxx} + \bar{u}N_1 v_{1x} - P_{1xx}v_1 - 2P_{1x}v_{1x} - P_1 v_{1xx} + \bar{u}P_1 v_1 \end{pmatrix}. \end{gathered} \tag{10}$$

Express the second, third, fourth, and fifth derivatives of functions v_i from system (8) and substitute the found values in (10). Let us group separately the terms with parameter λ and separately with functions v_i and derivatives v_{ix}:

$$(\hat{M} - \lambda E)\hat{B}_1 V = \begin{pmatrix} 0 & Q_1 \\ Q_2 & 0 \end{pmatrix}\begin{pmatrix} v_1 \\ v_2 \end{pmatrix} + \lambda \begin{pmatrix} Q_3 & 0 \\ 0 & Q_4 \end{pmatrix}\begin{pmatrix} v_1 \\ v_2 \end{pmatrix} + \begin{pmatrix} 0 & W_1 \\ W_2 & 0 \end{pmatrix}\begin{pmatrix} v_{1x} \\ v_{2x} \end{pmatrix} + \lambda \begin{pmatrix} W_3 & 0 \\ 0 & W_4 \end{pmatrix}\begin{pmatrix} v_{1x} \\ v_{2x} \end{pmatrix}, \tag{11}$$

where

$$Q_1 = -A_{2xx}u_x - 2A_{2x}(u_{xx} + u^2 + \lambda^2) - A_2(u_{xxx} + 3u_x u) - 2N_{2x}u - N_2 u_x - P_{2xx}, \tag{12}$$

$$Q_2 = -A_{1xx}\bar{u}_x - 2A_{1x}(\bar{u}_{xx} + \bar{u}^2 + \lambda^2) - A_1(\bar{u}_{xxx} + 3\bar{u}_x\bar{u}) - P_{1xx} - 2N_{1x}\bar{u} - N_1\bar{u}_x, \tag{13}$$

$$\begin{aligned} W_3 &= A_{2xx} + A_2\bar{u} - A_1\bar{u} - N_1 + N_2, \\ W_1 &= -A_{2xx}u - 4A_{2x}u_x - A_2(3u_{xx} + \lambda^2) + \lambda^2 A_1 - N_{2xx} - 2P_{2x}, \\ Q_3 &= 2A_{2x}(u + \bar{u}) + A_2(3u_x + \bar{u}_x) - A_1\bar{u}_x - P_1 + 2N_{2x} + P_2, \end{aligned} \tag{14}$$

$$\begin{aligned} W_2 &= -A_{1xx}\bar{u} - 4A_{1x}\bar{u}_x - A_1(\lambda^2 + 3\bar{u}_{xx}) + \lambda^2 A_2 - N_{1xx} - 2P_{1x}, \\ W_4 &= A_{1xx} + A_1 u - A_2 u - N_2 + N_1, \\ Q_4 &= 2A_{1x}(\bar{u} + u) + A_1(3\bar{u}_x + u_x) - A_2 u_x - P_2 + P_1 + 2N_{1x}. \end{aligned} \tag{15}$$

Let us choose the functions $A_k(\lambda, x, t)$, $N_k(\lambda, x, t)$, $P_k(\lambda, x, t)$, $k = 1, 2$ such that the coefficient at $\begin{pmatrix} v_{1x} \\ v_{2x} \end{pmatrix}$ is zero and the coefficients at $\begin{pmatrix} v_1 \\ v_2 \end{pmatrix}$ do not depend on λ. These requirements are equivalent to a system of equations:

$$0 = A_{2xx} + (A_2 - A_1)\bar{u} - N_1 + N_2, \tag{16}$$

$$0 = -A_{2xx}u - 4A_{2x}u_x - A_2(3u_{xx} + \lambda^2) + \lambda^2 A_1 - N_{2xx} - 2P_{2x} \tag{17}$$

$$0 = 2A_{2x}(u + \bar{u}) + A_2(3u_x + \bar{u}_x) - A_1\bar{u}_x - P_1 + 2N_{2x} + P_2, \tag{18}$$

$$0 = -A_{1xx}\bar{u} - 4A_{1x}\bar{u}_x - A_1(\lambda^2 + 3\bar{u}_{xx}) + \lambda^2 A_2 - N_{1xx} - 2P_{1x}, \tag{19}$$

$$0 = A_{1xx} + (A_1 - A_2)u - N_2 + N_1, \tag{20}$$

$$0 = 2A_{1x}(\bar{u} + u) + A_1(3\bar{u}_x + u_x) - A_2u_x - P_2 + P_1 + 2N_{1x}. \tag{21}$$

In order that Equations (17) and (19) do not depend on the parameter λ it is necessary to set

$$A_2 = A_1. \tag{22}$$

The sum of expressions (16), (20) leads to $A_{1xx} = 0$, which is easily solved by assuming $A_1 = a$ a constant value, and then the system (16)–(21) is simplified to four relations:

$$\begin{array}{l} -3au_{xx} - N_{1xx} - 2P_{2x} = 0,\ 3au_x - P_1 + 2N_{1x} + P_2 = 0, \\ -3a\bar{u}_{xx} - N_{1xx} - 2P_{1x} = 0,\ 3a\bar{u}_x - P_2 + P_1 + 2N_{1x} = 0. \end{array} \tag{23}$$

This system of equations is simultaneous if

$$a \in R, N_1 = -\frac{3}{4}a(u + \bar{u}) + \varphi(t),\ \bar{P}_1(\lambda, x, t) = P_2(\lambda, x, t) = \frac{3}{8}a(\bar{u} - 3u)_x + \psi(t). \tag{24}$$

For simplicity of further reasoning, let us assume that $\varphi(t) = \psi(t) = 0$.

The remaining part of Formula (11) $(\hat{M} - \lambda E)\hat{B}_1 v = \begin{pmatrix} 0 & Q_1 \\ Q_2 & 0 \end{pmatrix}\begin{pmatrix} v_1 \\ v_2 \end{pmatrix}$ gives the desired representation, where Q_1, Q_2 after substitution in (12)–(15) the found values take the following form:

$$Q_1 = -\frac{3}{2}au_xu - \frac{1}{8}a(3\bar{u} - u)_{xxx} + \frac{3}{2}a\bar{u}_xu + \frac{3}{4}a\bar{u}u_x, \tag{25}$$

$$Q_2 = -\frac{3}{2}a\bar{u}_x\bar{u} - \frac{1}{8}a(3u - \bar{u})_{xxx} + \frac{3}{2}au_x\bar{u} + \frac{3}{4}au\bar{u}_x. \tag{26}$$

Seen in $Q_1 = \bar{Q}_2$ and $F(x,t) = \begin{pmatrix} 0 & Q_1 \\ \bar{Q}_1 & 0 \end{pmatrix}$ is the 2×2 matrix, independent of λ. So, the desired form of operator $\hat{B}_1$ is found:

$$\hat{B}_1 = \begin{pmatrix} a & 0 \\ 0 & a \end{pmatrix}\frac{\partial^3}{\partial x^3} - \frac{3}{4}a\begin{pmatrix} u + \bar{u} & 0 \\ 0 & u + \bar{u} \end{pmatrix}\frac{\partial}{\partial x} + \frac{3}{8}a\begin{pmatrix} (u - 3\bar{u})_x & 0 \\ 0 & (\bar{u} - 3u)_x \end{pmatrix} \tag{27}$$

which confirms the Lemma. □

Lemma 2. *The operator* $\hat{H}_1 = \frac{\partial}{\partial t} + \hat{B}_1$ *converts the solution of the equation* $(\hat{M} - \lambda E)V = 0$ *into functions satisfying the inhomogeneous equation*

$$\left[\begin{pmatrix} 0 & \hat{L} \\ \bar{\hat{L}} & 0 \end{pmatrix} - \lambda \begin{pmatrix} 1 & 0 \\ 0 & 1 \end{pmatrix}\right] \hat{H}_1 V = R_1(u)V$$

where the operators have the following forms: $\hat{B}_1$ *in the form (27),* $\hat{L}$ *in the form (5), and*

$$R_1(u) = \begin{pmatrix} 0 & R_{11}(u) \\ \bar{R}_{11}(u) & 0 \end{pmatrix},\ R_{11}(u) = \frac{3}{2}a(\bar{u} - u)_x u + \frac{3}{4}a\bar{u}u_x - \frac{1}{8}a(3\bar{u} - u)_{xxx} - u_t.$$

Proof of Lemma 2. Differentiating the system (8) by t:

$$\begin{cases} -v_{1xxt} + \bar{u}v_{1t} - \lambda v_{2t} = -\bar{u}_t v_1, \\ -v_{2xxt} + uv_{2t} - \lambda v_{1t} = -u_t v_2, \end{cases}$$

we see that the operator $E\frac{\partial}{\partial t}$ converts the solutions of this system into functions $\frac{\partial v_1}{\partial t}, \frac{\partial v_2}{\partial t}$, satisfying the equation

$$\left[\begin{pmatrix} 0 & \hat{L} \\ \bar{\hat{L}} & 0 \end{pmatrix} - \lambda \begin{pmatrix} 1 & 0 \\ 0 & 1 \end{pmatrix}\right] \begin{pmatrix} v_{1t} \\ v_{2t} \end{pmatrix} = -\begin{pmatrix} 0 & u_t \\ \bar{u}_t & 0 \end{pmatrix} \begin{pmatrix} v_1 \\ v_2 \end{pmatrix}.$$

The operator $\hat{H}_1$ has the form

$$\hat{H}_1 = E\frac{\partial}{\partial t} + A\frac{\partial^3}{\partial x^3} + N\frac{\partial}{\partial x} + P, \tag{28}$$

and, by virtue of its linearity, given Lemma 1, $\hat{H}_1$ converts the solution of the equation $(\hat{M} - \lambda E)V = 0$ into

$$\left[\begin{pmatrix} 0 & \hat{L} \\ \bar{\hat{L}} & 0 \end{pmatrix} - \lambda \begin{pmatrix} 1 & 0 \\ 0 & 1 \end{pmatrix}\right] \hat{H}_1 V = \left\{F(x,t) - \begin{pmatrix} 0 & u_t \\ \bar{u}_t & 0 \end{pmatrix}\right\} V = R_1(u)V$$

where $R_1(u)$ has a matrix form:

$$R_1(u) = \begin{pmatrix} 0 & R_{11}(u) \\ \bar{R}_{11}(u) & 0 \end{pmatrix},\ R_{11} = \frac{3}{2}a(\bar{u} - u)_x u + \frac{3}{4}a\bar{u}u_x - \frac{1}{8}a(3\bar{u} - u)_{xxx} - u_t.$$

which was to be proved. □

Corollary 1. *For an operator* $\hat{H}_1$ *to transform a solution of an equation* $(\hat{M} - \lambda E)V = 0$ *into a solution of the same equation, it is necessary and sufficient that the complex function* $u(x,t)$ *of the operator* $\hat{L}$ *in the form (5) satisfy the equation:*

$$\frac{3}{2}a(\bar{u} - u)_x u + \frac{3}{4}a\bar{u}u_x - \frac{1}{8}a(3\bar{u} - u)_{xxx} = u_t. \tag{29}$$

At $a = 4$, (29) gives a complex-valued equation:

$$u_t = 3(\bar{u} - u)u_x + 6\bar{u}_x u - \frac{1}{2}(3\bar{u} - u)_{xxx}, \tag{30}$$

which was obtained earlier in [14–16] and for the real function turns into the Korteweg–de Vries equation

$$u_t = 6u_x u - u_{xxx},$$

and therefore is its complexification.

The proposed derivation differs from the one carried out earlier in [14–16] in that we find invariant transformations that translate solutions of the equation on the eigenvalues of the operator $\hat{M}$ into its own solutions. As a result, we can formulate the following conclusion.

Corollary 2. *The complexification of the Korteweg–de Vries Equation (30) has a Lax representation (1) with operators $\hat{M}$ and $\hat{B}_1$ of the form (4) and (27), respectively, at $a = 4$.*

Corollary 3. *The complex-valued nonlinear Equation (30) has an operator representation*

$$\hat{L}_t = \hat{L}\bar{A} - A\hat{L}, \tag{31}$$

with the operators $\hat{L}$ of the form (5) and

$$\hat{A} = 4\frac{\partial^3}{\partial x^3} + \frac{3}{2}(\bar{u} - 3u)\frac{\partial}{\partial x} + \frac{3}{2}\frac{\partial}{\partial x}(u - 3\bar{u}), \tag{32}$$

where $u(x,t)$ is some complex function of two independent variables.

Thus, for a function $u(x,t)$ to satisfy cKdV Equation (29), it is necessary and sufficient that the operator $\hat{H}_1$ transforms the solutions of the equation $(\hat{M} - \lambda E)V = 0$ into a solution of the same equation.

2.2. Higher-Order Transformation Operators

Let us now consider the possibility of constructing higher-order operators $\hat{H}_n$ that are invariant transformations for $(\hat{M} - \lambda E)V = 0$ and, in passing, obtain higher hierarchy equations (cKdV).

Theorem 1. *Operators*

$$\hat{H}_n = \begin{pmatrix} 1 & 0 \\ 0 & 1 \end{pmatrix}\frac{\partial}{\partial t} + \begin{pmatrix} A_{1(2n+1)} & 0 \\ 0 & A_{2(2n+1)} \end{pmatrix}\frac{\partial^{2n+1}}{\partial x^{2n+1}} + \sum_{k=0}^{2n-1}\begin{pmatrix} A_{1k} & 0 \\ 0 & A_{2k} \end{pmatrix}\frac{\partial^k}{\partial x^k} \tag{33}$$

transform the solutions of the equation $(\hat{M} - \lambda)V = 0$ into functions satisfying the equations

$$\left[\begin{pmatrix} 0 & \hat{L} \\ \bar{\hat{L}} & 0 \end{pmatrix} - \lambda\begin{pmatrix} 1 & 0 \\ 0 & 1 \end{pmatrix}\right]\hat{H}_n V = R_n(u)V$$

where $n \geq 1$ is a fixed natural number ($n \in N$), $R_n(u) = F_n(x,t) \begin{pmatrix} 0 & u_t \\ \bar{u}_t & 0 \end{pmatrix}$, $F_n(x,t) = \begin{pmatrix} 0 & Q_{1n} \\ Q_{2n} & 0 \end{pmatrix}$ is the 2×2 matrix, independent of λ, λ is an arbitrary complex parameter.

Proof of Theorem 1. We will prove the theorem by the method of mathematical induction. For $n = 1$ the theorem is proved in Lemmas 1, 2.

Now it is necessary to show that if the theorem is true for $n = m$, then it is also true for $n = m + 1$. To do this, it is necessary to determine how the structure of the system of Equations (16)–(21) changes as the order of the operator $\hat{H}_n$ increases. Obviously

$$\hat{H}_{m+1} = \begin{pmatrix} 1 & 0 \\ 0 & 1 \end{pmatrix}\frac{\partial}{\partial t} + \begin{pmatrix} A_{1(2m+3)} & 0 \\ 0 & A_{2(2m+3)} \end{pmatrix}\frac{\partial^{2m+3}}{\partial x^{2m+3}} + \sum_{k=0}^{2m+1}\begin{pmatrix} A_{1k} & 0 \\ 0 & A_{2k} \end{pmatrix}\frac{\partial^k}{\partial x^k},$$

or

$$\hat{H}_{m+1} = \begin{pmatrix} A_{1(2m+3)} & 0 \\ 0 & A_{2(2m+3)} \end{pmatrix} \frac{\partial^{2m+3}}{\partial x^{2m+3}} + \begin{pmatrix} A_{1(2m)} & 0 \\ 0 & A_{2(2m)} \end{pmatrix} \frac{\partial^{2m}}{\partial x^{2m}} + \hat{H}_n. \tag{34}$$

As a result of acting on the operator $\hat{H}_{m+1}$ by the operator $\hat{M} - \lambda E$, we have:

$$\begin{aligned} (\hat{M} - \lambda E)\hat{H}_{m+1}V = (\hat{M} - \lambda E)\hat{H}_n V + \left[\begin{pmatrix} 0 & \hat{L} \\ \bar{\hat{L}} & 0 \end{pmatrix} - \lambda \begin{pmatrix} 1 & 0 \\ 0 & 1 \end{pmatrix}\right] \begin{pmatrix} A_{1(2m+3)} & 0 \\ 0 & A_{2(2m+3)} \end{pmatrix} \frac{\partial^{2m+3}}{\partial x^{2m+3}} \begin{pmatrix} v_1 \\ v_2 \end{pmatrix} \\ + \left[\begin{pmatrix} 0 & \hat{L} \\ \bar{\hat{L}} & 0 \end{pmatrix} - \lambda \begin{pmatrix} 1 & 0 \\ 0 & 1 \end{pmatrix}\right] \begin{pmatrix} A_{1(2m)} & 0 \\ 0 & A_{2(2m)} \end{pmatrix} \frac{\partial^{2m}}{\partial x^{2m}} \begin{pmatrix} v_1 \\ v_2 \end{pmatrix} \end{aligned} \tag{35}$$

What new summands will arise in this case? By opening the brackets of the last terms of (35), we obtain:

$$\begin{pmatrix} -A_{2(2m+3)xx}v_{2x^{2m+3}} - 2A_{2(2m+3)x}v_{2x^{2m+4}} - A_{2(2m+3)}v_{2x^{2m+5}} + uA_{2(2m+3)}v_{2x^{2m+3}} - \lambda A_{1(2m+3)}v_{1x^{2m+3}} \\ -A_{1(2m+3)xx}v_{1x^{2m+3}} - 2A_{1(2m+3)x}v_{1x^{2m+4}} - A_{1(2m+3)}v_{1x^{2m+5}} + \bar{u}A_{1(2m+3)}v_{1x^{2m+3}} - \lambda A_{2(2m+3)}v_{2x^{2m+3}} \end{pmatrix}$$
$$+ \begin{pmatrix} -A_{2(2m)xx}v_{2x^{2m}} - 2A_{2(2m)x}v_{2x^{2m+1}} - A_{2(2m)}v_{2x^{2m+2}} + uA_{2(2m)}v_{2x^{2m}} - \lambda A_{1(2m)}v_{1x^{2m}} \\ -A_{1(2m)xx}v_{1x^{2m}} - 2A_{1(2m)x}v_{1x^{2m+1}} - A_{1(2m)}v_{1x^{2m+2}} + \bar{u}A_{1(2m)}v_{1x^{2m}} - \lambda A_{2(2m)}v_{2x^{2m}} \end{pmatrix}.$$

The notations $v_{jx^{2m+1}}, j = 1, 2$ denote the $(2m + 1)$-th order derivative of the function v_j by x. Here, we need to lower the degrees of the derivatives of functions v_j using Equation (8): $v_{2xx} = uv_2 - \lambda v_1$, $v_{1xx} = \bar{u}v_1 - \lambda v_2$. It is easy to see that decreasing by two orders results in the first degree of λ; hence, the terms with $v_{jx^{2m+3}}$ and $v_{jx^{2m+2}}$ will give λ^{m+1}, and the terms with functions $v_{jx^{2m+4}}$ and $v_{jx^{2m+5}}$ will give terms with a factor of λ^{m+2}. The first summand of expressions (35) $(\hat{M} - \lambda E)\hat{H}_n V$ contains terms of the highest degree λ^{m+1}, since the maximum derivative here is $2m + 3$. So, the terms with $v_{jx^{2m+4}}$ and $v_{jx^{2m+5}}$ form, after replacement (8), the following terms:

$$\lambda^{m+2}\left[\left(-A_{1(2m+3)} + A_{2(2m+3)}\right)v_{jx} + 2A_{j(2m+3)x}v_j\right] + \ldots, \; j = 1, 2.$$

They contain only newly added variables $A_{j(2m+3)}$ and are not related to the rest, so by imposing the condition $A_{1(2m+3)} = A_{2(2m+3)} = a_{2m+3}(t)$, these terms automatically disappear. The remaining elements, with powers λ^{m+1} and below, will fall into the system of equations previously created by the operator $(\hat{M} - \lambda E)\hat{H}_n$. Therefore, there will be no new equations, and by the assumption for $\hat{H}_n$ the theorem is correct. □

Corollary 4. *The Lax operator Equation (1), where $\hat{M}$ has the form (4), with an operator $\hat{L}$ of the form (5), and $\hat{B}_n$ is a family of differential operators written in symmetric form*

$$\begin{aligned} \hat{B}_n &= \begin{pmatrix} \hat{A}_n & 0 \\ 0 & \bar{\hat{A}}_n \end{pmatrix}, \\ \hat{A}_n &= r_n \frac{\partial^{2n+1}}{\partial x^{2n+1}} + \sum_{m=1}^{n} \left(p_m \frac{\partial^{2m-1}}{\partial x^{2m-1}} + \frac{\partial^{2m-1}}{\partial x^{2m-1}} \bar{p}_m\right), j = 2, 3, \ldots \end{aligned} \tag{36}$$

where r_n is a real constant number, $p_m(u, \bar{u}, u_x, \bar{u}_x, \ldots)$ are the functions of a complex variable $u(x,t)$ and its derivatives by the variable x are equivalent to the operator equation

$$\hat{L}_t = \hat{L}\hat{A}_n - \hat{A}_n\hat{L} \tag{37}$$

Corollary 5. *In order for operators* $\hat{H}_n$

$$\hat{H}_n = E\frac{\partial}{\partial t} + \hat{B}_n,$$

to be invariant transformations of the solution of the equation on eigenvalues $(\hat{M} - \lambda E)V = 0$, *it is necessary and sufficient that the potential function of the operator* $\hat{M}(4)$ *(the complex function* $u(x,t)$*), satisfies the equation* $R_n(u) = 0$, *i.e.,*

$$R_n(u) = \begin{pmatrix} 0 & Q_{1n} \\ Q_{2n} & 0 \end{pmatrix} - \begin{pmatrix} 0 & u_t \\ \bar{u}_t & 0 \end{pmatrix} = 0,$$

where $Q_{jn}, j = 1, 2$ *does not depend on* $\lambda, V = \begin{pmatrix} v_1(\lambda,x,t) \\ v_2(\lambda,x,t) \end{pmatrix}$ *is the vector-function,* λ *is an arbitrary parameter,* $\hat{B}_n$ *has the form (36).*

Let us show that each new operator $\hat{H}_{m+1}$ gives an equation of higher order that cannot be reduced to the previous one. To do this, it is sufficient to consider the third-order operator and the fifth-order operator and compare the results obtained. The third-order operator is considered in Lemma 1 and 2. Let us write down the fifth-order operator:

$$\hat{H}_2 = \begin{pmatrix} 1 & 0 \\ 0 & 1 \end{pmatrix}\frac{\partial}{\partial t} + \begin{pmatrix} A_{15} & 0 \\ 0 & A_{25} \end{pmatrix}\frac{\partial^5}{\partial x^5} + \begin{pmatrix} A_{13} & 0 \\ 0 & A_{23} \end{pmatrix}\frac{\partial^3}{\partial x^3} + \begin{pmatrix} A_{12} & 0 \\ 0 & A_{22} \end{pmatrix}\frac{\partial^2}{\partial x^2} + \begin{pmatrix} A_{11} & 0 \\ 0 & A_{21} \end{pmatrix}\frac{\partial}{\partial x} + \begin{pmatrix} A_{10} & 0 \\ 0 & A_{20} \end{pmatrix}.$$

Then, the expression $(\hat{M} - \lambda E)\hat{H}_2 V$ will take the following form. We write it down line by line.

First line:

$$\begin{aligned}
&-v_{2xxt} + uv_{2t} - A_{25xx}v_{2x^5} - 2A_{25x}v_{2x^6} - A_{25}v_{2x^7} + uA_{25}v_{2x^5} - A_{23xx}v_{2xxx} \\
&-2A_{23x}v_{2xxxx} - A_{23}v_{2x^5} + uA_{23}v_{2xxx} - A_{22xx}v_{2xx} - 2A_{22x}v_{2xxx} - A_{22}v_{2x^4} + uA_{22}v_{2xx} - A_{21xx}v_{2x} \\
&-2A_{21x}v_{2xx} - A_{21}v_{2xxx} + uA_{21}v_{2x} - A_{20xx}v_2 - 2A_{20x}v_{2x} - A_{20}v_{2xx} + uA_{20}v_2 - \lambda(A_{15}v_{1x^5} + A_{13}v_{1xxx} \\
&+A_{12}v_{1xx} + A_{11}v_{1x} + A_{10}v_1 + v_{1t}).
\end{aligned}$$

Second line:

$$\begin{aligned}
&-v_{1xxt} + \bar{u}v_{1t} - A_{15xx}v_{1x^5} - 2A_{15x}v_{1x^6} - A_{15}v_{1x^7} + \bar{u}A_{15}v_{1x^5} - A_{13xx}v_{1xxx} \\
&-2A_{13x}v_{1xxxx} - A_{13}v_{1x^5} + \bar{u}A_{13}v_{1xxx} - A_{12xx}v_{1xx} - 2A_{12x}v_{1xxx} - A_{12}v_{1x^4} + \bar{u}A_{12}v_{1xxx} - A_{11xx}v_{1x} \\
&-2A_{11x}v_{1xx} - A_{11}v_{1xxx} + \bar{u}A_{11}v_{1x} - A_{10xx}v_1 - 2A_{10x}v_{1x} - A_{10}v_{1xx} + \bar{u}A_{10}v_1 - \lambda(A_{25}v_{2x^5} + A_{23}v_{2xxx} \\
&+A_{22}v_{2xx} + A_{21}v_{2x} + A_{20}v_2 + v_{2t}).
\end{aligned}$$

Let us decrease the order of the functions' v_j derivatives using Equations (8) and group separately the expressions with v_1, v_2, v_{2x}, v_{1x} (we describe only the first one; for the second one we obtain a similar expression):

$$\begin{aligned}
v_{1x} :\ &\lambda[A_{25xx}(u+\bar{u}) + 4A_{25x}(2u_x + \bar{u}_x) + A_{25}(10u_{xx} + 3\bar{u}_{xx} + \bar{u}^2 + \lambda^2) + \bar{u}A_{23} + A_{23xx} + A_{21} \\
&-A_{15}(3\bar{u}_{xx} + \bar{u}^2 + \lambda^2) - A_{13}\bar{u} - A_{11} + 2A_{22x}] = 0, \\
v_{2x} :\ &A_{25xx}(3u_{xx} + u^2) + 4A_{25x}(2u_{xxx} + 3u_x u) + A_{25}(5u_{xxxx} + 10u_{xx}u + 10u_x^2) + A_{21xx} + 2(2A_{23x} + A_{22})u_x \\
&+(A_{23xx} + 2A_{22x})u + 3A_{23}u_{xx} + 2A_{20x} - \lambda^2[A_{15}(\bar{u}+u) + A_{13} - A_{25xx} - A_{23} - A_{25}(\bar{u}+u)] \\
&= 0,
\end{aligned}$$

$$v_1:\ \lambda[(A_{25xx}+A_{23})(3u_x+\bar{u}_x)+2A_{25x}(6u_{xx}+u(u+\bar{u})+\bar{u}_{xx}+\bar{u}^2+\lambda^2)+A_{25}(10u_{xxx}$$
$$+5u_x(u+\bar{u})+\bar{u}_{xxx}+4\bar{u}_x\bar{u})+2A_{23x}(u+\bar{u})+2A_{21x}+A_{22xx}+\bar{u}A_{22}+A_{20}-A_{15}(\bar{u}_{xxx}$$
$$+4\bar{u}_x\bar{u})-A_{13}\bar{u}_x-A_{10}-A_{12}\bar{u}]=0,$$
$$v_2:\ -u_t+(uA_{25}-A_{25xx}-A_{23})(u_{xxx}+4u_xu)-2A_{25x}\left[u_{xxxx}+6u_{xx}u+4u_x^2+u\left(u_{xx}+u^2\right)\right]-A_{25}(u_{x^5}$$
$$+11u_{xxx}u+15u_{xx}u_x+9u_xu^2)-(2A_{23x}+A_{22})\left(u_{xx}+u^2\right)+(uA_{23}-A_{23xx}-A_{21}-2A_{22x})u_x$$
$$+(uA_{22}-A_{22xx}-2A_{21x})u-A_{20xx}+\lambda^2[A_{15}(3\bar{u}_x+u_x)+A_{12}-2A_{25x}(2u+\bar{u})-3A_{25}(2u_x+\bar{u}_x)$$
$$-2A_{23x}-A_{22}]=0.$$

As it was assumed above in the proof, we shall set $A_{15}=A_{25}=a_5(t)$. Since the equations must be valid for any values of λ, we first get rid of the parameter λ in the obtained equations. For this purpose, we set

$$A_{13}=A_{23}=a_3(x,t), A_{13}=A_{23}=a_3(x,t),\ A_{22}-5a_5\bar{u}_x-2a_{3x}-A_{12}=0, \tag{38}$$

which completely defines the function $a_3(x,t)$ and the difference $A_{22}-A_{12}$ through $u(x,t)$:

$$a_3(x,t)=-\frac{5}{4}a_5(\bar{u}+u)+\varphi(t),\ A_{12}-A_{22}=\frac{5}{2}a_5(u-\bar{u})_x. \tag{39}$$

Here, $\varphi(t)$ is the integration constant (hereafter we assume $\varphi(t)=0$).

In order for the operator $\hat{H}_2$ to convert solutions of $(\hat{M}-\lambda E)\hat{H}_2V$ into functions $R_2(u)V$ it is necessary that the coefficients at v_{jx} turn to zero. As a result, the previously unknown functions are defined:

$$A_{11}=\bar{A}_{21}=\frac{5}{16}a_5\left[5\bar{u}u+\frac{1}{2}\left(u^2+\bar{u}^2\right)\right]-a_5\frac{5}{16}(u_{xx}+9\bar{u}_{xx}), \tag{40}$$

$$A_{10}=\bar{A}_{20}=a_5\frac{5}{32}(u_{xxx}-7\bar{u}_{xxx})+\frac{5}{64}a_5\left(3\bar{u}^2-u^2+10\bar{u}u\right)_x-\frac{5}{16}a_5(u_x\bar{u}-u\bar{u}_x) \tag{41}$$

(here the integration constant is zero).

As a result, all elements of the operator $\hat{H}_2$, which are expressed through the function $u(x,t)$ and $a_5(t)$, are found, leaving only two unused relations for the coefficients at v_j, which, after substituting the found values, form two complex conjugate expressions on the function $u(x,t)$:

$$\begin{aligned}R_{12}(u)=\tfrac{5}{16}a_5\Big(&\tfrac{3}{10}u_{x^5}-\tfrac{1}{2}\bar{u}_{x^5}-2(u^2+|u|^2)\bar{u}_x-\tfrac{1}{2}(\bar{u}^2+6|u|^2-3u^2)u_x+u_x(\bar{u}+3u)_{xx}\\&+2u\bar{u}_{xxx}+\tfrac{1}{4}(-3u^2+\bar{u}^2+2|u|^2)_{xxx}\Big)-u_t.\end{aligned} \tag{42}$$

As a result of these operations the following equation is obtained:

$$(\hat{M}-\lambda E)\hat{H}_2V=R_2(u)V,$$

where $R_2(u)$ has a matrix form:

$$R_2(u)=\begin{pmatrix}0 & R_{12}(u)\\ \bar{R}_{12}(u) & 0\end{pmatrix}$$

Comparing the results in Formulas (29) and (42), it should be noted that both expressions contain the first derivative by the variable t, but by the variable x in (29) the senior derivative is of order three, while in (42) it is of order five.

Corollary 6. For the operator $\hat{H}_2$ *to transform a solution of an equation* $(\hat{M} - \lambda E)V = 0$ *into a solution of the same equation, it is necessary and sufficient that the complex function* $u(x,t)$ *satisfies* $R_2(u) = 0$ *or satisfies the equation*

$$\begin{aligned}&\tfrac{5}{16}a_5\Big(\tfrac{3}{10}u_{x^5} - \tfrac{1}{2}\bar{u}_{x^5} - 2(u^2 + |u|^2)\bar{u}_x - \tfrac{1}{2}(\bar{u}^2 + 6|u|^2 - 3u^2)u_x + u_x(\bar{u} + 3u)_{xx} \\ &+ 2u\bar{u}_{xxx} + \tfrac{1}{4}(-3u^2 + \bar{u}^2 + 2|u|^2)_{xxx}\Big) = u_t.\end{aligned} \tag{43}$$

Assume in Equation (41) an arbitrary function $a_5(t)$ in the form of a constant $a_5 = -32$, then the equation will take the form

$$\begin{aligned}u_t &= 10(u^2 + |u|^2)\bar{u}_x + \tfrac{5}{2}(\bar{u}^2 + 6|u|^2 - 3u^2)u_x - 5u_x(\bar{u} + 3u)_{xx} - 10u\bar{u}_{xxx} \\ &- \tfrac{5}{4}(2|u|^2 - 3u^2 + \bar{u}^2)_{xxx} + \tfrac{1}{2}(5\bar{u} - 3u)_{xxxxx},\end{aligned} \tag{44}$$

which, under the assumption that $u(x,t)$ is a real function, passes into the second equation of the KdV hierarchy:

$$u_t = 30u^2u_x - 20u_xu_{xx} - 10uu_{xxx} + u_{xxxxx}.$$

Consequently, a complex extension of the second equation of the KdV is obtained.

Corollary 7. *The nonlinear equation (44) on the complex function* $u(x,t)$ *has the operator representation (37) with the operators* $\hat{L}$ *(Sturm–Liouville operator) and*

$$\begin{aligned}A_2 = &-16\tfrac{\partial^5}{\partial x^5} - 20(\bar{u} + u)\tfrac{\partial^3}{\partial x^3} - 10(u + 5\bar{u})_x\tfrac{\partial^2}{\partial x^2} + \Big(\tfrac{5}{2}(u^2 + \bar{u}^2 + 10|u|^2) - 5(9\bar{u} + u)_{xx}\Big)\tfrac{\partial}{\partial x} \\ &+ \tfrac{5}{2}(u - 7\bar{u})_{xxx} + \tfrac{5}{4}(3\bar{u}^2 - u^2 + 10|u|^2)_x + 5(u\bar{u}_x - \bar{u}u_x)\end{aligned}$$

and is a complexification of the second Korteweg–de Vries hierarchy equation.

Earlier, in [16], the construction of Equation (44) using the Lax operator equation with given operators was presented.

Thus, it is established that there exists a countable family of operators $\hat{H}_n = E\frac{\partial}{\partial t} + \hat{B}_n$ ($\hat{B}_n$ have the form (36) and depend on a complex function $u(x,t)$), which become invariant transformations of solutions of the homogeneous equation $(\hat{M} - \lambda E)\hat{H}_n V = 0$ only if the function $u(x,t)$ is a solution of one of the equations of the cKdV hierarchy.

All $\hat{H}_n$ are of odd order and determine the corresponding order of the equation of the cKdV hierarchy. The resulting complex equations are integrable since they possess a Lax pair with operators (4) and (6).

In particular, for Equation (30) the following takes place:

Proposition 1. *Equation (30) has a complex-valued solution*

$$u(\varsigma) = \frac{(ik)^2}{2}[1 + \tan^2(ik\varsigma) \mp \tan(ik\varsigma)],$$

where $\frac{1}{2}ik(x - 2(ik)^2t + \mu) = ik\varsigma$ *is a complex variable,* $k,\ \mu$ *are the arbitrary constants.*

The proof is obtained by simple substitution into Equation (30).

Functions of a complex argument can be represented using the Riemann sphere, by expressing the complex argument

$$\frac{1}{2}ik(x - 2(ik)^2t + \mu) = z = a + ib$$

in the polar coordinate system $a = \rho\cos\varphi$, $b = \rho\sin\varphi$ (ρ, φ polar coordinates of the complex plane Z), and then the third coordinate of the sphere should determine the value of the function with polar arguments $u(\rho\cos\varphi, \rho\sin\varphi)$.

Let us distinguish in the solution

$$u(a+ib) = -\frac{k^2}{2}\left[1+\tan^2(a+ib) \mp \tan(a+ib)\right]$$

the real and imaginary parts:

$$1+\tan^2 z \mp \tan z = \frac{4e^{2z} \pm i(e^{4z}-1)}{e^{4z}+2e^{2z}+1} = \frac{4e^{2a}(\cos 2b + i\sin 2b) \pm i\left[e^{4a}(\cos 4b + i\sin 4b) - 1\right]}{e^{4a}(\cos 4b + i\sin 4b) + 2e^{2a}(\cos 2b + i\sin 2b) + 1}.$$

We get rid of the imaginary unit in the denominator and go to hyperbolic functions:

$$\mathrm{Re}u = -k^2\left(\frac{\cos h2a\cos 2b+1}{(\cos h2a+\cos 2b)^2} \mp \frac{1}{2}\frac{\sin 2b}{\cos h2a+\cos 2b}\right),$$

$$\mathrm{Im}u = k^2\left(\frac{\sin h2a\sin 2b}{(\cos h2a+\cos 2b)^2} \mp \frac{1}{2}\frac{\sin h2a}{\cos h2a+\cos 2b}\right),$$

where $a = \rho\cos\varphi, b = \rho\sin\varphi$. The images of the real and imaginary parts, respectively, are shown in Figure 1a,b.

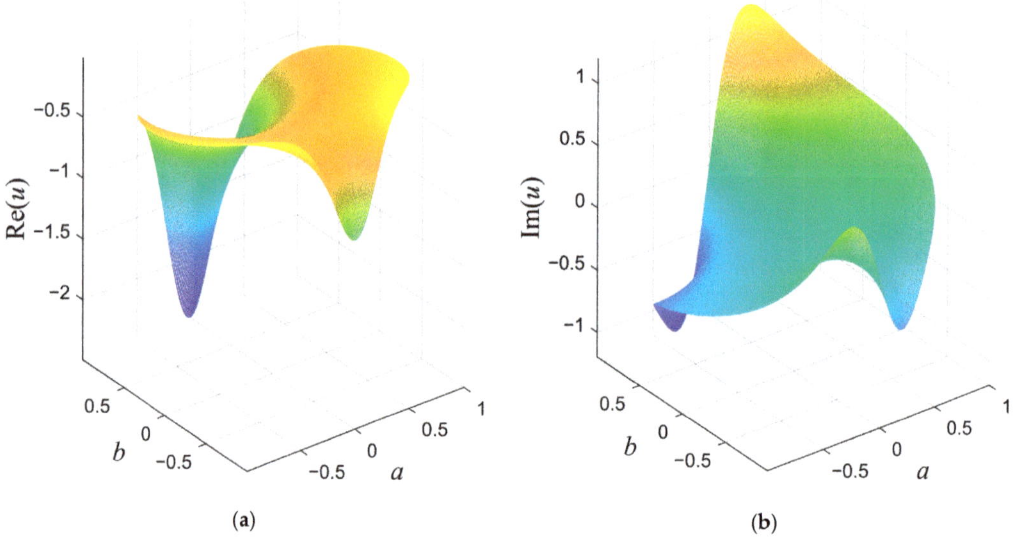

Figure 1. (**a**) Real part of u; (**b**) Imaginary part of u. Obtained at $k = 1$ and using "+" in corresponding equations.

3. Construction of the Hierarchy of Perturbed Korteweg–de Vries Equation

3.1. The perturbed Korteweg–de Vries Equation

In [14,15], the Lax Equation (1) is considered, where the operators $\hat{M}$ and $\hat{B}$ are matrices of the following form:

$$\hat{M} = \begin{pmatrix} \hat{L} & \mu\hat{N} \\ \hat{N} & -\delta\hat{L} \end{pmatrix}, \hat{B} = \begin{pmatrix} \hat{A} & \mu\delta\hat{R} \\ -\hat{R} & \hat{A} \end{pmatrix}, \quad (45)$$

where $\delta^2 = 1$, μ is an arbitrary parameter; $\hat{L}$, $\hat{A}$ are the linear differential operators; $\hat{N}$, $\hat{R}$ are the scalar operators. With this approach, the Lax Equation (1) is equivalent to a system of two operator equations:

$$\hat{L}_t = [\hat{L}, \hat{A}] - \mu(\hat{N}\hat{R} + \delta\hat{R}\hat{N}), \tag{46}$$

$$\hat{N}_t = [\hat{N}, \hat{A}] + \hat{R}\hat{L} + \delta\hat{L}\hat{R}. \tag{47}$$

The operators $\hat{L}$, $\hat{A}$ have the same form as for the Korteweg–de Vries equation, i.e.,

$$\hat{L} = -\frac{\partial^2}{\partial x^2} + u(x,t), \; \hat{A} = 4\frac{\partial^3}{\partial x^3} - 3\left(u\frac{\partial}{\partial x} + \frac{\partial}{\partial x}u\right). \tag{48}$$

$\hat{N}$ and $\hat{R}$, respectively, have the values

$$\hat{N} = w(x,t), \; \hat{R} = b(x,t), \tag{49}$$

where $u(x,t)$, $w(x,t)$, $b(x,t)$ are the unknown functions.

From Equations (46) and (47) at $\delta = 1$, $b(x,t) = -6w_x$ one can obtain a system of equations:

$$\begin{cases} u_t = 6uu_x - u_{xxx} + 12\mu w w_x, \\ \quad w_t = 2w_{xxx} - 6uw_x. \end{cases} \tag{50}$$

The resulting system can represent an example of the construction of the perturbed Korteweg–de Vries (KdV) equation

$$u_t + 6uu_x + u_{xxx} = \varepsilon f(u, u_x, \ldots), \; 0 < \varepsilon < 1$$

(at $w(x,t) = 0$ simply passing to KdV) with a special perturbation function $w(x,t)$, the dynamics of which are described by the second equation. Such a structure is satisfied by the first equation of system (50) at $0 < \mu << 1$, and the perturbation $w(x,t)$ itself satisfies some law—the second equation of this system.

Several similar systems are considered in [10]. The first super-integrable KdV equation was proposed in [18,19] and has the following form:

$$\begin{cases} u_t = 6uu_x - u_{xxx} - 3\xi\xi_{xx}, \\ \xi_t = -4\xi_{xxx} + 3u_x\xi + 6u\xi_x, \end{cases}$$

where $u(x, t)$ is a bosonic function and $\xi(x, t)$ is a fermionic function. It is bi-Hamiltonian and has an infinite number of conservation laws. Such systems are not unique; the following supersymmetric KdV system was proposed in [20]:

$$\begin{cases} u_t = 6uu_x - u_{xxx} - 3\xi\xi_{xx}, \\ \quad \xi_t = -4\xi_{xxx} + 3(u\xi)_x, \end{cases}$$

which is a reduction of the supersymmetric Kadomtsev–Petviashvili hierarchy [21]. In [22], another new system, the superextension of the KdV hierarchy was constructed:

$$\begin{cases} u_t = 6uu_x - u_{xxx} - 12\xi\xi_{xx} + 6u_x\xi\xi_x - 3\xi\xi_{xxxx} - 6\xi_x\xi_{xxx}, \\ \qquad \xi_t = -4\xi_{xxx} + 3u_x\xi + 6u\xi_x, \end{cases}$$

which is a super-integrable system describing a higher-order evolutionary perturbation.

Let us show that, as for the complex KdV expansion, there exists a hierarchy of perturbed systems associated with the higher KdV equations. For this purpose, we will use the existing operator system (46), (47), but replace the components of the operator $\hat{B}$ with higher derivatives, preserving its skew-symmetry. Since the elements of the hierarchies are united by a common scattering operator, at the derivation the operator $\hat{M}$ will retain the form specified in (45).

3.2. Hierarchy of the Perturbed Korteweg–de Vries Equation

Let us represent the operators (45) under the condition that $\delta = 1$, in the form:

$$\hat{M} = \begin{pmatrix} \hat{L} & \mu\hat{N} \\ \hat{N} & -\hat{L} \end{pmatrix}, \ \hat{B}_j = \begin{pmatrix} \hat{A}_j & \mu\hat{R}_j \\ -\hat{R}_j & \hat{A}_j \end{pmatrix}, \ j = 1,\ 2,\ 3,\ \ldots \tag{51}$$

Let us fix the operators $\hat{L}$, $\hat{N}$ in the form:

$$\hat{L} = -\frac{\partial^2}{\partial x^2} + u(x,t),\ \hat{N} = w(x,t). \tag{52}$$

Differential operators $\hat{A}_j$ and $\hat{R}_j$ have the following form:

$$\hat{A}_j = \alpha_j \frac{\partial^{2j+1}}{\partial x^{2j+1}} + \sum_{m=1}^{j} \left(p_m(x,t) \frac{\partial^{2m-1}}{\partial x^{2m-1}} + \frac{\partial^{2m-1}}{\partial x^{2m-1}} q_m(x,t) \right), j = 1,\ 2,\ 3,\ \ldots \tag{53}$$

$$\hat{R}_j = \sum_{m=0}^{2(j-1)} b_{2j-2-m}(x,t) \frac{\partial^{2j-2-m}}{\partial x^{2j-2-m}}, \tag{54}$$

where μ, α_j are arbitrary parameters, $p_m(x,t), q_m(x,t), b_m(x,t)$ are unknown functions, the form of which will be clarified in the course of research.

The proof of the existence of a countable hierarchy of perturbed KdV equations will be carried out by the method of mathematical induction. Let us find out in which case the result of the new operators (53), (54) in the operator equations

$$\hat{L}_t = [\hat{L}, \hat{A}_j] - \mu(\hat{N}\hat{R}_j + \delta\hat{R}_j\hat{N}), \tag{55}$$

$$\hat{N}_t = [\hat{N}, \hat{A}_j] + \hat{R}_j\hat{L} + \delta\hat{L}\hat{R}_j \tag{56}$$

leads to a system of two partial differential equations for two unknown functions $u(x,t)$, $w(x,t)$.

The proof of the first step of the method of mathematical induction for $j = 1$ was carried out in [14,15]. Now we need to show that the solvability of the system (55) and (56) for $j = n + 1$ with the operators $\hat{A}_{n+1}$ and $\hat{R}_{n+1}$ follows from the solvability of this system for $j = n$ with the operators $\hat{A}_n$ and $\hat{R}_n$ (the solvability of the system implies the reduction of the operator Equations (55) and (56) to two partial differential equations describing the dynamics of the functions $u(x,t)$ and $w(x,t)$, respectively).

Let us study in detail the structure of differential operators (53), (54). The operator $\hat{A}_n$ contains two consecutive odd higher derivatives; compare $\hat{A}_n$ and $\hat{A}_{n+1}$:

$$\hat{A}_n = \alpha_n \frac{\partial^{2n+1}}{\partial x^{2n+1}} + \sum_{m=1}^{n} \left(p_m(x,t) \frac{\partial^{2m-1}}{\partial x^{2m-1}} + \frac{\partial^{2m-1}}{\partial x^{2m-1}} q_m(x,t) \right) = \alpha_n \frac{\partial^{2n+1}}{\partial x^{2n+1}} + D_{2n-1}, \tag{57}$$

$$\hat{A}_{n+1} = \alpha_{n+1} \frac{\partial^{2n+3}}{\partial x^{2n+3}} + p_{n+1} \frac{\partial^{2n+1}}{\partial x^{2n+1}} + \frac{\partial^{2n+1}}{\partial x^{2n+1}} q_{n+1} + D_{2n-1}, \tag{58}$$

where D_{2n-1} is the differential terms from $2n-1$ order and below.

As can be seen for $\hat{A}_{n+1}$, increasing the index n by one increases the degree of the derivative by two orders of magnitude, adding two new unknown functions $p_{n+1}(x,t)$,

$q_{n+1}(x,t)$, which will be predetermined by transformations of the operator Equations (55) and (56).

Similarly, let us analyze for $\hat{R}_n$. $\hat{R}_n$ has a senior even derivative; when the index n increases by one $\hat{R}_{n+1}$, the degree of the differential terms increases by two orders of magnitude, so let us represent the two consecutive operators in the form:

$$\hat{R}_n = \sum_{m=0}^{2n-2} b_{2n-2-m}(x,t)\frac{\partial^{2n-2-m}}{\partial x^{2n-2-m}}, \qquad \hat{R}_{n+1} = b_{2n}(x,t)\frac{\partial^{2n}}{\partial x^{2n}} + b_{2n-1}(x,t)\frac{\partial^{2n-1}}{\partial x^{2n-1}} + \hat{R}_n. \tag{59}$$

As the order of the linear differential operator increases, the number of unknown functions also increases, and two new functions $b_{2n}(x,t), b_{2n-1}(x,t)$ arise that can also be further predetermined.

Let us show that as the order of the differential operators of the given form (58), (59) increases, the resulting systems for the unknown coefficients $p_m(x,t), q_m(x,t), b_m(x,t)$, $m = 0, 1, \ldots, 2n-2$ do not become overdetermined.

For this, we write the system (55), (56) for for $j = n$:

$$u_t = \left[\hat{L}, D_{2n-1}\right] + \alpha_n u\frac{\partial^{2n+1}}{\partial x^{2n+1}} - \alpha_n \sum_{j=0}^{2n+1} C_{2n+1}^{j} u_{x^j}\frac{\partial^{2n+1-j}}{\partial x^{2n+1-j}} - \mu\left(w\hat{R}_n + \hat{R}_n w\right), \tag{60}$$

$$w_t = \alpha_n w\frac{\partial^{2n+1}}{\partial x^{2n+1}} - \alpha_n \sum_{j=0}^{2n+1} C_{2n+1}^{j} w_{x^j}\frac{\partial^{2n+1-j}}{\partial x^{2n+1-j}} + [w, D_{2n-1}] + \hat{R}_n\hat{L} + \hat{L}\hat{R}_n. \tag{61}$$

Let us group the elements with differential operators of the same order and equate these coefficients to zero:

$$\frac{\partial^{2n}}{\partial x^{2n}} : \begin{cases} -\alpha_n(2n+1)u_x - 2p_{nx} - 2q_{nx} = 0, \\ -\alpha_n(2n+1)w_x - 2b_{2n-2} = 0, \end{cases} \tag{62}$$

$$\frac{\partial^{2n-1}}{\partial x^{2n-1}} : \begin{cases} (4n-1)q_{nxx} + p_{nxx} + (2n+1)n\alpha_n u_{xx} = 0, \\ \alpha_n(2n+1)nw_{xx} + 2b_{2n-3} + 2b_{(2n-2)x} = 0, \end{cases} \tag{63}$$

...

$$1 : \begin{cases} u_t = \sum_{j=1}^{n}\left[uq_{jx^{2j-1}} - q_{jx^{2j+1}} - p_j u_{x^{2j-1}} - (q_j u)_{x^{2j-1}}\right] - \alpha_n u_{x^{2n+1}} - \mu\left[wb_0 + \sum_{j=0}^{2n-2} b_j w_{x^j}\right], \\ w_t = -\alpha_n w_{x^{2n+1}} + \sum_{j=1}^{n}\left[wq_{jx^{2j-1}} - p_j w_{x^{2j-1}} - (q_j w)_{x^{2j-1}}\right] + \sum_{j=0}^{2n-2} b_j u_{x^j} - b_{0xx} + ub_0. \end{cases} \tag{64}$$

Non-trivial equations are obtained, from which the previously unknown functions are redefined $p_m(x,t), q_m(x,t), b_m(x,t)$:

$$b_{2n-2} = -\frac{\alpha_n}{2}(2n+1)w_x, b_{2n-3} = \frac{\alpha_n}{2}(2n+1)(1-n)w_{xx}, p_n = q_n = -\frac{\alpha_n}{4}(2n+1)u.$$

The last pair of (64) gives the desired system on functions $u(x,t)$ and $w(x,t)$.

Now let us perform a similar action for $j = n+1$ and make a grouping of coefficients at differential operators:

$$\frac{\partial^{2n+2}}{\partial x^{2n+2}} : \begin{cases} -\alpha_{n+1}(2n+3)u_x - 2p_{(n+1)x} - 2q_{(n+1)x} = 0, \\ -\alpha_{n+1}(2n+3)w_x - 2b_{2n} = 0, \end{cases} \tag{65}$$

$$\frac{\partial^{2n+1}}{\partial x^{2n+1}}:\begin{cases}(4n+3)q_{(n+1)xx}+p_{(n+1)xx}+(2n+3)(n+1)\alpha_{n+1}u_{xx}=0,\\ \alpha_{n+1}(2n+3)(n+1)w_{xx}+2b_{2n-1}+2b_{2nx}=0,\end{cases}\tag{66}$$

...

$$1:\begin{cases}u_t=\sum_{j=1}^{n+1}\left[uq_{jx^{2j-1}}-q_{jx^{2j+1}}-p_ju_{x^{2j-1}}-(q_ju)_{x^{2j-1}}\right]-\alpha_{n+1}u_{x^{2n+3}}-\mu\left[wb_0+\sum_{j=0}^{2n}b_jw_{x^j}\right],\\ w_t=-\alpha_{n+1}w_{x^{2n+3}}+\sum_{j=1}^{n+1}\left[wq_{jx^{2j-1}}-p_jw_{x^{2j-1}}-(q_jw)_{x^{2j-1}}\right]+\sum_{j=0}^{2n}b_ju_{x^j}-b_{0xx}+ub_0.\end{cases}\tag{67}$$

Comparing the differential operators obtained at $j=n$ and $j=n+1$, we see that only two non-trivial systems are added, corresponding to $\frac{\partial^{2n+2}}{\partial x^{2n+2}}$, $\frac{\partial^{2n+1}}{\partial x^{2n+1}}$. We have a total of four equations from which the functions are uniquely defined:

$$\begin{gathered}p_{n+1}(x,t)=q_{n+1}(x,t)=-\tfrac{\alpha_{n+1}}{2}(2n+3)u,\\ b_{2n}(x,t)=-\tfrac{\alpha_{n+1}}{2}(2n+3)w_x,\qquad b_{2n-1}(x,t)=-\tfrac{\alpha_{n+1}}{2}n(2n+3)w_{xx}.\end{gathered}\tag{68}$$

The number of remaining differential operators from $\frac{\partial^{2n}}{\partial x^{2n}}$ and below coincides with their number for $j=n$ and corresponds to the number of unknown functions $p_m(x,t)$, $q_m(x,t)$, $b_m(x,t)$ (by conjecture); hence, the overdetermination of the system does not arise. As a result, the following theorem is proved.

Theorem 2. *The system (55), (56) with operators of the form (52)–(54) generates a hierarchy of the perturbed Korteweg–de Vries equation on functions $u(x,t)$ and $w(x,t)$ of the form (64), where all functions $p_j(x,t), q_j(x,t), b_j(x,t), j=1,2,\ldots,n$, being coefficients of operators $\hat{A}_n$, $\hat{R}_n$, are defined uniquely from system (62), (63); and μ is an arbitrary parameter.*

Analyzing the structure of obtained systems at higher derivatives (60)–(63), one can notice that the first equations in pairs define the dependence of operator $\hat{A}_n$ coefficients $p_m(x,t), q_m(x,t)$ on function $u(x,t)$ and its derivatives, and the second equations in pairs define operator $\hat{R}_n$ coefficients $b_m(x,t)$ via function $w(x,t)$ and its derivatives (68). Assuming that there is no perturbation $w(x,t)=0$, the operators (51) $\hat{M}$ and $\hat{B}_n$ are transformed into operators $\hat{L}$, and $\hat{A}_n$ ($\hat{N}=0$, $\hat{R}_n=0$), which are Lax pairs for the KdV hierarchy equations. Consequently, all systems (64) will be transformed to higher KdV hierarchy equations.

In addition, from system (64) we can now obtain at once all the equations of the KdV hierarchy expressed through the operator $\hat{A}_n$ coefficients:

$$u_t=\sum_{j=1}^{n}\left[uq_{jx^{2j-1}}-q_{jx^{2j+1}}-p_ju_{x^{2j-1}}-(q_ju)_{x^{2j-1}}\right]-\alpha_nu_{x^{2n+1}}.\tag{69}$$

Theorem 3. *If the functions $u(x,t)$ and $w(x,t)$ satisfy the system (64), then the invariant transformations exist for solutions of the eigenvalue equation $(\hat{M}-\lambda E)V=0$ with operator $\hat{M}$ (45) of the form*

$$\hat{H}_n=\begin{pmatrix}\hat{A}_n & \mu\hat{R}_n\\ -\hat{R}_n & \hat{A}_n\end{pmatrix}-\begin{pmatrix}1&0\\0&1\end{pmatrix}\frac{\partial}{\partial t}, n=1,2,3,\ldots\tag{70}$$

where $V=\begin{pmatrix}v_1(\lambda,x,t)\\ v_2(\lambda,x,t)\end{pmatrix}$ is the vector-function, $\hat{A}_j$, $\hat{R}_j$ have the form (53), (54), λ, μ are the arbitrary parameters.

Proof of Theorem 3. Consider the action of operators $\hat{M}$ and $\hat{H}_n$ on the vector-function $V = \begin{pmatrix} v_1(\lambda, x, t) \\ v_2(\lambda, x, t) \end{pmatrix}$:

$$\begin{pmatrix} \hat{L} - \lambda & \mu\hat{N} \\ \hat{N} & -\hat{L} - \lambda \end{pmatrix} \left[\begin{pmatrix} \hat{A}_1 & \mu\hat{R}_1 \\ -\hat{R}_1 & \hat{A}_1 \end{pmatrix} + \frac{\partial}{\partial t} \right] \begin{pmatrix} v_1 \\ v_2 \end{pmatrix}$$
$$= \begin{pmatrix} (\hat{L}\hat{A}_1 - \lambda\hat{A}_1 - \mu\hat{N}\hat{R}_1)v_1 + \mu(\hat{L}\hat{R}_1 - \lambda\hat{R}_1 + \hat{N}\hat{A}_1)v_2 + (\hat{L} - \lambda)v_{1t} + \mu\hat{N}v_{2t} \\ (\hat{N}\hat{A}_1 + \hat{L}\hat{R}_1 + \lambda\hat{R}_1)v_1 + (\mu\hat{N}\hat{R}_1 - \hat{L}\hat{A}_1 - \lambda\hat{A}_1)v_2 - (\hat{L} + \lambda)v_{2t} + \hat{N}v_{1t} \end{pmatrix}. \tag{71}$$

Since the functions v_1, v_2 are solutions of a homogeneous equation

$$\begin{pmatrix} \hat{L} & \mu\hat{N} \\ \hat{N} & -\hat{L} \end{pmatrix} \begin{pmatrix} v_1 \\ v_2 \end{pmatrix} - \lambda \begin{pmatrix} 1 & 0 \\ 0 & 1 \end{pmatrix} \begin{pmatrix} v_1 \\ v_2 \end{pmatrix} = 0,$$

the following equations take place

$$\hat{L}v_1 + \mu\hat{N}v_2 = \lambda v_1, \hat{N}v_1 - \hat{L}v_2 = \lambda v_2. \tag{72}$$

Let us differentiate (72) by t, and determine the result of the operator $\hat{M} - \lambda E$ action on the functions $v_{1t}(\lambda, x, t), v_{2t}(\lambda, x, t)$:

$$\begin{aligned} v_{1xxt} &= u_t v_1 + \mu w_t v_2 + u v_{1t} + \mu w v_{2t} - \lambda v_{1t}, \\ v_{2xxt} &= u_t v_2 + u v_{2t} + \lambda v_{2t} - w_t v_1 - w v_{1t}, \end{aligned}$$

or in operator form

$$\begin{pmatrix} \hat{L} - \lambda & \mu\hat{N} \\ \hat{N} & -\hat{L} - \lambda \end{pmatrix} \begin{pmatrix} v_{1t} \\ v_{2t} \end{pmatrix} = - \begin{pmatrix} u_t & \mu w_t \\ w_t & -u_t \end{pmatrix} \begin{pmatrix} v_1 \\ v_2 \end{pmatrix} = - \begin{pmatrix} \hat{L}_t & \mu\hat{N}_t \\ \hat{N}_t & -\hat{L}_t \end{pmatrix} \begin{pmatrix} v_1 \\ v_2 \end{pmatrix}. \tag{73}$$

Then, using (72), (73) in (71) we can get rid of the parameter λ and the derivatives $v_{1t}(\lambda, x, t), v_{2t}(\lambda, x, t)$.

The equation $(\hat{M} - \lambda E)\hat{H}_n V = 0$ will take the form of a system

$$\begin{aligned} (\hat{L}\hat{A}_n - \mu\hat{N}\hat{R}_n - \hat{L}_t)v_1 - \hat{A}_n(\hat{L}v_1 + \mu\hat{N}v_2) + \mu(\hat{L}\hat{R}_n + \hat{N}\hat{A}_n - \hat{N}_t)v_2 - \mu\hat{R}_n(\hat{N}v_1 - \hat{L}v_2) = 0, \\ (\hat{N}\hat{A}_n + \hat{L}\hat{R}_n - \hat{N}_t)v_1 + \hat{R}_n(\hat{L}v_1 + \mu\hat{N}v_2) + (\mu\hat{N}\hat{R}_n - \hat{L}\hat{A}_n + \hat{L}_t)v_2 - \hat{A}_n(\hat{N}v_1 - \hat{L}v_2) = 0. \end{aligned}$$

Let us group the terms with v_1, v_2:

$$\begin{aligned} &([\hat{L}, \hat{A}_n] - \mu\hat{N}\hat{R}_n - \hat{L}_t - \mu\hat{R}_n\hat{N})v_1 + \mu(\hat{L}\hat{R}_n + \hat{R}_n\hat{L} + [\hat{N}, \hat{A}_n] - \hat{N}_t)v_2 = 0, \\ &([\hat{N}, \hat{A}_n] + \hat{L}\hat{R}_n - \hat{N}_t + \hat{R}_n\hat{L})v_1 + (\mu\hat{N}\hat{R}_n - [\hat{L}, \hat{A}_n] + \hat{L}_t + \mu\hat{R}_n\hat{N})v_2 = 0. \end{aligned} \tag{74}$$

It is easy to see that in (74) the coefficients at v_1, v_2 are operators of structures (55), (56) at $\delta = 1$, which reduce to the system (64), which proves the theorem. □

3.3. *Perturbation of the Second Korteweg–de Vries Hierarchy*

Let us construct an explicit form of the system describing the perturbation of the second KdV equation. Let us write the elements of operators $\hat{B}_2$, $\hat{R}_2$, and $\hat{A}_2$ in the form (53), (54), and the remaining elements (51), (52) retain the same form

$$\hat{R}_2 = b_2(x, t)\frac{\partial^2}{\partial x^2} + b_1(x, t)\frac{\partial}{\partial x} + b_0(x, t), \tag{75}$$

$$\hat{A}_2 = \alpha_2\frac{\partial^5}{\partial x^5} + p_2\frac{\partial^3}{\partial x^3} + \frac{\partial^3}{\partial x^3}q_2 + p_1\frac{\partial}{\partial x} + \frac{\partial}{\partial x}q_1, \tag{76}$$

where $b_i(x,t), i = 0,1,2, p_j(x,t), q_j(x,t), j = 1, 2$ are unknown functions, the form of which we will specify later, α_2 is an arbitrary constant.

Let us define the form of the system (55), (56). Let us expand the differentiation operators (55) and equate the coefficients at $\frac{\partial^4}{\partial x^4}, \frac{\partial^3}{\partial x^3}, \frac{\partial^2}{\partial x^2}, \frac{\partial}{\partial x}$ to zero; then, we obtain the system:

$$\begin{aligned} &\frac{\partial^4}{\partial x^4} : 2q_{2x} + 2p_{2x} + 5\alpha_2 u_x = 0, \\ &\frac{\partial^3}{\partial x^3} : 10\alpha_2 u_{xx} + p_{2xx} + 7q_{2xx} = 0, \\ &\frac{\partial^2}{\partial x^2} : 9q_{2xxx} + 10\alpha_2 u_{xxx} + 2p_{1x} + 2q_{1x} + 3p_2 u_x + 3q_2 u_x + \mu b_2 w(1+\delta) = 0, \\ &\frac{\partial}{\partial x} : 5q_{2x^4} + 3q_{1xx} - 3uq_{2xx} + 3(q_2 u)_{xx} + p_{1xx} + 3p_2 u_{xx} + \mu(\delta+1) b_1 w \\ &+2\mu\delta b_2 w_x + 5\alpha_2 u_{x^4} = 0, \\ &1: u_t(x,t) = uq_{1x} - q_{2x^5} - q_{1xxx} + uq_{2xxx} - \alpha_2 u_{x^5} - p_2 u_{xxx} - (q_2 u)_{xxx} \\ &-p_1 u_x - (q_1 u)_x - \mu b_0 w(1+\delta) - \mu\delta b_2 w_{xx} - \mu\delta b_1 w_x. \end{aligned} \tag{77}$$

From the first four equations of the system (77) the following functions are defined (the integration constants are assumed to be equal to zero):

$$q_2 = p_2 = -\frac{5}{4}\alpha_2 u, \quad p_{1x} = \frac{5}{8}\alpha_2 u_{xxx} + \frac{15}{4}\alpha_2 u u_x - \frac{\mu(1+\delta)}{2} b_2 w - q_{1x}, \tag{78}$$

$$q_{1xx} = \frac{5}{16}\alpha_2 u_{xxxx} + \frac{15}{16}\alpha_2 u_{xx}^2 + \frac{\mu(1+\delta)}{4}(b_2 w)_x - \frac{\mu(1+\delta)}{2} b_1 w - \mu\delta b_2 w_x. \tag{79}$$

Let us perform a similar procedure with the operator equation (56), resulting in the following system:

$$\begin{aligned} &\frac{\partial^4}{\partial x^4} : 5\alpha_2 w_x + (1+\delta) b_2 = 0, \\ &\frac{\partial^3}{\partial x^3} : 10\alpha_2 w_{xx} + (1+\delta) b_1 + 2\delta b_{2x} = 0, \\ &\frac{\partial^2}{\partial x^2} : 3wq_{2x} + (1+\delta)(ub_2 - b_0) - 10\alpha_2 w_{xxx} - 3p_2 w_x - 3(q_2 w)_x - \delta b_{2xx} - 2\delta b_{1x} = 0, \\ &\frac{\partial}{\partial x} : 3wq_{2xx} - 5\alpha_2 w_{x^4} + 2b_2 u_x + (1+\delta) b_1 u - 3p_2 w_{xx} - 3(q_2 w)_{xx} - \delta b_{1xx} - 2\delta b_{0x} = 0, \\ &1: w_t = wq_{2xxx} - \alpha_2 w_{x^5} - \delta b_{0xx} + b_2 u_{xx} + b_1 u_x + b_0 u - p_2 w_{xxx} + \delta u b_0 - (q_2 w)_{xxx} \\ &-p_1 w_x - q_1 w_x. \end{aligned} \tag{80}$$

The values of the functions are uniquely defined:

$$b_2(x,t) = -5\frac{\alpha_2}{\delta+1} w_x, \; b_1(x,t) = -\frac{10\alpha_2}{(\delta+1)^2} w_{xx}, \tag{81}$$

$$b_0(x,t) = \frac{5\alpha_2}{2(1+\delta)} u w_x + 5\alpha_2 \frac{4\delta - (\delta+1)(\delta+2)}{(\delta+1)^3} w_{xxx}, \tag{82}$$

$$5\alpha_2\left(2\delta\frac{\delta^2+3}{(\delta+1)^3} - 1\right) w_{x^4} + \frac{5\alpha_2}{\delta+1}\frac{1}{2}(\delta-1)(u_x w_x + u w_{xx}) = 0. \tag{83}$$

For (83) to be true identically, it is necessary to put the coefficients equal to zero:

$$2\delta\frac{\delta^2+3}{(\delta+1)^3} - 1 = 0, \;\; \delta - 1 = 0.$$

It is possible at $\delta = 1$.

As a result, from the two systems (77), (80) only the last equations that form the dynamical system remain. Let us substitute the found values of the functions by putting $\alpha_2 = -16$, and we obtain the system:

$$\begin{aligned} u_t &= \left[u_{xxxx} - 10uu_{xx} - 5u_x^2 + 10u^3 - 20\mu(w_{xx}w - w^2u)\right]_x, \\ w_t &= -4w_{x^5} + 20uw_{xxx} + 20w_{xx}u_x + 10w_xu_{xx} + 10(2\mu w^2 - u^2)w_x. \end{aligned} \tag{84}$$

As a result of this reasoning, the following corollary is proven.

Corollary 8. *The nonlinear system of Equation (84) has the operator representation (55), (56) with operators of the form (52), where $\hat{L}$ is the Sturm–Liouville operator, and the other operators have the form*

$$\hat{R}_2 = 40\left(w_x\frac{\partial^2}{\partial x^2} + w_{xx}\frac{\partial}{\partial x} + \frac{1}{2}[uw_x - w_{xxx}]\right), \ \hat{N} = w(x,t), \tag{85}$$

$$\hat{A}_2 = -16\frac{\partial^5}{\partial x^5} + 20u\frac{\partial^3}{\partial x^3} + 20\frac{\partial^3}{\partial x^3}u - 5(u_{xx} + 3u^2 + 2\mu w^2)\frac{\partial}{\partial x} - 5\frac{\partial}{\partial x}(u_{xx} + 3u^2 + 2\mu w^2), \tag{86}$$

where $\delta = 1$, $u(x,t), w(x,t)$ are arbitrary real functions, μ is an arbitrary parameter.

The system (84) is a perturbation of the second equation of the KdV hierarchy, since when $w = 0$ and at replacement $u(x,t) \to -u(x,t)$ the system is reduced to one equation, and this is the second equation of the KdV hierarchy:

$$u_t = (u_{xxxx} + 5u_x^2 + 10uu_{xx} + 10u^3)_x.$$

In the particular case when $\mu = 1$, and the functions $u(x,t), w(x,t)$ represent, respectively, the real and imaginary parts of some complex function $q(x,t) = u(x,t) + iw(x,t)$, the system (84) describes the behavior of the real and imaginary parts of the second equation of the KdV complexification hierarchy:

$$\begin{aligned} q_t = {} & 10\left(q^2 + |q|^2\right)\bar{q}_x + \tfrac{5}{2}\left(\bar{q}^2 + 6|q|^2 - 3q^2\right)q_x - 5q_x(\bar{q} + 3q)_{xx} - 10q\bar{q}_{xxx} \\ & -\tfrac{5}{4}\left(2|q|^2 - 3q^2 + 3\bar{q}^2\right)_{xxx} + \tfrac{1}{2}(5\bar{q} - 3q)_{xxxxx} \end{aligned}$$

4. Conclusions

In this paper we use the Lax operator equation, where the scattering operator is a Hermitian differential operator of the fourth order and the operator determining the dynamics of the eigenfunctions is a skew-symmetric differential operator with an odd higher order. We consider the possibility of constructing a hierarchy of the complex extension of the Korteweg–de Vries equation and a hierarchy of its perturbation with a special perturbation function. The first and second parts are based on the Lax method with operators having a matrix structure.

It is proved that for the equation on the eigenvalues of the fourth-order scattering operator, there exists a countable number of $\hat{H}_n$ operators that translate its solution into its other solution. Moreover, $\hat{H}_n$ operators are considered as differential operators of order $2n + 1$, which generate a hierarchy of cKdV and a hierarchy of pKdV.

All obtained equations describe nonlinear waves arising in various media with dispersion, and mainly these are problems of gas and hydrodynamics.

The obtained new nonlinear equations and systems possess a Lax pair, and hence one can expect the following properties: an infinite number of conservation laws, Painlevé coupling of the partial differential equation with the system of ordinary differential equations, Hamiltonian structure, Hirota formalism for constructing n-soliton solutions, Bäcklund transformations, etc.

Author Contributions: Conceptualization, T.V.R.; methodology, T.V.R.; validation, O.B.S.; formal analysis, A.R.Z. and R.G.Z.; investigation, T.V.R.; writing—original draft preparation, T.V.R.; writing—review and editing, A.R.Z. and R.G.Z.; project administration, A.R.Z. All authors have read and agreed to the published version of the manuscript.

Funding: This research was funded by North-Caucasus Center for Mathematical Research under agreement No. 075-02-2023-938 with the Ministry of Science and Higher Education of the Russian Federation.

Data Availability Statement: No new data were created.

Conflicts of Interest: The authors declare no conflict of interest.

References

1. Gardner, C.S.; Greene, J.M.; Kruskal, M.D.; Miura, R.M. Method for solving the Korteweg-de Vries equation. *Phys. Rev. Lett.* **1967**, *19*, 1095–1097. [CrossRef]
2. Liu, X.-K.; Wen, X.-Y. A discrete KdV equation hierarchy: Continuous limit, diverse exact solutions and their asymptotic state analysis. *Commun. Theor. Phys.* **2022**, *74*, 065001. [CrossRef]
3. Li, F.; Yao, Y. Multisoliton and rational solutions for the extended fifth-order KdV equation in fluids with self-consistent sources. *Theor. Math. Phys.* **2022**, *210*, 184–197. [CrossRef]
4. Zemlyanukhin, A.I.; Bochkarev, A.V. The perturbation method and exact solutions of nonlinear dynamics equations for media with microstructure. *Comput. Contin. Mech.* **2016**, *9*, 182–191. [CrossRef]
5. Kudryashov, N.A. Remarks on rational solutions for the Korteweg-de Vries hierarchy. *arXiv* **2007**, arXiv:nlin/0701034.
6. Clarkson, P.A.; Joshi, N.; Mazzocco, M. The Lax pair for the mKdV hierarchy. *Sémin. Congrès* **2006**, *14*, 53–64.
7. Ye, S.; Zeng, Y. Integration of the modified Korteweg-de Vries hierarchy with an integral type of source. *J. Phys. A Math. Gen.* **2002**, *35*, L283–L291. [CrossRef]
8. Joshi, N. The second Painlevé hierarchy and the stationary KdV hierarchy. *Publ. Res. Inst. Math. Sci.* **2004**, *40*, 1039–1061. [CrossRef]
9. Zabrodin, A.V. Kadomtsev–Petviashvili hierarchies of types B and C. *Theor. Math. Phys.* **2021**, *208*, 865–885. [CrossRef]
10. Zhang, Y.; Rui, W. A few super-integrable hierarchies and some re-ductions, super-Hamiltonian structures. *Rep. Math. Phys.* **2015**, *75*, 231–255. [CrossRef]
11. Liu, J.-G.; Yang, X.-J.; Feng, Y.-Y.; Cui, P.; Geng, L.-L. On integrability of the higher dimensional time fractional KdV-type equation. *J. Geom. Phys.* **2021**, *160*, 104000. [CrossRef]
12. Kundu, A. Integrable twofold hierarchy of perturbed equations and application to optical soliton dynamics. *Theor. Math. Phys.* **2011**, *167*, 800–810. [CrossRef]
13. Redkina, T.V.; Zakinyan, R.G.; Zakinyan, A.R.; Surneva, O.B.; Yanovskaya, O.S. Bäcklund Transformations for Nonlinear Differential Equations and Systems. *Axioms* **2019**, *8*, 45. [CrossRef]
14. Bogoyavlenskiĭ, O.I. Breaking solitons II. *Math. USSR Izv.* **1990**, *35*, 245–248. [CrossRef]
15. Bogoyavlenskiĭ, O.I. Breaking solitons III. *Math. USSR Izv.* **1991**, *36*, 129–137. [CrossRef]
16. Redkina, T.V. Some properties of the complexification of the Korteweg-de Vries equation. *Izv. Acad. Sci. USSR Ser. Math.* **1991**, *55*, 1300–1311.
17. Lax, P.D. Integrals of nonlinear equation of evolution and solitary waves. *Commun. Pure Appl. Math.* **1968**, *21*, 467–490. [CrossRef]
18. Kuperschmidt, B.A. *Integrable and Super-Integrable Systems*; World Scientific: Singapore, 1990.
19. Kuperschmidt, B.A. A super Korteweg-de Vries equation: An integrable system. *Phys. Lett. A* **1984**, *102*, 213–215. [CrossRef]
20. Manin, Y.I.; Radul, A.O. A supersymmetric extension of the Kadomtsev-Petviashvili hierarchy. *Commun. Math. Phys.* **1985**, *98*, 65–77. [CrossRef]
21. Magnot, J.P.; Rubtsov, V.N. On the Kadomtsev-Petviashvili hierarchy in an extended class of formal pseudo-differential operators. *Theor. Math. Phys.* **2021**, *207*, 458–488. [CrossRef]
22. Geng, X.; Wu, L. A new super-extension of the KdV hierarchy. *Appl. Math. Lett.* **2010**, *23*, 716–721. [CrossRef]

Disclaimer/Publisher's Note: The statements, opinions and data contained in all publications are solely those of the individual author(s) and contributor(s) and not of MDPI and/or the editor(s). MDPI and/or the editor(s) disclaim responsibility for any injury to people or property resulting from any ideas, methods, instructions or products referred to in the content.

axioms

MDPI

Article

Hyers–Ulam and Hyers–Ulam–Rassias Stability for Linear Fractional Systems with Riemann–Liouville Derivatives and Distributed Delays

Hristo Kiskinov [1], Ekaterina Madamlieva [2] and Andrey Zahariev [1,*]

[1] Department of Mathematical Analysis, Faculty of Mathematics and Informatics, University of Plovdiv, 4000 Plovdiv, Bulgaria; kiskinov@uni-plovdiv.bg
[2] Department of Mathematical Analysis and Differential Equations, Faculty of Applied Mathematics and Informatics, Technical University of Sofia, 1756 Sofia, Bulgaria; ekk.m@tu-sofia.bg
* Correspondence: zandrey@uni-plovdiv.bg

Abstract: The aim of the present paper is to study the asymptotic properties of the solutions of linear fractional system with Riemann–Liouville-type derivatives and distributed delays. We prove under natural assumptions (similar to those used in the case when the derivatives are first (integer) order) the existence and uniqueness of the solutions in the initial problem for these systems with discontinuous initial functions. As a consequence, we also prove the existence of a unique fundamental matrix for the homogeneous system, which allows us to establish an integral representation of the solutions to the initial problem for the corresponding inhomogeneous system. Then, we introduce for the studied systems a concept for Hyers–Ulam in time stability and Hyers–Ulam–Rassias in time stability. As an application of the obtained results, we propose a new approach (instead of the standard fixed point approach) based on the obtained integral representation and establish sufficient conditions, which guarantee Hyers–Ulam-type stability in time. Finally, it is proved that the Hyers–Ulam-type stability in time leads to Lyapunov stability in time for the investigated homogeneous systems.

Keywords: Riemann–Liouville fractional derivative; distributed delay; fundamental matrix; stability

MSC: 34A08; 34A12; 34D05; 34D20

Citation: Kiskinov, H.; Madamlieva, E.; Zahariev, A. Hyers–Ulam and Hyers–Ulam–Rassias stability for Linear Fractional Systems with Riemann–Liouville Derivatives and Distributed Delays. *Axioms* **2023**, *12*, 637. https://doi.org/10.3390/axioms12070637

Academic Editors: Hatıra Günerhan, Francisco Martínez González and Mohammed K. A. Kaabar

Received: 4 June 2023
Revised: 24 June 2023
Accepted: 25 June 2023
Published: 27 June 2023

Copyright: © 2023 by the authors. Licensee MDPI, Basel, Switzerland. This article is an open access article distributed under the terms and conditions of the Creative Commons Attribution (CC BY) license (https://creativecommons.org/licenses/by/4.0/).

1. Introduction

Practically, it is established that many real-world phenomena in various fields of science can be represented more accurately through mathematical models, including fractional differential equations. For more detailed information on fractional calculus theory and fractional differential equations, see the monographs of Kilbas et al. [1] and Podlubny [2]. It is well known that the existence of an integral representation (variation of constants formula) of the solutions of linear fractional differential equations and/or systems (ordinary or delayed) is a main tool in executing their qualitative analysis. In this aspect, the problem of establishing such integral representations (for which the existence of a fundamental matrix is needed) is an important task for stability analysis. It is no surprise that there exist many papers devoted to this problem.

A good historical overview concerning the stability results for fractional differential equations obtained till 2011 can be found in the excellent survey [3] and the references therein. For more recent works, for fractional differential equations and systems without delay, see [4,5]. Integral representation and the stability results in the autonomous case of delayed fractional differential equations mainly with Caputo-type derivatives are given in [6,7] and for the neutral case in [8–10]. For the nonautonomous case with variable delay, we refer to [11–13] and for the neutral case, to [14,15]. The case with Riemann–Liouville (RL)-type derivatives is studied significantly less often, but the works [16–20], and the references therein, give a good overview of the research in this area. To expand the information concerning the scope of the studied objects, we refer to the new works [21–24] devoted to the stability analysis of other important kinds of equations such as integro-differential, fuzzy, neural networks, etc.

It must be noted that the difference between the fractional Caputo derivatives and the fractional Riemann–Liouville (RL) derivatives are not only technical but also fundamental, since the Caputo fractional derivative of a constant is equal to zero, while the Riemann–Liouville fractional derivative of a constant is different from zero when the constant is not equal to zero. Thus, the main theorem of integral calculus is not true for the case of fractional Riemann–Liouville derivatives. This fact leads to large complications in many technical and fundamental aspects.

Our work is primarily motivated by the works [17,20]. In the present work, we consider a linear fractional system with distributed delay and derivatives in the RL sense. For these systems, we study two important problems. The first of them is to clear the problem with existence and the uniqueness of the solutions of the initial problem (IP) in the case of discontinuous initial functions. As far as we know (except in the autonomous case), there are no results concerning the initial problem for fractional differential equations with derivatives in the RL sense and distributed delay with discontinuous initial function. This result allows as a consequence to establish a variation of the constants formula for this initial problem. The second one is to introduce a concept for Hyers–Ulam (HU) in time stability and Hyers–Ulam–Rassias (HUR) in time stability (based on the concept of time stability in the Lyapunov sense introduced in the remarkable work [20]) for these systems and to establish some sufficient conditions which guaranty their Hyers–Ulam in time stability.

As far we know this paper is the first to study Hyers–Ulam-type stability and Hyers–Ulam–Rassias-type stability for linear fractional systems with distributed delay and derivatives in the Riemann–Liouville sense.

The paper is organized as follows: In Section 2, we recall some needed definitions and properties concerning the RL and Caputo fractional derivatives and present the problem statement. Section 3 is devoted to the existence and the uniqueness of the solutions of the initial (Cauchy) problem for the linear fractional differential system with distributed delays and RL-type derivatives in the case when the initial function is discontinuous. In Section 4, as a consequence, we prove the existence and uniqueness of a fundamental matrix, which allows us to establish an integral representation of the solution to the initial problem for the corresponding inhomogeneous system. In Section 5, we introduce a concept for HU in time stability and HUR in time stability for the investigated systems. In addition, as an application of the obtained in the previous section's results, we introduce a new approach via the obtained integral representation (replacing the standard fixed point approach) to establish sufficient conditions for HU in the time stability of these systems. Finally, for the homogeneous systems it is proved that the HU in time stability implies time stability in the Lyapunov sense. As usual, in the last Section 6, we provide some conclusions concerning the obtained results, and some open problems are proposed.

2. Preliminaries and Problem Statement

As is usual to avoid misunderstandings, below we provide the definitions of RL (RL) and Caputo fractional derivatives. For more details and other properties, we refer to [1].

Let $a \in \mathbb{R}, \alpha \in (0,1)$ be arbitrary and $g \in L_1^{loc}(\mathbb{R},\mathbb{R})$, where $L_1^{loc}(\mathbb{R},\mathbb{R})$ is the linear space of all locally Lebesgue integrable functions $g : \mathbb{R} \to \mathbb{R}$ and let $BL_1^{loc}(\mathbb{R},\mathbb{R}) \subset L_1^{loc}(\mathbb{R},\mathbb{R})$ be the subspace of all locally bounded functions.

The left-sided fractional integral operators of order $\alpha \in (0,1)$ for arbitrary $g \in L_1^{loc}(\mathbb{R},\mathbb{R})$ is defined by $(I_{a+}^{\alpha}g)(t) = \frac{1}{\Gamma(\alpha)}\int\limits_a^t (t-s)^{\alpha-1}g(s)ds$, and the corresponding left-side RL fractional derivative by $({}_{RL}D_{a+}^{\alpha}g)(t) = \frac{d}{dt}(I_{a+}^{1-\alpha}g)(t)$, $(D_{a+}^{0}g)(t) = g(t)$ for every $t > a$.

By ${}_CD^{\alpha}_{a+}g(t) = ({}_{RL}D^{\alpha}_{a+}[g(s) - g(a)])(t)$, we define the Caputo fractional derivative of the same order (see [1]).

Consider the fractional linear system with RL-type derivatives and distributed delays in the following general form:

$$ {}_{RL}D^{\alpha}_{a+}X(t) = \int\limits_{-h}^{0} [\mathrm{d}_{\theta}U(t,\theta)]X(t+\theta) + F(t), \tag{1} $$

where $J = [a,\infty)$, $J^0 = (a,\infty)$, $a \in \mathbb{R}$, $k \in \langle n \rangle = \{1,2,...,n\}$, $\langle m \rangle_0 = \langle m \rangle \cup \{0\}$, $h > 0$, $\alpha \in (0,1)$, $X(t) = col(x_1(t),...,x_n(t)) : J^0 \to \mathbb{R}^n$, $F(t) = col(f_1(t),...,f_n(t)) : J \to \mathbb{R}^n$ (the notation col mean column), $U(t,\theta) = \sum\limits_{i\in\langle m\rangle_0} U^i(t,\theta)$, $U^i : J \times \mathbb{R} \to \mathbb{R}^{n\times n}$, $U^i(t,\theta) = \{u^i_{kj}(t,\theta)\}^n_{k,j=1}$, ${}_{RL}D^{\alpha}_{a+}X(t) = col({}_{RL}D^{\alpha}_{a+}x_1(t),......, {}_{RL}D^{\alpha}_{a+}x_n(t))$, ${}_{RL}D^{\alpha}_{a+}$ denotes the left-side RL fractional derivative and $\alpha \in (0,1)$. A more detailed description of the homogenous case of system (1) (i.e., $f_k(t) \equiv 0$, $k \in \langle n \rangle$) has the form

$$ {}_{RL}D^{\alpha}_{a+}x_k(t) = \sum_{i\in\langle m\rangle_0}^{m} (\sum_{j=1}^{n} \int\limits_{-\sigma}^{0} x_j(t+\theta)\mathrm{d}_{\theta}u^i_{kj}(t,\theta)\,),\ k \in \langle n \rangle,\ n \in \mathbb{N}. \tag{2} $$

The following standard notations will be used too: $\mathbb{R}^0_+ = (0,\infty)$, $J_{-h} = [a-h,\infty)$, $J_b^{-h} = [a-h, a+b]$, $b,h \in \mathbb{R}^0_+$, $J_b = [a,a+b]$, $J_b^0 = (a,a+b]$, $\mathbf{0} \in \mathbb{R}^n$ is the zero vector, and by $\mathrm{I}, \Theta \in \mathbb{R}^{n\times n}$ are denoted the identity and the zero matrices. For $Y : J_a \times \mathbb{R} \to \mathbb{R}^{n\times n}$, $Y(t,\theta) = \{y^i_j(t,\theta)\}^n_{i,j=1}$, $|Y(t,\theta)| = \sum\limits_{k,j=1}^{n} |y^j_k(t,\theta)|$, $BV^{loc}(J\times\mathbb{R},\mathbb{R}^{n\times n})$, we denote the linear space of matrix valued functions $Y(t,\theta)$ with bounded variation in θ on every compact subinterval $K \subset \mathbb{R}$, and $Var_K Y(t,\cdot) = \{Var_K y^j_k(t,\cdot)\}^n_{k,j=1}$.

With $\mathbf{PC} = PC([-h,0],\mathbb{R}^n)$($\mathbf{PC}^* = \mathbf{PC} \cap BV([-h,0],\mathbb{R}^n)$), we denote the Banach spaces of all vector-valued piecewise continuous (piecewise continuous with bounded variation) functions, $\Phi = (\phi_1,...,\phi_n)^T : [-h,0] \to \mathbb{R}^n$ with norm $||\Phi|| = \sum\limits_{k\in\langle n\rangle} \sup\limits_{s\in[-h,0]} |\phi_k(s)| < \infty$ and for each $\Phi \in \mathbf{PC}$ by S^{Φ}, we denote the set of all jump points. In addition, for $\Phi \in \mathbf{PC}$, we assume that they are right continuous at $t \in S^{\Phi}$.

For arbitrary $\Phi \in \mathbf{PC}$, we introduce the following initial condition for the system (1):

$$ X(t) = \Phi(t-a)(x_k(t) = \phi_k(t-a),\ k \in \langle n \rangle),\ t \in [a-h,a], {}_{RL}D^{\alpha-1}_{a}X(a+0) = \Phi(0),\ h \in \mathbb{R}_+. \tag{3} $$

For other types of initial conditions, see [25].

Definition 1 ([26] p. 12, [27] p. 167, and [28] p. 100). *We say that for the kernels $U^i : \overline{\mathbb{R}}_+ \times \mathbb{R} \to \mathbb{R}^{n\times n}$, the conditions (S) are fulfilled if for $i \in \langle m \rangle_0$, the following conditions hold:*

(S1) *The function $(t,\theta) \to U^i(t,\theta)$ is measurable in $(t,\theta) \in J \times \mathbb{R}$ and normalized so that $U^i(t,\theta) = 0$ for $\theta \geq 0$ and $U^i(t,\theta) = U^i(t,-h)$ for $\theta \leq -h$, $t \in J$.*

(S2) *For any $t \in J$, the kernel $U^i(t,\theta)$ is continuous from the left in θ on $(-\sigma,0)$, $U^i(t,\cdot) \in BV^{loc}(J\times\mathbb{R},\mathbb{R}^{n\times n})$ in θ and $\left|Var_{[-h,0]}U^i(t,\cdot)\right| \in BL^{loc}_1(J_a,\mathbb{R}_+)$.*

(S3) *The Lebesgue decomposition of the kernel $U^i(t,\theta)$ for $t \in J$ and $\theta \in [-h,0]$ for each $i \in \langle m \rangle_0$ have the form: $U^i(t,\theta) = U^i_j(t,\theta) + U^i_{ac}(t,\theta) + U^i_s(t,\theta)$, where the jump part $U^i_j(t,\theta) = \{a^i_{kj}(t)H(\theta + \sigma^i_{kj}(t))\}^n_{k,j=1}$, $A^i(t) = \{a^i_{kj}(t)\}^n_{k,j=1} \in BL^{loc}_1(J,\mathbb{R}^n)$, $H(t)$ is the Heaviside function and the delays $\sigma^i_{kj}(t) \in C(J_a,[0,h])$, $\sigma^0_{kj}(t) \equiv 0, k,j \in \langle n \rangle$, $t \in J_a$. For every fixed $t \in J$, the functions $U^i_{ac}(t,\cdot) \in AC([-h,0],\mathbb{R}^{n\times n})$ and $U^i_s(t,\cdot) \in C([-h,0],\mathbb{R}^{n\times n})$ in $\theta \in \mathbb{R}$.*

(**S4**) *The sets* $S^i_{\Phi} = \{t \in J |\ t - \sigma_i(t) \in S_{\Phi}\}$ *do not have limit points and for any* $t, t_* \in J$, *the relation* $\int\limits_{-\sigma}^{0} |U^i(t,\theta) - U^i(t_*,\theta)| \mathrm{d}\theta \to 0$ *hold.*

Definition 2. *The vector function col* $X(t) = (x_1(t), \ldots, x_n(t))$ *is a solution of the IP* (1), (3) *in* $J^0_b(J^0)$, *if* $X|_{J^0_b} \in C(J^0_b, \mathbb{R}^n)(X|_{J^0} \in C(J^0, \mathbb{R}^n))$ *satisfies the system* (1) *for all* $t \in J^0_b(J^0)$ *and the initial condition* (3).

Consider the following auxiliary system for $k \in \langle n \rangle$

$$x_k(t) = \frac{\phi_k(0)(t-a)^{\alpha-1}}{\Gamma(\alpha)} + \frac{1}{\Gamma(\alpha)}[\int\limits_{a}^{t} (t-\eta)^{\alpha-1}[\sum_{i\in\langle m\rangle_0} (\sum_{j\in\langle n\rangle} \int\limits_{-h}^{0} x_j(\eta+\theta) \mathrm{d}_\theta u^i_{kj}(\eta,\theta))] \,d\eta$$
$$+ \int\limits_{a}^{t} (t-\eta)^{\alpha-1} f_k(\eta) \mathrm{d}\eta]. \tag{4}$$

Definition 3. *The vector function col* $X(t) = (x_1(t), ..., x_n(t))$ *is a solution of the IP* (4), (3) *in* $J^0_b(J^0)$ *if* $X|_{J^0_b} \in C(J^0_b, \mathbb{R}^n)(X|_{J^0} \in C(J^0, \mathbb{R}^n))$ *satisfies the system* (4) *for all* $t \in J^0_b(J^0)$ *and the initial condition* (3).

Let $G(t) = (g_1(t), \ldots, g_n(t)) : J^0_b \to \mathbb{R}^n$, $b \in \mathbb{R}_+$ and $\gamma \in [0,1]$ be arbitrary.

Definition 4. *The function* $G(t) = (g_1(t), \ldots, g_n(t)) \in C(J^0_b, \mathbb{R}^n)$, $b \in \mathbb{R}_+$, $\gamma \in [0,1]$ *will be called* $\gamma-$*continuous at a if the function* $I_\gamma(t-a)G(t) = col((t-a)^\gamma g_1(t), \ldots, (t-a)^\gamma g_n(t)) \in C(J_b, \mathbb{R}^n)$.

With $\mathbf{C}^\gamma_b$, we will denote the real linear space of all γ-continuous at a functions $G(t) \in C(J^0_b, \mathbb{R}^n)$ and with $\mathbf{C}^\gamma$ the linear space of all functions $G(t) \in C(J^0, \mathbb{R}^n)$, which are γ-continuous at a.

In our exposition below we will need the following auxiliary results:

Theorem 1 ([29] Fixpunktsatz). *Let* Ω *be a complete metric space endowed with metric* d_Ω, *the operator* $T : \Omega \to \Omega$ *and let the following conditions hold:*

1. *There exists a sequence* $\{\varepsilon_q \geq 0\}_{q\in\mathbb{N}}$, *with* $\sum\limits_{q=1}^{\infty} \varepsilon_q < \infty$.
2. *For each* $q \in \mathbb{N}$ *and for arbitrary* $x, y \in \Omega$, *the inequality* $d_\Omega(T^q x, T^q y) \leq \varepsilon_q d_\Omega(x,y)$ *hold.*

Then, the operator T has a uniquely fixed point $x^* \in \Omega$, *and for every* $x^0 \in \Omega$, *we have that* $\lim\limits_{q\to\infty} T^q x^0 = x^*$.

Lemma 1 (Lemma 1 [7]). *Let the following conditions be fulfilled.*

1. *The conditions (S) hold.*
2. *The functions* $F \in BL^{loc}_1(J, \mathbb{R}^n)$.

Then, every solution $X(t)$ *of IP* (1), (3) *is a solution of the IP* (4), (3) *and vice versa.*

Lemma 2 (Lemma 3.2 [1]). *Let* $\alpha \in (0,1)$, *and let* $y(t)$ *be a Lebesgue measurable function on* J_b.

(a) *If there exists a.e. (almost everywhere) the limit* $\lim\limits_{t\to a+0}[(t-a)^{1-\alpha} y(t)] = c \in \mathbb{R}$, *then there also exists a.e. the limit* $(D^{\alpha-1}_a y)(a+0) = (I^{1-\alpha}_a y)(a+0) = \lim\limits_{t\to a+0} (I^{1-\alpha}_a y)(t) = c\Gamma(\alpha)$.

(b) *If there exist a.e. the limit* $\lim\limits_{t\to a+0}[(t-a)^{1-\alpha} y(t)]$ *and* $\lim\limits_{t\to a+0} (I^{1-\alpha}_a y)(t) = c^*$, *then we have that* $\lim\limits_{t\to a+0}[(t-a)^{1-\alpha} y(t)] = \frac{c^*}{\Gamma(\alpha)}$.

Let $\overline{\Phi}(t) \in \mathbf{PC}^*$ be an arbitrary function. Define the set

$$\overline{M} = \{\Phi(t) \in \mathbf{PC}^* |\ \Phi(0) = \overline{\Phi}(0)\}$$

and introduce for arbitrary $\Phi^1(t), \Phi^2(t) \in \overline{M}$ the following metric functions:

$$d_{Var}(\Phi^1, \Phi^2) = \left|Var_{t\in[-h,0]}(\Phi^1(t) - \Phi^2(t))\right| \text{ and } d_{\sup}(\Phi^1, \Phi^2) = \sup_{t\in[-h,0]} \left|\Phi^1(t) - \Phi^2(t)\right|.$$

Lemma 3 (Lemma 1 [30]). *The set $\overline{M}$ is a complete metric space concerning both metrics and they are equivalent, i.e., there exist constant $C \in \mathbb{R}_+^0$ such that $d_{Var}(\Phi^1, \Phi^2) \leq C d_{\sup}(\Phi^1, \Phi^2)$ for arbitrary $\Phi^1(t), \Phi^2(t) \in \overline{M}$ (the inequality $d_{\sup}(\Phi^1, \Phi^2) \leq d_{Var}(\Phi^1, \Phi^2)$ obviously holds).*

3. The Initial Problem with Discontinuous Initial Function

Let $\Phi \in \mathbf{PC}$ be a fixed arbitrary initial function and introduce the set

$$\begin{aligned}\mathbf{M}^{1-\alpha} =&\{G : [a-h, \infty) \to \mathbb{R}^n |\ G|_J \in \mathbf{C}^{1-\alpha},\\ &G(t) = \Phi(t),\ t \in [a-h, a],\ {}_{RL}D_a^{\alpha-1}G(a+0) = \Phi(0)\}.\end{aligned}$$

For every $b \in \mathbb{R}_+$, define the sets

$$\mathbf{M}_b^{1-\alpha} = \{G^b = (g_1^b(t), ..., g_n^b(t)) | G^b = G|_{[a-h,a+b]}, G \in \mathbf{M}^{1-\alpha}\}$$

and the metric function $d_b^{\Phi} : \mathbf{M}_b^{1-\alpha} \times \mathbf{M}_b^{1-\alpha} \to \overline{\mathbb{R}}_+$ with

$$d_b^{\Phi}(G^b, \overline{G}^b) = \sum_{k=1}^{n} \sup_{t\in J_b}(t-a)^{1-\alpha}|g_k^b(t) - \overline{g}_k^b(t)|$$

for each $G^b, \overline{G}^b \in \mathbf{M}_b^{\Phi}$. It is not so hard to check that the set $\mathbf{M}_b^{\Phi}$ endowed with the metric d_b^{Φ} is a complete metric space. Note that for arbitrary $G^b, \overline{G}^b \in \mathbf{M}_b^{\Phi}$, according Lemma 2, we have that

$$\lim_{t\to a+0} (t-a)^{1-\alpha}G^b(t) = \Phi(0) = \lim_{t\to a+0} (t-a)^{1-\alpha}\overline{G}^b(t) \text{ and } G^b(a) = \overline{G}^b(a) = \Phi(0).$$

For every $G^b \in \mathbf{M}_b^{1-\alpha}$, we define for $t \in J_0$ the operator $\Re = (\Re_1, ..., \Re_n)$ as follows:

$$\begin{aligned}\Re_k g_k^b(t) =& \frac{\phi_k(0)(t-a)^{\alpha-1}}{\Gamma(\alpha)} + \frac{1}{\Gamma(\alpha)}\int_a^t (t-\eta)^{\alpha-1} f_k(\eta) d\eta]\\ &+ \frac{1}{\Gamma(\alpha)}\int_a^t (t-\eta)^{\alpha-1}\left(\sum_{i\in\langle m\rangle_0}\left(\sum_{j\in\langle n\rangle}\int_{-h}^{0} g_j^b(\eta+\theta) d_\theta u_{kj}^i(\eta,\theta))\right] d\eta\right)\right)\end{aligned} \tag{5}$$

$$\Re_k g_k^b(t) = \phi_k(t),\ t \in [a-h, a],\ k \in \langle n\rangle. \tag{6}$$

Theorem 2. *Let the following conditions be fulfilled.*

1. *The conditions (S) hold.*
2. *The kernels $U_s^i(t,\theta) \equiv \Theta$ in $J \times \mathbb{R}$, $i \in \langle m\rangle_0$, (i.e., in the Lebesgue decomposition of $U^i(t,\theta)$ did not exist a singular part) and $\sum_{i\in\langle m\rangle_0} \sup_{\theta\in[-h,0]} \left|\frac{\partial U^i}{\partial\theta}(\cdot,\theta)\right| \in BL_1^{loc}(J, \mathbb{R}^{n\times n})$.*
3. *The functions $F \in BL_1^{loc}(J, \mathbb{R}^n)$.*

Then, the IP (1), (3) has a unique solution $X(t) \in \mathbf{M}_b^{1-\alpha}$ for arbitrary $b \in \mathbb{R}$.

Proof. According to Lemma 1, we can instead (1), (3) study the IP (4), (3).

Let $\Phi \in \mathbf{PC}$ be an arbitrary fixed initial function and $b \in \mathbb{R}_+$ be an arbitrary fixed number. First, we will prove that $\Re(\mathbf{M}_b^{1-\alpha}) \subseteq \mathbf{M}_b^{1-\alpha}$. From condition 2 of Theorem 2, it follows that the function $t \to \int\limits_a^t (t-\eta)^{\alpha-1} f_k(\eta)\mathrm{d}\eta$ is a continuous function in J_b for each $k \in \langle n \rangle$.

Let $G^b \in \mathbf{M}_b^{1-\alpha}$, $k, j \in \langle n \rangle$, $i \in \langle m \rangle_0$ be arbitrary and consider the function $\tilde{g}^b(t) := \int\limits_{-h}^0 g_j^b(t+\theta)\mathrm{d}_\theta u_{kj}^i(t,\theta)$. Since $G^b \in \mathbf{M}_b^{1-\alpha}$, then from the conditions (S), it follows that $\tilde{g}^b(t) \in L_1^{loc}(J_b, \mathbb{R})$. From (5), it follows that $\Re_k g_k(t)$ is a continuous function in $t \in J_b^0$, $k \in \langle n \rangle$. Moreover, the second and third addend in the right side of (5) tends to zero when $t \to a+0$ and then taking into account this fact, from (5), it follows that

$$\begin{aligned}
&\lim_{t\to a+0}((t-a)^{1-\alpha}\Re g_k)(t) = \lim_{t\to a+0}\left((t-a)^{1-\alpha}\frac{\phi_k(0)(t-a)^{\alpha-1}}{\Gamma(\alpha)}\right) \\
&+ \lim_{t\to a+0}\left(\frac{1}{\Gamma(\alpha)}(t-a)^{1-\alpha}[\int\limits_a^t (t-\eta)^{\alpha-1}\left(\sum_{i\in\langle m\rangle_0}(\sum_{j\in\langle n\rangle}\int\limits_{-h}^0 g_j^b(\eta+\theta)\mathrm{d}_\theta u_{kj}^i(\eta,\theta))d\eta)\right)\right) \\
&+ \lim_{t\to a+0}\left(\frac{1}{\Gamma(\alpha)}(t-a)^{1-\alpha}\int\limits_a^t (t-\eta)^{\alpha-1} f_k(\eta)\mathrm{d}\eta]\right) = \frac{\phi_k(0)}{\Gamma(\alpha)}
\end{aligned} \tag{7}$$

and hence $\Re G^b(t) \in \mathbf{C}_b^{1-\alpha}$. Since from (7) it follows that $\lim_{t\to a+0}((t-a)^{1-\alpha}\Re g_k)(t) = \frac{\phi_k(0)}{\Gamma(\alpha)}$, then applying Lemma 2, we obtain that $(D_a^{\alpha-1}\Re g_k)(a+0) = \lim_{t\to a+0}(I_a^{1-\alpha}\Re g_k)(t) = \phi_k(0)$ and thus $\Re G^b(t) \in \mathbf{M}_b^{1-\alpha}$ and satisfies (6). Therefore, the operator $\Re$ maps $\mathbf{M}_b^{1-\alpha}$ into $\mathbf{M}_b^{1-\alpha}$.

The rest of the proof is based on some ideas introduced in [15]. In our exposition below, we need the values of the integral

$$\Im_q(t) = \int\limits_a^t (t-\eta)^{\alpha-1}(\eta-a)^{q\alpha}\mathrm{d}\eta$$

for each $q \in \mathbb{N}$ and $t \in J$. Via the substitution $\eta - a = z(t-a)$ and using the relation between the beta and gamma functions we obtain

$$\begin{aligned}
\Im_q(t) &= \int\limits_a^t (t-\eta)^{\alpha-1}(\eta-a)^{q\alpha}\mathrm{d}\eta = (t-a)^{q\alpha}\int\limits_0^1 (t-\eta)^{\alpha-1}\left(\frac{\eta-a}{t-a}\right)^{q\alpha}\mathrm{d}\eta \\
&= (t-a)^{q\alpha+1+\alpha-1}\int\limits_0^1 (1-z)^{\alpha-1}z^{2\alpha+1-1}\mathrm{d}z = (t-a)^{(1+q)\alpha}\frac{\Gamma(\alpha)\Gamma(1+q\alpha)}{\Gamma(1+(1+q)\alpha)}
\end{aligned} \tag{8}$$

Let us denote $U_b = \max\left(\sum_{i\in\langle m\rangle_0}\sup_{t\in[a,a+b]}\left|Var_{\theta\in[-h,0]}U^i(t,\cdot)\right|, \sum_{i\in\langle m\rangle_0}\sup_{\substack{t\in[a,a+b],\\ \theta\in[-h,0]}}\left|\frac{\partial U^i}{\partial\theta}(t,\theta)\right|\right)$,

and then for arbitrary $G^b(t), \overline{G}^b(t) \in \mathbf{M}_b^{1-\alpha}$, $k \in \langle n\rangle$ and $t \in J_b^0$ from (5) and (8) we obtain

$$\begin{aligned}
&|\Re_k g_k^b(t) - \Re_k \overline{g}_k^b(t)| \\
&\leq \frac{1}{\Gamma(\alpha)}\int_a^t (t-\eta)^{\alpha-1}\sum_{i\in\langle m\rangle_0}\left(\sum_{j\in\langle n\rangle}\left|\int_{-h}^0 (g_j^b(\eta+\theta) - \overline{g}_j^b(\eta+\theta))\mathrm{d}_\theta u_{kj}^i(\eta,\theta))\right|\right)\mathrm{d}\eta \\
&\leq \frac{1}{\Gamma(\alpha)}\int_a^t (t-\eta)^{\alpha-1}\sum_{i\in\langle m\rangle_0}(\sum_{j\in\langle n\rangle}|\int_{a-\eta}^0 |(\eta+\theta-a)^{1-\alpha}(g_j^b(\eta+\theta) \\
&-\overline{g}_j^b(\eta+\theta))||\frac{\partial u_{kj}^i}{\partial\theta}(t,\theta)\Big|(\eta+\theta-a)^{\alpha-1}\mathrm{d}\theta)\Big|\mathrm{d}\eta \qquad (9)\\
&\leq \frac{U_b}{\alpha\Gamma(\alpha)}\sum_{j\in\langle n\rangle}\left(\sup_{t\in J_b}(t-a)^{1-\alpha}|g_j^b(t) - \overline{g}_j^b(t)|\right)\left|\int_a^t (t-\eta)^{\alpha-1}(\int_{a-\eta}^0 \mathrm{d}_\theta(\eta+\theta-a)^\alpha)\mathrm{d}\eta\right| \\
&\leq \frac{U_b}{\Gamma(1+\alpha)}d_b^\Phi(G^b,\overline{G}^b)\left|\int_a^t (t-\eta)^{\alpha-1}(\eta-a)^\alpha\mathrm{d}\eta\right| \\
&\leq \frac{U_b}{\Gamma(1+\alpha)}d_b^\Phi(G^b,\overline{G}^b)(t-a)^{2\alpha}\frac{\Gamma(\alpha)\Gamma(1+\alpha)}{\Gamma(1+2\alpha)} = (t-a)^{2\alpha}\frac{\Gamma(\alpha)U_b}{\Gamma(1+2\alpha)}d_b^\Phi(G^b,\overline{G}^b)
\end{aligned}$$

Note that for $\eta+\theta \leq a$ we have that $g_j^b(\eta+\theta) - \overline{g}_j^b(\eta+\theta) = 0$ for $j \in \langle n\rangle$.

We will prove that for each $t \in J_b^0$ and $k \in \langle n\rangle$ the inequalities

$$\left|\Re_k^q g_k^b(t) - \Re_k^q\overline{g}_k^b(t)(t)\right| \leq \frac{(t-a)^{(1+q)\alpha}\Gamma(\alpha)U_b^q}{\Gamma(1+(1+q)\alpha)}d_b^\Phi(G^b,\overline{G}^b) \qquad (10)$$

hold for any $q \in \mathbb{N}$. From (9), it follows that the hypothesis (10) holds for $q = 1$, $t \in J_b^0$, and suppose that for each $t \in J_b^0$ and $k \in \langle n\rangle$, the inequality (10) holds for some $q \geq 1$. Then for arbitrary $G^b(t), \overline{G}^b(t) \in \mathbf{M}_b^{1-\alpha}$, $k \in \langle n\rangle$ and $t \in J_b^0$ from (5), (8) and (10) for $q+1$, we obtain that

$$\begin{aligned}
&|\Re_k^{q+1}g_k^b(t) - \Re_k^{q+1}\overline{g}_k^b(t)| = |\Re(\Re_k^q g_k^b)(t) - \Re(\Re_k^q\overline{g}_k^b)(t)| \\
&\leq \frac{1}{\Gamma(\alpha)}\int_a^t (t-\eta)^{\alpha-1}\sum_{i\in\langle m\rangle_0}\left(\sum_{j\in\langle n\rangle}\left|\int_{-h}^0 (\Re_j\left(\Re_j^q g_j^b\right)(\eta+\theta) - \Re_j\left(\Re_j^q\overline{g}_j^b\right)(\eta+\theta))\mathrm{d}_\theta u_{kj}^i(\eta,\theta)\right|\right)\mathrm{d}\eta \\
&\leq \frac{1}{\Gamma(\alpha)}\int_a^t (t-\eta)^{\alpha-1}\sum_{i\in\langle m\rangle_0}\left(\sum_{j\in\langle n\rangle}\left|\int_{a-\eta}^0 \left|\Re_j^q g_j^b(\eta+\theta) - \Re_j^q\overline{g}_j^b(\eta+\theta))\right|\left|\frac{\partial u_{kj}^i(\eta,\theta)}{\partial\theta}\right|d\theta\right|\right)\mathrm{d}\eta \\
&\leq \frac{U_bU_b^q\Gamma(\alpha)}{\Gamma(\alpha)\Gamma(1+q\alpha)}d_b^\Phi(G^b,\overline{G}^b)\int_a^t (t-\eta)^{\alpha-1}\left(\int_{a-\eta}^0 (\eta+\theta-a)^{q\alpha}\mathrm{d}\theta\right)\mathrm{d}\eta \qquad (11)\\
&\leq \frac{U_b^{1+q}}{(1+(1+q)\alpha)\Gamma(\alpha)\Gamma(1+(1+q)\alpha)}d_b^\Phi(G^b,\overline{G}^b)\int_a^t (t-\eta)^{\alpha-1}(\eta-a)^{(1+q)\alpha}\mathrm{d}\eta \\
&\leq \frac{U_b^{1+q}(t-a)^{(2+q)\alpha}}{\Gamma(2+(1+q)\alpha)}d_b^\Phi(G^b,\overline{G}^b)\frac{\Gamma(\alpha)\Gamma(2+(1+q)\alpha)}{\Gamma(1+(2+q)\alpha)} = \frac{U_b{}^{1+q}\Gamma(\alpha)(t-a)^{(2+q)\alpha}}{\Gamma(1+(2+q)\alpha)}.
\end{aligned}$$

Thus, (11) implies that hypothesis (10) holds for each $q \in \mathbb{N},\ t \in J_b$, and hence, from (10), it follows that for any $q \in \mathbb{N}$ the estimation

$$d_b^{\Phi}(\Re^q G^b, \Re^q \overline{G}^b) \leq \frac{n\Gamma(\alpha)(b-a)^{(1+q)\alpha} U_b^q}{\Gamma(1+\alpha(q+1))} d_b^{\Phi}(G, \overline{G}), \tag{12}$$

holds.

Then, consider the Mittag–Leffler function $E_{\alpha,1}(z) = \sum_{q=1}^{\infty} \frac{z^q}{\Gamma(1+\alpha q)}$; using (12), we define the sequence $\{\varepsilon_q\}_{q\in\mathbb{N}}$ appearing in Theorem 1 for each $q \in \mathbb{N}$ as follows:

$$\varepsilon_{q+1} = \left(\frac{n\Gamma(\alpha)}{U_b}\right) \frac{((b-a)^{\alpha} U_b)^{q+1}}{\Gamma(1+\alpha(q+1))} \tag{13}$$

It is simple to see that the series $\sum_{q=1}^{\infty} \frac{((b-a)^{\alpha} U_b)^{q+1}}{\Gamma(1+\alpha(q+1))}$ is the value of the considered Mittag–Leffler function calculated at the point $z = (b-a)^{\alpha} U_b$, and hence, it is convergent. Thus, for the series $\sum_{q=1}^{\infty} \varepsilon_q$ defined with (13), we have that $\sum_{q=1}^{\infty} \varepsilon_q = \left(\frac{n\Gamma(\alpha)}{U_b}\right)\left(\sum_{q=1}^{\infty} \frac{((b-a)^{\alpha} U_b)^{q+1}}{\Gamma(1+\alpha(q+1))}\right) < \infty$.

Therefore, from Theorem 1, it follows that the IP (4), (3), and according to Lemma 1, the IP (1), (3), has a unique solution $X(t) \in \mathbf{M}_b^{1-\alpha}$ for arbitrary $b \in \mathbb{R}_+$. □

Corollary 1. *Let the conditions of Theorem 2 hold.*
Then, the IP (1), (3) *has a unique solution* $X(t) \in \mathbf{M}^{1-\alpha}$.

Proof. Denote for each $q \in \mathbb{N}$ the unique solution of the IP (1), (3) by $X_q(t) \in \mathbf{M}_q^{1-\alpha}$ with the interval of existence J_q^0 existing according to Theorem 2. From the uniqueness, it follows that the solution $X_{(q+1)}(t)$ is a continuous prolongation of the solution $X_q(t)$. Then, we define for arbitrary $t \in J^0$ global solution $X(t)$ as $X(t)|_{t\in J_{q+1}^0} = X_{q+1}(t)$, where $q = [t]$ and hence $X(t) \in \mathbf{M}^{1-\alpha}$ is the unique solution of IP (1), (3), with the interval of existence J^0. □

4. Fundamental Matrix and Integral Representation

Consider for every arbitrary fixed number $s \in J$ the following matrix system

$${}_{RL}D_{a+}^{\alpha} W(t,s) = \int_{-h}^{0} [d_{\theta} U(t,\theta)] W(t+\theta, s), t > s \tag{14}$$

and the initial condition:

$$W(t,s) = \Theta,\ t \in [s-h, s)\ ; \quad W(t,s) = I,\ t = s \tag{15}$$

For every arbitrary fixed number $\bar{s} \in (-\infty, a]$, define

$$\Phi(t,\bar{s}) = \begin{cases} \mathbf{I},\ a-h \leq \bar{s} \leq t \leq a \\ \Theta,\ t < \bar{s} \\ \Theta,\ \bar{s} < a-h \end{cases}$$

and with $\Phi^j(t,\bar{s})$, denote the j-th column of the $\Phi(t,\bar{s})$.

Introduce the following initial condition:

$$W(t,\bar{s}) = \Phi(t,\bar{s}),\ \text{where}\ \bar{s} \in (-\infty, a]\ \text{is an arbitrary fixed number.} \tag{16}$$

Definition 5. *For some fixed $s \in J$, the matrix valued function $t \to C(t,s) = \{c_{kj}(t,s)\}_{k,j=1}^{n}$ is called a solution of the IP (14), (15) if $C(\cdot,s) : J_s^0 = (s,\infty) \to \mathbb{R}^{n\times n}$ is continuous for $t \in J_s^0$ and satisfies the matrix equation (14) in J_s^0, as well as the initial condition (15). The matrix $C(t,s)$ will be called the fundamental (or Cauchy) matrix for the system (2).*

Remark 1. *Since $C(a,s) = \Theta$, according the condition (15) for all $s \in J^0$, then we have that ${}_{RL}D_{a+}^{\alpha}C(t,s) = {}_{C}D_{a+}^{\alpha}C(t,s)$ (i.e., both derivatives coincide when $s \in J^0$). Then, Theorem 6 in [31] implies that for any $j \in \langle n\rangle$, $C^j(t,s) = col(c_{1j}(t,s),...,c_{nj}(t,s))$ is the unique solution of IP (2), (3) with initial function $\Phi(0) = I^j$, $\Phi(t-a) = \mathbf{0}$, $t \in [a-h,a)$, where I^j denotes the j-th column of the identity matrix $\mathbf{I} \in \mathbb{R}^{n\times n}$ and hence the IP (14), (15) has a unique solution $C(t,s) = (C^1(t,s),...,C^n(t,s))$. In the case when $\bar{s} = a$ for arbitrary $j \in \langle n\rangle$, according to Corollary 1, the IP (2), (3) has a unique solution $C^j(t,s) = col(c_{1j}(t,s),...,c_{nj}(t,s)) \in \mathbf{M}^{1-\alpha}$ with initial function $\Phi^j(t,a) \in \mathbf{PC}^*$; then $C(t,s) = (C^1(t,s),...,C^n(t,s))$, is obviously the unique solution of IP (14), (15) in this case.*

Let $\bar{s} \in [a-h,a]$ be an arbitrary fixed number and consider the matrix IP (14), (16).

Definition 6. *The matrix-valued function $t \to Q(t,\bar{s}) = \{q_{kj}(t,\bar{s})\}_{k,j=1}^{n} : \mathbb{R} \times (-\infty,a] \to \mathbb{R}^{n\times n}$ is called a solution of the IP (14), (16) for any fixed $\bar{s} \in [a-h,a]$, if $Q(\cdot,\bar{s}) \in \mathbf{M}^{1-\alpha}$ and satisfies the matrix equation (14) for $t \in J^0$, as well as the initial condition (16).*

Since $\Phi^j(t,s) \in \mathbf{PC}^*$ for any fixed $s \in (-\infty,a]$ and $j \in \langle n\rangle$ then in virtue of the IP (4), (3), it has a unique solution $Q^j(t,s) = col(q_{1j}(t,s),...,q_{nj}(t,s)) \in \mathbf{M}^{1-\alpha}$ with $\Phi_a^j(t,s)$ as the initial function. Since $j \in \langle n\rangle$ is arbitrary, then the matrix $Q(t,s) = (Q^1(t,s),...,Q^n(t,s))$ is the unique solution of the IP (14), (16) with $(\Phi^1(t,s),...,\Phi^n(t,s))$ as the initial matrix function.

Note that $C(t,a) = Q(t,a)$ since the Equations (14) and (16) are the same and the initial functions of both IP coincide with $s = a$.

Define the vector function

$$X_F^0(t)(t) = \int_a^t C(t,s)_{RL}D^{1-\alpha}F(s)ds \tag{17}$$

and for shortness denote $Z(t,s) = C(t,s)R(s)$, $R(s) = {}_{RL}D^{1-\alpha}F(s)$.

As in the Caputo case (see [13]), we will prove that $X_F^0(t)$ is the unique solution of the IP (1), (3) with initial function $\Phi(t-a) \equiv 0$, $t \in [-h,0]$.

Theorem 3. *Let the conditions of Theorem 2 be fulfilled and $F(a) = \mathbf{0}$.*

Then, the function $X_F^0(t)$ defined with the equality (17) is the unique solution of the IP (1), (3) with initial condition $\Phi(t-a) \equiv 0$, $t-a \in [-h,0]$.

Proof. Let us denote with $Z^*(t,s) = \frac{1}{\Gamma(1-\alpha)}\int_a^t (t-\eta)^{-\alpha}Z(\eta,s)d\eta$. Then, since $C(t,s) = 0$ for $t < s$, via the Fubini–Tonelli theorem and (Formula (2.211) [2]), we obtain that

$$
\begin{aligned}
&{}_{RL}D^{\alpha}_{a+}X^{0}_{F}(t) = \left({}_{RL}D^{\alpha}_{a+}\int_{a}^{t} Z(t,s)\mathrm{d}s \right)(t) = \frac{1}{\Gamma(1-\alpha)}\frac{d}{dt}\int_{a}^{t}(t-\eta)^{-\alpha}(\int_{a}^{\eta} Z(\eta,s))\mathrm{d}s)\mathrm{d}\eta \\
&= \frac{1}{\Gamma(1-\alpha)}\frac{d}{dt}\int_{a}^{t}(\int_{s}^{t}(t-\eta)^{-\alpha}Z(\eta,s)\mathrm{d}\eta)\mathrm{d}s = \frac{\mathrm{d}}{\mathrm{d}t}\int_{a}^{t}(\frac{1}{\Gamma(1-\alpha)}\int_{a}^{t}(t-\eta)^{-\alpha}Z(\eta,s)\mathrm{d}\eta)\mathrm{d}s \\
&= \frac{\mathrm{d}}{\mathrm{d}t}\int_{a}^{t} Z^{*}(t,s)\mathrm{d}s = \int_{a}^{t}\frac{\partial}{\partial t}Z^{*}(t,s)\mathrm{d}s + \lim_{s\to t-0} Z^{*}(t,s) = \int_{a}^{t} {}_{RL}D^{\alpha}_{a+}Z(t,s)\mathrm{d}s \\
&+ \lim_{s\to t-0} D^{\alpha-1}_{a+}Z(t,s) = \int_{a}^{t} R(s)\,{}_{RL}D^{\alpha}_{a+}C(t,s)\mathrm{d}s + \lim_{s\to t-0} D^{\alpha-1}_{a+}Z(t,s).
\end{aligned} \tag{18}
$$

Taking into account that $C(t,s)$ is the unique solution of IP (14), (15) and $C(a,s) = 0$ when $a < s$ for the first addend on the right side of (18), we obtain

$$
\begin{aligned}
&\int_{a}^{t} R(s)\,{}_{RL}D^{\alpha}_{a+}C(t,s)\mathrm{d}s = \int_{a}^{t} R(s)\int_{-h}^{0}[\mathrm{d}_{\theta}U(t,\theta)]C(t+\theta,s)\mathrm{d}s \\
&= \int_{-h}^{0}[\mathrm{d}_{\theta}U(t,\theta)](\int_{a}^{t} C(t+\theta,s)R(s)\mathrm{d}s = \int_{-h}^{0}[\mathrm{d}_{\theta}U(t,\theta)]X^{0}_{F}(t+\theta).
\end{aligned} \tag{19}
$$

For the second addend in the right side of (19), taking into account that $F(a) = \mathbf{0}$ and using (Lemma 3.2 [1]), we obtain that

$$
\begin{aligned}
&\lim_{s\to t-0} D^{\alpha-1}_{a+}Z(t,s) = \lim_{s\to t-0} I^{1-\alpha}_{a+}Z(t,s) = \frac{1}{\Gamma(1-\alpha)}\int_{a+}^{t}(t-\eta)^{-\alpha}\lim_{s\to\eta-0} Z(\eta,s)\mathrm{d}\eta \\
&= \frac{1}{\Gamma(1-\alpha)}\int_{a+}^{t}(t-\eta)^{-\alpha}C(\eta,\eta)R(\eta)\mathrm{d}\eta = \frac{1}{\Gamma(1-\alpha)}\int_{a+}^{t}(t-\eta)^{-\alpha}D^{1-\alpha}_{a+}F(\eta)\mathrm{d}\eta \\
&= D^{\alpha-1}_{a+}\,{}_{RL}D^{1-\alpha}_{a+}F(t) = F(t).
\end{aligned} \tag{20}
$$

Then, from (18)–(20), it follows that $X^{0}_{F}(t)$ defined with the equality (17) is the unique solution of the IP (1), (3) with initial condition $\Phi(t-a) \equiv 0,\ t-a \in [-h,0]$. □

Let $s \in [a-h,a]$ be an arbitrary number, $Q(t,s)$ be the corresponding unique solution of IP (14), (16) similar to the case of Caputo derivatives (see [15]), we introduce the vector function

$$
X^{\Phi}_{0}(t) = \int_{a-h}^{a} Q(t,s)\mathrm{d}_{s}\overline{\Phi}(s-a) \tag{21}
$$

for all $\Phi \in \mathbf{PC}^{*}$, where $\overline{\Phi}(s-a) \equiv \Phi(s-a)$ for $s \in (a-h,a]$ and $\overline{\Phi}(-h) = \mathbf{0}$.

Theorem 4. *Let the following conditions be fulfilled.*

1. *The conditions of Theorem 2 hold.*
2. *The function $F(t) \equiv 0$ for $t \in J$.*

Then, for each initial function $\Phi \in \mathbf{PC}^{*}$ and $t \in J^{0}$, the vector function $X^{\Phi}_{0}(t)$ defined by equality (21) is a unique solution of the IP (2), (3).

Proof. Since $Q(t,s)$ is a continuous function for $t \in J^0$, $\Phi \in \mathbf{PC}^*$ and hence according to (Lemma 1 [26]) $X_0^{\Phi}(t)$ defined via (21) is continuous in the same interval too. Then, similar as in (18), via the Fubini–Tonelli theorem, we obtain that

$$\begin{aligned}
{}_{RL}D_{a+}^{\alpha} X_0^{\Phi}(t) &= \left({}_{RL}D_{a+}^{\alpha} \int_{a-h}^{a} Q(t,s) \mathrm{d}_s \overline{\Phi}(s-a) \right)(t) \\
&= \frac{1}{\Gamma(1-\alpha)} \frac{\mathrm{d}}{\mathrm{d}t} \int_{a}^{t} (t-\eta)^{-\alpha} \Big(\int_{a-h}^{a} Q(\eta,s) d_s \overline{\Phi}(s-a) \Big) \mathrm{d}\eta \\
&= \int_{a-h}^{a} \left(\frac{1}{\Gamma(1-\alpha)} \frac{\mathrm{d}}{\mathrm{d}t} \int_{s}^{t} (t-\eta)^{-\alpha} Q(\eta,s) \mathrm{d}\eta \right) \mathrm{d}_s \overline{\Phi}(s-a) \\
&= \int_{a-h}^{a} {}_{RL}D_{a+}^{\alpha} Q(t,s) \mathrm{d}_s \overline{\Phi}(s-a)
\end{aligned} \tag{22}$$

For arbitrary fixed $t \in J^0$, denote by m_θ and m_s the Lebesgue–Stieltjes measures corresponding to $U(t,\theta)$ and $\overline{\Phi}(s)$. Then, for the rectangle $\rho = [-h,0] \times [a-h,a]$ and the product measure $m_\theta \times m_s$, the equality $m_\theta \times m_s(\rho) = m_\theta(\rho) m_s(\rho)$ holds. Thus,

$$\left| \iint_{\rho} Q(t+\theta,s) m_\theta \times m_s(\rho) \right| < \infty$$

and for each fixed $t \in J^0$, $(\theta,s) \in \rho$ the matrix function $Q(t+\theta,s) \in L_1^{loc}(\rho,\mathbb{R})$ is locally bounded. Then, in virtue of (Proposition 5.4 [32]), we can correctly apply the Fubini-Tonelli theorem and for the right side of (2) we obtain

$$\begin{aligned}
&\int_{-h}^{0} [\mathrm{d}_\theta U^i(t,\theta)] X_\Phi(t+\theta) = \int_{-h}^{0} [\mathrm{d}_\theta U^i(t,\theta)] \left(\int_{a-h}^{a} Q(t+\theta,s) \mathrm{d}_s \Phi(s-a) \right) \\
&= \int_{a-h}^{a} \left(\int_{-h}^{0} [d_\theta U^i(t,\theta)] Q(t+\theta,s) \right) \mathrm{d}_s \Phi(s-a),
\end{aligned} \tag{23}$$

and hence from (22), (23) it follows that $X_0^{\Phi}(t)$ satisfies (2) for $t \in J^0$.

Let $s^* \in [a-h,a]$ be an arbitrary fixed number. Then, for $t = s^*$ from (22), we have that

$$\begin{aligned}
X_0^{\Phi}(s^*) &= \int_{a-h}^{a} Q(t,s) \mathrm{d}_s \overline{\Phi}(s-a) = \int_{s^*}^{a} Q(t,s) \mathrm{d}_s \overline{\Phi}(s-a) + \int_{a-h}^{s^*} Q(t,s) \mathrm{d}_s \overline{\Phi}(s-a) \\
&= -\int_{s^*}^{a-h} I \mathrm{d}_s \overline{\Phi}(s-a) = -\overline{\Phi}(-h) + \overline{\Phi}(s^*-a) = \Phi(s^*-a),
\end{aligned}$$

i.e., $X_0^{\Phi}(t)$ satisfies the initial condition (3), which completes the proof. □

Corollary 2. *Let the following conditions hold.*

1. *The conditions of Theorem 4 hold.*
2. *The Lebesgue decomposition of the function $\Phi \in \mathbf{PC}^*$ does not possess a singular term.*

Then, the vector function $X_0^{\Phi}(t)$ *defined by equality* (21) *has the representation in the form*

$$X_0^{\Phi}(t) = (Q(t,a)(\Phi(0+) - \Phi(0)) + \sum_i Q(t,s_i)(\Phi(s_i - a + 0) - \Phi(s_i - a - 0)) + \int_{a-h}^{a} Q(t,s)\Phi'_{ac}(s-a)\mathrm{d}s), \tag{24}$$

where the summation is over all jump points $s_i \in [a-h, a)$ *and the sum is finite.*

Proof. Since $\Phi \in \mathbf{PC}^*$ has finite many jump points then (24) immediately follows from (21). □

Corollary 3. *Let the conditions of Theorem 4 hold.*

Then, for each initial function $\Phi \in \mathbf{PC}^*$, *the unique solution* $X_{\Phi}^F(t)$ *of the IVP* (1), (3) *for every* $t \in J^0$ *has the following representation*

$$X_F^{\Phi}(t) = \int_a^t C(t,s)_{RL}D^{1-\alpha}F(s)\mathrm{d}s + \int_{a-h}^{a} Q(t,s)\mathrm{d}_s\overline{\Phi}(s-a),$$

where $\overline{\Phi}(s-a) \equiv \Phi(s-a)$ *for* $s \in (a-h, a]$ *and* $\overline{\Phi}(-h) = \mathbf{0}$.

Proof. The statement of Corollary 3 immediately follows from the superposition principle and Theorems 3 and 4. □

5. Hyers–Ulam and Hyers–Ulam–Rassias in Time Stability

It is well known that the standard definitions of stability used in the systems with integer order or fractional Caputo-type derivatives are not directly applicable to the systems with fractional Riemann–Liouville-type derivatives, since the modulus of the solutions of the systems with Riemann–Liouville-type derivatives tends to infinity, when the independent variable tends to the initial point from the right, i.e., $\lim_{t \to a+0} |X(t)| = \infty$. That is why new types of definitions for the different kinds of stabilities applicable to systems with Riemann–Liouville-type derivatives are needed.

The aim of this section is to introduce definitions of time stability, Hyers–Ulam (HU) in time stability, and Hyers–Ulam–Rassias (HUR) in time stability for fractional systems (equations) with RL-type derivatives and to establish some sufficient conditions which guarantee the HU in time stability of the studied systems.

As was mentioned, our concept uses the idea of the concept "stability in time" in the Lyapunov sense introduced in the remarkable work [20] for fractional equations with Riemann–Liouville-type derivatives.

Definition 7 ([20]). *The zero solution of the IP* (2), (3) *(i.e., with* $\Phi(t-a) \equiv \mathbf{0}$, $t - a \in [-h, 0]$ *as initial function) is said to be:*

(i) *Stable in time in (Lyapunov in time stable) if for arbitrary* $\varepsilon > 0$, *there exist a point* $t_\varepsilon \in J^0$ *and number* $\delta(\varepsilon, t_\varepsilon) > 0$ *such that for any initial functions* $\Phi(t) \in \mathbf{PC}$ *with* $\|\Phi\| < \delta$, *the corresponding solution* $X_{\Phi}^0(t)$ *of the IP* (2), (3) *satisfies* $|X_{\Phi}^0(t)| \leq \varepsilon$ *for* $t \geq t_\varepsilon$.
(ii) *Asymptotically stable in time if it is stable in time and additionally* $\lim_{t \to \infty} |X_{\Phi}^0(t)| = 0$.

With the next definitions, we introduce a concept for HU and HUR in time stability for fractional systems (equations) with RL-type derivatives.

Definition 8. *The system* (1) *is said to be Hyers–Ulam (HU) in time stable on* $J_b^0(J^0)$, $b \in \mathbb{R}_+^0$ *if there exists a constant* $C > 0$ *such that for any* $\varepsilon > 0$ *and function* $Y(t) : J_b^{-h} \to \mathbb{R}^n (J^{-h} \to \mathbb{R}^n)$, *with* $Y(t)|_{[a-h,a]} = \Psi(t-a) \in \mathbf{PC}^*$, $t \in [a-h,a]$, $Y(t)|_{J^0} = Z_Y(t) \in \mathbf{M}_b^{1-\alpha}(\mathbf{M}^{1-\alpha})$ *for which there exists a function* $\Phi^\varepsilon(t) \in \mathbf{PC}^*$ *with* $|\Psi(t-a) - \Phi^\varepsilon(t-a)| \le \varepsilon$ *for* $t \in [a-h,a]$ *and* $t_\varepsilon \in (a,a+b)$, $(t_\varepsilon \in J^0)$ *such that for* $t \in [t_\varepsilon, a+b]$ $(t \in [t_\varepsilon, \infty))$, *the following inequalities hold*

$$\left| {}_{RL}D^{\alpha}_{a+}Y(t) - \int_{-h}^{0} [\mathrm{d}_\theta U(t,\theta)]Y(t+\theta) - F(t) \right| \le \varepsilon \tag{25}$$

then, there exists a unique solution $X^F_{\Phi^\varepsilon}(t)$ *of the IP* (1), (3) *(with initial function* $\Phi^\varepsilon(t)$*) for which the inequality*

$$\left| Y(t) - X^F_{\Phi^\varepsilon}(t) \right| \le C\varepsilon, \tag{26}$$

holds for any $t \in [t_\varepsilon, a+b]$ $(t \in [t_\varepsilon, \infty))$.

Let $b \in \mathbb{R}^0_+$ and $\varphi(t) \in C(J_b^{-h}, \mathbb{R}^0_+)(C(J^{-h}, \mathbb{R}^0_+))$ be arbitrary.

Definition 9. *The system* (1) *is said to be Hyers–Ulam–Rassias (HUR) in time stable on* $J_b^0(J^0)$, $b \in \mathbb{R}^0_+$ *with respect to* $\varphi(t)$ *if there exists a constant* $c_\varphi > 0$ *such that for arbitrary function* $Y(t) : J_b^{-h} \to \mathbb{R}^n(J^{-h} \to \mathbb{R}^n)$, *with* $Y(t)|_{J^0} \in \mathbf{M}_b^{1-\alpha}(\mathbf{M}^{1-\alpha})$, $Y(t)|_{[a-h,a]} = \Psi(t-a) \in \mathbf{PC}^*$ *for which there exist a function* $\Phi^\varphi(t) \in \mathbf{PC}^*$ *with* $|\Psi(t-a) - \Phi^\varphi(t-a)| \le c_\phi \phi(t)$, $t \in [a-h,a]$ *and* $t_\varphi \in J_b^0$ $(t_\varphi \in J^0)$ *such that for* $t \in [t_\varphi, a+b]$ $(t \in [t_\varphi, \infty))$ *the following inequality holds*

$$\left| {}_{RL}D^{\alpha}_{a+}Y(t) - \int_{-h}^{0} [\mathrm{d}_\theta U(t,\theta)]Y(t+\theta) - F(t) \right| \le \varphi(t), \tag{27}$$

then, there exists a unique solution $X^F_{\Phi^\varphi}(t)$ *of the IP* (1), (3) *(with initial function* $\Phi^\varphi(t)$*) such that the inequality*

$$\left| Y(t)|_{J^0} - X^F_{\Phi^\varphi}(t) \right| \le c_\phi \varphi(t),$$

holds for any $t \in [t_\varphi, a+b]$ $(t \in [t_\varphi, \infty))$.

Remark 2. *We note that in* (25) *and* (27), *we assume that as initial function is used* $Y(t)|_{[a-h,a]} = \Psi(t-a)$, *which is mentioned explicitly. It seems that our Definitions 8 and 9 are stated in the sense of the classical definitions for delayed equations with integer-order derivatives (see [33,34]).*

Theorem 5. *Let the following conditions be fulfilled.*

1. *The conditions of Theorem 4 hold.*
2. $b \in \mathbb{R}^0_+$ *is an arbitrary number.*

   Then, the system (1) *is HU and time stable on* J_b^0.

Proof. Let $t, s \in J_b$, and consider the fundamental matrix $C(t,s)$. Accordingly (Theorem 6 [14]), $C(t,s)$ is a continuous function in s and t for $s > a$ and $s \ne t$. When $s > a$ and $s = t$, then $C(t,s)$ has a first-kind jump. If $s = a$, and $s \ne t$, then $C(t,s)$ has a first kind jump at $s = a$, and if $t = s = a$ and $C(t,s)$ has a second kind jump at $t = a$ but is Lebesgue integrable (more precisely, for $t \to a+0$) we have that $C(t,s) = O((t-a)^{\alpha-1})$. Since $Q(t,a) = C(t,a)$, then $Q(t,a)$ has the same properties as $C(t,a)$. When $s \in [a-h,a)$, then $Q(t,s)$ has an integrable second kind jump at $t = a$, i.e., for $t \to a+0$ we have that $Q(t,s) = O((t-a)^{\alpha-1})$. Taking into account (16) for $t \in J^0 \cup [a-h,a)$ and $s \ne t$, $Q(t,s)$ is a continuous function in s and t. When $s = t$, then $Q(t,s)$ has a first kind jump. Thus, we can conclude that for every $\bar{t} \in J^0$, $C(t,s)$ is bounded for $t \in [\bar{t}, b]$, $s \in J_b$ and Lebesgue integrable in s on J_b. For every $\bar{t} \in J^0$ $Q(t,s)$ is bounded for $t \in [\bar{t}, b]$, $s \in [a-h,a]$ and Lebesgue integrable in s on $s \in [a-h,a]$. Note that $C(t,s)$ and $Q(t,s)$ are constructed via the system (2) and do not depend on the choice of the vector function $F(t)$ in system (1).

Let $b \in \mathbb{R}^0_+$, $\varepsilon > 0$ and the arbitrary function $Y(t) : J_b^{-h} \to \mathbb{R}^n$, with $Y(t)|_{[a-h,a]} = \Psi(t-a) \in \mathbf{PC}^*$, and $Y(t)|_{J_b^0} = Z_Y(t) \in \mathbf{M}_b^{1-\alpha}$ and satisfy the inequality (25) for $t \in [t_\varepsilon, a+b]$, $t_\varepsilon \in (a, a+b)$. Since $\Psi(t-a) \in \mathbf{PC}^*$, then defining $\Phi^\varepsilon(t-a) = \Psi(t-a) + col\,(\underbrace{\frac{\varepsilon}{2n}, \ldots, \frac{\varepsilon}{2n}}_{n})$, we obtain that $\Phi^\varepsilon(t-a) \in \mathbf{PC}^*$ and for $t \in [a-h, a]$, the functions satisfy the inequality $|\Psi(t-a) - \Phi^\varepsilon(t-a)| \le \varepsilon$.

Denote for $t \in [t_\varepsilon, a+b]$

$$\mathrm{H}(t) = {}_{RL}D^\alpha_{a+}Y(t) - \int\limits_{-h}^{0} [\mathrm{d}_\theta U(t,\theta)]Y(t+\theta) - F(t) \tag{28}$$

and assume that $H(t)$ is prolonged on $[a, t_\varepsilon]$ as a continuous function with $\mathrm{H}(a) = \mathbf{0}$ and $|\mathrm{H}(t)| \le \varepsilon$ for $t \in [a, t_\varepsilon]$.

Consider the IP (1), (3) with right side (1) $\widetilde{F}(t) = \mathrm{H}(t) + F(t)$ for $t \in J_b^0$, and initial function $\Psi(t-a)$. Note that from (25) and the prolongation, it follows that $|\mathrm{H}(t)| \le \varepsilon$ for $t \in [a, a+b]$. Since $\widetilde{F}(t) \in BL_1^{loc}(J_b, \mathbb{R}^n)$ in virtue of Theorem 2, we obtain that the considered IP (1), (3) has a unique solution $\widetilde{X}(t) \in \mathbf{M}_b^{1-\alpha}$. Thus, $\widetilde{X}(t)$ coincides with $Z_Y(t)$ for $t \in J_b^0$ and hence in virtue of Corollary 3, it has the following integral representation

$$\begin{aligned}\widetilde{X}(t) = Z_Y(t) &= \int\limits_a^t C(t,s)_{RL}D^{1-\alpha}\widetilde{F}(s)\mathrm{d}s + \int\limits_{a-h}^{a} Q(t,s)\mathrm{d}_s\overline{\Psi}(s-a) \\ &= \int\limits_a^t C(t,s)_{RL}D^{1-\alpha}F(s)\mathrm{d}s + \int\limits_a^t C(t,s)_{RL}D^{1-\alpha}\mathrm{H}(s)\mathrm{d}s + \int\limits_{a-h}^{a} Q(t,s)\mathrm{d}_s\overline{\Psi}(s-a)\end{aligned} \tag{29}$$

Analogically in virtue of Theorem 2, we obtain that the IP (1), (3) with right side (1) $F(t)$ for $t \in J_b^0$, and initial function $\Phi^\varepsilon(t-a)$, has a unique solution $X^F_{\Phi^\varepsilon}(t) \in \mathbf{M}_b^{1-\alpha}$ for $t \in J_b^0$ which it has the representation

$$X_F^{\Phi^\varepsilon}(t) = \int\limits_a^t C(t,s)_{RL}D^{1-\alpha}F(s)\mathrm{d}s + \int\limits_{a-h}^{a} Q(t,s)\mathrm{d}_s\overline{\Phi}^\varepsilon(s-a), \tag{30}$$

where $\overline{\Phi}^\varepsilon(s-a) \equiv \Phi^\varepsilon(s-a)$, $\overline{\Psi}(t-a) \equiv \Psi(t-a)$ for $s \in (a-h, a]$ and $\overline{\Phi}(-h) = \overline{\Psi}(-h) = \mathbf{0}$.

Denote

$$\overline{C}_b = \sup_{t\in[t_\varepsilon,a+b], s\in J_b} |C(t,s)|, \quad \overline{Q_b} = \sup_{t\in[t_\varepsilon,a+b], s\in[a-h,a]} |Q(t,s)|$$

and from (29) and (30), we obtain for $t \in [t_\varepsilon, a+b]$ that

$$\left|Y(t)|_{J^0} - X^F_{\Phi^\varphi}(t)\right| \le \left|\int\limits_a^t C(t,s)_{RL}D^{1-\alpha}\mathrm{H}(s)\mathrm{d}s\right| + \left|\int\limits_{a-h}^{a} Q(t,s)\mathrm{d}_s(\overline{\Psi}(s-a) - \overline{\Phi}^\varepsilon(s-a))\right|. \tag{31}$$

For the second addend in the right side of (31) in virtue of Lemma 3, we have

$$\begin{aligned}\left|\int\limits_{a-h}^{a} Q(t,s)\mathrm{d}_s(\overline{\Phi}(s-a) - \overline{\Psi}(s-a))\right| &\le \overline{Q}_b\left|Var_{s\in[a-h,a]}(\overline{\Phi}(s-a) - \overline{\Psi}(s-a))\right| \\ &\le CQ_{t_\varepsilon}\sup_{s\in[a-h,a]}\left|\overline{\Phi}(s-a) - \overline{\Psi}(s-a)\right| \le CQ_b\varepsilon.\end{aligned} \tag{32}$$

Estimating the first addend on the right side of (31), we obtain that

$$\begin{aligned}
&\left|\int_a^t C(t,s)_{RL}D^{1-\alpha}H(s)\mathrm{d}s\right| = \frac{1}{\Gamma(1-\alpha)}\left|\int_a^t C(t,s)\left(\frac{\mathrm{d}}{\mathrm{d}s}\int_a^s (s-z)^{-\alpha}H(z)dz\right)\mathrm{d}s\right| \\
&= \frac{1}{\Gamma(2-\alpha)}\left|\int_a^t C(t,s)\left(\frac{\mathrm{d}}{\mathrm{d}s}\int_a^s H(z)d_z(s-z)^{1-\alpha}\right)\mathrm{d}s\right| \\
&= \frac{1}{\Gamma(2-\alpha)}\left|\int_a^t C(t,s)\mathrm{d}_s\left(\int_a^s H(z)\mathrm{d}_z(s-z)^{1-\alpha}\right)\right| \\
&\le \frac{\varepsilon\overline{C}_b}{\Gamma(2-\alpha)}\int_a^t d_s Var_{\eta\in[a,s]}\left(\int_a^\eta \mathrm{d}_z(\eta-z)^{1-\alpha}\right) \le \frac{\varepsilon\overline{C}_b}{\Gamma(3-\alpha)}\int_a^t \mathrm{d}_s Var_{\eta\in[a,s]}(\eta-a)^{2-\alpha} \\
&\le \frac{\varepsilon\overline{C}_b}{\Gamma(3-\alpha)}Var_{\eta\in[a,t]}\int_a^t \mathrm{d}_s(s-a)^{2-\alpha} \\
&\le \frac{\varepsilon\overline{C}_b}{\Gamma(3-\alpha)}(t-a)^{2-\alpha} \le \frac{\varepsilon\overline{C}_b b^{2-\alpha}}{\Gamma(3-\alpha)}
\end{aligned} \tag{33}$$

Then, from (31)–(33), we obtain that

$$\left|Y(t)|_{J^0} - X^F_{\Phi^\varepsilon}(t)\right| \le \left(C\overline{Q}_b + \frac{\overline{C}_b b^{2-\alpha}}{\Gamma(3-\alpha)}\right)\varepsilon$$

and then (26) holds for $t \in [t_\varepsilon, a+b]$, with $\widetilde{C} = C\overline{Q}_b + \frac{\overline{C}_b b^{2-\alpha}}{\Gamma(3-\alpha)}$. □

Theorem 6. *Let the following conditions be fulfilled.*

1. *The conditions of Theorem 4 hold.*
2. *For some $r \in \mathbb{R}^0_+$, we have that $Q_r = \sup_{t\in[a+r,\infty)}\left(\sup_{s\in[a-h,a]}|Q(t,s)|\right) < \infty$.*
3. *For some $r \in \mathbb{R}^0_+$, the relation $C_\infty = \sup_{t\in[a+r,\infty)}(t-a)^{2-\alpha}C(t) < \infty$ hold where $C(t) = \sup_{s\in[a+r,t]}|C(t,s)|$.*

Then, the system (1) *is HU in time stable on J^0.*

Proof. This proof uses the same approach as the proof of Theorem 5, and hence, the matching details will only be sketched. First, we see that condition 3 implies that $C_r = \sup_{t\in[a+r,\infty)} C(t) < \infty$.

Let $\varepsilon > 0$ and the function $Y(t) : J_b^{-h} \to \mathbb{R}^n$, with $Y(t)|_{J^0} = Z_Y(t) \in \mathbf{M}_b^{1-\alpha}$ and $Y(t)|_{[a-h,a]} = \Psi(t-a) \in \mathbf{PC}^*$, be arbitrary, which satisfies the inequality (25) for $t \in [t_\varepsilon, \infty)$ and define the function $\Phi^\varepsilon(t-a)$ in the same way as in Theorem 5. Since $Z_Y(t)$ satisfies (25), for $t \in [t_\varepsilon, \infty)$, we can define the function $H(t)$ via (28) and as in the above, we assume that $H(t)$ is prolonged on $[a, t_\varepsilon]$ as a continuous function with $H(a) = \mathbf{0}$ and $|\mathrm{H}(t)| \le \varepsilon$ for $t \in [a, t_\varepsilon]$. Then, from (25) and the prolongation, it follows that $|\mathrm{H}(t)| \le \varepsilon$ for $t \in J$.

As above, consider the IP (1), (3) with right side (1), the function $\widetilde{F}(t) = \mathrm{H}(t) + F(t)$ for $t \in J$, and initial function $\Psi(t-a)$.

Since $\widetilde{F}(t) \in BL_1^{loc}(J, \mathbb{R}^n)$ in virtue of Corollary 1, we obtain that the considered IP (1), (3) has a unique solution $\widetilde{X}(t) \in \mathbf{M}^{1-\alpha}$. From the uniqueness, it follows that $\widetilde{X}(t)$ coincides with $Z_Y(t)$ for $t \in J^0$, and hence, in virtue of Corollary 3, it has the integral representation (29). Analogically, in virtue of Corollary 3, we obtain that the IP (1), (3) with right side (1)

$F(t)$ for $t \in J^0$, and initial function $\Phi^\varepsilon(t-a)$, has a unique solution $X^F_{\Phi^\varepsilon}(t) \in \mathbf{M}^{1-\alpha}$ for $t \in J^0$, which has the representation (30).

Note that for arbitrary $\overline{r} \in [a, r]$, according the consideration at the beginning of the proof of Theorem 5, we conclude that $C_{\overline{r}} = \sup_{t\in[a+\overline{r},\infty)}\left(\sup_{s\in[a+\overline{r},t]}|C(t,s)|\right) < \infty$, $Q_{\overline{r}} = \sup_{t\in[a+\overline{r},\infty)}\left(\sup_{s\in[a-h,a]}|Q(t,s)|\right) < \infty$ and hence from conditions 2 and 3 of Theorem 5, it follows that $C_{t_\varepsilon} = \sup_{t\in[t_\varepsilon,\infty)}\left(\sup_{s\in[t_\varepsilon,t]}|C(t,s)|\right) < \infty$ and $Q_{t_\varepsilon} = \sup_{t\in[t_\varepsilon,\infty)}\left(\sup_{s\in[a-h,a]}|Q(t,s)|\right) < \infty$.

Then, as above, we obtain the estimation (31), and hence, for the second addend in the right side of (31) in virtue of Lemma 3, we have that

$$\left|\int_{a-h}^{a} Q(t,s)\mathrm{d}_s\left(\overline{\Phi}(s-a) - \overline{\Psi}(s-a)\right)\right| \leq Q_{t_\varepsilon}\left|Var_{s\in[a-h,a]}\left(\overline{\Phi}(s-a) - \overline{\Psi}(s-a)\right)\right| \leq CQ_{t_\varepsilon}\varepsilon \tag{34}$$

For the second addend in the right side of (31) taking into account condition 3 of Theorem 5, we obtain

$$\begin{aligned}
&\left|\int_a^t C(t,s)\,{}_{RL}D^{1-\alpha}H(s)\mathrm{d}s\right| = \frac{1}{\Gamma(1-\alpha)}\left|\int_a^t C(t,s)\left(\frac{\mathrm{d}}{\mathrm{d}s}\int_a^s (s-z)^{-\alpha}H(z)\mathrm{d}z\right)\mathrm{d}s\right| \\
&= \frac{1}{\Gamma(2-\alpha)}\left|\int_a^t C(t,s)\left(\frac{\mathrm{d}}{\mathrm{d}s}\int_a^s H(z)\mathrm{d}(s-z)^{1-\alpha}\right)\mathrm{d}s\right| \\
&= \frac{1}{\Gamma(2-\alpha)}\left|\int_a^t C(t,s)\mathrm{d}_s\left(\int_a^s H(z)\mathrm{d}(s-z)^{1-\alpha}\right)\right| \\
&\leq \frac{\varepsilon C(t)}{\Gamma(2-\alpha)}Var_{s\in[a,t]}\left(\int_a^s (s-z)^{1-\alpha}\mathrm{d}z\right) \leq \frac{\varepsilon C(t)}{\Gamma(3-\alpha)}Var_{s\in[a,t]}(s-a)^{2-\alpha} \\
&\leq \frac{\varepsilon C(t)}{\Gamma(3-\alpha)}(t-a)^{2-\alpha} \leq \frac{\varepsilon C_\infty}{\Gamma(3-\alpha)}
\end{aligned} \tag{35}$$

Then, from (31), (34), and (35), it follows that for $t \in [t_\varepsilon, \infty)$, we obtain the estimation

$$\left|Y(t)|_{J^0} - X^F_{\Phi^\varepsilon}(t)\right| \leq \left(CQ_{t_\varepsilon} + \frac{C_\infty}{\Gamma(3-\alpha)}\right)\varepsilon$$

and then (26) holds for $t \in [t_\varepsilon, \infty)$ with $\widetilde{C} = \left(CQ_{t_\varepsilon} + \frac{C_\infty}{\Gamma(3-\alpha)}\right)$. □

Theorem 7. *Let the system* (2) *be HU in time stable on* J^0.
Then, the system (2) *is time stable in the Lyapunov sense (in the sense of Definition 7).*

Proof. Let us consider the function $Z(t) : J^{-h} \to \mathbb{R}^n, Z(t) \equiv \mathbf{0}, t \in J^{-h}$ and let $\varepsilon > 0$, $\delta \in (0, \varepsilon]$ be arbitrary numbers.

Introduce the initial function $\Phi^\delta(t-a) \in \mathbf{PC}^*$ with $\|\Phi^\delta\| < \delta$ and then in virtue of Corollary 3, the IP (2), (3) has a unique solution $X^0_{\Phi^\delta}(t) \in \mathbf{M}^{1-\alpha}$, which has the representation

$$X^0_{\Phi^\delta}(t) = \int_{a-h}^{a} Q(t,s)\mathrm{d}_s\overline{\Phi}^\delta(s-a) \tag{36}$$

Since the function $Z(t)$ satisfies the inequality (25) for $t \in [t_\varepsilon, \infty)$ where $t_\varepsilon \in J^0$, $|\Phi^\delta(t-a)| < \delta$ for $t \in [a-h, a]$ and the system (2) is HU in time stable, then we obtain that

$X^0_{\Phi^\delta}(t)$ satisfies (26) for $t \in [t_\varepsilon, \infty)$. Thus, from (26) and (36), it follows that for the $t \in J_{t_\varepsilon}$, if follows the estimation

$$\left|X^0_{\Phi^\delta}(t)\right| = \left|\int_{a-h}^{a} Q(t,s)\mathrm{d}_s\overline{\Phi}^\delta(s-a)\right| \leq \varepsilon \tag{37}$$

and hence, $Q_\varepsilon = \sup_{t\in[t_\varepsilon,\infty)}\left(\sup_{s\in[a-h,a]}|Q(t,s)|\right) < \infty$. Then, choosing $\delta = \min(\varepsilon(Q_\varepsilon C)^{-1}, \varepsilon)$ and estimating the integral in (37) for $t \in [t_\varepsilon, \infty)$, we obtain that

$$\left|\int_{a-h}^{a} Q(t,s)\mathrm{d}_s\overline{\Phi}^\delta(s-a)\right| \leq Q_\varepsilon Var_{s\in[a-h,a]}\overline{\Phi}^\delta(s-a) \leq Q_\varepsilon C\left\|\Phi^\delta\right\| \leq Q_\varepsilon C\delta < \varepsilon,$$

holds for any function $\Phi^\delta(t-a) \in \mathbf{PC}^*$ with $\left\|\Phi^\delta\right\| < \delta = \min(\varepsilon(Q_\varepsilon C)^{-1}, \varepsilon)$ which implies that the zero solution of (2) is stable in time. □

6. Conclusions and Comments

In the present paper for linear fractional systems with Riemann–Liouville (RL)-type derivatives and distributed delays, we obtained three main results.

The first is that under natural assumptions we proved the existence and uniqueness of the solutions of the initial problem (IP) for these systems with discontinuous initial functions. Note that the used assumptions are similar to these used for the same result in the case when the derivatives in the system are first (integer) order. As a consequence of this result, we also prove the existence of a unique fundamental matrix for the homogeneous system.

The second main result is the existence of a unique fundamental matrix to obtain integral representations of the solutions of the IP for the inhomogeneous systems as well as the solutions of the IP for the corresponding inhomogeneous system.

To obtain our third main result, first we introduce concepts for HU in time stability and HUR in time stability for the studied systems with Riemann–Liouville fractional derivatives, in which concepts the are based on the concept for Lyapunov in time stability proposed in [20]. Furthermore, to obtain our stability results, instead of the standard approach based on some concrete fixed-point theorem chosen by the researcher, we introduce a new approach based on the integral representation of the solutions for the studied systems in the corresponding linear case, which is a consequence of our results obtained in Sections 3 and 4 above. Our approach can be used in all cases (without the case of fuzzy equations, where additional work must be done) in which the standard approach based on some fixed-point theorem is applicable and without the difference of fractional derivative types included in the studied class equations (systems). The only restriction is that the equation must possess at least one continuous solution of the Cauchy problem for a class initial function, which can also be discontinuous with finitely many jumps of the first kind. Moreover, the applicability of our approach is regardless of the chosen technique for the proof of the solution's existence (fixed point theorems, topological methods, successive approximations, etc.). Generally speaking, the nonlinear case can be considered with the proposed approach in a similar way, after transforming it in the form of the nonlinear perturbed linear system under some natural assumptions on the nonlinearity term as in the integer case. As a third main result, using the proposed approach, we establish sufficient conditions which guarantee HU in time stability of the investigated systems. Finally, we prove that the HU in time stability leads to Lyapunov in time stability for the studied homogeneous systems.

As a comment, we note that the fact of existence and uniqueness of the fundamental matrix established in the present work, as well as the introduced new approach based on the integral presentations of the solutions of IP for the studied systems with initial function $\Phi \in \mathbf{PC}^*$, lead to some interesting open problems:

1. To establish sufficient conditions, which guarantee system (1) to be HUR in time stable on J_b^0 for arbitrary $b \in \mathbb{R}_+^0$, with respect to some $\varphi(t) \in C(J_b^{-h}, \mathbb{R}_+^0)(C(J^{-h}, \mathbb{R}_+^0))$.
2. To establish sufficient conditions which guarantee system (1) to be HUR in time stable on J^0 with respect to some $\varphi(t) \in C(J_b^{-h}, \mathbb{R}_+^0)(C(J^{-h}, \mathbb{R}_+^0))$.
3. To prove or disprove the conjecture that if the system (2) is HUR in time stable on J^0 with respect to some appropriate $\varphi(t) \in C(J_b^{-h}, \mathbb{R}_+^0)(C(J^{-h}, \mathbb{R}_+^0))$, then the zero solution of (2) is asymptotically stable in time in sense of Definition 7.

Author Contributions: Conceptualization, H.K., E.M. and A.Z. Writing—review and editing, H.K., E.M. and A.Z. The authors contributions in the article are equal. All authors have read and agreed to the published version of the manuscript.

Funding: The authors of this research have been partially supported as follows: Hristo Kiskinov by Bulgarian National Science Fund, Grant KP-06-N52/9, Ekaterina Madamlieva by the Bulgarian Ministry of Education and Science under the National Program "Young Scientists and Postdoctoral Students–2" (approved with RMS No. 206/ 7.04.2022), Stage I, 2022/2023, at the Faculty of Applied Mathematics and Informatics, Technical University of Sofia, and Andrey Zahariev by Bulgarian National Science Fund under Grant KP-06-N52/4, 2021.

Data Availability Statement: Not applicable.

Acknowledgments: The authors are grateful to the anonymous reviewers for their very helpful comments.

Conflicts of Interest: The authors declare no conflict of interest.

Abbreviations

The following abbreviations are used in this manuscript:

BV	Bounded Variation
HU	Hyers–Ulam
HUR	Hyers–Ulam–Rassias
IP	Initial Problem
PC	Piecewise Continuous
RL	Riemann–Liouville

References

1. Kilbas, A.A.; Srivastava, H.M.; Trujillo, J.J. *Theory and Applications of Fractional Differential Equations*; Elsevier Science BV: Amsterdam, The Netherlands, 2006.
2. Podlubny, I. *Fractional Differential Equation*; Academic Press: San Diego, CA, USA, 1999.
3. Li, C.; Zhang, F. A survey on the stability of fractional differential equations. *Eur. Phys. J. Spec. Top.* **2011**, *193*, 27–47. [CrossRef]
4. Li, K.; Peng, J. Laplace transform and fractional differential equations. *Appl. Math. Lett.* **2011**, *24*, 2019–2023. [CrossRef]
5. Gomoyunov, M.I. On representation formulas for solutions of linear differential equations with Caputo fractional derivatives. *Fract. Calc. Appl. Anal.* **2020**, *23*, 1141–1160. [CrossRef]
6. Krol, K. Asymptotic properties of fractional delay differential equations. *Appl. Math. Comput.* **2011**, *218*, 1515–1532. [CrossRef]
7. Veselinova, M.; Kiskinov, H.; Zahariev, A. Stability analysis of linear fractional differential system with distributed delays. *AIP Conf. Proc.* **2015**, *1690*, 040013. [CrossRef]
8. Zhang, H.; Cao, J.; Jiang, W. General solution of linear fractional neutral differential difference equations. *Discret. Dyn. Nat. Soc.* **2013**, *2013*, 489521. [CrossRef]
9. Golev, A.; Milev, M. Integral representation of the solution of the Cauchy problem for autonomous linear neutral fractional system. *Int. J. Pure Appl. Math.* **2018**, *119*, 235–247. [CrossRef]
10. Madamlieva, E.; Konstantinov, M.; Milev, M.; Petkova, M. Integral representation for the solutions of autonomous linear neutral fractional systems with distributed delay. *Mathematics* **2020**, *8*, 364. [CrossRef]
11. Zhang, H.; Wu, D. Variation of constant formulae for time invariant and time varying Caputo fractional delay differential systems. *J. Math. Res. Appl.* **2014**, *34*, 549–560. [CrossRef]
12. Veselinova, M.; Kiskinov, H.; Zahariev, A. About stability conditions for retarded fractional differential systems with distributed delays. *Commun. Appl. Anal.* **2016**, *20*, 325–334.
13. Boyadzhiev, D.; Kiskinov, H.; Zahariev, A. Integral representation of solutions of fractional system with distributed delays. *Integral Transform. Spec. Funct.* **2018**, *29*, 725–744. [CrossRef]

14. Kiskinov, H.; Madamlieva, E.; Veselinova, M.; Zahariev, A. Existence of absolutely continuous fundamental matrix of linear fractional system with distributed delays. *Mathematics* **2021**, *9*, 150. [CrossRef]
15. Kiskinov, H.; Madamlieva, E.; Veselinova, M.; Zahariev, A. Integral representation of the solutions for neutral linear fractional system with distributed delays. *Fractal Fract.* **2021**, *5*, 222. [CrossRef]
16. Liu, S.; Wu, X.; Zhou, X.F.; Jiang, W. Asymptotical stability of Riemann-Liouville fractional nonlinear systems. *Nonlinear Dyn.* **2016**, *86*, 65–71. [CrossRef]
17. Li, M.; Wang, J. Representation of solution of a Riemann–Liouville fractional differential equation with pure delay. *Appl. Math. Lett.* **2018**, *85*, 118–124. [CrossRef]
18. Liang, C., Wang, J., O'Regan, D. Representation of a solution for a fractional linear system with pure delay. *Appl. Math. Lett.* **2018**, *77*, 72–78. [CrossRef]
19. Matychyn, I. Analytical solution of linear fractional systems with variable coefficients involving Riemann–Liouville and Caputo derivatives. *Symmetry* **2019**, *11*, 1366. [CrossRef]
20. Agarwal, R.; Hristova, S.; O'Regan, D. Stability concepts of Riemann-Liouville fractional-order delay nonlinear systems. *Mathematics* **2021**, *9*, 435. [CrossRef]
21. Yan, S.; Gu, Z.; Park, J.H.; Xie, X. Synchronization of delayed fuzzy neural networks with probabilistic communication delay and its application to image encryption. *IEEE Trans. Fuzzy Syst.* **2023**, *31*. [CrossRef]
22. Tunç, O.; Tunç, C. Ulam stabilities of nonlinear iterative integro-differential equations. *Rev. Real Acad. Cienc. Exactas Fis. Nat. Ser. A-Mat.* **2023**, *117*, 118. [CrossRef]
23. Yan, S.; Gu, Z.; Park, J.H.; Xie, X. A delay-kernel-dependent approach to saturated control of linear systems with mixed delays. *Automatica* **2023**, *152*, 110984. [CrossRef]
24. Bohner, M.; Tunç, O.; Tunç, C. Qualitative analysis of Caputo fractional integro-differential equations with constant delays. *Comp. Appl. Math.* **2021**, *40*, 214. [CrossRef]
25. Kiskinov, H.; Zahariev, A. On fractional systems with Riemann-Liouville derivatives and distributed delays-Choice of initial conditions, existence and uniqueness of the solutions - Choice of initial conditions, existence and uniqueness of the solutions. *Eur. Phys. J. Spec. Top.* **2017**, *9*, 3473–3487. [CrossRef]
26. Myshkis, A. *Linear Differential Equations with Retarded Argument*; Nauka: Moscow, Russia, 1972. (In Russian)
27. Hale, J.; Lunel, S. *Introduction to Functional Differential Equations*; Springer: New York, NY, USA, 1993.
28. Kolmanovskii, V.; Myshkis, A. *Introduction to the Theory and Applications of Functional Differential Equations*; Kluwer Academic Publishers: Dordrecht, The Netherlands, 1999.
29. Weissinger, J. Zur Theorie und Anwendung des Iterationsverfahrens. *Math. Nachr.* **1952**, *8*, 193–212. [CrossRef]
30. Zahariev, A.; Kiskinov, H.; Angelova, E. Smoothness of the fundamental matrix of linear fractional system with variable delays. *Neural Parall. Sci. Comput.* **2019**, *27*, 71–83. [CrossRef]
31. Zahariev, A.; Kiskinov, H. Existence of fundamental matrix for neutral linear fractional system with distributed delays. *Int. J. Pure Appl. Math.* **2018**, *1*, 31–51. [CrossRef]
32. Reitano, R.R. *Foundations of Quantitative Finance: 5. General Measure and Integration Theory*; International Business School: Waltham, MA, USA, 2018.
33. Otrocol, D.; Ilea, V. Ulam stability for a delay differential equation. *Cent. Eur. J. Math.* **2013**, *7*, 1296–1303. [CrossRef]
34. Tunç, C.; Biçer, E. Hyers-Ulam-Rassias stability for a first order functional differential equation. *J. Math. Fund. Sci.* **2015**, *47*, 143–153. [CrossRef]

Disclaimer/Publisher's Note: The statements, opinions and data contained in all publications are solely those of the individual author(s) and contributor(s) and not of MDPI and/or the editor(s). MDPI and/or the editor(s) disclaim responsibility for any injury to people or property resulting from any ideas, methods, instructions or products referred to in the content.

axioms
MDPI
Article

Solvability of Iterative Classes of Nonlinear Elliptic Equations on an Exterior Domain

Xiaoming Wang [1], Jehad Alzabut [2,3,*], Mahammad Khuddush [4] and Michal Fečkan [5,6]

1 School of Mathematics and Computer Science, Shangrao Normal University, Shangrao 334001, China; wxmsuda03@163.com
2 Department of Mathematics and Sciences, Prince Sultan University, Riyadh 11586, Saudi Arabia
3 Department of Industrial Engineering, OSTİM Technical University, Ankara 06374, Türkiye
4 Department of Mathematics, Dr. Lankapalli Bullayya College of Engineering, Visakhapatnam 530013, Andhra Pradesh, India; khuddush89@gmail.com
5 Department of Mathematical Analysis and Numerical Mathematics, Faculty of Mathematics, Physics and Informatics, Comenius University in Bratislava, Mlynská Dolina, 842 48 Bratislava, Slovakia; michal.feckan@fmph.uniba.sk
6 Mathematical Institute, Slovak Academy of Sciences, Štefánikova 49, 814 73 Bratislava, Slovakia
* Correspondence: jalzabut@psu.edu.sa

Abstract: This work explores the possibility that iterative classes of elliptic equations have both single and coupled positive radial solutions. Our approach is based on using the well-known Guo–Krasnoselskii and Avery–Henderson fixed-point theorems in a Banach space. Furthermore, we utilize Rus' theorem in a metric space, to prove the uniqueness of solutions for the problem. Examples are constructed for the sake of verification.

Keywords: iterative class; elliptic equations; exterior domain; radial solutions; Banach space; complete metric space; fixed-point theorem

MSC: 35J66; 35J60; 34B18; 47H10

Citation: Wang, X.; Alzabut, J.; Khuddush, M.; Fečkan, M. Solvability of Iterative Classes of Nonlinear Elliptic Equations on an Exterior Domain. *Axioms* **2023**, *12*, 474. https://doi.org/10.3390/axioms12050474

Academic Editor: Chris Goodrich

Received: 25 March 2023
Revised: 8 May 2023
Accepted: 10 May 2023
Published: 14 May 2023

Copyright: © 2023 by the authors. Licensee MDPI, Basel, Switzerland. This article is an open access article distributed under the terms and conditions of the Creative Commons Attribution (CC BY) license (https://creativecommons.org/licenses/by/4.0/).

1. Introduction

The study of nonlinear elliptic systems has a strong motivation, and important research efforts have been made undertaken recently for these systems, aiming to apply the results of the existence and asymptotic behavior of positive solutions in applied fields (see [1–5]). The investigation of the following system of nonlinear elliptic equations in a bounded domain $\mho \subset \mathbb{R}^N$,

$$\triangle \mathfrak{z}_\beta + \lambda \mathrm{F}_\beta(\mathfrak{z}_{\beta+1}) = 0, \tag{1}$$

where $\mathfrak{z}_\beta = 0$ on $\partial\mho$ and $\mathfrak{z}_1 = \mathfrak{z}_{\eth+1}$, $\beta \in \{1, 2, 3, \cdots, \eth\}$, has an important application in science and technology [6,7]. In [8], Dalmasso discussed the existence of positive solutions to such systems for $\eth = 2$ when the $\mathrm{F}(0)'s$ are non-negative with at least one $\mathrm{F}(0) > 0$ (positone problems). In [7], when $\eth = 2$, Ali–Ramaswamy–Shivaji discussed the existence of multiple positive solutions to such positone problems. In particular, in cases where one of $\frac{\mathfrak{z}}{\mathrm{F}_1(\mathfrak{z})}$ or $\frac{\mathfrak{z}}{\mathrm{F}_2(\mathfrak{z})}$ decreases for some range of $\mathfrak{z}$, they established conditions for the existence of at least three positive solutions for a certain range of λ. In [9], Hai–Shivaji discussed the existence of positive solutions for $\lambda >> 1$ for cases where no sign conditions are assumed on $\mathrm{F}(0)$, $\beta \in \{1, 2\}$ (semipositone problems). In [10], again for $\eth = 2$, Ali–Shivaji discussed the existence of multiple positive solutions for $\lambda >> 1$ when $\mathrm{F}(0) = 0 = \mathrm{F}'(0)$ for $\beta \in \{1, 2\}$. In addition, in [11–20], relevant references to the most recent works on (1) can be found. Next, we quote some recent works on elliptic equations.

In [21], Padhi et al. derived sufficient conditions to the following problem in an annular domain:

$$\triangle \mathfrak{z} = \lambda F(|\nu|, \mathfrak{z}),\ \mathfrak{z} \in \mho = \{\nu \in \mathbb{R}^N : a_1 < |\nu| < a_2\},$$
$$\mathfrak{z} = 0,\ \mathfrak{z} \in \partial\mho,$$

for the existence of positive radial solutions, by utilizing Gustafson and Schmitt fixed-point theorems. In [22], Chrouda and Hassine established the uniqueness of positive radial solutions to the following Dirichlet boundary value problem for the semilinear elliptic equation in an annulus:

$$\triangle \mathfrak{z} = F(\mathfrak{z}),\ \mathfrak{z} \in \mho = \{\nu \in \mathbb{R}^N : a_1 < |\nu| < a_2\},$$
$$\mathfrak{z} = 0,\ \mathfrak{z} \in \mathfrak{z} \in \partial\mho,$$

for any dimension $N \geq 1$. In [23], Dong and Wei established the existence of radial solutions for the following nonlinear elliptic equations with gradient terms in annular domains:

$$\triangle \mathfrak{z} + g\left(|\nu|, \mathfrak{z}, \frac{\nu}{|\nu|} \cdot \nabla \mathfrak{z}\right) = 0 \ \text{ in } \ \Omega_a^b,$$
$$\mathfrak{z} = 0 \ \text{ on } \ \partial\Omega_a^b,$$

by using Schauder's fixed-point theorem and contraction mapping theorem. In [24], R. Kajikiya and E. Ko established the existence of positive radial solutions for a semipositone elliptic equation of the form

$$\triangle \mathfrak{z} + \lambda g(\mathfrak{z}) = 0 \ \text{ in } \ \Omega,$$
$$\mathfrak{z} = 0 \ \text{ on } \ \partial\Omega,$$

where Ω is a ball or an annulus in $\mathbb{R}^N$. Recently, Son and Wang [25] considered the following system in an exterior ball $\mho_{\mathfrak{x}}$:

$$\triangle \mathfrak{z}_\beta + \lambda K_\beta(|\nu|) F_\beta(\mathfrak{z}_{\beta+1}) = 0,$$
$$\mathfrak{z}_\beta \to 0 \text{ as } |\nu| \to +\infty$$
$$\mathfrak{z}_\beta = 0 \text{ on } |\nu| = r_0,$$

where $\beta \in \{1, 2, 3, \cdots, \eth\}$, $\mathfrak{z}_1 = \mathfrak{z}_{\eth+1}$, and derived sufficient conditions for the existence of positive radial solutions. The above-mentioned works motivated us to study the following iterative classes of nonlinear elliptic equations on an exterior domain:

$$\left.\begin{aligned} \triangle \mathfrak{z}_\beta - \frac{(N-2)^2 r_0^{2N-2}}{|\nu|^{2N-2}} \mathfrak{z}_\beta + \varrho(|\nu|) F_\beta(\mathfrak{z}_{\beta+1}) = 0,\ \nu \in \mho, \\ \lim_{|\nu| \to \infty} \mathfrak{z}_\beta(\nu) = 0,\ \mathfrak{z}_\beta|_{\partial\mho} = 0, \end{aligned}\right\} \tag{2}$$

where $\beta \in \{1, 2, 3, \cdots, n\}$, $\mathfrak{z}_1 = \mathfrak{z}_{n+1}$, $\Delta\mathfrak{z} = \mathrm{div}(\nabla\mathfrak{z})$, $N > 2$, $\mho = \{\mathfrak{z} \in \mathbb{R}^N |\ |\mathfrak{z}| > r_0\}$, $\varrho = \prod_{i=1}^{\kappa} \varrho_i$, each $\varrho_i \in C((r_0, +\infty), (0, +\infty))$, $r^{N-1}\varrho$ is integrable. The Guo–Krasnoselskii cone fixed-point theorem is a key tool for obtaining single positive radial solutions, whereas the Avery–Henderson cone fixed-point theorem is utilized to obtain the coupled solutions. We further study the uniqueness of solutions of the problem (2) via Rus' theorem in a metric space.

The study of the positive solutions to the iterative classes of ordinary differential equations with two-point boundary conditions,

$$\left.\begin{aligned} \mathfrak{z}_\beta''(\hat{r}) - r_0^2 \mathfrak{z}_\beta(\hat{r}) + \varrho(\hat{r}) F_\beta(\mathfrak{z}_{\beta+1}(\hat{r})) = 0,\ 0 < \hat{r} < 1, \\ \mathfrak{z}_\beta(0) = 0,\ \mathfrak{z}_\beta(1) = 0, \end{aligned}\right\} \tag{3}$$

where $\beta \in \{1,2,3,\cdots,\eth\}$, $\mathfrak{z}_1 = \mathfrak{z}_{\eth+1}$, $r_0 > 0$ and $\varrho(\hat{\mathfrak{r}}) = \frac{r_0^2}{(N-2)^2}\hat{\mathfrak{r}}^{\frac{2(N-1)}{2-N}}\prod_{i=1}^{\kappa}\varrho_i(\hat{\mathfrak{r}})$, $\varrho_i(\hat{\mathfrak{r}}) = \varrho_i(r_0\hat{\mathfrak{r}}^{\frac{1}{2-N}})$ by a Kelvin-type transformation [26,27] through the change of variables $\mathfrak{m} = |\nu|$ and $\hat{\mathfrak{r}} = \left(\frac{\mathfrak{m}}{r_0}\right)^{2-N}$, facilitates the investigation of the positive radial solutions of (2).

We impose the below-mentioned presumptions whenever necessary:

($\mathcal{J}_1$) $F_\beta : [0,+\infty) \to [0,+\infty)$ is continuous.

($\mathcal{J}_2$) For $1 \le i \le \eth$, $\varrho_i \in L^{p_i}[0,1](1 \le p_i \le +\infty)$ and $\exists\, \varrho_i^\star > 0 \ni \varrho_i^\star < \varrho_i(\hat{\mathfrak{r}}) < \infty$ almost everywhere on the interval $[0,1]$.

The remainder of the paper is structured as follows: The problem (3) is transformed into an analogous integral equation involving the kernel in Section 2. Additionally, we calculate the kernel boundaries that are crucial to our major findings. In Section 3, we employ Guo–Krasnoselskii's cone fixed-point theorem, to provide a criterion for the single positive radial solution. In Section 4, the coupled solutions are established by the Avery–Henderson cone fixed-point theorem. The final portion deals with a unique solution. Meanwhile, some numerical examples are provided.

2. Preliminaries

The essential results are stated here, prior to proceeding to the main results in the subsequent sections.

Lemma 1. *For every $\wp \in C[0,1]$, the BVP*

$$-\mathfrak{z}_1''(\hat{\mathfrak{r}}) + r_0^2\mathfrak{z}_1(\hat{\mathfrak{r}}) = \wp(\hat{\mathfrak{r}}),\ 0 < \hat{\mathfrak{r}} < 1,$$

$$\mathfrak{z}_1(0) = \mathfrak{z}_1(1) = 0,$$

has a unique solution

$$\mathfrak{z}_1(\hat{\mathfrak{r}}) = \int_0^1 Q(\hat{\mathfrak{r}},\zeta)\wp(\zeta)d\zeta,$$

where

$$Q(\hat{\mathfrak{r}},\zeta) = \frac{1}{r_0\sinh(r_0)}\begin{cases}\sinh(r_0\hat{\mathfrak{r}})\sinh(r_0(1-\zeta)), & 0 \le \hat{\mathfrak{r}} \le \zeta \le 1,\\ \sinh(r_0\zeta)\sinh(r_0(1-\hat{\mathfrak{r}})), & 0 \le \zeta \le \hat{\mathfrak{r}} \le 1.\end{cases}$$

Lemma 2. *The kernel $Q(\hat{\mathfrak{r}},\zeta)$ has the subsequent characteristics:*

(i) $Q(\hat{\mathfrak{r}},\zeta) \ge 0$ *and continuous on* $[0,1]\times[0,1]$;

(ii) $Q(\hat{\mathfrak{r}},\zeta) \le Q(\zeta,\zeta)$, $\hat{\mathfrak{r}},\zeta \in [0,1]$;

(iii) there exists $\xi \in (0,\frac{1}{2})$ *such that* $\sigma(\xi)Q(\zeta,\zeta) \le Q(\hat{\mathfrak{r}},\zeta)$, $(\hat{\mathfrak{r}},\zeta) \in [\xi,1-\xi]\times[0,1]$, *where* $\sigma(\xi) = \frac{\sinh(r_0\xi)}{\sinh(r_0)}$.

Proof. (i) is evident. The following proves (ii):

$$\frac{Q(\hat{\mathfrak{r}},\zeta)}{Q(\zeta,\zeta)} = \begin{cases}\dfrac{\sinh(r_0\hat{\mathfrak{r}})}{\sinh(r_0\zeta)}, & 0 \le \hat{\mathfrak{r}} \le \zeta \le 1,\\ \dfrac{\sinh(r_0(1-\hat{\mathfrak{r}}))}{\sinh(r_0(1-\zeta))}, & 0 \le \zeta \le \hat{\mathfrak{r}} \le 1,\end{cases}$$
$$\le \begin{cases}1, & 0 \le \hat{\mathfrak{r}} \le \zeta \le 1,\\ 1, & 0 \le \zeta \le \hat{\mathfrak{r}} \le 1,\end{cases}$$

For (iii), we consider

$$
\begin{aligned}
\frac{\mathtt{Q}(\hat{\mathbf{r}},\zeta)}{\mathtt{Q}(\zeta,\zeta)} &= \begin{cases} \dfrac{\sinh(r_0\hat{\mathbf{r}})}{\sinh(r_0\zeta)}, & 0 \le \hat{\mathbf{r}} \le \zeta \le 1, \\ \dfrac{\sinh(r_0(1-\hat{\mathbf{r}}))}{\sinh(r_0(1-\zeta))}, & 0 \le \zeta \le \hat{\mathbf{r}} \le 1, \end{cases} \\
&\ge \begin{cases} \dfrac{\sinh(r_0\xi)}{\sinh(r_0)}, & 0 \le \hat{\mathbf{r}} \le \zeta \le 1,\ \xi \le \hat{\mathbf{r}} \le 1-\xi, \\ \dfrac{\sinh(r_0\xi)}{\sinh(r_0)}, & 0 \le \zeta \le \hat{\mathbf{r}} \le 1,\ \xi \le \hat{\mathbf{r}} \le 1-\xi, \end{cases} \\
&= \sigma.
\end{aligned}
$$

The proof is now completed. □

We observe that a $\eth$-tuple $(\mathfrak{z}_1, \mathfrak{z}_2, \cdots, \mathfrak{z}_\eth)$ is a solution of BVP (3) from Lemma 1 if and only if

$$
\begin{aligned}
\mathfrak{z}_1(\hat{\mathbf{r}}) = \int_0^1 \mathtt{Q}(\hat{\mathbf{r}},\zeta_1)\varrho(\zeta_1)\mathtt{F}_1\Bigg[\int_0^1 \mathtt{Q}(\zeta_1,\zeta_2)\varrho(\zeta_2)\mathtt{F}_2\Bigg[\int_0^1 \mathtt{Q}(\zeta_2,\zeta_3)\varrho(\zeta_3)\mathtt{F}_4\cdots \\
\mathtt{F}_{\eth-1}\Bigg[\int_0^1 \mathtt{Q}(\zeta_{\eth-1},\zeta_\eth)\varrho(\zeta_\eth)\mathtt{F}_\eth(\mathfrak{z}_1(\zeta_\eth))\mathrm{d}\zeta_\eth\Bigg]\cdots\Bigg]\mathrm{d}\zeta_3\Bigg]\mathrm{d}\zeta_2\Bigg]\mathrm{d}\zeta_1.
\end{aligned}
$$

In general,

$$
\begin{aligned}
&\mathfrak{z}_\beta(\hat{\mathbf{r}}) = \int_0^1 \mathtt{Q}(\hat{\mathbf{r}},\zeta)\varrho(\zeta)\mathtt{F}_\beta(\mathfrak{z}_{\beta+1}(\zeta))\mathrm{d}\zeta,\ \beta = 1,2,3,\cdots,\eth, \\
&\mathfrak{z}_1(\hat{\mathbf{r}}) = \mathfrak{z}_{\eth+1}(\hat{\mathbf{r}}).
\end{aligned}
$$

Let $\aleph := \mathtt{C}((0,1),\mathbb{R})$ be a Banach space equipped with a norm $\|\mathfrak{z}\| = \max_{\hat{\mathbf{r}}\in[0,1]} |\mathfrak{z}(\hat{\mathbf{r}})|$, and

$$
\mathfrak{X}_\xi = \left\{\mathfrak{z} \in \aleph : \mathfrak{z}(\hat{\mathbf{r}}) \ge 0 \text{ on } [0,1],\ \min_{\hat{\mathbf{r}}\in[\xi,1-\xi]} \mathfrak{z}(\hat{\mathbf{r}}) \ge \sigma(\xi)\|\mathfrak{z}\|\right\}
$$

be a cone, for $\xi \in (0,\frac{1}{2})$. For any $\mathfrak{z}_1 \in \mathfrak{X}$, define an operator $\pounds : \mathfrak{X} \to \aleph$ by

$$
\begin{aligned}
(\pounds\mathfrak{z}_1)(\hat{\mathbf{r}}) = \int_0^1 \mathtt{Q}(\hat{\mathbf{r}},\zeta_1)\varrho(\zeta_1)\mathtt{F}_1\Bigg[\int_0^1 \mathtt{Q}(\zeta_1,\zeta_2)\varrho(\zeta_2)\mathtt{F}_2\Bigg[\int_0^1 \mathtt{Q}(\zeta_2,\zeta_3)\varrho(\zeta_3)\cdots \\
\mathtt{F}_{\eth-1}\Bigg[\int_0^1 \mathtt{Q}(\zeta_{\eth-1},\zeta_\eth)\varrho(\zeta_\eth)\mathtt{F}_\eth(\mathfrak{z}_1(\zeta_\eth))\mathrm{d}\zeta_\eth\Bigg]\cdots\Bigg]\mathrm{d}\zeta_3\Bigg]\mathrm{d}\zeta_2\Bigg]\mathrm{d}\zeta_1. \quad (4)
\end{aligned}
$$

Lemma 3. *$\pounds$ is self-mapping on $\mathfrak{X}_\xi$ and $\pounds : \mathfrak{X}_\xi \to \mathfrak{X}_\xi$ is completely continuous.*

Proof. As $\mathtt{F}_\beta(\mathfrak{z}_{\beta+1}(\hat{\mathbf{r}})) \ge 0$ and $\mathtt{Q}(\hat{\mathbf{r}},\zeta) \ge 0$ for $\hat{\mathbf{r}},\zeta \in [0,1]$, we have $\pounds(\mathfrak{z}_1(\hat{\mathbf{r}})) \ge 0$ for $\hat{\mathbf{r}} \in [0,1]$, $\mathfrak{z}_1 \in \mathfrak{X}_\xi$. Applying Lemmas 1 and 2, we obtain

$$\min_{\hat{r}\in[\xi,1-\xi]}(\pounds\mathfrak{z}_1)(\hat{r}) = \min_{\hat{r}\in[\xi,1-\xi]}\Bigg\{\int_0^1 Q(\hat{r},\zeta_1)\varrho(\zeta_1)F_1\Bigg[\int_0^1 Q(\zeta_1,\zeta_2)\varrho(\zeta_2)F_2\Bigg[\int_0^1 Q(\zeta_2,\zeta_3)\varrho(\zeta_3)F_4\cdots$$

$$F_{\eth-1}\Bigg[\int_0^1 Q(\zeta_{\eth-1},\zeta_\eth)\varrho(\zeta_\eth)F_\eth(\mathfrak{z}_1(\zeta_\eth))d\zeta_\eth\Bigg]\cdots\Bigg]d\zeta_3\Bigg]d\zeta_2\Bigg]d\zeta_1\Bigg\}$$

$$\geq \sigma(\xi)\Bigg\{\int_0^1 Q(\zeta_1,\zeta_1)\varrho(\zeta_1)F_1\Bigg[\int_0^1 Q(\zeta_1,\zeta_2)\varrho(\zeta_2)F_2\Bigg[\int_0^1 Q(\zeta_2,\zeta_3)\varrho(\zeta_3)F_4\cdots$$

$$F_{\eth-1}\Bigg[\int_0^1 Q(\zeta_{\eth-1},\zeta_\eth)\varrho(\zeta_\eth)F_\eth(\mathfrak{z}_1(\zeta_\eth))d\zeta_\eth\Bigg]\cdots\Bigg]d\zeta_3\Bigg]d\zeta_2\Bigg]d\zeta_1\Bigg\}$$

$$\geq \sigma(\xi)\Bigg\{\int_0^1 Q(\hat{r},\zeta_1)\varrho(\zeta_1)F_1\Bigg[\int_0^1 Q(\zeta_1,\zeta_2)\varrho(\zeta_2)F_2\Bigg[\int_0^1 Q(\zeta_2,\zeta_3)\varrho(\zeta_3)F_4\cdots$$

$$F_{\eth-1}\Bigg[\int_0^1 Q(\zeta_{\eth-1},\zeta_\eth)\varrho(\zeta_\eth)F_\eth(\mathfrak{z}_1(\zeta_\eth))d\zeta_\eth\Bigg]\cdots\Bigg]d\zeta_3\Bigg]d\zeta_2\Bigg]d\zeta_1\Bigg\}$$

$$\geq \sigma(\xi)\max_{\hat{r}\in[0,1]}|\pounds\mathfrak{z}_1(\hat{r})|.$$

Thus, $\pounds(\mathfrak{X}_\xi) \subset \mathfrak{X}_\xi$. In light of this, the operator $\pounds$ is fully continuous according to the Arzela–Ascoli theorem. □

The following theorems are key tools for the existence of positive solutions:

Theorem 1 (Hölder's [28]). *For $\ell = 1,2,\cdots,\kappa$, and $p_\ell > 1$, let $\hbar \in L^{p_\ell}[0,1]$ with $\sum_{\ell=1}^{\kappa}\frac{1}{p_\ell} = 1$; then, $\prod_{\ell=1}^{\kappa}\hbar_\ell \in L^1[0,1]$ and $\|\prod_{\ell=1}^{\kappa}\hbar_\ell\|_1 \leq \prod_{\ell=1}^{\kappa}\|\hbar_\ell\|_{p_\ell}$. Furthermore, if $\hbar \in L^1[0,1]$ and $\bar{g} \in L^\infty[0,1]$ then $\hbar\bar{g} \in L^1[0,1]$ and $\|\hbar\bar{g}\|_1 \leq \|\hbar\|_1\|\bar{g}\|_\infty$.*

Theorem 2 (Guo–Krasnoselskii [29]). *Let $\mathfrak{G}$ be a Banach space, and let $\mathfrak{N}_1, \mathfrak{N}_2$ be bounded open subsets of $\mathfrak{G}$ with $0 \in \mathfrak{N}_1 \subset \overline{\mathfrak{N}_1} \subset \mathfrak{N}_2$ and $\aleph : \mathfrak{X} \cap (\overline{\mathfrak{N}_2}\backslash\mathfrak{N}_1) \to \mathfrak{X}$ ($\mathfrak{X} \subset \mathfrak{G}$ is a cone) as a completely continuous operator, such that*

(i) $\|\aleph\mathfrak{z}\| \leq \|\mathfrak{z}\|$, $\mathfrak{z} \in \mathfrak{X} \cap \partial\mathfrak{N}_1$, and $\|\aleph\mathfrak{z}\| \geq \|\mathfrak{z}\|$, $\mathfrak{z} \in \mathfrak{X} \cap \partial\mathfrak{N}_2$, or
(ii) $\|\aleph\mathfrak{z}\| \geq \|\mathfrak{z}\|$, $\mathfrak{z} \in \mathfrak{X} \cap \partial\mathfrak{N}_1$, and $\|\aleph\mathfrak{z}\| \leq \|\mathfrak{z}\|$, $\mathfrak{z} \in \mathfrak{X} \cap \partial\mathfrak{N}_2$;

then, $\aleph$ has a fixed point in $\mathfrak{X} \cap (\overline{\mathfrak{N}_2}\backslash\mathfrak{N}_1)$.

Let $\psi \geq 0$ be a continuous functional on a cone $\mathfrak{X}$, and let $\mathfrak{f} > 0$ and $\mathfrak{h} > 0$. Define $\mathfrak{X}(\psi,\mathfrak{h}) = \{\mathfrak{z} \in \mathfrak{X} : \psi(\mathfrak{z}) < \mathfrak{h}\}$ and $\mathfrak{X}_\mathfrak{f} = \{\mathfrak{z} \in \mathfrak{X} : \|\mathfrak{z}\| < \mathfrak{f}\}$.

Theorem 3 (Avery–Henderson [30]). *If $\gamma_1 \geq 0$, $\gamma_2 \geq 0$, $\gamma_3 \geq 0$ continuous and increasing functionals on $\mathfrak{X}$, $\gamma_3(0) = 0$, such that, for some positive numbers $\mathfrak{h}$ and k, $\gamma_2(\mathfrak{z}) \leq \gamma_3(\mathfrak{z}) \leq \gamma_1(\mathfrak{z})$ and $\|\mathfrak{z}\| \leq k\gamma_2(\mathfrak{z})$, for all $\mathfrak{z} \in \overline{\mathfrak{X}(\gamma_2,\mathfrak{h})}$, and there exist $\mathfrak{f} > 0$ and $\mathfrak{g} > 0$ with $\mathfrak{f} < \mathfrak{g} < \mathfrak{h}$, such that $\gamma_3(\lambda\mathfrak{z}) \leq \lambda\gamma_3(\mathfrak{z})$, for $0 \leq \lambda \leq 1$ and $\mathfrak{z} \in \partial\mathfrak{X}(\gamma_3,\mathfrak{g})$. Furthermore, if $\pounds : \overline{\mathfrak{X}(\gamma_2,\mathfrak{h})} \to \mathfrak{X}$ is a completely continuous operator, such that*

(a) $\gamma_2(\pounds\mathfrak{z}) > \mathfrak{h}$, for all $\mathfrak{z} \in \partial\mathfrak{X}(\gamma_2,\mathfrak{h})$,
(b) $\gamma_3(\pounds\mathfrak{z}) < \mathfrak{g}$, for all $\mathfrak{z} \in \partial\mathfrak{X}(\gamma_3,\mathfrak{g})$,
(c) $\mathfrak{X}(\gamma_1,\mathfrak{f}) \neq \emptyset$ and $\gamma_1(\pounds\mathfrak{z}) > \mathfrak{f}$, for all $\partial\mathfrak{X}(\gamma_1,\mathfrak{f})$,

then $\pounds$ has at least two fixed points ${}^1\mathfrak{z}, {}^2\mathfrak{z} \in P(\gamma_2,\mathfrak{h})$, such that $\mathfrak{f} < \gamma_1({}^1\mathfrak{z})$ with $\gamma_3({}^1\mathfrak{z}) < \mathfrak{g}$ and $\mathfrak{g} < \gamma_3({}^2\mathfrak{z})$ with $\gamma_2({}^2\mathfrak{z}) < \mathfrak{h}$.

Define the non-negative, increasing, continuous functional γ_2, γ_3, and γ_1 by

$$\gamma_2(\mathfrak{z}) = \min_{\hat{r}\in[\xi,1-\xi]}\mathfrak{z}(\hat{r}),\ \gamma_3(\mathfrak{z}) = \max_{\hat{r}\in[0,1]}\mathfrak{z}(\hat{r}),\ \gamma_1(\mathfrak{z}) = \max_{\hat{r}\in[0,1]}\mathfrak{z}(\hat{r}).$$

It is obvious that for each $\mathfrak{z} \in \mathfrak{X}$, $\gamma_2(\mathfrak{z}) \leq \gamma_3(\mathfrak{z}) = \gamma_1(\mathfrak{z})$, and $\gamma_2(\mathfrak{z}) \geq \sigma(\xi)\|\mathfrak{z}\|$. Thus, $\|\mathfrak{z}\| \leq \frac{1}{\sigma(\xi)}\gamma_2(\mathfrak{z})$ for all $\mathfrak{z} \in \mathfrak{X}$. Furthermore, we observe that $\gamma_3(\lambda\mathfrak{z}) = \lambda\gamma_3(\mathfrak{z})$, for $0 \leq \lambda \leq 1$, $\mathfrak{z} \in \mathfrak{X}$.

3. Single Positive Radial Solution

In accordance with Guo–Krasnoselskii's theorem, we demonstrate in this section that problem (3) has a single positive radial solution.

For $\varrho_i \in L^{p_i}[0,1]$, we have the following cases:

$$\sum_{i=1}^{\kappa} \frac{1}{p_i} < 1, \quad \sum_{i=1}^{\kappa} \frac{1}{p_i} = 1, \quad \sum_{i=1}^{\kappa} \frac{1}{p_i} > 1.$$

We discuss the positive radial solutions for $\sum_{i=1}^{\kappa} \frac{1}{p_i} < 1$, in the following theorem:

Theorem 4. *Suppose that $(\mathcal{J}_1)$–$(\mathcal{J}_2)$ hold, and there exist positive constants $a_2 > a_1 > 0$, such that*

$(\mathcal{J}_3)$ $F_\beta(\mathfrak{z}(\hat{\mathfrak{r}})) \leq \mathfrak{R}_2 a_2$ *for* $0 \leq \hat{\mathfrak{r}} \leq 1$, $0 \leq \mathfrak{z} \leq a_2$, *where* $\mathfrak{R}_2 = \left[\frac{r_0^2}{(N-2)^2}\|\widehat{Q}\|_q \prod_{i=1}^{\kappa} \|\varrho_i\|_{p_i}\right]^{-1}$

and $\widehat{Q}(\zeta) = Q(\zeta,\zeta)\zeta^{\frac{2(N-1)}{2-N}}$,

$(\mathcal{J}_4)$ $F_\beta(\mathfrak{z}(\hat{\mathfrak{r}})) \geq \mathfrak{R}_1 a_1$ *for* $\xi \leq \hat{\mathfrak{r}} \leq 1-\xi$, $\sigma(\xi)a_1 \leq \mathfrak{z} \leq a_1$, *where*

$$\mathfrak{R}_1 = \left[\frac{\sigma(\xi) r_0^2}{(N-2)^2}\prod_{i=1}^{\kappa} \varrho_i^\star \int_{\xi}^{1-\xi} Q(\zeta,\zeta)\zeta^{\frac{2(N-1)}{2-N}}\,d\zeta\right]^{-1},$$

then the BVP (3) *has a solution* $(\mathfrak{z}_1, \mathfrak{z}_2, \cdots, \mathfrak{z}_\eth)$, *such that* $\mathfrak{z}_\beta > 0$, $a_1 \leq \|\mathfrak{z}_\beta\| \leq a_2$, $\beta = 1, 2, \cdots, \eth$.

Proof. Let $\mathfrak{N}_1 = \{\mathfrak{z} \in \aleph : \|\mathfrak{z}\| < a_1\}$ and $\mathfrak{N}_2 = \{\mathfrak{z} \in \aleph : \|\mathfrak{z}\| < a_2\}$. For $\mathfrak{z}_1 \in \partial\mathfrak{N}_2$, $0 \leq \mathfrak{z}_1 \leq a_2$ for $\hat{\mathfrak{r}} \in [0,1]$. For $\zeta_{\eth-1} \in [0,1]$, and from $(\mathcal{J}_3)$, we obtain

$$\begin{aligned}
\int_0^1 Q(\zeta_{\eth-1},\zeta_\eth)\varrho(\zeta_\eth)F_\eth(\mathfrak{z}_1(\zeta_\eth))\,d\zeta_\eth &\leq \int_0^1 Q(\zeta_\eth,\zeta_\eth)\varrho(\zeta_\eth)F_\eth(\mathfrak{z}_1(\zeta_\eth))\,d\zeta_\eth \\
&\leq \mathfrak{R}_2 a_2 \int_0^1 Q(\zeta_\eth,\zeta_\eth)\varrho(\zeta_\eth)\,d\zeta_\eth \\
&\leq \mathfrak{R}_2 a_2 \frac{r_0^2}{(N-2)^2}\int_0^1 Q(\zeta_\eth,\zeta_\eth)\zeta_\eth^{\frac{2(N-1)}{2-N}} \prod_{i=1}^{\kappa} \varrho_i(\zeta_\eth)\,d\zeta_\eth.
\end{aligned}$$

Now, there exists $q > 1$, such that $\sum_{i=1}^{\kappa} \frac{1}{p_i} + \frac{1}{q} = 1$. From Theorem 1, we have

$$\begin{aligned}
\int_0^1 Q(\zeta_{\eth-1},\zeta_\eth)\varrho(\zeta_\eth)F_\eth(\mathfrak{z}_1(\zeta_\eth))\,d\zeta_\eth &\leq \mathfrak{R}_2 a_2 \frac{r_0^2}{(N-2)^2}\|\widehat{Q}\|_q \prod_{i=1}^{\kappa} \|\varrho_i\|_{p_i} \\
&\leq a_2.
\end{aligned}$$

Similarly, for $0 < \zeta_{\eth-2} < 1$,

$$\begin{aligned}\int_0^1 \mathtt{Q}(\zeta_{\eth-2},\zeta_{\eth-1})\varrho(\zeta_{\eth-1})\mathtt{F}_{\eth-1}\left[\int_0^1 \mathtt{Q}(\zeta_{\eth-1},\zeta_\eth)\varrho(\zeta_\eth)\mathtt{F}_\eth\big(\mathfrak{z}_1(\zeta_\eth)\big)d\zeta_\eth\right]d\zeta_{\eth-1} &\le \int_0^1 \mathtt{Q}(\zeta_{\eth-1},\zeta_{\eth-1})\varrho(\zeta_{\eth-1})\mathtt{F}_{\eth-1}(a_2)d\zeta_{\eth-1}\\ &\le \mathfrak{R}_2 a_2\int_0^1 \mathtt{Q}(\zeta_{\eth-1},\zeta_{\eth-1})\varrho(\zeta_{\eth-1})d\zeta_{\eth-1}\\ &\le \mathfrak{R}_2 a_2\frac{r_0^2}{(\mathrm{N}-2)^2}\|\widehat{\mathtt{Q}}\|_{\mathtt{q}}\prod_{i=1}^{\kappa}\|\varrho_i\|_{\mathtt{p}_i}\\ &\le a_2.\end{aligned}$$

Following this bootstrapping reasoning, we arrive at

$$\begin{aligned}(\pounds\mathfrak{z}_1)(t) = \int_0^1 \mathtt{Q}(\mathfrak{r},\zeta_1)\varrho(\zeta_1)\mathtt{F}_1\left[\int_0^1 \mathtt{Q}(\zeta_1,\zeta_2)\varrho(\zeta_2)\mathtt{F}_2\left[\int_0^1 \mathtt{Q}(\zeta_2,\zeta_3)\varrho(\zeta_3)\mathtt{F}_4\cdots\right.\right.\\ \left.\left.\mathtt{F}_{\eth-1}\left[\int_0^1 \mathtt{Q}(\zeta_{\eth-1},\zeta_\eth)\varrho(\zeta_\eth)\mathtt{F}_\eth\big(\mathfrak{z}_1(\zeta_\eth)\big)d\zeta_\eth\right]\cdots\right]d\zeta_3\right]d\zeta_2\right]d\zeta_1\\ \le a_2.\end{aligned}$$

As $\mathfrak{N}_2 = \|\mathfrak{z}_1\|$ for $\mathfrak{z}_1 \in \mathfrak{X}\cap\partial\mathfrak{N}_2$, we obtain

$$\|\pounds\mathfrak{z}_1\| \le \|\mathfrak{z}_1\|. \tag{5}$$

Let $\mathfrak{r} \in [\xi, 1-\xi]$; then, $a_1 = \|\mathfrak{z}_1\| \ge \mathfrak{z}_1(\mathfrak{r}) \ge \min_{\mathfrak{r}\in[\xi,1-\xi]} \mathfrak{z}_1(t) \ge \sigma(\xi)\,\|\mathfrak{z}_1\| \ge \sigma(\xi)a_1$. By $(\mathcal{J}_4)$ and for $\zeta_{\eth-1} \in [\xi, 1-\xi]$, we have

$$\begin{aligned}\int_0^1 \mathtt{Q}(\zeta_{\eth-1},\zeta_\eth)\varrho(\zeta_\eth)\mathtt{F}_\eth\big(\mathfrak{z}_1(\zeta_\eth)\big)d\zeta_\eth &\ge \int_\xi^{1-\xi} \mathtt{Q}(\zeta_{\eth-1},\zeta_\eth)\varrho(\zeta_\eth)\mathtt{F}_\eth\big(\mathfrak{z}_1(\zeta_\eth)\big)d\zeta_\eth\\ &\ge \sigma(\xi)\int_\xi^{1-\xi} \mathtt{Q}(\zeta_\eth,\zeta_\eth)\varrho(\zeta_\eth)\mathtt{F}_\eth\big(\mathfrak{z}_1(\zeta_\eth)\big)d\zeta_\eth\\ &\ge \sigma(\xi)\mathfrak{R}_1 a_1\int_\xi^{1-\xi} \mathtt{Q}(\zeta_\eth,\zeta_\eth)\varrho(\zeta_\eth)d\zeta_\eth\\ &\ge \mathfrak{R}_1 a_1\frac{\sigma(\xi)r_0^2}{(\mathrm{N}-2)^2}\int_\xi^{1-\xi} \mathtt{Q}(\zeta_\eth,\zeta_\eth)\zeta_\eth^{\frac{2(\mathrm{N}-1)}{2-\eth}}\prod_{i=1}^{\kappa}\varrho_i(\zeta_\eth)d\zeta_\eth\\ &\ge \mathfrak{R}_1 a_1\frac{\sigma(\xi)r_0^2}{(\mathrm{N}-2)^2}\prod_{i=1}^{\kappa}\varrho_i^\star\int_\xi^{1-\xi} \mathtt{Q}(\zeta_\eth,\zeta_\eth)\zeta_\eth^{\frac{2(\mathrm{N}-1)}{2-\mathrm{N}}}d\zeta_\eth\\ &\ge a_1.\end{aligned}$$

Similarly, for $0 < \zeta_{\eth-2} < 1$,

$$\int_0^1 Q(\zeta_{\eth-2},\zeta_{\eth-1})\varrho(\zeta_{\eth-1})F_{\eth-1}\left[\int_0^1 Q(\zeta_{\eth-1},\zeta_\eth)\varrho(\zeta_\eth)F_\eth(\mathfrak{z}_1(\zeta_\eth))d\zeta_\eth\right]d\zeta_{\eth-1}$$
$$\geq \int_\xi^{1-\xi} Q(\zeta_{\eth-2},\zeta_{\eth-1})\varrho(\zeta_{\eth-1})F_{\eth-1}(a_1)d\zeta_{\eth-1}$$
$$\geq \sigma(\xi)\int_\xi^{1-\xi} Q(\zeta_{\eth-1},\zeta_{\eth-1})\varrho(\zeta_{\eth-1})F_{\eth-1}(a_1)d\zeta_{\eth-1}$$
$$\geq \sigma(\xi)\mathfrak{N}_1 a_1\int_\xi^{1-\xi} Q(\zeta_{\eth-1},\zeta_{\eth-1})\varrho(\zeta_{\eth-1})d\zeta_{\eth-1}$$
$$\geq \mathfrak{N}_1 a_1\frac{\sigma(\xi)r_0^2}{(N-2)^2}\int_\xi^{1-\xi} Q(\zeta_{\eth-1},\zeta_{\eth-1})\zeta_{\eth-1}^{\frac{2(N-1)}{2-\eth}}\prod_{i=1}^{\kappa}\varrho_i(\zeta_{\eth-1})d\zeta_{\eth-1}$$
$$\geq \mathfrak{N}_1 a_1\frac{\sigma(\xi)r_0^2}{(N-2)^2}\prod_{i=1}^{\kappa}\varrho_i^\star\int_0^1 Q(\zeta_{\eth-1},\zeta_{\eth-1})\zeta_{\eth-1}^{\frac{2(N-1)}{2-N}}d\zeta_{\eth-1}$$
$$\geq a_1.$$

It follows that

$$(\pounds\mathfrak{z}_1)(\hat{r}) = \int_0^1 Q(\hat{r},\zeta_1)\varrho(\zeta_1)F_1\left[\int_0^1 Q(\zeta_1,\zeta_2)\varrho(\zeta_2)F_2\left[\int_0^1 Q(\zeta_2,\zeta_3)\varrho(\zeta_3)F_4\cdots\right.\right.$$
$$\left.\left.F_{\eth-1}\left[\int_0^1 Q(\zeta_{\eth-1},\zeta_\eth)\varrho(\zeta_\eth)F_\eth(\mathfrak{z}_1(\zeta_\eth))d\zeta_\eth\right]\cdots\right]d\zeta_3\right]d\zeta_2\Big]d\zeta_1$$
$$\geq a_1.$$

Thus, for $\mathfrak{z}_1 \in \mathfrak{X}\cap\partial\mathfrak{N}_1$, we have

$$\|\pounds\mathfrak{z}_1\| \geq \|\mathfrak{z}_1\|. \tag{6}$$

It can be seen that $0\in\mathfrak{N}_1\subset\overline{\mathfrak{N}}_1\subset\mathfrak{N}_2$, and from (5), (6), and Theorem 2, the operator £ has a fixed point $\mathfrak{z}_1\in\mathfrak{X}\cap(\overline{\mathfrak{N}}_2\backslash\mathfrak{N}_1)$ and $\mathfrak{z}_1(\hat{r})\geq 0$ on $(0,1)$. Now, put $\mathfrak{z}_1 = \mathfrak{z}_{\eth+1}$, to obtain an infinite number of solutions:

$$\mathfrak{z}_\beta(\hat{r}) = \int_0^1 Q(\hat{r},s)\varrho(s)F_\beta(\mathfrak{z}_{\beta+1}(s))ds,\ \beta = 1,2,\cdots,\eth-1,\eth,$$
$$\mathfrak{z}_{\eth+1}(\hat{r}) = \mathfrak{z}_1(\hat{r}),\ \hat{r}\in(0,1).$$

□

For the cases $\sum_{i=1}^{\kappa}\frac{1}{p_i} = 1$ and $\sum_{i=1}^{\kappa}\frac{1}{p_i} > 1$, we have the following theorems:

Theorem 5. *Suppose* $(\mathcal{J}_1)$–$(\mathcal{J}_2)$ *hold, and there exist constants* $b_2 > b_1 > 0$ *with* F_β $(\beta = 1,2,\cdots,\eth)$ *satisfies* $(\mathcal{J}_4)$ *and*

$(\mathcal{J}_5)$ $F_\beta(\mathfrak{z}(\hat{r}))\leq\mathfrak{N}_2 b_2$ *for* $0\leq\hat{r}\leq 1$, $0\leq\mathfrak{z}\leq b_2$, *where* $\mathfrak{N}_2 = \left[\frac{r_0^2}{(N-2)^2}\|\widehat{Q}\|_\infty\prod_{i=1}^{\kappa}\|\varrho_i\|_{p_i}\right]^{-1}$

and $\widehat{Q}(\zeta) = Q(\zeta,\zeta)\zeta^{\frac{2(N-1)}{2-N}}$;

then the BVP (3) has a solution $(\mathfrak{z}_1,\mathfrak{z}_2,\cdots,\mathfrak{z}_\eth)$, *such that* $\mathfrak{z}_\beta > 0$, $b_1\leq\|\mathfrak{z}_\beta\|\leq b_2$, $\beta = 1,2,\cdots,\eth$.

Proof. The proof is similar to the proof of Theorem 4; therefore, we omit the details here. □

Theorem 6. *Suppose* $(\mathcal{J}_1)$–$(\mathcal{J}_2)$ *hold, and there exist constants* $c_2 > c_1 > 0$ *with* F_β $(\beta = 1,2,\cdots,\eth)$ *satisfying* $(\mathcal{J}_4)$ *and*

($\mathcal{J}_6$) $F_\beta(\mathfrak{z}(\hat{\mathfrak{r}})) \le \mathfrak{M}_2 c_2$ *for all* $0 \le \hat{\mathfrak{r}} \le 1$, $0 \le \mathfrak{z} \le c_2$, *where* $\mathfrak{M}_2 = \left[\frac{r_0^2}{(N-2)^2}\|\widehat{Q}\|_\infty \prod_{i=1}^{\kappa}\|\varrho_i\|_1\right]^{-1}$ *and* $\widehat{Q}(\zeta) = Q(\zeta,\zeta)\zeta^{\frac{2(N-1)}{2-N}}$,

then the BVP (3) has a solution $(\mathfrak{z}_1, \mathfrak{z}_2, \cdots, \mathfrak{z}_\mathfrak{d})$, *such that* $\mathfrak{z}_\beta > 0$, $c_1 \le \|\mathfrak{z}_\beta\| \le c_2$, $\beta = 1, 2, \cdots, \mathfrak{d}$.

Proof. The proof is similar to the proof of Theorem 4; therefore, we omit the details here. □

Example 1. *Consider the problem*

$$\triangle \mathfrak{z}_\beta - \frac{(N-2)^2 r_0^{2N-2}}{|\nu|^{2N-2}}\mathfrak{z}_\beta + \varrho(|\nu|)F_\beta(\mathfrak{z}_{\beta+1}) = 0,\ 1 < |\nu| < 3, \tag{7}$$

$$\mathfrak{z}_\beta(0) = 0,\ \mathfrak{z}_\beta(1) = 0, \tag{8}$$

where $r_0 = 1$, $N = 3$, $\beta \in \{1,2\}$, $\mathfrak{z}_3 = \mathfrak{z}_1$, $\varrho(\hat{\mathfrak{r}}) = \frac{1}{\hat{\mathfrak{r}}^4}\prod_{i=1}^{2}\varrho_i(\hat{\mathfrak{r}})$, $\varrho_i(\hat{\mathfrak{r}}) = \varrho_i\left(\frac{1}{\hat{\mathfrak{r}}}\right)$, *in which* $\varrho_1(t) = \frac{2}{t^2+1}$ *and* $\varrho_2(t) = \frac{1}{\sqrt{t+2}}$, *then* $\varrho_1, \varrho_2 \in L^p[0,1]$ *and* $\prod_{i=1}^{2}\varrho_i^* = \frac{1}{\sqrt{3}}$. *Let* $\xi = \frac{1}{3}$, $F_1(\mathfrak{z}) = F_2(\mathfrak{z}) = 1 + \frac{1}{3}|\sin(1+\mathfrak{z})| + \frac{1}{1+\mathfrak{z}}$.

$$Q(\hat{\mathfrak{r}}, \zeta) = \frac{1}{\sinh(1)}\begin{cases} \sinh(\hat{\mathfrak{r}})\sinh(1-\zeta), & 0 \le \hat{\mathfrak{r}} \le \zeta \le 1, \\ \sinh(\zeta)\sinh(1-\hat{\mathfrak{r}}), & 0 \le \zeta \le \hat{\mathfrak{r}} \le 1, \end{cases}$$

and $\sigma(\xi) = \frac{\sinh(\xi)}{\sinh(1)} = \frac{\sinh(\frac{1}{3})}{\sinh(1)} = 0.2889212153$. *In addition,*

$$\mathfrak{N}_1 = \left[\frac{\sigma(\xi)r_0^2}{(N-2)^2}\prod_{i=1}^{\kappa}\varrho_i^*\int_\xi^{1-\xi} Q(\zeta,\zeta)\zeta^{\frac{2(N-1)}{2-N}}\,d\zeta\right]^{-1} \approx 2.932844681.$$

Let $p_1 = 2, p_2 = 3$ *and* $q = 6$, *then* $\frac{1}{p_1} + \frac{1}{p_2} + \frac{1}{q} = 1$ *and*

$$\mathfrak{N}_2 = \left[\frac{r_0^2}{(N-2)^2}\|\widehat{Q}\|_q \prod_{i=1}^{\kappa}\|\varrho_i\|_{p_i}\right]^{-1} \approx 4.284821634.$$

Choose $a_1 = \frac{1}{2}$ *and* $a_2 = 1$. *Then,*

$$F_1(\mathfrak{z}) = F_2(\mathfrak{z}) = 1 + \frac{1}{3}|\sin(1+\mathfrak{z})| + \frac{1}{1+\mathfrak{z}} \le 4.284821634 = \mathfrak{N}_2 a_2,\ 0 \le \mathfrak{z} \le 1,$$
$$F_1(\mathfrak{z}) = F_2(\mathfrak{z}) = 1 + \frac{1}{3}|\sin(1+\mathfrak{z})| + \frac{1}{1+\mathfrak{z}} \ge 1.466422340 = \mathfrak{N}_1 a_1,\ 0.1444606076 \le \mathfrak{z} \le \frac{1}{2}.$$

Thus, by Theorem 4, BVP (7) and (8) has at least one positive solution $(\mathfrak{z}_1, \mathfrak{z}_2)$, *such that* $\frac{1}{2} \le \|\mathfrak{z}_\beta\| \le 1$ *for* $\beta = 1, 2$.

4. Existence of Coupled Positive Radial Solutions

By utilizing the Avery–Henderson cone fixed-point theorem, we demonstrate in this section that there are coupled positive solutions for (3). Denote

$$\beta_1 = \frac{\sigma(\xi)r_0^2}{(N-2)^2}\prod_{i=1}^{\kappa}\varrho_i^*\int_0^1 Q(\zeta,\zeta)\zeta^{\frac{2(N-1)}{2-N}}\,d\zeta,$$

$$\beta_2 = \frac{r_0^2}{(N-2)^2}\|\widehat{Q}\|_q \prod_{i=1}^{\kappa} \|\varrho_i\|_{p_i},$$

$$\beta_3 = \frac{r_0^2}{(N-2)^2}\|\widehat{Q}\|_\infty \prod_{i=1}^{\kappa} \|\varrho_i\|_{p_i},$$

$$\beta_4 = \frac{r_0^2}{(N-2)^2}\|\widehat{Q}\|_\infty \prod_{i=1}^{\kappa} \|\varrho_i\|_1.$$

Theorem 7. *Suppose that* $(\mathcal{J}_1)$–$(\mathcal{J}_2)$ *hold, and that there exist three positive real numbers* $\mathfrak{f} < \mathfrak{g} < \mathfrak{h}$ *with* $F_\beta(\beta = 1, 2, \cdots, \eth)$ *satisfying*

$(\mathcal{J}_7)$ $F_\beta(\mathfrak{z}) > \frac{\mathfrak{h}}{\beta_1}, \mathfrak{h} \le \mathfrak{z} \le \frac{\mathfrak{h}}{\sigma(\xi)}$,

$(\mathcal{J}_8)$ $F_\beta(\mathfrak{z}) < \frac{\mathfrak{g}}{\beta_2}, 0 \le \mathfrak{z} \le \frac{\mathfrak{g}}{\sigma(\xi)}$,

$(\mathcal{J}_9)$ $F_\beta(\mathfrak{z}) > \frac{\mathfrak{f}}{\beta_1}, \mathfrak{f} \le \mathfrak{z} \le \frac{\mathfrak{f}}{\sigma(\xi)}$,

then the BVP (3) *has coupled positive solutions* $\{({}^1\mathfrak{z}_1, {}^1\mathfrak{z}_2, \cdots, {}^1\mathfrak{z}_\eth)\}$ *and* $\{({}^2\mathfrak{z}_1, {}^2\mathfrak{z}_2, \cdots, {}^2\mathfrak{z}_\eth)\}$ *satisfying*

$$\mathfrak{f} < \gamma_1({}^1\mathfrak{z}_\beta) \ \textit{with}\ \gamma_3({}^1\mathfrak{z}_\beta) < \mathfrak{g},\ \beta = 1, 2, \cdots, \eth$$

and

$$\mathfrak{g} < \gamma_3({}^2\mathfrak{z}_\beta) \ \textit{with}\ \gamma_2({}^2\mathfrak{z}_\beta) < \mathfrak{h},\ \beta = 1, 2, \cdots, \eth.$$

Proof. It is easy to demonstrate that $\pounds : \overline{\mathfrak{X}(\gamma_2, \mathfrak{h})} \to \mathfrak{X}$ and $\pounds$ are completely continuous from (4): first, we check that the condition (a) of Theorem 3 holds; for this, we choose $\mathfrak{z}_1 \in \partial\mathfrak{X}(\gamma_2, \mathfrak{h})$; then, $\gamma_2(\mathfrak{z}_1) = \min_{\hat{\mathfrak{r}} \in [\xi, 1-\xi]} \mathfrak{z}_1(\hat{\mathfrak{r}}) = \mathfrak{h}$, so $\mathfrak{h} \le \mathfrak{z}_1(\hat{\mathfrak{r}})$ for $\hat{\mathfrak{r}} \in [\xi, 1-\xi]$. As $\|\mathfrak{z}_1\| \le \frac{1}{\sigma(\xi)}\gamma_2(\mathfrak{z}_1) = \frac{1}{\sigma(\xi)}\mathfrak{h}$, we have $\mathfrak{h} \le \mathfrak{z}_1(\hat{\mathfrak{r}}) \le \frac{\mathfrak{h}}{\sigma(\xi)}$, $\hat{\mathfrak{r}} \in [\xi, 1-\xi]$. Let $\zeta_{\eth-1} \in [\xi, 1-\xi]$. Then, by $(\mathcal{J}_7)$, we have

$$\begin{aligned}
\int_0^1 Q(\zeta_{\eth-1}, \zeta_\eth)\varrho(\zeta_\eth)F_\eth(\mathfrak{z}_1(\zeta_\eth))d\zeta_\eth &\ge \sigma(\xi)\int_\xi^{1-\xi} Q(\zeta_\eth, \zeta_\eth)\varrho(\zeta_\eth)F_\eth(\mathfrak{z}_1(\zeta_\eth))d\zeta_\eth \\
&\ge \frac{\sigma(\xi)\mathfrak{h}}{\beta_1}\int_\xi^{1-\xi} Q(\zeta_\eth, \zeta_\eth)\varrho(\zeta_\eth)d\zeta_\eth \\
&\ge \frac{\sigma(\xi)\mathfrak{h}r_0^2}{(N-2)^2\beta_1}\int_\xi^{1-\xi} Q(\zeta_\eth, \zeta_\eth)\zeta_\eth^{\frac{2(N-1)}{2-N}}\prod_{i=1}^{\kappa}\varrho_i(\zeta_\eth)d\zeta_\eth \\
&\ge \frac{\sigma(\xi)\mathfrak{h}r_0^2}{(N-2)^2\beta_1}\prod_{i=1}^{\kappa}\varrho_i^\star\int_\xi^{1-\xi} Q(\zeta_\eth, \zeta_\eth)\zeta_\eth^{\frac{2(N-1)}{2-N}}d\zeta_\eth \\
&\ge \mathfrak{h}.
\end{aligned}$$

Following this, we arrive at

$$\begin{aligned}
\gamma_2(\pounds\mathfrak{z}_1) = \min_{\hat{\mathfrak{r}} \in [0,1]} \int_0^1 & Q(\hat{\mathfrak{r}}, \zeta_1)\varrho(\zeta_1)F_1\left[\int_0^1 Q(\zeta_1, \zeta_2)\varrho(\zeta_2)F_2\left[\int_0^1 Q(\zeta_2, \zeta_3)\varrho(\zeta_3)F_4 \cdots\right.\right. \\
&\left.\left. F_{\eth-1}\left[\int_0^1 Q(\zeta_{\eth-1}, \zeta_\eth)\varrho(\zeta_\eth)F_\eth(\mathfrak{z}_1(\zeta_\eth))d\zeta_\eth\right]\cdots\right]d\zeta_3\right]d\zeta_2\Bigg]d\zeta_1 \\
\ge \mathfrak{h}.&
\end{aligned}$$

Condition (a) of Theorem 3 is proved. To prove (b), choose $\mathfrak{z}_1 \in \partial\mathfrak{X}(\gamma_3, \mathfrak{g})$. Then, $\gamma_3(\mathfrak{z}_1) = \max_{\hat{\mathfrak{r}} \in [0,1]} \mathfrak{z}_1(\hat{\mathfrak{r}}) = \mathfrak{g}$, so that $0 \le \mathfrak{z}_1(\hat{\mathfrak{r}}) \le \mathfrak{g}$ for $\hat{\mathfrak{r}} \in [0, 1]$. As $\|\mathfrak{z}_1\| \le \frac{1}{\sigma(\xi)}\gamma_2(\mathfrak{z}_1) \le$

$\frac{1}{\sigma(\xi)}\gamma_3(\mathfrak{z}_1) = \frac{\mathfrak{g}}{\sigma(\xi)}$, we have $0 \leq \mathfrak{z}_1(\hat{\mathfrak{r}}) \leq \sigma(\xi)^2\mathfrak{g}$, $\hat{\mathfrak{r}} \in [0,1]$. Let $0 < \zeta_{\mathfrak{d}-1} < 1$. Then, by $(\mathcal{J}_8)$, we have

$$\begin{aligned}\int_0^1 \mathtt{Q}(\zeta_{\mathfrak{d}-1},\zeta_{\mathfrak{d}})\varrho(\zeta_{\mathfrak{d}})\mathtt{F}_{\mathfrak{d}}(\mathfrak{z}_1(\zeta_{\mathfrak{d}}))d\zeta_{\mathfrak{d}} &\leq \sigma(\xi)\int_0^1 \mathtt{Q}(\zeta_{\mathfrak{d}},\zeta_{\mathfrak{d}})\varrho(\zeta_{\mathfrak{d}})\mathtt{F}_{\mathfrak{d}}(\mathfrak{z}_1(\zeta_{\mathfrak{d}}))d\zeta_{\mathfrak{d}}\\ &\leq \frac{\sigma(\xi)\mathfrak{g}}{\beta_2}\int_0^1 \mathtt{Q}(\zeta_{\mathfrak{d}},\zeta_{\mathfrak{d}})\varrho(\zeta_{\mathfrak{d}})d\zeta_{\mathfrak{d}}\\ &\leq \frac{\sigma(\xi)\mathfrak{g}r_0^2}{(\mathrm{N}-2)^2\beta_2}\int_0^1 \mathtt{Q}(\zeta_{\mathfrak{d}},\zeta_{\mathfrak{d}})\zeta_{\mathfrak{d}}^{\frac{2(\mathrm{N}-1)}{2-\mathrm{N}}}\prod_{i=1}^{\kappa}\varrho_i(\zeta_{\mathfrak{d}})d\zeta_{\mathfrak{d}}.\end{aligned}$$

For some $\mathrm{q} > 1$, we have $\frac{1}{\mathrm{q}} + \sum_{i=1}^{\kappa}\frac{1}{\mathrm{p}_i} = 1$. From Theorem 1, we have

$$\int_0^1 \mathtt{Q}(\zeta_{\mathfrak{d}-1},\zeta_{\mathfrak{d}})\varrho(\zeta_{\mathfrak{d}})\mathtt{F}_{\mathfrak{d}}(\mathfrak{z}_1(\zeta_{\mathfrak{d}}))d\zeta_{\mathfrak{d}} \leq \frac{\sigma(\xi)\mathfrak{g}r_0^2}{(\mathrm{N}-2)^2\beta_2}\|\widehat{\mathtt{Q}}\|_{\mathrm{q}}\prod_{i=1}^{\kappa}\|\varrho_i\|_{\mathrm{p}_i} \leq \mathfrak{g}.$$

It follows that

$$\begin{aligned}\gamma_3(\pounds\mathfrak{z}_1) = \max_{\hat{\mathfrak{r}}\in[0,1]}\int_0^1 \mathtt{Q}(\hat{\mathfrak{r}},\zeta_1)\varrho(\zeta_1)\mathtt{F}_1\Bigg[\int_0^1 \mathtt{Q}(\zeta_1,\zeta_2)\varrho(\zeta_2)\mathtt{F}_2\Bigg[\int_0^1 \mathtt{Q}(\zeta_2,\zeta_3)\varrho(\zeta_3)\mathtt{F}_4\cdots\\ \mathtt{F}_{\mathfrak{d}-1}\Bigg[\int_0^1 \mathtt{Q}(\zeta_{\mathfrak{d}-1},\zeta_{\mathfrak{d}})\varrho(\zeta_{\mathfrak{d}})\mathtt{F}_{\mathfrak{d}}(\mathfrak{z}_1(\zeta_{\mathfrak{d}}))d\zeta_{\mathfrak{d}}\Bigg]\cdots\Bigg]d\zeta_3\Bigg]d\zeta_2\Bigg]d\zeta_1\\ \leq \mathfrak{g}.\end{aligned}$$

Thus, (b) holds. Finally, we also check that (c) of Theorem 3 holds. Observe that $\mathfrak{z}_1(\hat{\mathfrak{r}}) = \mathfrak{f}/4 \subset \mathfrak{X}(\gamma_1,\mathfrak{f})$ and $\mathfrak{f}/4 < \mathfrak{f}$, so that $\mathfrak{X}(\gamma_1,\mathfrak{f}) \neq \emptyset$. Next, if $\mathfrak{z}_1 \in \mathfrak{X}(\gamma_1,\mathfrak{f})$, then $\mathfrak{f} = \gamma_1(\mathfrak{z}_1) = \max_{\hat{\mathfrak{r}}\in[0,1]}\mathfrak{z}_1(\hat{\mathfrak{r}}) = \|\mathfrak{z}_1\| = \frac{1}{\sigma(\xi)}\gamma_2(\mathfrak{z}_1) \leq \frac{1}{\sigma(\xi)}\gamma_3(\mathfrak{z}_1) = \frac{1}{\sigma(\xi)}\gamma_1(\mathfrak{z}_1) = \frac{\mathfrak{f}}{\sigma(\xi)}$, i.e., $\mathfrak{f} \leq \mathfrak{z}_1(\hat{\mathfrak{r}}) \leq \frac{\mathfrak{f}}{\sigma(\xi)}$ for $\hat{\mathfrak{r}} \in [0,1]$. Let $0 < \zeta_{\mathfrak{d}-1} < 1$. Then, by $(\mathcal{J}_9)$, we have

$$\begin{aligned}\int_0^1 \mathtt{Q}(\zeta_{\mathfrak{d}-1},\zeta_{\mathfrak{d}})\varrho(\zeta_{\mathfrak{d}})\mathtt{F}_{\mathfrak{d}}(\mathfrak{z}_1(\zeta_{\mathfrak{d}}))d\zeta_{\mathfrak{d}} &\geq \sigma(\xi)\int_{\xi}^{1-\xi} \mathtt{Q}(\zeta_{\mathfrak{d}},\zeta_{\mathfrak{d}})\varrho(\zeta_{\mathfrak{d}})\mathtt{F}_{\mathfrak{d}}(\mathfrak{z}_1(\zeta_{\mathfrak{d}}))d\zeta_{\mathfrak{d}}\\ &\geq \frac{\sigma(\xi)\mathfrak{f}}{\beta_1}\int_{\xi}^{1-\xi} \mathtt{Q}(\zeta_{\mathfrak{d}},\zeta_{\mathfrak{d}})\varrho(\zeta_{\mathfrak{d}})d\zeta_{\mathfrak{d}}\\ &\geq \frac{\sigma(\xi)\mathfrak{f}r_0^2}{(\mathrm{N}-2)^2\beta_1}\int_{\xi}^{1-\xi} \mathtt{Q}(\zeta_{\mathfrak{d}},\zeta_{\mathfrak{d}})\zeta_{\mathfrak{d}}^{\frac{2(\mathrm{N}-1)}{2-\mathrm{N}}}\prod_{i=1}^{\kappa}\varrho_i(\zeta_{\mathfrak{d}})d\zeta_{\mathfrak{d}}\\ &\geq \frac{\sigma(\xi)\mathfrak{f}r_0^2}{(\mathrm{N}-2)^2\beta_1}\prod_{i=1}^{\kappa}\varrho_i^{\star}\int_{\xi}^{1-\xi} \mathtt{Q}(\zeta_{\mathfrak{d}},\zeta_{\mathfrak{d}})\zeta_{\mathfrak{d}}^{\frac{2(\mathrm{N}-1)}{2-\mathrm{N}}}d\zeta_{\mathfrak{d}}\\ &\geq \mathfrak{f}.\end{aligned}$$

Following this bootstrapping reasoning, we arrive at

$$
\begin{aligned}
\gamma_1(\pounds_{\mathfrak{z}_1}) &= \max_{\hat{\mathfrak{r}}\in[0,1]} \int_0^1 \mathtt{Q}(\hat{\mathfrak{r}},\zeta_1)\varrho(\zeta_1)\mathtt{F}_1\left[\int_0^1 \mathtt{Q}(\zeta_1,\zeta_2)\varrho(\zeta_2)\mathtt{F}_2\left[\int_0^1 \mathtt{Q}(\zeta_2,\zeta_3)\varrho(\zeta_3)\mathtt{F}_4\cdots\right.\right.\\
&\qquad \left.\left.\mathtt{F}_{\eth-1}\left[\int_0^1 \mathtt{Q}(\zeta_{\eth-1},\zeta_\eth)\varrho(\zeta_\eth)\mathtt{F}_\eth(\mathfrak{z}_1(\zeta_\eth))d\zeta_\eth\right]\cdots\right]d\zeta_3\right]d\zeta_2\Bigg]d\zeta_1\\
&\geq \min_{\hat{\mathfrak{r}}\in[0,1]} \int_0^1 \mathtt{Q}(\hat{\mathfrak{r}},\zeta_1)\varrho(\zeta_1)\mathtt{F}_1\left[\int_0^1 \mathtt{Q}(\zeta_1,\zeta_2)\varrho(\zeta_2)\mathtt{F}_2\left[\int_0^1 \mathtt{Q}(\zeta_2,\zeta_3)\varrho(\zeta_3)\mathtt{F}_4\cdots\right.\right.\\
&\qquad \left.\left.\mathtt{F}_{\eth-1}\left[\int_0^1 \mathtt{Q}(\zeta_{\eth-1},\zeta_\eth)\varrho(\zeta_\eth)\mathtt{F}_\eth(\mathfrak{z}_1(\zeta_\eth))d\zeta_\eth\right]\cdots\right]d\zeta_3\right]d\zeta_2\Bigg]d\zeta_1\\
&\geq \mathfrak{f}.
\end{aligned}
$$

Thus, assumption (c) of Theorem 3 holds. Hence, by Theorem 3, there exist coupled positive solutions as mentioned in the hypothesis. □

The following theorems are for the cases, $\sum_{i=1}^{\kappa} \frac{1}{\mathrm{p}_i} = 1$ and $\sum_{i=1}^{\kappa} \frac{1}{\mathrm{p}_i} > 1$, respectively:

Theorem 8. *Suppose that* $(\mathcal{J}_1)$–$(\mathcal{J}_2)$ *hold, and there exist three positive real numbers* $\mathfrak{f} < \mathfrak{g} < \mathfrak{h}$ *with* $\mathtt{F}_\beta(\beta = 1, 2, \cdots, \eth)$ *satisfying* $(\mathcal{J}_7)$, $(\mathcal{J}_9)$, *and*
$(\mathcal{J}_{10})\mathtt{F}_\beta(\mathfrak{z}) < \frac{\mathfrak{g}}{\beta_3}, 0 \leq \mathfrak{z} \leq \frac{\mathfrak{g}}{\sigma(\xi)}$,

then the BVP (3) *has coupled positive solutions* $\{({}^1\mathfrak{z}_1, {}^1\mathfrak{z}_2, \cdots, {}^1\mathfrak{z}_\eth)\}$ *and* $\{({}^2\mathfrak{z}_1, {}^2\mathfrak{z}_2, \cdots, {}^2\mathfrak{z}_\eth)\}$ *satisfying*

$$\mathfrak{f} < \gamma_1({}^1\mathfrak{z}_\beta) \text{ with } \gamma_3({}^1\mathfrak{z}_\beta) < \mathfrak{g},\ \beta = 1, 2, \cdots, \eth$$

and

$$\mathfrak{g} < \gamma_3({}^2\mathfrak{z}_\beta) \text{ with } \gamma_2({}^2\mathfrak{z}_\beta) < \mathfrak{h},\ \beta = 1, 2, \cdots, \eth.$$

Proof. The proof is similar to the proof of Theorem 7; therefore, we omit the details here. □

Theorem 9. *Suppose that* $(\mathcal{J}_1)$–$(\mathcal{J}_3)$ *hold, and there exist three positive real numbers* $0 < \mathfrak{f} < \mathfrak{g} < \mathfrak{h}$ *with* $\mathtt{F}_\beta(\beta = 1, 2, \cdots, \eth)$ *satisfying* $(\mathcal{J}_7)$, $(\mathcal{J}_9)$ *and*
$(\mathcal{J}_{11})\mathtt{F}_\beta(\mathfrak{z}) < \frac{\mathfrak{g}}{\beta_4}, 0 \leq \mathfrak{z} \leq \frac{\mathfrak{g}}{\sigma(\xi)}$,

then the BVP (3) *has coupled positive solutions* $\{({}^1\mathfrak{z}_1, {}^1\mathfrak{z}_2, \cdots, {}^1\mathfrak{z}_\eth)\}$ *and* $\{({}^2\mathfrak{z}_1, {}^2\mathfrak{z}_2, \cdots, {}^2\mathfrak{z}_\eth)\}$ *satisfying*

$$\mathfrak{f} < \gamma_1({}^1\mathfrak{z}_\beta) \text{ with } \gamma_3({}^1\mathfrak{z}_\beta) < \mathfrak{g},\ \beta = 1, 2, \cdots, \eth$$

and

$$\mathfrak{g} < \gamma_3({}^2\mathfrak{z}_\beta) \text{ with } \gamma_2({}^2\mathfrak{z}_\beta) < \mathfrak{h},\ \beta = 1, 2, \cdots, \eth.$$

Proof. The proof is similar to the proof of Theorem 7; therefore, we omit the details here. □

Example 2. *Consider the problem*

$$\triangle \mathfrak{z}_\beta - \frac{(\mathrm{N}-2)^2 r_0^{2\mathrm{N}-2}}{|\nu|^{2\mathrm{N}-2}} \mathfrak{z}_\beta + \varrho(|\nu|)\mathtt{F}_\beta(\mathfrak{z}_{\beta+1}) = 0,\ 1 < |\nu| < 3, \tag{9}$$

$$\mathfrak{z}_\beta(0) = \mathfrak{z}_\beta(1) = 0, \tag{10}$$

where $r_0 = 1$, $\mathrm{N} = 3$, $\beta \in \{1,2\}$, $\mathfrak{z}_3 = \mathfrak{z}_1$, $\varrho(\hat{\mathfrak{r}}) = \frac{1}{\hat{\mathfrak{r}}^4}\prod_{i=1}^{2}\varrho_i(\hat{\mathfrak{r}})$, $\varrho_i(\hat{\mathfrak{r}}) = \varrho_i\left(\frac{1}{\hat{\mathfrak{r}}}\right)$, *in which* $\varrho_1(\hat{\mathfrak{r}}) = \frac{1}{\hat{\mathfrak{r}}+2}$ *and* $\varrho_2(\hat{\mathfrak{r}}) = \frac{3}{\hat{\mathfrak{r}}^2+1}$, *then* $\varrho_1, \varrho_2 \in L^{\mathrm{p}}[0,1]$, $\prod_{i=1}^{2}\varrho_i^* = \frac{1}{2}$, *and* $\sigma(\xi) = \frac{\sinh(\xi)}{\sinh(1)} = \frac{\sinh(\frac{1}{3})}{\sinh(1)} = 0.2889212153$. *In addition,*

$$\beta_1 = \frac{\sigma(\xi)r_0^2}{(\mathrm{N}-2)^2}\prod_{i=1}^{\kappa}\varrho_i^\star\int_{\xi}^{1-\xi}\mathrm{Q}(\zeta,\zeta)\zeta^{\frac{2(\mathrm{N}-1)}{2-\mathrm{N}}}\mathrm{d}\zeta \approx 0.1704829453.$$

Let $\mathrm{p}_1 = 6, \mathrm{p}_2 = 3$ *and* $\mathrm{q} = 2$, *then* $\frac{1}{\mathrm{p}_1} + \frac{1}{\mathrm{p}_2} + \frac{1}{\mathrm{q}} = 1$ *and*

$$\beta_2 = \frac{r_0^2}{(\mathrm{N}-2)^2}\|\widehat{\mathrm{Q}}\|_{\mathrm{q}}\prod_{i=1}^{\kappa}\|\varrho_i\|_{\mathrm{p}_i} \approx 0.1255931381.$$

Let

$$\mathrm{F}_1(\mathfrak{z}) = \mathrm{F}_2(\mathfrak{z}) = \begin{cases} 3.9, & \mathfrak{z} \le 1.8, \\ 3.9(\mathfrak{z}-0.8)^2 + \mathfrak{z} - 1.8, & \mathfrak{z} > 1.8. \end{cases}$$

Choose $\mathfrak{f} = \frac{1}{3}$, $\mathfrak{g} = \frac{1}{2}$ *and* $\mathfrak{h} = \frac{3}{5}$. *Then,*

$$\begin{aligned}
\mathrm{F}_1(\mathfrak{z}) = \mathrm{F}_2(\mathfrak{z}) &\ge 3.519413622 = \frac{\mathfrak{h}}{\beta_1}, \quad \mathfrak{z} \in \left[\frac{3}{5}, 3.461 \times \frac{3}{5}\right], \\
\mathrm{F}_1(\mathfrak{z}) = \mathrm{F}_2(\mathfrak{z}) &\le 3.981109220 = \frac{\mathfrak{g}}{\beta_2}, \quad \mathfrak{z} \in \left[0, 3.461 \times \frac{1}{2}\right], \\
\mathrm{F}_1(\mathfrak{z}) = \mathrm{F}_2(\mathfrak{z}) &\ge 1.955229790 = \frac{\mathfrak{f}}{\beta_1}, \quad \mathfrak{z} \in \left[\frac{1}{3}, 3.461 \times \frac{1}{3}\right].
\end{aligned}$$

Hence, by an application of Theorem 4, the BVP (9) *and* (10) *has coupled positive solutions* $({}^{\beta}\mathfrak{z}_1, {}^{\beta}\mathfrak{z}_2)$, $\beta = 1,2$, *such that*

$$\frac{1}{3} < \max_{\hat{\mathfrak{r}}\in[0,1]} {}^{\beta}\mathfrak{z}_1(\hat{\mathfrak{r}}) \ \textit{with} \ \max_{\hat{\mathfrak{r}}\in[0,1]} {}^{\beta}\mathfrak{z}_1(\hat{\mathfrak{r}}) < \frac{1}{2}, \ \textit{for} \ \beta = 1,2,$$

$$\frac{1}{2} < \max_{\hat{\mathfrak{r}}\in[0,1]} {}^{\beta}\mathfrak{z}_2(\hat{\mathfrak{r}}) \ \textit{with} \ \min_{\hat{\mathfrak{r}}\in[0,1]} {}^{\beta}\mathfrak{z}_2(\hat{\mathfrak{r}}) < \frac{3}{5}, \ \textit{for} \ \beta = 1,2.$$

5. Uniqueness of Positive Radial Solution

We use two metrics, in accordance with Rus' theorem [31,32], in this part, to test if there is a unique positive solution to the BVP (3). Consider the collection of continuous, real-valued functions defined on $[0,1]$: this space is symbolised by the letter X. Take into account the below metrics on X, for functions $\mathfrak{y}, \mathfrak{z} \in \mathrm{X}$:

$$\mathrm{d}(\mathfrak{y},\mathfrak{z}) = \max_{\hat{\mathfrak{r}}\in[0,1]} |\mathfrak{y}(\hat{\mathfrak{r}}) - \mathfrak{z}(\hat{\mathfrak{r}})|; \tag{11}$$

$$\rho(\mathfrak{y},\mathfrak{z}) = \left[\int_0^1 |\mathfrak{y}(\hat{\mathfrak{r}}) - \mathfrak{z}(\hat{\mathfrak{r}})|^{\mathrm{p}}\mathrm{d}\hat{\mathfrak{r}}\right]^{\frac{1}{\mathrm{p}}}, \ \mathrm{p} > 1. \tag{12}$$

The combination (X, d) creates a complete metric space for d in (11). Then, (X, ρ) constitutes a metric space for the value of ρ in (12). The equation expressing the connection between the two measures on X is

$$\rho(\mathfrak{y},\mathfrak{z}) \le \mathrm{d}(\mathfrak{y},\mathfrak{z}) \ \text{for all} \ \mathfrak{y},\mathfrak{z} \in \mathrm{X}. \tag{13}$$

Theorem 10 (Rus [32]). *Let* $F : X \to X$ *be a continuous with respect to* d *on* X *and*

$$d(F\mathfrak{y}, F\mathfrak{z}) \leq \alpha_1 \rho(\mathfrak{y}, \mathfrak{z}), \tag{14}$$

for some $\alpha_1 > 0$ *and for all* $\mathfrak{y}, \mathfrak{z} \in X$,

$$\rho(F\mathfrak{y}, F\mathfrak{z}) \leq \alpha_2 \rho(\mathfrak{y}, \mathfrak{z}), \tag{15}$$

for some $0 < \alpha_2 < 1$ *for all* $\mathfrak{y}, \mathfrak{z} \in X$, *then there is a unique* $\mathfrak{y}^* \in X$ *such that* $F\mathfrak{y}^* = \mathfrak{y}^*$.

Denote $Y(\zeta) = Q(\zeta, \zeta)\zeta^{\frac{2(N-1)}{2-N}} \prod_{i=1}^{\kappa} \varrho_i(\zeta)$.

Theorem 11. *Suppose that* $(\mathcal{J}_1)$ *and* $(\mathcal{J}_2)$ *and the following*
$(\mathcal{J}_{12})\, |F_\beta(\mathfrak{z}) - F_\beta(\mathfrak{y})| \leq K|\mathfrak{z} - y|$ *for* $\mathfrak{z}, \mathfrak{y} \in X$, *for some* $K > 0$
are satisfied. Furthermore, there are two real numbers $p > 1$, $q > 1$ *satisfying* $\frac{1}{p} + \frac{1}{q} = 1$, *and the following holds:*

$$\left[\frac{\sigma(\xi) K r_0^2}{(N-2)^2}\right]^{\eth+1} \left[\int_0^1 |Y(\zeta)| d\zeta\right]^{\eth} \left[\int_0^1 |Y(\zeta)|^q d\zeta\right]^{\frac{1}{q}} < 1; \tag{16}$$

then the BVP (3) *has a unique positive solution in* X.

Proof. Let $\mathfrak{z}_1, \mathfrak{y}_1 \in X$ and $\zeta_{n-1} \in [0,1]$. The Hölder's inequality gives

$$\begin{aligned}
&\left|\int_0^1 Q(\zeta_{\eth-1}, \zeta_\eth)\varrho(\zeta_\eth) F_\eth(\mathfrak{z}_1(\zeta_\eth)) d\zeta_\eth - \int_0^1 Q(\zeta_{\eth-1}, \zeta_\eth)\varrho(\zeta_\eth) F_\eth(\mathfrak{y}_1(\zeta_\eth)) d\zeta_\eth\right| \\
&\leq \int_0^1 |Q(\zeta_{\eth-1}, \zeta_\eth)\, \varrho(\zeta_\eth)||F_\eth(\mathfrak{z}_1(\zeta_\eth)) - F_\eth(\mathfrak{y}_1(\zeta_\eth))| d\zeta_\eth \\
&\leq \int_0^1 |Q(\zeta_\eth, \zeta_\eth)\, \varrho(\zeta_\eth)|\, K|\mathfrak{z}_1(\zeta_\eth) - \mathfrak{y}_1(\zeta_\eth)| d\zeta_\eth \leq \frac{K r_0^2}{(\eth-2)^2} \int_0^1 |Y(\zeta_\eth)||\mathfrak{z}_1(\zeta_\eth) - \mathfrak{y}_1(\zeta_\eth)| d\zeta_\eth \\
&\leq \frac{K r_0^2}{(N-2)^2} \left[\int_0^1 |Y(\zeta_\eth)|^q d\zeta_\eth\right]^{\frac{1}{q}} \left[\int_0^1 |\mathfrak{z}_1(\zeta_\eth) - \mathfrak{y}_1(\zeta_\eth)|^p d\zeta_\eth\right]^{\frac{1}{p}} \\
&\leq \frac{K r_0^2}{(N-2)^2} \left[\int_0^1 |Y(\zeta_\eth)|^q d\zeta_\eth\right]^{\frac{1}{q}} \rho(\mathfrak{z}_1, \mathfrak{y}_1) \leq \alpha_1^\star \rho(\mathfrak{z}_1, \mathfrak{y}_1),
\end{aligned}$$

where

$$\alpha_1^\star = \frac{K r_0^2}{(N-2)^2} \left[\int_0^1 |Y(\zeta_\eth)|^q d\zeta\right]^{\frac{1}{q}}.$$

Similarly, for $0 < \zeta_{\eth-2} < 1$, we obtain

$$\begin{aligned}
&\left|\int_0^1 Q(\zeta_{\eth-2}, \zeta_{\eth-1})\varrho(\zeta_{\eth-1}) F_{\eth-1}\left[\int_0^1 Q(\zeta_{\eth-1}, \zeta_\eth)\varrho(\zeta_\eth) F_\eth(\mathfrak{z}_1(\zeta_\eth)) d\zeta_\eth\right] d\zeta_{\eth-1}\right. \\
&\qquad \left. - \int_0^1 Q(\zeta_{\eth-2}, \zeta_{\eth-1})\varrho(\zeta_{\eth-1}) F_{\eth-1}\left[\int_0^1 Q(\zeta_{\eth-1}, \zeta_\eth)\varrho(\zeta_\eth) F_\eth(\mathfrak{y}_1(\zeta_\eth)) d\zeta_\eth\right] d\zeta_{\eth-1}\right| \\
&\leq \frac{K r_0^2}{(N-2)^2} \int_0^1 |Y(\zeta_{\eth-1})| \alpha_1 \rho(\mathfrak{z}_1, \mathfrak{y}_1) d\zeta_{\eth-1} \leq \widehat{\alpha}_1 \alpha_1^\star \rho(\mathfrak{z}_1, \mathfrak{y}_1),
\end{aligned}$$

where

$$\widehat{\alpha}_1 = \frac{K r_0^2}{(N-2)^2} \int_0^1 |Y(\zeta)| d\zeta.$$

Thus, we have

$$|F\mathfrak{z}_1(\zeta) - F\mathfrak{y}_1(\zeta)| \leq \widehat{\alpha}_1^{\eth} \alpha_1^\star \rho(\mathfrak{z}_1, \mathfrak{y}_1);$$

that is,

$$\mathrm{d}(F\mathfrak{z}_1, F\mathfrak{y}_1) \leq \alpha_1 \rho(\mathfrak{z}_1, \mathfrak{y}_1), \tag{17}$$

for some $\alpha_1 = \widehat{\alpha}_1^{\mathfrak{d}} \alpha_1^{\star} > 0$ for all $\mathfrak{z}_1, \mathfrak{y}_1 \in X$, this proves (14). Next, let $\mathfrak{z}_1, \mathfrak{y}_1 \in X$, and from (13) and (17), we obtain

$$\mathrm{d}(F\mathfrak{z}_1, F\mathfrak{y}_1) \leq \alpha_1 \rho(\mathfrak{z}_1, \mathfrak{y}_1) \leq \alpha_1 \mathrm{d}(\mathfrak{z}_1, \mathfrak{y}_1).$$

Thus, for $\varepsilon > 0$, select $\eta = \varepsilon/\alpha_1$, we obtain $\mathrm{d}(F\mathfrak{z}_1, F\mathfrak{y}_1) < \varepsilon$, whenever $\mathrm{d}(\mathfrak{z}_1, \mathfrak{y}_1) < \eta$, which shows that F is continuous on X with metric d. It remains to be shown that F is contractive on X with metric ρ. For each $\mathfrak{z}_1, \mathfrak{y}_1 \in X$, and from (17), we have

$$\begin{aligned} \left[\int_0^1 |(F\mathfrak{z}_1)(\zeta) - (F\mathfrak{y}_1)(\zeta)|^p d\zeta\right]^{\frac{1}{p}} &\leq \left[\int_0^1 |\widehat{\alpha}_1^{\mathfrak{d}} \alpha_1^{\star} \rho(\mathfrak{z}_1, \mathfrak{y}_1)|^p d\zeta\right]^{\frac{1}{p}} \\ &\leq \left[\frac{Kr_0^2}{(N-2)^2}\right]^{\mathfrak{d}+1} \left[\int_0^1 |Y(\zeta)| d\zeta\right]^{\mathfrak{d}} \left[\int_0^1 |Y(\zeta)|^q d\zeta\right]^{\frac{1}{q}} \rho(\mathfrak{z}_1, \mathfrak{y}_1); \end{aligned}$$

that is

$$\rho(F\mathfrak{z}_1, F\mathfrak{y}_1) \leq \left[\frac{Kr_0^2}{(N-2)^2}\right]^{\mathfrak{d}+1} \left[\int_0^1 |Y(\zeta)| d\zeta\right]^{\mathfrak{d}} \left[\int_0^1 |Y(\zeta)|^q d\zeta\right]^{\frac{1}{q}} \rho(\mathfrak{z}_1, \mathfrak{y}_1).$$

From assumption (16), we have

$$\rho(F\mathfrak{z}_1, F\mathfrak{y}_1) \leq \alpha_2 \rho(\mathfrak{z}_1, \mathfrak{y}_1)$$

for some $\alpha_2 < 1$ and all $\mathfrak{z}_1, \mathfrak{y}_1 \in X$. It follows from Theorem 10 that F has a unique fixed point in X. Moreover, from Lemma 3, F is positive. Hence, the BVP (1) has a unique positive solution. □

Example 3. *Consider the problem,*

$$\triangle \mathfrak{z}_\beta - \frac{(N-2)^2 r_0^{2N-2}}{|\nu|^{2N-2}} \mathfrak{z}_\beta + \varrho(|\nu|) F_\beta(\mathfrak{z}_{\beta+1}) = 0,\ 1 < |\nu| < 2, \tag{18}$$

$$\mathfrak{z}_\beta(0) = \mathfrak{z}_\beta(1) = 0, \tag{19}$$

where $r_0 = 1$, $N = 3$, $\beta \in \{1,2\}$, $\mathfrak{z}_3 = \mathfrak{z}_1$, $\varrho(\hat{r}) = \frac{1}{\hat{r}^4} \prod_{i=1}^2 \varrho_i(\hat{r})$, $\varrho_i(\hat{r}) = \varrho_i\left(\frac{1}{\hat{r}}\right)$, *in which* $\varrho_1(\hat{r}) = \varrho_2(\hat{r}) = \frac{\hat{r}^3}{\sqrt{\hat{r}+1}}$. *Let* $F_1(\mathfrak{z}) = \frac{3}{2}\sin(\mathfrak{z})$ *and* $F_2(\mathfrak{z}) = \frac{3}{2(\mathfrak{z}+1)}$; *then,*

$$|F_1(\mathfrak{z}) - F_1(y)| = \frac{|\sin(\mathfrak{z}) - \sin(y)|}{10^3} \leq \frac{3}{2}|\mathfrak{z} - y|$$

and

$$|F_2(\mathfrak{z}) - F_2(y)| = \frac{3}{2}\left|\frac{1}{\mathfrak{z}+1} - \frac{1}{y+1}\right| \leq \frac{3}{2}|\mathfrak{z} - y|.$$

Thus, $K = \frac{3}{2}$. *Let* $\mathfrak{d} = 2$ *and* $p = q = 2$; *then,*

$$\left[\frac{Kr_0^2}{(N-2)^2}\right]^{\mathfrak{d}+1} \left[\int_0^1 |Y(\zeta)| d\zeta\right]^{\mathfrak{d}} \left[\int_0^1 |Y(\zeta)|^q d\zeta\right]^{\frac{1}{q}} \approx 0.1508078067 < 1.$$

Hence, as an application of Theorem 11, the BVP (18) *and* (19) *has a unique positive radial solution.*

6. Conclusions

In this paper, we developed a theory to study the existence of single and coupled positive radial solutions for a certain type of iterative system of nonlinear elliptic equations, by applying Krasnoselskii's and Avery–Henderson's fixed-point theorems in a Banach space. In the future, we will study the existence of positive radial solutions for an iterative system of elliptic equations with a logarithmic nonlinear term. In addition, we will study global existence and ground-state solutions to the addressed problem.

Author Contributions: Conceptualization, X.W. and J.A.; methodology, M.K.; software, validation, M.F.; writing—original draft preparation, M.K.; writing—review and editing, J.A. and M.K. All authors have read and agreed to the published version of the manuscript.

Funding: This research is supported by the National Natural Science Foundation of China (Grant No. 11861053).

Institutional Review Board Statement: This article does not contain any studies, performed by any of the authors, involving human participants or animals.

Data Availability Statement: Data sharing not applicable to this paper, as no data sets were generated or analyzed during the current study.

Acknowledgments: The authors would like to thank the referees for their valuable suggestions and comments for the improvement of the paper. Xiaoming Wang is thankful to the National Natural Science Foundation of China (Grant No. 11861053). J. Alzabut is thankful to Prince Sultan University and OSTİM Technical University, and Mahammad Khuddush is thankful to Lankapalli Bullayya College of Engineering for their tireless support during work on this paper. M. Fečkan is thankful to the Slovak Research and Development Agency, under contract No. APVV-18-0308, and to the Slovak Grant Agency VEGA No. 1/0084/23 and No. 2/0127/20.

Conflicts of Interest: The authors declare no conflict of interest.

References

1. Alsaedi, R. Positive solutions for some nonlinear elliptic systems in exterior domains of $\mathbb{R}^2$. *Abstr. Appl. Anal.* **2012**, *2012*, 273017. [CrossRef]
2. Boulbrachene, M. L^∞ error estimate for a class of semilinear elliptic systems of quasi-variational inequalities. *J. Nonlinear Var. Anal.* **2021**, *5*, 429–440.
3. Chen, H. A new two-grid P_0^2–P_1 mixed finite element algorithm for general elliptic optimal control problems. *J. Nonlinear Funct. Anal.* **2022**, *2022*, 41.
4. Ni, W.M. *Some Aspects of Semilinear Elliptic Equations on $\mathbb{R}^n$, in Nonlinear Diffusion Equations and Their Equilibrium States II*; Ni, W.M., Peletier, L.A., Serrin, J., Eds.; Springer: New York, NY, USA, 1988; pp. 171–205.
5. Yanagida, E. Uniqueness of positive radial solutions of $\Delta u + g(|\mathbf{x}|)u + g(|\mathbf{x}|)u^p = 0$ in $\mathbb{R}^n$. *Arch. Rational Mech. Anal.* **1991**, *115*, 257–274. [CrossRef]
6. Ali, J.; Brown, K.; Shivaji, R. Positive solutions for $n \times n$ elliptic systems with combined nonlinear effects. *Differ. Integral Equ.* **2011**, *24*, 307–324. [CrossRef]
7. Ali, J.; Shivaji, R.; Ramaswamy, M. Multiple positive solutions for classes of elliptic systems with combined nonlinear effects. *Differ. Integral Equ.* **2006**, *19*, 669–680. [CrossRef]
8. Dalmasso, R. Existence and uniqueness of positive solutions of semilinear elliptic systems. *Nonlinear Anal.* **2000**, *39*, 559–568. [CrossRef]
9. Hai, D.D.; Shivaji, R. An existence result on positive solutions for a class of pLaplacian systems. *Nonlinear Anal. Theory Methods Appl.* **2004**, *56*, 1007–1010. [CrossRef]
10. Ali, J.; Shivaji, R. Positive solutions for a class of p-Laplacian systems with multiple parameters. *J. Math. Anal. Appl.* **2007**, *335*, 1013–1019. [CrossRef]
11. Ali, J.; Padhi, S. Existence of multiple positive radial solutions to elliptic equations in an annulus. *Commun. Appl. Anal.* **2018**, *22*, 695–710. [CrossRef]
12. Beldzinski, M.; Galewski, M. On solvability of elliptic boundary value problems via global invertibility. *Opusc. Math.* **2020**, *40*, 37–47. [CrossRef]
13. Gala, S.; Galakhov, E.; Ragusa, M.A.; Salieva, O. Beale-Kato-Majda regularity criterion of smooth solutions for the Hall-MHD equations with zero viscosity. *Bull. Braz. Math. Soc.* **2022**, *53*, 229–241. [CrossRef]
14. Hai, D.D.; Shivaji, R. An existence result on positive solutions for a class of semilinear elliptic systems. *Proc. R. Soc. Edinb. Sect. A* **2004**, *134*, 137–141. [CrossRef]

15. Hai, D.D.; Shivaji, R. Uniqueness of positive solutions for a class of semipositone elliptic systems. *Nonlinear Anal.* **2007**, *66*, 396–402. [CrossRef]
16. Khuddush, M.; Prasad, K.R. Positive Solutions for an Iterative System of Nonlinear Elliptic Equations. *Bull. Malays. Math. Sci. Soc.* **2022**, *45*, 245–272. [CrossRef]
17. Khuddush, M.; Prasad, K.R. Existence of infinitely many positive radial solutions for an iterative system of nonlinear elliptic equations on an exterior domain. *Afr. Mat.* **2022**, *33*, 93. [CrossRef]
18. Khuddush, M.; Prasad, K.R.; Bharathi, B. Denumerably many positive radial solutions to iterative system of nonlinear elliptic equations on the exterior of a ball. *Nonlinear Dyn. Syst. Theory* **2023**, *1*, 95–106.
19. Li, Y. Positive radial solutions for elliptic equations with nonlinear gradient terms in an annulus. *Complex Var. Elliptic Equ.* **2018**, *63*, 171–187. [CrossRef]
20. Mei, L. Structure of positive radial solutions of a quasilinear elliptic problem with singular nonlinearity. *Complex Var. Elliptic Equ.* **2018**, *63*, 1595–1603. [CrossRef]
21. Padhi, S.; Graef, J.R.; Kanaujiya, A. Positive solutions to nonlinear elliptic equations depending on a parameter with Dirichlet boundary conditions. *Differ. Equ. Dyn. Syst.* **2023**, *31*, 319–336. [CrossRef]
22. Chrouda, M.B.; Hassine, K. Uniqueness of positive radial solutions for elliptic equations in an annulus. *Proc. Am. Math. Soc.* **2020**, *149*, 649–660. [CrossRef]
23. Dong, X.; Wei, Y. Existence of radial solutions for nonlinear elliptic equations with gradient terms in annular domains. *Nonlinear Anal.* **2019**, *187*, 93–109. [CrossRef]
24. Kajikiya, R.; Ko, E. Existence of positive radial solutions for a semipositone elliptic equation. *J. Math. Anal. Appl.* **2020**, *484*, 123735. [CrossRef]
25. Son, B.; Wang, P. Positive radial solutions to classes of nonlinear elliptic systems on the exterior of a ball. *J. Math. Anal. Appl.* **2020**, *488*, 124069. [CrossRef]
26. Lan, K.; Webb, J.R.L. Positive solutions of semilinear differential equations with singularities. *J. Differ. Equ.* **1998**, *148*, 407–421. [CrossRef]
27. Lee, Y.H. Multiplicity of positive radial solutions for multiparameter semilinear elliptic systems on an annulus. *J. Differ. Equ.* **2001**, *174*, 420–441. [CrossRef]
28. Cheung, W.S. Generalizations of Hölder's inequality. *Int. Math. Math. Sci.* **2001**, *26*, 7–10. [CrossRef]
29. Guo, D.; Lakshmikantham, V. *Nonlinear Problems in Abstract Cones*; Academic Press: San Diego, CA, USA, 1988.
30. Avery, R.I.; Henderson, J. Two positive fixed points of nonlinear operators on ordered Banach spaces. *Comm. Appl. Nonlinear Anal.* **2001**, *8*, 27–36.
31. Prasad, K.R.; Khuddush, M.; Leela, D. Existence, uniqueness and Hyers–Ulam stability of a fractional order iterative two-point boundary value problems. *Afr. Mat.* **2021**, *32*, 1227–1237. [CrossRef]
32. Rus, I.A. On a fixed point theorem of Maia. *Stud. Univ.-Babes-Bolyai Math.* **1977**, *1*, 40–42.

Disclaimer/Publisher's Note: The statements, opinions and data contained in all publications are solely those of the individual author(s) and contributor(s) and not of MDPI and/or the editor(s). MDPI and/or the editor(s) disclaim responsibility for any injury to people or property resulting from any ideas, methods, instructions or products referred to in the content.

axioms

MDPI

Article

Study of the Hypergeometric Equation via Data Driven Koopman-EDMD Theory

Evangelos Melas [1], Costas Poulios [1], Elias Camouzis [2,*], John Leventides [1] and Nick Poulios [3]

1 Department of Economics, National and Kapodistrian University of Athens, 1, Sofokleous Str., 10559 Athens, Greece
2 Department of Business Administration, National and Kapodistrian University of Athens, 1, Sofokleous Str., 10559 Athens, Greece
3 Lehrstuhl Wirtschafts-und Betribswissenschaften (wBw), Montanuniversität Leoben, Franz Josef Straße 18, A-8700 Leoben, Austria
* Correspondence: ecamouzis@ba.uoa.gr

Abstract: We consider a data-driven method, which combines Koopman operator theory with Extended Dynamic Mode Decomposition. We apply this method to the hypergeometric equation which is the Fuchsian equation with three regular singular points. The space of solutions at any of its singular points is a two-dimensional linear vector space on the field of reals when the independent variable is restricted to take values in the real axis and the unknown function is restricted to be a real-valued function of a real variable. A basis of the linear vector space of solutions is spanned by the hypergeometric function and its products with appropriate powers of the independent variable or the logarithmic function depending on the roots of the indicial equation of the hypergeometric equation. With our work, we obtain a new representation of the fundamental solutions of the hypergeometric equation and relate them to the spectral analysis of the finite approximation of the Koopman operator associated with the hypergeometric equation. We expect that the usefulness of our results will come more to the fore when we extend our study into the complex domain.

Keywords: hypergeometric equation; Koopman operators; EDMD

MSC: 37P99; 34A45; 34M99

Citation: Melas, E.; Poulios, C.; Camouzis, E.; Leventides, J.; Poulios, N. Study of the Hypergeometric Equation via Data Driven Koopman-EDMD Theory. *Axioms* **2023**, *12*, 134. https://doi.org/10.3390/axioms12020134

Academic Editors: Hatıra Günerhan, Francisco Martínez González and Mohammed K. A. Kaabar

Received: 24 December 2022
Revised: 22 January 2023
Accepted: 23 January 2023
Published: 29 January 2023

Copyright: © 2023 by the authors. Licensee MDPI, Basel, Switzerland. This article is an open access article distributed under the terms and conditions of the Creative Commons Attribution (CC BY) license (https://creativecommons.org/licenses/by/4.0/).

1. Introduction

The study of complex nonlinear dynamical systems appears in many disciplines, such as physics, engineering, biology, social sciences, etc. The high degree of complexity of such systems makes their analysis quite a challenge. From this point of view, data-driven mathematical methods might be of high importance. These methods aspire to exploit measurement data, which form a relatively small subset of the original state space. However, they might describe the evolution of the original system, even if its dynamics are complicated or unknown. In recent years, it seems that advances in numerical techniques and the broader availability of data have brought data-driven methods to the forefront of scientific research. For example, one such technique might as well be Koopman operator theory in connection with Dynamic Mode Decomposition (DMD), and especially with Extended Dynamic Mode Decomposition (EDMD).

Firstly, in the Koopman operator framework (initiated in [1], see also [2,3]), the central objects are complex-valued functions defined on the state space (these functions are called observables of the systems). The Koopman operator describes the evolution of the observables according to the evolution of the system. This approach enables us to "lift" the dynamical system from its original state space to new spaces spanned by observables.

The main advantage is that the Koopman operator is linear. Hence, powerful methods from operator theory, such as spectral analysis, can be applied. The Koopman operator might be quite useful especially when we study in high-dimensional and strongly nonlinear systems. In these cases, the phase space is quite large and its dynamics are so complicated that very little can be concluded about its corresponding geometrical properties. Applications of this approach range from, among others, fluid dynamics (see [4,5]), energy modeling in buildings (see [6]), oceanography (see [7]) and molecular kinetics (see [8]).

Despite its advantages, the Koopman operator converts a finite-dimensional system to an infinite-dimensional linear system. In other words, we "pay" in dimensions, in order to gain "linearity". Being infinite-dimensional, the Koopman operator cannot be calculated while its spectral properties are difficult to explore. In practice, this amounts to a simplification only when one can handle the operator numerically. Consequently, the need for numerical methods that generate finite dimensional approximations of the Koopman operator is emerging.

In this direction, dynamic mode decomposition (DMD) (see [9,10]) and its generalization, the extended-DMD (EDMD) have been proven very efficient. Since these methods depend on data and rely only on least square regression, they are very easy to implement.

The EDMD method algorithm starts by choosing a finite set of observables, which is called a dictionary. Then, we approximate the Koopman operator as a linear map on the span of this finite set. Note that the finite-dimensional linear map which emerges in such a case is numerically tractable. Furthermore, its spectral properties can approximate those of the Koopman operator (see [11]).

Critical to the success of the EDMD algorithm is the appropriate choice of the dictionary. The choice of a suitable dictionary significantly impacts the approximation quality of the spectral properties of the system (see [11–13]). However, in many practical applications, it is often not so easy to make such a selection without some prior information on the dynamics of the system.

The Koopman operator-EDMD algorithm has been applied to several ODEs and PDEs. For example, see [14] for an application to Burgers' equation and the nonlinear Scrödinger equation. Moreover, see [15] for an application to Kuramoto–Sivashinsky PDE. In this paper, we demonstrate the use of the Koopman-EDMD method when applied to the hypergeometric equation. The effectiveness of our approach is based on the choice of the appropriate dictionary.

The hypergeometric equation is a linear second-order homogeneous differential equation that falls into the Fuchsian class and has three regular singular points at 0, 1, and ∞. In this paper, we restrict the independent variable to be real and the dependent variable to be a real−valued function of a real variable. At each singular point, there is a fundamental set of two solutions that span the two-dimensional linear vector solution space.

Summarizing our discussion, the innovation and contribution of this paper are summarized as follows: We address the trajectory approximation of a hypergeometric equation via EDMD methods. The EDMD method gives rise to a linear system on an enhanced state space that can approximate a given trajectory. Having data of a given trajectory in a finite horizon allows us to construct a discrete linear system of dimension $n > m$, where m is the dimension of the state space of the original nonlinear system. We demonstrate the approximation of a single trajectory of a hypergeometric equation via EDMD methods. In particular, we solve a hypergeometric equation in the vicinity of 0, which is one of its singular points, by using the Koopman-EDMD theory. Finally, we show that we can improve the approximation of the solution of a hypergeometric equation in the vicinity of 0, by using successive trajectory reconstruction via Koopman-EDMD theory with moving horizon.

The EDMD method is data-driven. Consequently, depending on a suitable choice, the method can be applied to any dynamical system for which probably the dynamical law is unknown and data, in the form of time series, can be collected for some of its trajectories in the state space. Moreover, our approach can be used for any nonlinear dynamical system with known dynamics. However, in such a case a linearization of the dynamics via the EDMD method may be required in order, for example, to study the control theory of this linearized system; the control theory of linear systems is much better understood than the control theory of nonlinear systems.

The rest of the paper is organized as follows. In Section 2, we briefly present some basic facts about the Koopman operator theory and EDMD method. In Section 3, we give an example of a hypergeometric equation and its exact solution via hypergeometric series. In Section 4, we solve the hypergeometric equation in the interval $(-0.9, -0.001)$ via Koopman-EDMD theory. In Section 5, we solve the hypergeometric equation in the interval $(0.2, 1)$ via Koopman-EDMD theory. In Section 6, we present a successive trajectory reconstruction via Koopman-EDMD theory with a moving horizon. Finally, Section 7 contains our conclusions about this paper.

2. Koopman Operator and EDMD

Koopman operator theory has been extensively used in the analysis, prediction, and control of nonlinear dynamical systems. To define this class of operators, we start with a continuous dynamical system $\mathcal{M}, f$, where $\mathcal{M}$ is the state space (usually a manifold in $\mathbb{R}^n$) and f is the evolution map. The system is described by the differential equation $\dot{\mathbf{x}} = f(\mathbf{x})$. We also denote by $\Phi_t(\mathbf{x}_0)$ the flow map, which is defined as the state of the system in time t when the initial condition is x_0.

In the literature of Koopman operators, complex-valued functions $g\colon \mathcal{M} \to \mathbb{C}$ defined on $\mathcal{M}$ are called *observables* of the system $(\mathcal{M}, f)$. We now consider a function space $\mathcal{F}$ of observables which is closed under composition with the flow map. This means that $g \circ \Phi_t$ belongs to $\mathcal{F}$ whenever $g \in \mathcal{F}$. (In many applications, $\mathcal{F}$ is the space $L^2(\mathcal{M})$ of complex valued square integrable functions on $\mathcal{M}$. However, other function spaces can also be considered.) Then, for any $t \geq 0$, the operator $K_t\colon \mathcal{F} \to \mathcal{F}$ is defined by $K_t(g) = g \circ \Phi_t$. The term Koopman operator usually refers to the whole class of operators, i.e., $\mathcal{K} = (K_t)_{t\geq 0}$. The linearity of composition implies that K_t is a linear operator for any $t \geq 0$.

In a similar way, the Koopman operator can be defined for discrete dynamical systems, which, in some sense, are more natural. Indeed, in many practical applications, the differential equations that describe the evolution of the system are completely unknown and we have only measurement data that are provided in discrete time. So, let us assume that we are given a discrete system, $x_{k+1} = f(x_k)$, where x_k belongs to the state space $\mathcal{M}$. The Koopman operator is defined as the composition of any observable with the evolution map f. Thus, $\mathcal{K}\colon \mathcal{F} \to \mathcal{F}$ is given by $\mathcal{K}(g) = g \circ f$, for any $g \in \mathcal{F}$. (Again, $\mathcal{F}$ is a function space of observables closed under composition with f).

By its definition, the Koopman operator updates every observable according to the evolution of the dynamical system. A new system $(\mathcal{F}, \mathcal{K})$ is defined which is a global linearization of the original system $(\mathcal{M}, f)$ (i.e., it does not hold only to the area of some attractor or fixed point). Furthermore, many properties of $(\mathcal{M}, f)$ can be related to the eigenstructure of $\mathcal{K}$ (see [16]). Consequently, one can utilize tools from functional analysis and operator theory in order to study the system $(\mathcal{M}, f)$ even if this is a nonlinear one.

The main advantage of the Koopman operator is its linearity. However, it is infinite-dimensional and, except in some cases, we can calculate neither the operator nor its eigenstructure. In order to address the problems that infinite dimensionality poses, we have to look for finite-dimensional linear approximations of the Koopman operator. Towards this direction, the Dynamic Mode Decomposition (DMD) and, mainly, its generalization the Extended Dynamic Mode Decomposition (EDMD) have been proven very successful.

Extended Dynamic Mode Decomposition (EDMD)

We next give a brief description of the EDMD algorithm. The first step is to fix a set of observables $\{g_1, g_2, \ldots, g_p\}$, which is usually called a *dictionary*. In the case of DMD (Dynamic Mode Decomposition), we use only the observables $g_i(\mathbf{x}) = x_i$, for $i = 1, 2, \ldots, n$. On the contrary, in EDMD any observable can be chosen. In this way, we construct an augmented state space and; hence, EDMD gives better approximation properties than

DMD. The augmented state space is denoted by $\overline{\mathcal{M}}$ and its elements are denoted by $\mathbf{y} = [g_1(\mathbf{x}), \ldots, g_p(\mathbf{x})]^T$.

The second step involves data collection. To this end, we consider a trajectory of the original system with some initial condition $\mathbf{x}_0$ and some finite time horizon T. Then, we collect sampling points at a fixed time interval ΔT (although, uniform sampling is not mandatory and one can apply other sampling methods). Therefore, we consider $n_0 = \frac{T}{\Delta T}$ points in this trajectory, which are denoted by $(\mathbf{x}_s)_{s=0}^{n_0}$. These points generate data $(\mathbf{y}_s)_{s=0}^{n_0}$ in the augmented space $\overline{\mathcal{M}}$. Finally, the data are organized in data matrices as follows

$$\mathbf{Y}_{[0,n_0-1]} = \left[\mathbf{y}_0, \mathbf{y}_1, \ldots, \mathbf{y}_{n_0-1}\right] \quad \text{and} \quad \mathbf{Y}_{[1,n_0]} = \left[\mathbf{y}_1, \mathbf{y}_2, \ldots, \mathbf{y}_{n_0}\right].$$

The last step is to obtain a $p \times p$ matrix $\mathbf{A}$ (using, for instance, least square regression methods) such that $\mathbf{Y}_{[1,n_0]} \sim \mathbf{A}\mathbf{Y}_{[0,n_0-1]}$. Therefore,

$$\mathbf{A} = \underset{\tilde{\mathbf{A}} \in \mathbb{R}^{p \times p}}{\operatorname{argmin}} \left\| \mathbf{Y}_{[1,n_0]} - \tilde{\mathbf{A}}\mathbf{Y}_{[0,n_0-1]} \right\|,$$

where $\|\cdot\|$ is some matrix norm.

The procedure described above can be applied to several trajectories. Hence, we may fix k trajectories and, following the previous steps, we obtain data matrices $\mathbf{Y}_{j[0,n_0-1]}$ and $\mathbf{Y}_{j[01,n_0]}$ for every $j = 1, 2, \ldots, k$. In this case, the matrix $\mathbf{A}$ is chosen such that

$$\mathbf{A} = \underset{\tilde{\mathbf{A}} \in \mathbb{R}^{p \times p}}{\operatorname{argmin}} \sum_{j=1}^{k} \left\| \mathbf{Y}_{j[1,n_0]} - \tilde{\mathbf{A}}\mathbf{Y}_{j[0,n_0-1]} \right\|.$$

Consequently, $\mathbf{A}$ is a best-fit matrix that relates the two data matrices in every trajectory. The matrix $\mathbf{A}$ generates a finite-dimensional linear system that advances spatial measurements from one time to the next and it provides approximations to the Koopman operator and to the original nonlinear system.

One of the main advantages of EDMD is that it is a purely data-driven method. Therefore, there is actually no restriction to its applicability and it can be utilized even if the dynamics of the system are completely unknown. However, the success of this method depends on the a priori chosen dictionary. In many problems, the most difficult part is to choose a dictionary that will give good approximations. There is no generic algorithm for this problem, however, some recent studies use artificial intelligence methods in order to "train" the dictionary (see [15,17]).

3. An Example of Hypergeometric Equation and Its Exact Solution via Hypergeometric Series

We consider the hypergeometric equation

$$t(t-1)\frac{\mathrm{d}^2 x}{\mathrm{d}t^2} + (2t-1)\frac{\mathrm{d}x}{\mathrm{d}t} + x = 0, \tag{1}$$

with initial conditions $t = -0.9$, $x(-0.9) = 0.1$, $\left.\frac{\mathrm{d}x}{\mathrm{d}t}\right|_{t=-0.9} = 1$. The solution of the complexification of (1) with the aforementioned initial conditions is given by

$$\begin{aligned}(-16.9355 + 11.3861i)\Big(&\mathit{LegendreP}\left(\frac{1}{2}i\left(i+\sqrt{3}\right), -1+2t\right) \quad + \\ (0.00524496 - 0.649963i)&\mathit{LegendreQ}\left(\frac{1}{2}i\left(i+\sqrt{3}\right), -1+2t\right)\Big)\end{aligned} \tag{2}$$

where *LegendreP* denotes the Legendre function of the first kind and *LegendreQ* denotes the Legendre function of the second kind. Figure 1 depicts the plot of the real part of the solution (2). We observe that the solution has vertical asymptotes at the singular points

$t = 0, t = 1$ of (1). In the next section, we numerically integrate (1) and reproduce the solution of (1) in the connected interval $t \in (-0.9, -0.001)$.

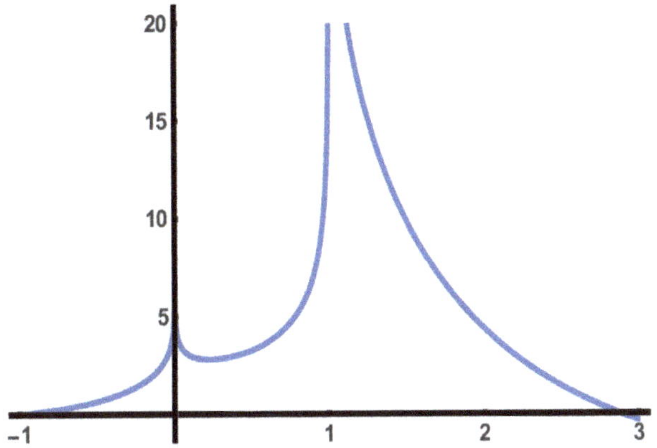

Figure 1. Graph of the real part of the solution (2).

4. Solving the Hypergeometric Equation in the Interval $(-0.9, -0.001)$ via Koopman-EDMD Theory

We numerically integrate

$$t(t-1)\frac{\mathrm{d}^2x}{\mathrm{d}t^2} + (2t-1)\frac{\mathrm{d}x}{\mathrm{d}t} + x = 0,$$

with initial conditions $t = -0.9$, $x(-0.9) = 0.1$, $\left.\frac{\mathrm{d}x}{\mathrm{d}t}\right|_{t=-0.9} = 1$ in the interval $t \in (-0.9, -0.001)$. Subsequently, we sample the trajectory with a time step $\Delta t = 0.01$. Figure 2 depicts the graph of the sampled points showing the asymptotic trend at $t = 0$.

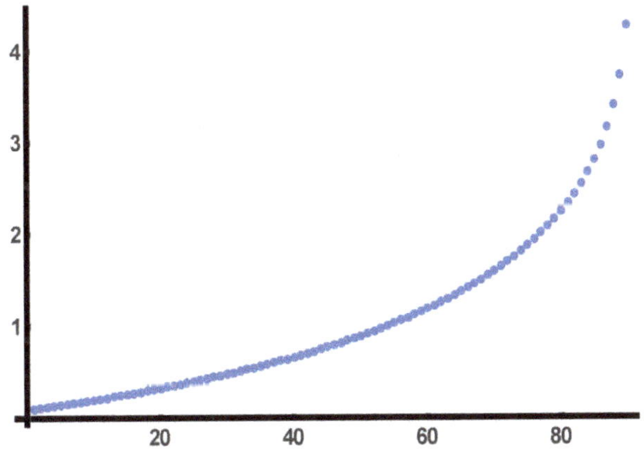

Figure 2. The graph of the sampled points of the hypergeometric Equation (1).

We then apply EDMD interpolation, as described in Section 2, using a dictionary of 4 observables, namely x, $\frac{1}{x}$, tx, $\frac{t}{x}$. The EDMD algorithm provides the following 4×4 transition matrix

$$\begin{bmatrix} 1.08228 & 0.401294 & 0.145089 & 0.131762 \\ 0.00886136 & 1.01576 & -0.00552547 & -0.00574604 \\ 0.0075471 & -0.35145 & 0.628826 & -0.252387 \\ -0.0127506 & 0.332983 & 0.354283 & 1.23706 \end{bmatrix}$$

The above matrix has 4 eigenvalues, two of which are real and the other two are complex numbers. In particular, the eigenvalues are

$$1.11249, \quad 0.987529 + 0.00693293i, \quad 0.987529 - 0.00693293i, \quad 0.876376.$$

Figure 3 shows the position of these eigenvalues in the complex plane.

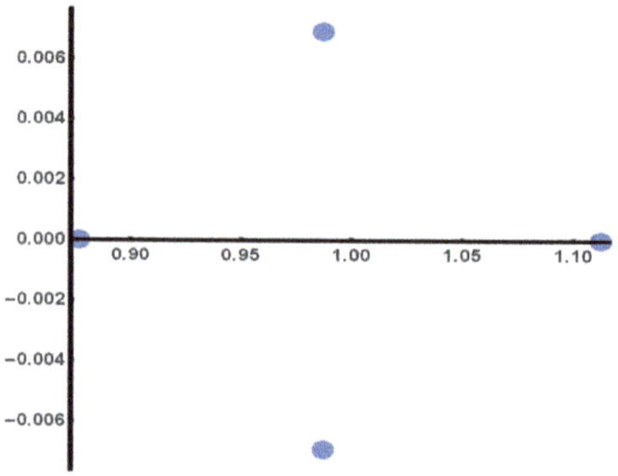

Figure 3. The eigenvalues of the EDMD transition matrix depicted in the complex plane.

The above matrix gives rise to a (finite-dimensional) linear dynamical system, whose trajectory (for the specific initial conditions) approximates the real trajectory. The comparison between the two trajectories approximated (orange line) and real data (blue line) is shown in Figure 4. Despite the low dimensions of this approximation, the Koopman-EDMD curve approximates well the given data away from the singularity at $t = 0$ and fails to do so near $t = 0$. It is possible to considerably improve the approximation by augmenting the dictionary both quantitatively and qualitatively.

Improving the Trajectory Approximation via Koopman-EDMD Theory

We follow on by augmenting the dictionary and repeating the trajectory approximation via EDMD. The dictionary that produces the best results and at the same time the dimension of the augmented space is kept comparatively low (equal to 5) is given by x, $\frac{1}{x}$, tx, $\frac{t}{x}$, xt^{15}. The comparison between the real trajectory and the approximation provided by the EDMD algorithm is presented in Figure 5. We notice that the approximation is significantly improved.

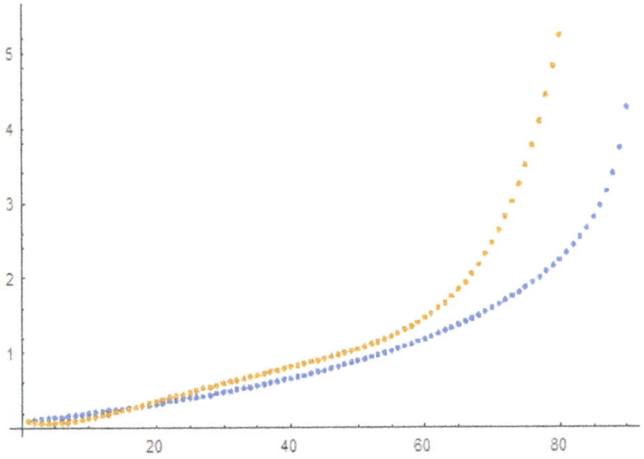

Figure 4. The real data (blue line) and the approximate trajectory (orange line).

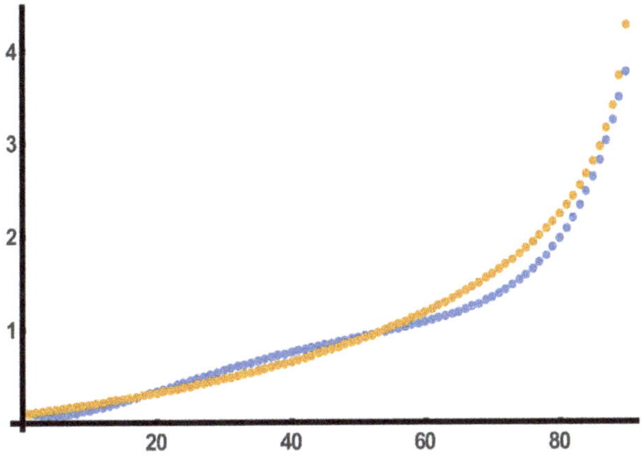

Figure 5. Comparison between the real trajectory (blue line) and the trajectory (orange line) given by the EDMD algorithm with a dictionary of five observables.

The matrix provided by the EDMD algorithm is now given by

$$\begin{bmatrix} 1.08292 & 0.387515 & 0.126814 & 0.119021 & 1.67268 \\ 0.00887233 & 1.01553 & -0.00583752 & -0.0059636 & 0.0285622 \\ 0.0162179 & -0.537512 & 0.382055 & -0.424438 & 22.5875 \\ -0.0213778 & 0.518112 & 0.599816 & 1.40825 & -22.4742 \\ -0.0000448427 & 0.00187752 & 0.00186914 & 0.00143044 & 0.799134 \end{bmatrix}$$

This matrix has two complex eigenvalues and three real eigenvalues, namely

$$1.11308, \quad 0.986969 + 0.00680815i, \quad 0.986969 - 0.00680815i, \quad 0.901002, \quad 0.699867.$$

Their positions in the complex plane are depicted in Figure 6.

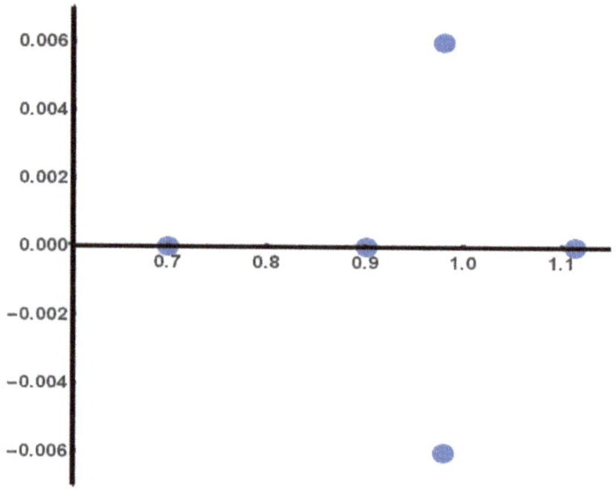

Figure 6. Eigenvalues of the 5×5 matrix produced by the EDMD methodology.

5. Solving the Hypergeometric Equation in the Interval $(0.2, 1)$ via Koopman-EDMD Theory

Figure 7 shows the plot of the real part of the solution (2) in the interval $[0, 1]$ (this is also depicted in Figure 1).

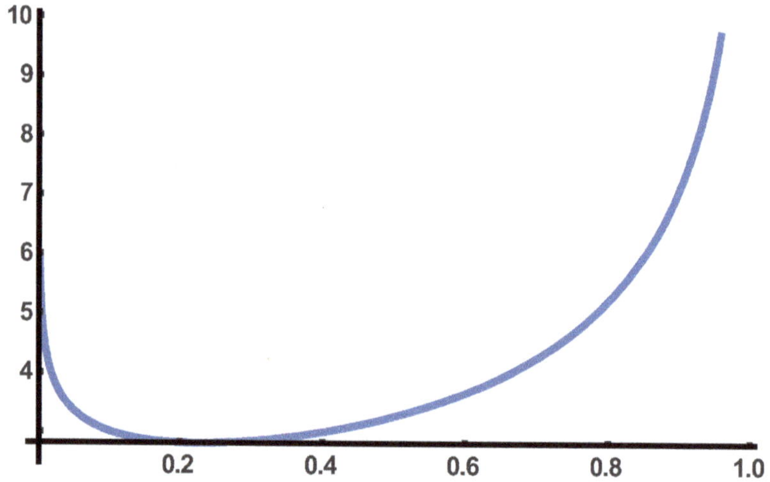

Figure 7. Graph of the real part of the solution (2) in the interval $[0, 1]$.

This solution has vertical asymptotes at the singular points of (1), that is, at $t = 0, t = 1$. We are going to numerically integrate (1) and reproduce the solution of (1) by Koopmman-EDMD theory in the connected interval $(0.2, 1)$.

We approximate this solution in the interval $(0.2, 1)$ by using the EDMD basis x, $\frac{1}{x}$, tx, $\frac{t}{x}$, $xt^{0.1}$. The five-dimensional discrete linear system obtained this way approximates satisfactorily the trajectory in the interval $(0.2, 1)$ as shown in Figure 8.

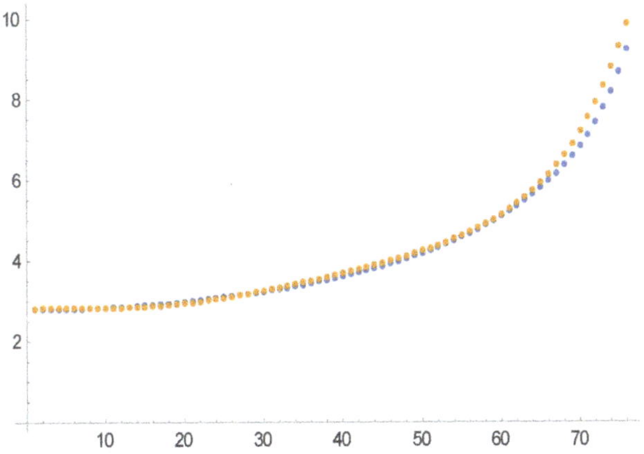

Figure 8. Comparison between approximated (orange line) and real data (blue line) in the interval $(0.2, 1)$.

The EDMD matrix is given by

$$\begin{bmatrix} 8.03736 & 3.0825 & 5.23571 & 6.45347 & -10.0906 \\ 7.37378 & 4.18128 & 5.39554 & 6.58341 & -10.5197 \\ -0.0144556 & -0.00620308 & 0.978249 & 0.00396585 & 0.0199957 \\ -0.00137726 & -0.00686054 & -0.020928 & 0.975436 & 0.00765612 \\ 7.15414 & 3.10723 & 5.294 & 6.46348 & -9.23167 \end{bmatrix}$$

which has the following eigenvalues

$$1.10972, \quad 0.984838 + 0.0194333i, \quad 0.984838 - 0.0194333i, \quad 0.959174, \quad 0.902077.$$

6. Successive Trajectory Reconstruction via Koopman-EDMD Theory with Moving Horizon

We apply EDMD trajectory reconstruction for $t \in (0,1)$ of the real part of the solution (2) of the differential Equation (1) whose graph is depicted in Figure 1.

We consider a four-dimensional EDMD basis consisting of x, $\frac{1}{x}$, tx, $\frac{t}{x}$, and we cover the interval $[0.05, 0.95]$ with 14 overlapping windows each of which contains 41 sample points of the hypergeometric solution. We then apply 14 EDMD computations for the 14 moving windows and produce 14 approximating trajectories as well as an equal number of EDMD matrices. The errors between these approximations compared to the real data and measured by the l_2 (Euclidean) norm for all 14 horizons are depicted in Figure 9 and, thus, the approximation is considered very satisfactory.

The 14 successive approximating trajectories to the hypergeometric solution (2) of Equation (1) which cover the interval $[0.05, 0.95]$ are given by

$$P_x A_k^n x_{ok} = a_{1k}\lambda_{1k}^n + a_{2k}\lambda_{2k}^n + a_{3k}\overline{\lambda}_{2k}^n + a_{4k}\lambda_{4k}^n, \tag{3}$$

where $k = 0, \ldots, 14$ enumerates the 14 EDMD computations for the 14 moving windows and the resulting approximating trajectories, $n = 0, \ldots, 40$ enumerates the 41 sample points at each window, x_{ok} is a 4×1 vector of initial conditions for the basis functions x, $\frac{1}{x}$, tx, $\frac{t}{x}$, for each one of the EDMD computations, A_k is the 4×4 EDMD matrix for each of the moving windows, P_x is the 1×4 projection matrix to the one-dimensional space spanned by x, $\overline{\lambda}_{2k}$ is the complex conjugate of λ_{2k}, λ_{1k}, λ_{2k}, $\overline{\lambda}_{2k}$, λ_{4k} are the eigenvalues of the matrices A_k, and $a_{1k}, a_{2k}, a_{3k}, a_{4k}$ are real coefficients. In the three diagrams of Figure 10, we depict from left to right the real eigenvalue λ_{1k}, which is the largest, versus k, the modulus

$|\lambda_{2k}| = |\overline{\lambda}_{2k}|$ of the complex conjugate eigenvalues $\lambda_{2k}, \overline{\lambda}_{2k}$, which are the intermediate, versus k, and the real eigenvalue λ_{4k}, which is the smallest, versus k. It becomes evident from the diagrams that the largest real eigenvalue λ_{1k} dominates in the approximating trajectory at the vicinity of the $t = 1$ asymptote.

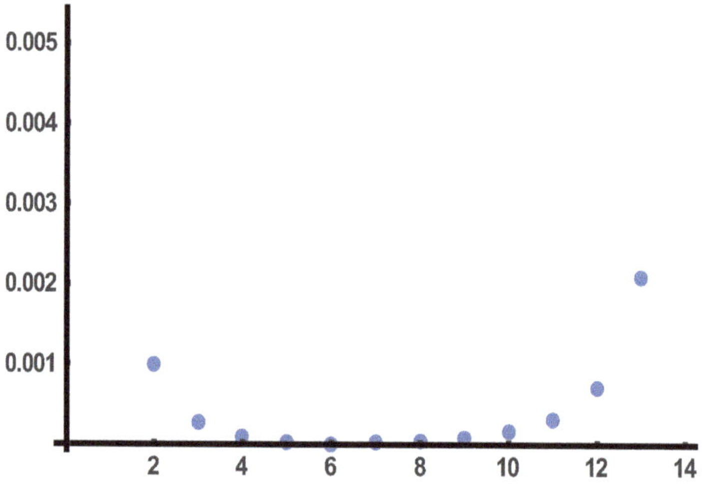

Figure 9. Errors between the 14 EDMD approximating trajectories and real data measured by the l_2 (Euclidean) norm.

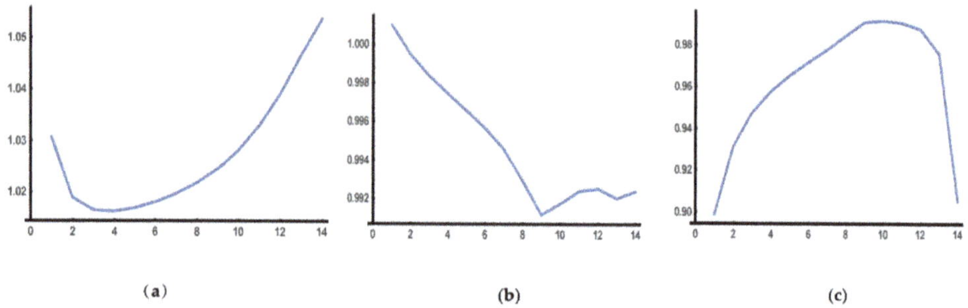

Figure 10. The graph of (**a**) the largest real eigenvalue; (**b**) the modulus of the complex conjugate eigenvalues; (**c**) the smallest real eigenvalue versus k.

7. Conclusions

The hypergeometric equation is a linear second-order homogeneous differential equation that falls into the Fuchsian class and has three regular singular points at 0, 1, and ∞. The solution space of the hypergeometric equation is two-dimensional with basis vectors hypergeometric series. We present an alternative data-driven method in order to solve the hypergeometric equation. This method, the Koopman-EDMD method, whose popularity has increased over the last years, does not use power series but it uses instead a basis of functions, remarkably 4 or 5. The Koopman-EDMD method is data-driven and we use it in order to approximate a trajectory of the hypergeometric equation at hand in the vicinity of 0 which is one of its singular points. Having data of a given trajectory in a finite horizon allows us to construct with the Koopman-EDMD theory a discrete linear system of dimension $n > m$, where $m = 2$ is the dimension of the state space of the hypergeometric equation. In our approach, we have $n = 4$ or $n = 5$ depending on how accurate we want to be the approximation to the real trajectory of the hypergeometric equation. It is noteworthy that we approximate with great accuracy the real trajectory of the hypergeometric equation by a small increase in the number of dimensions of the state space (2 is increased only to 4 or 5 in the Koopman-EDMD theory. The Koopman-EDMD theory can be used as an alternative theory in order to study the solution space of both ordinary differential equations and of partial differential equations. Our results are amenable for application and generalization to these other cases of differential equations as well.

Author Contributions: All authors contributed equally. All authors have read and agreed to the published version of the manuscript.

Funding: This research received no external funding.

Data Availability Statement: No new data were created or analyzed in this study. Data sharing is not applicable to this article.

Conflicts of Interest: The authors declare no conflict of interest.

References

1. Koopman, B.O. Hamiltonian systems and transformation in Hilbert space. *Proc. Natl. Acad. Sci. USA* **1931**, *17*, 315–318. [CrossRef] [PubMed]
2. Brunton, S.; Kutz, N. *Data-Driven Science and Engineering: Machine Learning, Dynamical Systems, and Control*; Cambridge Univerisy Press: Cambridge, UK, 2019.
3. Mauroy, A.; Mezić, I.; Susuki, Y. (Eds.) *The Koopman Operator in Systems and Control*; **358** Lecture Notes in Control and Information Sciences; Springer: Berlin/Heidelberg, Germany, 2020; p. 358.
4. Mezić, I. Analysis of fluid flows via spectral properties of the koopman operator. *Annu. Fluid Mech.* **2013**, *45*, 357–378. [CrossRef]
5. Sharma, A.S.; Mezić, I.; McKeon, B.J. Correspondence between koopman mode decomposition, resolvent mode decomposition, and invariant solutions of the navier-stokes equations. *Phys. Rev. Fluids* **2016**, *1*, 032402. [CrossRef]
6. Georgescu, M.; Mezić, I. Building energy modeling: A systematic approach to zoning and model reduction using koopman mode analysis. *Energy Build.* **2015**, *86*, 794–802. [CrossRef]
7. Giannakis, D.; Slawinska, J.; Zhao, Z. Spatiotemporal feature extraction with datadriven Koopman operators. *J. Mach. Learn. Res. Proc.* **2015**, *44*, 103–115.
8. Wu, H.; Nüske, F.; Paul, F.; Klus, S.; Koltai, P.; Noé, F. Variational koopman models: Slow collective variables and molecular kinetics from short off-equilibrium simulations. *J. Chem. Phys.* **2017**, *146*, 154104. [CrossRef] [PubMed]
9. Rowley, C.W.; Mezić, I.; Bagheri, S.; Schlatter, P.; Henningson, D.S. Spectral analysis of nonlinear flows. *J. Fluid Mech.* **2009**, *641*, 115–127. [CrossRef]
10. Schmid, P.J. Dynamic mode decomposition of numerical and experimental data. *J. Fluid Mech.* **2010**, *656*, 5–28. [CrossRef]
11. Korda, M.; Mezić, I. On convergence of extended dynamic mode decomposition to the Koopman operator. *J. Nonlinear Sci.* **2018**, *28*, 687–710. [CrossRef]
12. Williams, M.O.; Kevrekidis, I.G.; Rowley, C.W. A DataDriven Approximation of the Koopman Operator: Extending Dynamic Mode Decomposition. *J. Nonlinear Sci.* **2015**, *25*, 1307–1346. [CrossRef]
13. Williams, M.O.; Rowley, C.W.; Kevrekidis, I.G. A kernel approach to data-driven koopman spectral analysis. *arXiv* **2014**, arXiv:1411.2260.
14. Nathan Kutz, J.; Proctor, J.L.; Brunton, S.L. Applied Koopman Theory for Partial Differential Equations and Data-Driven Modeling of Spatio-Temporal Systems. *Complexity* **2018**, *2018*, 6010634. [CrossRef]
15. Li, Q.; Dietrich, F.; Bollt, E.M.; Kevrekidis, I.G. Extended dynamic mode decomposition with dictionary learning: A data-driven adaptive spectral decomposition of the Koopman operator. *Chaos* **2017**, *27*, 103111. [CrossRef] [PubMed]
16. Mezić, I. Spectral properties of dynamical systems, model reduction and decompositions. *Nonlinear Dyn.* **2005**, *41*, 309–325. [CrossRef]
17. Folkestad, C.; Pastor, D.; Mezic, I.; Mohr, R.; Fonoberova, M.; Burdick, J. Extended Dynamic Mode Decomposition with Learned Koopman Eigenfunctions for Prediction and Control. In Proceedings of the 2020 American Control Conference (ACC), Denver, CO, USA, 1–3 July 2020; pp. 3906–3913. [CrossRef]

Disclaimer/Publisher's Note: The statements, opinions and data contained in all publications are solely those of the individual author(s) and contributor(s) and not of MDPI and/or the editor(s). MDPI and/or the editor(s) disclaim responsibility for any injury to people or property resulting from any ideas, methods, instructions or products referred to in the content.

axioms

Article

A Fractional Rheological Model of Viscoanelastic Media

Armando Ciancio [1], Vincenzo Ciancio [2] and Bruno Felice Filippo Flora [3,*]

1 Department of Biomedical and Dental Sciences and Morphofunctional Imaging (BIOMORF), University of Messina, Via Consolare Valeria c/o A.O.U. Policlinico 'G.Martino', 98126 Messina, Italy
2 Accademia Peloritana dei Pericolanti, Piazza S. Pugliatti 1, 98122 Messina, Italy
3 Azienda Ospedaliera "Papardo", Viale F. Stagno d'Alcontres 34, 98158 Messina, Italy
* Correspondence: brunoflora@aopapardo.it

Abstract: The mechanical behaviour of materials can be described by a phenomenological relationship that binds strain to stress, by the complex modulus function: $\mathfrak{M}(\omega)$, which represents the frequency response of the medium in which a transverse mechanical wave is propagated. From the experimental measurements of the internal friction obtained when varying the frequency of a transverse mechanical wave, the parameters that characterize the complex module are determined. The internal friction or loss tangent is bound to the dissipation of the specific mechanical energy. The non-equilibrium thermodynamics theory leads to a general description of irreversible phenomena such as relaxation and viscosity that can coexist in a material. Through the state variables introduced by Ciancio and Kluitenberg, and applying the fractional calculation due to a particular memory mechanism, a model of a viscoanelastic medium is obtained in good agreement with the experimental results.

Keywords: viscoanelastic media; derivative fractional; state variables; reologic coefficients; internal friction; differential evolution

Citation: Ciancio, A.; Ciancio, V.; Flora, B.F.F. A Fractional Rheological Model of Viscoanelastic Media. *Axioms* **2023**, *12*, 243. https://doi.org/10.3390/axioms12030243

Academic Editors: Hatıra Günerhan, Francisco Martínez González, Mohammed K. A. Kaabar and Alexandr M. Khludnev

Received: 22 December 2022
Revised: 20 February 2023
Accepted: 24 February 2023
Published: 27 February 2023

Copyright: © 2023 by the authors. Licensee MDPI, Basel, Switzerland. This article is an open access article distributed under the terms and conditions of the Creative Commons Attribution (CC BY) license (https://creativecommons.org/licenses/by/4.0/).

1. Introduction

In the second half of the 20th century, a theory was proposed for the study of mechanical [1–16] and electromagnetic [17–21] phenomena in continuous media which is based on the general methods of non-equilibrium thermodynamics. In the hypothesis that different microscopic phenomena produce inelastic strains (instance slip, dislocation) and effects similar to the flow of ordinary viscous fluids, the entropy is characterized by internal energy and inelastic strain tensors; then the expression of entropy production obtained characterizes the state of non-equilibrium. Zener conducted experimental investigations on the mechanical behaviour of solids subject to the action of given stress [22]. In particular, by carrying out measurements of internal friction they were able to describe the process of relaxation due to the anelasticity media. The proposed anelastic media were only valid for some frequency values. Many years later, Caputo and Mainardi proposed a model of viscoanelastic media using Caputo's fractional derivative [23,24]. This is an integral operator whose kernel represents the memory effect. Viscoelastic media have been studied in the field of finite strains by Coleman and Noll [25,26]. An extension of the many viscoelastic models to the fractional calculation have been resumed as in [27]. In the case of elastic and viscoelastic means this effect is evanescent [28]. The Caputo–Mainardi model is very different at low frequencies from the experimental values. Concurrently with the study of systems with memory, fractional calculus theory has been developed and has been used in several applications, allowing a greater physical understanding of the problems. In particular, the use of local fractional derivatives [29–34] has made it possible to obtain models in good agreement with the experimental data highlighting, in relation to the physical problem studied, the dependence of the order of local fractional derivation from the processes of relaxation in the media with memory. To obtain a mechanical representation consistent with the description of the relaxation processes valid for many solid viscoanelastic materials and over a wide range of frequencies, in Section 2, from thermodynamic considerations of non-reversible processes synthesized in the definition of specific entropy and total strain tensor for small field displacements, the rheological equation is derived. The rheological equation allows the stress tensor to be determined by means of internal variables and phenomenological coefficients, when the strain tensor resulting from the displacement field and the rheological coefficients are known, the latter obtained by experimental measurements. In Section 3, from the rheological equation relating to viscoanelastic media, passing into the Laplace transform domain, a mechanical representation with four parameters is obtained, where the components of the model, responsible for the relaxation process, are characterized through two relaxation times, one due to the viscosity understood in solids as slipping of crystalline planes and the other due to the inelasticity. To evaluate the memory effect, we consider relaxation times expressible by means of real exponentials. For this purpose, in Section 4, in the rheological equation we use the Caputo fractional derivative to obtain a four-parameter fractional model. As pointed out by Berry, impurities and defects in the crystal lattice cause more relaxation processes independent of each other. In Section 5, the fractional model is extended to two relaxation processes, resulting in an eight-parameter model. Using the Zener experimental curves in tabular form, in Section 6, we show the results obtained for aluminium, brass and steel in relation to the eight-parameter model by applying the differential evolution (DE) algorithm. Unlike other works on viscoelastic media [35], we have taken into consideration the DE algorithm to determine the parameters of the fractional model of viscoanelastic media, the latter consistent with the principles of thermodynamics.

2. The Rheological Equation

If both elastic and inelastic deformations occur, for index $\alpha, \beta \in \{1, 2, 3\}$, we have:

$$\epsilon_{\alpha\beta} = \epsilon_{\alpha\beta}^{(0)} + \epsilon_{\alpha\beta}^{(1)} \tag{1}$$

where $\epsilon_{\alpha\beta}$ is the tensor of total strain and $\epsilon_{\alpha\beta}^{(0)}$ and $\epsilon_{\alpha\beta}^{(1)}$ are tensors describing the elastic and inelastic strain, respectively. Therefore the entropy will depend on the internal energy u, on the $\epsilon_{\alpha\beta}$. Hence [5–7]:

$$\mathfrak{s} = \mathfrak{s}\left(u, \epsilon_{\alpha\beta}, \epsilon_{\alpha\beta}^{(1)}\right) \tag{2}$$

where $\mathfrak{s}$ is specific entropy and u is internal energy. The temperature is:

$$T^{-1} = \frac{\partial}{\partial u} \mathfrak{s}\left(u, \epsilon_{\alpha\beta}, \epsilon_{\alpha\beta}^{(1)}\right) \tag{3}$$

and we define the equilibrium-stress tensor:

$$\tau_{\alpha\beta}^{(eq)} = -\rho T \frac{\partial}{\partial \epsilon_{\alpha\beta}} \mathfrak{s}\left(u, \epsilon_{\alpha\beta}, \epsilon_{\alpha\beta}^{(1)}\right) \tag{4}$$

and

$$\tau_{\alpha\beta}^{(1)} = \rho T \frac{\partial}{\partial \epsilon_{\alpha\beta}^{(1)}} \mathfrak{s}\left(u, \epsilon_{\alpha\beta}, \epsilon_{\alpha\beta}^{(1)}\right) \tag{5}$$

where ρ is the mass density and we will call $\tau_{\alpha\beta}^{(1)}$ the affinity stress tensor conjugate to $\epsilon_{\alpha\beta}^{(1)}$.

By using Equations (3)–(5) from (1) we obtain the differential $d\mathfrak{s}$ of $\mathfrak{s}$:

$$T d\mathfrak{s} = du - \nu \tau_{\alpha\beta}^{(eq)} d\epsilon_{\alpha\beta} + \nu \tau_{\alpha\beta}^{(1)} d\epsilon_{\alpha\beta}^{(1)} \tag{6}$$

where $v = \rho^{-1}$ is the specific volume (volume for unit of mass). Relation (6) is called the Gibbs relation in which the usual summation convention for the dummy index is used. In the following we will use the deviator $\tilde{A}_{\alpha\beta}$ of an arbitrary tensor field $A_{\alpha\beta}$, ie:

$$\tilde{A}_{\alpha\beta} = A_{\alpha\beta} - A \tag{7}$$

where

$$A = \frac{1}{3}A_{\alpha\alpha} = \frac{1}{3}(A_{11} + A_{22} + A_{33}) \tag{8}$$

and the specific free energy f:

$$f = u - T\mathfrak{s} \tag{9}$$

From (3) and (6) we have:

$$df = -\mathfrak{s}dT + v\tau_{\alpha\beta}^{(eq)}\, d\epsilon_{\alpha\beta} - v\tau_{\alpha\beta}^{(1)}\, d\epsilon_{\alpha\beta}^{(1)} \tag{10}$$

and, hence:

$$\tau_{\alpha\beta}^{(eq)} = \rho\,\frac{\partial}{\partial\epsilon_{\alpha\beta}} f\left(u, \epsilon_{\alpha\beta}, \epsilon_{\alpha\beta}^{(1)}\right) \tag{11}$$

$$\tau_{\alpha\beta}^{(1)} = -\rho\,\frac{\partial}{\partial\epsilon_{\alpha\beta}^{(1)}} f\left(u, \epsilon_{\alpha\beta}, \epsilon_{\alpha\beta}^{(1)}\right) \tag{12}$$

Assuming that the strains are small from a geometrical point of view:

$$\epsilon_{\alpha\beta} = \frac{1}{2}\left(\frac{\partial u_\alpha}{\partial x^\beta} + \frac{\partial u_\beta}{\partial x^\alpha}\right) \tag{13}$$

where u_α are the components of the displacement field and the stress tensors $\tau_{\alpha\beta}^{(eq)}$ and $\tau_{\alpha\beta}^{(1)}$ are linear functions of the strain tensors and of temperature; we suppose that f has the form [6,7]:

$$f = v_0 \cdot \left\{ f^{(a)}\left(\tilde{\epsilon}_{\alpha\beta}, \epsilon_{\alpha\beta}, \epsilon_{\alpha\beta}^{(1)}\right) + f^{(b)}\left(\tilde{\epsilon}_{\alpha\beta}, \epsilon_{\alpha\beta}, \epsilon_{\alpha\beta}^{(1)}\right) + 3(T - T_0)\left(c^{(0)}\epsilon_{\alpha\beta} - c^{(1)}\epsilon_{\alpha\beta}^{(1)}\right)\right\} - \psi(T) \tag{14}$$

where

$$f^{(a)}\left(\tilde{\epsilon}_{\alpha\beta}, \epsilon_{\alpha\beta}, \epsilon_{\alpha\beta}^{(1)}\right) = \frac{1}{2}a^{(0,0)}\tilde{\epsilon}_{\alpha\beta}\left(\tilde{\epsilon}_{\alpha\beta} - 2\epsilon_{\alpha\beta}^{(1)}\right) + \frac{1}{2}a^{(1,1)}\left(\tilde{\epsilon}_{\alpha\beta}^{(1)}\right)^2 \tag{15}$$

$$f^{(b)}\left(\tilde{\epsilon}_{\alpha\beta}, \epsilon_{\alpha\beta}, \epsilon_{\alpha\beta}^{(1)}\right) = \frac{1}{2}b^{(0,0)}\epsilon_{\alpha\beta}\left(\epsilon_{\alpha\beta} - 2\epsilon_{\alpha\beta}^{(1)}\right) + \frac{3}{2}b^{(1,1)}\left(\epsilon_{\alpha\beta}^{(1)}\right)^2 \tag{16}$$

In (14) the strain is measured with respect to a reference state, v_0 is specific volume, T_0 is the temperature of the media in the reference state and $a^{(0,0)}$, $a^{(1,1)}$, $b^{(0,0)}$, $b^{(1,1)}$, $c^{(0)}$, $c^{(1)}$ are scalar constants [6–9]. Finally, $\psi(T)$ is same function of the temperature. Using (11) and (12) from (14) one obtains the following expression for the deviators of tensors $\tilde{\tau}_{\alpha\beta}^{(eq)}$ and $\tilde{\tau}_{\alpha\beta}^{(1)}$:

$$\tilde{\tau}_{\alpha\beta}^{(eq)} = a^{(0,0)}\,\tilde{\epsilon}_{\alpha\beta}^{(0)} \tag{17}$$

$$\tilde{\tau}_{\alpha\beta}^{(eq)} = a^{(0,0)}\,\tilde{\epsilon}_{\alpha\beta} - a^{(1,1)}\,\tilde{\epsilon}_{\alpha\beta}^{(1)} \tag{18}$$

Making $\tilde{\tau}_{\alpha\beta}$ the mechanical stress tensor which occurs in the equation of motion and in the first law of thermodynamics, the viscous stress tensor $\tilde{\tau}_{\alpha\beta}^{(vi)}$ is defined by:

$$\tau_{\alpha\beta}^{(vi)} = \tau_{\alpha\beta} - \tau_{\alpha\beta}^{(eq)} \tag{19}$$

Furthermore, we introduce [9] the following flow laws for slicer phenomena in isotropic media:

$$\frac{d}{dt}\tilde{\epsilon}^{(1)}_{\alpha\beta} = \eta_s^{(1,1)}\,\tilde{\tau}^{(1)}_{\alpha\beta} + \eta_s^{(1,0)}\,\frac{d}{dt}\tilde{\epsilon}_{\alpha\beta} \tag{20}$$

$$\tau^{(vi)}_{\alpha\beta} = \eta_s^{(0,1)}\,\tilde{\tau}^{(1)}_{\alpha\beta} + \eta_s^{(0,0)}\,\frac{d}{dt}\tilde{\epsilon}_{\alpha\beta} \tag{21}$$

The scalar $\eta_s^{(i,j)}$ $(i,j = 0,1)$ are called phenomenological coefficients. Using (2) and (19) one may eliminate $\tilde{\epsilon}^{(0)}_{\alpha\beta}$, $\tilde{\epsilon}^{(1)}_{\alpha\beta}$, $\tilde{\tau}^{(eq)}_{\alpha\beta}$, $\tilde{\tau}^{(1)}_{\alpha\beta}$, and $\tilde{\tau}^{(vi)}_{\alpha\beta}$, from the Equations of state (17) and (18) and the phenomenological Equations (20) and (21) one has:

$$R^{(\tau)}_{(d)0}\tilde{\tau}_{\alpha\beta} + \frac{d}{dt}\tilde{\tau}_{\alpha\beta} = R^{(\epsilon)}_{(d)0}\tilde{\epsilon}_{\alpha\beta} + R^{(\epsilon)}_{(d)1}\frac{d}{dt}\tilde{\epsilon}_{\alpha\beta} + R^{(\epsilon)}_{(d)2}\frac{d^2}{dt^2}\tilde{\epsilon}_{\alpha\beta} \tag{22}$$

where

$$R^{(\epsilon)}_{(d)0} = a^{(1,1)}\eta_s^{(1,1)} \tag{23}$$

$$R^{(\epsilon)}_{(d)0} = a^{(0,0)}\left(a^{(1,1)} - a^{(0,0)}\right)\eta_s^{(1,1)} \tag{24}$$

$$R^{(\epsilon)}_{(d)1} = a^{(0,0)}\left(1 + 2\eta_s^{(0,1)}\right) + a^{(1,1)}\left\{\eta_s^{(0,0)}\eta_s^{(1,1)} + \left(\eta_s^{(0,1)}\right)^2\right\} \tag{25}$$

$$R^{(\epsilon)}_{(d)2} = \eta_s^{(0,0)} \tag{26}$$

3. Mechanical Representation of the Viscoanelastic Media According to the Ciancio–Kluitenberg Model

Several mechanical representations of the media have been given regarding the binding between stress and deformation [29]. In this section, we apply the Ciancio–Kluitenberg theory to the problem of determining the deformation to which a viscoanelastic medium is subject under the action of a stress. Subsequently we provide a mechanical representation of the viscoanelastic medium in a Laplace domain. For elastic materials, the binding between the strain deviator tensor $\tilde{\epsilon}_{\alpha\beta}$ and the stress one $\tilde{\tau}_{\alpha\beta}$ is of the type:

$$\tilde{\epsilon}_{\alpha\beta}(k,\omega) = -\mathfrak{M}_0\tilde{\tau}_{\alpha\beta}(k,\omega) \tag{27}$$

where Equation (27) represents the equivalent Hooke's law and $\mathfrak{M}_0^{-1} = cost.^{te}$ is the elastic constant that depends on the material and is a real number. In the case of anelastic, viscoelastic, and viscoanelastic material, the constitutive binding between the strain deviator tensor $\tilde{\epsilon}_{\alpha\beta}$ and the stress tensor $\tilde{\tau}_{\alpha\beta}$ is of the type:

$$\tilde{\epsilon}_{\alpha\beta}(k,\omega) = (\mathfrak{M}(\omega) - \mathfrak{M}_0)\tilde{\tau}_{\alpha\beta}(k,\omega) \tag{28}$$

where $\mathfrak{M}(\omega)$ is the complex modulus, while $\tilde{\mathfrak{M}}(\omega) = \mathfrak{M}(\omega) - \mathfrak{M}_0$ is the non-elastic component of the complex modulus at the ω angular frequency produced by the displacement field u_α with $\alpha = 1,2,3$:

$$\epsilon_{\alpha\beta} = \tilde{\epsilon}_{\alpha\beta} = \frac{1}{2}\left(\partial_{x_\beta}u_\alpha + \partial_{x_\alpha}u_\beta\right) \tag{29}$$

Considering small displacements, the substantial derivative coincides with the local one:

$$\frac{d}{dt} = \partial_t$$

The rheological equation of a viscoanelastic medium for Equation (22) becomes:

$$R^{(\tau)}_{(d)0}\tilde{\tau}_{\alpha\beta} + \partial_t\tilde{\tau}_{\alpha\beta} = R^{(\epsilon)}_{(d)0}\tilde{\epsilon}_{\alpha\beta} + R^{(\epsilon)}_{(d)1}\partial_t\tilde{\epsilon}_{\alpha\beta} + R^{(\epsilon)}_{(d)2}\partial^2_{tt}\tilde{\epsilon}_{\alpha\beta} \tag{30}$$

where the parameters $R^{(\tau)}_{(d)0}$, $R^{(\epsilon)}_{(d)0}$, $R^{(\epsilon)}_{(d)1}$, and $R^{(\epsilon)}_{(d)2}$ are the reological coefficients. Therefore the Ciancio–Kluitenberg model characterizes a single relaxation process with four parameters, i.e., the four rheological coefficients.

Transforming both members of Equation (30) according to Laplace we obtain:

$$R^{(\tau)}_{(d)0}\tilde{\tau}^*_{\alpha\beta} + s\tilde{\tau}^*_{\alpha\beta} = R^{(\epsilon)}_{(d)0}\tilde{\epsilon}^*_{\alpha\beta} + sR^{(\epsilon)}_{(d)1}\tilde{\epsilon}^*_{\alpha\beta} + s^2R^{(\epsilon)}_{(d)2}\tilde{\epsilon}^*_{\alpha\beta} \tag{31}$$

where

$$\tilde{\tau}^*_{\alpha\beta} = \int_0^\infty \tilde{\tau}_{\alpha\beta}e^{-st}\,dt \tag{32}$$

$$\tilde{\epsilon}^*_{\alpha\beta} = \int_0^\infty \tilde{\epsilon}_{\alpha\beta}e^{-st}\,dt \tag{33}$$

rearranging the terms present in the Equation (31), we obtain

$$\tilde{\epsilon}^*_{\alpha\beta}(s) = \left(\frac{R^{(\tau)}_{(d)0} + s}{R^{(\epsilon)}_{(d)0} + sR^{(\epsilon)}_{(d)1} + s^2R^{(\epsilon)}_{(d)2}}\right)\tilde{\tau}^*_{\alpha\beta}(s) \tag{34}$$

that we rewrite as:

$$\tilde{\epsilon}^*_{\alpha\beta}(s) = \left(\frac{R^{(\tau)}_{(d)0}}{R^{(\epsilon)}_{(d)0}}\right)\left(\frac{1 + s\left(\dfrac{1}{R^{(\tau)}_{(d)0}}\right)}{1 + s\left(\dfrac{R^{(\epsilon)}_{(d)1}}{R^{(\epsilon)}_{(d)0}}\right) + s^2\left(\dfrac{R^{(\epsilon)}_{(d)2}}{R^{(\epsilon)}_{(d)0}}\right)}\right)\tilde{\tau}^*_{\alpha\beta}(s) \tag{35}$$

It is observed that by placing:

$$t_1 = \left(\frac{1}{R^{(\tau)}_{(d)0}}\right) \tag{36}$$

$$t_2 = \left(\frac{\mathfrak{M}_0}{R^{(\epsilon)}_{(d)0}}\right) \tag{37}$$

$$\mathfrak{M}_0 = \left[R^{(\epsilon)}_{(d)1}\right]^{-1} \tag{38}$$

$$\omega_0^2 = \frac{\mathfrak{M}_0}{t_2R^{(\epsilon)}_{(d)2}} \tag{39}$$

Equation (35) becomes:

$$\tilde{\epsilon}^*_{\alpha\beta}(s) = \mathfrak{M}_0\left(\frac{t_2}{t_1}\right)\left(\frac{1 + t_1s}{1 + t_2s + \left(\dfrac{s}{\omega_0}\right)^2}\right)\tilde{\tau}^*_{\alpha\beta}(s) \tag{40}$$

From the comparison with Equation (28), we obtain:

$$\mathfrak{M}(\omega) = \mathfrak{M}_0\left(1 + \left(\frac{t_2}{t_1}\right)\left(\frac{1 + t_1s}{1 + t_2s + \left(\dfrac{s}{\omega_0}\right)^2}\right)\right) \tag{41}$$

Figure 1 shows the mechanical representation of viscoanelastic media in the Laplace domain. Here, we observe how the spring, compliance, and resistance have the electrical equivalent of resistance, capacitance, and inductance, respectively. R' and R'' represent the parameters that characterize the elastic component of the medium, indicated with the spring symbol, C represents the compliance denoted by means of the vibration damper, and L represents the resistance that opposes the medium to deformation. All parameters are constant: $t_1 = \frac{L}{R'}$, $t_2 = R'C$, $\omega_0 = \frac{1}{\sqrt{LC}}$, $\mathfrak{M}_0 = R''$ and $\mathfrak{M}_0\left(\frac{t_2}{t_1}\right) = R'$ where $\tilde{\varepsilon}^*_{\alpha\beta}(s) = \varepsilon = \varepsilon' + \varepsilon''$ and $\tilde{\tau}^*_{\alpha\beta}(s) = \tilde{\tau}^* = \tilde{\tau}^{*'} + \tilde{\tau}^{*''}$. If $L = 0$ and $R'' = 0$ then the mechanical representation coincides with that of a viscoelastic medium, where the viscosity part is given by compliance C and the elastic part is given by R'. Hence the anelastic part is characterized by branch $R' + Ls$, whereas the viscosity part is characterized by branch $1/Cs$.

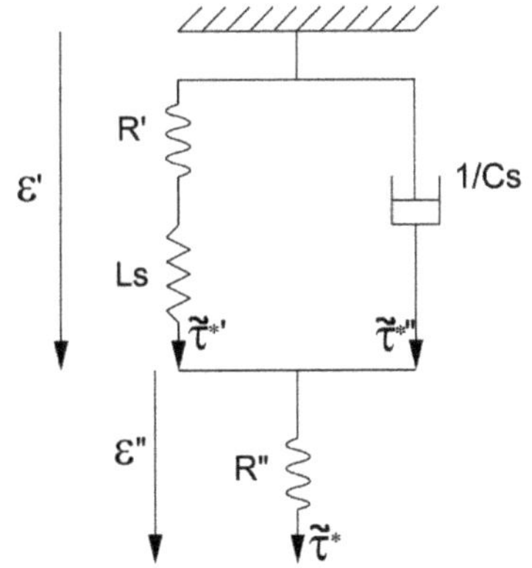

Figure 1. Mechanical representation of the viscoanelastic medium. Ciancio–Kluitenberg model.

4. Fractional Rheological Model with Four Parameters of a Viscoanelastic Medium for a Single Relaxation Process

It is experimentally verifiable that, with the passage of time, the elastic or viscoelastic material tends to forget its more remote history; that is the deformations to which it has been subjected in the past tend to have less and less influence on the current deformation [28]. In viscoanelastic media the memory effect is permanent. From a mathematical point of view, this implies that relaxation time is a power of fractional order. It is preferred not to proceed with the dimensionless method, as in [36], to highlight that relaxation time is a real power of fractional order. From Ciancio–Kluitenberg's theory and fractional calculation, we obtain the following rheological equation:

$$R^{(\tau)}_{(d)0}\tilde{\tau}_{\alpha\beta} + \partial^{\gamma}_t\tilde{\tau}_{\alpha\beta} = R^{(\epsilon)}_{(d)0}\tilde{\varepsilon}_{\alpha\beta} + R^{(\epsilon)}_{(d)1}\partial^{\gamma}_t\tilde{\varepsilon}_{\alpha\beta} + R^{(\epsilon)}_{(d)2}\partial^{2\gamma}_{tt}\tilde{\varepsilon}_{\alpha\beta} \tag{42}$$

where $\partial^{\gamma}_t(\cdot)$ is fractional derivative of order γ with respect to time and $0 < \gamma \leq 1$. From a physical point of view it is natural to apply the fractional derivative of Caputo [23] that characterizes the means with memory in which the relaxation process is observed:

$${}^{C}\partial^{\gamma}_t f(x,t) = \frac{1}{\Gamma(1-\gamma)} \int_0^t \frac{\partial_w f(x,w)}{(t-w)^{\gamma}} dw \tag{43}$$

Applying the Fourier transform to the rheological Equation (42), we obtain:

$$\tilde{\varepsilon}_{\alpha\beta}(k,\omega) = \mathfrak{M}_0\left(\frac{t_2}{t_1}\right)\left(\frac{1 + t_1(-i\omega)^{\gamma}}{1 + t_2(-i\omega)^{\gamma} + (-i\omega/\omega_0)^{2\gamma}}\right)\tilde{\tau}_{\alpha\beta}(k,\omega) \tag{44}$$

From comparison with the constitutive Equation (28), the complex module is obtained:

$$\mathfrak{M}(\omega) = \mathfrak{M}_0\left(1 + \left(\frac{t_2}{t_1}\right)\left(\frac{1 + t_1(-i\omega)^\gamma}{1 + t_2(-i\omega)^\gamma + (-i\omega/\omega_0)^{2\gamma}}\right)\right) \quad (45)$$

Identification of rheological parameters:

- $R^{(\tau)}_{(d)0} = \frac{1}{t_1}$, depends on the stress time constant $t_1^{'}$, with:

$$t_1^{'} = (t_1/2\pi)^\gamma$$

- $R^{(\epsilon)}_{(d)0} = \frac{\mathfrak{M}_0}{t_2}$, depends on the stress relaxation time $t_2^{'}$, with:

$$t_2^{'} = (t_2/2\pi)^\gamma$$

- $\left[R^{(\epsilon)}_{(d)1}\right]^{-1} = \mathfrak{M}_0$, coincides with the complex module due to the impulsive stress applied at the initial instant.
- $R^{(\epsilon)}_{(d)2} = \frac{\mathfrak{M}_0}{t_2\omega_0^{2\gamma}}$, depends on natural angular frequency ω_0

We observe how the rheological coefficients depend on the characteristic parameters, i.e., by relaxation time due to the stress and deformation, respectively, and natural angular frequency. Determining the parameters experimentally it will therefore be possible to obtain the values of state variables.

5. Fractional Rheological Model with Eight Parameters of a Viscoanelastic Medium for Two Single Relaxation Processes

Although the behaviour of viscoanelastic media can be described using models developed by Zener [37] and other authors such as Caputo and Mainardi [24], they present a significant discrepancy with experimental values of internal friction (IF) [38–40]. This discrepancy can be reduced by considering the presence of several independent relaxation processes that also take into account the impurity of materials at the microscopic level due to the presence of defects in the crystalline lattice or different atomic configuration characteristics of other materials. It is natural to think of an extension of the theory by applying the principle of superposition to n relaxation processes [40]. Applying the principle of superposition in the case of n relaxation processes, we obtain:

$$\frac{\mathfrak{M}(\omega)}{\mathfrak{M}_0} = 1 + \sum_{q=1}^{m}\left(\frac{t_{2,q}}{t_{1,q}}\right)\left(\frac{1 + t_{1,q}(-i\omega)^{\gamma_q}}{1 + t_{2,q}(-i\omega)^{\gamma_q} + (-i\omega/\omega_{0,q})^{2\gamma_q}}\right) \quad (46)$$

a model with $4m$ parameters. For $m = 2$, i.e., with two relaxation processes, we obtain a rheological model with eight parameters (Figure 2):

$$\mathbf{p} = [t_{1,1}, t_{2,1}, \gamma_1, \omega_{0,1}, t_{1,2}, t_{2,2}, \gamma_2, \omega_{0,2}]$$

where $t_{11} = \frac{L_1}{R_1^{'}}$, $t_{21} = R_1^{'}C_1$, $\omega_{01} = \frac{1}{\sqrt{L_1C_1}}$, $\mathfrak{M}_0\left(\frac{t_{21}}{t_{11}}\right) = R_1^{'}$, $t_{12} = \frac{L_2}{R_2^{'}}$, $t_{22} = R_2^{'}C_2$, $\omega_{02} = \frac{1}{\sqrt{L_2C_2}}$, $\mathfrak{M}_0\left(\frac{t_{22}}{t_{12}}\right) = R_2^{'}$, $\mathfrak{M}_0 = R^{''}$ with $\tilde{\epsilon}^*_{\alpha\beta}(s) = \varepsilon = \varepsilon_1^{'} + \varepsilon_2^{'} + \varepsilon^{''}$ and $\tilde{\tau}^*_{\alpha\beta}(s) = \tilde{\tau}^* = \tilde{\tau}_1^{*'} + \tilde{\tau}_1^{*''} = \tilde{\tau}_2^{*'} + \tilde{\tau}_2^{*''}$. The eight parameters, four for each of the two relaxation processes, bound to the corresponding rheological coefficients, are obtained by applying the differential evolution (DE) algorithm from experimental measurements of the so-called internal friction, IF(ω), or loss tangent: $IF(\omega) = \frac{Imag(\mathfrak{M}(\omega))}{Real(\mathfrak{M}(\omega))}$, relating to the dissipation of mechanical energy due to internal friction as the frequency changes. This function is given by the relationship between the imaginary and the real part of the complex module, which for small losses of the medium coincides with the specific dissipation function.

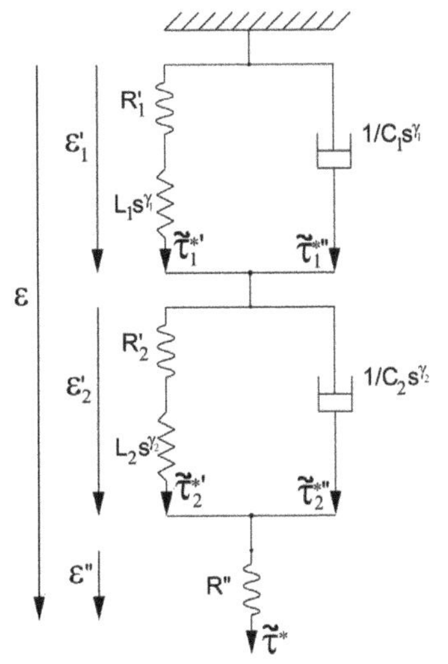

Figure 2. Mechanical representation of the viscoanelastic medium. Fractional model at two relaxation processes.

6. Numerical Results

In this section, we simulate the eight-parameter fractional model considering the experimental data [38]. The IF experimental data are given in the figure on page 55 of [37] and from this are appropriately extracted and shown in Table 1, corresponding to certain frequency values and relative to the metals: steel, brass, and aluminium.

Table 1. Internal friction for steel, brass, and aluminium with respect to frequency.

i	f_i	IF_{Steel}	IF_{Brass}	$IF_{Aluminium}$
1	1	0.440	0.205	0.910
2	2	0.570	0.325	0.780
3	3	0.650	0.435	0.735
4	4	0.725	0.520	0.725
5	5	0.770	0.620	0.720
6	10	0.975	0.975	0.770
7	20	1.200	1.530	1.070
8	25	1.213	1.650	1.150
9	30	1.180	1.880	1.380
10	40	1.065	2.090	1.691
11	46	1.025	2.100	1.775
12	50	0.975	2.080	1.965
13	60	0.900	1.965	2.180
14	70	0.840	1.840	2.360
15	80	0.790	1.740	2.450
16	93	0.750	1.605	2.510
17	100	0.730	1.575	2.505
18	200	0.590	1.090	2.040
19	300	0.540	0.860	1.675
20	400	0.495	0.690	1.375
21	500	0.480	0.565	1.140

To this end we use the differential evolution (DE) algorithm [41] that minimizes the objective function $J(\mathbf{p})$ for determining the parameters $\mathbf{p} = [t_{1,1}, t_{2,1}, \gamma_1, \omega_{0,1}, t_{1,2}, t_{2,2}, \gamma_2, \omega_{0,2}]$ of the model. The DE algorithm [42] is an iterative method of a stochastic nature for the search for the possible optimal solutions on a large space of the parameters. In this work, it has been used in the Python language with the use of the scipy library [43,44]. The DE was chosen for its ability to provide optimal possible solutions without resorting to classical methods of finding solutions such as the gradient method or Newton's method with which it is easy to fall into local minimums, where use requires differentiation of functions. The objective function $J(\mathbf{p})$ taken into account is the mean square relative error between the experimental values of the internal friction $\widehat{IF}(f_i)$ and the values related to the eight-parameter fractional model $IF(f_i)$ at frequencies $f_i, i = 1, 2, \ldots, m$:

$$J(\mathbf{p}) = \frac{1}{m+1}\sum_{i=1}^{m}\left(\frac{\widehat{IF}(f_i) - IF(f_i;\mathbf{p})}{\widehat{IF}(f_i)}\right)^2 \tag{47}$$

In Tables 2 and 3, we obtain the model parameters and the rheological coefficients of the aluminium, respectively. In Figure 3, to the variation of the frequency, it is brought back in the panel of left the shape of the internal friction while in the one of right the relative percentage error for aluminium. In Figure 4, it is brought back in the panel of left the real part while in the one right the imaginary part of the modulus complex for aluminium. In Tables 4 and 5, we obtain the model parameters and the rheological coefficients of the brass, respectively. In Figure 5, to the variation of the frequency, it is brought back in the panel of left the shape of the internal friction while in the one of right the relative percentage error for brass. In Figure 6, it is brought back in the panel of left the real part while in the one right the imaginary part of the modulus complex for brass. Finally, in Tables 6 and 7 we obtain the model parameters and the rheological coefficients of the steel, respectively. In Figure 7, to the variation of the frequency, it is brought back in the panel of left the shape of the internal friction while in the one of right the relative percentage error for steel. In Figure 8, it is brought back in the panel of left the real part while in the one right the imaginary part of the modulus complex for steel.

Table 2. Parameters of the model—aluminium.

i	γ_q	$t_{1,i}$	$t_{2,i}$	$\omega_{0,i}$
1	0.575515	0.001006	0.022103	172.96
2	0.360071	0.000229	0.077811	0.57

Table 3. Rheological coefficients—aluminium.

i	$R^{(\tau)}_{(d)0,i}$	$R^{(\epsilon)}_{(d)0,i}$	$R^{(\epsilon)}_{(d)1,i}$	$R^{(\epsilon)}_{(d)2,i}$
1	994.035785	45.242727	1.000000	0.120119
2	4366.812227	12.851653	1.000000	19.272905

Table 4. Parameters of the model—brass.

i	γ_i	$t_{1,i}$	$t_{2,i}$	$\omega_{0,i}$
1	0.561151	0.001453	0.072381	64.97
2	0.158946	0.005930	0.077555	0.99

Table 5. Rheological coefficients—brass.

i	$R^{(\tau)}_{(d)0,i}$	$R^{(\epsilon)}_{(d)0,i}$	$R^{(\epsilon)}_{(d)1,i}$	$R^{(\epsilon)}_{(d)2,i}$
1	688.231246	13.815780	1.000000	0.127644
2	168.634064	12.894075	1.000000	12.952460

Table 6. Parameters of the model—steel.

i	γ_i	$t_{1,i}$	$t_{2,i}$	$\omega_{0,i}$
1	0.806110	0.003680	0.069378	73.54
2	0.206638	0.000088	0.017235	0.03

Table 7. Rheological coefficients—steel.

i	$R^{(\tau)}_{(d)0,i}$	$R^{(\epsilon)}_{(d)0,i}$	$R^{(\epsilon)}_{(d)1,i}$	$R^{(\epsilon)}_{(d)2,i}$
1	271.739130	14.413791	1.000000	0.014111
2	11,363.636364	58.021468	1.000000	257.802147

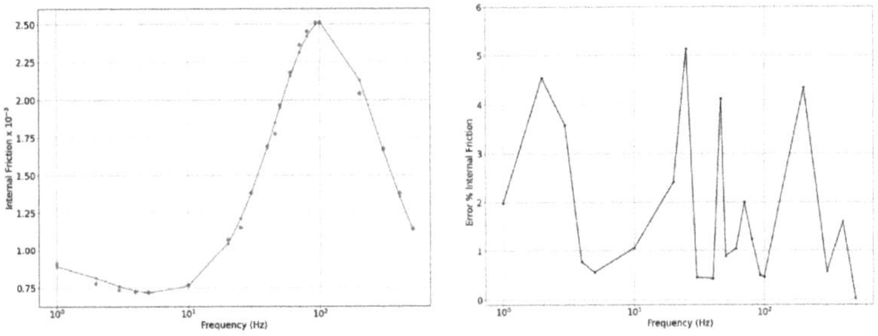

Figure 3. Left panel: internal friction of aluminium—the experimental values for aluminium are represented with the diamond marker in red. The continuous blue line represents the model. **Right** panel: percentage error between the experimental values of the internal friction of the aluminium and the rheological model.

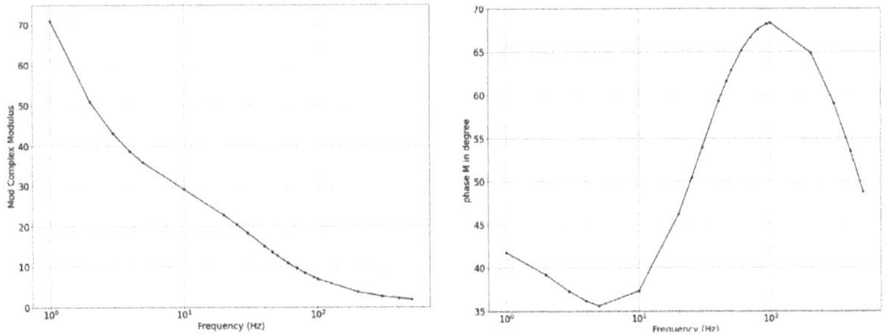

Figure 4. Left panel: mod complex modulus of aluminium. **Right** panel: phase complex modulus of Aluminium.

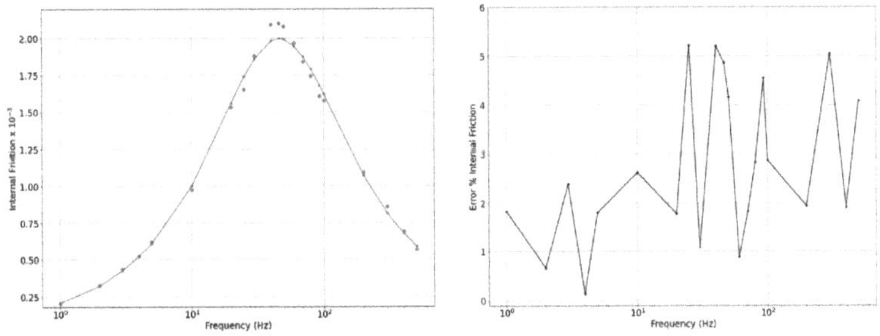

Figure 5. Left panel: internal friction of brass—the experimental values for brass are represented with the diamond marker in red. The continuous blue line represents the model. **Right** panel: percentage error between the experimental values of the internal friction of the brass and the rheological model.

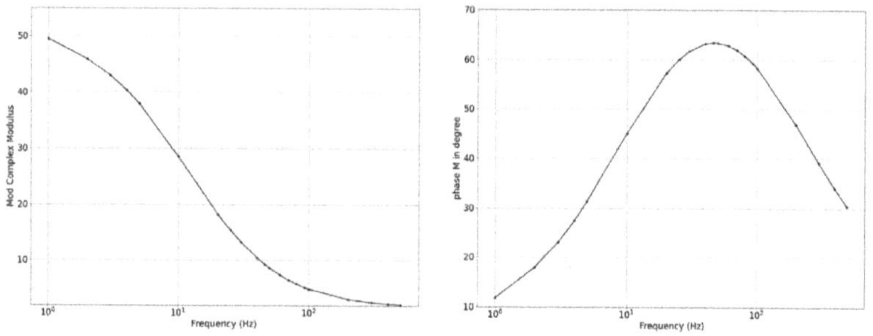

Figure 6. Left panel: mod complex modulus of brass. **Right** panel: phase complex modulus of brass.

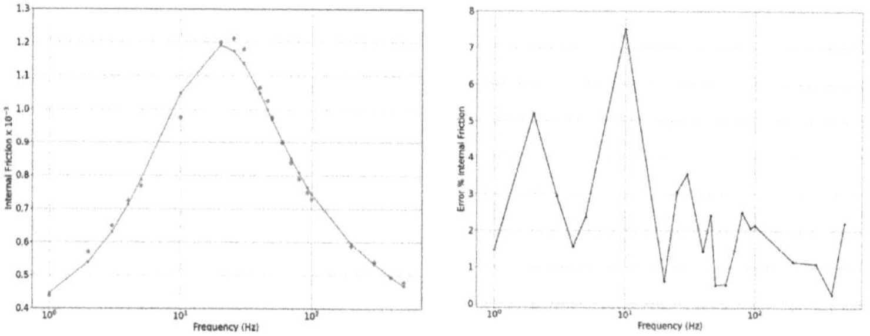

Figure 7. Left panel: internal friction of steel—the experimental values for steel are represented with the diamond marker in red. The continuous blue line represents the model. **Right** panel: percentage error between the experimental values of the internal friction of the steel and the rheological model.

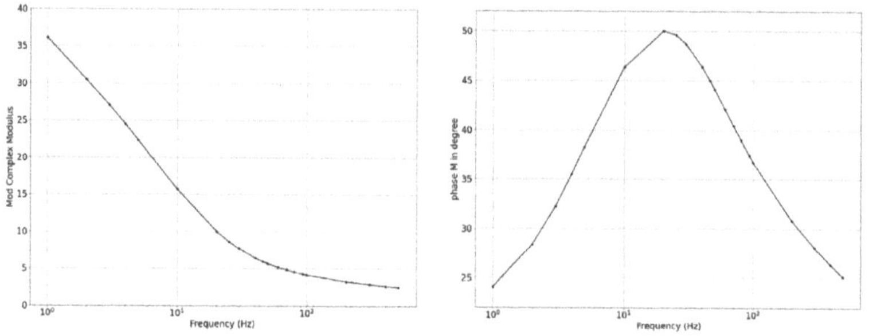

Figure 8. Left panel: mod complex modulus of steel. **Right** panel: phase complex modulus of steel.

7. Conclusions

Applying the Ciancio–Kluitenberg theory, in this work a mechanical representation of a viscoanelastic medium has been found that allows the problem to be solved of determining the state of the system solicited by a stress. Unlike previous models, the mechanical representation found is consistent with the relaxation processes observed in relation to the type of material considered. Moreover, it is very general in that the case of viscoelastic media is obtained as a limit case of inelastic media. Using the DE algorithm, which minimizes the relative quadratic error in the calculation of internal friction (IF), the values of the eight parameters or eight rheological coefficients have been determined. The results obtained confirm the validity of the eight-parameter model whose relative percentage error does not exceed 5% over almost the entire frequency range. In addition, it was possible to obtain the trend of the complex module $\mathfrak{M}$ (module and phase). In all metals it is observed that the fractional order is less than 1; this characteristic is typical in the propagation of mechanical waves at low frequency from 0 to 500 Hz. Finally, the values obtained of the rheological coefficients, for all the metals considered here, are positive in accordance with the second principle of thermodynamics.

Author Contributions: Conceptualization, A.C., V.C. and B.F.F.F.; methodology, A.C., V.C. and B.F.F.F.; software, B.F.F.F.; validation, A.C., V.C. and B.F.F.F. ; formal analysis, A.C., V.C. and B.F.F.F.; data curation, A.C., V.C. and B.F.F.F.; writing—original draft preparation, B.F.F.F.; visualization, A.C., V.C. and B.F.F.F. All authors have read and agreed to the published version of the manuscript.

Funding: This research received no external funding.

Institutional Review Board Statement: Not applicable.

Informed Consent Statement: Not applicable.

Data Availability Statement: The data presented in this study are available in the article.

Conflicts of Interest: The authors declare no conflict of interest.

References

1. Kluitenberg, G. On rheology and thermodynamics of irreversible processes. *Physica* **1962**, *28*, 1173–1183. [CrossRef]
2. Kluitenberg, G. A note on the thermodynamics of Maxwell bodies, Kelvin bodies (Voigt bodies), and fluids. *Physica* **1962**, *28*, 561–568. [CrossRef]
3. Kluitenberg, G. On the thermodynamics of viscosity and plasticity. *Physica* **1963**, *29*, 633–652. [CrossRef]
4. Kluitenberg, G. On heat dissipation due to irreversible mechanical phenomena in continuous media. *Physica* **1967**, *35*, 177–192. [CrossRef]
5. Kluitenberg, G. A thermodynamic derivation of the stress–strain relations for burgers media and related substances. *Physica* **1968**, *38*, 513–548. [CrossRef]
6. Kluitenberg, G.; Ciancio, V. On linear dynamical equations of state for isotropic media I: General formalism. *Phys. Stat. Mech. Appl.* **1978**, *93*, 273–286. [CrossRef]
7. Cianco, V.; Kluitenberg, G. On linear dynamical equations of state for isotropic media II. *Phys. Stat. Mech. Appl.* **1979**, *99*, 592–600. [CrossRef]
8. Ciancio, V. Propagation and attenuation of singular wave surfaces in linear inelastic media. *Phys. Stat. Mech. Appl.* **1979**, *97*, 127–138. [CrossRef]
9. Turrisi, E.; Ciancio, V.; Kluitenberg, G. On the propagation of linear transverse acoustic waves in isotropic media with mechanical relaxation phenomena due to viscosity and a tensorial internal variable II. Some cases of special interest (Poynting-Thomson, Jeffreys, Maxwell, Kelvin-Voigt, Hooke and Newton media). *Phys. Stat. Mech. Appl.* **1982**, *116*, 594–603. [CrossRef]
10. Ciancio, V.; Bartolotta, A.; Farsaci, F. Experimental confirmations on a thermodynamical theory for viscoanelastic media with memory. *Phys. Condens. Matter* **2007**, *394*, 8–13. [CrossRef]
11. Ciancio, A.; Ciancio, V.; Farsaci, F. Wave propagation in media obeying a thermoviscoanelastic model. *UPB Sci. Bull. Ser. A* **2007**, *69*, 69–79.
12. Ciancio, V.; Ciancio, A.; Farsaci, F. On general properties of phenomenological and state coefficients for isotropic viscoanelastic media. *Phys. Condens. Matter* **2008**, *403*, 3221–3227. [CrossRef]
13. Ciancio, A. An approximate evalutation of the phenomenological and state coefficients for viscoanelastic media with memory. *U.P.B. Sci. Bull.* **2011**, *73*, 3–14.
14. Ciancio, V; Restuccia, L. On heat equation in the framework of classic irreversible thermodynamics with internal variables. *Int. J. Geom. Methods Mod. Phys.* **2016**, *13*, 1640003. [CrossRef]
15. Ciancio, V.; Palumbo, A. A thermodynamical theory with internal variables describing thermal effects in viscous fluids. *J. -Non-Equilib. Thermodyn.* **2018**, *43*, 171–184. [CrossRef]
16. Ciancio, V. On the temperature equation in classical irreversible thermodinamics. *Appl. Sci.* **2022**, *24*, 71–86.
17. Ciancio, V. On the Generalized Debye Equation for Media with Dielectric Relaxation Phenomena Described by Vectorial Internal Thermodynamic Variables. *J. Non-Equilib. Thermodyn.* **1989**, *14*, 239–250. [CrossRef]
18. Ciancio, V.; Kluitenberg, G. On electromagnetic waves in isotropic media with dielectric relaxation. *Acta Phys. Hung.* **1989**, *66*, 251–276. [CrossRef]
19. Ciancio, V.; Restuccia, L.; Kluitenberg, G. A Thermodynamic Derivation of Equations for Dielectric Relaxation Phenomena in Anisotropic Polarizable Media. *J. Non.-Equil. Thermodyn.* **1990**, *15*, 157–172. [CrossRef]
20. Ciancio, V.; Farsaci, F.; Di Marco, G. A method for experimental evaluation of phenomenological coefficients in media with dielectric relaxation. *Phys. Condens. Matter* **2007**, *387*, 130–135. [CrossRef]
21. Ciancio, V.; Verhás, J. A Thermodynamic Theory for Heat Radiation Through the Atmosphere. *J. Non.-Equil. Thermodyn.* **1991**, *16*, 57–66. [CrossRef]
22. Zener, C. Internal friction in solids. *Proc. Phys. Soc.* **1940**, *52*, 152. [CrossRef]

23. Caputo, M. Linear Models of Dissipation whose Q is almost Frequency Independent—II. *Geophys. J. Int.* **1967**, *13*, 529–539. [CrossRef]
24. Caputo, M.; Mainardi, F. A new dissipation model based on memory mechanism. *Pure Appl. Geophys.* **1971**, *91*, 134–147. [CrossRef]
25. Coleman, B.D.; Noll, W. The thermodynamics of elastic materials with heat conduction and viscosity. *Arch. Ration. Mech. Anal.* **1963**, *13*, 167–178. [CrossRef]
26. Coleman, B.D.; Noll, W. Foundations of linear viscoelasticity. *Rev. Mod. Phys.* **1961**, *33*, 239. [CrossRef]
27. Shen, L.J. Fractional derivative models for viscoelastic materials at finite deformations. *Int. J. Solids Struct.* **2020**, *190*, 226–237. [CrossRef]
28. Fichera, G. Sul principio della memoria evanescente. *Rend. Semin. Mat. Della Univ. Padova* **1982**, *68*, 245–259.
29. Mainardi, F.; Spada, G. Creep, relaxation and viscosity properties for basic fractional models in rheology. *Eur. Phys. J. Spec. Top.* **2011**, *193*, 133–160. [CrossRef]
30. Ciancio, A.; Flora, B.F.F. A Fractional Complex Permittivity Model of Media with Dielectric Relaxation. *Fractal Fract.* **2017**, *1*, 1–11. [CrossRef]
31. Ciancio, A.; Ciancio, V.; d'Onofrio, A.; Flora, B.F.F. A Fractional Model of Complex Permittivity of Conductor Media with Relaxation: Theory vs. Experiments. *Fractal Fract.* **2022**, *6*, 390. [CrossRef]
32. Caputo, M.; Fabrizio, M. A new definition of fractional derivative without singular kernel. *Prog. Fract. Differ. Appl.* **2015**, *1*, 73–85.
33. Tarasov, V.E.; Tarasova, S.S. Fractional derivatives and integrals: What are they needed for? *Mathematics* **2020**, *8*, 164. [CrossRef]
34. Tarasov, V.E. No nonlocality. No fractional derivative. *Commun. Nonlinear Sci. Numer. Simul.* **2018**, *62*, 157–163. [CrossRef]
35. Di Paola, M.; Pirrotta, A.; Valenza, A. Visco-elastic behavior through fractional calculus: An easier method for best fitting experimental results. *Mech. Mater.* **2011**, *43*, 799–806. [CrossRef]
36. Ebaid, A.; El-Zahar, E.; Aljohani, A.; Salah, B.; Krid, M.; Machado, J.T. Analysis of the two-dimensional fractional projectile motion in view of the experimental data. *Nonlinear Dyn.* **2019**, *97*, 1711–1720. [CrossRef]
37. Zener, C.M.; Siegel, S. Elasticity and Anelasticity of Metals. *J. Phys. Chem.* **1949**, *53*, 1468. [CrossRef]
38. Bennewitz, K.; Rötger, H. Ueber die innere Reibung fester Körper; Absorptionsfrequenzen von Metallen im akustischen Gebiet. *Physik. Zeitschr.* **1936**, *37*, 578–588.
39. Nowick, A.S. Internal friction in metals. *Prog. Met. Phys.* **1953**, *4*, 1–70. [CrossRef]
40. Berry, B. Precise investigation of the theory of damping by transverse thermal currents. *J. Appl. Phys.* **1955**, *26*, 1221–1224. [CrossRef]
41. Storn, R.; Price, K. Differential evolution—A simple and efficient heuristic for global optimization over continuous spaces. *J. Glob. Optim.* **1997**, *11*, 341–359. [CrossRef]
42. Price, K.; Storn, R.M.; Lampinen, J.A. *Differential Evolution: A Practical Approach to Global Optimization*; Springer Science & Business Media: Berlin/Heidelberg, Germany, 2006.
43. Johansson, R. *Numerical Python: A Practical Techniques Approach for Industry*; Apress: Berkeley, CA, USA, 2015.
44. SciPy v1.9.3 Manual. Available online: https://docs.scipy.org/doc/scipy/reference/generated/scipy.optimize.differential_evolution.html (accessed on 10 December 2022).

Disclaimer/Publisher's Note: The statements, opinions and data contained in all publications are solely those of the individual author(s) and contributor(s) and not of MDPI and/or the editor(s). MDPI and/or the editor(s) disclaim responsibility for any injury to people or property resulting from any ideas, methods, instructions or products referred to in the content.

axioms

MDPI

Article

Two Reliable Computational Techniques for Solving the MRLW Equation

Kamel Al-Khaled * and Haneen Jafer

Department of Mathematics and Statistics, Jordan University of Science and Technology, P.O. Box 3030, Irbid 22110, Jordan
* Correspondence: kamel@just.edu.jo

Abstract: In this paper, a numerical solution of the modified regularized long wave (MRLW) equation is obtained using the Sinc-collocation method. This approach approximates the space dimension of the solution with a cardinal expansion of Sinc functions. First, discretizing the time derivative of the MRLW equation by a classic finite difference formula, while the space derivatives are approximated by a $\theta-$weighted scheme. For comparison purposes, we also find a soliton solution using the Adomian decomposition method (ADM). The Sinc-collocation method was were found to be more accurate and efficient than the ADM schemes. Furthermore, we show that the number of solitons generated can be approximated using the Maxwellian initial condition. The proposed methods' results, analytical solutions, and numerical methods are compared. Finally, a variety of graphical representations for the obtained solutions makes the dynamics of the MRLW equation visible and provides the mathematical foundation for physical and engineering applications.

Keywords: MRLW equation; soliton solutions; sinc-collocation method; Adomian decomposition method

MSC: 65R20; 26A33; 46F12; 74G10

Citation: Al-Khaled, K.; Jafer, H. Two Reliable Computational Techniques for Solving the MRLW Equation. *Axioms* **2023**, *12*, 174. https://doi.org/10.3390/axioms12020174

Academic Editors: Hatıra Günerhan, Francisco Martínez González and Mohammed K. A. Kaabar

Received: 22 December 2022
Revised: 25 January 2023
Accepted: 6 February 2023
Published: 8 February 2023

Copyright: © 2023 by the authors. Licensee MDPI, Basel, Switzerland. This article is an open access article distributed under the terms and conditions of the Creative Commons Attribution (CC BY) license (https://creativecommons.org/licenses/by/4.0/).

1. Introduction

Partial differential equations, especially non-linear ones, are used in the study of many natural phenomena that often arise in the physical sciences and engineering applications. For nonlinear equations, there is a difficulty, if not an impossibility, in finding exact solutions to the equation, and researchers often resort to finding a solution with approximate methods. Here, we will use two different schemes to solve the modified equation for the long wave known as MRLW equation (see, [1–3]).

$$\frac{\partial u}{\partial t} + \frac{\partial u}{\partial x} + \epsilon u^p \frac{\partial u}{\partial x} - \mu \frac{\partial}{\partial t}\left(\frac{\partial^2 u}{\partial x^2}\right) = 0 \tag{1}$$

With the following boundary and initial conditions

$$u(a,t) = \alpha_1(t), \quad u(b,t) = \alpha_2(t) \tag{2}$$

$$u(x,0) = f(x), \quad x \in [a,b] \subset \mathbb{R}. \tag{3}$$

where ϵ and μ in Equation (1) are positive constants that describe the undular bore's behavior, and p is a positive integer greater than or equal to 1, while the function $f(x)$ is a localized disturbance inside the interval $[a,b]$ subject to physical boundary conditions $u \to \infty$ as $x \to \mp\infty$. The functions that appeared on both sides in Equation (2) are also continuous. Equation (1), which we will abbreviate with MRLW, was originally a mathematical model to describe a physical phenomenon with weak scattering waves, and in another application it describes the movement of transverse waves in shallow water.

There are many previous studies that dealt with the use of numerical methods to find approximate solutions to the equation under consideration, the MRLW equation. In the paper [4], the collocation method was used to find an approximate solution to the MRLW equation. The method relied mainly on the use of the Sinc function as a basis. The B-splines finite element method of order 3 was used in [5] to solve the MRLW equation numerically, the numerical results proved the accuracy of the used method. In [6], two different bases are used to solve numerically the MRLW equation, in which the finite difference method is used along the time derivatives, while the delta-shaped basis was used to discretize the space direction. It should be noted here that there are many previous studies in which the Sinc method was used or those that dealt with approximate solutions to the equation under study, among which we mention [7–9]. Recently published papers in [10–14] dealt with the use of different methods to find numerical solutions to various forms of the generalized RLW equation. For more knowledge, there are other previous studies that discussed the same ideas presented in this paper, but in different ways, such as [1,15,16].

The Sinc methodology is one of the most powerful tools for solving various types of equations that model various physical phenomena. This method is used to solve integral equations, partial differential equations, and integro-differential equations. The most important motive of this research work is the use of the Sinc method because the convergence of the approximate solution is of exponential type. For some positive constants c, h the Sinc method yields an iterative scheme with an error of order $\mathcal{O}(\exp(-c/h)$, which is much faster than other traditional methods.

The main objective of this paper is to find an approximate solution to the MRLW equation in (1)–(3), where the basis of the Sinc function on the variable x will be used, while we will use the regular finite difference method when talking about the time variable t. Moreover, the Adomian decomposition method will be used for comparison purposes.

The main idea of using the Sinc function is that in the process of replacing the partial derivatives that appeared in (1), in terms of the variable x, with the corresponding formulas that have been proven in both references Stenger [17] and by Lund [18], followed by the use of the Sinc quadrature formula for integration with some simple manipulations, we end up with a discrete system of the general form $Ax = b$ that can be solved iteratively via the use of iterative techniques, such as Newton's method. What encourages us to use the Sinc function is its ease of use, and most importantly, the fast exponential convergence property when using the Sinc function as a basis. For the purpose of comparing the solution that will be obtained by the Sinc methodology, we will use the Adomian analysis method, the so-called Adomian decomposition method (ADM) [19,20], to find another solution in an approximate (not numerical) way. The ADM method was created and developed at the beginning of the 1980s of the last century, and it has proven its worth when used in various nonlinear, ordinary and partial differential equations. There are many previous studies that dealt with finding a solution to linear or nonlinear, ordinary or partial differential equations, via the use of ADM, see for example [21–23]. Those equations represented a mathematical model in several fields, including physics, chemistry, biology, engineering in its various forms and medical sciences. The ADM is summarized as finding a solution in the form of a convergent series, and often we need a number that does not exceed the number of fingers on one hand to obtain an appropriate solution, knowing that in previous studies there is sufficient and convincing evidence for the convergence of the method to an accurate solution.

The general structure of this paper can be reviewed as follows: In Section 2, we present the main concepts of the Sinc function and all the theories we need in writing the solution to Equation (1). As for Section 3, we will discuss the formulation of the solution using the Sinc-collocation method, while Section 4 is limited to talking about the stability of the calculated solution. Section 5 is where we will present the alternative method, which is ADM. The effectiveness of the solution presented by the two methods in this paper is discussed in Section 6 by taking two different values of the constant p. The credibility of the methods used will be shown by presenting the numerical results in the form of tables and graphs, and finally, a summary of what happened with some recommendations in Section 7.

2. Sinc-Collocation

The Sinc function method has proven its effectiveness in finding approximate solutions to many problems with physical and engineering applications. The Sinc function is considered to be some kind of wavelet that has been used effectively in recent years to find solutions to many problems. Here, we will review some important characteristics that we will use to formulate the solution using the basis of the Sinc function. These are discussed in [17,18]. It is known that the Sinc function is defined in the domain of all real numbers as follows

$$\text{sinc}\,(x) = \frac{\sin(\pi x)}{\pi x}, x \in \mathbb{R}. \tag{4}$$

We will use the Sinc function for the purposes of interpolation, over the defined interval of the question under consideration. To do so, we first divide the interval into sub-intervals, each of which is h, and then redefine the Sinc function as follows:

$$S_j(x) = \text{sinc}\left(\frac{x - jh}{h}\right), \quad j = 0, \mp 1, \mp 2, \cdots \tag{5}$$

In order to use the formula in Equation (5) as a basis, then for every continuous function $f(x)$, we define an infinite series, known as Whittaker cardinal function, denoted by $C(f,h)$, and defined to be

$$C(f,h)(x) = \sum_{j=-\infty}^{\infty} f(ih)S_j(x).$$

We know very well that we cannot deal with an infinite series, so we will deal with a finite series, ensuring its convergence within certain conditions, which we will impose on the function to be approximated, so N can be a positive integer, we define the series of $2N+1$ terms as

$$C_N(f,h)(x) = \sum_{j=-N}^{N} f_j S_j(x). \tag{6}$$

We use the above series to approximate the nth derivative of the function f, and is given by the relationship

$$f^{(n)} \approx \sum_{j=-N}^{N} f(jh)\frac{d^n}{dx^n}[S_j(x)]. \tag{7}$$

In fact, we need the derivatives of the Sinc function computed at the nodes on which the period was divided, and in this paper we need the first and second derivatives only, so that we can write the solution in the form of a system of linear equations, as we will see in detail later. We also require derivatives of composite Sinc functions evaluated at the nodes. The expressions are required for the present discussion, so the following convenient notation will be needed [17].

$$\delta^{(0)}_{j-k} = [S_j(x)]\Big|_{x=x_k} = \begin{cases} 1, & j = k \\ 0, & j \neq k \end{cases} \tag{8}$$

$$\delta^{(1)}_{j-k} = \frac{d}{dx}[S_j(x)]\Big|_{x=x_k} = \begin{cases} 0, & j = k \\ \frac{(-1)^{jk}}{h(k-j)}, & j \neq k \end{cases} \tag{9}$$

$$\delta_{j-k}^{(2)} = \frac{d^2}{dx^2}[S_j(x)]\Big|_{x=x_k} = \begin{cases} \frac{-\pi^2}{3}, \; j = k \\ \\ \frac{-2(-1)^{k-j}}{(k-j)^2}, \; j \neq k. \end{cases} \tag{10}$$

where the points x_k appeared above, they are all those points that have been divided into the period and are called collocation points, and they will be used in the approximation process. So, we need to use a finite series that starts from the integer $-N$ and ends with the number N, but there must be a constraint or conditions that the function f, to be approximated, must fulfill or its derivatives. The next definition provides us with a property called exponentially decaying that the function must achieve for this purpose.

Definition 1. *We define a domain $\mathcal{D}_d$, in the form of an infinite strip of width $2d, d > 0$, as*

$$\mathcal{D}_d = \{z \in \mathbb{C} : z = x + iy, \; |y| < d \leq \pi/2\}.$$

When $0 < \epsilon < 1$, we define the rectangular domain $\mathcal{D}_d(\epsilon)$ by

$$\mathcal{D}_d(\epsilon) = \{z \in \mathbb{C} : z = x + iy, \; |x| < 1/\epsilon, \; |y| < d(1-\epsilon)\}. \tag{11}$$

In the region $\mathcal{D}_d$, we define the Hardy space, denoted by $\mathcal{B}(\mathcal{D}_d)$, to be the set of all functions f that satisfy the following boundedness condition.

$$\lim_{\epsilon \to 0} \int_{\partial \mathcal{D}_d(\epsilon)} |f(z)| \, |dz| < \infty. \tag{12}$$

There are a lot of characteristics related to the family $\mathcal{B}(\mathcal{D}_d)$ mentioned in [17]. Below we write a theorem that we will need when talking about the convergence of the Sinc method.

Theorem 1 ([17]). *For the positive constants α, β and d, suppose the following conditions hold true*

1. *f belongs to the class $\mathcal{B}(\mathcal{D}_d)$.*
2. *the function f satisfy the decaying condition $|f(x)| \leq \alpha \exp(-\beta|x|)$, valid for all real-valued of x. We conclude that*

$$\sup \left| f^{(n)}(x) - \sum_{j=N}^{N} f_j S_j^{(n)}(x) \right| \leq C_1 N^{(n+1)/2} \exp(-\sqrt{\pi d \beta N})$$

for some constant c_1, where $h = \sqrt{\pi d/(\beta N)}$.

It can be summarized what the previous theorem stipulated as follows, if the analytic function f fulfills the vanishing condition, then we can use the Sinc function to approximate f and its nth-derivatives $f^{(n)}$, so that the error in the approximation is of the exponential type, which is considered to be one of the fastest types of convergence. Thus, in order for us to find an approximate solution to Equation (1), there must be a hypothesis that the initial condition belongs to the family $\mathcal{B}(\mathcal{D}_d)$. Now, we will define some matrices that we will need to describe the solution as a discrete system.

Define three Toeplitz matrices, each of size $m \times m, (m = 2N+1)$, as $I_m^{(q)} = [\delta_{j-k}^{(q)}]$, for values of $q = 0, 1, 2$, which means the matrix whose $jkth$ entry is given by $\delta_{j-k}^{(q)}, q = 0, 1, 2$. The diagonal matrix $\mathcal{D}(g)$ is defined to be $\mathcal{D}(g) = \text{diag}\,[g(x_{-N}), \cdots, g(x_N)]$. It is known that the matrix $I^{(2)}$ is symmetric, and $I^{(1)}$ is skew-symmetric, i.e., $I_{jk}^{(1)} = -I_{kj}^{(1)}$ and they take the form

$$I_m^{(2)} = \begin{pmatrix} \frac{-\pi^2}{3} & 2 & \vdots & \frac{(-1)^{m-1}}{m-1} \\ 2 & \cdot & \cdot & \cdot \\ \vdots & \cdot & \cdot & \vdots \\ \frac{(-1)^{m-1}}{m-1} & \vdots & 2 & \frac{-\pi^2}{3} \end{pmatrix}, \text{ and } I_m^{(1)} = \begin{pmatrix} 0 & -1 & \dots & \frac{(-1)^{m-1}}{m-1} \\ 1 & 0 & & \vdots \\ \vdots & & & \vdots \\ \frac{(-1)^{m-1}}{m-1} & \dots & 1 & 0 \end{pmatrix} \tag{13}$$

It is noted that $I^{(0)}$ is the identity matrix. Because these matrices will appear in the final discrete solution, and for the purpose of demonstrating the stability property of the solution, it is necessary to find some bounds for the eigenvalues, as stated in [17]. If $\{i\lambda_j^{(1)}\}_{j=-N}^{N}$ indicate to be the eigenvalues of the matrix $I^{(1)}$, then $-\pi \leq \lambda_{-N}^{(1)} \leq \cdots \leq \lambda_N^{(1)} \leq \pi$. Similarly, $\{i\lambda_j^{(2)}\}_{j=-N}^{N}$ indicate to be the eigenvalues of the matrix $I^{(2)}$, then $-\pi^2 \leq \lambda_{-N}^{(2)} \leq \cdots \leq \lambda_N^{(2)} \leq \pi^2$.

3. Setting Up the Scheme

To accomplish the goal of finding an approximate solution for the Equation (1), using Sinc-collocation, without losing anything of importance, but for reasons related to facilitating the calculations, we will discuss the solution by the Sinc methodology when $p = 2$ only. We discretize the time derivatives that appeared on the left side and the last term in Equation (1) via the use of the regular finite-difference scheme, secondly, we apply $\theta-$metric $(0 \leq \theta \leq 1)$ scheme to the x derivatives evaluated at two time levels n and $n+1$, so we obtain

$$\begin{aligned} \left(\tfrac{u^{(n+1)}-u^{(n)}}{\delta t}\right) + \theta\left[\left(\tfrac{\partial u}{\partial x}\right)^{(n+1)} + \epsilon(u)^{(n+1)}\left(\tfrac{\partial u}{\partial x}\right)^{(n+1)}\right] + (1-\theta)\left[\left(\tfrac{\partial u}{\partial x}\right)^{(n)} + \epsilon(u)^{(n)}\left(\tfrac{\partial u}{\partial x}\right)^{(n)}\right] \\ -\tfrac{\mu}{\delta t}\left[\left(\tfrac{\partial^2 u}{\partial x^2}\right)^{(n+1)} - \left(\tfrac{\partial^2 u}{\partial x^2}\right)^{(n)}\right] = 0, \end{aligned} \tag{14}$$

where the notation $u^{(n)}$ is to represent the value of the solution at time level n, i.e., $u^{(n)} = u(x, t^{(n)})$, and for the time step size δt, we denote $t^{(n)} = t^{(n-1)} + \delta t$. Before going into the process of writing the solution, it is necessary to convert the non-linear term in Equation (14) into a linear quantity and the conversion process is achieved through the use of Taylor expansion, as follows:

$$(u^2)^{(n+1)}\left(\frac{\partial u}{\partial x}\right)^{(n+1)} \approx (u^{(n)})^2\left(\frac{\partial u}{\partial x}\right)^{(n+1)} + 2u^{(n)}\left(\frac{\partial u}{\partial x}\right)^{(n)} u^{(n+1)} - 2\left(u^{(n)}\right)^2\left(\frac{\partial u}{\partial x}\right)^{(n)} \tag{15}$$

From Equations (14) and (15), we arrive at

$$\begin{aligned} u^{(n+1)} + \delta t\theta\left[\left(\tfrac{\partial u}{\partial x}\right)^{(n+1)} + \epsilon\left\{(u^{(n)})^2\left(\tfrac{\partial u}{\partial x}\right)^{(n+1)} + 2u^{(n)}\left(\tfrac{\partial u}{\partial x}\right)^{(n)} u^{(n+1)}\right\}\right] - \mu\left(\tfrac{\partial^2 u}{\partial x^2}\right)^{(n+1)} \\ = u^{(n)} + \delta t\left[\epsilon(3\theta - 1)(u^{(n)})^2\left(\tfrac{\partial u}{\partial x}\right)^{(n)} - (1-\theta)\left(\tfrac{\partial u}{\partial x}\right)^{(n)}\right] - \mu\left(\tfrac{\partial^2 u}{\partial x^2}\right)^{(n)} \end{aligned} \tag{16}$$

where $u^{(n)}$ represent the nth iteration in the obtained approximate solution. Next, we use the Sinc-collocation method along the space variable, for that we discretize the interval $[a, b]$ as follows: For the positive integer $N > 2$, take the step-size $h = \frac{(b-a)}{N-1}$, then points of interpolation are

$$x_0 = a, x_N = b,\ x_i = \frac{ih}{N},\ i = 1, 2, \cdots, N-1. \tag{17}$$

To find a solution for Equation (14), using Sinc basis, we plug in,

$$u(x, t_n) \equiv u^n(x) = \sum_{j=1}^{N} u_j^n S_j(x), \tag{18}$$

where the basis Sinc functions are given by

$$S_j(x) = \text{sinc}\left(\frac{x-(j-1)h-a}{h}\right). \tag{19}$$

The constants u_j in Equation (18) are to be determined. Hence, for each collocation point x_i in (17), Equation (18) can be written as

$$u^n(x_i) = \sum_{j=1}^{N} u_j^n S_j(x_i), i = 1, \cdots, N. \tag{20}$$

Replacing Equation (20) into Equation (16), the approximation evaluated at those nodes inside the interval is given by

$$\begin{aligned}
&\textstyle\sum_{j=1}^N u_j^{n+1} S_j^{(0)}(x_i) + \delta t\theta\Big[\Big(\sum_{j=1}^N u_j^{n+1} S_j^{(1)}(x_i)\Big) + \epsilon\Big\{(\sum_{j=1}^N u_j^n S_j(x_i))^2\Big(\sum_{j=1}^N u_j^{n+1} S_j^{(1)}(x_i)\Big) \\
&\quad +2\textstyle\sum_{j=1}^N u_j^n S_j(x_i)\Big(\sum_{j=1}^N u_j^n S_j^{(1)}(x_i)\Big)\sum_{j=1}^N u_j^{n+1} S_j(x_i)\Big\}\Big] - \mu\Big(\sum_{j=1}^N u_j^{n+1} S_j^{(2)}(x_i)\Big) \\
&\quad = \textstyle\sum_{j=1}^N u_j^n S_j(x_i) + \delta t\Big[\epsilon(3\theta-1)(\sum_{j=1}^N u_j^n S_j(x_i))^2\Big(\sum_{j=1}^N u_j^n S_j^{(1)}(x_i)\Big) \\
&\quad -(1-\theta)\Big(\textstyle\sum_{j=1}^N u_j^n S_j^{(1)}(x_i)\Big)\Big] - \mu\Big(\sum_{j=1}^N u_j^n S_j^{(2)}(x_i)\Big).
\end{aligned} \tag{21}$$

The above Equation (21) is used for all interior points $x = x_i$, $i = 2, \cdots, N-1$. The boundary conditions are given by Equation (2) for the boundary points x_1 and x_N can be formulated as

$$\sum_{j=1}^{N} u_j^{n+1} S_j(x_i) = \alpha_1(t^{n+1}), \quad \sum_{j=1}^{N} u_j^{n+1} S_j(x_i) = \alpha_2(t^{n+1}). \tag{22}$$

In order to write the solution as stated in the previous two equations, and in the form of a system of matrices, we redefine the following matrices and vectors:

$$U^n = [u_1^n, u_2^n, \cdots, n_N^n]^T, I^{(0)} = (S_j(x_i), \quad I^{(1)} = (S_j'(x_i), \quad I^{(2)} = (S_j''(x_i), \quad i,j = 1, \cdots, N. \tag{23}$$

Therefore, in matrix form, Equation (21) becomes as

$$\begin{aligned}
&\Big[I^{(0)} - \mu I^{(2)} + \theta\delta t\Big\{I^{(1)} + \epsilon\Big(\Big(u^{(n)}\Big)^2 \star I^{(1)} + 2\Big(u^{(n)} \circ u_x^{(n)}\Big) \star I^{(0)}\Big)\Big\}\Big]u^{n+1} \\
&= \Big[I^{(0)} - \mu I^{(2)} + \delta t\Big\{\epsilon(3\theta-1)\Big(u^{(n)}\Big)^2 \star I^{(2)} - (1-\theta)I^{(2)}\Big\}\Big]u^n + F^{n+1}.
\end{aligned} \tag{24}$$

where the multiplication of the *ith* component of the vector $u^{(n)}$ by every element of the *ith* row of the matrix $I^{(q)}, q = 0,1,2$ is denoted by the symbolic notations $\star$, that has been used above. While the symbol $\circ$ is to denote the Hadamard matrix multiplication. The discrete system in Equation (24) represents a system of $N+1$ equations in $N+1$ unknowns, which can be written in a more compact form as

$$Mu^{n+1} = R \tag{25}$$

where

$$M = [A_d + A_b - \mu C + \theta\delta t\{B + \epsilon(E + D)\}]$$
$$R = [A_d - \mu C + \delta t\{\epsilon(3\theta-1)E - (1-\theta)B\}]u^n + F^{n+1},$$

in which the matrices A_d, A_d, B and C each of size $N \times N$ and can be written as

$$A_d = [I_{ij}^{(0)}, \ i = 2, \cdots, N-1; j = 1, \cdots, N, \textit{otherwise } 0], \ A_b = [I_{ij}^{(0)}, \ i = 1, N; j = 1, \cdots, N, \textit{otherwise } 0]$$

$$B = [I_{ij}^{(1)},\ i = 2, \cdots, N-1; j = 1, \cdots, N, otherwise\ 0],\ C = [I_{ij}^{(2)},\ i = 2, \cdots, N-1; j = 1, \cdots, N, otherwise\ 0].$$

Moreover, $u_x^n = Bu^n$, $D = 2u^n \star u_x^n \star D_d$, $E = (u^n)^2 \star B$, and $F^{n+1} = [\alpha_1(t^{n+1}), 0, ..., \alpha_2(t^{n+1})]^T$. The approximate solution can be found from Equation (25) at any point in the interval $[a, b]$ at each time level, which can be solved by any iterative techniques. It should be noted that a previous study for a system of partial differential equations using the same method, (Sinc-collocation) was published by the first author in [24]. For the purposes of facilitating the computing process, we offer the following algorithm, which summarizes what was stated in this section.

Algorithm Stages

We follow the following steps to write the program:

1. Select collocation points inside the interval $[a, b]$.
2. Select the parameters δt and θ.
3. Setup the initial solution $u^{(0)}$, then use Equation (24).
4. Evaluate the matrix M and the vector R in Equation (25).
5. The approximate solution $u^{(n+1)}$ at the successive time level is obtained.
6. If $n\delta t < T$ stop, otherwise go to step 4.

4. Stability Analysis

Here, we study briefly and in an analytical way the stability of the solution by the Sinc method for the MRLW equation. Imitation of what was performed in [4,25], if $\mathbf{U}$ represent the exact solution, while $\tilde{\mathbf{U}}$, is taken to be the numerical solution of the MRLW equation in (1). If we define the error $\varepsilon_u^n = \mathbf{U} - \tilde{\mathbf{U}}$.

Then, the error ε_u^{n+1} can be written as

$$\varepsilon_u^{n+1} = \mathbf{U}^{\mathbf{n+1}} - \tilde{\mathbf{U}}^{\mathbf{n+1}} = I^{(0)} A_d{}^{-1} A_b \varepsilon_u^n \tag{26}$$

For the stability of the method, we need $\varepsilon_u^n \to 0$, provided n is large enough. We may conclude that the scheme is stable in a numerical sense, if $\rho(I^{(0)} A_d{}^{-1} A_b) < 1$, where the notation $\rho(.)$ represents the spectral radius. Upon passing simple calculations, it is easy to verify stability if the following two conditions are fulfilled

$$\left| \frac{1 + \alpha\delta t\theta\lambda_3 + 6\alpha\delta t\theta[\lambda_{1N} + \lambda_{2N}]}{1 - \alpha(1-\theta)\delta t\lambda_3 - 6\alpha(1-\theta)\delta t\lambda_{1N} + 6\alpha\delta t\theta\lambda_{1N} + 2\mu\delta t\lambda_{1N}} \right| < 1 \tag{27}$$

and

$$\left| \frac{1 + \beta\delta t\theta\lambda_3}{1 - \beta(1-\theta)\delta t\lambda_3 - 3\beta\delta t\lambda_{1N}} \right| < 1 \tag{28}$$

where we have used the numbers 1, $\lambda_1, \lambda_3, \lambda_{1N}, \lambda_{2N}$ being eigenvalues of the matrices $I^{(0)}, I^{(1)}, I^{(3)}, \mathbf{U}^n * I^{(1)}, \mathbf{U}^n * I^{(0)}$, respectively. We use some known facts about the upper bounds for the matrices $I^{(1)}, I^{(2)}$, together with the fact that $\lambda_1 = i|\lambda_1|$, $\lambda_3 = i|\lambda_3|$, and $\lambda_{1N}, \lambda_{2N}$ are complex, after algebraic manipulation (see, [4,25]), the condition (27) must hold for all eigenvalues of the respective matrices, for the method to be stable, and for $1/2 \leq \theta < 1$ is a necessary condition for stability, but not sufficient.

5. Adomian Decomposition Method

Our goal in this section is to introduce the performance of the second scheme, namely, the Adomian decomposition method (ADM) [19,20], and give a detailed description to setup a solution for the MRLW equation [26]. The ADM is a technique to find solutions for differential equations (partial, ordinary), linear and nonlinear, homogeneous and nonhomogeneous. First, we look at the problem under consideration in general, so any nonlinear partial differential equation can be written as

$$\mathbf{L}_t u(x,t) = \mathbf{L}_x u(x,t) + R(u(x,t)) + F(u(x,t)) + g(x,t) \tag{29}$$

where the operator $\mathbf{L}_x$ is to represent the highest order derivative with respect to the variable x, $\mathbf{L}_t$ represent the time operator, $R(u(x,t))$ contains the remaining linear terms of lower derivatives in x, $F(u(x,t))$ is an analytic nonlinear term, and $g(x,t)$ is the forcing inhomogeneous term. Applying the inverse operator $\mathbf{L}_t^{-1}$ to Equation (29), we arrive at

$$u(x,t) = u(x,0) + \mathbf{L}_t^{-1}\{\mathbf{L}_x u(x,t) + R(u(x,t)) + F(u(x,t)) + g(x,t)\} \tag{30}$$

For the use of ADM, we express the solution $u(x,t)$ of (30) by the decomposition series

$$u(x,t) = \sum_{n=0}^{\infty} u_n(x,t) \tag{31}$$

while we express the nonlinear term $F(u(x,t))$ with an infinite sum of polynomials given by

$$F(u(x,t)) = \sum_{n=0}^{\infty} A_n(u_0, u_1, \cdots, u_n), \tag{32}$$

where the terms $u_n(x,t)$ are calculated recurrently so that the zeroth term $u_0(x,t)$ is chosen from those terms arises from the initial condition, or from the source term. Then, followed by finding the first term $u_1(x,t)$, which depends on the zeroth term, followed by finding the second term, which also depends on the first term, and so on until we reach the nth component. As for calculating Adomian polynomials A_n, there is a general formula written by Adomian [19,20,27], and another in a famous paper for Wazwaz [27], here we present the Adomian's formula

$$A_n = \frac{1}{n!}\frac{d^n}{d\lambda^n}\left[F(\sum_{i=0}^{n} \lambda^i u_i)\right]_{\lambda=0}, \quad n \geq 0.$$

The substitution of (31) and (32) into (30) yields

$$\sum_{n=0}^{\infty} u_n(x,t) = u(x,0) + \mathbf{L}_t^{-1}\left\{\mathbf{L}_x \sum_{n=0}^{\infty} u_n(x,t) + R(\sum_{n=0}^{\infty} u_n(x,t)) + (\sum_{n=0}^{\infty} A_n(x,t)) + g(x,t)\right\}. \tag{33}$$

As mentioned above, the components are computed in a recursive manner as

$$\begin{aligned} u_0(x,t) &= u(x,0) + \mathbf{L}_t^{-1}[g(x,t)], \\ u_{k+1}(x,t) &= \mathbf{L}_t^{-1}\Big[\mathbf{L}_x(u_k(x,t)) + R(u_k(x,t)) + (A_k(x,t))\Big], \quad k \geq 0. \end{aligned} \tag{34}$$

Looking at the above relationships, we can say that all terms depend largely on the zeroth term, so it is desirable that the zeroth term contain the least possible number of terms. If the series converges in a suitable way, then we see that

$$u_A(x,t) = \lim_{M\to\infty} \sum_{n=0}^{M} u_n(x,t) \tag{35}$$

where M is the number of terms that we found. Previous studies showed the convergence of the solution series presented in the Equation (35), see for example [28,29]. In order to understand more about the above explanation and presentation of the ADM method, we present in the next subsection the method applied to the equation under consideration.

Analysis of ADM

We rewrite Equation (1) in an operator form as (see, [30])

$$L_t u = -u_x - \epsilon N(u) + \mu L_{xx}(u_t) \tag{36}$$

with the initial condition $u(x,0) = f(x)$, where the linear operators are defined by $L_t(.) = \frac{\partial}{\partial t}(.)$ and $L_{xx}(.) = \frac{\partial^2}{\partial x^2}(.)$. While the term $N(u)$ represents the non-linear term $u^p u_x$. To start, we operate on both sides of Equation (36) with the inverse of L_t, denoted by $L_t^{-1}(.) = \int_0^t . \, dt$ yields

$$u(x,t) = u(x,0) - L_t^{-1}(u_x) - \epsilon L_t^{-1}(N(u)) + \mu L_t^{-1}(L_{xx}(u_t)). \tag{37}$$

Assume the solution $u(x,t)$ can be represented as an infinite sum of components of the form:

$$u(x,t) = \sum_{n=0}^{\infty} u_n(x,t).$$

While the nonlinear operator $N(u)$ can be expressed as

$$N(u) = u^p u_x = \left(\frac{u^{p+1}}{p+1}\right)_x = \sum_{n=0}^{\infty} A_n(u_0, u_1, \cdots, u_n).$$

In our case, as the nonlinear part in the PDE is $N(u)$, then Adomian polynomials A_n can be evaluated by a formula set by Adomian

$$A_n = \frac{1}{n!}\frac{d^n}{d\lambda^n}\left[N\Big(\sum_{i=0}^{\infty} \lambda^i u_i\Big)\right]\Big|_{\lambda=0}.$$

In the next, we just state the first three Adomian polynomials as:

$$A_0 = \left(\frac{u_0^{p+1}}{p+1}\right)_x, \quad A_1 = \left(u_0^p u_1\right)_x, \quad A_2 = \left(p u_0^{p-1}\frac{u_1^2}{2!} + u_0^p u_2\right)_x,$$

$$A_3 = \left((p-1)p u_0^{p-2}\frac{u_1^3}{3!} + p u_0^{p-1} u_1 u_2 + u_0^p u_3\right)_x$$

and so on. In the same way, additional polynomials can be calculated. Now, Equation (37) reduces to

$$\begin{aligned} \textstyle\sum_{n=0}^{\infty} u_n(x,t) &= u(x,0) - L_t^{-1}(\textstyle\sum_{n=0}^{\infty} u_{nx}(x,t)) - \epsilon L_t^{-1}(\textstyle\sum_{n=0}^{\infty} A_n(u_0,u_1,\cdots,u_n)) \\ &+ \mu L_t^{-1}(L_{xx}(\textstyle\sum_{n=0}^{\infty} u_{nt}(x,t))), \end{aligned} \tag{38}$$

Now, set $n = 0$ into the left-hand-side to identify the zero component to be $u_0(x,t) = u(x,0)$, and for $n \geq 1$ we obtain the subsequent components as

$$u_{n+1}(x,t) = -L_t^{-1}(u_n)_x - \epsilon L_t^{-1}(A_n) + \mu L_t^{-1}(L_{xx}(u_n)_t), \; n \geq 1.$$

Then, we see that the approximate solution is given by

$$u_A(x,t) = \lim_{M\to\infty} \sum_{n=0}^{M} u_n(x,t) \tag{39}$$

where M is the number of terms that we found.

6. Numerical Experiments and Results

This section provides numerical solutions to the MRLW equation for three standard problems: solitary wave motion and the development of the Maxwellian initial condition into solitary waves. In order to be able to determine the accuracy and effectiveness of the method, we will deal with specific values of the constants that appeared in Equation (1), and here if the value of $\epsilon = 6, \mu = 1$ and $p = 2$, then for these values, the exact solution to

Equation (1) is known and this allows us to know the exact error, and so we discuss the effectiveness of the proposed schemes in this paper.

Example 1. *Let us examine the problem*

$$\frac{\partial u}{\partial t} + \frac{\partial u}{\partial x} + 6u^2\frac{\partial u}{\partial x} - \frac{\partial}{\partial t}\left(\frac{\partial^2 u}{\partial x^2}\right) = 0 \tag{40}$$

with boundary conditions $u \to 0$, *as* $x \to \mp\infty$, *and the initial condition*

$$u(x,0) = \sqrt{c}\, sech[\sqrt{\frac{c}{\mu(c+1)}}(x + x_0)], \tag{41}$$

here, the constants c, x_0 *are free. The exact solution is given by [31]*

$$u(x,t) = \sqrt{c}\, sech[\sqrt{\frac{c}{\mu(c+1)}}(x - (c+1)t + x_0)]. \tag{42}$$

Equation (40) has three polynomial invariants that are related to mass, momentum and energy and is given by [32],

$$I_1 = \int_a^b u(x,t)dx, \; I_2 = \int_a^b (u^2(x,t) + \mu u_x^2(x,t))dx, \; I_3 = \int_a^b (u^4(x,t) - 6\mu u_x^2(x,t))dx. \tag{43}$$

The invariants I_1, I_2, I_3 are considered to be an excellent tool to measure the success of the numerical solution, especially for cases where we do not know the exact solution to the problem. The quantities I_1, I_2 and I_3 are applied to measure the conservation properties of the collocation scheme. The integrals in (43) are approximated by sums to obtain numerical values of invariants in Equation (43) at the finite domain $[a,b]$ as follows:

$$I_1 \simeq h\sum_{j=0}^{N} u_j^{(n)}, \; I_2 \simeq h\sum_{j=0}^{N}\Big((u_j^{(n)})^2 + \mu((u')_j^{(n)})^2\Big), \; I_3 \simeq h\sum_{j=0}^{N}\Big((u_j^{(n)})^4 - \mu((u')_j^{(n)})^2\Big) \tag{44}$$

The computations associated with the example were performed using Mathematica. The accuracy of ADM is demonstrated for the absolute errors $|u(x,t) - u_A(x,t)|$. We compute the quantities I_1, I_2 and I_3 to ensure the conservation laws in using ADM as an approximate tool for MRLW. In the computational work, we take $c = 1, \mu = 1, \epsilon = 6$, and the simulation is performed up to $t = 1, n = 8$. Table 1 shows the difference between the exact and the ADM solution $u_A(x,t)$. From Table 1, we can read that results show a high degree of accuracy and efficiency of the ADM. Since the changes of invariants I_1, I_2 and I_3 are less than $10^{-4}, 10^{-5}$ and 10^{-6}, respectively, our scheme is sensibly conservative, and our results are recorded in Table 1.

In our computational work for the Sinc-collocation method, we take $\alpha = 1.5$, $\mu = 0.1$, $\epsilon = 6$, and two different values of the time step sizes $\delta t = 0.1$ and $\delta t = 0.05$, where our interval is taken to be $[-30,30]$ and, the $N = 160$ for the points in Equation (17). We use the L_2, L_∞ [4,33], defined below to measure the accuracy of our schemes

$$L_2 = \| \mathbf{u} - \tilde{\mathbf{u}} \|_2 = \sqrt{h\sum_{j=1}^{N} |\mathbf{u}_j - \tilde{\mathbf{u}}_j|^2}, \quad L_\infty = \| \mathbf{u} - \tilde{\mathbf{u}} \|_\infty = \max_{1 \le j \le N} |\mathbf{u}_j - \tilde{\mathbf{u}}_j|$$

where $\mathbf{u}$ and $\tilde{\mathbf{u}}$ represent the exact and approximate solutions, respectively, and h is the minimum distance between any two points in Equation (18). We calculate the convergence with respect to time t, according to the following relationship [4,33]

$$\text{Order} = \frac{\log_{10}\Big(\| u_{exact} - u_{\delta t_j} \| \,/\, \| u_{exact} - u_{\delta t_{j+1}} \| \Big)}{\log_{10}(\delta t_j / \delta t_{j+1})},$$

where the numerical solution with step size δt_j is denoted by $u_{\delta t_j}$. The numerical solutions are shown in Tables 2 and 3, where invariant and error norms for solitary waves are presented. Looking at the last column in Table 2, we see that the order of convergence is almost 2. The numerical solutions that are shown in Figures 1–3. Figure 1 shows the plot of a single soliton solution for different values of time T using the Sinc-collocation method. These solutions are the bell-shaped waves, which agree with the results of [4–6]. Figures 2 and 3 illustrate that the series solution is very close to the exact solution.

Table 1. Invariants for MRLW equation using ADM when $c = 0.01$ and $0 \le x \le 60$. We used xEy to denote $x \times 10^y$.

t	I_1	I_2	I_3	$\lvert u(x,t) - u_A(x,t) \rvert$
0	3.082210	0.201518	0.000678011	6.28820E−08
0.1	3.082210	0.201518	0.000678015	1.22231E−08
0.2	3.082208	0.201518	0.000678019	6.32709E−07
0.3	3.082205	0.201517	0.000678021	2.72210E−07
0.4	3.082202	0.201515	0.000678025	3.77219E−06
0.5	3.082201	0.201515	0.000678027	1.70010E−06
0.6	3.082201	0.201512	0.000678029	6.00899E−05
0.7	3.082200	0.201512	0.000678029	3.91129E−05
0.8	3.082196	0.201510	0.000678032	5.59981E−04
0.9	3.082190	0.201510	0.000678036	3.72210E−04
1.0	3.082184	0.201506	0.000678039	1.00287E−04

Table 2. Estimated error for the Sinc solution of Equation (1) : $t = 16, \theta = \frac{1}{2}, N = 60, -30 \le x \le 30$. We used xEy to denote $x \times 10^y$.

δt	L_∞	**Order**	L_2	**Order**
0.8	3.10524E−03	–	1.10518E−02	–
0.4	1.22201E−03	1.96166	3.22148E−03	1.96453
0.2	5.35209E−04	1.99086	8.35020E−04	1.99486
0.1	1.49743E−04	1.99748	4.49278E−04	1.99782
0.05	8.66014E−05	1.99835	1.65082E−04	1.99892
0.025	6.84252E−05	1.99809	5.82611E−05	1.99212
0.010	2.04701E−05	1.98971	1.02058E−05	1.98775

Table 3. Invariants and errors using Sinc-collocation when $\delta t = 0.1, c = 0.01, N = 80$ and $-40 \le x \le 60$. We used xEy to denote $x \times 10^y$.

Time	L_∞	L_2	I_1	I_2	I_3	**CPU Time**
4	1.65338E−05	3.54902E−05	3.985214	0.810673	2.597800	0.437 s
8	2.85221E-05	7.50021E-05	3.985216	0.810673	2.597800	0.901 s
12	3.85008E-05	1.25882E-04	3.985217	0.810673	2.597800	1.642 s
16	5.54338E-05	1.57520E-04	3.985202	0.810673	2.597800	1.860 s
20	1.65338E-05	3.54902E-04	3.985192	0.810673	2.597800	2.145 s

Example 2. *In this example, we will take the value of p that appeared in Equation (1) to be 3, while keeping the values μ, ϵ as they are in the previous example.*

We noticed from the graphics in the first example that the type of solution is of soliton types, but in this second example, a new feature called bifurcation will appear, where the wave starts to bifurcate into two waves after some time close to $t = 0.4$, as shown in Figure 4.

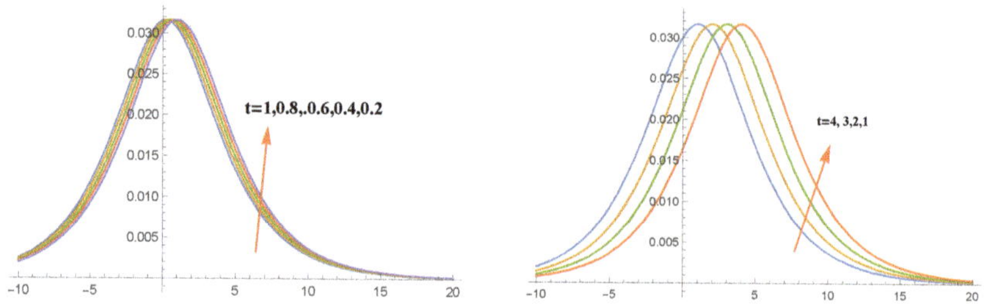

Figure 1. The soliton solution by Sinc-collocation method for different values of time t, and $-10 \leq x \leq 20$.

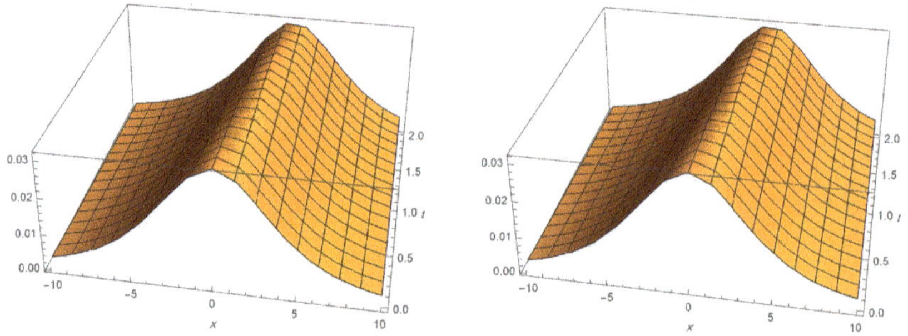

Figure 2. The ADM soliton solution (**left**) with exact (**right**) for MRLW for $c = 0.01$ and $0 \leq t \leq 2$.

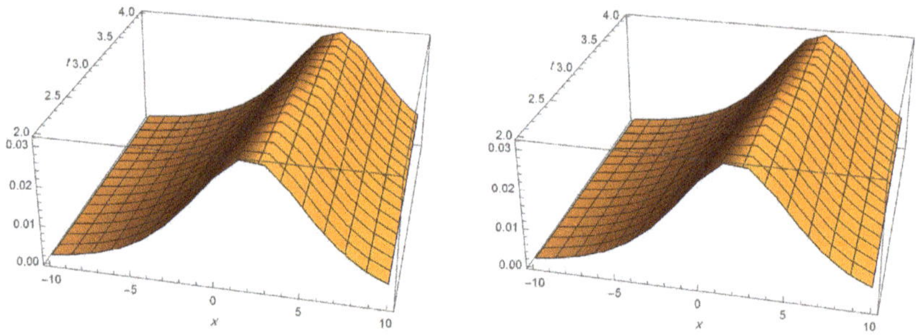

Figure 3. The ADM soliton solution (**left**) with exact (**right**) for MRLW for $c = 0.01$ and $2 \leq t \leq 4$.

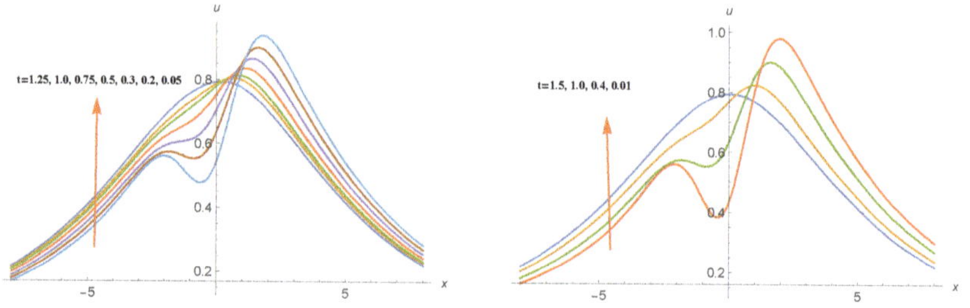

Figure 4. The solution of Equation (1) using ADM when $p = 3$ for different values of t.

Example 3. *In this last example, we examined the evolution of an initial Maxwellian pulse into solitary waves, arising as the initial condition of the form*

$$u(x, 0) = exp[-(x - 40)^2]$$

When solving Equation (1) for $p = 2$, and $\epsilon = 6$. It is known that the behavior of the solution with the Maxwellian condition depends on the values of μ. So, we study each of the three cases: $\mu = 0.5$, where only a single soliton is generated as shown in Figure 5, and $\mu = 0.05$. When μ is reduced more and more, such as in the case of $\mu = 0.05$, two single solitons are generated as in Figure 5, and for the case $\mu = 0.005$, the Maxwellian initial condition has decayed into three stable solitary waves as generated and shown in Figure 5.

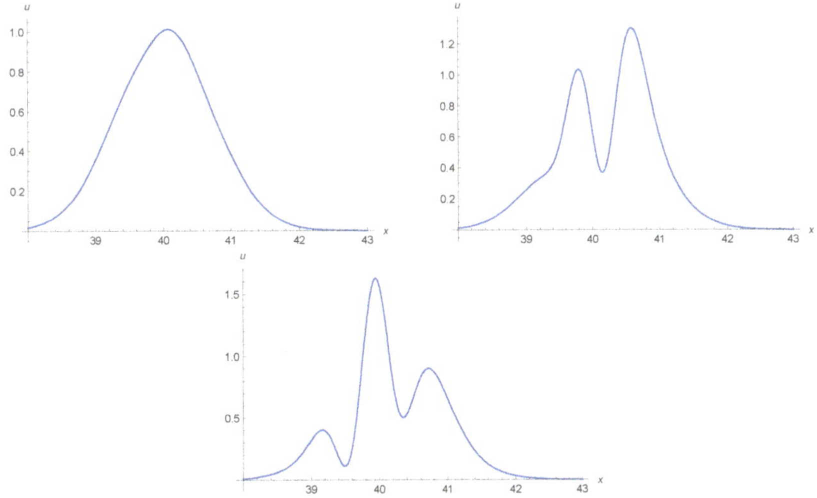

Figure 5. The solution of Equation (1) using ADM when $p = 2, \epsilon = 6$ when $t = 2$ and $\mu = 0.5$ (Single soliton), $\mu = 0.05$ (two solitons), $\mu = 0.005$ (three solitons).

7. Discussion and Conclusions

Two algorithms have been proposed to find a numerical solution to the MRLW equation, which often appears in physical applications. Whereas the first method, which is known as Sinc-collocation, is described in detail, with a simple proof of the stability of the obtained numerical solution, with an indication of an insufficient necessary condition. The other method, known as ADM, was presented in general first, and then the method was allocated to Equation (1). For the effectiveness of the two algorithms, we use one example with a known solution of soliton type, and the accuracy is investigated via the use of the L_∞, L_2 error norms. The numerical results we obtained in the last section prove the effectiveness and accuracy of the two methods to a large extent. However, we would like to point out that the Sinc method is numerical, and the solution was obtained and evaluated at some nodes. The scheme was found to be stable, and it converges exponentially in space direction. On the other hand, the other scheme used to solve the MRLW equation is ADM, which was found to be highly efficient, and it provides accurate approximate solutions without spatial discretization as in the Sinc method. We used a few terms from the series solution obtained by the ADM and obtained a suitable accuracy. However, we may easily increase the accuracy using ADM by adding more terms to the series. The biggest benefit of using this method is the speed of its convergence to the exact solution, as well as the ease of use. Finally, a Maxwellian initial condition was used, and the relationship between μ and the number of solitons was discussed.

Author Contributions: Conceptualization, K.A.-K.; methodology, K.A.-K. and H.J.; software, K.A.-K.; validation, K.A.-K.; formal analysis, K.A.-K. and H.J.; data curation, K.A.-K.; writing—original draft preparation, K.A.-K.; writing—review and editing, K.A.-K.; visualization, K.A.-K. and H.J. All authors have read and agreed to the published version of the manuscript.

Funding: This research received no external funding.

Institutional Review Board Statement: Not applicable.

Informed Consent Statement: Not applicable.

Data Availability Statement: Not applicable.

Acknowledgments: Both authors give all thanks to Jordan University of Science and Technology, where one part of this paper (Sections 5 and 6) was done as a master's thesis for the second author.

Conflicts of Interest: The authors declare no conflict of interest.

References

1. Karakoç, S.B.G.; Ak, T.; Zeybek, H. An Efficient Approach to Numerical Study of the MRLW Equation with B-Spline Collocation Method. *Abstr. Appl. Anal.* **2014**, *2014*, 596406. [CrossRef]
2. Pindza, E.; Maré, E. Solving the Generalized Regularized Long Wave Equation Using a Distributed Approximating Functional Method. *Int. J. Comput. Math.* **2014**, *2014*, 178024. [CrossRef]
3. Karakoç, S.B.G.; Mei, L.; Ali, K.K. Two efficient methods for solving the generalized regularized long wave equation. *Appl. Anal.* **2022**, *101*, 4721–4742.
4. Mokhtari, R.; Mohammad, M. Numerical solution of GRLW equation using Sinc-collocation method. *Computer Phys. Commun.* **2010**, *181*, 1266–1274.
5. Khalifa, A.K.; Raslan, K.R.; Alzubaidi, H. A collocation method with cubic B-spline for solving the MRLW eqution. *J. Comput. Appl. Math.* **2008**, *212*, 406–418. [CrossRef]
6. Omer, O. Numerical investigation of nonlinear generalized regularized long wave equation via delta-shaped basis functions. *Int. J. Optim. Control. Theor. Appl. (IJOCTA)* **2020**, *10*, 244–258.
7. Mei, L.; Chen, Y. Numerical solutions of RLW equation using Galerkin method with extrapolation techniques. *Comput. Phys. Commun.* **2012**, *183*, 1609–1616.
8. Ali, M.R.; Ma, W.; Sadat, R. Lie symmetry analysis and invariant solutions for (2+1) dimensional Bogoyavlensky-Konopelchenko equation with variable-coefficient in wave propagation. *J. Ocean. Eng. Sci.* **2022**, *7*, 248–254. [CrossRef]
9. Al-Khaled, K. Solving a Generalized Fractional Nonlinear Integro-Differential Equations via Modified Sumudu Decomposition Transform. *Axioms* **2022**, *11*, 398.
10. Kumar, S.; Kumar, A. Abundant closed-form wave solutions and dynamical structures of soliton solutions to the (3+1)-dimensional BLMP equation in mathematical physics. *J. Ocean Eng. Sci.* **2022**, *7*, 178–187. [CrossRef]
11. H. Zeybek, and S. Battal Gazi Karakoc, A collocation algorithm based on quintic B-splines for the solitary wave simulation of the GRLW equation. *Sci. Iran. B* **2019**, *26*, 3356–3368.
12. Kukreja, S.V.K. Analysis of RLW and MRLW equation using an improvised collocation technique with SSP-RK43. scheme. *Wave Motion* **2021**, *105*, 102761.
13. Avazzadeh, Z.; Nikan, O.; Machado, J.A.T. Solitary Wave Solutions of the Generalized Rosenau-KdV-RLW Equation. *Mathematics* **2020**, *8*, 1601. http://doi.org10.3390/math8091601. [CrossRef]
14. Jena, S.R.; Senapati, A.; Gebremedhin, G.S. Approximate solution of MRLW equation in B-spline environment. *Math. Sci.* **2020**, *14*, 345–357.
15. Rafiq, M.; Singh, B.; Arifa, S.; Nazeer, M.; Usman, M.; Arif, S.; Bibi, M.; Jahangir, A. Harmonic waves solution in dual-phase-lag magneto-thermoelasticity. *Open Phys.* **2019**, *17*, 8–15. [CrossRef]
16. Al-Khaled, K. Theory and computation in singular boundary value problems. *Chaos Soliton Fract.* **2007**, *33*, 678–684. [CrossRef]
17. Stenger, F. *Numerical Methods Based on Sinc and Analytic Functions*; Springer: New York, NY, USA, 1993.
18. Lund, J.; Bowers, K.L. *Sinc Methods for Quadrature and Differential Equations*; SIAM: Philadelphia, PA, USA, 1992.
19. Adomian, G. A review of the decomposition method in applied mathematics. *J. Math. Anal. Appl.* **1988**, *135*, 501–544.
20. Adomian, G. *Solving Frontier Problems of Physics: The Decompsition Method*; Kluwer Academic Publishers: Boston, MA, USA,1994.
21. Danaf, T.E.; Ramadan, M.A.; Alaal, F.A. The use of adomian decomposition method for solving the regularized long-wave equation. *Chaos Solitons Fractals* **2005**, *26*, 747–757. [CrossRef]
22. Al-Zaid, N.A.; Bakodah, H.O.; Hendi, F.A. Numerical Solutions of the Regularized Long-Wave (RLW) Equation Using New Modification of Laplace-Decomposition Method . *Adv. Pure Math.* **2013**, *3*, 159–163. [CrossRef]
23. Khalifa, A.K.; Raslan, K.R.; Alzubaidi, H. Numerical study using ADM for the modified regularized long wave equation. *Appl. Math. Model.* **2008**, *32*, 2962–2972. [CrossRef]
24. Al-Khaled, K. Numerical Wave Solutions for Nonlinear Coupled Equations using Sinc-Collocation Method. *J. Sci.* **2015**, *20*, 19–30.
25. Ma, W.-X.; Seoud, E.Y.A.E.; Ali, M.R.; Sadat, R. Dynamical Behavior and Wave Speed Perturbations in the $(2+1)$ PKP Equation. *Qual. Theory Dyn. Syst.* **2023**, *22*, 2. [CrossRef]
26. Jafer, H. Soliton Solutions for the Generalized Regularized Long Wave Equation Using ADM. Master's Thesis, Jordan University of Science and Technology, Irbid, Jordan, 2021.

27. Wazwaz, A.-M. A new algorithm for calculating Adomian polynomials for nonlinear operators. *Appl. Math. Comput.* **2000**, *111*, 53–69. [CrossRef]
28. Cherruault, Y.; Adomian, G. Decomposition methods: A new proof of convergence. *Math. Comput. Model.* **1993**, *18*, 103–106. [CrossRef]
29. Abbaoui, K.; Cherruault, Y. Convergence of Adomian's method applied to nonlinear equations. *Math. Comput. Model.* **1994**, *20*, 69–73.
30. Hajji, M.A.; Al-Khaled, K. Two reliable methods for solving nonlinear evolution equations. *Appl. Math. Comput.* **2007**, *186*, 1151–1162. [CrossRef]
31. Dereli, Y. Numerical solutions of the MRLW equation using Meshless kernel based method of lines. *Int. J. Nonlinear Sci.* **2012**, *13*, 28–38.
32. Khan, Y.; Taghipour, R.; Falahian, M.; Nikkar, A. A new approach to modified regularized long wave equation. *Neural Comput. Appl.* **2013**, *23*, 1335–1341.
33. Alia, A.; Siraj-ul-Islamb; Haq, S. A Computational Meshfree Technique for the Numerical Solution of the Two-Dimensional Coupled Burgers' Equations. *Int. J. Comput. Methods Eng. Sci. Mech.* **2009**, *10*, 406–422. [CrossRef]

Disclaimer/Publisher's Note: The statements, opinions and data contained in all publications are solely those of the individual author(s) and contributor(s) and not of MDPI and/or the editor(s). MDPI and/or the editor(s) disclaim responsibility for any injury to people or property resulting from any ideas, methods, instructions or products referred to in the content.

axioms

Article

Solutions of Time Fractional (1 + 3)-Dimensional Partial Differential Equations by the Natural Transform Decomposition Method (NTDM)

Musa Rahamh Gadallah and Hassan Eltayeb *

Mathematics Department, College of Science, King Saud University, P.O. Box 2455, Riyadh 11451, Saudi Arabia; magal@ksu.edu.sa
* Correspondence: hgadain@ksu.edu.sa

Abstract: The current study employs the natural transform decomposition method (NTDM) to test fractional-order partial differential equations (FPDEs). The present technique is a mixture of the natural transform method and the Adomian decomposition method. For the purpose of checking the precis of our technique, some examples are offered, and the series solutions of these equations are introduced by using NTDM. The outcome shows that the suggested approach is very active and straightforward for obtaining a series solutions of FPDEs and is more accurate if we compare it with existing methods.

Keywords: natural transform; fractional-order linear and nonlinear; approximate solution; inverse natural transform

MSC: 35A22; 44A30

Citation: Gadallah, M.R.; Eltayeb, H. Solutions of Time Fractional (1 + 3)-Dimensional Partial Differential Equations by the Natural Transform Decomposition Method (NTDM). *Axioms* **2023**, *12*, 958. https://doi.org/10.3390/axioms12100958

Academic Editors: Hatıra Günerhan, Francisco Martínez González and Mohammed K. A. Kaabar

Received: 12 September 2023
Revised: 3 October 2023
Accepted: 4 October 2023
Published: 11 October 2023

Copyright: © 2023 by the authors. Licensee MDPI, Basel, Switzerland. This article is an open access article distributed under the terms and conditions of the Creative Commons Attribution (CC BY) license (https://creativecommons.org/licenses/by/4.0/).

1. Introduction

During the last decades, various numerical methods have been improved in the field of fractional calculus. The fractional differentiation equations play a crucial role in several theoretical physical, biological, and applied engineering problems, such as electromagnetics, viscoelasticity, fluid mechanics, electrochemistry, and biological population models [1–5]. The ADSTM method can be applied to solve the energy balance equations of the porous fin with several temperature dependent properties—see [6]. The authors in [7] discussed the approximate solution of the atmospheric internal waves model by applying FRDTM method. Various approximation and numerical techniques have been utilized to solve fractional differential equations [8,9]. Recently, different new methods for fractional differential equations have been suggested, for example, the fractional differential transform method (FDTM) [10,11], fractional variational iteration method (FVIM) [4], fractional Adomian decomposition method (FROM) [12,13], natural transform decomposition method (NTDM) [14–18], homotopy perturbation method (HPM) [19], and Sumudu transform method (STM) [20,21]. The definition of the natural transform, including its properties, was introduced by Khan in [22], which was later used by Belgacem and his colleagues to obtain the relation between this transform and the Laplace and Sumudu transforms [23]. Some physical problems have been modeled by fractional PDEs and solved by utilizing NTDM, for example, the analytical solution of the system of nonlinear PDEs is proposed in [24]. The main goal of this work is to apply the natural transform decomposition method (NTDM) to solve some types of fractional linear and nonlinear partial differential equations (PDEs). The organization of this work is divided into five sections. In Section 2, definitions and properties of the natural transform method (NTM) are addressed. In Section 3, we discuss the methodology of FNTDM. In Section 4, we offered three examples of fractional PDEs and solved them by NTDM. Finally, Section 5 contains the concluding notions.

2. Basic Definitions and Properties of the Natural Transform Method (NTM)

In this part, some definitions and properties of fractional calculus with natural transform are addressed.

Definition 1. *The natural transform (NT) of a function $g(\nu)$ is defined by the integral [22]*

$$\mathbb{N}^{+}[g(\nu)] = \varphi(s,\mu) = \int_{0}^{\infty} g(\mu\nu)e^{-s\nu}d\nu, \qquad \mu > 0,\ s > 0 \tag{1}$$

where s and μ are transform variables.

Definition 2. *If $n \in \mathbb{N}$, where $n-1 \leq \gamma < n$ and $\varphi(s,\mu)$ is natural transform of a function $g(\nu)$, then the (NT) of Caputo fractional derivative of $\frac{\partial^{\gamma} g(\zeta,\nu)}{\partial \nu^{\gamma}}$ is denoted by [18]*

$$\mathbb{N}^{+}\left[\frac{\partial^{\gamma} g(\zeta,\nu)}{\partial \nu^{\gamma}}\right] = \frac{s^{\gamma}}{\mu^{\gamma}}\varphi(s,\mu) - \sum_{k=0}^{n-1}\frac{s^{\gamma-(k+1)}}{\mu^{\gamma-k}}\left[\frac{\partial^{\gamma} g(\zeta,\nu)}{\partial \nu^{\gamma}}\right]_{\nu=0} \tag{2}$$

Definition 3. *The inverse natural transform (INTM) of $\varphi(s,\mu)$ is defined by*

$$\mathbb{N}^{-1}[\varphi(s,\mu)] = g(\nu) = \frac{1}{2\pi i}\int_{\varepsilon-i\infty}^{\varepsilon+i\infty} \varphi(s,\mu)e^{\frac{s\nu}{\mu}}ds, \qquad \mu > 0,\ s > 0 \tag{3}$$

Definition 4. *The Caputo operator of order γ for a fractional derivative [25] is presented by the following mathematical expression for $n \in \mathbb{N}, \zeta > 0, g \in \mathbb{C}_{\nu}$:*

$$D^{\gamma} g(\zeta) = \frac{\partial^{\gamma} g(\zeta)}{\partial \zeta^{\gamma}} = I^{n-\gamma}\left[\frac{\partial^{\gamma} g(\zeta)}{\partial \zeta^{\gamma}}\right], \text{ if } n-1 < \gamma \leq n \in \mathbb{N} \tag{4}$$

Definition 5. *Riemann–Liouville fractional order integral [26]:*

$$I_{\zeta}^{\gamma} g(\zeta) = \left\{\begin{array}{ll} g(\zeta) & \text{if } \gamma = 0 \\ \frac{1}{\Gamma(\gamma)}\int_0^{\zeta}(\zeta-\mu)^{\gamma-1}g(\mu)d\mu & \text{if } \gamma > 0 \end{array}\right\} \tag{5}$$

where Γ describes the concept of the gamma variable by

$$\Gamma(\Phi)\int_0^{\infty} e^{-\zeta}\zeta^{\Phi-1}d\zeta, \qquad \Phi \in \mathbb{C} \tag{6}$$

Important properties: some basic properties of the natural transform method (NTM) are given as follows:

$$\begin{aligned} \mathbb{N}^{+}[v''(\nu)] &= \frac{s^2}{\mu^2}\varphi(s,\mu) - \frac{s}{\mu^2}v(0) - \frac{1}{\mu}v'(0). \\ \mathbb{N}^{+}[v'''(\nu)] &= \frac{s^3}{\mu^3}\varphi(s,\mu) - \frac{s^2}{\mu^3}v(0) - \frac{s}{\mu^3}v'(0) - \frac{1}{\mu}v''(0). \end{aligned}$$

3. Natural Transform and Decomposition Method (NTDM)

Here, we demonstrate the pertinence of the (NTDM) to obtain the general solution of FPDEs.

$$D_{\nu}^{\alpha}\Psi(\zeta,\nu) + L\Psi(\zeta,\nu) + N\Psi(\zeta,\nu) = g(\zeta,\nu), \quad 0 < \alpha \leq 2, \zeta, \nu \geq 0 \tag{7}$$

subject to the initial conditions

$$\Psi(\zeta,0) = g_1(\zeta), \quad \Psi_\nu(\zeta,0) = g_2(\zeta), \tag{8}$$

where symbols L and N indicate the linear and nonlinear operators, respectively, g is the source function, and $D_\nu^\alpha = \frac{\partial^\alpha}{\partial \nu^\alpha}$ is the Caputo operator. By applying the natural transform method (NTM) to both sides of Equation (7), we obtain

$$\mathbb{N}^+[D_\nu^\alpha \Psi(\zeta,\nu)] + \mathbb{N}^+[L\Psi(\zeta,\nu)] + \mathbb{N}^+[N\Psi(\zeta,\nu)] = \mathbb{N}^+[g(\zeta,\nu)], \tag{9}$$

By employing the differentiation property of the natural transform method, one can obtain

$$\frac{s^\alpha}{\mu^\alpha}\mathbb{N}^+[\Psi(\zeta,\nu)] - \frac{s^{\alpha-1}}{\mu^\alpha}\Psi(\zeta,0) - \frac{s^{\alpha-2}}{\mu^{\alpha-1}}\Psi_\nu(\zeta,0) = \mathbb{N}^+[g(\zeta,\nu)] - \mathbb{N}^+[L\Psi(\zeta,\nu) + N\Psi(\zeta,\nu)], \tag{10}$$

and

$$\mathbb{N}^+[\Psi(\zeta,\nu)] = \frac{1}{s}g_1(\zeta) + \frac{\mu}{s^2}g_2(\zeta) + \frac{\mu^\alpha}{s^\alpha}\mathbb{N}^+[g(\zeta,\nu)] - \frac{\mu^\alpha}{s^\alpha}\mathbb{N}^+[L\Psi(\zeta,\nu) + N\Psi(\zeta,\nu)], \tag{11}$$

taking the inverse NT for both sides of Equation (11), we obtain

$$\Psi(\zeta,\nu) = g_1(\zeta) + \nu g_2(\zeta) + \mathbb{N}^{-1}\left[\frac{\mu^\alpha}{s^\alpha}\mathbb{N}^+[g(\zeta,\nu)]\right] - \mathbb{N}^{-1}\left[\frac{\mu^\alpha}{s^\alpha}\mathbb{N}^+[L\Psi(\zeta,\nu) + N\Psi(\zeta,\nu)]\right] \tag{12}$$

The NTDM solution $\Psi(\zeta,\nu)$ is described by the following infinite series:

$$\Psi(\zeta,\nu) = \sum_{n=0}^{\infty}\Psi_n(\zeta,\nu), \tag{13}$$

The nonlinear term $N\Psi(\zeta,\nu)$ satisfies the property

$$N\Psi(\zeta,\nu) = \sum_{n=0}^{\infty} B_n, \tag{14}$$

$$B_n = \frac{1}{n!}\left[\frac{d^n}{d\mu^n}\left[N\sum_{n=0}^{\infty}(\mu^n\Psi_n)\right]\right]_{\mu=0}, \quad n = 0,1,2,\ldots \tag{15}$$

Substituting Equations (13) and (14) into Equation (12), we obtain

$$\begin{aligned}\mathbb{N}^+\left[\sum_{n=0}^{\infty}\Psi(\zeta,\nu)\right] &= g_1(\zeta) + \nu g_2(\zeta) + \mathbb{N}^{-1}\left[\frac{\mu^\alpha}{s^\alpha}\mathbb{N}^+[g(\zeta,\nu)]\right] \\ &\quad -\mathbb{N}^{-1}\left[\frac{\mu^\alpha}{s^\alpha}\mathbb{N}^+\left[L\sum_{n=0}^{\infty}\Psi_n(\zeta,\nu) + \sum_{n=0}^{\infty}B_n\right]\right]\end{aligned} \tag{16}$$

We define the repetition relation

$$\begin{aligned}
\Psi_0(\zeta,\nu) &= g_1(\zeta) + \nu g_2(\zeta) + \mathbb{N}^{-1}\left[\frac{\mu^\alpha}{s^\alpha}\mathbb{N}^+[g(\zeta,\nu)]\right] \\
\Psi_1(\zeta,\nu) &= -\mathbb{N}^{-1}\left[\frac{\mu^\alpha}{s^\alpha}\mathbb{N}^+[\Psi_0(\zeta,\nu) + B_0]\right] \\
\Psi_2(\zeta,\nu) &= -\mathbb{N}^{-1}\left[\frac{\mu^\alpha}{s^\alpha}\mathbb{N}^+[\Psi_1(\zeta,\nu) + B_1]\right] \\
\Psi_3(\zeta,\nu) &= -\mathbb{N}^{-1}\left[\frac{\mu^\alpha}{s^\alpha}\mathbb{N}^+[\Psi_2(\zeta,\nu) + B_2]\right] \\
&\vdots \\
\Psi_{n+1}(\zeta,\nu) &= -\mathbb{N}^{-1}\left[\frac{\mu^\alpha}{s^\alpha}\mathbb{N}^+[\Psi_n(\zeta,\nu) + B_n]\right]
\end{aligned} \tag{17}$$

Therefore, the precise solution is denoted by

$$\Psi(\zeta,\nu) = \Psi_0(\zeta,\nu) + \Psi_1(\zeta,\nu) + \Psi_2(\zeta,\nu) + \Psi_3(\zeta,\nu) + \Psi_4(\zeta,\nu) + \Psi_5(\zeta,\nu) + \cdots \tag{18}$$

4. Illustrative Examples

In this part, we examine the above method using three examples and then compare the approximate solutions with the exact solutions.

Example 1. *Consider the following one-dimensional nonlinear wave-like equation with variable coefficients:*

$$\begin{aligned}
\frac{\partial^\alpha \Psi(\zeta,\nu)}{\partial \nu^\alpha} &= \zeta^2 \frac{\partial}{\partial \zeta}\left[\frac{\partial \Psi(\zeta,\nu)}{\partial \zeta}\frac{\partial^2 \Psi(\zeta,\nu)}{\partial \zeta^2}\right] - \zeta^2\left[\left(\frac{\partial^2 \Psi(\zeta,\nu)}{\partial \zeta^2}\right)^2 - \Psi(\zeta,\nu)\right] \\
0 &< \alpha \leq 2,\ \nu > 0,
\end{aligned} \tag{19}$$

subject to the initial condition

$$\Psi(\zeta,0) = 0, \qquad \Psi_\nu(\zeta,0) = \zeta^2, \tag{20}$$

By employing the NTM for both sides of Equation (19), we have

$$\begin{aligned}
&\frac{s^\alpha}{\mu^\alpha}\mathbb{N}^+[\Psi(\zeta,\nu)] - \frac{s^{\alpha-1}}{\mu^\alpha}\Psi(\zeta,0) - \frac{s^{\alpha-2}}{\mu^{\alpha-1}}\Psi_\nu(\zeta,0) \\
&= \mathbb{N}^+\left[\zeta^2 \frac{\partial}{\partial \zeta}\left[\frac{\partial \Psi(\zeta,\nu)}{\partial \zeta}\frac{\partial^2 \Psi(\zeta,\nu)}{\partial \zeta^2}\right] - \zeta^2\left[\left(\frac{\partial^2 \Psi(\zeta,\nu)}{\partial \zeta^2}\right)^2 - \Psi(\zeta,\nu)\right]\right]
\end{aligned} \tag{21}$$

Using the initial conditions in Equation (20) and rearranging the terms, we have

$$\Psi(\zeta,\nu) = \frac{\mu}{s^2}\zeta^2 + \mathbb{N}^+\left[\zeta^2 \frac{\partial}{\partial \zeta}\left[\frac{\partial \Psi(\zeta,\nu)}{\partial \zeta}\frac{\partial^2 \Psi(\zeta,\nu)}{\partial \zeta^2}\right] - \zeta^2\left[\left(\frac{\partial^2 \Psi(\zeta,\nu)}{\partial \zeta^2}\right)^2 - \Psi(\zeta,\nu)\right]\right] \tag{22}$$

On using the inverse NTM of Equation (22), we have

$$\Psi(\zeta,\nu)=\zeta^2\nu+\mathbb{N}^{-1}\left[\frac{\mu^\alpha}{s^\alpha}\mathbb{N}^+\left[\zeta^2\frac{\partial}{\partial\zeta}\left[\frac{\partial\Psi(\zeta,\nu)}{\partial\zeta}\frac{\partial^2\Psi(\zeta,\nu)}{\partial\zeta^2}\right]-\zeta^2\left[\left(\frac{\partial^2\Psi(\zeta,\nu)}{\partial\zeta^2}\right)^2-\Psi(\zeta,\nu)\right]\right]\right] \tag{23}$$

Now, we assume an infinite series solution for the Equation (23) which is defined by Equation (13); then, Equation (23) becomes

$$\begin{aligned}\sum_{n=0}^{\infty}\Psi_n(\zeta,\nu) &= \zeta^2\nu+\mathbb{N}^{-1}\left[\frac{\mu^\alpha}{s^\alpha}\mathbb{N}^+\left[\zeta^2\sum_{n=0}^{\infty}\frac{\partial}{\partial\zeta}[H(\Psi_\zeta\Psi_{\zeta\zeta})]\right]\right]\\ &\quad -\mathbb{N}^{-1}\left[\frac{\mu^\alpha}{s^\alpha}\mathbb{N}^+\left[\zeta^2\sum_{n=0}^{\infty}F(\Psi^2_{\zeta\zeta})\right]\right]\\ &\quad -\mathbb{N}^{-1}\left[\frac{\mu^\alpha}{s^\alpha}\mathbb{N}^+\left[\sum_{n=0}^{\infty}\Psi_n(\zeta,\nu)\right]\right]\end{aligned} \tag{24}$$

where $H(\Psi_\zeta\Psi_{\zeta\zeta})$ and $F(\Psi^2_{\zeta\zeta})$ are the Adomian polynomials, which represent the nonlinear terms. The few nonlinear terms are as follows:

$$\begin{aligned}H_0(\Psi_\zeta\Psi_{\zeta\zeta}) &= \Psi_{0\zeta}\Psi_{0\zeta\zeta},\\ H_1(\Psi_\zeta\Psi_{\zeta\zeta}) &= \Psi_{0\zeta}\Psi_{1\zeta\zeta}+\Psi_{1\zeta}\Psi_{0\zeta\zeta},\\ H_2(\Psi_\zeta\Psi_{\zeta\zeta}) &= \Psi_{0\zeta}\Psi_{2\zeta\zeta}+\Psi_{1\zeta}\Psi_{1\zeta\zeta}+\Psi_{2\zeta}\Psi_{0\zeta\zeta},\\ H_3(\Psi_\zeta\Psi_{\zeta\zeta}) &= \Psi_{0\zeta}\Psi_{3\zeta\zeta}+\Psi_{1\zeta}\Psi_{2\zeta\zeta}+\Psi_{2\zeta}\Psi_{1\zeta\zeta}+\Psi_{3\zeta}\Psi_{0\zeta\zeta},\\ &\vdots\end{aligned} \tag{25}$$

and

$$\begin{aligned}F_0(\Psi^2_{\zeta\zeta}) &= \Psi^2_{0\zeta\zeta},\\ F_1(\Psi^2_{\zeta\zeta}) &= 2\Psi_{0\zeta\zeta}\Psi_{1\zeta\zeta},\\ F_2(\Psi^2_{\zeta\zeta}) &= 2\Psi_{0\zeta\zeta}\Psi_{2\zeta\zeta}+\Psi^2_{1\zeta\zeta},\\ F_3(\Psi^2_{\zeta\zeta}) &= 2\Psi_{0\zeta\zeta}\Psi_{3\zeta\zeta}+2\Psi_{1\zeta\zeta}\Psi_{2\zeta\zeta},\\ &\vdots\end{aligned} \tag{26}$$

Comparing both sides of Equation (24), we can obtain

$$
\begin{aligned}
\Psi_0(\zeta,\nu) &= \zeta^2\nu, \\
\Psi_1(\zeta,\nu) &= \mathbb{N}^{-1}\left[\frac{\mu^\alpha}{s^\alpha}\mathbb{N}^{+}\left[\zeta^2\sum_{n=0}^{\infty}\frac{\partial}{\partial\zeta}(\Psi_{0\zeta}\Psi_{0\zeta\zeta}) - \zeta^2\sum_{n=0}^{\infty}\Psi_{0\zeta\zeta}^2 - \sum_{n=0}^{\infty}\Psi_0\right]\right] \\
&= -\zeta^2\frac{\nu^{\alpha+1}}{\Gamma(\alpha+2)}, \\
\Psi_2(\zeta,\nu) &= \mathbb{N}^{-1}\left[\frac{\mu^\alpha}{s^\alpha}\mathbb{N}^{+}\left[\zeta^2\frac{\partial}{\partial\zeta}(\Psi_{0\zeta}\Psi_{1\zeta\zeta} + \Psi_{1\zeta}\Psi_{0\zeta\zeta}) - \zeta^2(2\Psi_{0\zeta\zeta}\Psi_{1\zeta\zeta}) - \Psi_1\right]\right] \\
&= \zeta^2\frac{\nu^{2\alpha+1}}{\Gamma(2\alpha+2)}, \\
\Psi_3(\zeta,\nu) &= \mathbb{N}^{-1}\left[\frac{\mu^\alpha}{s^\alpha}\mathbb{N}^{+}\left[\zeta^2\frac{\partial}{\partial\zeta}(\Psi_{0\zeta}\Psi_{2\zeta\zeta} + \Psi_{2\zeta}\Psi_{0\zeta\zeta} + \Psi_{1\zeta}\Psi_{1\zeta\zeta})\right]\right] \\
&\quad \mathbb{N}^{-1}\left[\frac{\mu^\alpha}{s^\alpha}\mathbb{N}^{+}\left[-\zeta^2\left(2\Psi_{0\zeta\zeta}\Psi_{2\zeta\zeta} + \Psi_{1\zeta\zeta}^2\right) - \Psi_2\right]\right] \\
&= -\zeta^2\frac{\nu^{3\alpha+1}}{\Gamma(3\alpha+2)}, \\
\Psi_4(\zeta,\nu) &= \mathbb{N}^{-1}\left[\frac{\mu^\alpha}{s^\alpha}\mathbb{N}^{+}\left[\zeta^2\frac{\partial}{\partial\zeta}(\Psi_{0\zeta}\Psi_{3\zeta\zeta} + \Psi_{1\zeta}\Psi_{2\zeta\zeta} + \Psi_{2\zeta}\Psi_{1\zeta\zeta} + \Psi_{3\zeta}\Psi_{0\zeta\zeta})\right]\right] \\
&\quad -\mathbb{N}^{-1}\left[\frac{\mu^\alpha}{s^\alpha}\mathbb{N}^{+}\left[\zeta^2(2\Psi_{0\zeta\zeta}\Psi_{3\zeta\zeta} + 2\Psi_{1\zeta\zeta}\Psi_{2\zeta\zeta})\right]\right] - \mathbb{N}^{-1}\left[\frac{\mu^\alpha}{s^\alpha}\mathbb{N}^{+}[\Psi_3]\right] \\
&= \zeta^2\frac{\nu^{4\alpha+1}}{\Gamma(4\alpha+2)}, \\
&\ \ \vdots
\end{aligned}
$$

The NTDM solution for the above equation is

$$\Psi(\zeta,\nu) = \zeta^2\left[\nu - \frac{\nu^{\alpha+1}}{\Gamma(\alpha+2)} + \frac{\nu^{2\alpha+1}}{\Gamma(2\alpha+2)} - \frac{\nu^{3\alpha+1}}{\Gamma(3\alpha+2)} + \frac{\nu^{4\alpha+1}}{\Gamma(4\alpha+2)} - \frac{\nu^{5\alpha+1}}{\Gamma(5\alpha+2)} + \cdots\right]. \tag{27}$$

If we substitute $\alpha = 2$ in Equation (27), the approximate solution of Equation (19) becomes

$$\Psi(\zeta,\nu) = \zeta^2\left[\nu - \frac{\nu^3}{3!} + \frac{\nu^5}{5!} - \frac{\nu^7}{7!} + \frac{\nu^9}{9!} - \cdots\right]. \tag{28}$$

Therefore, the solution of Equation (19) in a closed form is

$$\Psi(\zeta,\nu) = \zeta^2\sin(\nu).$$

Figure 1: The solution $\Psi(\zeta,\nu)$ for Example 1 when $\alpha = 2$.

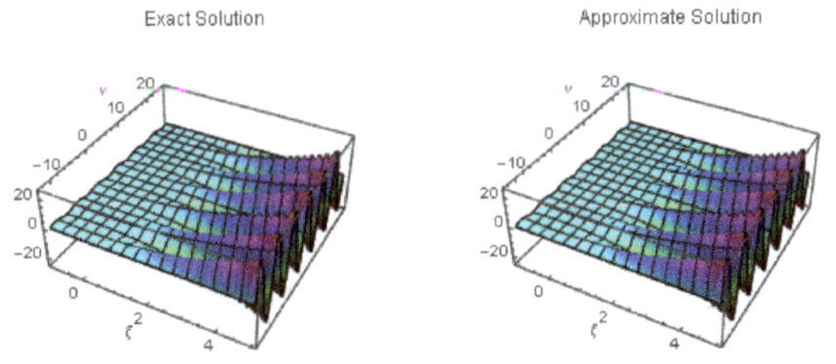

Figure 1. $\psi(\zeta,\nu) = \zeta^2\sin\nu$.

Figure 2: The solution $\Psi(\zeta, \nu)$ for Example 1 when $\alpha = 2, 1.80, 1.50$.

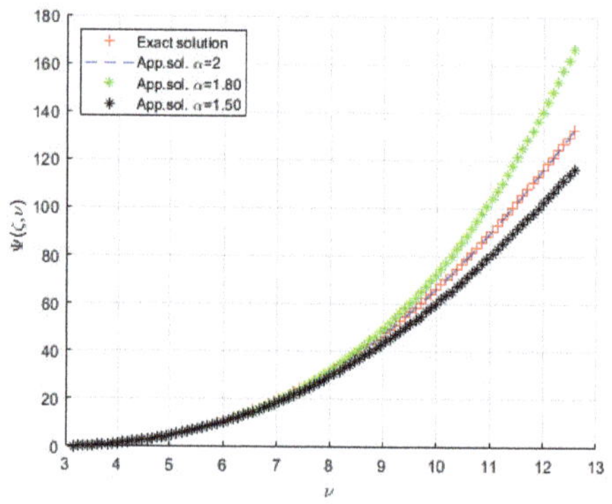

Figure 2. $\psi(\zeta, \nu) = \zeta^2 \sin \nu$.

In the next example, we apply the natural transform decomposition method to solve a non-constant coefficient two-dimensional partial differential equation.

Example 2. *Consider the following two-dimensional fractional wave-like equation [19]:*

$$\frac{\partial^\alpha \Psi(\zeta, \eta, \nu)}{\partial \nu^\alpha} = \frac{1}{12}\left[\zeta^2 \frac{\partial^2 \Psi(\zeta, \eta, \nu)}{\partial \zeta^2} + \eta^2 \frac{\partial^2 \Psi(\zeta, \eta, \nu)}{\partial \eta^2}\right], \ 0 < \alpha \leq 2, \nu > 0 \tag{29}$$

subject to conditions

$$\Psi(\zeta, \eta, 0) = \zeta^4, \qquad \Psi_\nu(\zeta, \eta, 0) = \eta^4 \tag{30}$$

Utilizing the NTM for both sides of Equation (29), we can obtain

$$\frac{s^\alpha}{\mu^\alpha} \mathrm{N}^+[\Psi(\zeta, \eta, \nu)] - \frac{s^{\alpha-1}}{\mu^\alpha} \Psi(\zeta, \eta, 0) - \frac{s^{\alpha-2}}{\mu^{\alpha-1}} \Psi_\nu(\zeta, \eta, 0) = \frac{1}{12} \mathrm{N}^+\left[\zeta^2 \frac{\partial^2 \Psi(\zeta, \eta, \nu)}{\partial \zeta^2} + \eta^2 \frac{\partial^2 \Psi(\zeta, \eta, \nu)}{\partial \eta^2}\right], \tag{31}$$

By placing conditions Equation (30) into Equation (31), we obtain

$$\Psi(\zeta, \eta, \nu) = \frac{1}{s}\zeta^4 + \frac{\mu}{s^2}\eta^4 + \frac{1}{12} \mathrm{N}^+\left[\zeta^2 \frac{\partial^2 \Psi(\zeta, \eta, \nu)}{\partial \zeta^2} + \eta^2 \frac{\partial^2 \Psi(\zeta, \eta, \nu)}{\partial \eta^2}\right], \tag{32}$$

Employing the inverse natural transform method of Equation (32), we have

$$\Psi(\zeta, \eta, \nu) = \zeta^4 + \eta^4 \nu + \mathrm{N}^{-1}\left[\frac{1}{12} \mathrm{N}^+\left[\zeta^2 \frac{\partial^2 \Psi(\zeta, \eta, \nu)}{\partial \zeta^2} + \eta^2 \frac{\partial^2 \Psi(\zeta, \eta, \nu)}{\partial \eta^2}\right]\right]. \tag{33}$$

Now, we suppose an infinite series solution for the Equation (13); then, Equation (33) becomes

$$\sum_{n=0}^{\infty} \Psi_n(\zeta, \eta, \nu) = \zeta^4 + \eta^4 \nu + \mathrm{N}^{-1}\left[\frac{1}{12} \mathrm{N}^+\left[\zeta^2 \sum_{n=0}^{\infty} \frac{\partial^2 \Psi_n(\zeta, \eta, \nu)}{\partial \zeta^2} + \eta^2 \sum_{n=0}^{\infty} \frac{\partial^2 \Psi_n(\zeta, \eta, \nu)}{\partial \eta^2}\right]\right] \tag{34}$$

Making both sides of Equation (34) equivalent, we have

$$\begin{aligned}
\Psi_0(\zeta,\eta,\nu) &= \zeta^4+\eta^4\nu,\\
\Psi_1(\zeta,\eta,\nu) &= \mathbb{N}^{-1}\left[\frac{1}{12}\mathbb{N}^{+}\left[\zeta^2\sum_{n=0}^{\infty}\frac{\partial^2\Psi_0(\zeta,\eta,\nu)}{\partial\zeta^2}+\eta^2\sum_{n=0}^{\infty}\frac{\partial^2\Psi_0(\zeta,\eta,\nu)}{\partial\eta^2}\right]\right]\\
&= \zeta^4\frac{\nu^{\alpha}}{\Gamma(\alpha+1)}+\eta^4\frac{\nu^{\alpha+1}}{\Gamma(\alpha+2)},\\
\Psi_2(\zeta,\eta,\nu) &= \mathbb{N}^{-1}\left[\frac{1}{12}\mathbb{N}^{+}\left[\zeta^2\sum_{n=0}^{\infty}\frac{\partial^2\Psi_1(\zeta,\eta,\nu)}{\partial\zeta^2}+\eta^2\sum_{n=0}^{\infty}\frac{\partial^2\Psi_1(\zeta,\eta,\nu)}{\partial\eta^2}\right]\right]\\
&= \zeta^4\frac{\nu^{2\alpha}}{\Gamma(2\alpha+1)}+\eta^4\frac{\nu^{2\alpha+1}}{\Gamma(2\alpha+2)},\\
\Psi_3(\zeta,\eta,\nu) &= \mathbb{N}^{-1}\left[\frac{1}{12}\mathbb{N}^{+}\left[\zeta^2\sum_{n=0}^{\infty}\frac{\partial^2\Psi_2(\zeta,\eta,\nu)}{\partial\zeta^2}+\eta^2\sum_{n=0}^{\infty}\frac{\partial^2\Psi_2(\zeta,\eta,\nu)}{\partial\eta^2}\right]\right]\\
&= \zeta^4\frac{\nu^{3\alpha}}{\Gamma(3\alpha+1)}+\eta^4\frac{\nu^{3\alpha+1}}{\Gamma(3\alpha+2)},\\
\Psi_4(\zeta,\eta,\nu) &= \mathbb{N}^{-1}\left[\frac{1}{12}\mathbb{N}^{+}\left[\zeta^2\sum_{n=0}^{\infty}\frac{\partial^2\Psi_3(\zeta,\eta,\nu)}{\partial\zeta^2}+\eta^2\sum_{n=0}^{\infty}\frac{\partial^2\Psi_3(\zeta,\eta,\nu)}{\partial\eta^2}\right]\right]\\
&= \zeta^4\frac{\nu^{4\alpha}}{\Gamma(4\alpha+1)}+\eta^4\frac{\nu^{4\alpha+1}}{\Gamma(4\alpha+2)},\\
\Psi_5(\zeta,\eta,\nu) &= \mathbb{N}^{-1}\left[\frac{1}{12}\mathbb{N}^{+}\left[\zeta^2\sum_{n=0}^{\infty}\frac{\partial^2\Psi_4(\zeta,\eta,\nu)}{\partial\zeta^2}+\eta^2\sum_{n=0}^{\infty}\frac{\partial^2\Psi_4(\zeta,\eta,\nu)}{\partial\eta^2}\right]\right]\\
&= \zeta^4\frac{\nu^{5\alpha}}{\Gamma(5\alpha+1)}+\eta^4\frac{\nu^{5\alpha+1}}{\Gamma(5\alpha+2)},\\
&\vdots
\end{aligned}$$

The NTDM solution is

$$\begin{aligned}
\Psi(\zeta,\eta,\nu) &= \Psi_0(\zeta,\eta,\nu)+\Psi_1(\zeta,\eta,\nu)+\Psi_2(\zeta,\eta,\nu)+\Psi_3(\zeta,\eta,\nu)+\Psi_4(\zeta,\eta,\nu)+\cdots\\
\Psi(\zeta,\eta,\nu) &= \zeta^4+\eta^4\nu+\zeta^4\frac{\nu^{\alpha}}{\Gamma(\alpha+1)}+\eta^4\frac{\nu^{\alpha+1}}{\Gamma(\alpha+2)}\\
&+\zeta^4\frac{\nu^{2\alpha}}{\Gamma(2\alpha+1)}+\eta^4\frac{\nu^{2\alpha+1}}{\Gamma(2\alpha+2)}+\zeta^4\frac{\nu^{3\alpha}}{\Gamma(3\alpha+1)}\\
&+\eta^4\frac{\nu^{3\alpha+1}}{\Gamma(3\alpha+2)}+\zeta^4\frac{\nu^{4\alpha}}{\Gamma(4\alpha+1)}+\eta^4\frac{\nu^{4\alpha+1}}{\Gamma(4\alpha+2)}\\
&+\zeta^4\frac{\nu^{5\alpha}}{\Gamma(5\alpha+1)}+\eta^4\frac{\nu^{5\alpha+1}}{\Gamma(5\alpha+2)}+\cdots
\end{aligned} \tag{35}$$

If we substitute $\alpha=2$, in Equation (35), the approximate solution of Equation (29) becomes

$$\begin{aligned}
\Psi(\zeta,\eta,\nu) &= \zeta^4\left[1+\frac{\nu^2}{2!}+\frac{\nu^4}{4!}+\frac{\nu^6}{6!}+\frac{\nu^8}{8!}+\cdots\right]\\
&+\eta^4\left[\nu+\frac{\nu^3}{3!}+\frac{\nu^5}{5!}+\frac{\nu^7}{7!}+\frac{\nu^9}{9!}+\cdots\right],
\end{aligned}$$

Hence, the exact solution of Equation (29) in a closed form is

$$\Psi(\zeta,\eta,\nu)=\zeta^4\cosh(\nu)+\eta^4\sinh(\nu)$$

Figure 3: The exact and approximate solutions $\Psi(\zeta,\eta,z,\nu)$ for Example 2 when $\alpha = 2$.

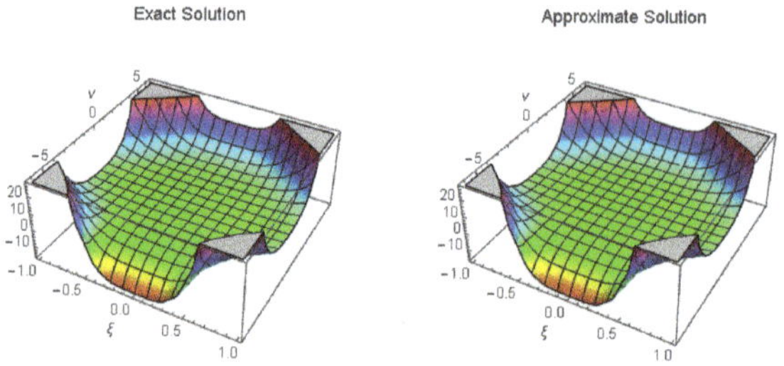

Figure 3. $\Psi(\zeta,\eta,\nu) = \zeta^4\cosh(\nu) + \eta^4\sinh(\nu)$

Figure 4: The exact and approximate solutions $\Psi(\zeta,\eta,z,\nu)$ for Example 2 when $\alpha = 2$, 1.5, 1.

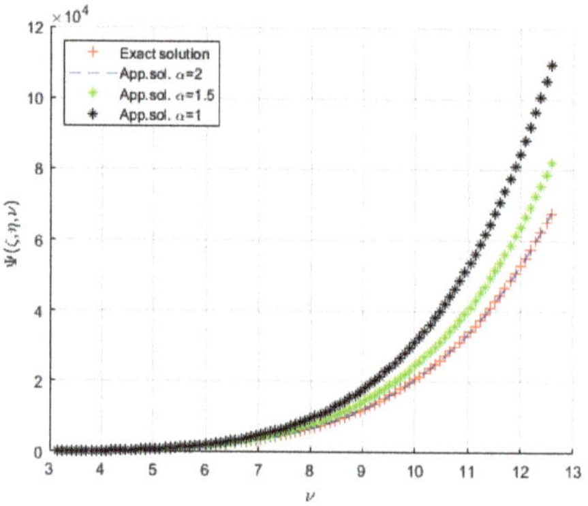

Figure 4. $\Psi(\zeta,\eta,\nu) = \zeta^4\cosh(\nu) + \eta^4\sinh(\nu)$.

Example 3. *Consider the 3D fractional heat equation [19]:*

$$\frac{\partial^\alpha\Psi(\zeta,\eta,z,\nu)}{\partial\nu^\alpha} = \frac{1}{36}\left[\zeta^2\frac{\partial^2\Psi(\zeta,\eta,z,\nu)}{\partial\zeta^2} + \eta^2\frac{\partial^2\Psi(\zeta,\eta,z,\nu)}{\partial\eta^2} + z^2\frac{\partial^2\Psi(\zeta,\eta,z,\nu)}{\partial z^2}\right] + \zeta^4\eta^4z^4$$
$$0 < \alpha \le 1, \tag{36}$$

with conditions

$$\Psi(\zeta,\eta,z,0) = 0. \tag{37}$$

Applying the NTM to both sides of Equation (36), we obtain

$$\frac{s^\alpha}{\mu^\alpha}\mathbb{N}^+[\Psi(\zeta,\eta,z,\nu)] - \frac{s^{\alpha-1}}{\mu^\alpha}\Psi(\zeta,\eta,z,0) =$$
$$\mathbb{N}^+\left[\frac{1}{36}\left[\zeta^2\frac{\partial^2\Psi(\zeta,\eta,z,\nu)}{\partial\zeta^2} + \eta^2\frac{\partial^2\Psi(\zeta,\eta,z,\nu)}{\partial\eta^2} + z^2\frac{\partial^2\Psi(\zeta,\eta,z,\nu)}{\partial z^2}\right]\right]$$
$$+\mathbb{N}^+\left[\zeta^4\eta^4z^4\right] \tag{38}$$

Taking the inverse NTM of Equation (38), we have

$$\begin{aligned}\Psi(\zeta,\eta,z,\nu) &= \mathbb{N}^{-1}\left[\frac{\Psi(\zeta,\eta,z,0)}{s}+\frac{\mu^{\alpha}}{s^{\alpha}}\mathbb{N}^{+}\left[\zeta^{4}\eta^{4}z^{4}\right]\right]\\ &+\mathbb{N}^{-1}\left[\frac{\mu^{\alpha}}{s^{\alpha}}\mathbb{N}^{+}\frac{1}{36}\left[\zeta^{2}\frac{\partial^{2}\Psi(\zeta,\eta,z,\nu)}{\partial\zeta^{2}}+\eta^{2}\frac{\partial^{2}\Psi(\zeta,\eta,z,\nu)}{\partial\eta^{2}}\right]\right]\\ &+\mathbb{N}^{-1}\left[\frac{\mu^{\alpha}}{s^{\alpha}}\mathbb{N}^{+}\frac{1}{36}\left[z^{2}\frac{\partial^{2}\Psi(\zeta,\eta,z,\nu)}{\partial z^{2}}\right]\right]\end{aligned} \tag{39}$$

Then, Equation (39) becomes

$$\begin{aligned}&\Psi_{0}(\zeta,\eta,z,\nu)=\zeta^{4}\eta^{4}z^{4}\frac{\nu^{\alpha}}{\Gamma(\alpha+1)},\\ &\sum_{n=0}^{\infty}\Psi_{n+1}(\zeta,\eta,z,\nu)=\mathbb{N}^{-1}\left[\frac{\mu^{\alpha}}{s^{\alpha}}\mathbb{N}^{+}\frac{1}{36}\left[\zeta^{2}\sum_{n=0}^{\infty}\frac{\partial^{2}\Psi_{n}}{\partial\zeta^{2}}+\eta^{2}\sum_{n=0}^{\infty}\frac{\partial^{2}\Psi_{n}}{\partial\eta^{2}}\right]\right]\\ &+\mathbb{N}^{-1}\left[\frac{\mu^{\alpha}}{s^{\alpha}}\mathbb{N}^{+}\frac{1}{36}\left[z^{2}\sum_{n=0}^{\infty}\frac{\partial^{2}\Psi_{n}}{\partial z^{2}}\right]\right]\end{aligned} \tag{40}$$

For $n=0$,

$$\begin{aligned}\Psi_{1}(\zeta,\eta,z,\nu) &= \mathbb{N}^{-1}\left[\frac{\mu^{\alpha}}{s^{\alpha}}\mathbb{N}^{+}\frac{1}{36}\left[\zeta^{2}\frac{\partial^{2}\Psi_{0}}{\partial\zeta^{2}}+\eta^{2}\frac{\partial^{2}\Psi_{0}}{\partial\eta^{2}}+z^{2}\frac{\partial^{2}\Psi_{0}}{\partial z^{2}}\right]\right]\\ &= \mathbb{N}^{-1}\left[\zeta^{4}\eta^{4}z^{4}\frac{\mu^{2\alpha}}{s^{2\alpha+1}}\right]\\ &= \zeta^{4}\eta^{4}z^{4}\frac{\nu^{2\alpha}}{\Gamma(2\alpha+1)},\end{aligned} \tag{41}$$

The subsequent terms are given as follows:

$$\begin{aligned}\Psi_{2}(\zeta,\eta,z,\nu) &= \mathbb{N}^{-1}\left[\frac{\mu^{\alpha}}{s^{\alpha}}\mathbb{N}^{+}\frac{1}{36}\left[\zeta^{2}\frac{\partial^{2}\Psi_{1}}{\partial\zeta^{2}}+\eta^{2}\frac{\partial^{2}\Psi_{1}}{\partial\eta^{2}}+z^{2}\frac{\partial^{2}\Psi_{1}}{\partial z^{2}}\right]\right]\\ &= \zeta^{4}\eta^{4}z^{4}\frac{\nu^{3\alpha}}{\Gamma(3\alpha+1)},\\ \Psi_{3}(\zeta,\eta,z,\nu) &= \mathbb{N}^{-1}\left[\frac{\mu^{\alpha}}{s^{\alpha}}\mathbb{N}^{+}\frac{1}{36}\left[\zeta^{2}\frac{\partial^{2}\Psi_{2}}{\partial\zeta^{2}}+\eta^{2}\frac{\partial^{2}\Psi_{2}}{\partial\eta^{2}}+z^{2}\frac{\partial^{2}\Psi_{2}}{\partial z^{2}}\right]\right]\\ &= \zeta^{4}\eta^{4}z^{4}\frac{\nu^{4\alpha}}{\Gamma(4\alpha+1)},\\ \Psi_{4}(\zeta,\eta,z,\nu) &= \mathbb{N}^{-1}\left[\frac{\mu^{\alpha}}{s^{\alpha}}\mathbb{N}^{+}\frac{1}{36}\left[\zeta^{2}\frac{\partial^{2}\Psi_{3}}{\partial\zeta^{2}}+\eta^{2}\frac{\partial^{2}\Psi_{3}}{\partial\eta^{2}}+z^{2}\frac{\partial^{2}\Psi_{3}}{\partial z^{2}}\right]\right]\\ &= \zeta^{4}\eta^{4}z^{4}\frac{\nu^{5\alpha}}{\Gamma(5\alpha+1)},\\ \Psi_{5}(\zeta,\eta,z,\nu) &= \mathbb{N}^{-1}\left[\frac{\mu^{\alpha}}{s^{\alpha}}\mathbb{N}^{+}\frac{1}{36}\left[\zeta^{2}\frac{\partial^{2}\Psi_{4}}{\partial\zeta^{2}}+\eta^{2}\frac{\partial^{2}\Psi_{4}}{\partial\eta^{2}}+z^{2}\frac{\partial^{2}\Psi_{4}}{\partial z^{2}}\right]\right]\\ &= \zeta^{4}\eta^{4}z^{4}\frac{\nu^{6\alpha}}{\Gamma(6\alpha+1)},\\ &\vdots\end{aligned} \tag{42}$$

The approximate solution of Equation (42) is denoted by

$$\begin{aligned}\Psi(\zeta,\eta,z,\nu) &= \Psi_0+\Psi_1+\Psi_2+\Psi_3+\Psi_4+\Psi_5+\Psi_6+\cdots\\ \Psi(\zeta,\eta,z,\nu) &= \zeta^4\eta^4z^4\left[\frac{\nu^{\alpha}}{\Gamma(\alpha+1)}+\frac{\nu^{2\alpha}}{\Gamma(2\alpha+1)}+\frac{\nu^{3\alpha}}{\Gamma(3\alpha+1)}\right]\\ &\quad+\zeta^4\eta^4z^4\left[\frac{\nu^{4\alpha}}{\Gamma(4\alpha+1)}+\frac{\nu^{5\alpha}}{\Gamma(5\alpha+1)}+\cdots\right]\end{aligned} \tag{43}$$

By letting $\alpha = 1$ in Equation (43), we have

$$\Psi(\zeta,\eta,z,\nu) = \zeta^4\eta^4z^4\left[\nu+\frac{\nu^2}{2}+\frac{\nu^3}{6}+\frac{\nu^4}{24}+\frac{\nu^5}{120}+\cdots\right] \tag{44}$$

Therefore, the solution of Equation (36) is provided by

$$\Psi(\zeta,\eta,z,\nu) = \zeta^4\eta^4z^4[e^{\nu}-1]$$

Figure 5: The exact and approximate solutions $\Psi(\zeta,\eta,z,\nu)$ for Example 3 when $\alpha = 2$.

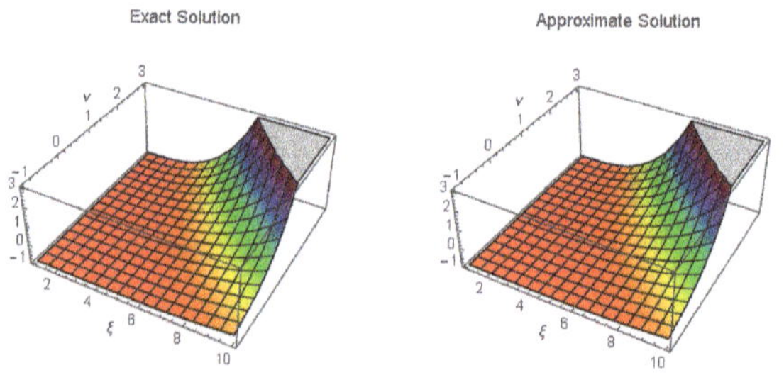

Figure 5. $\Psi(\zeta,\eta,z,\nu) = \zeta^4\eta^4z^4[e^{\nu}-1]$.

Figure 6: The exact and approximate solutions $\Psi(\zeta,\eta,z,\nu)$ for Example 3 when $\alpha =$ 1, 0.80, 0.50.

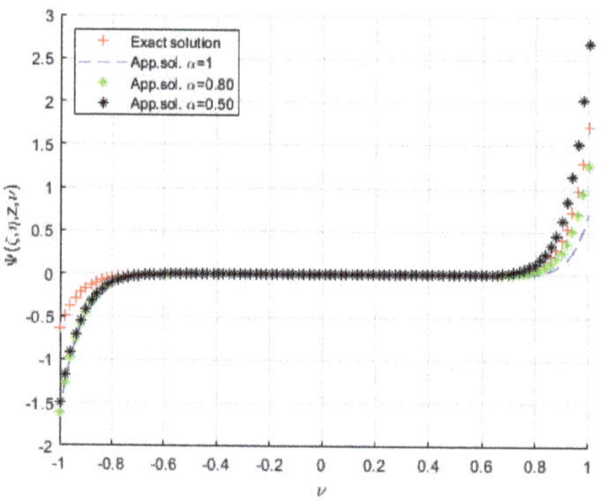

Figure 6. $\Psi(\zeta,\eta,z,\nu) = \zeta^4\eta^4z^4[e^{\nu}-1]$.

In the next example, we apply the natural transform decomposition method to solve the homogeneous time-fractional gas dynamics equation.

Example 4. *Consider the following homogeneous time-fractional gas dynamics equation [27]:*

$$\frac{\partial^{\alpha}\Psi(\zeta,\nu)}{\partial\nu^{\alpha}}+\Psi(\zeta,\nu)\frac{\partial\Psi(\zeta,\nu)}{\partial\zeta}-\Psi(\zeta,\nu)[1-\Psi(\zeta,\nu)]=0,\ \nu>0, 0<\alpha\leq 1, \tag{45}$$

with the initial condition

$$\Psi(\zeta,\nu)=e^{-\zeta},\quad \zeta\in\mathbb{R}. \tag{46}$$

Taking the NTM of Equation (45) and the initial condition in Equation (46), we have

$$\begin{aligned}\mathbb{N}^{+}\left[\frac{\partial^{\alpha}\Psi(\zeta,\nu)}{\partial\nu^{\alpha}}\right] &= \mathbb{N}^{+}\left[-\Psi(\zeta,\nu)\frac{\partial\Psi(\zeta,\nu)}{\partial\zeta}+\Psi(\zeta,\nu)-\Psi^{2}(\zeta,\nu)\right]\\ \mathbb{N}^{+}[\Psi(\zeta,\nu)] &= \frac{1}{s}e^{-\zeta}+\frac{\mu^{\alpha}}{s^{\alpha}}\mathbb{N}^{+}\left[-\Psi(\zeta,\nu)\frac{\partial\Psi(\zeta,\nu)}{\partial\zeta}\right]\\ &+\frac{\mu^{\alpha}}{s^{\alpha}}\mathbb{N}^{+}\left[\Psi(\zeta,\nu)-\Psi^{2}(\zeta,\nu)\right]\end{aligned} \tag{47}$$

Taking the inverse NTM of Equation (47), we obtain

$$\begin{aligned}\Psi(\zeta,\nu) &= e^{-\zeta}-\mathbb{N}^{-1}\left[\frac{\mu^{\alpha}}{s^{\alpha}}\mathbb{N}^{+}\left[\Psi(\zeta,\nu)\frac{\partial\Psi(\zeta,\nu)}{\partial\zeta}\right]\right]\\ &+\mathbb{N}^{-1}\left[\frac{\mu^{\alpha}}{s^{\alpha}}\mathbb{N}^{+}[\Psi(\zeta,\nu)]\right]-\mathbb{N}^{-1}\left[\frac{\mu^{\alpha}}{s^{\alpha}}\mathbb{N}^{+}\left[\Psi^{2}(\zeta,\nu)\right]\right]\end{aligned} \tag{48}$$

Now, we assume an infinite series solution for the Equation (48) given by the form

$$\begin{aligned}\Psi(\zeta,\nu) &= \sum_{n=0}^{\infty}\Psi_{n}(\zeta,\nu)\\ \Psi(\zeta,\nu) &= e^{-\zeta}-\mathbb{N}^{-1}\left[\frac{\mu^{\alpha}}{s^{\alpha}}\mathbb{N}^{+}\left[\Psi(\zeta,\nu)\frac{\partial\Psi(\zeta,\nu)}{\partial\zeta}\right]\right]\\ &+\mathbb{N}^{-1}\left[\frac{\mu^{\alpha}}{s^{\alpha}}\mathbb{N}^{+}[\Psi(\zeta,\nu)]\right]-\mathbb{N}^{-1}\left[\frac{\mu^{\alpha}}{s^{\alpha}}\mathbb{N}^{+}\left[\Psi^{2}(\zeta,\nu)\right]\right]\end{aligned} \tag{49}$$

The nonlinear terms $\Psi(\zeta,\nu)\frac{\partial\Psi(\zeta,\nu)}{\partial\zeta}$, and $\Psi^{2}(\zeta,\nu)$ are denoted by

$$\Psi\Psi_{\zeta}=\sum_{n=0}^{\infty}K_{n},\qquad \Psi^{2}=\sum_{n=0}^{\infty}M_{n} \tag{50}$$

where K_n and M_n are Adomian polynomials. Then, Equation (49) becomes

$$\begin{aligned}&\sum_{n=0}^{\infty}\Psi_{n}(\zeta,\nu)=e^{-\zeta}-\mathbb{N}^{-1}\left[\frac{\mu^{\alpha}}{s^{\alpha}}\mathbb{N}^{+}\left[\sum_{n=0}^{\infty}K_{n}\right]\right]\\ &+\mathbb{N}^{-1}\left[\frac{\mu^{\alpha}}{s^{\alpha}}\mathbb{N}^{+}[\Psi_{n}]\right]-\mathbb{N}^{-1}\left[\frac{\mu^{\alpha}}{s^{\alpha}}\mathbb{N}^{+}\left[\sum_{n=0}^{\infty}M_{n}\right]\right],\end{aligned} \tag{51}$$

The nonlinear term K_n and M_n are expressed as

$$\begin{aligned}K_{0} &= \Psi_{0}\Psi_{0\zeta},\\ K_{1} &= \Psi_{0}\Psi_{1\zeta}+\Psi_{1}\Psi_{0\zeta},\\ K_{2} &= \Psi_{0}\Psi_{2\zeta}+\Psi_{1}\Psi_{1\zeta}+\Psi_{2}\Psi_{0\zeta},\\ K_{3} &= \Psi_{0}\Psi_{3\zeta}+\Psi_{1}\Psi_{2\zeta}+\Psi_{2}\Psi_{1\zeta}+\Psi_{3}\Psi_{0\zeta},\\ &\vdots\end{aligned} \tag{52}$$

and

$$\begin{aligned} M_0 &= \Psi_0^2, \\ M_1 &= 2\Psi_0\Psi_1, \\ M_2 &= 2\Psi_0\Psi_2 + \Psi_1^2, \\ &\vdots \end{aligned} \tag{53}$$

Making both sides of Equation (51) equivalent, we can obtain

$$\begin{aligned} \Psi_0(\zeta,\nu) &= e^{-\zeta}, \\ \Psi_1(\zeta,\nu) &= -\mathrm{N}^{-1}\left[\frac{\mu^\alpha}{s^\alpha}\mathrm{N}^+[\Psi_0\Psi_{0\zeta}]\right] \\ &\quad +\mathrm{N}^{-1}\left[\frac{\mu^\alpha}{s^\alpha}\mathrm{N}^+[\Psi_0]\right] - \mathrm{N}^{-1}\left[\frac{\mu^\alpha}{s^\alpha}\mathrm{N}^+\left[\Psi_0^2\right]\right] \\ &= e^{-\zeta}\frac{\nu^\alpha}{\Gamma(\alpha+1)}, \\ \Psi_2(\zeta,\nu) &= -\mathrm{N}^{-1}\left[\frac{\mu^\alpha}{s^\alpha}\mathrm{N}^+[\Psi_0\Psi_{1\zeta}+\Psi_1\Psi_{0\zeta}]\right] \\ &\quad +\mathrm{N}^{-1}\left[\frac{\mu^\alpha}{s^\alpha}\mathrm{N}^+[\Psi_1]\right] - \mathrm{N}^{-1}\left[\frac{\mu^\alpha}{s^\alpha}\mathrm{N}^+[2\Psi_0\Psi_1]\right] \\ &= e^{-\zeta}\frac{\nu^{2\alpha}}{\Gamma(2\alpha+1)}, \\ \Psi_3(\zeta,\nu) &= -\mathrm{N}^{-1}\left[\frac{\mu^\alpha}{s^\alpha}\mathrm{N}^+[\Psi_0\Psi_{2\zeta}+\Psi_1\Psi_{1\zeta}+\Psi_2\Psi_{0\zeta}]\right] \\ &\quad +\mathrm{N}^{-1}\left[\frac{\mu^\alpha}{s^\alpha}\mathrm{N}^+[\Psi_3]\right] - \mathrm{N}^{-1}\left[\frac{\mu^\alpha}{s^\alpha}\mathrm{N}^+[\Psi_0\Psi_3+\Psi_1\Psi_2]\right] \\ &= e^{-\zeta}\frac{\nu^{3\alpha}}{\Gamma(3\alpha+1)}, \\ \Psi_4(\zeta,\nu) &= -\mathrm{N}^{-1}\left[\frac{\mu^\alpha}{s^\alpha}\mathrm{N}^+[\Psi_0\Psi_{3\zeta}+\Psi_1\Psi_{2\zeta}+\Psi_2\Psi_{1\zeta}+\Psi_3\Psi_{0\zeta}]\right] \\ &\quad +\mathrm{N}^{-1}\left[\frac{\mu^\alpha}{s^\alpha}\mathrm{N}^+[\Psi_3]\right] - \mathrm{N}^{-1}\left[\frac{\mu^\alpha}{s^\alpha}\mathrm{N}^+\left[2\Psi_0\Psi_2+\Psi_1^2\right]\right] \\ &= e^{-\zeta}\frac{\nu^{4\alpha}}{\Gamma(4\alpha+1)}, \\ &\vdots \end{aligned} \tag{54}$$

The above equation becomes

$$\begin{aligned} \Psi(\zeta,\nu) &= \sum_{n=0}^{\infty}\Psi_n(\zeta,\nu) \\ &= \Psi_0(\zeta,\nu)+\Psi_1(\zeta,\nu)+\Psi_2(\zeta,\nu)+\Psi_3(\zeta,\nu)+\Psi_4(\zeta,\nu)+\cdots \\ &= e^{-\zeta}\left[1+\frac{\nu^\alpha}{\Gamma(\alpha+1)}+\frac{\nu^{2\alpha}}{\Gamma(2\alpha+1)}+\frac{\nu^{3\alpha}}{\Gamma(3\alpha+1)}+\frac{\nu^{4\alpha}}{\Gamma(4\alpha+1)}+\cdots\right] \\ &= e^{-\zeta}\sum_{n=0}^{\infty}\frac{\nu^{n\alpha}}{\Gamma(n\alpha+1)}, \end{aligned} \tag{55}$$

take $\alpha = 1$, the approximate solution of Equation (55) given by

$$\Psi(\zeta,\nu) = e^{-\zeta}\left[1+\frac{\nu}{1!}+\frac{\nu^2}{2!}+\frac{\nu^3}{3!}+\frac{\nu^4}{4!}+\cdots\right]$$

the solution of Equation (45) is denoted by

$$\Psi(\zeta, \nu) = e^{-\zeta+\nu}$$

Figure 7: The exact and approximate solutions $\Psi(\zeta, \nu)$ for Example 4 when $\alpha = 2$.

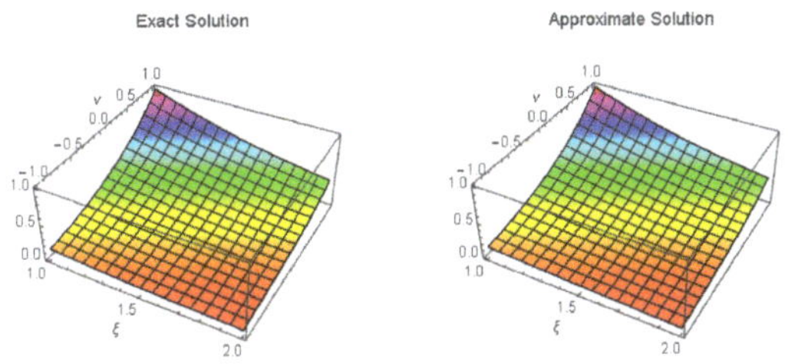

Figure 7. $\Psi(\zeta, \nu) = e^{-\zeta+\nu}$.

Figure 8: The exact and approximate solutions $\Psi(\zeta, \nu)$ for Example 4 when $\alpha = 1, 0.80, 0.50$.

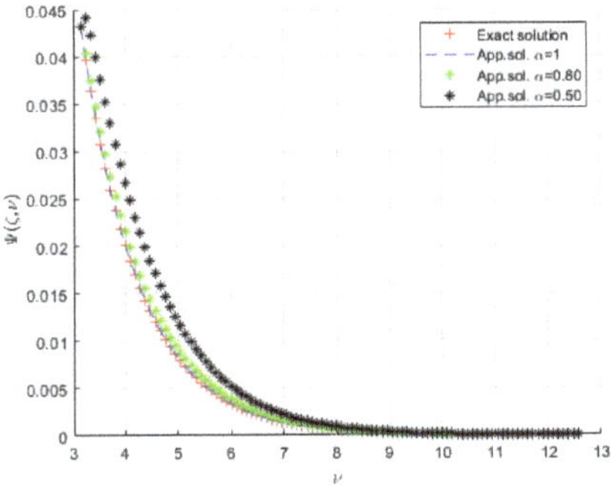

Figure 8. $\Psi(\zeta, \nu) = e^{-\zeta+\nu}$.

The introduced paper's purpose is to obtain analytical and numerical solutions for (NTDM) more precisely. In Tables 1–4, we show a comparison between the absolute errors for the obtained numerical results and the exact solution.

Table 1. Comparison of the absolute errors for the obtained numerical results and the exact solution for Example 1, for $\alpha = 2, 1.80$, and 1.5.

ζ	ν	$\alpha = 2$	$\alpha = 1.8$	$\alpha = 1.5$	Exact	Absolute Error
	0.5	0.0299640962	0.0293796164	0.0280835396	0.0299640962	0
0.25	0.75	0.0513947958	0.0452272241	0.0384946707	0.0426024225	0.0087923732
	1	0.0734500746	0.0501614436	0.0460926237	0.0010907754	0.0723592991
	0.5	0.1302738263	0.1175184656	0.1123341583	01198563846	0.0104174417
0.50	0.75	0.2055791830	0.1809088961	0.153976827	0.1704096900	0.035169493
	1	0.2938002984	0.2006457422	0.184370449	0.0043631016	0.2894371968
	0.5	0.5210953055	0.4700738629	0.4493366329	0.4794255386	0.0416697669
1	0.75	0.8223167320	0.7236355851	0.6159147310	0.6816387600	0.140677972
	1	1.175201193	0.8025829685	0.7374819794	0.0174524064	1.157748787

Table 2. Comparison of the absolute errors for the obtained numerical results and the exact solution for Example 2, when $\zeta = \eta = 0.25, 0.50$, and 1.

ζ	ν	$\alpha = 2$	$\alpha = 1.8$	$\alpha = 1.5$	Exact	Absolute Error
	0.5	0.0064403174	0.0066750912	0.0072013111	0.0064403174	1×10^{-12}
0.25	0.75	0.0082695312	0.0084681072	00096675856	0.0082695313	6.7×10^{-11}
	1	0.0106182872	0.0074431273	0.0128345819	0.0106182883	1.19×10^{-9}
	0.5	0.1030451762	0.1070299290	0.1152209783	0.0130450794	9.68×10^{-8}
0.50	0.75	0.1323130518	0.0885159904	0.1546813706	0.1323125010	5.508×10^{-7}
	1	0.1698925954	0.1190900375	0.2053533103	0.1698926143	1.89×10^{-8}
	0.5	1.648721270	1.708823359	1.843435654	1.648721270	0
1	0.75	2.117000000	2.232441653	2.474901931	2.117000017	1.7×10^{-8}
	1	2.718281526	1.905440600	3.285652963	2.718281828	3.02×10^{-7}

Table 3. Comparison of the absolute errors for the obtained numerical results and the exact solution for Example 3, when $\zeta = \nu = z = 0.25, 0.50, 1$.

ζ	ν	$\alpha = 1$	$\alpha = 0.80$	$\alpha = 0.50$	Exact	Absolute Error
	0.5	0.386654×10^{-7}	0.481388×10^{-7}	0.103833×10^{-6}	0.386668×10^{-7}	1.39203×10^{-12}
0.25	0.75	0.665619×10^{-7}	0.841673×10^{-7}	0.157573×10^{-6}	0.665783×10^{-7}	1.647378×10^{-11}
	1	0.102321×10^{-6}	0.129654×10^{-6}	0.219436×10^{-6}	1.024175×10^{-7}	9.62711×10^{-11}
	0.5	0.0001583735	0.0001971769	0.0004253023	1.583792×10^{-7}	5.7017×10^{-9}
0.50	0.75	0.0002726376	0.0003447496	0.0006454195	2.727050×10^{-7}	6.74765×10^{-8}
	1	0.0004191080	0.0005869575	0.0008988117	4.195023×10^{-7}	3.9432705×10^{-7}
	0.5	0.6486979167	0.8076367013	1.742038385	0.6487212707	2.3354×10^{-5}
1	0.75	1.116723633	1.412094400	2.643638290	1.117000017	2.76384×10^{-4}
	1	1.716666667	2.175242941	3.681533056	1.718281828	1.615161×10^{-3}

Table 4. Comparison of the absolute errors for the obtained numerical results and the exact solution for Example 4, with $\alpha = 1, 0.80$, and 0.5.

ζ	ν	$\alpha = 1$	$\alpha = 0.80$	$\alpha = 0.50$	Exact	Absolute Error
	0.5	1.284007229	1.501210297	2.135501642	1.284025417	1.8188×10^{-5}
0.25	0.75	1.648506023	1.968100996	2.837668354	1.648721271	2.15248×10^{-4}
	1	2.115742127	2.553826345	3.645981610	2.117000017	1.25789×10^{-3}
	0.5	0.999985352	1.169143755	1.663130351	1	1.415448×10^{-5}
0.50	0.75	1.283857782	1.532758597	2.209978336	1.284025417	1.67635×10^{-4}
	1	1.647741626	1.988921957	2.839493333	1.648721271	9.79645×10^{-4}
	0.5	0.6065220684	0.7091215329	1.008739549	0.6065306597	8.5913×10^{-6}
1	0.75	0.7786991072	0.9296650831	1.340419618	0.7788007831	1.01659×10^{-4}
	1	0.9994058152	1.206342147	1.722239764	1	5.941848×10^{-4}

5. Conclusions

The authors in this work successfully executed the natural transform decomposition method (NTDM) to acquire the approximate solutions of (1+3)-dimensional fractional nonlinear partial differential equations. We have also offered three test problems. The simplicity and high precision of the method show that this technique can be involved in many nonlinear partial differential equations. The NTDM presents a significant improvement in the field over the existing methods such as the optimal homotopy asymptotic method (OHAM) and fractional homotopy analysis transform method (FHATM). In addition to the currently presented methods, it is noteworthy to highlight the discontinuous Galerkin method [28] as a novel and efficient alternative for solving fractional-order linear and nonlinear partial differential equations. Its application to these equations holds substantial potential and can produce promising outcomes. Mathematica software package was applied to obtain the numerical results and graphs.

Author Contributions: Methodology, M.R.G. and H.E.; Writing—original draft, M.R.G.; Writing—review and editing, H.E. All authors have read and agreed to the published version of the manuscript.

Funding: The author would like to extend their sincere appreciation to Researchers Supporting Project number (RSPD 2023R948), King Saud University, Riyadh, Saudi Arabia.

Data Availability Statement: Not applicable.

Conflicts of Interest: The authors declare no conflict of interest.

References

1. Caputo, M. *Elasticitae Dissipazione*; Zanichelli: Bologna, Italy, 1969.
2. Caputo, M.; Mainardi, F. Linear models of dissipation in anelastic solids. *Riv. del Nuovo Cimento.* **1971**, *1*, 161–198. [CrossRef]
3. Garg, M.; Manohar, P. Numerical solution of fractional diffusion-wave equation with two space variables by matrix method. *Fract. Calc. Appl. Anal.* **2019**, *13*, 191–207.
4. Kilbas, A.A.; Srivastava, H.M.; Trujillo, J.J. *Theory and Applications of Fractional Differential Equations*; Elsevier: Amsterdam, The Netherlands, 2006.
5. Rawashdeh, M. An efficient approach for time-fractional damped Burger and time-sharma-tasso-Olver equations using the FRDTM. *Appl. Math. Inf. Sci.* **2015**, *9*, 1239–1246.
6. Patel, T.; Meher, R. Thermal Analysis of porous fin with uniform magnetic field using Adomian decomposition Sumudu transform method. *Nonlinear Eng.* **2017**, *6*, 191–200. [CrossRef]
7. Patel, T.; Patel, H.; Meher, R. Analytical study of atmospheric internal waves model with fractional approach. *JOES* **2022**. [CrossRef]
8. Omran, M.; Kiliçman, A. Natural transform of fractional order and some properties. *Cogent Math.* **2016**, *3*, 1251874. [CrossRef]
9. Kazem, S. Exact solution of some linear fractional differential equations by Laplace transform. *Int. J.Nonlinear Sci.* **2013**, *16*, 3–11.
10. Odibat, Z.; Momani, S.; Erturk, V.S. Generalized differential transform method: Application to differential equations of fractional order. *Appl. Math. Comput.* **2008**, *197*, 467–477. [CrossRef]
11. Inc, M. The approximate and exact solutions of the space- and time-fractional Burgers equations with initial conditions by variational iteration method. *J. Math. Anal. Appl.* **2008**, *345*, 476–484. [CrossRef]
12. Garg, M.; Sharma, A. Solution of space-time fractional telegraph equation by Adomian decomposition method. *J. Inequal. Spec. Funct.* **2011**, *2*, 1–7.
13. Ray, S.S.; Bera, R.K. An approximate solution of a nonlinear fractional differential equation by Adomian decomposition method. *Appl. Math. Comput.* **2005**, *167*, 561–571.
14. Rawashdeh, M.; Solving, M.S. Nonlinear ordinary differential equations using the NDM. *J. Appl. Anal. Comput.* **2015**, *5*, 77–88.
15. Rawashdeh, M.S.; Al-Jammal, H. New approximate solutions to fractional nonlinear systems of partial differential equations using the FNDM. *Adv. Differ. Equ.* **2016**, *2016*, 235. [CrossRef]
16. Rawashdeh, M.; Maitama, S. Finding exact solutions of nonlinear PDEs using the natural decomposition method. *Math. Methods Appl. Sci.* **2017**, *40*, 223–236. [CrossRef]
17. Cherif, M.H.; Ziane, D.; Belghaba, K. Fractional natural decomposition method for solving fractional system of nonlinear equations of unsteady flow of a polytropic gas. *Nonlinear Stud.* **2018**, *25*, 753–764.
18. Eltayeb, H.; Abdalla, Y.T.; Bachar, I.; Khabir, M.H. Fractional telegraph equation and its solution by natural transform decomposition method. *Symmetry* **2019**, *11*, 334. [CrossRef]
19. Sarwar, S.; Alkhalaf, S.; Iqbal, S.; Zahid, M.A. A note on optimal homotopy asymptotic method for the solutions of fractional order heat- and wave-like partial differential equations. *Comput. Math. Appl.* **2015**, *70*, 942–953. [CrossRef]
20. Katatbeh, Q.D.; Belgacem, F.B.M. Applications of the Sumudu transform to fractional differential equations. *Nonlinear Stud. J.* **2011**, *18*, 99–112.
21. Kumar, D.; Singh, J.; An, K.A. Efficient approach for fractional Harry Dym equation by using Sumudu transform. *Abstr. Appl. Anal.* **2013**, *2013*, 608943. [CrossRef]
22. Khan, Z.H.; Khan, W.A. N-transform properties and applications. *NUST J. Eng. Sci.* **2008**, *1*, 127–133.

23. Belgacem, F.B.M.; Silambarasan, R. Theory of natural transform. *Math. Eng. Sci. Aerosp. (MESA)* **2012**, *3*, 99–124.
24. Marin, M.; Marinescu, C. Thermoelasticity of initially stressed bodies, asymptotic equipartition of energies. *Int. J. Eng. Sci.* **1998**, *36*, 73–86. [CrossRef]
25. Rawashdeh, M.S.; Al-Jammal, H. Theories and Applications of the Inverse Fractional Natural Transform Method. *Adv. Differ.* **2018**, *2018*, 222. [CrossRef]
26. Hilfer, R. *Applications of Fractional Calculus in Physics*; World Scientific: Singapore, 2000.
27. Kumar, S.; Rashidi, M. New analytical method for gas dynamics equation arising in shock fronts. *Comput. Phys. Commun.* **2014**, *185*, 1947–1954. [CrossRef]
28. Baccouch, M.; Temimi, H. A high-order space-time ultra-weak discontinuous Galerkin method for the second-order wave equation in one space dimension. *J. Comput. Appl. Math.* **2021**, *389*, 113331. [CrossRef]

Disclaimer/Publisher's Note: The statements, opinions and data contained in all publications are solely those of the individual author(s) and contributor(s) and not of MDPI and/or the editor(s). MDPI and/or the editor(s) disclaim responsibility for any injury to people or property resulting from any ideas, methods, instructions or products referred to in the content.

axioms

Article

More Effective Criteria for Testing the Asymptotic and Oscillatory Behavior of Solutions of a Class of Third-Order Functional Differential Equations

Fahd Masood [1], Osama Moaaz [2,*], Ghada AlNemer [3] and Hamdy El-Metwally [1]

1 Department of Mathematics, Faculty of Science, Mansoura University, Mansoura 35516, Egypt; fahdmasoud22@gmail.com (F.M.); helmetwally@mans.edu.eg (H.E.-M.)
2 Department of Mathematics, College of Science, Qassim University, P.O. Box 6644, Buraydah 51452, Saudi Arabia
3 Department of Mathematical Science, College of Science, Princess Nourah bint Abdulrahman University, P.O. Box 105862, Riyadh 11656, Saudi Arabia; gnnemer@pnu.edu.sa
* Correspondence: o_moaaz@mans.edu.eg

Abstract: This paper delves into the investigation of quasi-linear neutral differential equations in the third-order canonical case. In this study, we refine the relationship between the solution and its corresponding function, leading to improved preliminary results. These enhanced results play a crucial role in excluding the existence of positive solutions to the investigated equation. By building upon the improved preliminary results, we introduce novel criteria that shed light on the nature of these solutions. These criteria help to distinguish whether the solutions exhibit oscillatory behavior or tend toward zero. Moreover, we present oscillation criteria for all solutions. To demonstrate the relevance of our results, we present an illustrative example. This example validates the theoretical framework we have developed and offers practical insights into the behavior of solutions for quasi-linear third-order neutral differential equations.

Keywords: oscillatory; nonoscillatory; delay differential equation; third-order; canonical

MSC: 34C10; 34K11

Citation: Masood, F.; Moaaz, O.; AlNemer, G.; El-Metwally, H. More Effective Criteria for Testing the Asymptotic and Oscillatory Behavior of Solutions of a Class of Third-Order Functional Differential Equations. *Axioms* **2023**, *12*, 1112. https://doi.org/10.3390/axioms12121112

Academic Editors: Hatıra Günerhan, Francisco Martínez González, Mohammed K. A. Kaabar and Behzad Djafari-Rouhani

Received: 15 September 2023
Revised: 25 October 2023
Accepted: 30 November 2023
Published: 11 December 2023

Copyright: © 2023 by the authors. Licensee MDPI, Basel, Switzerland. This article is an open access article distributed under the terms and conditions of the Creative Commons Attribution (CC BY) license (https://creativecommons.org/licenses/by/4.0/).

1. Introduction

Third-order quasi-linear NDEs, while sounding complex, play a pivotal role in various practical applications, addressing a wide array of real-world problems. These equations emerge in fields such as engineering, physics, and biology, where they are instrumental in modeling dynamic systems exhibiting intricate interactions and time delays. By delving into their solutions and properties, we gain insights into phenomena ranging from electrical circuits with distributed parameters to the behavior of biochemical systems with feedback loops. In this paper, understanding and solving third-order quasi-linear NDEs become invaluable tools for engineers, scientists, and researchers seeking to unravel the mysteries of dynamic systems and optimize their performance in the face of delays and nonlinearities [1–3].

Delay-neutral differential equations are considered one of the most important tools used to describe and represent life models and systems with extreme accuracy. This is due to the nature of the delay-neutral differential equation, which contains both delayed and non-delayed functions. Therefore, many mechanical, physical, chemical, and other science models use delay-neutral differential equations. For example, these equations are used in describing population growth dynamics and in modeling physiological processes with neurotransmission delays, see [4]. For more applications in various sciences, please see [5–7].

In this paper, we study the oscillatory behavior of quasi-linear third-order NDEs. These equations are expressed in the following form:

$$\left(a_2(\ell)\left(\left(a_1(\ell)z'(\ell)\right)'\right)^{\alpha}\right)' + q(\ell)x^{\alpha}(\sigma(\ell)) = 0,\ \ell \geq \ell_0, \tag{1}$$

where $z(\ell) = x(\ell) + \mathrm{p}(\ell)x(\tau(\ell))$. Throughout this study, we make the following assumptions:

(H_1) α is a ratio of two positive odd integers and $\alpha > 1$;
(H_2) $q, \mathrm{p} \in C([\ell_0, \infty))$, $q(\ell) \geq 0$, and $0 \leq \mathrm{p}(\ell) < \mathrm{p}_0 < \infty$;
(H_3) $\tau, \sigma \in C^1([\ell_0, \infty))$, $\tau(\ell) \leq \ell$, $\sigma(\ell) \leq \ell$, $\tau'(\ell) \geq \tau_0 > 0$, $\sigma'(\ell) > 0$, $(\sigma^{-1}(\ell))' \geq \sigma_0 > 0$, $\tau \circ \sigma = \sigma \circ \tau$, $\lim_{\ell\to\infty} \tau(\ell) = \infty$, and $\lim_{\ell\to\infty} \sigma(\ell) = \infty$;
(H_4) $a_2 \in C^1([\ell_0, \infty))$, $a_1 \in C^2([\ell_0, \infty))$, $a_1 > 0$, $a_2 > 0$,

$$\int_{\ell_0}^{\infty} \frac{1}{a_1(s)} \mathrm{d}s = \infty, \text{ and } \int_{\ell_0}^{\infty} \frac{1}{a_2^{1/\alpha}(s)} \mathrm{d}s = \infty. \tag{2}$$

By a solution to (1), we mean a nontrivial function, $x \in C([L_x, \infty), \mathbb{R})$, $L_x \geqslant \ell_0$, which has the property z, $a_1 z'$, $a_2\left((a_1 z')'\right)^{\alpha} \in C^1([L_x, \infty), \mathbb{R})$, and satisfies (1) on $[L_x, \infty)$. We consider only those solutions x of (1) that exist on some half-line $[L_x, \infty)$ and satisfy the condition

$$\sup\{|x(\ell)| : \ell \geqslant L\} > 0, \text{ for all } L \geq L_x.$$

Differential equations (DEs) form a fundamental framework in mathematics, encompassing a variety of applications across science and engineering. Within this field, NDEs hold a special place due to their ability to model systems where the rate of change of a function is affected not only by its past behavior but also by the behavior of the delayed intermediate. This property allows NDEs to capture real-world phenomena that exhibit inherent time lags, making them invaluable tools in various fields, including biology, control theory, economics, and physics, see [8–10].

Oscillation theory, a pivotal facet of differential equation analysis, offers crucial insights into solution behaviors. Oscillatory solutions, reflecting dynamic and periodic phenomena, pervade many natural systems. Hence, investigating oscillation criteria, particularly for third-order NDEs, holds paramount importance in both theoretical and practical contexts. This paper delves into obtaining oscillation criteria for third-order NDEs, aiming to establish more precise conditions governing the occurrence of oscillations in the solutions, see [11–14].

The study of oscillation criteria for higher-order DEs has long captured significant interest within the field, see [15–18]. Notably, the analysis of third-order NDEs has received attention due to its importance in diverse scientific and engineering fields, from control theory to population dynamics. Several preceding studies have contributed valuable insights into the oscillation behavior of such equations. Researchers have proposed varied techniques and methodologies to establish conditions under which solutions of third-order NDEs either oscillate or remain nonoscillatory. These criteria often involve intricate mathematical analyses, including inequalities, integral inequalities, and comparisons with auxiliary functions, see [19–21].

Hanan [22], in 1961, studied third-order differential equations in the linear case, that is, by setting $a_1(\ell) = a_2(\ell) = 1, \alpha = 1$ in (1). She provides one of the most important conditions that cannot be weakened for (1) in the linear case by introducing the condition

$$\liminf_{t\to\infty} t^3 q(t) > \frac{2}{3\sqrt{3}}.$$

Thereafter, many works focused on this type of equation. In 2010, Saker and Džurina [23], extended the study to include the presence of α, i.e., they were interested in studying the oscillatory behavior of the delay differential equation

$$\left(a_2(\ell)(x''(\ell))^{\alpha}\right)' + q(\ell)x^{\alpha}(\sigma(\ell)) = 0.$$

They presented sufficient conditions ensuring that every solution of previous equations either oscillates or converges to zero. On the other hand, by using Riccati transformation, Thandapani and Li [24] investigated some asymptotic properties for the neutral differential equation

$$\left(a_2(\ell)(z''(\ell))^{\alpha}\right)' + q(\ell)x^{\alpha}(\sigma(\ell)) = 0, \tag{3}$$

with $0 \leq \mathrm{p}(\ell) \leq \mathrm{p}_0 < 0$. They established certain sufficient conditions guaranteeing that every solution of (3) either oscillates or converges to zero.

In 2019, Džurina et al. [25] established necessary conditions for the nonexistence of Kneser solutions in oscillation results for third-order NDEs of the following form

$$\left(a_2(\ell)(a_1(\ell)z'(\ell))'\right)' + q(\ell)x(\sigma(\ell)) = 0. \tag{4}$$

By combining their recently acquired results with pre-existing research, they ensured oscillation for all solutions of (4). In the same year, Jadlovská et al. [26] investigated the effective oscillatory criteria associated with third-order delay differential equations, represented by the form

$$\left(a_2(\ell)(a_1(\ell)x'(\ell))'\right)' + q(\ell)x(\sigma(\ell)) = 0,$$

with a specific focus on the canonical case, aiming to establish that any nonoscillatory solution converges to zero.

Following a different approach, Chatzarakis et al. [27] introduced improved criteria for oscillatory behavior in third-order NDEs with unbounded neutral coefficients, presented by the form

$$z'''(\ell) + q(\ell)x^{\alpha}(\sigma(\ell)) = 0,$$

where they introduced sharp criteria that demonstrate the nonexistence of Kneser solutions.

On the other hand, higher order equations have been studied using many methods and techniques, see for example [28,29].

This paper aims to establish more stringent and improved criteria that guarantee the oscillation of all solutions of (1) through the use of advanced mathematical tools and techniques. The proposed criteria extend current results and facilitate a deeper understanding of the oscillatory nature of tertiary NDEs, providing more space when modeling.

The rest of this paper is structured as follows. In Section 2, we introduce a set of definitions and lemmas essential for simplifying mathematical operations in our work. Section 3 is dedicated to a series of lemmas that pertain to the asymptotic properties of solutions within the class N_2. These lemmas play a pivotal role in illustrating oscillation results. Section 4 provides results that ensure the asymptotic convergence to zero of any Kneser solution. Moving on to Section 5, we combine the results from the preceding sections to articulate the main results of this paper. Finally, in Section 6, we offer an example that supports and illustrates the validity of our results.

2. Preliminary Results

In this section, we present a set of definitions and assumptions that are needed in this paper to simplify the mathematical calculations. For the sake of brevity, we define

$$\mathrm{p}_0(\ell) := (1 - \mathrm{p}(\sigma(\ell)))^{\alpha},$$

$$\phi(\ell) := \min\{q(\ell), q(\tau(\ell))\},$$

$$L_0 z = z,\ L_1 z = a_1 z',\ L_2 z = a_2\Big(\big(a_1 z'\big)'\Big)^{\alpha}, L_3 z = \Big(a_2\Big(\big(a_1 z'\big)'\Big)^{\alpha}\Big)',$$

$$\pi_1(\ell) := \int_{\ell_0}^{\ell} \frac{1}{a_1(s)} \mathrm{d}s,\ \pi_2(\ell) := \int_{\ell_0}^{\ell} \frac{1}{a_2^{1/\alpha}(s)} \mathrm{d}s,\ \pi_{12}(\ell) := \int_{\ell_0}^{\ell} \frac{\pi_2(s)}{a_1(s)} \mathrm{d}s,$$

$$\pi_1(\varsigma, \varrho) := \int_{\varrho}^{\varsigma} \frac{1}{a_1(s)} \mathrm{d}s,\ \pi_2(\varsigma, \varrho) := \int_{\varrho}^{\varsigma} \frac{1}{a_2^{1/\alpha}(s)} \mathrm{d}s,\ \pi_{12}(\varsigma, \varrho) := \int_{\varrho}^{\varsigma} \frac{\pi_2(s)}{a_1(s)} \mathrm{d}s,$$

$$F^{[0]}(\ell) := F(\ell) \text{ and } F^{[j]}(\ell) := F\Big(F^{[j-1]}(\ell)\Big), \text{ for } j = 1, 2, \ldots, n,$$

$$\mathrm{p}_1(\ell; n) := \sum_{k=0}^{n} \left(\prod_{i=0}^{2k} \mathrm{p}\Big(\tau^{[i]}(\ell)\Big) \right) \left[\frac{1}{\mathrm{p}(\tau^{[2k]}(\ell))} - 1 \right] \frac{\pi_{12}(\tau^{[2k]}(\ell))}{\pi_{12}(\ell)},$$

$$\widehat{\mathrm{p}}_1(\ell, n) := \sum_{k=1}^{n} \left(\prod_{i=1}^{2k-1} \frac{1}{\mathrm{p}(\tau^{[-i]}(\ell))} \right) \left[\frac{\pi_{12}\Big(\tau^{[-2k+1]}(\ell)\Big)}{\pi_{12}(\tau^{[-2k]}(\ell))} - \frac{1}{\mathrm{p}(\tau^{[-2k]}(\ell))} \right],$$

$$\mathrm{B}(\ell, n) := \begin{cases} \max\{\mathrm{p}_0(\ell), \mathrm{p}_1(\ell; n)\} & \text{for } p_0 < 1, \\ \widehat{\mathrm{p}}_1(\ell; n) & \text{for } p_0 > R_{12}(\ell, \ell_1)/R_{12}(\tau(\ell), \ell_1), \end{cases}$$

$$\lambda_* := \liminf_{\ell \to \infty} \frac{\pi_{12}(\ell)}{\pi_{12}(\sigma(\ell))},$$

$$\beta_* := \liminf_{\ell \to \infty} \frac{1}{\alpha} a_2^{1/\alpha}(\ell) \pi_{12}^{\alpha}(\sigma(\ell)) \pi_2(\ell) q(\ell) \mathrm{B}^{\alpha}(\sigma(\ell), n),$$

and

$$k_* := \liminf_{\ell \to \infty} \frac{\pi_2^{\beta_*}(\ell)}{\pi_{12}(\ell)} \int_{\ell_0}^{\ell} \frac{\pi_2^{1-\beta_*}(s)}{a_1(s)} \mathrm{d}s, \text{ for } \beta_* \in (0, 1).$$

Remark 1. *For our purposes, we must define the following conditions*

$$\frac{\pi_{12}(\ell)}{\pi_{12}(\sigma(\ell))} \geq \lambda, \textit{ where } \lambda \in (1, \lambda_*), \tag{5}$$

$$\frac{1}{\alpha} a_2^{1/\alpha}(\ell) \pi_{12}^{\alpha}(\sigma(\ell)) \pi_2(\ell) q(\ell) \mathrm{B}^{\alpha}(\sigma(\ell), n) \geq \beta, \textit{ where } \beta \in (0, \beta_*), \tag{6}$$

and

$$\frac{\pi_2^{\beta}(\ell)}{\pi_{12}(\ell)} \int_{\ell_0}^{\ell} \frac{\pi_2^{1-\beta}(s)}{a_1(s)} \mathrm{d}s \geq k, \textit{ where } k \in [1, \infty). \tag{7}$$

Lemma 1 ([30]). *Assume that A and B are real numbers, $A > 0$, then,*

$$BU - AU^{(\alpha+1)/\alpha} \leq \frac{\alpha^{\alpha}}{(\alpha+1)^{\alpha+1}} \frac{B^{\alpha+1}}{A^{\alpha}}. \tag{8}$$

Lemma 2 ([31]). *Assume that $x_1,\ x_2 \in [0, \infty)$. Then,*

$$(x_1 + x_2)^{\alpha} \leq \mu(x_1^{\alpha} + x_2^{\alpha})$$

and

$$\mu = \begin{cases} 1 & \textit{for } 0 < \alpha \leq 1; \\ 2^{\alpha-1} & \textit{for } \alpha > 1. \end{cases}$$

Lemma 3 ([32]). *Let $y \in C^n([\ell_0,\infty),(0,\infty))$, $y^{(i)}(\ell) > 0$ for $i = 1,2,\dots,n$, and $y^{(n+1)}(\ell) \leq 0$, eventually. Then, eventually,*

$$\frac{y(\ell)}{y'(\ell)} \geq \frac{\epsilon}{n}\ell,$$

for every $\epsilon \in (0,1)$.

Lemma 4 ([33]). *Suppose that x is a solution to (1) that is positive eventually. In such a case, z satisfies one of the following cases*

$$\begin{aligned} \mathrm{N}_1 &: \quad z > 0,\ L_1 z < 0,\ L_2 z > 0, \text{ and } L_3 z \leq 0, \\ \mathrm{N}_2 &: \quad z > 0,\ L_1 z > 0, \text{ and } L_2 z > 0, \end{aligned}$$

for ℓ large enough. The symbol Ω_i (Category Ω_i) represents the set of all solutions that are positive eventually and where the corresponding function fulfills condition (N_i) for $i = 1,2$. The solutions within the category Ω_1 are referred to as Kneser solutions.

Lemma 5 ([34]). *Assume that x is an eventually positive solution of (1). If $\mathrm{p}_0 < 1$, then, eventually*

$$x(\ell) > \sum_{k=0}^{n}\left(\prod_{i=0}^{2k} \mathrm{p}\left(\tau^{[i]}(\ell)\right)\right)\left[\frac{z\left(\tau^{[2k]}(\ell)\right)}{\mathrm{p}\left(\tau^{[2k]}(\ell)\right)} - z\left(\tau^{[2k+1]}(\ell)\right)\right],$$

for any integer $n \geq 0$.

Lemma 6. *Assume that x is an eventually positive solution of (1). If $\mathrm{p}_0 > 1$, then,*

$$x(\ell) > \sum_{k=1}^{n}\left(\prod_{i=1}^{2k-1} \frac{1}{\mathrm{p}\left(\tau^{[-k]}(\ell)\right)}\right)\left[z\left(\tau^{[-2k+1]}(\ell)\right) - \frac{1}{\mathrm{p}\left(\tau^{[-2k]}(\ell)\right)} z\left(\tau^{[-2k]}(\ell)\right)\right].$$

Proof. From

$$z(\ell) = x(\ell) + \mathrm{p}(\ell)x(\tau(\ell)),$$

we deduce that

$$\begin{aligned} x(\ell) &= \frac{1}{\mathrm{p}(\tau^{-1}(\ell))}\left[z\left(\tau^{-1}(\ell)\right) - x\left(\tau^{-1}(\ell)\right)\right] \\ &= \frac{1}{\mathrm{p}(\tau^{[-1]}(\ell))} z\left(\tau^{[-1]}(\ell)\right) \\ &\quad - \frac{1}{\mathrm{p}(\tau^{[-1]}(\ell))}\frac{1}{\mathrm{p}(\tau^{[-2]}(\ell))}\left[z\left(\tau^{[-2]}(\ell)\right) - x\left(\tau^{[-2]}(\ell)\right)\right] \\ &= \frac{1}{\mathrm{p}(\tau^{[-1]}(\ell))} z\left(\tau^{[-1]}(\ell)\right) - \prod_{i=1}^{2}\frac{1}{\mathrm{p}(\tau^{[-i]}(\ell))} z\left(\tau^{[-2]}(\ell)\right) \\ &\quad + \prod_{i=1}^{3}\frac{1}{\mathrm{p}(\tau^{[-i]}(\ell))}\left[z\left(\tau^{[-3]}(\ell)\right) - x\left(\tau^{[-3]}(\ell)\right)\right]. \end{aligned}$$

By repeating the same technique a number of times, we obtain

$$x(\ell) > \sum_{k=1}^{n}\left(\prod_{i=1}^{2k-1} \frac{1}{\mathrm{p}\left(\tau^{[i]}(\ell)\right)}\right)\left[z\left(\tau^{[-2k+1]}(\ell)\right) - \frac{1}{\mathrm{p}\left(\tau^{[-2k]}(\ell)\right)} z\left(\tau^{[-2k]}(\ell)\right)\right].$$

Therefore, we have successfully demonstrated the proof. □

3. Nonexistence of N_2-Type Solutions

In this section, we introduce several lemmas that pertain to the asymptotic properties of solutions within the class N_2. These lemmas will play a pivotal role in demonstrating our primary results regarding oscillations.

Lemma 7. *Suppose that $\beta_* > 0$ and $x \in \Omega_2$. Then for ℓ sufficiently large*
$(A_{1,1})$ $\lim_{\ell\to\infty} L_2z(\ell) = \lim_{\ell\to\infty} L_1z(\ell)/\pi_2(\ell) = \lim_{\ell\to\infty} z(\ell)/\pi_{12}(\ell) = 0$;
$(A_{1,2})$ *L_1z/π_2 is decreasing and $L_1z \geq \pi_2(L_2z)^{1/\alpha}$;*
$(A_{1,3})$ *z/π_{12} is decreasing and $x > (\pi_{12}/\pi_2)L_1z$.*

Proof. Let $x \in \Omega_2$ and choose $\ell_1 \geq \ell_0$, such that $x(\tau(\ell)) > 0$ and β satisfies (6) for $\ell \geq \ell_1$.
$(A_{1,1})$: Since L_2z is a positive decreasing function, obviously

$$\lim_{\ell\to\infty} L_2z = l \geq 0.$$

If $l > 0$, then $L_2z \geq l > 0$, and so for any $\varepsilon \in (0,1)$, we have

$$z(\ell) \geq l^{1/\alpha}\int_{\ell_1}^{\ell}\frac{1}{a_1(u)}\int_{\ell_1}^{u}\frac{1}{a_2^{1/\alpha}(s)}\mathrm{d}s\mathrm{d}u \geq \tilde{l}\pi_{12}(\ell),\ \tilde{l} = \varepsilon l^{1/\alpha}. \tag{9}$$

Since

$$z(\ell) = x(\ell) + \mathrm{p}(\ell)x(\tau(\ell)),$$

then $z(\ell) \geq x(\ell)$ and

$$\begin{aligned} x(\ell) &= z(\ell) - \mathrm{p}(\ell)x(\tau(\ell)) \\ &\geq z(\ell) - \mathrm{p}(\ell)z(\tau(\ell)). \end{aligned}$$

Since $z' > 0$, then

$$x(\ell) \geq (1 - \mathrm{p}(\ell))z(\ell).$$

Using this in (1), we obtain

$$\begin{aligned} -L_3z(\ell) &= q(\ell)x^{\alpha}(\sigma(\ell)) \\ &\geq q(\ell)(1 - \mathrm{p}(\sigma(\ell)))^{\alpha}z(\sigma(\ell))^{\alpha}. \end{aligned}$$

From (9), we find

$$-L_3z(\ell) \geq -\tilde{l}^{\alpha}q(\ell)\mathrm{B}(\ell)\pi_{12}^{\alpha}(\sigma(\ell)).$$

Integrating from ℓ_1 to ℓ, we have

$$\begin{aligned} L_2z(\ell_1) &\geq \tilde{l}^{\alpha}\int_{\ell_1}^{\ell} q(s)\mathrm{B}(s)\pi_{12}^{\alpha}(\sigma(s))\mathrm{d}s \\ &\geq \alpha\beta\tilde{l}^{\alpha}\int_{\ell_1}^{\ell}\frac{1}{a_2^{1/\alpha}(s)\pi_2(s)}\mathrm{d}s \\ &= \alpha\beta\tilde{l}^{\alpha}\ln\frac{\pi_2(\ell)}{\pi_2(\ell_1)} \to \infty \text{ as } \ell \to \infty, \end{aligned}$$

which is a contradiction. Hence, $l = 0$. Applying l'Hôpital's rule, we see that $(A_{1,1})$ holds.
$(A_{1,2})$: Using the fact that L_2z is positive and decreasing, we see that

$$\begin{aligned} L_1z(\ell) &= L_1z(\ell_1) + \int_{\ell_1}^{\ell} (L_1z(s))'\mathrm{d}s \\ &\geq L_1z(\ell_1) + \int_{\ell_1}^{\ell} \frac{L_2^{1/\alpha}z(s)}{a_2^{1/\alpha}(s)}\mathrm{d}s \\ &\geq L_1z(\ell_1) + L_2^{1/\alpha}z(\ell) \int_{\ell_1}^{\ell} \frac{1}{a_2^{1/\alpha}(s)}\mathrm{d}s \\ &= L_1z(\ell_1) + L_2^{1/\alpha}z(\ell) \int_{\ell_1}^{\ell} \frac{1}{a_2^{1/\alpha}(s)}\mathrm{d}s - L_2^{1/\alpha}z(\ell) \int_{\ell_0}^{\ell_1} \frac{1}{a_2^{1/\alpha}(s)}\mathrm{d}s. \end{aligned}$$

In view of $(A_{1,1})$, there is a $\ell_2 > \ell_1$, such that

$$L_1z(\ell_1) - L_2^{1/\alpha}z(\ell) \int_{\ell_0}^{\ell_1} \frac{1}{a_2^{1/\alpha}(s)}\mathrm{d}s > 0, \ \ell \geq \ell_2.$$

Thus

$$L_1z(\ell) > \pi_2(\ell)L_2^{1/\alpha}z(\ell),$$

and consequently

$$\left(\frac{L_1z}{\pi_2}\right)'(\ell) = \frac{\pi_2(\ell)L_2^{1/\alpha}z(\ell) - L_1z(\ell)}{a_2^{1/\alpha}(\ell)\pi_2^2(\ell)} < 0.$$

$(A_{1,3})$: Since L_1z/π_2 is a decreasing function tending to zero, then

$$\begin{aligned} z(\ell) &= z(\ell_2) + \int_{\ell_2}^{\ell} \frac{L_1z(s)}{\pi_2(s)}\frac{\pi_2(s)}{a_1(s)}\mathrm{d}s \\ &\geq z(\ell_2) + \frac{L_1z(\ell)}{\pi_2(\ell)} \int_{\ell_2}^{\ell} \frac{\pi_2(s)}{a_1(s)}\mathrm{d}s \\ &\geq z(\ell_2) + \frac{L_1z(\ell)}{\pi_2(\ell)}\pi_{12}(\ell) + \frac{L_1z(\ell)}{\pi_2(\ell)} \int_{\ell_0}^{\ell_2} \frac{\pi_2(s)}{a_1(s)}\mathrm{d}s \\ &> \frac{L_1z(\ell)}{\pi_2(\ell)}\pi_{12}(\ell). \end{aligned}$$

Therefore

$$\left(\frac{z}{\pi_{12}}\right)'(\ell) = \frac{L_1z(\ell)\pi_{12}(\ell) - z(\ell)\pi_2(\ell)}{a_1(\ell)\pi_{12}^2(\ell)} < 0.$$

□

Lemma 8. *Assume that $x \in \Omega_2$. Then*

$$x(\ell) > \mathrm{B}(\ell, n)z(\ell) \tag{10}$$

and

$$\left(a_2(\ell)\left(\left(a_1(\ell)z'(\ell)\right)'\right)^{\alpha}\right)' \leq -q(\ell)\mathrm{B}^{\alpha}(\sigma(\ell), n)z^{\alpha}(\sigma(\ell)). \tag{11}$$

Proof. If $\mathrm{p}_0 < 1$, then, due to the fact that $z(\ell)$ is increasing and $\tau^{[2k]}(\ell) \geq \tau^{[2k+1]}(\ell)$, we have

$$z(\tau^{[2k]}(\ell)) \geq z(\tau^{[2k+1]}(\ell)),$$

which, along with Lemma 5, implies that

$$\begin{aligned} x(\ell) &> \sum_{k=0}^{n} \left(\prod_{i=0}^{2k} \mathrm{p}\left(\tau^{[i]}(\ell)\right)\right) \left[\frac{z(\tau^{[2k]}(\ell))}{\mathrm{p}(\tau^{[2k]}(\ell))} - z(\tau^{[2k+1]}(\ell))\right] \\ &\geq \sum_{k=0}^{n} \left(\prod_{i=0}^{2k} \mathrm{p}\left(\tau^{[i]}(\ell)\right)\right) \left[\frac{1}{\mathrm{p}(\tau^{[2k]}(\ell))} - 1\right] z(\tau^{[2k]}(\ell)). \end{aligned} \tag{12}$$

Moreover, as z/π_{12} is decreasing and $\tau^{[2k]}(\ell) \leq \ell$, we have

$$\frac{z(\tau^{[2k]}(\ell))}{\pi_{12}(\tau^{[2k]}\ell)} \geq \frac{z(\ell)}{\pi_{12}(\ell)}$$

and

$$z(\tau^{[2k]}(\ell)) \geq \frac{\pi_{12}(\tau^{[2k]}(\ell))}{\pi_{12}(\ell)} z(\ell).$$

Thus, using the above inequality and substituting in (12), we obtain

$$\begin{aligned} x(\ell) &> \sum_{k=0}^{n} \left(\prod_{i=0}^{2k} \mathrm{p}\left(\tau^{[i]}(\ell)\right) \right) \left[\frac{1}{\mathrm{p}(\tau^{[2k]}(\ell))} - 1 \right] \frac{\pi_{12}(\tau^{[2k]}(\ell))}{\pi_{12}(\ell)} z(\ell) \\ &= \mathrm{p}_1(\ell; n) z(\ell). \end{aligned} \tag{13}$$

On the other hand, if $\mathrm{p}_0 > 1$, then z/π_{12} is decreasing and $\tau^{[-2k]}(\ell) \geq \tau^{[-2k+1]}(\ell)$, implying that

$$\frac{z\left(\tau^{[-2k+1]}(\ell)\right)}{\pi_{12}(\tau^{[-2k+1]}(\ell))} \geq \frac{z\left(\tau^{[-2k]}(\ell)\right)}{\pi_{12}(\tau^{[-2k]}(\ell))}$$

and

$$z\left(\tau^{[-2k+1]}(\ell)\right) \geq \frac{\pi_{12}\left(\tau^{[-2k+1]}(\ell)\right)}{\pi_{12}(\tau^{[-2k]}(\ell))} z\left(\tau^{[-2k]}(\ell)\right).$$

Using Lemma 6, we can conclude that

$$x(\ell) > \sum_{k=1}^{n} \left(\prod_{i=1}^{2k-1} \frac{1}{\mathrm{p}(\tau^{[-i]}(\ell))} \right) \left[\frac{\pi_{12}\left(\tau^{[-2k+1]}(\ell)\right)}{\pi_{12}(\tau^{[-2k]}(\ell))} - \frac{1}{\mathrm{p}(\tau^{[-2k]}(\ell))} \right] z\left(\tau^{[-2k]}(\ell)\right).$$

As $z(\ell)$ is increasing and $\tau^{[-2k]}(\ell) \geq \ell$, we have

$$\begin{aligned} x(\ell) &> \sum_{k=1}^{n} \left(\prod_{i=1}^{2k-1} \frac{1}{\mathrm{p}(\tau^{[-i]}(\ell))} \right) \left[\frac{\pi_{12}\left(\tau^{[-2k+1]}(\ell)\right)}{\pi_{12}(\tau^{[-2k]}(\ell))} - \frac{1}{\mathrm{p}(\tau^{[-2k]}(\ell))} \right] z(\ell) \\ &= \widehat{\mathrm{p}}_1(\ell, n) z(\ell). \end{aligned} \tag{14}$$

From (1), we have

$$L_3 z(\ell) = -q(\ell) x^{\alpha}(\sigma(\ell)).$$

Using (13) and (14), we obtain

$$L_3 z(\ell) \leq -q(\ell) \mathrm{B}^{\alpha}(\sigma(\ell), n) z^{\alpha}(\sigma(\ell)).$$

Hence, we have successfully demonstrated the proof of the lemma. □

The following lemma gives some additional properties of solutions belonging to the class N_2.

Lemma 9. *Assume that $\beta_* > 0$ and $x \in \Omega_2$. Then for $\beta \in (0, \beta_*)$ and ℓ sufficiently large*
$(A_{2,1})$ $L_1 z/\pi_2^{1-\beta_*}$ *is decreasing and* $(1 - \beta_*) L_1 z > \pi_2 (L_2 z)^{1/\alpha}$;
$(A_{2,2})$ $\lim_{\ell \to \infty} L_1 z(\ell)/\pi_2^{1-\beta_*}(\ell) = 0$;
$(A_{2,3})$ $z/\pi_{12}^{1/k}$ *is decreasing and* $z > k(\pi_{12}/\pi_2) L_1 z$.

Proof. Let $x \in \Omega_2$ and choose $\ell_1 \geq \ell_0$, such that $z(\sigma(\ell)) > 0$ and parts $(A_{1,1})$–$(A_{1,3})$ in Lemma 7 hold for $\ell \geq \ell_1 \geq \ell_0$ and choose fixed but arbitrarily large $\beta \in (\beta_*/(1+\beta_*), \beta_*)$

and $k \leq k_*$ satisfying (6) and (7), respectively, for $\ell \geq \ell_1$.
Since

$$\frac{\beta}{1-\beta} > \beta_*,$$

there exist constants $c_1 \in (0,1)$ and $c_2 > 0$, such that

$$\frac{c_1\beta}{1-\beta} > \beta_* + c_2. \tag{15}$$

$(A_{2,1})$: Define

$$w(\ell) = L_1 z(\ell) - \pi_2(\ell)(L_2 z(\ell))^{1/\alpha}, \tag{16}$$

which is clearly positive by $(A_{1,2})$. Differentiating w and using (11) and (6), we see that

$$\begin{aligned} w'(\ell) &= \left(L_1 z(\ell) - (L_2 z(\ell))^{1/\alpha}\pi_2(\ell)\right)' \\ &= -\frac{1}{\alpha}\pi_2(\ell)(L_2 z(\ell))^{1/\alpha-1} L_3 z(\ell) \\ &\geq \frac{1}{\alpha} q(\ell)\pi_2(\ell)\mathrm{B}^{\alpha}(\sigma(\ell),n) z^{\alpha}(\sigma(\ell))(L_2 z(\ell))^{1/\alpha-1} \\ &\geq \beta\frac{z^{\alpha}(\sigma(\ell))}{a_2^{1/\alpha}(\ell)\pi_{12}^{\alpha}(\sigma(\ell))}(L_2 z(\ell))^{1/\alpha-1}. \end{aligned} \tag{17}$$

By virtue of $(A_{1,3})$, we have

$$w'(\ell) \geq \beta\frac{z^{\alpha}(\ell)}{a_2^{1/\alpha}(\ell)\pi_{12}^{\alpha}(\ell)}(L_2 z(\ell))^{1/\alpha-1}. \tag{18}$$

Considering $(A_{1,2})$ and $(A_{1,3})$, we obtain the following inequality:

$$\frac{z(\ell)}{\pi_{12}(\ell)} > \frac{L_1 z(\ell)}{\pi_2(\ell)} > (L_2 z(\ell))^{1/\alpha}.$$

Since $\alpha > 1$, then

$$\left(\frac{z(\ell)}{\pi_{12}(\ell)}\right)^{1-\alpha} < \left(\frac{L_1 z(\ell)}{\pi_2(\ell)}\right)^{1-\alpha} < (L_2 z(\ell))^{(1-\alpha)/\alpha}. \tag{19}$$

Substituting the previous inequality in (18), we obtain

$$w'(\ell) \geq \beta\frac{z^{\alpha}(\ell)}{a_2^{1/\alpha}(\ell)\pi_{12}^{\alpha}(\ell)}\left(\frac{z(\ell)}{\pi_{12}(\ell)}\right)^{1-\alpha} = \beta\frac{z(\ell)}{a_2^{1/\alpha}(\ell)\pi_{12}(\ell)} \geq \beta\frac{L_1 z(\ell)}{a_2^{1/\alpha}(\ell)\pi_2(\ell)}.$$

Integrating from ℓ_2 to ℓ and using the fact that $L_1 z/\pi_2$ is decreasing and tends to zero asymptotically, we have

$$\begin{aligned} w(\ell) &\geq w(\ell_2) + \beta\int_{\ell_2}^{\ell}\frac{L_1 z(s)}{a_2^{1/\alpha}(s)\pi_2(s)}\mathrm{d}s \geq w(\ell_2) + \beta\frac{L_1 z(\ell)}{\pi_2(\ell)}\int_{\ell_2}^{\ell}\frac{1}{a_2^{1/\alpha}(s)}\mathrm{d}s \\ &= z(\ell_2) + \beta\frac{L_1 x(\ell)}{\pi_2(\ell)}\pi_2(\ell) - \beta\frac{L_1 x(\ell)}{\pi_2(\ell)}\int_{\ell_0}^{\ell_2}\frac{1}{a_2^{1/\alpha}(s)}\mathrm{d}s > \beta L_1 x(\ell). \end{aligned} \tag{20}$$

Then

$$(1-\beta)L_1 z(\ell) > \pi_2(\ell)(L_2 z(\ell))^{1/\alpha}$$

and

$$\left(\frac{L_1 z(\ell)}{\pi_2^{1-\beta}(\ell)}\right)' = \frac{(L_2 z(\ell))^{1/\alpha}\pi_2(\ell) - (1-\beta)L_1 z(\ell)}{a_2^{1/\alpha}(\ell)\pi_2^{2-\beta}(\ell)} < 0. \tag{21}$$

It can be deduced straightforwardly from (21) and the observation that $L_1 z$ is increasing that $\beta < 1$. Using this in (20) and taking (15) into account, we find that

$$\begin{aligned} w(\ell) &\geq w(\ell_3) + \beta \int_{\ell_3}^{\ell} \frac{L_1 z(s)}{a_2^{1/\alpha}(s)\pi_2(s)} \mathrm{d}s \\ &\geq w(\ell_3) + \beta \frac{L_1 z(\ell)}{\pi_2^{1-\beta}(\ell)} \int_{\ell_3}^{\ell} \frac{1}{a_2^{1/\alpha}(s)\pi_2^{\beta}(s)} \mathrm{d}s \\ &\geq \frac{\beta}{1-\beta} \frac{L_1 z(\ell)}{\pi_2^{1-\beta}(\ell)} \left(\pi_2^{1-\beta}(\ell) - \pi_2^{1-\beta}(\ell_3) \right) \\ &\geq \frac{c_1 \beta}{1-\beta} L_1 z(\ell) \\ &\geq (\beta_* + c_2) L_1 z(\ell), \end{aligned}$$

which implies

$$(1-\beta_*) L_1 z(\ell) > (1-\beta_* - c_2) L_1 z(\ell) > (L_2 z(\ell))^{1/\alpha} \pi_2(\ell)$$

and

$$\left(\frac{L_1 z(\ell)}{\pi_2^{1-\beta_*-c_2}(\ell)} \right)' < 0, \tag{22}$$

the conclusion then immediately follows.

$(A_{2,2})$: Obviously, (22) also implies that $L_1 z / \pi_2^{1-\beta_*} \to 0$ as $\ell \to \infty$, since otherwise

$$\frac{L_1 z(\ell)}{\pi_2^{1-\beta_*-c_2}(\ell)} = \frac{L_1 z(\ell)}{\pi_2^{1-\beta_*}(\ell)} \pi_2^{c_2}(\ell) \to \infty \text{ as } \ell \to \infty, \tag{23}$$

which is a contradiction.

$(A_{2,3})$: By utilizing $(A_{2,1})$ and $(A_{2,2})$, as well as $L_1 z / \pi_2^{1-\beta_*}$ as a decreasing function tending towards zero, we can derive:

$$\begin{aligned} z(\ell) &= z(\ell_4) + \int_{\ell_4}^{\ell} \frac{L_1 z(s)}{\pi_2^{1-\beta_*}(s)} \frac{\pi_2^{1-\beta_*}(s)}{a_1(s)} \mathrm{d}s \\ &\geq z(\ell_4) + \frac{L_1 z(\ell)}{\pi_2^{1-\beta_*}(\ell)} \int_{\ell_4}^{\ell} \frac{\pi_2^{1-\beta_*}(s)}{a_1(s)} \mathrm{d}s \\ &= z(\ell_4) + \frac{L_1 z(\ell)}{\pi_2^{1-\beta_*}(\ell)} \int_{\ell_0}^{\ell} \frac{\pi_2^{1-\beta_*}(s)}{a_1(s)} \mathrm{d}s - \frac{L_1 z(\ell)}{\pi_2^{1-\beta_*}(\ell)} \int_{\ell_0}^{\ell_4} \frac{\pi_2^{1-\beta_*}(s)}{a_1(s)} \mathrm{d}s \\ &> \frac{L_1 z(\ell)}{\pi_2^{1-\beta_*}(\ell)} \int_{\ell_0}^{\ell} \frac{\pi_2^{1-\beta_*}(s)}{a_1(s)} \mathrm{d}s \\ &\geq k \frac{\pi_{12}(\ell)}{\pi_2(\ell)} L_1 z(\ell). \end{aligned}$$

Therefore

$$\left(\frac{z(\ell)}{\pi_{12}^{1/k}(\ell)} \right)' = \frac{k\pi_{12}(\ell) L_1 z(\ell) - \pi_2(\ell) z(\ell)}{k a_1(\ell) \pi_2^{1/k+1}(\ell)} < 0.$$

As a result, we have successfully concluded the proof of the Lemma. □

Corollary 1. *If* $\beta_* \geq 1$ *then* $\Omega_2 = \varnothing$.

Proof. This can be deduced from the inequality:

$$(1-\beta_*)L_1z(\ell) > (L_2z(\ell))^{1/\alpha}\pi_2(\ell),$$

taking into account the positivity of L_2z. □

Corollary 2. *If $\beta_* > 0$ and $\lambda_* = \infty$, then $\Omega_2 = \varnothing$.*

Proof. Let $x \in \Omega_2$, and choose $\ell_1 \geq \ell_0$, such that $z(\sigma(\ell)) > 0$ and parts $(A_{2,1})$–$(A_{2,3})$ in Lemma 7 hold for $\ell \geq \ell_1 \geq \ell_0$ and choose fixed but arbitrarily large $\lambda \leq \lambda_*$, $\beta \leq \beta_*$, and $k \leq k_*$ satisfying (5), (6), and (7), respectively, for $\ell \geq \ell_1$. Using (17), and the decreasing of $z/\pi_{12}^{1/k}$, we have

$$\begin{aligned} w'(\ell) &\geq \beta\frac{z^\alpha(\sigma(\ell))}{a_2^{1/\alpha}(\ell)\pi_{12}^{\alpha/k}(\sigma(\ell))\pi_{12}^{\alpha(1-1/k)}(\sigma(\ell))}(L_2z(\ell))^{1/\alpha-1} \\ &\geq \beta\frac{z^\alpha(\ell)}{\pi_{12}^{\alpha/k}(\ell)}\frac{1}{a_2^{1/\alpha}(\ell)\pi_{12}^{\alpha(1-1/k)}(\sigma(\ell))}(L_2z(\ell))^{1/\alpha-1}. \end{aligned}$$

Using $(A_{2,3})$, (19), and (5), we obtain

$$\begin{aligned} w'(\ell) &\geq \beta\frac{z^\alpha(\ell)}{\pi_{12}^{\alpha/k}(\ell)}\frac{1}{a_2^{1/\alpha}(\ell)\pi_{12}^{\alpha(1-1/k)}(\sigma(\ell))}\left(\frac{z(\ell)}{\pi_{12}(\ell)}\right)^{1-\alpha} \\ &= \beta\frac{\pi_{12}^{\alpha(1-1/k)}(\ell)}{a_2^{1/\alpha}(\ell)\pi_{12}^{\alpha(1-1/k)}(\sigma(\ell))}\frac{z(\ell)}{\pi_{12}(\ell)} \\ &\geq \beta\frac{\lambda^{\alpha(1-1/k)}}{a_2^{1/\alpha}(\ell)}\frac{z(\ell)}{\pi_{12}(\ell)} \geq \beta k\lambda^{\alpha(1-1/k)}\frac{L_1z(\ell)}{a_2^{1/\alpha}(\ell)\pi_2(\ell)}. \end{aligned}$$

Integrating the last inequality from ℓ_2 to ℓ and using that L_1z/π_2 is a decreasing function tending to zero, we obtain

$$w(\ell) \geq k\beta\lambda^{\alpha(1-1/k)}L_1z(\ell). \tag{24}$$

Thus

$$\left(1-k\beta\lambda^{\alpha(1-1/k)}\right)L_1z(\ell) \geq (L_2z(\ell))^{1/\alpha}\pi_2(\ell).$$

As λ can assume arbitrarily large values, we can choose λ such that $\lambda > (1/k\beta)^{k/\alpha(k-1)}$, thereby leading to a contradiction with the positivity L_2z. This concludes the proof of Corollary 2. □

Corollary 3. *Assume that $\beta_* > 0$ and $k_* = \infty$. Then, $\Omega_2 = \varnothing$.*

Proof. The proof follows with the same steps from Corollary 2, and the fact that k can be arbitrarily large, we omit it. □

Definition 1. *For our purposes, let us define the following sequence $\{\beta_n\}_{n=0}^\infty$, assuming it exists:*

$$\beta_0 = \beta_*, \text{ where } \beta_* \in (0,1),$$

$$\beta_n = \frac{\beta_0 k_{n-1}\lambda_*^{\alpha(1-1/k_{n-1})}}{1-\beta_{n-1}}, \text{ where } \lambda_* \in [1,\infty), \tag{25}$$

and k_n satisfies the condition:

$$k_n = \liminf_{\ell\to\infty}\frac{\pi_2^{\beta_n}(\ell)}{\pi_{12}(\ell)}\int_{\ell_0}^{\ell}\frac{\pi_2^{1-\beta_n}(s)}{a_1(s)}\mathrm{d}s,\ n \in \mathbb{N}_0. \tag{26}$$

Remark 2. *Clearly, β_{n+1} exists if $\beta_i < 1$ and $k_i \in [1, \infty)$ for $i = 0, 1, \ldots, n$. In this scenario, we can derive the following inequality:*

$$\frac{\beta_1}{\beta_0} = \frac{k_0 \lambda^{\alpha(1-1/k_0)}}{1-\beta_0} > 1$$

and

$$k_1 \geq k_0.$$

We can easily establish, through the use of mathematical induction on n, the following inequality

$$\frac{\beta_{n+1}}{\beta_n} \geq l_n > 1, \tag{27}$$

where

$$l_0 := \frac{k_0 \lambda_*^{\alpha(1-1/k_{n-1})}}{1-\beta_0},$$

$$l_n := \frac{k_n \lambda_*^{\alpha(1/k_{n-1}-1/k_n)}(1-\beta_{n-1})}{k_{n-1}(1-\beta_n)}, \; n \in \mathbb{N}, \tag{28}$$

with

$$k_n \geq k_{n-1}.$$

Next, we will demonstrate how iterative improvements can be made to the results presented in Lemma 9.

Lemma 10. *Suppose that $\delta_* > 0$ and $x \in \Omega_2$. Then, for any $n \in \mathbb{N}_0$ and ℓ sufficiently large*
$(A_{n,1})$ $L_1 z / \pi_2^{1-\beta_n}$ *is decreasing and* $(1-\beta_n) L_1 z > (L_2 z)^{1/\alpha} \pi_2$;
$(A_{n,2})$ $\lim_{\ell \to \infty} L_1 z(\ell) / \pi_n^{1-\beta_n}(\ell) = 0$;
$(A_{n,3})$ $z / \pi_{12}^{1/\varepsilon_n k_n}$ *is decreasing and* $z > \varepsilon_n k_n (\pi_{12}/\pi_2) L_1 z$ *for any* $\varepsilon_n \in (0,1)$.

Proof. Let $x \in \Omega_2$ with $z(\sigma(\ell)) > 0$ and parts $(A_{1,1})$–$(A_{1,3})$ in Lemma 7 hold for $\ell \geq \ell_1 \geq \ell_0$ and choose fixed but arbitrarily large $\beta \leq \beta_*$, and $k \leq k_*$ satisfying (6) and (7), respectively, for $\ell \geq \ell_1$. We will proceed by induction on n. For $n = 0$, the conclusion follows from Lemma 9 with $\varepsilon_0 = k/k_*$. Next, assume that $(A_{n,1})$–$(A_{n,3})$ hold for $n \geq 1$ for $\ell \geq \ell_n \geq \ell_1$. We need to show that they each hold for $n+1$.
$(A_{n+1,1})$: Using $(A_{n,3})$ in (17), we obtain

$$\begin{aligned} w'(\ell) &\geq \beta \frac{z^\alpha(\sigma(\ell))}{a_2^{1/\alpha}(\ell) \pi_{12}^{\alpha/\varepsilon_n k_n}(\sigma(\ell)) \pi_{12}^{\alpha(1-1/\varepsilon_n k_n)}(\sigma(\ell))} (L_2 z(\ell))^{1/\alpha - 1} \\ &\geq \beta \frac{z^\alpha(\ell)}{a_2^{1/\alpha}(\ell) \pi_{12}^{\alpha/\varepsilon_n k_n}(\ell) \pi_{12}^{\alpha(1-1/\varepsilon_n k_n)}(\sigma(\ell))} \left(\frac{z(\ell)}{\pi_{12}(\ell)} \right)^{1-\alpha} \\ &= \beta \frac{\pi_{12}^{\alpha(1-1/\varepsilon_n k_n)}(\ell)}{\pi_{12}^{\alpha(1-1/\varepsilon_n k_n)}(\sigma(\ell))} \frac{z(\ell)}{a_2^{1/\alpha}(\ell) \pi_{12}(\ell)} \\ &\geq \varepsilon_n k_n \beta \lambda^{\alpha(1-1/\varepsilon_n k_n)} \frac{L_1 z(\ell)}{a_2^{1/\alpha}(\ell) \pi_2(\ell)}. \end{aligned}$$

By integrating the aforementioned inequality from ℓ_n to ℓ and employing $(A_{n,1})$ and $(A_{n,2})$, we obtain

$$
\begin{aligned}
w(\ell) &\geq w(\ell_n) + \varepsilon_n k_n \beta \lambda^{\alpha(1-1/\varepsilon_n k_n)} \int_{\ell_n}^{\ell} \frac{L_1 z(s)}{a_2^{1/\alpha}(s)\pi_2(s)} ds \\
&\geq w(\ell_n) + \varepsilon_n k_n \beta \lambda^{\alpha(1-1/\varepsilon_n k_n)} \frac{L_1 z(\ell)}{\pi_2^{1-\beta_n}(\ell)} \int_{\ell_n}^{\ell} \frac{1}{a_2^{1/\alpha}(s)\pi_2^{\beta_n}(s)} ds \\
&\geq w(\ell_n) + \frac{\varepsilon_n k_n \beta \lambda^{\alpha(1-1/\varepsilon_n k_n)}}{1-\beta_n} \frac{L_1 z(\ell)}{\pi_2^{1-\beta_n}(\ell)} \left[\pi_2^{1-\beta_n}(\ell) - \pi_2^{1-\beta_n}(\ell_n)\right] \\
&> \frac{\varepsilon_n k_n \beta \lambda^{\alpha(1-1/\varepsilon_n k_n)}}{1-\beta_n} L_1 z(\ell) = \eta \beta_{n+1} L_1 z(\ell),
\end{aligned}
\tag{29}
$$

where

$$
\eta = \frac{\beta}{\beta_*} \varepsilon_n \frac{\lambda^{\alpha(1-1/\varepsilon_n k_n)}}{\lambda_*^{\alpha(1-1/k_n)}} \in (0,1),
$$

and $\eta \to 1$ where $(\lambda, \varepsilon_n, \beta) \to (\lambda_*, 1, \beta_*)$. Choose η, such that

$$
\eta > \frac{1}{1-\beta_n+\beta_{n+1}} = \frac{1}{1+\beta_n(l_n-1)}, \tag{30}
$$

where l_n satisfies (27). Then

$$
\frac{\eta\beta_{n+1}}{1-\eta\beta_{n+1}} > \frac{\beta_{n+1}}{(1+\beta_n(l_n-1))\left(1-\frac{l_n\beta_n}{1+\beta_n(l_n-1)}\right)} = \frac{\beta_{n+1}}{1-\beta_n},
$$

and there exist two constants, $c_1 \in (0,1)$ and $c_2 > 0$, such that

$$
c_1 \frac{\eta(1-\beta_n)\beta_{n+1}}{1-\eta\beta_{n+1}} > \beta_{n+1} + c_2.
$$

According to the definition (16) of w, we deduce that

$$
(1-\eta\beta_{n+1}) L_1 z(\ell) = (L_2 z(\ell))^{1/\alpha} \pi_2(\ell)
$$

and

$$
\left(\frac{L_1 z(\ell)}{\pi_2^{1-\eta\beta_{n+1}}(\ell)}\right)' < 0.
$$

Using the above monotonicity in (29), we see that

$$
\begin{aligned}
w(\ell) &\geq w(\ell_n) + \varepsilon_n k_n \beta \lambda^{\alpha(1-1/\varepsilon_n k_n)} \int_{\ell_n}^{\ell} \frac{L_1 z(s)}{a_2^{1/\alpha}(s)\pi_2(s)} ds \\
&\geq \frac{\varepsilon_n k_n \beta \lambda^{\alpha(1-1/\varepsilon_n k_n)}}{1-\eta\beta_{n+1}} \frac{L_1 z(\ell)}{\pi_2^{1-\eta\beta_{n+1}}(\ell)} \left(\pi_2^{1-\eta\beta_{n+1}}(\ell) - \pi_2^{1-\eta\beta_{n+1}}(\ell_n)\right) \\
&\geq \frac{c_1 \varepsilon_n k_n \beta \lambda^{\alpha(1-1/\varepsilon_n k_n)}}{1-\eta\beta_{n+1}} L_1 z(\ell) \\
&= c_1 \eta \beta_{n+1} \frac{1-\beta_n}{1-\eta\beta_{n+1}} L_1 z(\ell) \\
&> (\beta_{n+1} + c_2) L_1 z(\ell).
\end{aligned}
$$

Then

$$
(1-\beta_{n+1}-c_2) L_1 x(\ell) > (L_2 x(\ell))^{1/\alpha} \pi_2(\ell), \tag{31}
$$

and

$$
\left(\frac{L_1 x(\ell)}{\pi_2^{1-\beta_{n+1}-c_2}(\ell)}\right)' < 0, \tag{32}
$$

which leads to the conclusion.
$(A_{n+1,2})$: Obviously, (32) also implies that $L_1z/\pi_2^{1-\beta_{n+1}} \to 0$ as $\ell \to \infty$, since otherwise

$$\frac{L_1z(\ell)}{\pi_2^{1-\beta_{n+1}-c_2}(\ell)} = \frac{L_1(z\ell)}{\pi_2^{1-\beta_{n+1}}(\ell)}\pi_2^{c_2}(\ell) \to \infty \text{ as } \ell \to \infty, \tag{33}$$

which is a contradiction.
$(A_{n+1,3})$: By utilizing that $(A_{n+1,1})$ and $(A_{n+1,2})$, as well as $L_1z/\pi_2^{1-\beta_{n+1}}$ as a decreasing function tending towards zero, we can derive:

$$\begin{aligned} z(\ell) &= z(\ell_n'') + \int_{\ell_n''}^{\ell} \frac{L_1z(s)}{\pi_2^{1-\beta_{n+1}}(s)} \frac{\pi_2^{1-\beta_{n+1}}(s)}{a_1(s)} \mathrm{d}s \\ &\geq z(\ell_n'') + \frac{L_1z(\ell)}{\pi_2^{1-\beta_{n+1}}(\ell)} \int_{\ell_n''}^{\ell} \frac{\pi_2^{1-\beta_{n+1}}(s)}{a_1(s)} \mathrm{d}s \\ &= z(\ell_n'') + \frac{L_1z(\ell)}{\pi_2^{1-\beta_{n+1}}(\ell)} \int_{\ell_0}^{\ell} \frac{\pi_2^{1-\beta_{n+1}}(s)}{a_1(s)} \mathrm{d}s - \frac{L_1z(\ell)}{\pi_2^{1-\beta_{n+1}}(\ell)} \int_{\ell_0}^{\ell_n''} \frac{\pi_2^{1-\beta_{n+1}}(s)}{a_1(s)} \mathrm{d}s \\ &> \frac{L_1z(\ell)}{\pi_2^{1-\beta_{n+1}}(\ell)} \int_{\ell_0}^{\ell} \frac{\pi_2^{1-\beta_{n+1}}(s)}{a_1(s)} \mathrm{d}s \\ &\geq \varepsilon_{n+1}k_{n+1}\frac{\pi_{12}(\ell)}{\pi_2(\ell)}L_1z(\ell), \end{aligned}$$

and

$$\begin{aligned} \left(\frac{z(\ell)}{\pi_{12}^{1/\varepsilon_{n+1}k_{n+1}}(\ell)}\right)' &= \frac{\varepsilon_{n+1}k_{n+1}\pi_{12}^{1/\varepsilon_{n+1}k_{n+1}}(\ell)L_1z(\ell) - \pi_{12}^{1/\varepsilon_{n+1}k_{n+1}-1}(\ell)\pi_2(\ell)z(\ell)}{\varepsilon_{n+1}k_{n+1}a_1(\ell)\pi_{12}^{2/\varepsilon_{n+1}k_{n+1}}(\ell)} \\ &= \frac{\varepsilon_{n+1}k_{n+1}\pi_{12}(\ell)L_1z(\ell) - \pi_2(\ell)z(\ell)}{\varepsilon_{n+1}k_{n+1}a_1(\ell)\pi_{12}^{1/\varepsilon_{n+1}k_{n+1}+1}(\ell)} < 0, \end{aligned}$$

for any $\varepsilon_n \in (0,1)$. The proof of this Lemma is complete. □

Corollary 4. *Assume that $\beta_i < 1, i = 0,1,2,\ldots,n-1$, and $\beta_n \geq 1$. Then, $\Omega_2 = \varnothing$.*

Proof. This follows directly from

$$(1-\beta_n)L_1z(\ell) > (L_2z(\ell))^{1/\alpha}\pi_2(\ell),$$

and the fact that L_2 is positive. □

In view of the previous corollary and (27), the sequence $\{\beta_n\}$ given by (25) is increasing and bounded from above, i.e, there exists a limit

$$\lim_{n\to\infty} \beta_n = \beta_j \in (0,1),$$

satisfying the equation

$$\beta_j = \frac{\beta_* k_j \lambda_*^{\alpha(1-1/k_j)}}{1-\beta_j}, \tag{34}$$

where

$$k_j = \liminf_{\ell\to\infty} \frac{\pi_2^{\beta_j}(\ell)}{\pi_{12}(\ell)} \int_{\ell_0}^{\ell} \frac{\pi_2^{1-\beta_j}(s)}{a_1(s)} \mathrm{d}s.$$

Then, the next important resulting in the nonexistence of N_2-type solutions are direct.

Lemma 11. *Assume that $\lambda_* < \infty$ and (34) does not possess a root on $(0,1)$. Then, $\Omega_2 = \varnothing$.*

Corollary 5. *Assume that $\lambda_* < \infty$. If*

$$\beta_* > \max\left\{ \frac{\beta_j(1-\beta_j)\lambda_*^{\alpha(1/k_j-1)}}{k_j} : 0 < \beta_j < 1 \right\}. \tag{35}$$

Then, $\Omega_2 = \varnothing$.

Lemma 12. *Assume that (2) holds. Furthermore, assume that there exists $\rho \in C^1([\ell_0,\infty),(0,\infty))$, such that*

$$\limsup_{\ell\to\infty} \int_{\ell_0}^{\ell} \left(\rho(s)q(s)B^{\alpha}(\sigma(s),n)\left(\frac{\sigma(s)}{s}\right)^{2\alpha/\epsilon} - \frac{a_1^{\alpha}(s)(\rho'(s))_+^{\alpha+1}}{(\alpha+1)^{\alpha+1}\pi_2^{\alpha}(s)\rho^{\alpha}(s)} \right) ds = \infty, \tag{36}$$

where $(\rho'(\ell))_+ = \max\{0,\rho'(\ell)\}$. Then, $\Omega_2 = \varnothing$.

Proof. Assume the contrary, that $x \in \Omega_2$. Now define

$$w(\ell) = \rho(\ell)\frac{L_2 z(\ell)}{z^{\alpha}(\ell)},\ \ell \geq \ell_1, \tag{37}$$

then, $w(\ell) > 0$ and

$$\begin{aligned} w'(\ell) &= \rho'(\ell)\frac{L_2 z(\ell)}{z^{\alpha}(\ell)} + \rho(\ell)\frac{L_3 z(\ell)}{z^{\alpha}(\ell)} - \alpha\rho(\ell)\frac{L_2 z(\ell)}{z^{\alpha}(\ell)}\frac{z'(\ell)}{z(\ell)} \\ &= \rho'(\ell)\frac{L_2 z(\ell)}{z^{\alpha}(\ell)} + \rho(\ell)\frac{L_3 z(\ell)}{z^{\alpha}(\ell)} - \alpha\rho(\ell)\frac{L_2 z(\ell)}{z^{\alpha}(\ell)}\frac{1}{a_1(\ell)}\frac{L_1 z(\ell)}{z(\ell)} \\ &\leq -\rho(\ell)q(\ell)B^{\alpha}(\sigma(\ell),n)\frac{z^{\alpha}(\sigma(\ell))}{z^{\alpha}(\ell)} + \frac{\rho'(\ell)}{\rho(\ell)}w(\ell) - \alpha w(\ell)\frac{1}{a_1(\ell)}\frac{L_1 z(\ell)}{z(\ell)}. \end{aligned}$$

Then, in view of (11) and $(A_{1,2})$-part of Lemma 7, we have

$$\begin{aligned} w'(\ell) &\leq -\rho(\ell)q(\ell)B^{\alpha}(\sigma(\ell),n)\frac{z^{\alpha}(\sigma(\ell))}{z^{\alpha}(\ell)} + \frac{\rho'(\ell)}{\rho(\ell)}w(\ell) - \alpha\frac{\pi_2(\ell)}{a_1(\ell)}w(\ell)\frac{(L_2 z)^{1/\alpha}}{z(\ell)} \\ &= -\rho(\ell)q(\ell)B^{\alpha}(\sigma(\ell),n)\frac{z^{\alpha}(\sigma(\ell))}{z^{\alpha}(\ell)} + \frac{\rho'(\ell)}{\rho(\ell)}w(\ell) - \frac{\alpha\pi_2(\ell)}{a_1(\ell)\rho^{1/\alpha}(\ell)}w^{1+1/\alpha}(\ell). \end{aligned}$$

Since $z > 0$, $L_1 z > 0$, and $L_2 z > 0$, then from Lemma 3 we obtain

$$\frac{z(\ell)}{z'(\ell)} \geq \frac{\varepsilon}{2}\ell.$$

By integrating the preceding inequality over the interval from $\tau(\ell)$ to ℓ, we obtain

$$\frac{z(\sigma(\ell))}{z(\ell)} \geq \left(\frac{\sigma(\ell)}{\ell}\right)^{2/\epsilon},$$

which implies that

$$w'(\ell) \leq -\rho(\ell)q(\ell)B^{\alpha}(\sigma(\ell),n)\left(\frac{\sigma(\ell)}{\ell}\right)^{2\alpha/\epsilon} + \frac{(\rho'(\ell))_+}{\rho(\ell)}w(\ell) - \frac{\alpha\pi_2(\ell)}{a_1(\ell)\rho^{1/\alpha}(\ell)}w^{1+1/\alpha}(\ell). \tag{38}$$

Setting

$$B = \frac{(\rho'(\ell))_+}{\rho(\ell)} \text{ and } A = \frac{\alpha\pi_2(\ell)}{a_1(\ell)\rho^{1/\alpha}(\ell)},$$

and using Lemma 1, we see that

$$\frac{(\rho'(\ell))_+}{\rho(\ell)}\mathrm{w}(\ell) - \frac{\alpha\pi_2(\ell)}{a_1(\ell)\rho^{1/\alpha}(\ell)}\mathrm{w}^{1+1/\alpha}(\ell) \le \frac{a_1^\alpha(\ell)(\rho'(\ell))_+^{\alpha+1}}{(\alpha+1)^{\alpha+1}\pi_2^\alpha(\ell)\rho^\alpha(\ell)}. \tag{39}$$

Thus, from (38) and (39), we obtain

$$\mathrm{w}'(\ell) \le -\left(\rho(\ell)q(\ell)\mathrm{B}^\alpha(\sigma(\ell),n)\left(\frac{\sigma(\ell)}{\ell}\right)^{2\alpha/\epsilon} - \frac{a_1^\alpha(\ell)(\rho'(\ell))_+^{\alpha+1}}{(\alpha+1)^{\alpha+1}\pi_2^\alpha(\ell)\rho^\alpha(\ell)}\right). \tag{40}$$

Integrating (40) from ℓ_1 to ℓ, we obtain

$$\int_{\ell_1}^{\ell}\left(\rho(s)q(s)\mathrm{B}^\alpha(\sigma(s),n)\left(\frac{\sigma(s)}{s}\right)^{2/\epsilon} - \frac{a_1^\alpha(s)(\rho'(s))_+^{\alpha+1}}{(\alpha+1)^{\alpha+1}\pi_2^\alpha(s)\rho^\alpha(s)}\right)\mathrm{d}s \le w(\ell_1),$$

for all large ℓ. This is a contradiction to (36). □

4. Convergence to Zero of Kneser Solutions

In this section, we establish certain conditions that guarantee the absence of Kneser solutions satisfying (N_1) within Category Ω_1.

Theorem 1. *If there exists a function $\zeta \in C([\ell_0,\infty),(0,\infty))$ satisfying $\sigma(\ell) < \zeta(\ell)$ and $\tau^{-1}(\zeta(\ell)) < \ell$, such that the differential equation*

$$\omega'(\ell) + \frac{1}{\mu}\frac{\tau_0}{\tau_0 + \mathrm{p}_0^\alpha}\phi(\ell)\pi_{12}^\alpha(\zeta(\ell),\sigma(\ell))\omega\left(\tau^{-1}(\zeta(\ell))\right) \le 0, \tag{41}$$

is oscillatory, then $\Omega_1 = \varnothing$.

Proof. Let $x \in \Omega_1$, say $x(\ell) > 0$ and $x(\sigma(\ell)) > 0$ for $\ell \ge \ell_1 \ge \ell_0$. This implies that

$$z > 0,\ L_1 z < 0,\ L_2 z > 0,\ \text{and } L_3 z \le 0. \tag{42}$$

From (1), we see that

$$\begin{aligned} 0 &\ge \frac{\mathrm{p}_0^\alpha}{\tau'(\ell)}\left(a_2(\tau(\ell))\left((a_1(\tau(\ell))z'(\tau(\ell)))'\right)^\alpha\right)' + \mathrm{p}_0^\alpha q(\tau(\ell))x^\alpha(\sigma(\tau(\ell))) \\ &\ge \frac{\mathrm{p}_0^\alpha}{\tau_0}L_3 z(\tau(\ell)) + \mathrm{p}_0^\alpha q(\tau(\ell))x^\alpha(\sigma(\tau(\ell))) \\ &= \frac{\mathrm{p}_0^\alpha}{\tau_0}L_3 z(\tau(\ell)) + \mathrm{p}_0^\alpha q(\tau(\ell))x^\alpha(\tau(\sigma(\ell))). \end{aligned} \tag{43}$$

Combining (1) and (43), we obtain

$$\begin{aligned} 0 &\ge L_3 z(\ell) + \frac{\mathrm{p}_0^\alpha}{\tau_0}L_3 z(\tau(\ell)) + q(\ell)x^\alpha(\sigma(\ell)) + \mathrm{p}_0^\alpha q(\tau(\ell))x^\alpha(\tau(\sigma(\ell))) \\ &\ge L_3 z(\ell) + \frac{\mathrm{p}_0^\alpha}{\tau_0}L_3 z(\tau(\ell)) + \phi(\ell)(x^\alpha(\sigma(\ell)) + \mathrm{p}_0^\alpha x^\alpha(\tau(\sigma(\ell)))). \end{aligned}$$

Using Lemma (2), we obtain

$$0 \ge L_3 z(\ell) + \frac{\mathrm{p}_0^\alpha}{\tau_0}L_3 z(\tau(\ell)) + \frac{1}{\mu}\phi(\ell)(x(\sigma(\ell)) + \mathrm{p}_0 x(\tau(\sigma(\ell))))^\alpha. \tag{44}$$

From the definition of z, we have

$$z(\sigma(\ell)) = x(\sigma(\ell)) + p(\sigma(\ell))x(\tau(\sigma(\ell))) \leq x(\sigma(\ell)) + p_0 x(\tau(\sigma(\ell))).$$

By using the latter inequality in (44), we find

$$0 \geq L_3 z(\ell) + \frac{p_0^\alpha}{\tau_0} L_3 z(\tau(\ell)) + \frac{1}{\mu}\phi(\ell) z^\alpha(\sigma(\ell)).$$

That is

$$\left(L_2 z(\ell) + \frac{p_0^\alpha}{\tau_0} L_2 z(\tau(\ell))\right)' + \frac{1}{\mu}\phi(\ell) z^\alpha(\sigma(\ell)) \leq 0. \tag{45}$$

However, it can be deduced from the monotonicity of $L_2 z(\ell)$ that

$$\begin{aligned} -L_1 z(\varrho) &\geq L_1 z(\varsigma) - L_1 z(\varrho) = \int_\varrho^\varsigma (L_1 z(s))' \mathrm{d}s = \int_\varrho^\varsigma \frac{L_2^{1/\alpha} z(s)}{a_2^{1/\alpha}(s)} \mathrm{d}s \\ &\geq L_2^{1/\alpha} z(\varsigma) \int_\varrho^\varsigma \frac{1}{a_2^{1/\alpha}(s)} \mathrm{d}s = L_2^{1/\alpha} z(\varsigma) \pi_2(\varsigma, \varrho). \end{aligned} \tag{46}$$

Integrating (46) from ϱ to ς, and using (42), we obtain

$$z(\varrho) \geq L_2^{1/\alpha} z(\varsigma) \pi_{12}(\varsigma, \varrho). \tag{47}$$

Thus, we have

$$z(\sigma(\ell)) \geq L_2^{1/\alpha} z(\zeta(\ell)) \pi_{12}(\zeta(\ell), \sigma(\ell)),$$

which, by virtue of (45), yields that

$$\left(L_2 z(\ell) + \frac{p_0^\alpha}{\tau_0} L_2 z(\tau(\ell))\right)' + \frac{1}{\mu}\phi(\ell) \pi_{12}^\alpha(\zeta(\ell), \sigma(\ell)) L_2 z(\zeta(\ell)) \leq 0. \tag{48}$$

Now, set

$$\omega(\ell) = L_2 z(\ell) + \frac{p_0^\alpha}{\tau_0} L_2 z(\tau(\ell)) > 0.$$

From the fact that $L_2 z(\ell)$ is non-increasing, we have

$$\omega(\ell) \leq L_2 z(\tau(\ell)) \left(1 + \frac{p_0^\alpha}{\tau_0}\right),$$

or equivalently,

$$L_2 z(\zeta(\ell)) \geq \frac{\tau_0}{\tau_0 + p_0^\alpha} \omega\left(\tau^{-1}(\zeta(\ell))\right). \tag{49}$$

Using (49) in (48), we show that ω is a positive solution of the differential inequality

$$\omega'(\ell) + \frac{1}{\mu} \frac{\tau_0}{\tau_0 + p_0^\alpha} \phi(\ell) \pi_{12}^\alpha(\zeta(\ell), \sigma(\ell)) \omega\left(\tau^{-1}(\zeta(\ell))\right) \leq 0.$$

Considering ([35], Theorem 1), we can deduce that (41) also possesses a positive solution, which contradicts our previous assertion. Thus, we can conclude that the proof is now fully established. □

Corollary 6. *If there exists a function $\zeta \in C([\ell_0, \infty), (0, \infty))$ satisfying $\sigma(\ell) < \zeta(\ell)$ and $\tau^{-1}(\zeta(\ell)) < \ell$, such that*

$$\liminf_{\ell \to \infty} \int_{\tau^{-1}(\zeta(\ell))}^{\ell} \phi(s) \pi_{12}^\alpha(\zeta(s), \sigma(s)) \mathrm{d}s > \frac{\mu(\tau_0 + p_0^\alpha)}{\tau_0 \mathrm{e}}, \tag{50}$$

then, $\Omega_1 = \varnothing$.

Theorem 2. *If there exists a function* $\delta \in C([\ell_0, \infty), (0, \infty))$ *satisfying* $\delta(\ell) < \ell$, *and* $\sigma(\ell) < \tau(\delta(\ell))$, *such that*

$$\limsup_{\ell \to \infty} \pi_{12}^{\alpha}(\tau(\delta(\ell)), \sigma(\ell)) \int_{\delta(\ell)}^{\ell} \phi(s) ds > \frac{\mu(\tau_0 + p_0^{\alpha})}{\tau_0}, \tag{51}$$

then, $\Omega_1 = \varnothing$.

Proof. Using the same method as demonstrated in the proof of Theorem 1, we obtain the following inequality:

$$0 \geq \left(L_2 z(\ell) + \frac{p_0^{\alpha}}{\tau_0} L_2 z(\tau(\ell)) \right)' + \frac{1}{\mu} \phi(\ell) z^{\alpha}(\sigma(\ell)).$$

By integrating the previous inequality from $\delta(\ell)$ to ℓ, and considering the fact that z is a decreasing function, we derive:

$$\begin{aligned} L_2 z(\delta(\ell)) + \frac{p_0^{\alpha}}{\tau_0} L_2 z(\tau(\delta(\ell))) &\geq L_2 z(\ell) + \frac{p_0^{\alpha}}{\tau_0} L_2 z(\tau(\ell)) + \frac{1}{\mu} z^{\alpha}(\sigma(\ell)) \int_{\delta(\ell)}^{\ell} \phi(s) ds \\ &\geq \frac{1}{\mu} z^{\alpha}(\sigma(\ell)) \int_{\delta(\ell)}^{\ell} \phi(s) ds. \end{aligned}$$

Since $\tau(\delta(\ell)) < \tau(\ell)$, and $L_2 z(\ell)$ is non-increasing, we have

$$L_2 z(\tau(\delta(\ell))) \left(1 + \frac{p_0^{\alpha}}{\tau_0} \right) \geq \frac{1}{\mu} z^{\alpha}(\sigma(\ell)) \int_{\delta(\ell)}^{\ell} \phi(s) ds. \tag{52}$$

By using (47) with $\varsigma = \tau(\delta(\ell))$ and $\varrho = \sigma(\ell)$ in (52), we obtain

$$L_2 z(\tau(\delta(\ell))) \left(1 + \frac{p_0^{\alpha}}{\tau_0} \right) \geq \frac{1}{\mu} L_2 z(\tau(\delta(\ell))) \pi_{12}^{\alpha}(\tau(\delta(\ell)), \sigma(\ell)) \int_{\delta(\ell)}^{\ell} \phi(s) ds.$$

That is

$$\frac{\tau_0 + p_0^{\alpha}}{\tau_0} \geq \frac{1}{\mu} \pi_{12}^{\alpha}(\tau(\delta(\ell)), \sigma(\ell)) \int_{\delta(\ell)}^{\ell} \phi(s) ds.$$

Next, we calculate the lim sup for both sides of the preceding inequality, which leads to a contradiction with (51). This concludes the proof. □

5. Oscillation Theorems

In this section, we are prepared to present the main results of this paper. By combining the results from the preceding two sections, we can readily derive the following theorems without providing proof.

Theorem 3. *Assume that* $\beta_* \geq 1$, *and either (50) or (51) holds. Then, (1) is oscillatory.*

Theorem 4. *Assume that* $\beta_* > 0$, $\lambda_* = \infty$, *and either (50) or (51) holds. Then, (1) is oscillatory.*

Theorem 5. *Assume that* $\beta_i < 1, i = 0, 1, 2, \ldots, n-1$, *and* $\beta_n \geq 1$ *and either (50) or (51) holds. Then, (1) is oscillatory.*

Theorem 6. *Assume that* $\lambda_* < \infty$, *(35), and either (50) or (51) holds. Then, (1) is oscillatory.*

Theorem 7. *Assume that (36) and either (50) or (51) holds. Then, (1) is oscillatory.*

In the following, we provide an example that supports and illustrates our results.

Example 1. *Consider*

$$\left(\left(\left((x(\ell) + p_0 x(\tau_0 \ell))''\right)^5\right)\right)' + \frac{q_0}{\ell^{11}} x^5(\sigma_0 \ell) = 0, \tag{53}$$

where $0 \leq p_0 < 1$, *and* $\tau_0, \sigma_0 \in (0,1)$. *Clearly,*

$$a_1(\ell) = 1, \ a_2(\ell) = 1, \ \pi_1(\ell) \sim \ell, \ \pi_2(\ell) \sim \ell, \ \pi_{12}(\ell) \sim \ell^2/2.$$

We can calculate:

$$\lambda_* = \liminf_{\ell \to \infty} \frac{\pi_{12}(\ell)}{\pi_{12}(\sigma(\ell))} = \frac{1}{\sigma_0^2},$$

$$p_1(\ell;n) = [1 - p_0] \sum_{k=0}^{n} p_0^{2k} \tau_0^{4k},$$

$$\widehat{p}_1(\ell, n) = \left[p_0 \tau_0^2 - 1\right] \sum_{k=1}^{n} \frac{1}{p_0^{2k}},$$

and

$$B(\ell, n) = B_0 = \begin{cases} p_1(\ell;n) & \text{for } p_0 < 1, \\ \widehat{p}_1(\ell;n) & \text{for } p_0 > 1/\tau_0^2. \end{cases}$$

Then

$$\begin{aligned}\beta_* &= \liminf_{\ell \to \infty} \frac{1}{\alpha} a_2^{1/\alpha}(\ell) \pi_{12}^{\alpha}(\sigma(\ell)) \pi_2(\ell) q(\ell) B_0^{\alpha}(\sigma(\ell), n) \\ &= \liminf_{\ell \to \infty} \frac{1}{5} \frac{\sigma_0^{10} \ell^{10}}{2^5} \ell \frac{q_0}{\ell^{11}} B_0^5 = \frac{1}{160} \sigma_0^{10} q_0 B_0^5.\end{aligned}$$

For $\beta_* \geq 1$, *we have*

$$q_0 > \frac{160}{\sigma_0^{10} B_0^5}. \tag{54}$$

Now, for $\rho(\ell) = \ell^\nu$, *where* $\nu \geq 10$, *condition (36) leads to*

$$\begin{aligned}&\limsup_{\ell \to \infty} \int_{\ell_0}^{\ell} \left(\rho(s) q(s) B^{\alpha}(\sigma(s), n) \left(\frac{\sigma(s)}{s}\right)^{2\alpha/\epsilon} - \frac{a_1^{\alpha}(s)(\rho'(s))_+^{\alpha+1}}{(\alpha+1)^{\alpha+1} \pi_2^{\alpha}(s) \rho^{\alpha}(s)} \right) ds \\ &= \limsup_{\ell \to \infty} \int_{\ell_0}^{\ell} \left(s^\nu \frac{q_0}{s^{11}} B_0^5 \sigma_0^{10/\epsilon} - \frac{1}{6^6} \frac{\nu^6 s^{6\nu-6}}{s^5 s^{5\nu}} \right) ds \\ &= \limsup_{\ell \to \infty} \int_{\ell_0}^{\ell} \left(q_0 B_0^5 \sigma_0^{10/\epsilon} - \frac{\nu^6}{6^6} \right) s^{\nu-11} ds = \infty,\end{aligned}$$

Which is satisfied when

$$q_0 > \frac{\nu^6}{6^6 B_0^5 \sigma_0^{10/\epsilon}}. \tag{55}$$

Condition (50) leads to:

$$\begin{aligned}\liminf_{\ell \to \infty} \int_{\tau^{-1}(\zeta(\ell))}^{\ell} \phi(s) \pi_{12}^{\alpha}(\zeta(s), \sigma(s)) ds &= \liminf_{\ell \to \infty} \int_{\tau_0^{-1} \zeta_0 \ell}^{\ell} \frac{q_0}{s^{11}} \frac{(\zeta_0^2 - \sigma_0^2)^5}{2^5} s^{10} ds \\ &= \frac{1}{32} q_0 \left(\zeta_0^2 - \sigma_0^2\right)^5 \ln \frac{\tau_0}{\zeta_0}.\end{aligned}$$

which is satisfied when:

$$q_0 > \frac{32\mu(\tau_0 + p_0^{\alpha})}{\tau_0 e(\zeta_0^2 - \sigma_0^2)^5 \ln \frac{\tau_0}{\zeta_0}} \tag{56}$$

Condition (51) leads to:

$$\begin{aligned}
\limsup_{\ell\to\infty} \pi_{12}^{\alpha}(\tau(\delta(\ell)),\sigma(\ell)) \int_{\delta(\ell)}^{\ell} \phi(s)\mathrm{d}s &= \limsup_{\ell\to\infty} \pi_{12}^{5}(\tau_0\delta_0\ell,\sigma_0\ell) \int_{\delta_0\ell}^{\ell} \frac{q_0}{s^{11}}\mathrm{d}s \\
&= \limsup_{\ell\to\infty} \frac{(\tau_0^2\delta_0^2 - \sigma_0^2)^5 (1-\delta_0^{10})\ell^{10}}{320\delta_0^{10}} \frac{q_0}{\ell^{10}} \\
&= \frac{(\tau_0^2\delta_0^2 - \sigma_0^2)^5 (1-\delta_0^{10})}{320\delta_0^{10}} q_0,
\end{aligned}$$

which is satisfied when:

$$q_0 > \frac{320(\tau_0 + p_0^5)\delta_0^{10}}{(\tau_0^2\delta_0^2 - \sigma_0^2)^5 (1-\delta_0^{10})}. \tag{57}$$

Now, by applying conditions (54)–(57), *we can show that Theorems (3) and (7) exhibit oscillatory behavior. This can be confirmed by assigning particular values to (53).*

Example 2. *Consider*

$$(x(\ell) + 0.5x(0.9\ell))''' + \frac{q_0}{\ell^3} x(0.5\ell) = 0. \tag{58}$$

Clearly,

$$\lambda_* = 4,$$

$$p_1(\ell;10) = (1-0.5) \sum_{k=0}^{10} (0.5)^{2k} (0.9)^{4k} = 0.5981,$$

and

$$B(\ell,10) = B_0 = p_1(\ell;10) = 0.5981.$$

Then

$$\beta_* = \liminf_{\ell\to\infty} \frac{(0.5)^2\ell^2}{2} \ell \frac{q_0}{\ell^3} (0.5981) = 0.07476 q_0.$$

For $\beta_* \geq 1$, we have

$$q_0 > 13.376.$$

Conditions (36) and (51) are satisfied when

$$q_0 > 26.751,\ \rho(\ell) = \ell^2,\ \epsilon = 0.5$$

and

$$q_0 > 22.274,\ \delta_0 = 0.7, \tag{59}$$

respectively. Thus, from Theorems 3 and 7, we conclude that (58) is oscillatory.

6. Conclusions

This paper has studied the oscillatory behavior of a quasi-linear NDE of the third order. Through our research efforts, we have significantly enhanced the understanding of the relationship between the solution, x, and the corresponding function, z. This improvement has led to the derivation of improved preliminary results, which play a crucial role in excluding positive solutions for the studied equation. Building upon these refined preliminary results, we have developed novel criteria for determining the nature of the solutions, whether they exhibit oscillatory behavior or tend towards zero. These criteria contribute to a deeper comprehension of the dynamic behavior of the systems described by these equations. In the future, an intriguing avenue for research involves broadening the scope of this study to encompass NDEs of higher orders.

Author Contributions: Conceptualization, F.M., O.M., G.A. and H.E.-M.; methodology, F.M., O.M., G.A. and H.E.-M.; investigation, F.M., O.M., G.A. and H.E.-M.; writing—original draft, F.M. and G.A.; writing—review and editing, O.M. and H.E.-M. All authors have read and agreed to the published version of the manuscript.

Funding: This research was funded by Princess Nourah bint Abdulrahman University Researchers Supporting Project number (PNURSP2023R45), Princess Nourah bint Abdulrahman University, Riyadh, Saudi Arabia.

Data Availability Statement: No new data were created or analyzed in this study.

Acknowledgments: Princess Nourah bint Abdulrahman University Researchers Supporting Project number (PNURSP2023R45), Princess Nourah bint Abdulrahman University, Riyadh, Saudi Arabia.

Conflicts of Interest: The authors declare no conflict of interest.

References

1. Jayaraman, G.; Padmanabhan, N.; Mehrotra, R. Entry flow into a circular tube of slowly varying cross-section. *Fluid Dyn. Res.* **1986**, *1*, 131. [CrossRef]
2. Vreeke, S.A.; Sandquist, G.M. Phase space analysis of reactor kinetics. *Nucl. Sci. Eng.* **1970**, *42*, 295–305. [CrossRef]
3. Gregus, M. *Third Order Linear Differential Equations*; Springer Science & Business Media: Berlin, Germany, 2012; Volume 22.
4. Villagomez, A.N.; Muoz, F.M.; Peterson, R.L.; Colbert, A.M.; Gladstone, M.; MacDonald, B. Collaboration Neurodevelopmental Delay Working Group. Neurodevelopmental delay: Case definition and guidelines for data collection, analysis, and presentation of immunization safety data. *Vaccine* **2019**, *37*, 7623. [CrossRef]
5. Liu, M.; Dassios, I.; Tzounas, G.; Milano, F. Stability analysis of power systems with inclusion of realistic-modeling WAMS delays. *IEEE Trans. Power Syst.* **2018**, *34*, 627–636. [CrossRef]
6. Milano, F.; Dassios, I. Small-signal stability analysis for non-index 1 Hessenberg form systems of delay differential-algebraic equations. *IEEE Trans. Circuits Syst. Regul. Pap.* **2016**, *63*, 1521–1530. [CrossRef]
7. Agarwal, R.P.; Berezansky, L.; Braverman, E.; Domoshnitsky, A. *Nonoscillation Theory of Functional Differential Equations with Applications*; Springer Science and Business Media: Berlin, Germany, 2012.
8. Norkin, S.B. *Second Order Differential Equations with Retarded Argument*; Nauk: Moscow, Russia, 1965.
9. Braun, M. *Qualitative Theory of Differential Equations: Differential Equations and Their Applications*; Springer: New York, NY, USA, 1993.
10. Hale, J.K. *Functional Differential Equation*; Springer: New York, NY, USA; Berlin/Heidelberg, Germany, 1971.
11. Agarwal, R.P.; Bohner, M.; Li, W.T. *Nonoscillation and Oscillation: Theory for Functional Differential Equations*; Marcel Dekker, Inc.: New York, NY, USA, 2004.
12. Bainov, D.D.; Mishev, D.P. *Oscillation Theory for Neutral Differential Equations with Delay*; CRC Press: Boca Raton, FL, USA, 1991.
13. Gyori, I.; Ladas, G. *Oscillation Theory of Delay Differential Equations*; Oxford University Press: New York, NY, USA, 1991.
14. Moaaz, O.; Masood, F.; Cesarano, C.; Alsallami, S.A.M.; Khalil, E.M.; Bouazizi, M.L. Neutral Differential Equations of Second-Order: Iterative Monotonic Properties. *Mathematics* **2022**, *10*, 1356. [CrossRef]
15. Baculíková, B.; Džurina, J. Oscillation theorems for higher order neutral differential equations. *Appl. Math. Comput.* **2012**, *219*, 3769–3778. [CrossRef]
16. Jadlovská, I.; Džurina, J.; Graef, J.R.; Grace, S.R. Sharp oscillation theorem for fourth-order linear delay differential equations. *J. Inequal. Appl.* **2022**, *2022*, 122. [CrossRef]
17. Masood, F.; Moaaz, O.; Santra, S.S.; Fernandez-Gamiz, U.; El-Metwally, H.A. Oscillation theorems for fourth-order quasi-linear delay differential equations. *AIMS Math.* **2023**, *8*, 16291–16307. [CrossRef]
18. Alnafisah, Y.; Masood, F.; Muhib, A.; Moaaz, O. Improved Oscillation Theorems for Even-Order Quasi-Linear Neutral Differential Equations. *Symmetry* **2023**, *15*, 1128. [CrossRef]
19. Baculikova, B.; Rani, B.; Selvarangam, S.; Thandapani, E. Properties of Kneser's solution for half-linear third order neutral differential equations. *Acta Math. Hung.* **2017**, *152*, 525–533. [CrossRef]
20. Chatzarakis, G.E.; Grace, S.R.; Jadlovská, I. Oscillation criteria for third-order delay differential equations. *Adv. Differ. Equ.* **2017**, *2017*, 330. [CrossRef]
21. Chatzarakis, G.E.; Grace, S.R. Third-order nonlinear differential equations with nonlinear neutral terms. *Funct. Differ. Equ.* **2020**, *27*, 3–13. [CrossRef]
22. Hanan, M. Oscillation criteria for third-order linear differential equations. *Pac. J. Math.* **1961**, *11*, 919–944. [CrossRef]
23. Saker, S.H.; Džurina, J. On the oscillation of certain class of third-order nonlinear delay differential equations. *Math. Bohem.* **2010**, *135*, 225–237. [CrossRef]

24. Thandapani, E.; Li, T. On the oscillation of third-order quasi-linear neutral functional differential equations. *Arch. Math.* **2011**, *47*, 181–199.
25. Džurina, J.; Grace, S.R.; Jadlovská, I. On nonexistence of Kneser solutions of third-order neutral delay differential equations. *Appl. Math. Lett.* **2019**, *88*, 193–200. [CrossRef]
26. Jadlovská, I.; Chatzarakis, G.E.; Džurina, J.; Grace, S.R. On sharp oscillation criteria for general third-order delay differential equations. *Mathematics* **2021**, *9*, 1675. [CrossRef]
27. Chatzarakis, G.E.; Grace, S.R.; Jadlovská, I.; Li, T.; Tunç, E. Oscillation criteria for third-order Emden–Fowler differential equations with unbounded neutral coefficients. *Complexity* **2019**, *2019*, 5691758. [CrossRef]
28. Karpuz, B.; Ocalan, O.; Ozturk, S. Comparison theorems on the oscillation and asymptotic behavior of higher-order neutral differential equations. *Glasg. Math. J.* **2010**, *52*, 107–114. [CrossRef]
29. Xing, G.; Li, T.; Zhang, C. Oscillation of higher-order quasi-linear neutral differential equations. *Adv. Differ. Equ.* **2011**, *2011*, 45. [CrossRef]
30. Zhang, C.; Agarwal, R.; Bohner, M.; Li, T. New results for oscillatory behavior of even-order half-linear delay differential equations. *Appl. Math. Lett.* **2013**, *26*, 179–183. [CrossRef]
31. Hilderbrandt, T.H. *Introduction to the Theory of Integration*; Academic Press: New York, NY, USA, 1963.
32. Kiguradze, I.T.; Chanturiya, T.A. *Asymptotic Properties of Solutions of Nonautonomous Ordinary Differential Equations*; Kluwer Academic Publishers: Dordrecht, The Netherlands, 1993.
33. Kusano, T.; Naito, M. Comparison theorems for functional differential equations with deviating arguments. *J. Math. Soc. Jpn.* **1981**, *33*, 509–532. [CrossRef]
34. Moaaz, O.; Cesarano, C.; Almarri, B. An Improved Relationship between the Solution and Its Corresponding Function in Fourth-Order Neutral Differential Equations and Its Applications. *Mathematics* **2023**, *11*, 1708. [CrossRef]
35. Philos, C. On the existence of nonoscillatory solutions tending to zero at ∞ for differential equations with positive delays. *Arch. Math.* **1981**, *36*, 168–178. [CrossRef]

Disclaimer/Publisher's Note: The statements, opinions and data contained in all publications are solely those of the individual author(s) and contributor(s) and not of MDPI and/or the editor(s). MDPI and/or the editor(s) disclaim responsibility for any injury to people or property resulting from any ideas, methods, instructions or products referred to in the content.

axioms

MDPI

Article

New Conditions for Testing the Asymptotic Behavior of Solutions of Odd-Order Neutral Differential Equations with Multiple Delays

Fahd Masood [1,*], Osama Moaaz [1,2,*], Sameh S. Askar [3] and Ahmad Alshamrani [3]

[1] Department of Mathematics, Faculty of Science, Mansoura University, Mansoura 35516, Egypt
[2] Section of Mathematics, International Telematic University Uninettuno, Corso Vittorio Emanuele II, 39, 00186 Roma, Italy
[3] Department of Statistics and Operations Research, College of Science, King Saud University, P.O. Box 2455, Riyadh 11451, Saudi Arabia; saskar@ksu.edu.sa (S.S.A.); ahmadm@ksu.edu.sa (A.A.)
* Correspondence: fahdmasoud22@gmail.com (F.M.); o_moaaz@mans.edu.eg (O.M.)

Abstract: The purpose of this research is to investigate the asymptotic and oscillatory characteristics of odd-order neutral differential equation solutions with multiple delays. The relationship between the solution and its derivatives of different orders, as well as their related functions, must be understood in order to determine the oscillation terms of the studied equation. In order to contribute to this subject, we create new and significant relationships and inequalities. We use these relationships to create conditions in which positive and N-Kneser solutions of the considered equation are excluded. To obtain these terms, we employ the comparison method and the Riccati technique. Furthermore, we use the relationships obtained to create new criteria, so expanding the existing literature on the field. Finally, we provide an example from the general case to demonstrate the results' significance. The findings given in this work provide light on the behavior of odd-order neutral differential equation solutions with multiple delays.

Keywords: neutral differential equation; asymptotic properties; odd-order; several delays

MSC: 34C10; 34K11

Citation: Masood, F.; Moaaz, O.; Askar, S.S.; Alshamrani, A. New Conditions for Testing the Asymptotic Behavior of Solutions of Odd-Order Neutral Differential Equations with Multiple Delays. *Axioms* **2023**, *12*, 658. https://doi.org/10.3390/axioms12070658

Academic Editors: Hatıra Günerhan, Francisco Martínez González and Mohammed K. A. Kaabar

Received: 27 May 2023
Revised: 20 June 2023
Accepted: 22 June 2023
Published: 2 July 2023

Copyright: © 2023 by the authors. Licensee MDPI, Basel, Switzerland. This article is an open access article distributed under the terms and conditions of the Creative Commons Attribution (CC BY) license (https://creativecommons.org/licenses/by/4.0/).

1. Introduction

Differential equations (DEs) are a powerful and useful mathematical tool for understanding and analyzing many natural and technological processes. Differential equations are made up of functions and their derivatives. These equations are important tools in engineering, physics, computer science, natural sciences, economics, and other domains. It is used to research the motion and dynamics of things, to analyze biological growth and disease spread, and to advance technology in sectors like electrical engineering, mechanics, and others. Differential equations aid in the study of natural occurrences, as well as the development of scientific and technical models and forecasts. Differential equations are crucial in scientific research and practical applications, see [1–4].

Neutral differential equations are an important branch of differential equations because they contain time delays, functions, and their derivatives. These equations are crucial in understanding and analyzing occurrences and processes in various domains, from engineering and physics to medical and economic sciences. Using neutral differential equations, we may develop a scientific understanding in the field of dynamic analysis and control, as well as better technological and economic systems and processes (see [5–7]).

The oscillation theorem is a mathematical branch that studies the behavior of oscillating solutions in differential equations. This theorem helps to comprehend the pattern and form that the solution to the equation takes, such as regular vibration and oscillation. Oscillations are a phenomenon that occurs in many domains, including physics, engineering, and economics, and they play a significant part in integrated systems in electronic systems. Understanding oscillation theory allows us to collaborate, stabilize, and control it more efficiently (see [8–10]).

The stability of a time-delay force feedback teleoperation system based on a scattering matrix is crucial. It ensures reliable and robust communication between the operator and the remote robot, preventing delays or disruptions that could compromise control. By analyzing the system's scattering matrix, key stability properties can be assessed, such as stability margins and robustness to external disturbances, enabling the development of more efficient and dependable teleoperation systems (see [11,12]).

The main objective of this investigation is to investigate the oscillatory characteristics exhibited by solutions of a non-linear DE of odd order, represented by the following expression

$$\left(b(\mathrm{s})\left(\mathcal{U}^{(n-1)}(\mathrm{s})\right)^{\alpha}\right)' + \sum_{i=1}^{m} \mathrm{q}_i(\mathrm{s})x^{\alpha}(v_i(\mathrm{s}))) = 0,\ \mathrm{s} \geq \mathrm{s}_0, \tag{1}$$

where $\mathcal{U}(\mathrm{s}) = x(\mathrm{s}) + p(\mathrm{s})x(\mathfrak{y}(\mathrm{s}))$. In this paper, we make the following assumptions:

(H_1) n is an odd natural number, while α represents the ratio of two positive odd integers;
(H_2) $b, \mathfrak{y}, v_i \in C^1([\mathrm{s}_0,\infty),\mathbb{R}^+)$, $b'(\mathrm{s}) \geq 0$, and $0 \leq p(\mathrm{s}) < p_0 < \infty$;
(H_3) $\mathfrak{y}(\mathrm{s}) < \mathrm{s}$, $v_i(\mathrm{s}) \leq \mathrm{s}$, $v_i'(\mathrm{s}) > 0$, $\left(v_i^{-1}(\mathrm{s})\right)' \geq v_0 > 0$, $\mathfrak{y}'(\mathrm{s}) \geq \mathfrak{y}_0 > 0$, and $\lim_{\mathrm{s}\to\infty} \mathfrak{y}(\mathrm{s}) = \lim_{\mathrm{s}\to\infty} v_i(\mathrm{s}) = \infty$;
(H_4) $\mathfrak{y} \circ v_i = v_i \circ \mathfrak{y}$, for $i = 1,2,...,m$;
(H_5) $\mathrm{q}_i \in C([\mathrm{s}_0,\infty),[0,\infty))$, for $i = 1,2,...,m$.

Moreover, we consider the canonical case, i.e.,

$$\int_{\mathrm{s}_0}^{\infty} \frac{1}{b^{1/\alpha}(\nu)} \mathrm{d}\nu = \infty. \tag{2}$$

A function $x \in C^{n-1}([\mathrm{S}_x,\infty))$, $\mathrm{S}_x \geqslant \mathrm{s}_0$, is considered a solution of (1) which has the property $b(\mathcal{U}^{(n-1)})^{\alpha} \in C^1[\mathrm{s}_x,\infty)$, and it satisfies the Equation (1) for all $x \in [\mathrm{S}_x,\infty)$. We examine, exclusively, the solutions x from (1) that are present on a half-line $[\mathrm{S}_x,\infty)$ and fulfill the requirement:

$$\sup\{|x(\mathrm{s})| : \mathrm{s} \geqslant \mathrm{S}\} > 0, \text{ for all } \mathrm{S} \geq \mathrm{S}_x.$$

A solution is referred to as oscillatory if it does not eventually positive or negative. Otherwise, it is considered non-oscillatory. Equation (1) is considered oscillatory when all of its solutions exhibit oscillatory behavior.

Previous works on the subject of neutral DEs opened the path for advances in our understanding of delayed systems. Researchers have extensively researched neutral DEs of various orders, making substantial contributions to the theoretical foundations and practical applications of these equations.

In the canonical case, multiple studies have explored the oscillation behavior of even-order quasilinear neutral functional differential equations. Baculikova et al. [13], Dzurina [14], Graef et al. [15], and Bohner et al. [16] have specifically delved into this topic, shedding light on the properties of these equations. In the non-canonical case, several studies have concentrated on analyzing the oscillation criteria for even-order neutral delay differential equations. These studies include the works of Moaaz et al. [17], Almari et al. [18], another study by Bohner et al. [19], and Jadlovska [20]. The investigations conducted have provided valuable insights regarding the oscillatory behavior and dynamics exhibited by these equations.

Dzurina and Baculıkova [21] introduced a generalized version of Philos and Staikos lemmas, which aimed to examine the oscillatory behavior and asymptotic characteristics of a higher-order DDE

$$\left(b(\mathrm{s})\left(x'(\mathrm{s})\right)^{\alpha}\right)^{(n-1)}+q(\mathrm{s})x^{\alpha}(v(\mathrm{s}))=0.$$

They employed a comparison theory to obtain their results.

Karpuz et al. [22] focused on higher-order neutral DEs of the form:

$$(x(\mathrm{s})+\mathrm{p}(\mathrm{s})x(\mathfrak{y}(\mathrm{s})))^{(n)}+q(\mathrm{s})x(v(\mathrm{s}))=0,\ \mathrm{s}\geq\mathrm{s}_0,$$

The authors compared the asymptotic and oscillatory behaviors of all solutions of higher-order neutral DEs with those of first-order delay DEs.

Sun et al. [23] investigated the oscillatory behavior of neutral DEs of the form

$$\left(b(\mathrm{s})(x(\mathrm{s})+\mathrm{p}(\mathrm{s})x(\mathfrak{y}(\mathrm{s})))^{(n-1)}\right)'+q(\mathrm{s})K(x(v(\mathrm{s})))=0,$$

under two conditions, the canonical condition (2) and non-canonical condition

$$\int_{\mathrm{s}_0}^{\infty}\frac{1}{b^{1/\alpha}(\nu)}\mathrm{d}\nu<\infty,$$

where $K(x)/x\geq k>0$.

Baculková et al. [24] examined the oscillation behavior and asymptotic properties of the equation

$$\left(b(\mathrm{s})\left(x^{(n-1)}(\mathrm{s})\right)^{\alpha}\right)'+q(\mathrm{s})K(x(v(\mathrm{s})))=0,$$

when K is a non-decreasing function satisfying:

$$-K(-\mathrm{s}_1\mathrm{s}_2)\geq K(\mathrm{s}_1\mathrm{s}_2)\geq K(\mathrm{s}_1)K(\mathrm{s}_2)\text{ for }\mathrm{s}_1\mathrm{s}_2>0.$$

Xing et al. [25] developed several oscillation criteria for a particular higher-order quasi-linear NDE

$$\left(b(\mathrm{s})\left((x(\mathrm{s})+\mathrm{p}(\mathrm{s})x(\mathfrak{y}(\mathrm{s})))^{(n-1)}\right)^{\alpha}\right)'+q(\mathrm{s})x^{\alpha}(v(\mathrm{s}))=0. \tag{3}$$

Moaaz et al. [26] focused on the oscillatory characteristics of the neutral DE (3) in the non-canonical case.

This work aims to look into the oscillatory behavior of solutions in odd-order neutral DEs with multiple delays. The study aims to establish new relationships and terms within this field. Additionally, a novel approach is employed to derive new criteria that guarantee the oscillatory nature of the solutions for the considered equation.

2. Preliminary Results

This section will introduce several essential lemmas that will be utilized to demonstrate the main results. To simplify our notation, let us denote the following:

$$\rho'_{+}(\mathrm{s}):=\max\{0,\ \rho'(\mathrm{s})\},$$

$$\widetilde{v}(\mathrm{s}):=\min\{v_i(\mathrm{s}),\ i=1,2,...,m\},\ v(\mathrm{s}):=\max\{v_i(\mathrm{s}),\ i=1,2,...,m\},$$

$$\pi_0(\varsigma,\varrho):=\int_{\varrho}^{\varsigma}b^{-1/\alpha}(\nu)\mathrm{d}\nu,\ \pi_i(\varsigma,\varrho):=\int_{\varrho}^{\varsigma}\pi_{i-1}(\varsigma,\nu)\mathrm{d}\nu,$$

$$\pi_0(\mathrm{s}):=\int_{\mathrm{s}_0}^{\mathrm{s}}b^{-1/\alpha}(\nu)\mathrm{d}\nu,\ \pi_i(\mathrm{s}):=\int_{\mathrm{s}_0}^{\mathrm{s}}\pi_{i-1}(\nu)\mathrm{d}\nu,\ i=1,2,...,n-2,$$

$$Q_0(s) := \sum_{i=1}^{m} q_i(s)(1 - p(v_i(s)))^{\alpha},$$

$$Q(s) := \sum_{i=1}^{m} \widetilde{q}_i(s),\ \widehat{Q}(s) := \sum_{i=1}^{m} \widehat{q}_i(s),$$

and

$$\widetilde{q}_i(s) := \min\{q_i(s), q_i(\eta(s))\},\ \widehat{q}_i(s) := \min\{q_i\left(v_i^{-1}(s)\right), q_i\left(v_i^{-1}(\eta(s))\right)\}.$$

Lemma 1 ([27]). *Assume that* $x_1,\ x_2 \in [0,\infty)$. *Then,*

$$(x_1 + x_2)^{\alpha} \le \mu(x_1^{\alpha} + x_2^{\alpha}),$$

and

$$\mu = \begin{cases} 2^{\alpha-1} & \text{for } \alpha > 1; \\ 1 & \text{for } 0 < \alpha \le 1. \end{cases}$$

Lemma 2 ([28]). *For* $A > 0$ *and* B *is any real number, the following inequality holds:*

$$B\psi - A\psi^{(\alpha+1)/\alpha} \le \frac{\alpha^{\alpha}}{(\alpha+1)^{\alpha+1}} \frac{B^{\alpha+1}}{A^{\alpha}}. \tag{4}$$

Lemma 3 ([29]). *Assume that* $\psi \in C^n([s_0,\infty),(0,\infty))$. *Additionally,* $\psi^{(n)}(s)$ *has a fixed sign and is not equal to zero throughout* $[s_0,\infty)$. *Furthermore, there exists* $s_1 \ge s_0$ *satisfying the condition* $\psi^{(n-1)}(s)\psi^{(n)}(s) \le 0$ *for all* $s \ge s_1$. *If* $\lim_{s\to\infty}\psi(s) \ne 0$, *then for any* $\lambda \in (0,1)$, *there exists* $s_{\mu} \ge s_1$ *satisfying the inequality:*

$$\psi(s) \ge \frac{\lambda}{(n-1)!} s^{n-1} \left|\psi^{(n-1)}(s)\right| \text{ for } s \ge s_{\mu}.$$

Lemma 4 ([30]). *Consider* $x(s)$ *as a positive solution of (1). Consequently,* $b(s)\left(\mathcal{U}^{(n-1)}(s)\right)^{\alpha}$ *is a decreasing function. Furthermore, all derivatives* $\mathcal{U}^{(i)}(s)$, $1 \le i \le n-1$ *have constant signs. Additionally,* $\mathcal{U}(s)$ *satisfies one of the following cases:*

$$\begin{aligned} &C_1: \quad \mathcal{U}(s) > 0,\ \mathcal{U}'(s) > 0,\ \mathcal{U}''(s) > 0, \mathcal{U}^{(n-1)}(s) > 0,\ (b(s)(\mathcal{U}^{(n-1)}(s))^{\alpha})' < 0; \\ &C_2: \quad (-1)^k \mathcal{U}^{(k)}(s) > 0, \text{ for } k = 0,1,2,\ldots,n. \end{aligned}$$

Notation 1. *The symbols* K_1 *and* K_2 *represent sets of solutions that are eventually positive and satisfy the corresponding function conditions* (C_1) *and* (C_2), *respectively.*

Definition 1 ([31]). *We define a* ***Kneser solution*** *for Equation (1) as a solution* x *that satisfies the following condition, there exists a* $s_* \in [s_0,\infty)$ *such that* $\mathcal{U}(s)\mathcal{U}'(s) < 0$ *for all* $s \in [s_*,\infty)$..

3. Criteria for Non-Existence of N-Kneser Solutions

In this section, we introduce specific criteria that ensure the non-existence of N-Kneser solutions that satisfy condition (C_2).

Theorem 1. *If* $\zeta \in C([s_0,\infty),(0,\infty))$ *fulfilling* $v(s) < \zeta(s)$ *and* $\eta^{-1}(\zeta(s)) < s$, *such that the DE*

$$G'(s) + \frac{1}{\mu} \frac{\eta_0}{\eta_0 + p_0^{\alpha}} \pi_{n-2}^{\alpha}(\zeta(s), v(s)) Q(s) G\left(\eta^{-1}(\zeta(s))\right) = 0, \tag{5}$$

is oscillatory, then $K_2 = \varnothing$.

Proof. Let $x \in \mathrm{K}_2$, say $x(\mathrm{s}) > 0$ and $x(v_i(\mathrm{s})) > 0$ for $\mathrm{s} \geq \mathrm{s}_1 \geq \mathrm{s}_0$. This implies that

$$(-1)^k \mathcal{U}^{(k)}(\mathrm{s}) > 0, \text{ for } k = 0, 1, 2, ..., n. \tag{6}$$

From (1), we see that:

$$\begin{aligned} 0 \geq & \frac{\mathrm{p}_0^\alpha}{\mathfrak{y}'}\left(b(\mathfrak{y})\left(\mathcal{U}^{(n-1)}(\mathfrak{y})\right)^\alpha\right)' + \mathrm{p}_0^\alpha \sum_{i=1}^m \mathrm{q}_i(\mathfrak{y}) x^\alpha(v_i(\mathfrak{y})) \\ \geq & \frac{\mathrm{p}_0^\alpha}{\mathfrak{y}_0}\left(b(\mathfrak{y})\left(\mathcal{U}^{(n-1)}(\mathfrak{y})\right)^\alpha\right)' + \mathrm{p}_0^\alpha \sum_{i=1}^m \mathrm{q}_i(\mathfrak{y}) x^\alpha(v_i(\mathfrak{y})) \\ = & \frac{\mathrm{p}_0^\alpha}{\mathfrak{y}_0}\left(b(\mathfrak{y})\left(\mathcal{U}^{(n-1)}(\mathfrak{y})\right)^\alpha\right)' + \mathrm{p}_0^\alpha \sum_{i=1}^m \mathrm{q}_i(\mathfrak{y}) x^\alpha(\mathfrak{y}(v_i)). \end{aligned} \tag{7}$$

When we combine (1) with (7), we obtain:

$$\begin{aligned} 0 &\geq (b(\mathcal{U}^{(n-1)})^\alpha)' + \frac{\mathrm{p}_0^\alpha}{\mathfrak{y}_0}\left(b(\mathfrak{y})\left(\mathcal{U}^{(n-1)}(\mathfrak{y})\right)^\alpha\right)' + \sum_{i=1}^m \mathrm{q}_i x^\alpha(v_i) + \mathrm{p}_0^\alpha \sum_{i=1}^n \mathrm{q}_i(\mathfrak{y}) x^\alpha(\mathfrak{y}(v_i)) \\ &= (b(\mathcal{U}^{(n-1)})^\alpha)' + \frac{\mathrm{p}_0^\alpha}{\mathfrak{y}_0}\left(b(\mathfrak{y})\left(\mathcal{U}^{(n-1)}(\mathfrak{y})\right)^\alpha\right)' + \sum_{i=1}^m [\mathrm{q}_i x^\alpha(v_i) + \mathrm{p}_0^\alpha \mathrm{q}_i(\mathfrak{y}) x^\alpha(\mathfrak{y}(v_i))] \\ &\geq (b(\mathcal{U}^{(n-1)})^\alpha)' + \frac{\mathrm{p}_0^\alpha}{\mathfrak{y}_0}\left(b(\mathfrak{y})\left(\mathcal{U}^{(n-1)}(\mathfrak{y})\right)^\alpha\right)' + \sum_{i=1}^m \widetilde{\mathrm{q}}_i [x^\alpha(v_i) + \mathrm{p}_0^\alpha x^\alpha(\mathfrak{y}(v_i))]. \end{aligned}$$

Using Lemma 1, we have:

$$\begin{aligned} 0 \geq & (b(\mathcal{U}^{(n-1)})^\alpha)' + \frac{\mathrm{p}_0^\alpha}{\mathfrak{y}_0}\left(b(\mathfrak{y})\left(\mathcal{U}^{(n-1)}(\mathfrak{y})\right)^\alpha\right)' \\ & + \frac{1}{\mu} \sum_{i=1}^m \widetilde{\mathrm{q}}_i (x(v_i) + \mathrm{p}_0 x(\mathfrak{y}(v_i))))^\alpha. \end{aligned} \tag{8}$$

From definition of $\mathcal{U}$, we have:

$$\mathcal{U}(v_i) = x(v_i) + \mathrm{p}(v_i) x(\mathfrak{y}(v_i)) \leq x(v_i) + \mathrm{p}_0 x(\mathfrak{y}(v_i)).$$

From (8), we obtain:

$$0 \geq (b(\mathcal{U}^{(n-1)})^\alpha)' + \frac{\mathrm{p}_0^\alpha}{\mathfrak{y}_0}\left(b(\mathfrak{y})\left(\mathcal{U}^{(n-1)}(\mathfrak{y})\right)^\alpha\right)' + \frac{1}{\mu} \sum_{i=1}^m \widetilde{\mathrm{q}}_i \mathcal{U}^\alpha(v_i).$$

Since $\mathcal{U}$ is decreasing, then:

$$\begin{aligned} 0 \geq & (b(\mathcal{U}^{(n-1)})^\alpha)' + \frac{\mathrm{p}_0^\alpha}{\mathfrak{y}_0}\left(b(\mathfrak{y})\left(\mathcal{U}^{(n-1)}(\mathfrak{y})\right)^\alpha\right)' + \frac{1}{\mu} \mathcal{U}^\alpha(v) \sum_{i=1}^m \widetilde{\mathrm{q}}_i \\ = & (b(\mathcal{U}^{(n-1)})^\alpha)' + \frac{\mathrm{p}_0^\alpha}{\mathfrak{y}_0}\left(b(\mathfrak{y})\left(\mathcal{U}^{(n-1)}(\mathfrak{y})\right)^\alpha\right)' + \frac{1}{\mu} \mathrm{Q} \mathcal{U}^\alpha(v). \end{aligned}$$

That is

$$\left(b(\mathcal{U}^{(n-1)})^\alpha + \frac{\mathrm{p}_0^\alpha}{\mathfrak{y}_0} b(\mathfrak{y})\left(\mathcal{U}^{(n-1)}(\mathfrak{y})\right)^\alpha\right)' + \frac{1}{\mu} \mathrm{Q} \mathcal{U}^\alpha(v) \leq 0. \tag{9}$$

It follows from $\left(b\left(\mathcal{U}^{(n-1)}\right)^\alpha\right)' \leq 0$ that

$$-\mathcal{U}^{(n-2)}(\varrho) \geq \int_\varrho^\varsigma \frac{b^{1/\alpha}(\nu)\mathcal{U}^{(n-1)}(\nu)}{b^{1/\alpha}(\nu)} \mathrm{d}\nu \geq b^{1/\alpha}(\varsigma)\mathcal{U}^{(n-1)}(\varsigma)\pi_0(\varsigma, \varrho). \tag{10}$$

By integrating (10) over (ϱ, ς), we arrive at

$$-\mathcal{U}^{(n-3)}(\varrho) \leq b^{1/\alpha}(\varsigma)\mathcal{U}^{(n-1)}(\varsigma)\pi_1(\varsigma, \varrho). \tag{11}$$

By applying the integration process $n-3$ times to (11) over (ϱ, ς) and then using (6), we obtain

$$\mathcal{U}(\varrho) \geq b^{1/\alpha}(\varsigma)\mathcal{U}^{(n-1)}(\varsigma)\pi_{n-2}(\varsigma, \varrho). \tag{12}$$

Therefore, we obtain:

$$\mathcal{U}(v) \geq b^{1/\alpha}(\zeta)\mathcal{U}^{(n-1)}(\zeta)\pi_{n-2}(\zeta, v).$$

By virtue of (9), it follows that

$$\begin{aligned} 0 \geq & \left(b(\mathcal{U}^{(n-1)})^\alpha + \frac{\mathrm{p}_0^\alpha}{\mathfrak{y}_0} b(\mathfrak{y})\left(\mathcal{U}^{(n-1)}(\mathfrak{y})\right)^\alpha\right)' \\ & + \frac{1}{\mu} \mathrm{Q} b(\zeta)\left(\mathcal{U}^{(n-1)}(\zeta)\right)^\alpha \pi_{n-2}^\alpha(\zeta, v). \end{aligned} \tag{13}$$

Now, set

$$G = b(\mathcal{U}^{(n-1)})^\alpha + \frac{\mathrm{p}_0^\alpha}{\mathfrak{y}_0} b(\mathfrak{y})\left(\mathcal{U}^{(n-1)}(\mathfrak{y})\right)^\alpha > 0.$$

From $\left(b\left(\mathcal{U}^{(n-1)}\right)^\alpha\right)' \leq 0$, we have

$$G \leq b(\mathfrak{y})\left(\mathcal{U}^{(n-1)}(\mathfrak{y})\right)^\alpha \left(1 + \frac{\mathrm{p}_0^\alpha}{\mathfrak{y}_0}\right),$$

or, equivalently,

$$b(\zeta)(\mathcal{U}^{(n-1)}(\zeta))^\alpha \geq \frac{\mathfrak{y}_0}{\mathfrak{y}_0 + \mathrm{p}_0^\alpha} G\left(\mathfrak{y}^{-1}(\zeta)\right). \tag{14}$$

By applying (14) within (13), it becomes evident that G represents a positive solution of the differential inequality

$$G' + \frac{1}{\mu}\frac{\mathfrak{y}_0}{\mathfrak{y}_0 + \mathrm{p}_0^\alpha} \pi_{n-2}^\alpha(\zeta, v) \mathrm{Q} G\left(\mathfrak{y}^{-1}(\zeta)\right) \leq 0.$$

Considering [32] (Theorem 1), it can be inferred that (5) also possesses a positive solution, which contradicts the previous inequality. As a result, the proof is concluded. □

Corollary 1. *If $\zeta \in \mathrm{C}([\mathrm{s}_0, \infty), (0, \infty))$ fulfilling $v(\mathrm{s}) < \zeta(\mathrm{s})$ and $\mathfrak{y}^{-1}(\zeta(\mathrm{s})) < \mathrm{s}$, such that*

$$\liminf_{\mathrm{s}\to\infty} \int_{\mathfrak{y}^{-1}(\zeta(\mathrm{s}))}^{\mathrm{s}} \pi_{n-2}^\alpha(\zeta(\nu), v(\nu)) \mathrm{Q}(\nu) \mathrm{d}\nu > \frac{\mu(\mathfrak{y}_0 + \mathrm{p}_0^\alpha)}{\mathfrak{y}_0 \mathrm{e}}, \tag{15}$$

then $\mathrm{K}_2 = \varnothing$.

Theorem 2. *If $\delta(\mathrm{s}) \in \mathrm{C}([\mathrm{s}_0, \infty),\ (0, \infty))$ fulfilling $\delta(\mathrm{s}) < \mathrm{s}$ and $v(\mathrm{s}) < \mathfrak{y}(\delta(\mathrm{s}))$ such that*

$$\limsup_{\mathrm{s}\to\infty} \frac{\pi_{n-2}^\alpha(\mathfrak{y}(\delta(\mathrm{s})), v(\mathrm{s}))}{b(\mathfrak{y}(\delta(\mathrm{s})))} \int_{\delta(\mathrm{s})}^{\mathrm{s}} \mathrm{Q}(\nu) \mathrm{d}\nu > \frac{\mu(\mathfrak{y}_0 + \mathrm{p}_0^\alpha)}{\mathfrak{y}_0}, \tag{16}$$

then $\mathrm{K}_2 = \varnothing$.

Proof. Using the same procedure as in the proof of Theorem 1, we obtain

$$0 \geq \left(b(\mathrm{s})(\mathcal{U}^{(n-1)}(\mathrm{s}))^{\alpha} + \frac{\mathrm{p}_0^{\alpha}}{\mathfrak{y}_0} b(\mathfrak{y}(\mathrm{s}))\left(\mathcal{U}^{(n-1)}(\mathfrak{y}(\mathrm{s}))\right)^{\alpha}\right)' + \frac{1}{\mu}\mathrm{Q}(\mathrm{s})\mathcal{U}^{\alpha}(v(\mathrm{s})).$$

Integrating the previous inequality over $(\delta(\mathrm{s}),\mathrm{s})$ and utilizing the property that $\mathcal{U}$ is decreasing, we have

$$\begin{aligned} & b(\delta(\mathrm{s}))(\mathcal{U}^{(n-1)}(\delta(\mathrm{s})))^{\alpha} + \frac{\mathrm{p}_0^{\alpha}}{\mathfrak{y}_0} b(\mathfrak{y}(\delta(\mathrm{s})))\left(\mathcal{U}^{(n-1)}(\mathfrak{y}(\delta(\mathrm{s})))\right)^{\alpha} \\ \geq\ & b(\mathrm{s})(\mathcal{U}^{(n-1)}(\mathrm{s}))^{\alpha} + \frac{\mathrm{p}_0^{\alpha}}{\mathfrak{y}_0} b(\mathfrak{y}(\mathrm{s}))\left(\mathcal{U}^{(n-1)}(\mathfrak{y}(\mathrm{s}))\right)^{\alpha} + \frac{1}{\mu}\mathcal{U}^{\alpha}(v(\mathrm{s}))\int_{\delta(\mathrm{s})}^{\mathrm{s}} \mathrm{Q}(\nu)\mathrm{d}\nu \\ \geq\ & \frac{1}{\mu}\mathcal{U}^{\alpha}(v(\mathrm{s}))\int_{\delta(\mathrm{s})}^{\mathrm{s}} \mathrm{Q}(\nu)\mathrm{d}\nu. \end{aligned}$$

Since $\mathfrak{y}(\delta(\mathrm{s})) < \mathfrak{y}(\mathrm{s})$ and $\left(b(\mathrm{s})(\mathcal{U}^{(n-1)}(\mathrm{s}))^{\alpha}\right)' \leq 0$, we obtain

$$b(\mathfrak{y}(\delta(\mathrm{s})))(\mathcal{U}^{(n-1)}(\mathfrak{y}(\delta(\mathrm{s}))))^{\alpha}\left(1 + \frac{\mathrm{p}_0^{\alpha}}{\mathfrak{y}_0}\right) \geq \frac{1}{\mu}\mathcal{U}^{\alpha}(v(\mathrm{s}))\int_{\delta(\mathrm{s})}^{\mathrm{s}} \mathrm{Q}(\nu)\mathrm{d}\nu. \tag{17}$$

By utilizing (12) with $\varsigma = \mathfrak{y}(\delta(\mathrm{s}))$ and $\varrho = v(\mathrm{s})$ into (17), we derive the following inequality

$$\begin{aligned} & b(\mathfrak{y}(\delta(\mathrm{s})))(\mathcal{U}^{(n-1)}(\mathfrak{y}(\delta(\mathrm{s}))))^{\alpha}\left(1 + \frac{\mathrm{p}_0^{\alpha}}{\mathfrak{y}_0}\right) \\ \geq\ & \frac{1}{\mu}\left(\mathcal{U}^{(n-1)}(\mathfrak{y}(\delta(\mathrm{s})))\right)^{\alpha}\pi_{n-2}^{\alpha}(\mathfrak{y}(\delta(\mathrm{s})), v(\mathrm{s}))\int_{\delta(\mathrm{s})}^{\mathrm{s}} \mathrm{Q}(\nu)\mathrm{d}\nu. \end{aligned}$$

That is

$$\frac{\mathfrak{y}_0 + \mathrm{p}_0^{\alpha}}{\mathfrak{y}_0} \geq \frac{1}{\mu}\frac{\pi_{n-2}^{\alpha}(\mathfrak{y}(\delta(\mathrm{s})), v(\mathrm{s}))}{b(\mathfrak{y}(\delta(\mathrm{s})))}\int_{\delta(\mathrm{s})}^{\mathrm{s}} \mathrm{Q}(\nu)\mathrm{d}\nu.$$

By considering the lim sup of both sides of the aforementioned inequality, it becomes apparent that it contradicts (16). As a result, we can conclude the proof. □

Theorem 3. *Assume that $v_i(\mathfrak{y}(\mathrm{s})) < \mathrm{s}$, $i = 1,2,...,n$ holds. If the DE*

$$\Psi'(\mathrm{s}) + \widehat{\mathrm{Q}}(\mathrm{s})\pi_{n-2}^{\alpha}(\mathfrak{y}(\mathrm{s}),\mathrm{s})\left(\frac{v_0\mathfrak{y}_0}{\mathfrak{y}_0 + \mathrm{p}_0^{\alpha}}\right)\Psi(v(\mathrm{s})) = 0, \tag{18}$$

is oscillatory, then $\mathrm{K}_2 = \varnothing$.

Proof. Suppose $u \in \mathrm{K}_2$, with $x(\mathrm{s}) > 0$, $x(\mathfrak{y}(\mathrm{s})) > 0$ and $x(v_i(\mathrm{s})) > 0$ for $\mathrm{s} \geq \mathrm{s}_1 \geq \mathrm{s}_0$. Consequently, it follows that

$$(-1)^k\mathcal{U}^{(k)}(\mathrm{s}) > 0, \text{ for } k = 0,1,2,...,n.$$

Utilising (1), we can be observed that

$$\begin{aligned} 0 \ \geq\ & \frac{1}{\left(v_i^{-1}(\mathrm{s})\right)'}\left(b\left(v_i^{-1}(\mathrm{s})\right)\left(\mathcal{U}^{(n-1)}\left(v_i^{-1}(\mathrm{s})\right)\right)^{\alpha}\right)' + \sum_{i=1}^{m}\mathrm{q}_i\left(v_i^{-1}(\mathrm{s})\right)x^{\alpha}(\mathrm{s}) \\ \geq\ & \frac{1}{v_0}\left(b\left(v_i^{-1}(\mathrm{s})\right)\left(\mathcal{U}^{(n-1)}\left(v_i^{-1}(\mathrm{s})\right)\right)^{\alpha}\right)' + \sum_{i=1}^{m}\mathrm{q}_i\left(v_i^{-1}(\mathrm{s})\right)x^{\alpha}(\mathrm{s}). \end{aligned}$$

Similarly,

$$\begin{aligned} 0 &\geq \frac{p_0^{\alpha}}{\left(v_i^{-1}(\eta(s))\right)'}\left(b\left(v_i^{-1}(\eta(s))\right)\left(\mathcal{U}^{(n-1)}\left(v_i^{-1}(\eta(s))\right)\right)^{\alpha}\right)' \\ &\quad + p_0^{\alpha}\sum_{i=1}^{m} q_i\left(v_i^{-1}(\eta(s))\right)x^{\alpha}(\eta(s)) \\ &\geq \frac{p_0^{\alpha}}{v_0\eta_0}\left(b\left(v_i^{-1}(\eta(s))\right)\left(\mathcal{U}^{(n-1)}\left(v_i^{-1}(\eta(s))\right)\right)^{\alpha}\right)' \\ &\quad + p_0^{\alpha}\sum_{i=1}^{m} q_i\left(v_i^{-1}(\eta(s))\right)x^{\alpha}(\eta(s)). \end{aligned}$$

Combining the above inequalities yields that

$$\begin{aligned} 0 &\geq \frac{1}{v_0}\left(b\left(v_i^{-1}(s)\right)\left(\mathcal{U}^{(n-1)}\left(v_i^{-1}(s)\right)\right)^{\alpha}\right)' \\ &\quad + \frac{p_0^{\alpha}}{v_0\eta_0}\left(b\left(v_i^{-1}(\eta(s))\right)\left(\mathcal{U}^{(n-1)}\left(v_i^{-1}(\eta(s))\right)\right)^{\alpha}\right)' \\ &\quad + \sum_{i=1}^{m}\left[q_i\left(v_i^{-1}(s)\right)x^{\alpha}(s) + p_0^{\alpha}q_i\left(v_i^{-1}(\eta(s))\right)x^{\alpha}(\eta(s))\right] \\ &\geq \frac{1}{v_0}\left(b\left(v_i^{-1}(s)\right)\left(\mathcal{U}^{(n-1)}\left(v_i^{-1}(s)\right)\right)^{\alpha}\right)' \\ &\quad + \frac{p_0^{\alpha}}{v_0\eta_0}\left(b\left(v_i^{-1}(\eta(s))\right)\left(\mathcal{U}^{(n-1)}\left(v_i^{-1}(\eta(s))\right)\right)^{\alpha}\right)' \\ &\quad + \sum_{i=1}^{m}\widehat{q}_i(s)\left[x^{\alpha}(s) + p_0^{\alpha}x^{\alpha}(\eta(s))\right]. \end{aligned}$$

That is

$$\begin{aligned} 0 &\geq \left[\left(\frac{1}{v_0}b\left(v_i^{-1}(s)\right)\left(\mathcal{U}^{(n-1)}\left(v_i^{-1}(s)\right)\right)^{\alpha}\right)\right. \\ &\quad \left. + \frac{p_0^{\alpha}}{v_0\eta_0}b\left(v_i^{-1}(\eta(s))\right)\left(\mathcal{U}^{(n-1)}\left(v_i^{-1}(\eta(s))\right)\right)^{\alpha}\right]' + \widehat{Q}(s)\mathcal{U}^{\alpha}(s). \end{aligned} \tag{19}$$

Now, we set

$$\begin{aligned} \Psi(s) &= \frac{1}{v_0}b\left(v_i^{-1}(s)\right)\left(\mathcal{U}^{(n-1)}\left(v_i^{-1}(s)\right)\right)^{\alpha} \\ &\quad + \frac{p_0^{\alpha}}{v_0\eta_0}b\left(v_i^{-1}(\eta(s))\right)\left(\mathcal{U}^{(n-1)}\left(v_i^{-1}(\eta(s))\right)\right)^{\alpha}. \end{aligned} \tag{20}$$

Since $\left(b(s)(\mathcal{U}^{(n-1)}(s))^{\alpha}\right)' \leq 0$, it is clear that

$$\begin{aligned} \Psi(s) &\leq \frac{b\left(\left(v_i^{-1}(\eta(s))\right)\right)\left(\mathcal{U}^{(n-1)}\left(v_i^{-1}(\eta(s))\right)\right)^{\alpha}}{v_0}\left(1 + \frac{p_0^{\alpha}}{\eta_0}\right) \\ &\leq \frac{b\left(\left(v^{-1}(\eta(s))\right)\right)\left(\mathcal{U}^{(n-1)}\left(v^{-1}(\eta(s))\right)\right)^{\alpha}}{v_0}\left(1 + \frac{p_0^{\alpha}}{\eta_0}\right). \end{aligned} \tag{21}$$

By using (12) with $\varsigma = \mathfrak{y}(s)$ and $\varrho = s$ and (21), we have $\mathcal{U}(\varrho) \geq b^{1/\alpha}(\varsigma)\mathcal{U}^{(n-1)}(\varsigma)\pi_{n-2}(\varsigma,\varrho)$, and

$$\mathcal{U}^{\alpha}(s) \geq b(\mathfrak{y}(s))\left(\mathcal{U}^{(n-1)}(\mathfrak{y}(s))\right)^{\alpha}\pi_{n-2}^{\alpha}(\mathfrak{y}(s),s) \geq \Psi(v(s))\pi_{n-2}^{\alpha}(\mathfrak{y}(s),s)\left(\frac{v_0\mathfrak{y}_0}{\mathfrak{y}_0+p_0^{\alpha}}\right).$$

Using the preceding inequality and the definition of Ψ in (19), we obtain

$$\Psi'(s) + \widehat{Q}(s)\pi_{n-2}^{\alpha}(\mathfrak{y}(s),s)\left(\frac{v_0\mathfrak{y}_0}{\mathfrak{y}_0+p_0^{\alpha}}\right)\Psi(v(s)) \leq 0.$$

Based on [32] (Theorem 1), it can be inferred that Equation (18) also has a positive solution, which contradicts the previous inequality. As a result, the proof is concluded. □

Corollary 2. *Suppose that* $v_i(\mathfrak{y}(s)) < s$, $i = 1,2,...,n$ *holds. If*

$$\liminf_{s\to\infty}\int_{v(s)}^{s}\pi_{n-2}^{\alpha}(\mathfrak{y}(\nu),\nu)\widehat{Q}(\nu)d\nu > \frac{\mathfrak{y}_0+p_0^{\alpha}}{v_0\mathfrak{y}_0 e}, \tag{22}$$

then $K_2 = \varnothing$.

4. Non-Existence of Solutions from the Class C_1

The main objective of this section is to analyze the asymptotic and monotonic properties displayed by the positive solutions of the examined equation. Additionally, we present limitations to guarantee that none of the positive solutions meet the criteria stated as condition (C_1).

Lemma 5. *Assume that* $x \in K_1$. *Then, eventually*

$$x(s) > (1-p(s))\mathcal{U}(s),$$

and (1) becomes

$$\left(b(s)\left(\mathcal{U}^{(n-1)}(s)\right)^{\alpha}\right)' + Q_0(s)\mathcal{U}^{\alpha}(\widetilde{v}(s)) \leq 0, \tag{23}$$

eventually.

Proof. Since

$$\mathcal{U}(s) = x(s) + p(s)x(\mathfrak{y}(s)),$$

then $\mathcal{U}(s) \geq x(s)$ and

$$x(s) = \mathcal{U}(s) - p(s)x(\mathfrak{y}(s)) \geq \mathcal{U}(s) - p(s)\mathcal{U}(\mathfrak{y}(s)).$$

Since $\mathcal{U}(s)$ is increasing, then

$$x(s) \geq (1-p(s))\mathcal{U}(s). \tag{24}$$

From (1), we have

$$\begin{aligned} 0 &= \left(b(s)\left(\mathcal{U}^{(n-1)}(s)\right)^{\alpha}\right)' + \sum_{i=1}^{m} q_i(s)x^{\alpha}(v_i(s)) \\ &\geq \left(b(s)\left(\mathcal{U}^{(n-1)}(s)\right)^{\alpha}\right)' + \sum_{i=1}^{n} q_i(s)(1-p(v_i(s)))^{\alpha}\mathcal{U}^{\alpha}(v_i(s)) \\ &\geq \left(b(s)\left(\mathcal{U}^{(n-1)}(s)\right)^{\alpha}\right)' + \mathcal{U}^{\alpha}(\widetilde{v}(s))\sum_{i=1}^{n} q_i(s)(1-p(v_i(s)))^{\alpha} \\ &\geq \left(b(s)\left(\mathcal{U}^{(n-1)}(s)\right)^{\alpha}\right)' + Q_0(s)\mathcal{U}^{\alpha}(\widetilde{v}(s)). \end{aligned}$$

Therefore, the proof is concluded. □

Theorem 4. *Assume that there is a* $\rho \in C^1([s_0,\infty),(0,\infty))$ *such that*

$$\limsup_{s\to\infty}\int_{s_0}^{s}\left(\rho(v)Q_0(v)-\frac{((n-2)!)^{\alpha}}{(\alpha+1)^{\alpha+1}}\frac{b(\tilde{v}(v))(\rho'(v))^{\alpha+1}}{(\lambda\rho(v)\tilde{v}^{n-2}(v)\tilde{v}'(v))^{\alpha}}\right)dv=\infty. \tag{25}$$

Then $K_1=\varnothing$.

Proof. Suppose the opposite that $x\in K_1$. We introduce w defined as

$$w(s)=\rho(s)\frac{b(s)\left(\mathcal{U}^{(n-1)}(s)\right)^{\alpha}}{\mathcal{U}^{\alpha}(\tilde{v}(s))}. \tag{26}$$

Then $w(s)>0$. Differentiating (26), we have

$$\begin{aligned} w'(s) &= \rho'(s)\frac{b(s)\left(\mathcal{U}^{(n-1)}(s)\right)^{\alpha}}{\mathcal{U}^{\alpha}(\tilde{v}(s))}+\rho(s)\frac{\left(b(s)\left(\mathcal{U}^{(n-1)}(s)\right)^{\alpha}\right)'}{\mathcal{U}^{\alpha}(\tilde{v}(s))}\\ &\quad -\alpha\tilde{v}'(s)\rho(s)\frac{b(s)\left(\mathcal{U}^{(n-1)}(s)\right)^{\alpha}\mathcal{U}'(\tilde{v}(s))}{\mathcal{U}^{\alpha+1}(\tilde{v}(s))}\\ &\le \frac{\rho'(s)}{\rho(s)}w(s)-\rho(s)Q_0(s)\frac{\mathcal{U}^{\alpha}(\tilde{v}(s))}{\mathcal{U}^{\alpha}(\tilde{v}(s))}-\alpha\tilde{v}'(s)w(s)\frac{\mathcal{U}'(\tilde{v}(s))}{\mathcal{U}(\tilde{v}(s))}. \end{aligned} \tag{27}$$

Using Lemma 3 with $\psi(s)=\mathcal{U}'(s)$, we see that

$$\mathcal{U}'(s)\ge\frac{\lambda}{(n-2)!}s^{n-2}\mathcal{U}^{(n-1)}(s),\ \text{for all}\ \lambda\in(0,1),$$

and

$$\mathcal{U}'(\tilde{v}(s))\ge\frac{\lambda}{(n-2)!}\tilde{v}^{n-2}(s)\mathcal{U}^{(n-1)}(\tilde{v}(s)).$$

Putting the last inequality into (27), we obtain

$$w'(s)\le\frac{\rho'(s)}{\rho(s)}w(s)-\rho(s)Q_0(s)-\frac{\alpha\lambda}{(n-2)!}\frac{\tilde{v}'(s)\tilde{v}^{n-2}(s)}{b^{1/\alpha}(\tilde{v}(s))}\frac{b^{1/\alpha}(\tilde{v}(s))\mathcal{U}^{(n-1)}(\tilde{v}(s))w(s)}{\mathcal{U}(\tilde{v}(s))}. \tag{28}$$

Since $b^{1/\alpha}(s)\mathcal{U}^{(n-1)}(s)$ is decreasing, then

$$b^{1/\alpha}(\tilde{v}(s))\mathcal{U}^{(n-1)}(\tilde{v}(s))\ge b^{1/\alpha}(s)\mathcal{U}^{(n-1)}(s).$$

Therefore, (28) can be expressed as

$$\begin{aligned} w'(s) &\le \frac{\rho'(s)}{\rho(s)}w(s)-\rho(s)Q_0(s)-\frac{\alpha\lambda}{(n-2)!}\frac{\tilde{v}'(s)\tilde{v}^{n-2}(s)}{b^{1/\alpha}(\tilde{v}(s))}\frac{b^{1/\alpha}(s)\mathcal{U}^{(n-1)}(s)w(s)}{\mathcal{U}(\tilde{v}(s))}\\ &= \frac{\rho'(s)}{\rho(s)}w(s)-\rho(s)Q_0(s)-\frac{\alpha\lambda}{(n-2)!}\frac{\tilde{v}'(s)\tilde{v}^{n-2}(s)}{(\rho(s)b(\tilde{v}(s)))^{1/\alpha}}w^{(\alpha+1)/\alpha}(s). \end{aligned} \tag{29}$$

Using Lemma 2 where $B=\rho'(s)/\rho(s)$, $B=\alpha\lambda\tilde{v}'(s)\tilde{v}^{n-2}(s)/(\rho(s)b(\tilde{v}(s)))^{1/\alpha}$, and $\psi=w$, we obtain

$$\begin{aligned}&\frac{\rho'(s)}{\rho(s)}w(s)-\frac{\alpha\lambda}{(n-2)!}\frac{\widetilde{v}'(s)\widetilde{v}^{n-2}(s)}{(\rho(s)b(\widetilde{v}(s)))^{1/\alpha}}w^{(\alpha+1)/\alpha}(s)\\ \leq\;&\frac{((n-2)!)^{\alpha}}{(\alpha+1)^{\alpha+1}}\frac{(\rho'(s))^{\alpha+1}b(\widetilde{v}(s))}{(\lambda\rho(s)\widetilde{v}'(s)\widetilde{v}^{n-2}(s))^{\alpha}}.\end{aligned}$$

Substituting the previous inequality into (29), we obtain

$$w'(s)\leq-\rho(s)Q_0(s)+\frac{((n-2)!)^{\alpha}}{(\alpha+1)^{\alpha+1}}\frac{(\rho'(s))^{\alpha+1}b(\widetilde{v}(s))}{(\lambda\rho(s)\widetilde{v}'(s)\widetilde{v}^{n-2}(s))^{\alpha}}. \tag{30}$$

Integrating (30) from s_1 to s, we have

$$\int_{s_1}^{s}\left(\rho(\nu)Q_0(\nu)-\frac{((n-2)!)^{\alpha}}{(\alpha+1)^{\alpha+1}}\frac{b(\widetilde{v}(\nu))(\rho'(\nu))^{\alpha+1}}{(\lambda\rho(\nu)\widetilde{v}^{n-2}(\nu)\widetilde{v}'(\nu))^{\alpha}}\right)d\nu\leq w(s_1),$$

which contradicts (25). □

Theorem 5. *If*

$$\liminf_{s\to\infty}\int_{\widetilde{v}(s)}^{s}Q_0(\nu)\left(\widetilde{v}^{n-1}(\nu)\right)^{\alpha}d\nu>\frac{((n-1)!)^{\alpha}}{e}, \tag{31}$$

then $K_1=\varnothing$.

Proof. Let us assume the opposite, that $x\in K_1$. It is clear from the use of the Lemma 3 that

$$\mathcal{U}(s)\geq\frac{\lambda}{(n-1)!}s^{n-1}\mathcal{U}^{(n-1)}(s),\ \text{for all}\ \lambda\in(0,1). \tag{32}$$

Substituting from (32) into (23), we conclude that

$$\left(b(s)\left(\mathcal{U}^{(n-1)}(s)\right)^{\alpha}\right)'+\left(\frac{\lambda}{(n-1)!}\widetilde{v}^{n-1}(s)\right)^{\alpha}Q_0(s)\left(\mathcal{U}^{(n-1)}(\widetilde{v}(s))\right)^{\alpha}\leq 0.$$

Let us define $\varphi(s)=b(s)\left(\mathcal{U}^{(n-1)}(s)\right)^{\alpha}>0$, It follows that φ is a positive solution to the inequality

$$\varphi'(s)+\frac{\lambda^{\alpha}}{((n-1)!)^{\alpha}}\left(\widetilde{v}^{n-1}(s)\right)^{\alpha}Q_0(s)\varphi(\widetilde{v}(s))\leq 0.$$

However, from Theorem 2.1.1 in [33], condition (31) confirms the oscillatory nature of all solutions to Equation (32). This contradicts the previous inequality. □

Theorem 6. *If the DE*

$$\theta'(s)+\frac{\mathfrak{y}_0\lambda^{\alpha}}{\mathfrak{y}_0+p_0^{\alpha}}\frac{(\widetilde{v}^{n-1}(s))^{\alpha}Q(s)}{((n-1)!)^{\alpha}b(\widetilde{v}(s))}\theta\left(\mathfrak{y}^{-1}(\widetilde{v}(s))\right)=0 \tag{33}$$

is oscillatory, then $K_1=\varnothing$.

Proof. Assume that $x\in K_1$. Similar to the proof of Theorem 1, we observe that (9) can be expressed as

$$0\geq\left(b(s)(\mathcal{U}^{(n-1)}(s))^{\alpha}+\frac{p_0^{\alpha}}{\mathfrak{y}_0}b(\mathfrak{y}(s))\left(\mathcal{U}^{(n-1)}(\mathfrak{y}(s))\right)^{\alpha}\right)'+\frac{1}{\mu}Q(s)\mathcal{U}^{\alpha}(\widetilde{v}(s)). \tag{34}$$

Applying Lemma 3, we obtain

$$\mathcal{U}(s) \geq \frac{\lambda}{(n-1)!b^{1/\alpha}(s)} s^{n-1} b^{1/\alpha}(s) \mathcal{U}^{(n-1)}(s). \tag{35}$$

Therefore, by setting $w(s) = b(s)(\mathcal{U}^{(n-1)}(s))^{\alpha}$ in (34) and employing (35), it becomes evident that w is a positive solution of the equation

$$\left(w(s) + \frac{p_0^{\alpha}}{\mathfrak{y}_0} w(\mathfrak{y}(s))\right)' + \left(\frac{\lambda}{(n-1)!b^{1/\alpha}(\tilde{v}(s))} \tilde{v}^{n-1}(s)\right)^{\alpha} Q(s) w(\tilde{v}(s)) = 0. \tag{36}$$

Since $w(s) = b(s)(\mathcal{U}^{(n-1)}(s))^{\alpha}$ is decreasing and it satisfies (36). Let us denote

$$\theta(s) = w(s) + \frac{p_0^{\alpha}}{\mathfrak{y}_0} w(\mathfrak{y}(s)).$$

It follows from $\mathfrak{y}(s) < s$,

$$\theta(s) \leq w(\mathfrak{y}(s)) \left(1 + \frac{p_0^{\alpha}}{\mathfrak{y}_0}\right).$$

By replacing these expressions into (36), we discover that θ is a positive solution of

$$\theta'(s) + \frac{\mathfrak{y}_0 \lambda^{\alpha}}{\mathfrak{y}_0 + p_0^{\alpha}} \frac{(\tilde{v}^{n-1}(s))^{\alpha} Q(s)}{((n-1)!)^{\alpha} b(\tilde{v}(s))} \theta\left(\mathfrak{y}^{-1}(\tilde{v}(s))\right) \leq 0.$$

According to [32] (Theorem 1), it implies that (33) has a positive solution as well, resulting in a contradiction with (33). □

Corollary 3. *If*

$$\liminf_{s \to \infty} \int_{\mathfrak{y}^{-1}(\tilde{v}(s))}^{s} \frac{(\tilde{v}^{n-1}(v))^{\alpha} Q(v)}{b(\tilde{v}(v))} dv > \frac{(\mathfrak{y}_0 + p_0^{\alpha})((n-1)!)^{\alpha}}{\lambda^{\alpha} \mathfrak{y}_0 e}, \tag{37}$$

then $K_1 = \varnothing$.

5. Oscillation Theorem

This section builds on the preceding section's findings to establish new criteria for investigating the oscillatory behavior of all solutions in (1). By merging the established conditions that eliminate positive solutions for both cases (C_1) and (C_2), we can formulate criteria outlined in the next theorem to determine the oscillation characteristics of the studied equation.

Theorem 7. *One of conditions (15), (16), or (22), together with one of conditions (25), (31), or (37), ensure that all solutions of Equation (1) oscillate.*

Proof. Let us assume the opposite scenario, that x is a solution to Equation (1). that eventually becomes positive. Based on Lemma 4, we can deduce that there are two potential situations for the behavior of z and its derivatives. Applying Corollary 1 and Theorem 4, it can be determined that conditions (15) and (25) guarantee that there are no solutions to (1) satisfy (C_1) and (C_2), respectively. The same approach is used for the remaining conditions mentioned in the theorem. As a result, we can conclude that the proof is finished. □

6. Application

In this section, we will utilize the derived findings to address a specific case of the (1). Let us examine the non-linear differential equation (NDE) given by:

$$\left(\left((x(s)+p_0x(\eta_0 s))''\right)^{\alpha}\right)' + \sum_{i=1}^{m}\frac{q_i}{s^{2\alpha+1}}x^{\alpha}(v_i s) = 0,\ s \geq 1. \tag{38}$$

From (38) we have $n = 3$, $b(s) = 1$, $p(s) = p_0$, $\eta(s) = \eta_0 s$, $v(s) = v_0 s = \max\{v_i(s),\ i = 1,2,...,m\}$, $\tilde{v}(s) = \tilde{v}_0 s = \min\{v_i s,\ i = 1,2,...,m\}$, $q_i(s) = q_i/s^{2\alpha+1}$,

$$\pi_0(s) = s,\ \pi_1(s) = \frac{s^2}{2},$$

$$\pi_0(\eta(s), v(s)) = (\eta_0 - v_0)s,\ \pi_1(\eta(s), v(s)) = (\eta_0 - v_0)^3\frac{s^2}{2},$$

and

$$Q_0(s) = \frac{(1-p_0)^{\alpha}}{s^{3\alpha+1}}\sum_{i=1}^{m} q_i.$$

The condition described in (15) is fulfilled when:

$$(\zeta_0 - v_0)^{3\alpha}2^{-\alpha}\left(\sum_{i=1}^{n} q_i\right)\ln\frac{\eta_0}{\zeta_0} > \frac{\mu(\eta_0 + p_0^{\alpha})}{\eta_0 e}. \tag{39}$$

The condition stated in (16) is satisfied when:

$$(\eta_0\delta_0 - v_0)^{3\alpha}2^{-\alpha}\left(1-\delta_0^{2\alpha}\right)\sum_{i=1}^{n} q_i > \frac{2\alpha\mu\delta_0^{2\alpha}(\eta_0 + p_0^{\alpha})}{\eta_0}. \tag{40}$$

The condition presented in (22) is met when

$$(1-\eta_0)^{3\alpha}\sum_{i=1}^{m} q_i \ln\frac{1}{v_0} > \frac{2^{\alpha}(\eta_0 + p_0^{\alpha})}{v_0\eta_0 e}. \tag{41}$$

The condition described in (25) is satisfied when

$$(1-p_0)^{\alpha}\sum_{i=1}^{m} q_i > \left(\frac{2\alpha}{\alpha+1}\right)^{\alpha+1}\left(\frac{1}{\lambda\tilde{v}_0^2}\right)^{\alpha},\ \rho(s) = s^{2\alpha}. \tag{42}$$

The condition given in (31) is met when

$$\tilde{v}^{2\alpha}(1-p_0)^{\alpha}\left(\sum_{i=1}^{m} q_i\right)\ln\frac{1}{\tilde{v}_0} > \frac{2^{\alpha}}{e}. \tag{43}$$

The condition presented in (31) is satisfied when

$$\tilde{v}^{2\alpha}\left(\sum_{i=1}^{m} q_i\right)\ln\frac{\eta_0}{\tilde{v}_0} > \frac{2^{\alpha}(\eta_0 + p_0^{\alpha})}{\lambda^{\alpha}\eta_0 e}. \tag{44}$$

Now, by applying conditions (39)–(44), we observe that the Theorem 7 demonstrates oscillatory behavior. This can be verified by assigning specific values to Equation (38).

Remark 1. *If we substitute $p = 0$, $\alpha = 1$, and $m = 1$ into (38), we obtain a third-order Euler-type equation in the given form:*

$$x'''(s) + \frac{q_1}{s^3}x(v_1 s) = 0,\ s \geq 1.$$

7. Conclusions

This research aims to investigate the oscillatory and asymptotic characteristics of solutions to odd-order NDEs with multiple delays. By comprehending the relationship between the solution, its derivatives of various orders, and its corresponding function, we have significantly advanced the research of oscillation conditions in neutral differential equations. We derived criteria that eliminate N-Kneser solutions and positive solutions of the studied equation by deducing novel relationships and inequalities. These inferred relationships and variances also enable the development of additional criteria that contribute to the expansion of the literature and provide a better understanding of the behavior of NDE solutions containing multiple delays. To demonstrate the importance of our findings, We provided a general example. The obtained results provide useful insights into the behavior of solutions in odd-order NDEs and emphasize the necessity for future study to investigate the state when the equation:

$$\left(b(\mathrm{s})\left(\mathcal{U}^{(n-1)}(\mathrm{s})\right)^{\alpha}\right)' + \sum_{i=1}^{m} \mathrm{q}_i(\mathrm{s})x^{\beta}(v_i(\mathrm{s}))) = 0,$$

Moreover, one of the interesting open research points is obtaining oscillation criteria for all solutions of Equation (1) without the need for constraint (H_4).

Author Contributions: Conceptualization, O.M.; methodology, F.M.; validation, F.M., S.S.A. and A.A.; formal analysis, O.M.; investigation, S.S.A. and A.A.; writing-original draft preparation, F.M.; writing-review and editing, S.S.A. and A.A. All authors have read and agreed to the published version of the manuscript.

Funding: This project is funded by King Saud University, Riyadh, Saudi Arabia.

Data Availability Statement: Data is contained within the article.

Acknowledgments: Researchers Supporting Project number (RSPD2023R533), King Saud University, Riyadh, Saudi Arabia.

Conflicts of Interest: The authors declare no conflict of interest.

References

1. Braun, M. *Qualitative Theory of Differential Equations: Differential Equations and Their Applications*; Springer: New York, NY, USA, 1993.
2. Cooke, K.L. *Differential Difference Equations*; Academic Press: New York, NY, USA, 1963.
3. Myshkis, A.D. On solutions of linear homogeneous differential equations of the first order of stable type with a retarded argument. *Mat. Sb.* **1951**, *70*, 641–658.
4. Tunç, O.; Atan, Ö.; Tunç, C.; Yao, J. Qualitative analyses of integro-fractional differential equations with Caputo derivatives and retardations via the Lyapunov–Razumikhin method. *Axioms* **2021**, *10*, 58. [CrossRef]
5. Hale, J.K. *Theory of Functional Differential Equations*; Springer: New York, NY, USA, 1977.
6. Agarwal, R.P.; Bohner, M.; Li, T.; Zhang, C. A new approach in the study of oscillatory behavior of even-order neutral delay differential equations. *Appl. Math. Comput.* **2013**, 225, 787–794. [CrossRef]
7. Zafer, A.; Oscillation criteria for even order neutral differential equations, *Appl. Math. Lett.* **1998**, *11*, 21–25.
8. Gyori, I.; Ladas, G. *Oscillation Theory of Delay Differential Equations with Applications*; Clarendon Press: Oxford, UK, 1991.
9. Zafer, A. *Oscillatory and Nonoscillatory Properties of Solutions of Functional Differential Equations and Difference Equations*; Iowa State University: Ames, IA, USA, 1992.
10. Grace, S.R.; Dzurina, J.; Jadlovska, I.; Li, T. On the oscillation of fourth-order delay differential equations. *Adv. Differ. Equ.* **2019**, *2019*, 118. [CrossRef]
11. Wang, C.; Shi, F.; Li, L.; Alhamami, M. Research on Stability of Time-delay Force Feedback Teleoperation System Based on Scattering Matrix. *Appl. Math. Nonlinear Sci.* **2022**. [CrossRef]
12. Zhang, H.; Katib, I.; Hasan, H. Research on the Psychological Distribution Delay of Artificial Neural Network Based on the Analysis of Differential Equation by Inequality Expansion and Contraction Method. *Appl. Math. Nonlinear Sci.* **2022**, *7*, 343–352. [CrossRef]
13. Baculikova, B.; Dzurina, J.; Li, T. Oscillation results for even-order quasilinear neutral functional differential equations. *Electron. J. Differ. Equ* **2011**, *2011*, 1–9.

14. Dzurina, J. Oscillation theorems for second order advanced neutral differential equations. *Tatra Mt. Math. Publ.* **2011**, *48*, 61–71. [CrossRef]
15. Graef, J.R.; Grace, S.R.; Tunç, E. Oscillatory behavior of even-order nonlinear differential equations with a sublinear neutral term. *Opusc. Math.* **2019**, *39*, 39–47. [CrossRef]
16. Bohner, M.; Grace, S.; Jadlovská, I. Oscillation criteria for second-order neutral delay differential equations. *Electron. J. Differ. Equ.* **2017**, *2017*, 1–12. [CrossRef]
17. Moaaz, O.; Masood, F.; Cesarano, C.; Alsallami, S.A.M.; Khalil, E.M.; Bouazizi, M.L. Neutral Differential Equations of Second-Order: Iterative Monotonic Properties. *Mathematics* **2022**, *10*, 1356. [CrossRef]
18. Almarri, B.; Masood, F.; Moaaz, O.; Muhib, A. Amended Criteria for Testing the Asymptotic and Oscillatory Behavior of Solutions of Higher-Order Functional Differential Equations. *Axioms* **2022**, *11*, 718. [CrossRef]
19. Bohner, M.; Grace, S.R.; Jadlovská, I. Sharp results for oscillation of second-order neutral delay differential equations. *Electron. J. Qual. Theory Differ. Equ.* **2023**, *4*, 1–23. [CrossRef]
20. Jadlovská, I.; Dzurina, J.; Graef, J. R.; Grace, S.R. Sharp oscillation theorem for fourth-order linear delay differential equations. *J. Inequalities Appl.* **2022**, *2022*, 122. [CrossRef]
21. Baculikova, B.; Dzurina, J. Asymptotic and oscillatory behavior of higher order quasilinear delay differential equations. *Electron. J. Qual. Theory Differ. Equ.* **2012**, *2012*, 1–10. [CrossRef]
22. Karpuz, B.; Ocalan, O.; Ozturk, S. Comparison theorems on the oscillation and asymptotic behaviour of higher-order neutral differential equations. *Glasgow Math. J.* **2010**, *52*, 107–114. [CrossRef]
23. Sun, Y.; Han, Z.; Sun, S.; Zhang, C. Oscillation criteria for even order nonlinear neutral differential equations. *Electron. J. Qual. Theory Differ. Equ.* **2012**, *30*, 1–12. [CrossRef]
24. Baculíková, B.; Džurina, J.; Graef, J.R.; On the oscillation of higher-order delay differential equations. *J. Math. Sci.* **2012**, *187*, 387–400. [CrossRef]
25. Xing, G.; Li, T.; Zhang, C. Oscillation of higher-order quasi-linear neutral differential equations. *Adv. Differ. Equat.* **2011**, *2011*, 45. [CrossRef]
26. Moaaz, O.; Almarri, B.; Masood, F.; Atta, D. Even-order neutral delay differential equations with noncanonical operator: New oscillation criteria. *Fractal Fract.* **2022**, *6*, 313. [CrossRef]
27. Hilderbrandt, TH. *Introduction to the Theory of Integration*; Academic Press: New York, NY, USA, 1963.
28. Zhang, C.; Agarwal, R.; Bohner, M.; Li, T. New results for oscillatory behavior of even-order half-linear delay differential equations. *Appl. Math. Lett.* **2013**, *26*, 179–183. [CrossRef]
29. Agarwal, R.P.; Grace, S.R.; O'Regan, D. *Oscillation Theory for Difference and Functional Differential Equations*; Kluwer Academic: Dordrecht, The Netherlands, 2000.
30. Baculíková, B.; Džurina, J. On the oscillation of odd order advanced differential equations. *Bound. Value Probl.* **2014**, *2014*, 214. [CrossRef]
31. Muhib, A.; Khashan, M. M.; Moaaz, O. Even-order differential equation with continuous delay: Nonexistence criteria of Kneser solutions. *Adv. Differ. Equ.* **2021**, *2021*, 250. [CrossRef]
32. Philos, C. On the existence of nonoscillatory solutions tending to zero at ∞ for differential equations with positive delays. *Arch. Math.* **1981**, *36*, 168–178. [CrossRef]
33. Ladde, G.S.; Lakshmikantham, V.; Zhang, B.G. *Oscillation Theory of Differential Equations with Deviating Arguments*; Marcel Dekker: New York, NY, USA, 1987.

Disclaimer/Publisher's Note: The statements, opinions and data contained in all publications are solely those of the individual author(s) and contributor(s) and not of MDPI and/or the editor(s). MDPI and/or the editor(s) disclaim responsibility for any injury to people or property resulting from any ideas, methods, instructions or products referred to in the content.

axioms

MDPI

Article

Ground State Solutions for a Non-Local Type Problem in Fractional Orlicz Sobolev Spaces

Liben Wang [1], Xingyong Zhang [2,*] and Cuiling Liu [2]

[1] School of Computer Science and Technology, Dongguan University of Technology, Dongguan 523808, China; wanglbdgust@163.com
[2] Faculty of Science, Kunming University of Science and Technology, Kunming 650500, China; 20191111001@stu.kust.edu.cn
* Correspondence: zhangxingyong1@163.com

Abstract: In this paper, we study the following non-local problem in fractional Orlicz–Sobolev spaces: $(-\Delta_\Phi)^s u + V(x)a(|u|)u = f(x,u), \quad x \in \mathbb{R}^N$, where $(-\Delta_\Phi)^s (s \in (0,1))$ denotes the non-local and maybe non-homogeneous operator, the so-called fractional Φ-Laplacian. Without assuming the Ambrosetti–Rabinowitz type and the Nehari type conditions on the non-linearity f, we obtain the existence of ground state solutions for the above problem with periodic potential function $V(x)$. The proof is based on a variant version of the mountain pass theorem and a Lions' type result in fractional Orlicz–Sobolev spaces.

Keywords: fractional Orlicz–Sobolev spaces; fractional Φ-Laplacian; critical point; ground state

MSC: 35R11; 46E30; 35A15

Citation: Wang, L.; Zhang, X.; Liu, C. Ground State Solutions for a Non-Local Type Problem in Fractional Orlicz Sobolev Spaces. *Axioms* **2024**, *13*, 294. https://doi.org/10.3390/axioms13050294

Academic Editors: Francisco Martínez González, Mohammed K. A. Kaabar and Hatıra Günerhan

Received: 13 March 2024
Revised: 21 April 2024
Accepted: 22 April 2024
Published: 27 April 2024

Copyright: © 2024 by the authors. Licensee MDPI, Basel, Switzerland. This article is an open access article distributed under the terms and conditions of the Creative Commons Attribution (CC BY) license (https://creativecommons.org/licenses/by/4.0/).

1. Introduction and Main Results

In recent decades, much attention has been devoted to the study of the non-linear Schrödinger equations involving non-local operators. These types of operators can be used to model many phenomena in the natural sciences, such as fluid dynamics, quantum mechanics, phase transitions, finance, and so on, see [1–4] and the references therein. Due to the important work of Fernández Bonder and Salort [5], a new generalized fractional Φ-Laplacian operator has caused great interest among scholars in recent years, since it allows to model non-local problems involving a non-power behavior, see [6–13] and the references therein.

In this paper, we are interested in studying the following non-local problem involving fractional Φ-Laplacian:

$$(-\Delta_\Phi)^s u + V(x)a(|u|)u = f(x,u), \quad x \in \mathbb{R}^N, \tag{1}$$

where $s \in (0,1)$, $N \in \mathbb{N}$, the function $a : [0,+\infty) \to \mathbb{R}$ is such that $\phi : \mathbb{R} \to \mathbb{R}$ defined by:

$$\phi(t) = \begin{cases} a(|t|)t & \text{for } t \neq 0, \\ 0 & \text{for } t = 0, \end{cases} \tag{2}$$

is an increasing homeomorphism from $\mathbb{R}$ onto $\mathbb{R}$, and $\Phi : [0,+\infty) \to [0,+\infty)$ defined by:

$$\Phi(t) = \int_0^t \phi(\tau)d\tau$$

is an N-function (see Section 2 for details), which together with the potential V and the non-linearity f satisfy the following basic assumptions:

(ϕ_1) $1 < l := \inf\limits_{t>0}\frac{t\phi(t)}{\Phi(t)} \leq \sup\limits_{t>0}\frac{t\phi(t)}{\Phi(t)} =: m < \min\{\frac{N}{s}, l^*\}$ where $l^* := \frac{Nl}{N-sl}$;

(V) $V \in C(\mathbb{R}^N, \mathbb{R}_+)$ is 1-periodic in $x_1, \cdots, x_N$ (called 1-periodic in x for short), and so, there exist two constants $\alpha_1, \alpha_2 > 0$ such that $\alpha_1 \leq V(x) \leq \alpha_2$ for all $x \in \mathbb{R}^N$;

(f_1) $f \in C(\mathbb{R}^N \times \mathbb{R})$ is 1-periodic in x satisfying:

$$\lim_{|t|\to 0}\frac{f(x,t)}{\phi(|t|)} = 0 \quad \text{and} \quad \lim_{|t|\to\infty}\frac{f(x,t)}{\Phi'_*(|t|)} = 0, \quad \text{uniformly in } x \in \mathbb{R}^N,$$

where Φ_* denotes the Sobolev conjugate function of Φ (see Section 2 for details).

For $s \in (0,1)$, the so-called fractional Φ-Laplacian operator is defined as:

$$(-\Delta_\Phi)^s u(x) := P.V. \int_{\mathbb{R}^N} a(|D_s u|)\frac{D_s u}{|x-y|^{N+s}}dy, \quad \text{where} \quad D_s u := \frac{u(x)-u(y)}{|x-y|^s} \tag{3}$$

and $P.V.$ denotes the principal value of the integral. Notice that if $\Phi(t) = |t|^p (p > 1)$, then the fractional Φ-Laplacian operator reduces to the following fractional p-Laplacian operator:

$$(-\Delta_p)^s u(x) := P.V. \int_{\mathbb{R}^N} \frac{|u(x)-u(y)|^{p-2}(u(x)-u(y))}{|x-y|^{N+ps}}dy.$$

To study this class of non-local problem involving fractional p-Laplacian, the variational method has become one of the important tools over the past several decades, see [14–20] and the references therein. In many studies on p-superlinear elliptic problems, to ensure the boundedness of the Palais–Smale sequence or Cerami sequence of the energy functional, the following (AR) type condition for the non-linearity f due to Ambrosetti–Rabinowitz [21] was always assumed:

For (AR), there exists a constant $\mu > p$ such that:

$$0 < \mu F(x,t) \leq t f(x,t), \quad \text{for all } t \neq 0,$$

where the following is true: $F(x,t) = \int\limits_0^t f(x,\tau)d\tau$.

In fact, (AR) implies that there exist two positive constants c_1, c_2 such that:

$$F(x,t) \geq c_1|t|^\mu - c_2, \quad \text{for all } (x,t) \in \mathbb{R}^N \times \mathbb{R},$$

which is obviously stronger than the following p-superlinear growth condition:

(F_1) $\lim\limits_{|t|\to\infty}\frac{F(x,t)}{|t|^p} = +\infty$, uniformly in $x \in \mathbb{R}^N$.

(F_1) was first introduced by Liu and Wang in [22] for the case $p = 2$ and has since been commonly used in recent papers. With the development of the variational theory and application, certain new restrictive conditions have been established in order to weaken (AR). However, the majority of these conditions are just complementary to (AR). For example, one can replace (AR) with (F_1) and the following Nehari type condition:

(Ne) $\frac{f(x,t)}{|t|^{p-1}}$ is (strictly) increasing in t for all $x \in \mathbb{R}^N$.

For the case $p = 2$, Li, Wang and Zeng proved the existence of ground state by Nehari method in [23]. Besides, for the case $p = 2$, Ding and Szulkin in [24] replaced (AR) with (F_1) and the following condition:

(F_2) $\mathcal{F}(x,t) > 0$ for all $t \neq 0$, and $|f(x,t)|^\sigma \leq c_3\mathcal{F}(x,t)|t|^\sigma$ for some $c_3 > 0, \sigma > \max\{1, \frac{N}{2}\}$ and all (x,t) with $|t|$ larger enough, where $\mathcal{F}(x,t) = tf(x,t) - 2F(x,t)$.

They demonstrated that (F_1) and (F_2) are valid when the non-linearity f satisfies both (AR) and a subcritical growth condition that $|f(x,t)| \leq c_4(|t| + |t|^{q-1})$ for some $c_4 > 0, q \in (2, 2^*)$ and all $(x,t) \in \mathbb{R}^N \times \mathbb{R}$, where $2^* = \frac{2N}{N-2}$ if $N \geq 3$ and $2^* = \infty$ if $N = 1$ or $N = 2$. In [25,26], some conditions similar to (F_2) were introduced for the case $p > 1$. Moreover, in [27], Tang introduced the following new and weaker super-quadratic condition:

(F_3) there exists a $\theta_0 \in (0,1)$ such that:

$$\frac{1-\theta^2}{2} tf(x,t) \geq \int_{\theta t}^{t} f(x,\tau)d\tau = F(x,t) - F(x,\theta t), \text{ for all } \theta \in [0,\theta_0], (x,t) \in \mathbb{R}^N \times \mathbb{R}.$$

Tang proved that (F_3) is weaker than both (AR) and (Ne) and also different from (F_2). It is worth noting that (F_3) has been extended for the case $p > 1$ in [28].

To the best of our knowledge, some conditions mentioned above have been successfully generalized to the non-local problem involving fractional Φ-Laplacian. In [29], for Equation (1) with potential $V(x) \equiv 1$, by applying the mountain pass theorem, Sabri, Ounaies, and Elfalah proved the existence of a non-trivial solution when the autonomous non-linearity $f(u)$ satisfies an (AR) type condition. On the whole space $\mathbb{R}^N$, to overcome the difficulty due to the lack of compactness of the Sobolev embedding, the authors reconstructed the compactness by choosing a radially symmetric function subspace as the working space. In [13], for Equation (1) with unbounded or bounded potentials V, by applying the Nehari manifold method, Silva, Carvalho, de Albuquerque, and Bahrouni proved the existence of ground state solutions when the non-linearity f satisfies the following both (AR) and (Ne) type conditions:

For (AR)*, there exists $\theta > m$ such that $\theta F(x,t) \leq tf(x,t)$, for $(x,t) \in \mathbb{R}^N \times \mathbb{R}$;

For (Ne)*, the map $t \to \frac{f(x,t)}{|t|^{m-1}}$ is strictly increasing for $t > 0$ and strictly decreasing for $t < 0$.

To be precise, for the case when V is unbounded, the authors reconstructed the compactness by assuming that V is coercive and then choosing a subspace depending on V as the working space. For the case when V is bounded, to overcome the difficulty due to the lack of compactness and obtain a non-trivial solution, the authors assumed that V and f are 1-periodic in x and introduced an important Lions' type result for fractional Orlicz–Sobolev spaces (see Theorem 1.6 in [13]). Since the ground state solution is obtained as a minimizer of the energy functional on the Nehari manifold $\mathcal{N}$, it is crucial to require that f is of class C^1. Otherwise $\mathcal{N}$ may not be a C^1-manifold and it is not clear that the minimizer on the Nehari manifold $\mathcal{N}$ is a critical point of the energy functional.

Motivated by [13], in this paper, we still study the existence of ground state for Equation (1) under the assumption that V and f are 1-periodic in x. We manage to extend the above p-superlinear growth conditions (F_2) and (F_3) to the non-local problem involving fractional Φ-Laplacian. Instead of applying the Nehari manifold method, we firstly prove that Equation (1) has a non-trivial solution by using a variant mountain pass theorem (see Theorem 3 in [30]). Subsequently, we prove the existence of ground state by using the Lions' type result for fractional Orlicz–Sobolev spaces and some techniques of Jeanjean and Tanaka (see Theorem 4.5 in [31]).

Next, we present our main results as follows.

Theorem 1. *Assume that (ϕ_1), (V), (f_1) and the following conditions hold:*

(ϕ_2) $\limsup_{t\to 0} \frac{|t|^l}{\Phi(|t|)} < +\infty$;

(f_2) $\lim_{|t|\to\infty} \frac{F(x,t)}{\Phi(|t|)} = +\infty$*, uniformly in* $x \in \mathbb{R}^N$;

(f_3) $\widehat{F}(x,t) > 0$ *for all* $t \neq 0$*, and* $|F(x,t)|^k \leq c\widehat{F}(x,t)|t|^{lk}$ *for some* $c > 0$, $k > \frac{N}{sl}$ *and all* (x,t) *with* $|t|$ *larger enough, where* $\widehat{F}(x,t) = tf(x,t) - mF(x,t)$.

Then, Equation (1) has at least one ground state solution.

Theorem 2. *Assume that (ϕ_1), (V), (f_1) and the following conditions hold:*

(f_4) $F(x,t) \geq 0$ *for all* $(x,t) \in \mathbb{R}^N \times \mathbb{R}$*, and* $\lim_{|t|\to\infty} \frac{F(x,t)}{|t|^m} = +\infty$*, uniformly in* $x \in \mathbb{R}^N$;

(f_5) *there exists a* $\theta_0 \in (0,1)$ *such that:*

$$\frac{1-\theta^l}{m} t f(x,t) \geq \int_{\theta t}^{t} f(x,\tau)d\tau = F(x,t) - F(x,\theta t), \text{ for all } \theta \in [0,\theta_0], (x,t) \in \mathbb{R}^N \times \mathbb{R}.$$

Then, Equation (1) has at least one ground state solution.

Remark 1. *To some extent, Theorem 2 improves the result of Theorem 1.8 in [13]. In fact, our results do not require the smoothness condition that functions f and a are of class C^1. Moreover, it is obvious that (φ_4) in [13] implies (ϕ_1) and (f_0) in [13] implies our subcritical growth condition given by (f_1). Furthermore, when $\Phi(t) = |t|^2$, (f_5) is weaker than both (AR) type condition (f_4) and (Ne) type condition (f_4) in [13] (see [27]).*

Remark 2. *Theorem 2 extends and improves the result of Theorem 1.1 in [32]. In fact, when $\Phi(t) = |t|^2$, our subcritical growth condition given by (f_1) reduces to:*

$$\lim_{|t|\to\infty} \frac{f(x,t)}{|t|^{2^*-1}} = 0, \quad \text{uniformly in } x \in \mathbb{R}^N, \tag{4}$$

which is weaker than (A_2) in [32]. For example, it is easy to check that function $f(t) = \frac{|t|^{2^*-2}t}{\log(e+|t|)}$ satisfies (4) but does not satisfy (A_2) in [32]. Moreover, it is obvious that Theorem 1 is different from Theorem 1.2 in [32] even when the fractional Φ-Laplacian Equation (1) reduces to the fractional Schrödinger equation.

The rest of this paper is organized as follows. In Section 2, we recall some definitions and basic properties on the Orlicz and fractional Orlicz–Sobolev spaces. In Section 3, we complete the proofs of the main results. In Section 4, we present some examples about the function ϕ defined by (2) and non-linearity f to illustrate our results.

2. Preliminaries

In this section, we make a brief introduction about Orlicz and fractional Orlicz–Sobolev spaces. For more details, we refer the reader to [5,33,34] and references therein.

To begin with, we recall the notion of N-function. Let $\phi : [0,+\infty) \to [0,+\infty)$ be a right continuous and monotone increasing function that satisfies the following conditions:

(1) $\phi(0) = 0$;
(2) $\lim_{t\to+\infty} \phi(t) = +\infty$;
(3) $\phi(t) > 0$ whenever $t > 0$.

Then, the function defined on $[0,+\infty)$ by $\Phi(t) = \int_0^t \phi(\tau)d\tau$ is called an N-function. It is obvious that $\Phi(0) = 0$ and Φ is strictly increasing and convex in $[0,+\infty)$.

An N-function Φ is said to satisfy the Δ_2-condition if there exists a constant $K > 0$ such that $\Phi(2t) \leq K\Phi(t)$ for all $t \geq 0$. Φ satisfies the Δ_2-condition if and only if for any given $c \geq 1$, there exists a constant $K_c > 0$ such that $\Phi(ct) \leq K_c\Phi(t)$ for all $t \geq 0$.

Given two N-functions A and B, B is said to dominate A globally if there exists a constant $K > 0$ such that $A(t) \leq B(Kt)$ for all $t \geq 0$. Furthermore, B is said to be essentially stronger than A, denoted by $A \prec\prec B$, if for each $c > 0$ it holds that:

$$\lim_{t\to+\infty} \frac{A(ct)}{B(t)} = 0.$$

For the N-function introduced above, the complement of Φ is defined by:

$$\widetilde{\Phi}(t) = \max_{\rho\geq 0}\{t\rho - \Phi(\rho)\}, \quad \text{for } t \geq 0.$$

Then, it holds that Young's inequality:

$$\rho t \leq \Phi(\rho) + \widetilde{\Phi}(t), \quad \text{for all } \rho, t \geq 0, \tag{5}$$

and the inequality (see Lemma A.2 in [35]):

$$\widetilde{\Phi}(\phi(t)) \leq \Phi(2t), \quad \text{for all } t \geq 0. \tag{6}$$

Now, we recall the Orlicz space $L^{\Phi}(\mathbb{R}^N)$ associated with Φ. When Φ satisfies the Δ_2-condition, the Orlicz space $L^{\Phi}(\mathbb{R}^N)$ is the vectorial space of the measurable functions $u : \mathbb{R}^N \to \mathbb{R}$ satisfying:

$$\int_{\mathbb{R}^N} \Phi(|u|)dx < +\infty.$$

The space $L^{\Phi}(\mathbb{R}^N)$ is a Banach space endowed with the Luxemburg norm:

$$\|u\|_{\Phi} = \|u\|_{L^{\Phi}(\mathbb{R}^N)} := \inf\left\{\lambda > 0 : \int_{\mathbb{R}^N} \Phi\left(\frac{|u|}{\lambda}\right)dx \leq 1\right\}.$$

Particularly, when $\Phi(t) = |t|^p (p > 1)$, the corresponding Orlicz space $L^{\Phi}(\mathbb{R}^N)$ reduces to the classical Lebesgue space $L^p(\mathbb{R}^N)$ endowed with the norm:

$$\|u\|_p = L^p(\mathbb{R}^N) := \left(\int_{\mathbb{R}^N} |u(x)|^p dx\right)^{\frac{1}{p}}.$$

The fact that Φ satisfies Δ_2-condition implies that:

$$u_n \to u \text{ in } L^{\Phi}(\Omega) \Longleftrightarrow \int_{\Omega} \Phi(|u_n - u|)dx \to 0, \tag{7}$$

where Ω is an open set of $\mathbb{R}^N$. Moreover, by the Young's inequality (5), the following generalized version of Hölder's inequality holds (see [33,34]):

$$\left|\int_{\mathbb{R}^N} uvdx\right| \leq 2\|u\|_{\Phi}\|v\|_{\widetilde{\Phi}}, \quad \text{for all } u \in L^{\Phi}(\mathbb{R}^N), v \in L^{\widetilde{\Phi}}(\mathbb{R}^N).$$

Given an N-function Φ and a fractional parameter $0 < s < 1$, we recall the fractional Orlicz–Sobolev space $W^{s,\Phi}(\mathbb{R}^N)$ defined as:

$$W^{s,\Phi}(\mathbb{R}^N) := \left\{u \in L^{\Phi}(\mathbb{R}^N) : \iint_{\mathbb{R}^{2N}} \Phi(|D_s u|)d\mu < +\infty\right\},$$

where $D_s u$ is defined by (3) and $d\mu(x,y) := \frac{dxdy}{|x-y|^N}$. The space $W^{s,\Phi}(\mathbb{R}^N)$ is a Banach space endowed with the following norm:

$$\|u\|_{s,\Phi} = \|u\|_{W^{s,\Phi}(\mathbb{R}^N)} := \|u\|_{\Phi} + [u]_{s,\Phi},$$

where the so-called (s,Φ)-Gagliardo semi-norm is defined as:

$$[u]_{s,\Phi} := \inf\left\{\lambda > 0 : \iint_{\mathbb{R}^{2N}} \Phi\left(\frac{|D_s u|}{\lambda}\right)d\mu \leq 1\right\}.$$

The following lemmas will be useful in the following.

Lemma 1. *(see [33,35]) Assume that Φ is an N-function. Then, the following conditions are equivalent:*

(1)

$$1 < l = \inf_{t>0} \frac{t\phi(t)}{\Phi(t)} \le \sup_{t>0} \frac{t\phi(t)}{\Phi(t)} = m < +\infty; \tag{8}$$

(2) *Let* $\zeta_1(t) = \min\{t^l, t^m\}$, $\zeta_2(t) = \max\{t^l, t^m\}$, *for* $t \ge 0$. *Then,* Φ *satisfies:*

$$\zeta_1(t)\Phi(\rho) \le \Phi(\rho t) \le \zeta_2(t)\Phi(\rho), \quad \text{for all } \rho, t \ge 0;$$

(3) Φ *satisfies the* Δ_2*-condition.*

Lemma 2. *(see [11,35]) Assume that* Φ *is an N-function and (8) holds. Then,* Φ *satisfies:*

(1)

$$\zeta_1(\|u\|_\Phi) \le \int_{\mathbb{R}^N} \Phi(|u|)dx \le \zeta_2(\|u\|_\Phi), \quad \text{for all } u \in L^\Phi(\mathbb{R}^N);$$

(2)

$$\zeta_1([u]_{s,\Phi}) \le \iint_{\mathbb{R}^{2N}} \Phi(|D_s u|)d\mu \le \zeta_2([u]_{s,\Phi}), \quad \text{for all } u \in W^{s,\Phi}(\mathbb{R}^N).$$

Lemma 3. *(see [35]) Assume that* Φ *is an N-function and (8) holds with* $l > 1$. *Let* $\widetilde{\Phi}$ *be the complement of* Φ *and* $\zeta_3(t) = \min\{t^{\widetilde{l}}, t^{\widetilde{m}}\}$, $\zeta_4(t) = \max\{t^{\widetilde{l}}, t^{\widetilde{m}}\}$, *for* $t \ge 0$, *where* $\widetilde{l} := \frac{l}{l-1}$ *and* $\widetilde{m} := \frac{m}{m-1}$. *Then,* $\widetilde{\Phi}$ *satisfies:*

(1)

$$\widetilde{m} = \inf_{t>0} \frac{t\widetilde{\Phi}'(t)}{\widetilde{\Phi}(t)} \le \sup_{t>0} \frac{t\widetilde{\Phi}'(t)}{\widetilde{\Phi}(t)} = \widetilde{l};$$

(2)

$$\zeta_3(t)\widetilde{\Phi}(\rho) \le \widetilde{\Phi}(\rho t) \le \zeta_4(t)\widetilde{\Phi}(\rho), \quad \text{for all } \rho, t \ge 0;$$

(3)

$$\zeta_3(\|u\|_{\widetilde{\Phi}}) \le \int_{\mathbb{R}^N} \widetilde{\Phi}(|u|)dx \le \zeta_4(\|u\|_{\widetilde{\Phi}}), \quad \text{for all } u \in L^{\widetilde{\Phi}}(\mathbb{R}^N).$$

Remark 3. *By Lemmas 1 and 3,* (ϕ_1) *implies that* Φ *and* $\widetilde{\Phi}$ *are two N-functions satisfying the* Δ_2*-condition. The fact that* Φ *and* $\widetilde{\Phi}$ *satisfy the* Δ_2*-condition implies that* $L^\Phi(\mathbb{R}^N)$ *and* $W^{s,\Phi}(\mathbb{R}^N)$ *are separable and reflexive Banach spaces. Moreover,* $C_c^\infty(\mathbb{R}^N)$ *is dense in* $W^{s,\Phi}(\mathbb{R}^N)$ *(see [5,33,34]).*

Next, we recall the Sobolev conjugate function of Φ, which is denoted by Φ_*. Suppose that:

$$\int_0^1 \frac{\Phi^{-1}(\tau)}{\tau^{\frac{N+s}{N}}} d\tau < +\infty \quad \text{and} \quad \int_1^{+\infty} \frac{\Phi^{-1}(\tau)}{\tau^{\frac{N+s}{N}}} d\tau = +\infty. \tag{9}$$

Then, Φ_* is defined by:

$$\Phi_*^{-1}(t) = \int_0^t \frac{\Phi^{-1}(\tau)}{\tau^{\frac{N+s}{N}}} d\tau, \quad \text{for } t \ge 0.$$

Lemma 4. *(see [6,36]) Assume that* Φ *is an N-function and (8) holds with* $l, m \in (1, \frac{N}{s})$. *Then, (9) holds. Let* $\zeta_5(t) = \min\{t^{l^*}, t^{m^*}\}$, $\zeta_6(t) = \max\{t^{l^*}, t^{m^*}\}$, *for* $t \ge 0$, *where* $l^* := \frac{Nl}{N-sl}$, $m^* := \frac{Nm}{N-sm}$. *Then,* Φ_* *satisfies:*

(1)

$$l^* = \inf_{t>0} \frac{t\Phi_*'(t)}{\Phi_*(t)} \le \sup_{t>0} \frac{t\Phi_*'(t)}{\Phi_*(t)} = m^*;$$

(2)
$$\zeta_5(t)\Phi_*(\rho) \le \Phi_*(\rho t) \le \zeta_6(t)\Phi_*(\rho), \quad \textit{for all } \rho, t \ge 0;$$

(3)
$$\zeta_5(\|u\|_{\Phi_*}) \le \int_{\mathbb{R}^N} \Phi_*(|u|)dx \le \zeta_6(\|u\|_{\Phi_*}), \quad \textit{for all } u \in L^{\Phi_*}(\mathbb{R}^N).$$

The conjugate function Φ_* plays a crucial role in the following embedding results, which will be used frequently in our proofs.

Lemma 5. *(see [13,33,36]) Assume that Φ is an N-function and (8) holds with $l, m \in (1, \frac{N}{s})$. Then, the following embedding results hold:*

(1) *the embedding $W^{s,\Phi}(\mathbb{R}^N) \hookrightarrow L^{\Phi_*}(\mathbb{R}^N)$ is continuous;*
(2) *the embedding $W^{s,\Phi}(\mathbb{R}^N) \hookrightarrow L^{\Phi}(\mathbb{R}^N)$ is continuous;*
(3) *the embedding $W^{s,\Phi}(\mathbb{R}^N) \hookrightarrow L^{\Psi}(\mathbb{R}^N)$ is continuous if Φ dominates Ψ globally;*
(4) *the embedding $W^{s,\Phi}(\mathbb{R}^N) \hookrightarrow L^{\Psi}(\mathbb{R}^N)$ is continuous if Ψ satisfies the Δ_2-condition, $\Psi \prec\prec \Phi_*$ and*
$$\lim_{t\to 0^+} \frac{\Psi(t)}{\Phi(t)} = 0;$$
(5) *when $\mathbb{R}^N$ is replaced by a $C^{0,1}$ bounded open subset D of $\mathbb{R}^N$, then the embedding $W^{s,\Phi}(D) \hookrightarrow L^{\Psi}(D)$ is compact if $\Psi \prec\prec \Phi_*$. Explicitly, when $m < l^*$, the embedding $W^{s,\Phi}(B_r) \hookrightarrow L^{\Phi}(B_r)$ is compact, where the following is true: $B_r := \{x \in \mathbb{R}^N : |x| < r\}$ for $r > 0$.*

Notation: Throughout this paper, C_d is used to denote a positive constant which depends only on the constant or function d.

3. Proofs

In fractional Orlicz–Sobolev space $W^{s,\Phi}(\mathbb{R}^N)$, denoted by W for simplicity, the energy functional I associated with Equation (1) is defined by:

$$I(u) := \iint_{\mathbb{R}^{2N}} \Phi(|D_s u|)d\mu + \int_{\mathbb{R}^N} V(x)\Phi(|u|)dx - \int_{\mathbb{R}^N} F(x,u)dx. \tag{10}$$

It follows (f_1) that for any given constant $\varepsilon > 0$, there exists a constant $C_\varepsilon > 0$ such that:

$$|f(x,t)| \le \varepsilon\phi(|t|) + C_\varepsilon \Phi_*'(|t|) \text{ and } |F(x,t)| \le \varepsilon\Phi(|t|) + C_\varepsilon\Phi_*(|t|), \text{ for all } (x,t) \in \mathbb{R}^N \times \mathbb{R}. \tag{11}$$

Thus, by using standard arguments as [8], we have that $I \in C^1(W,\mathbb{R})$ and its derivative is given by:

$$\langle I'(u), v\rangle = \iint_{\mathbb{R}^{2N}} a(|D_s u|)D_s u D_s v d\mu + \int_{\mathbb{R}^N} V(x)a(|u|)uv dx - \int_{\mathbb{R}^N} f(x,u)v dx, \text{ for all } u,v \in W. \tag{12}$$

Thus, the critical points of I are weak solutions of Equation (1).

Define $I_i (i = 1,2) : W \to \mathbb{R}$ by:

$$I_1(u) = \iint_{\mathbb{R}^{2N}} \Phi(|D_s u|)d\mu + \int_{\mathbb{R}^N} V(x)\Phi(|u|)dx \tag{13}$$

and:

$$I_2(u) = \int_{\mathbb{R}^N} F(x,u)dx. \tag{14}$$

Then:

$$I(u) = I_1(u) - I_2(u), \text{ for all } u,v \in W$$

and:

$$\begin{aligned}\langle I_1'(u),v\rangle &= \iint_{\mathbb{R}^{2N}} a(|D_s u|)D_s u D_s v d\mu + \int_{\mathbb{R}^N} V(x)a(|u|)uv dx, \text{ for all } u,v\in W, &(15)\\ \langle I_2'(u),v\rangle &= \int_{\mathbb{R}^N} f(x,u)v dx, \text{ for all } u,v\in W. &(16)\end{aligned}$$

Lemma 6. *Assume that* (ϕ_1), (V) *and* (f_1) *hold. Then, there exist two constants* $\rho,\eta>0$ *such that* $I(u)\geq\eta$ *for all* $u\in W$ *with* $\|u\|_{s,\Phi}=\rho$.

Proof. When $\|u\|_{s,\Phi}=\|u\|_\Phi+[u]_{s,\Phi}\leq 1$, by (10), (V), (11) with taking $\varepsilon<\alpha_1$, Lemma 2, (3) in Lemma 4 and (1) in Lemma 5, we have:

$$\begin{aligned}I(u) &\geq \iint_{\mathbb{R}^{2N}} \Phi(|D_s u|)d\mu + \alpha_1\int_{\mathbb{R}^N}\Phi(|u|)dx - \int_{\mathbb{R}^N}|F(x,u)|dx\\ &\geq \iint_{\mathbb{R}^{2N}} \Phi(|D_s u|)d\mu + (\alpha_1-\varepsilon)\int_{\mathbb{R}^N}\Phi(|u|)dx - C_\varepsilon\int_{\mathbb{R}^N}\Phi_*(|u|)dx\\ &\geq [u]_{s,\Phi}^m + (\alpha_1-\varepsilon)\|u\|_\Phi^m - C_\varepsilon\max\{\|u\|_{\Phi_*}^{l^*},\|u\|_{\Phi_*}^{m^*}\}\\ &\geq \min\{1,\alpha_1-\varepsilon\}C_m\|u\|_{s,\Phi}^m - C_\varepsilon C_{\Phi_*}^{l^*}\|u\|_{s,\Phi}^{l^*} - C_\varepsilon C_{\Phi_*}^{m^*}\|u\|_{s,\Phi}^{m^*}.\end{aligned}$$

Taking into account that $m<l^*\leq m^*$, it follows from the aforementioned inequality that there exist sufficiently small positive constants ρ and η such that $I(u)\geq\eta$ for all $u\in W$ with $\|u\|_{s,\Phi}=\rho$. □

Lemma 7. *Assume that* (ϕ_1), (V), (f_1) *and* (f_2) *(or* (f_4)*) hold. Then, there exists a* $u_0\in W$ *such that* $I(tu_0)\to-\infty$ *as* $t\to+\infty$.

Proof. For any given constant $M>\alpha_2$, by (f_1) and (f_2) (or combine (f_4) with (2) in Lemma 1), there exists a constant $C_M>0$ such that:

$$F(x,t)\geq M\Phi(|t|)-C_M, \text{ for all } (x,t)\in\mathbb{R}^N\times\mathbb{R}. \tag{17}$$

Now, choose $u_0\in C_c^\infty(B_r)\setminus\{\mathbf{0}\}$ with $0\leq u_0(x)\leq 1$. Then $u_0\in W$, and by (10), (V), (17), (2) in Lemma 1 and the fact $F(x,0)=0$ for all $x\in\mathbb{R}^N$, when $t>0$ we have:

$$\begin{aligned}I(tu_0) &= \iint_{\mathbb{R}^{2N}}\Phi(|D_s(tu_0)|)d\mu + \int_{\mathbb{R}^N}V(x)\Phi(|tu_0|)dx - \int_{\mathbb{R}^N}F(x,tu_0)dx\\ &= \iint_{\mathbb{R}^{2N}}\Phi(t|D_s u_0|)d\mu + \int_{\mathbb{R}^N}V(x)\Phi(t|u_0|)dx - \int_{B_r}F(x,tu_0)dx\\ &\leq \Phi(t)\iint_{\mathbb{R}^{2N}}\max\{|D_s u_0|^l,|D_s u_0|^m\}d\mu + \alpha_2\int_{\mathbb{R}^N}\Phi(t|u_0|)dx - M\int_{B_r}\Phi(t|u_0|)+C_M|B_r|\\ &\leq \Phi(t)\iint_{\mathbb{R}^{2N}}(|D_s u_0|^l+|D_s u_0|^m)d\mu - (M-\alpha_2)\Phi(t)\int_{\mathbb{R}^N}\min\{|u_0|^l,|u_0|^m\}dx + C_M|B_r|\\ &= \Phi(t)\left[\iint_{\mathbb{R}^{2N}}(|D_s u_0|^l+|D_s u_0|^m)d\mu-(M-\alpha_2)\|u_0\|_m^m\right]+C_M|B_r|.\end{aligned}$$

Note that $\lim_{t\to+\infty}\Phi(t)=+\infty$. We can choose $M>\frac{1}{\|u_0\|_m^m}\{\iint_{\mathbb{R}^{2N}}(|D_s u_0|^l+|D_s u_0|^m)d\mu\}+\alpha_2$ such that $I(tu_0)\to-\infty$ as $t\to+\infty$. What needs to be pointed out is that here we used the fact that $u_0\in W^{s,\Psi}(\mathbb{R}^N)$, where $\Psi(t)=|t|^l+|t|^m, t\geq 0$. So, $\iint_{\mathbb{R}^{2N}}(|D_s u_0|^l+|D_s u_0|^m)d\mu<+\infty$. □

Lemmas 6 and 7 and the fact that $I(\mathbf{0})=0$ show that the energy functional I has a mountain pass geometry; that is, setting:

$$\Gamma=\{\gamma\in C([0,1],W):\gamma(0)=\mathbf{0}, \|\gamma(1)\|_{s,\Phi}>\rho \text{ and } I(\gamma(1))\leq 0\},$$

we have $\Gamma \neq \emptyset$. Then, by using the variant version of the mountain pass theorem (see Theorem 3 in [30]), we deduce that I possesses a $(C)_c$-sequence $\{u_n\}$ with the level $c \geq \eta > 0$ given by:

$$c = \inf_{\gamma\in\Gamma} \max_{t\in[0,1]} I(\gamma(t)). \tag{18}$$

We recall that $(C)_c$-sequence $\{u_n\}$ of I in W means

$$I(u_n) \to c \quad \text{and} \quad (1 + \|u_n\|_{s,\Phi})\|I'(u_n)\|_{W^*} \to 0, \quad \text{as } n \to \infty. \tag{19}$$

To prove the boundedness of the $(C)_c$-sequence $\{u_n\}$ of I in W, we will use the Lions' type result for fractional Orlicz–Sobolev spaces (see Theorem 1.6 in [13]). We note that the claim $u_n \rightharpoonup 0$ in X of Theorem 1.6 in [13] is not necessary. With the same proof as Theorem 1.6 in [13], we can get the following result.

Lemma 8. *(Lions' type result for fractional Orlicz–Sobolev spaces). Suppose that the function ϕ defined by (2) satisfies (ϕ_1) and:*

$$\lim_{t\to 0^+} \frac{\Psi(t)}{\Phi(t)} = 0.$$

Let $\{u_n\}$ be a bounded sequence in $W^{s,\Phi}(\mathbb{R}^N)$ in such a way that:

$$\lim_{n\to\infty} \sup_{y\in\mathbb{R}^N} \int_{B_r(y)} \Phi(|u_n|)dx = 0,$$

for some $r > 0$. Then, $u_n \to \mathbf{0}$ in $L^{\Psi}(\mathbb{R}^N)$, where Ψ is an N-function such that $\Psi \prec\prec \Phi_*$.

Lemma 9. *Assume that (ϕ_1), (ϕ_2), (V) and (f_1)-(f_3) hold. Then, any $(C)_c$-sequence of I in W is bounded for all $c \geq 0$.*

Proof. Let $\{u_n\}$ be a $(C)_c$-sequence of I in W for $c \geq 0$. By (19), we have:

$$I(u_n) \to c \text{ and } \left|\left\langle I'(u_n), \frac{1}{m}u_n \right\rangle\right| \to 0, \text{ as } n \to \infty. \tag{20}$$

Then, by (10), (12), (ϕ_1), and (V), for n large, we have:

$$\begin{aligned} c+1 &\geq I(u_n) - \left\langle I'(u_n), \frac{1}{m}u_n \right\rangle \\ &= \iint_{\mathbb{R}^{2N}} \left(\Phi(|D_s u_n|) - \frac{1}{m}a(|D_s u_n|)|D_s u_n|^2\right) d\mu \\ &\quad + \int_{\mathbb{R}^N} V(x)\left(\Phi(|u_n|) - \frac{1}{m}a(|u_n|)u_n^2\right)dx \\ &\quad + \int_{\mathbb{R}^N} \left(\frac{1}{m}u_n f(x,u_n) - F(x,u_n)\right)dx \\ &\geq \frac{1}{m}\int_{\mathbb{R}^N} \widehat{F}(x,u_n)dx. \end{aligned} \tag{21}$$

To prove the boundedness of $\{u_n\}$, arguing by contradiction, we suppose that there exists a subsequence of $\{u_n\}$, still denoted by $\{u_n\}$, such that $\|u_n\|_{s,\Phi} \to \infty$, as $n \to \infty$. Let $\tilde{u}_n = \frac{u_n}{\|u_n\|_{s,\Phi}}$. Then $\|\tilde{u}_n\|_{s,\Phi} = 1$.

Firstly, we claim that:

$$\lambda_1 := \lim_{n\to\infty} \sup_{y\in\mathbb{R}^N} \int_{B_2(y)} \Phi(|\tilde{u}_n|)dx = 0. \tag{22}$$

Indeed, if $\lambda_1 \neq 0$, there exist a constant $\delta > 0$, a subsequence of $\{\tilde{u}_n\}$, still denoted by $\{\tilde{u}_n\}$, and a sequence $\{z_n\} \in \mathbb{Z}^N$ such that:

$$\int_{B_2(z_n)} \Phi(|\tilde{u}_n|)dx > \delta, \quad \text{for all } n \in \mathbb{N}. \tag{23}$$

Let $\bar{u}_n = \tilde{u}_n(\cdot + z_n)$. Then $\|\bar{u}_n\|_{s,\Phi} = \|\tilde{u}_n\|_{s,\Phi} = 1$, that is, $\{\bar{u}_n\}$ is bounded in W. Passing to a subsequence of $\{\bar{u}_n\}$, still denoted by $\{\bar{u}_n\}$, by Remark 3 and (5) in Lemma 5, we can assume that there exists a $\bar{u} \in W$ such that:

$$\bar{u}_n \rightharpoonup \bar{u} \text{ in } W, \quad \bar{u}_n \to \bar{u} \text{ in } L^{\Phi}(B_2) \quad \text{and} \quad \bar{u}_n(x) \to \bar{u}(x) \text{ a.e. in } B_2. \tag{24}$$

Note that:

$$\int_{B_2} \Phi(|\bar{u}_n|)dx = \int_{B_2(z_n)} \Phi(|\tilde{u}_n|)dx.$$

Then, by (23), (24), and (7), we obtain that $\bar{u} \neq \mathbf{0}$ in $L^{\Phi}(B_2)$, that is, $[\bar{u} \neq 0] := \{x \in B_2 : \bar{u}(x) \neq 0\}$ has non-zero Lebesgue measure. Let $u_n^* = u_n(\cdot + z_n)$. Then $\|u_n^*\|_{s,\Phi} = \|u_n\|_{s,\Phi}$, and it follows from the fact that V and f are 1-periodic in x that:

$$I(u_n^*) = I(u_n) \quad \text{and} \quad \|I'(u_n^*)\|_{W^*} = \|I'(u_n)\|_{W^*}, \quad \text{for all } n \in \mathbb{N},$$

which imply that $\{u_n^*\}$ is also a $(C)_c$-sequence of I. Then, by (21), for n large, we have:

$$\int_{\mathbb{R}^N} \widehat{F}(x, u_n^*)dx \leq m(c+1). \tag{25}$$

However, by (2) in Lemma 1, (f_2) and (f_3) imply:

$$\lim_{|t|\to\infty} \widehat{F}(x,t) = +\infty, \quad \text{uniformly in } x \in \mathbb{R}^N. \tag{26}$$

Moreover, by (24), $\bar{u}_n = \tilde{u}_n(\cdot + z_n) = \frac{u_n(\cdot+z_n)}{\|u_n\|_{s,\Phi}} = \frac{u_n^*}{\|u_n\|_{s,\Phi}}$ implies:

$$|u_n^*(x)| = |\bar{u}_n(x)|\|u_n\|_{s,\Phi} \to \infty, \quad \text{a.e. } x \in [\bar{u} \neq 0]. \tag{27}$$

Then, it follows from (f_3), (26), (27) and Fatou's Lemma that:

$$\int_{\mathbb{R}^N} \widehat{F}(x, u_n^*)dx \geq \int_{[\bar{u}\neq 0]} \widehat{F}(x, u_n^*)dx \to +\infty, \quad \text{as } n \to \infty,$$

which contradicts (25). Therefore, $\lambda_1 = 0$, and thus, (22) holds.

Next, for given $p \in (l, l^*)$ and $c > 0$, by (ϕ_1), (ϕ_2) and 2) in Lemma 4, we have:

$$\lim_{t\to 0^+} \frac{t^p}{\Phi(t)} = 0 \quad \text{and} \quad \lim_{t\to+\infty} \frac{(ct)^p}{\Phi_*(t)} \leq \lim_{t\to+\infty} \frac{c^p t^p}{\Phi_*(1)\min\{t^{l^*}, t^{m^*}\}} = 0. \tag{28}$$

Then, by Lemma 8, (22) and (28) imply that:

$$\tilde{u}_n \to \mathbf{0} \text{ in } L^p(\mathbb{R}^N), \quad \text{for all } p \in (l, l^*). \tag{29}$$

In addition, let $\Psi = |t|^l, t \geq 0$. Combining (ϕ_1) and (ϕ_2) with Lemma 1, we can easily check that Φ dominates Ψ globally. Then, it follows from 3) in Lemma 5 that the embedding $W \hookrightarrow L^l(\mathbb{R}^N)$ is continuous, which implies that there exists a constant $M_1 > 0$ such that:

$$\|\tilde{u}_n\|_l^l \leq M_1, \quad \text{for all } n \in \mathbb{N}. \tag{30}$$

Finally, to get a contradiction, we will divide both sides of formula $I(u_n) = I_1(u_n) - I_2(u_n)$ by $\|u_n\|^l_{s,\Phi_1}$ and let $n \to \infty$. On the ond hand, by (20), it is clear that:

$$\frac{I(u_n)}{\|u_n\|^l_{s,\Phi}} \to 0, \quad \text{as } n \to \infty. \tag{31}$$

On the other hand, by (13), (V) and Lemma 2, we have:

$$\begin{aligned}
\frac{I_1(u_n)}{\|u_n\|^l_{s,\Phi}} &= \frac{1}{\|u_n\|^l_{s,\Phi}}\{\iint_{\mathbb{R}^{2N}} \Phi(|D_s u_n|)d\mu + \int_{\mathbb{R}^N} V(x)\Phi(|u_n|)dx\} \\
&\geq \frac{\min\{[u_n]^l_{s,\Phi}, [u_n]^m_{s,\Phi}\} + \alpha_1 \min\{\|u_n\|^l_\Phi, \|u_n\|^m_\Phi\}}{\|u_n\|^l_{s,\Phi}} \\
&\geq \frac{[u_n]^l_{s,\Phi} + \alpha_1\|u_n\|^l_\Phi - 1 - \alpha_1}{\|u_n\|^l_{s,\Phi}} \\
&\geq \frac{\min\{1,\alpha_1\}C_l([u_n]_{s,\Phi} + \|u_n\|_\Phi)^l - 1 - \alpha_1}{\|u_n\|^l_{s,\Phi}} \to \min\{1,\alpha_1\}C_l, \text{ as } n \to \infty.
\end{aligned} \tag{32}$$

Moreover, by (2) in Lemma 1, (f_1) implies that:

$$\lim_{|t|\to 0} \frac{F(x,t)}{|t|^l} = 0, \quad \text{uniformly in } x \in \mathbb{R}^N.$$

Then, for any given constant $\varepsilon > 0$, there exists a constant $R_\varepsilon > 0$ such that:

$$\frac{|F(x,t)|}{|t|^l} \leq \varepsilon, \quad \text{for all } x \in \mathbb{R}^N, |t| \leq R_\varepsilon. \tag{33}$$

For the above $R_\varepsilon > 0$, by (f_1) and (f_3), there exists a constant $C_R > 0$ such that:

$$\left(\frac{|F(x,t)|}{|t|^l}\right)^k \leq C_R \widehat{F}(x,t), \quad \text{for all } x \in \mathbb{R}^N, |t| > R_\varepsilon. \tag{34}$$

Let:

$$X_n = \{x \in \mathbb{R}^N : |u_n(x)| \leq R_\varepsilon\} \text{ and } Y_n = \{x \in \mathbb{R}^N : |u_n(x)| > R_\varepsilon\}.$$

Then:

$$\frac{|I_2(u_n)|}{\|u_n\|^l_{s,\Phi}} \leq \int_{X_n} \frac{|F(x,u_n)|}{\|u_n\|^l_{s,\Phi}}dx + \int_{Y_n} \frac{|F(x,u_n)|}{\|u_n\|^l_{s,\Phi}}dx. \tag{35}$$

By (33) and (30), we have:

$$\int_{X_n} \frac{|F(x,u_n)|}{\|u_n\|^l_{s,\Phi}}dx = \int_{X_n} \frac{|F(x,u_n)|}{|u_n|^l}|\tilde{u}_n|^l dx \leq \varepsilon\|\tilde{u}_n\|^l_l \leq \varepsilon M_1. \tag{36}$$

The claim $k > \frac{N}{sl}$ given by (f_3) implies that $\frac{lk}{k-1} \in (l, l^*)$. Hence, by Hölder's inequality, (34), (21), (29), and the fact that $\widehat{F}(x,t) \geq 0$, we have:

$$\begin{aligned}
\int_{Y_n} \frac{|F(x,u_n)|}{\|u_n\|_{s,\Phi}^l} dx &= \int_{Y_n} \frac{|F(x,u_n)|}{|u_n|^l} |\tilde{u}_n|^l dx \\
&\le \left(\int_{Y_n} \left(\frac{|F(x,u_n)|}{|u_n|^l} \right)^k dx \right)^{\frac{1}{k}} \left(\int_{Y_n} |\tilde{u}_n|^{\frac{lk}{k-1}} dx \right)^{\frac{k-1}{k}} \\
&\le \left(\int_{Y_n} C_R \widehat{F}(x,u_n) dx \right)^{\frac{1}{k}} \|\tilde{u}_n\|_{\frac{lk}{k-1}}^l \\
&\le [C_R m(c+1)]^{\frac{1}{k}} \|\tilde{u}_n\|_{\frac{lk}{k-1}}^l \to 0, \quad \text{as } n \to \infty.
\end{aligned} \tag{37}$$

Since ε is arbitrary, it follows from (35), (36), and (37) that:

$$\frac{I_2(u_n)}{\|u_n\|_{s,\Phi}^l} \to 0, \quad \text{as } n \to \infty. \tag{38}$$

By dividing both sides of formula $I(u_n) = I_1(u_n) - I_2(u_n)$ by $\|u_n\|_{s,\Phi_1}^l$ and letting $n \to \infty$, we get a contradiction via (31), (32), and (38). Therefore, the $(C)_c$-sequence $\{u_n\}$ is bounded. □

Lemma 10. *Assume that (ϕ_1), (V), (f_1), (f_4) and (f_5) are satisfied. Then, for $u \in W$, it holds that:*

$$I(u) \ge I(tu) + \frac{1-t^l}{m} \langle I'(u), u \rangle, \quad \text{for all } t \in [0, \theta_0],$$

where θ_0 is given in (f_5).

Proof. When $u \in W$, $0 \le t \le 1$, by (10), (12), and Lemma 1, we have:

$$\begin{aligned}
& I(u) - I(tu) - \frac{1-t^l}{m} \langle I'(u), u \rangle \\
= & \iint_{\mathbb{R}^{2N}} \Phi(|D_s u|) d\mu + \int_{\mathbb{R}^N} V(x) \Phi(|u|) dx - \int_{\mathbb{R}^N} F(x,u) dx \\
& - \iint_{\mathbb{R}^{2N}} \Phi(|D_s tu|) d\mu - \int_{\mathbb{R}^N} V(x) \Phi(|tu|) dx + \int_{\mathbb{R}^N} F(x,tu) dx \\
& - \frac{1-t^l}{m} \iint_{\mathbb{R}^{2N}} a(|D_s u|) |D_s u|^2 d\mu - \frac{1-t^l}{m} \int_{\mathbb{R}^N} V(x) a(|u|) u^2 dx + \frac{1-t^l}{m} \int_{\mathbb{R}^N} u f(x,u) dx \\
\ge & \iint_{\mathbb{R}^{2N}} \Phi(|D_s u|) d\mu - \max\{t^l, t^m\} \iint_{\mathbb{R}^{2N}} \Phi(|D_s u|) d\mu - (1-t^l) \iint_{\mathbb{R}^{2N}} \Phi(|D_s u|) d\mu \\
& + \int_{\mathbb{R}^N} V(x) \Phi(|u|) dx - \max\{t^l, t^m\} \int_{\mathbb{R}^N} V(x) \Phi(|u|) dx - (1-t^l) \int_{\mathbb{R}^N} V(x) \Phi(|u|) dx \\
& + \int_{\mathbb{R}^N} \left[\frac{1-t^l}{m} u f(x,u) - F(x,u) + F(x,tu) \right] dx \\
= & \int_{\mathbb{R}^N} \left[\frac{1-t^l}{m} u f(x,u) - \int_{tu}^{u} f(x,\tau) d\tau \right] dx.
\end{aligned}$$

Then, it follows from (f_5) that:

$$I(u) \ge I(tu) + \frac{1-t^l}{m} \langle I'(u), u \rangle, \quad \text{for all } t \in [0, \theta_0],$$

for some $\theta_0 \in (0,1)$. □

Lemma 11. *Assume that (ϕ_1), (V), (f_1), (f_4) and (f_5) hold. Then any $(C)_c$-sequence of I in W is bounded for all $c \ge 0$.*

Proof. Let $\{u_n\}$ be a $(C)_c$-sequence of I in W for $c \geq 0$. By (19), we have:

$$I(u_n) \to c \text{ and } |\langle I'(u_n), u_n\rangle| \to 0, \text{ as } n \to \infty. \tag{39}$$

To prove the boundedness of $\{u_n\}$, arguing by contradiction, we suppose that there exists a subsequence of $\{u_n\}$, still denoted by $\{u_n\}$, such that $\|u_n\|_{s,\Phi} \to \infty$, as $n \to \infty$. Let $\tilde{u}_n = \frac{u_n}{\|u_n\|_{s,\Phi}}$. Then $\|\tilde{u}_n\|_{s,\Phi} = 1$.

Firstly, we claim that:

$$\lambda_2 := \lim_{n\to\infty} \sup_{y\in\mathbb{R}^N} \int_{B_2(y)} \Phi(|\tilde{u}_n|)dx = 0. \tag{40}$$

Indeed, if $\lambda_2 \neq 0$, there exist a constant $\delta > 0$, a subsequence of $\{\tilde{u}_n\}$, still denoted by $\{\tilde{u}_n\}$, and a sequence $\{z_n\} \in \mathbb{Z}^N$ such that:

$$\int_{B_2(z_n)} \Phi(|\tilde{u}_n|)dx > \delta, \quad \text{for all } n \in \mathbb{N}. \tag{41}$$

Let $\bar{u}_n = \tilde{u}_n(\cdot + z_n)$. Then $\|\bar{u}_n\|_{s,\Phi} = \|\tilde{u}_n\|_{s,\Phi} = 1$, that is, $\{\bar{u}_n\}$ is bounded in W. Passing to a subsequence of $\{\bar{u}_n\}$, still denoted by $\{\bar{u}_n\}$, by Remark 3 and (5) in Lemma 5, we can assume that there exists a $\bar{u} \in W$ such that:

$$\bar{u}_n \rightharpoonup \bar{u} \text{ in } W, \quad \bar{u}_n \to \bar{u} \text{ in } L^\Phi(B_2) \quad \text{and} \quad \bar{u}_n(x) \to \bar{u}(x) \text{ a.e. in } B_2. \tag{42}$$

Note that:

$$\int_{B_2} \Phi(|\bar{u}_n|)dx = \int_{B_2(z_n)} \Phi(|\tilde{u}_n|)dx.$$

Then, by (41), (42), and (7), we obtain that $\bar{u} \neq \mathbf{0}$ in $L^\Phi(B_2)$, that is, $[\bar{u} \neq 0] := \{x \in B_2 : \bar{u}(x) \neq 0\}$ has non-zero Lebesgue measure. Let $u_n^* = u_n(\cdot + z_n)$. Then $\|u_n^*\|_{s,\Phi} = \|u_n\|_{s,\Phi}$, and:

$$|u_n^*(x)| = |\bar{u}_n(x)|\|u_n\|_{s,\Phi} \to \infty, \quad \text{a.e. } x \in [\bar{u} \neq 0]. \tag{43}$$

Then, it follows from (14), (f_4), (43) and Fatou's Lemma that:

$$\begin{aligned} \frac{I_2(u_n)}{\|u_n\|^m_{s,\Phi}} &= \int_{\mathbb{R}^N} \frac{F(x,u_n)}{\|u_n\|^m_{s,\Phi}}dx \\ &= \int_{\mathbb{R}^N} \frac{F(x+z_n,u_n^*)}{|u_n^*|^m}|\bar{u}_n|^m dx \\ &\geq \int_{[\bar{u}\neq 0]} \frac{F(x+z_n,u_n^*)}{|u_n^*|^m}|\bar{u}_n|^m dx \to +\infty, \quad \text{as } n \to \infty. \end{aligned} \tag{44}$$

Moreover, it follows from (13), (V), and Lemma 2 that:

$$\begin{aligned} \limsup_{n\to\infty} \frac{I_1(u_n)}{\|u_n\|^m_{s,\Phi}} &= \limsup_{n\to\infty} \frac{1}{\|u_n\|^m_{s,\Phi}}\{\iint_{\mathbb{R}^{2N}} \Phi(|D_s u_n|)d\mu + \int_{\mathbb{R}^N} V(x)\Phi(|u_n|)dx\} \\ &\leq \limsup_{n\to\infty} \frac{\max\{[u_n]^l_{s,\Phi}, [u_n]^m_{s,\Phi}\} + \alpha_2 \max\{\|u_n\|^l_\Phi, \|u_n\|^m_\Phi\}}{\|u_n\|^m_{s,\Phi}} \\ &\leq 1 + \alpha_2. \end{aligned} \tag{45}$$

By dividing both sides of formula $I(u_n) = I_1(u_n) - I_2(u_n)$ by $\|u_n\|^m_{s,\Phi_1}$ and letting $n \to \infty$, we get a contradiction via (39), (44), and (45). Therefore, $\lambda_2 = 0$ and thus (40) holds.

Then, by using the Lions' type result for fractional Orlicz–Sobolev spaces, with the similar discussion as in Lemma 9, we have:

$$\tilde{u}_n \to \mathbf{0} \text{ in } L^p(\mathbb{R}^N), \quad \text{for all } p \in (m, l^*). \tag{46}$$

Besides, it follows from (1) in Lemma 2, (3) in Lemma 4, (1)–(2) in Lemma 5 and the fact $\|\tilde{u}_n\|_{s,\Phi} = 1$ that there exists a constant $M_2 > 0$ such that:

$$\begin{aligned} & \int_{\mathbb{R}^N} (\Phi(|\tilde{u}_n|) + \Phi_*(|\tilde{u}_n|))dx \\ \leq\ & \max\left\{\|\tilde{u}_n\|_{\Phi}^{l}, \|\tilde{u}_n\|_{\Phi}^{m}\right\} + \max\left\{\|\tilde{u}_n\|_{\Phi_*}^{l^*}, \|\tilde{u}_n\|_{\Phi_*}^{m^*}\right\} \\ \leq\ & M_2, \quad \text{for all } n \in \mathbb{N}. \end{aligned} \tag{47}$$

Next, for any given $R > 1$, let $t_n = \frac{R}{\|u_n\|_{s,\Phi}}$. Since $\|u_n\|_{s,\Phi} \to \infty$ as $n \to \infty$, it follows that $t_n \in (0, \theta_0)$ for n large enough. Thus, by (39) and Lemma 10, we have:

$$\begin{aligned} c + o_n(1) &= I(u_n) \\ &\geq I(t_n u_n) + \frac{1 - t_n^l}{m}\langle I'(u_n), u_n\rangle \\ &= I\left(\frac{R}{\|u_n\|_{s,\Phi}} u_n\right) + o_n(1) \\ &= I(R\tilde{u}_n) + o_n(1) \\ &= I_1(R\tilde{u}_n) - I_2(R\tilde{u}_n) + o_n(1). \end{aligned} \tag{48}$$

For the above R and any given $\varepsilon > 0$, by (f_1), the continuity of F and the fact that Φ and Φ_* satisfy the Δ_2-condition, there exist constants $C_\varepsilon > 0$ and $p \in (m, l^*)$ such that:

$$|F(x, Rt)| \leq \varepsilon(\Phi(|t|) + \Phi_*(|t|)) + C_\varepsilon |t|^p, \text{ for all } (x,t) \in \mathbb{R}^N \times \mathbb{R}. \tag{49}$$

Then, by (14), (46), (47), and (49), we have:

$$\begin{aligned} |I_2(R\tilde{u}_n)| &\leq \int_{\mathbb{R}^N} |F(x, R\tilde{u}_n)|dx \\ &\leq \varepsilon \int_{\mathbb{R}^N} (\Phi(|\tilde{u}_n|) + \Phi_*(|\tilde{u}_n|))dx + C_\varepsilon \int_{\mathbb{R}^N} |\tilde{u}_n|^p dx \\ &\leq \varepsilon M_2 + o_n(1). \end{aligned} \tag{50}$$

Since $\varepsilon > 0$ is arbitrary, (50) implies that:

$$I_2(R\tilde{u}_n) = o_n(1). \tag{51}$$

Moreover, for the above $R > 1$, by (13), Lemma 1 and the fact $\|\tilde{u}_n\|_{s,\Phi} = \|\tilde{u}_n\|_{\Phi} + [\tilde{u}_n]_{s,\Phi} = 1$, we have:

$$\begin{aligned} I_1(R\tilde{u}_n) &= \iint_{\mathbb{R}^{2N}} \Phi(|D_s(R\tilde{u}_n)|)d\mu + \int_{\mathbb{R}^N} V(x)\Phi(|R\tilde{u}_n|)dx \\ &\geq \min\{R^l, R^m\}\left(\min\{[\tilde{u}_n]_{s,\Phi}^{l}, [\tilde{u}_n]_{s,\Phi}^{m}\} + \alpha_1 \min\{\|\tilde{u}_n\|_{\Phi}^{l}, \|\tilde{u}_n\|_{\Phi}^{m}\}\right) \\ &= R^l\left([\tilde{u}_n]_{s,\Phi}^{m} + \alpha_1\|\tilde{u}_n\|_{\Phi}^{m}\right) \\ &\geq \min\{1, \alpha_1\}R^l\left([\tilde{u}_n]_{s,\Phi}^{m} + \|\tilde{u}_n\|_{\Phi}^{m}\right) \\ &\geq \min\{1, \alpha_1\}R^l C_m, \end{aligned} \tag{52}$$

where $C_m := \inf_{|u|+|v|=1}\{|u|^m + |v|^m\} > 0$. Then, by the arbitrariness of R, combining (51) and (52) with (48), we get a contradiction. Therefore, the $(C)_c$-sequence $\{u_n\}$ is bounded. □

Lemma 12. *Assume that* (ϕ_1), (V), *and* (f_1) *hold. Then* $I' : W \to W^*$ *is weakly sequentially continuous. Namely, if* $u_n \rightharpoonup u$ *in* W, *then* $I'(u_n) \rightharpoonup I'(u)$ *in the dual space* W^* *of* W.

Proof. Since W is reflexive, it is enough to prove $I'(u_n) \overset{w^*}{\rightharpoonup} I'(u)$ in W^*. Namely, to prove:

$$\lim_{n\to\infty} \langle I'(u_n), v\rangle = \langle I'(u), v\rangle, \text{ for all } v \in W. \tag{53}$$

Firstly, we prove that I' is bounded on each bounded subset of W. Indeed, by (12), (V), (5), (11), (6), Lemma 2, (3) in Lemma 4, (1) in Lemma 5, and the fact that Φ, $\widetilde{\Phi}$ and Φ_* satisfy the Δ_2-condition, we have:

$$\begin{aligned}
\|I'(u)\|_{W^*} &= \sup_{v\in W, \|v\|_{s,\Phi}=1} |\langle I'(u), v\rangle| \\
&\le \sup_{v\in W, \|v\|_{s,\Phi}=1} \Big(\iint_{\mathbb{R}^{2N}} a(|D_s u|)|D_s u||D_s v| d\mu + \int_{\mathbb{R}^N} V(x) a(|u|)|u||v| dx \\
&\quad + \int_{\mathbb{R}^N} |f(x,u)||v| dx \Big) \\
&\le \sup_{v\in W, \|v\|_{s,\Phi}=1} \Big(\iint_{\mathbb{R}^{2N}} \widetilde{\Phi}(a(|D_s u|)|D_s u|) d\mu + \iint_{\mathbb{R}^{2N}} \Phi(|D_s v|) d\mu \\
&\quad + (\alpha_2+\varepsilon) \int_{\mathbb{R}^N} \widetilde{\Phi}(a(|u|)|u|) dx + (\alpha_2+\varepsilon) \int_{\mathbb{R}^N} \Phi(|v|) dx \\
&\quad + C_\varepsilon \int_{\mathbb{R}^N} \widetilde{\Phi}_*(\Phi_*'(|u|)) dx + C_\varepsilon \int_{\mathbb{R}^N} \Phi_*(|v|) dx \Big) \\
&\le \Big(\iint_{\mathbb{R}^{2N}} \Phi(2|D_s u|) d\mu + (\alpha_2+\varepsilon) \int_{\mathbb{R}^N} \Phi(2|u|) dx + C_\varepsilon \int_{\mathbb{R}^N} \Phi_*(2|u|) dx \Big) \\
&\quad + \sup_{v\in W, \|v\|_{s,\Phi}=1} \Big(\max\{[v]_{s,\Phi}^l, [v]_{s,\Phi}^m\} + (\alpha_2+\varepsilon) \max\{\|v\|_{\Phi}^l, \|v\|_{\Phi}^m\} \\
&\quad + C_\varepsilon \max\{\|v\|_{\Phi_*}^{l^*}, \|v\|_{\Phi_*}^{m^*}\} \Big) \\
&\le K_2 \Big(\iint_{\mathbb{R}^{2N}} \Phi(|D_s u|) d\mu + (\alpha_2+\varepsilon) \int_{\mathbb{R}^N} \Phi(|u|) dx + C_\varepsilon \int_{\mathbb{R}^N} \Phi_*(|u|) dx \Big) \\
&\quad + 1 + \alpha_2 + \varepsilon + C_\varepsilon C_{\Phi_*} \\
&\le K_2 \Big((1+\alpha_2+\varepsilon)\|u\|_{s,\Phi}^m + C_\varepsilon C_{\Phi_*} \|u\|_{s,\Phi}^{m^*} \Big) + (K_2+1)(1+\alpha_2+\varepsilon+C_\varepsilon C_{\Phi_*}),
\end{aligned}$$

which implies that I' is bounded on each bounded subset of W. Moreover, $C_c^\infty(\mathbb{R}^N)$ is dense in W. Then, to prove (53) we only need to prove:

$$\lim_{n\to\infty} \langle I'(u_n), w\rangle = \langle I'(u), w\rangle, \text{ for all } w \in C_c^\infty(\mathbb{R}^N). \tag{54}$$

To get (54), arguing by contradiction, we suppose that there exist constant $\delta > 0$, $w_0 \in C_c^\infty(\mathbb{R}^N)$ with $\text{supp}\{w_0\} \subset B_r$ for some $r > 0$, and a subsequence of $\{u_n\}$, still denoted by $\{u_n\}$, such that:

$$|\langle I'(u_n), w_0\rangle - \langle I'(u), w_0\rangle| \ge \delta, \text{ for all } n \in \mathbb{R}^N. \tag{55}$$

Since $u_n \rightharpoonup u$ in W, by (5) in Lemma 5, there exists a subsequence of $\{u_n\}$, still denoted by $\{u_n\}$, such that

$$u_n \to u \text{ in } L_{loc}^{\Phi}(\mathbb{R}^N), \quad u_n(x) \to u(x) \text{ a.e. in } \mathbb{R}^N \quad \text{and} \quad D_s u_n \to D_s u \text{ a.e. in } \mathbb{R}^{2N}.$$

Next, we claim that

$$\lim_{n\to\infty}\int_{\mathbb{R}^N} f(x,u_n)w_0dx = \int_{\mathbb{R}^N} f(x,u)w_0dx. \tag{56}$$

Indeed, it follows (f_1) that for any given constant $\varepsilon > 0$, there exists a constant $C_\varepsilon > 0$ such that:

$$|f(x,t)| \leq C_\varepsilon + \varepsilon\Phi'_*(|t|), \text{ for all } (x,t) \in \mathbb{R}^N \times \mathbb{R}.$$

Then, by using standard arguments, we can obtain that the sequence $\{f(x,u_n)\}$ is bounded in $L^{\widetilde{\Phi}_*}(B_r)$. Moreover, $f(x,u_n) \to f(x,u)$ a.e. in B_r. Then, by applying Lemma 2.1 in [37], we get $f(x,u_n) \rightharpoonup f(x,u)$ in $L^{\widetilde{\Phi}_*}(B_r)$, and thus (56) holds because $w_0 \in L^{\Phi_*}(B_r)$.

Similarly, we can get:

$$\lim_{n\to\infty}\iint_{\mathbb{R}^{2N}} a(|D_su_n|)D_su_nD_sw_0d\mu = \iint_{\mathbb{R}^{2N}} a(|D_su|)D_suD_sw_0d\mu \tag{57}$$

and:

$$\lim_{n\to\infty}\int_{\mathbb{R}^N} V(x)a(|u_n|)u_nw_0dx = \int_{\mathbb{R}^N} V(x)a(|u|)uw_0dx, \tag{58}$$

which is based on the fact that the sequence $\{a(|D_su_n|)D_su_n\}$ is bounded in $L^{\widetilde{\Phi}}(\mathbb{R}^{2N},d\mu)$, $a(|D_su_n|)D_su_n \to a(|D_su|)D_su$ a.e. in $\mathbb{R}^{2N}$, $D_sw_0 \in L^{\Phi}(\mathbb{R}^{2N},d\mu)$, and the sequence $\{V(x)a(|u_n|)u_n\}$ is bounded in $L^{\widetilde{\Phi}}(\mathbb{R}^N)$, $V(x)a(|u_n|)u_n \to V(x)a(|u|)u$ a.e. in $\mathbb{R}^N$, $w_0 \in L^{\Phi}(\mathbb{R}^N)$, respectively.

Therefore, combining (56)–(58) with (12), we can conclude that:

$$\lim_{n\to\infty}|\langle I'(u_n),w_0\rangle - \langle I'(u),w_0\rangle| = 0,$$

which contradicts (55). Thus, (54) holds and the proof is completed. □

Lemma 13. *Equation (1) has at least a non-trivial solution under the assumptions of Theorem 1 and Theorem 2, respectively.*

Proof. Let $\{u_n\}$ be the $(C)_c$-sequence of I in W for the level $c > 0$ given in (18). Lemmas 9 and 11 show that the sequence $\{u_n\}$ is bounded in W under the assumptions of Theorem 1 and Theorem 2, respectively.

First, we claim that:

$$\lambda_3 := \lim_{n\to\infty}\sup_{y\in\mathbb{R}^N}\int_{B_2(y)}\Phi(|u_n|)dx > 0. \tag{59}$$

Indeed, if $\lambda_3 = 0$, by using the Lions' type result for fractional Orlicz–Sobolev spaces again, we have:

$$u_n \to \mathbf{0} \text{ in } L^p(\mathbb{R}^N), \quad \text{for all } p \in (m,l^*). \tag{60}$$

Given $p \in (m,l^*)$, by (f_1), (ϕ_1) and the definition $F(x,t) = \int_0^t f(x,\tau)d\tau$, for any given constant $\varepsilon > 0$, there exists a constant $C_\varepsilon > 0$ such that:

$$|F(x,t)| \leq \varepsilon(\Phi(|t|) + \Phi_*(|t|)) + C_\varepsilon|t|^p, \text{ for all } (x,t) \in \mathbb{R}^N \times \mathbb{R} \tag{61}$$

and:

$$|tf(x,t)| \leq \varepsilon(\Phi(|t|) + \Phi_*(|t|)) + C_\varepsilon|t|^p, \text{ for all } (x,t) \in \mathbb{R}^N \times \mathbb{R}. \tag{62}$$

Then, it follows from (60)–(62), (1) in Lemma 2, (3) in Lemma 4 and (1) in Lemma 5, the boundedness of $\{u_n\}$, and the arbitrariness of ε that:

$$\lim_{n\to\infty}\int_{\mathbb{R}^N} F(x,u_n)dx = \lim_{n\to\infty}\int_{\mathbb{R}^N} u_n f(x,u_n)dx = 0. \tag{63}$$

Hence, by (10), (12), (19), (ϕ_1), (V), and (63), we have:

$$\begin{aligned} c &= \lim_{n\to\infty}\left\{I(u_n) - \left\langle I'(u_n), \frac{1}{l}u_n\right\rangle\right\} \\ &= \lim_{n\to\infty}\left\{\iint_{\mathbb{R}^{2N}}\left(\Phi(|D_s u_n|) - \frac{1}{l}a(|D_s u_n|)|D_s u_n|^2\right)d\mu \right. \\ &\quad + \int_{\mathbb{R}^N} V(x)\left(\Phi(|u_n|) - \frac{1}{l}a(|u_n|)u_n^2\right)dx \\ &\quad \left. + \int_{\mathbb{R}^N}\left(\frac{1}{l}u_n f(x,u_n) - F(x,u_n)\right)dx\right\} \\ &\le \lim_{n\to\infty}\left\{\int_{\mathbb{R}^N}\left(\frac{1}{l}u_n f(x,u_n) - F(x,u_n)\right)dx\right\} = 0, \end{aligned}$$

which contradicts $c > 0$. Therefore, $\lambda_3 > 0$, and thus, (59) holds.

Then, it follows from (59) that there exist a constant $\delta > 0$, a subsequence of $\{u_n\}$, still denoted by $\{u_n\}$, and a sequence $\{z_n\} \subset \mathbb{Z}^N$ such that:

$$\int_{B_2(z_n)} \Phi(|u_n|)dx = \int_{B_2}(\Phi(|u_n^*|)dx > \delta, \quad \text{for all } n \in \mathbb{N}, \tag{64}$$

where $u_n^* := u_n(\cdot + z_n)$. Since V and F are 1-periodic in x, $\{u_n^*\}$ is also a $(C)_c$-sequence of I. Then, passing to a subsequence of $\{u_n^*\}$, still denoted by $\{u_n^*\}$, we can assume that there exists a $u^* \in W$ such that:

$$u_n^* \rightharpoonup u^* \text{ in } W \quad \text{and} \quad u_n^* \to u^* \text{ in } L^\Phi(B_2). \tag{65}$$

Thus, by (64), (65), and (7), we obtain that $u^* \neq \mathbf{0}$. Moreover, it follows from Lemma 12 and (19) that:

$$\|I'(u^*)\|_{W^*} \le \liminf_{n\to\infty}\|I'(u_n^*)\|_{W^*} = 0,$$

which implies $I'(u^*) = \mathbf{0}$, that is, u^* is a non-trivial solution of Equation (1). □

Lemma 14. *Assume that* (ϕ_1), (V) *and* (f_1) *hold. Then:*

$$\langle I'(u), u\rangle = \langle I_1'(u), u\rangle - o(\langle I_1'(u), u\rangle) \quad as \quad \|u\|_{s,\Phi} \to 0.$$

Proof. By using the continuity of $I_i'(i = 1,2)$ defined by (15) and (16), we can easily verify that $\langle I_i'(u), u\rangle = o(1)(i = 1,2)$ as $\|u\|_{s,\Phi} \to 0$. Then, it is sufficient to prove $\langle I_2'(u), u\rangle = o(\langle I_1'(u), u\rangle)$ as $\|u\|_{s,\Phi} \to 0$ because $\langle I'(u), u\rangle = \langle I_1'(u), u\rangle - \langle I_2'(u), u\rangle$.

For any given constant $\varepsilon > 0$, it follows (f_1), (ϕ_1) and (5) that there exists a constant $C_\varepsilon > 0$ such that:

$$|tf(x,t)| \le \varepsilon\Phi(|t|) + C_\varepsilon\Phi_*(|t|), \text{ for all } (x,t) \in \mathbb{R}^N \times \mathbb{R}. \tag{66}$$

Then, by (16) and (66), we have:

$$\begin{aligned} |\langle I_2'(u), u\rangle| &\le \int_{\mathbb{R}^N}|uf(x,u)|dx \\ &\le \varepsilon\int_{\mathbb{R}^N}\Phi(|u|)dx + C_\varepsilon\int_{\mathbb{R}^N}\Phi_*(|u|)dx. \end{aligned} \tag{67}$$

Moreover, by (15), (ϕ_1), and (V), we have:

$$\begin{aligned}\langle I_1'(u),u\rangle &= \iint_{\mathbb{R}^{2N}} a(|D_su|)|D_su|^2 d\mu + \int_{\mathbb{R}^N} V(x)a(|u|)u^2 dx \\ &\geq l\iint_{\mathbb{R}^{2N}} \Phi(|D_su|)d\mu + \alpha_1 l\int_{\mathbb{R}^N} \Phi(|u|)dx. \end{aligned} \tag{68}$$

Then, (67), (68), Lemma 2, (3) in Lemma 4, (1) in Lemma 5, and the fact that $1 < m < l^*$ imply that:

$$\begin{aligned}\lim_{\|u\|_{s,\Phi}\to 0} \frac{|\langle I_2'(u),u\rangle|}{\langle I_1'(u),u\rangle} &\leq \lim_{\|u\|_{s,\Phi}\to 0} \frac{\varepsilon\int_{\mathbb{R}^N}\Phi(|u|)dx + C_\varepsilon\int_{\mathbb{R}^N}\Phi_*(|u|)dx}{l\iint_{\mathbb{R}^{2N}}\Phi(|D_su|)d\mu + \alpha_1 l\int_{\mathbb{R}^N}\Phi(|u|)dx} \\ &\leq \frac{\varepsilon}{\alpha_1 l} + \lim_{\|u\|_{s,\Phi}\to 0} \frac{C_\varepsilon\int_{\mathbb{R}^N}\Phi_*(|u|)dx}{\min\{1,\alpha_1\}l(\iint_{\mathbb{R}^{2N}}\Phi(|D_su|)d\mu + \int_{\mathbb{R}^N}\Phi(|u|)dx)} \\ &\leq \frac{\varepsilon}{\alpha_1 l} + \lim_{\|u\|_{s,\Phi}\to 0} \frac{C_\varepsilon \max\{C_{\Phi_*}^{l^*}, C_{\Phi_*}^{m^*}\}\|u\|_{s,\Phi}^{l^*}}{\min\{1,\alpha_1\}lC_m\|u\|_{s,\Phi}^m} \\ &= \frac{\varepsilon}{\alpha_1 l}.\end{aligned}$$

Since ε is arbitrary, we conclude that $|\langle I_2'(u),u\rangle| = o(\langle I_1'(u),u\rangle)$ as $\|u\|_{s,\Phi}\to 0$, which implies that $\langle I_2'(u),u\rangle = o(\langle I_1'(u),u\rangle)$ as $\|u\|_{s,\Phi}\to 0$. □

Proof of Theorems 1 and 2. Lemma 13 shows that Equation (1) has at least a non-trivial solution under the assumptions of Theorem 1 and Theorem 2, respectively. Next, we prove Equation (1) has a ground state solution. Let:

$$\mathcal{N} := \{u \in W\setminus\{\mathbf{0}\} : I'(u) = \mathbf{0}\} \quad \text{and} \quad d := \inf_{u\in\mathcal{N}}\{I(u)\}.$$

First, we claim that $d \geq 0$. Indeed, for any given non-trivial critical point $u \in \mathcal{N}$, by (10), (12), (ϕ_1), (V) and (f_3) (or (f_5)), we have:

$$\begin{aligned} I(u) &= I(u) - \left\langle I'(u), \frac{1}{m}u\right\rangle \\ &= \iint_{\mathbb{R}^{2N}}\left(\Phi(|D_su|) - \frac{1}{m}a(|D_su|)|D_su|^2\right)d\mu \\ &\quad + \int_{\mathbb{R}^N} V(x)\left(\Phi(|u|) - \frac{1}{m}a(|u|)u^2\right)dx \\ &\quad + \int_{\mathbb{R}^N}\left(\frac{1}{m}uf(x,u) - F(x,u)\right)dx \\ &\geq \frac{1}{m}\int_{\mathbb{R}^N}\widehat{F}(x,u)dx \geq 0. \end{aligned}$$

Since the non-trivial critical point u of I is arbitrary, we conclude $d \geq 0$. Choose a sequence $\{u_n\} \subset \mathcal{N}$ such that $I(u_n) \to d$ as $n \to \infty$. Then, it is obvious that $\{u_n\}$ is a $(C)_d$-sequence of I for the level d. Lemmas 9 and 11 show that $\{u_n\}$ is bounded in W. Moreover, combining Lemma 14 with the fact that $\{u_n\} \subset \mathcal{N}$, we can conclude that there exists a constant $M_3 > 0$ such that:

$$\|u_n\|_{s,\Phi} \geq M_3, \quad \text{for all } n \in \mathbb{N}. \tag{69}$$

Now, we claim that:

$$\lambda_4 := \lim_{n\to\infty}\sup_{y\in\mathbb{R}^N}\int_{B_2(y)}\Phi(|u_n|)dx > 0. \tag{70}$$

Indeed, if $\lambda_4 = 0$, similar to (63), we can get:

$$\lim_{n\to\infty} \int_{\mathbb{R}^N} u_n f(x, u_n) dx = 0. \tag{71}$$

Then, by (12), (ϕ_1), (V), and (71), we have:

$$\begin{aligned} 0 &= \lim_{n\to\infty} \left\{ \langle I'(u_n), u_n \rangle + \int_{\mathbb{R}^N} u_n f(x, u_n) dx \right\} \\ &= \lim_{n\to\infty} \left\{ \iint_{\mathbb{R}^{2N}} a(|D_s u_n|) |D_s u_n|^2 d\mu + \int_{\mathbb{R}^N} V(x) a(|u_n|) u_n^2 dx \right\} \\ &\geq \lim_{n\to\infty} \left\{ l \iint_{\mathbb{R}^{2N}} \Phi(|D_s u_n|) d\mu + \alpha_1 l \int_{\mathbb{R}^N} \Phi(|u_n|) dx \right\} \\ &\geq 0, \end{aligned}$$

which together with Lemma 2 implies that $\|u_n\|_{s,\Phi} = \|u_n\|_\Phi + [u_n]_{s,\Phi} \to 0$ as $n \to \infty$, which contradicts (69). Therefore, $\lambda_4 > 0$, and thus, (70) holds.

Next, with similar arguments as those in Lemma 13, let $u_n^* := u_n(\cdot + z_n)$. Then, $\{u_n^*\}$ is also a $(C)_d$-sequence of I. Moreover, there exist a subsequence of $\{u_n^*\}$, still denoted by $\{u_n^*\}$, and a $u^* \in W$ such that $u_n^* \rightharpoonup u^*$ in W with $u^* \neq \mathbf{0}$ and $I'(u^*) = \mathbf{0}$. This shows that $u^* \in \mathcal{N}$, and thus, $I(u^*) \geq d$.

On the other hand, by (10), (12), (ϕ_1), (V), (f_3) (or (f_5)), and Fatou's Lemma, we have:

$$\begin{aligned} I(u^*) &= I(u^*) - \left\langle I'(u^*), \frac{1}{m} u^* \right\rangle \\ &= \iint_{\mathbb{R}^{2N}} \left(\Phi(|D_s u^*|) - \frac{1}{m} a(|D_s u^*|) |D_s u^*|^2 \right) d\mu \\ &\quad + \int_{\mathbb{R}^N} V(x) \left(\Phi(|u^*|) - \frac{1}{m} a(|u^*|) |u^*|^2 \right) dx \\ &\quad + \int_{\mathbb{R}^N} \left(\frac{1}{m} u^* f(x, u^*) - F(x, u^*) \right) dx \\ &\leq \liminf_{n\to\infty} \left\{ I(u_n^*) - \left\langle I'(u_n^*), \frac{1}{m} u_n^* \right\rangle \right\} \\ &= d. \end{aligned}$$

Therefore, $I(u^*) = d$, that is, u^* is a ground state solution of Equation (1). This finishes the proof. □

4. Examples

For Equation (1), when given $s \in (0,1)$ and $N \in \mathbb{N}$, the function ϕ defined by (2) can be selected from the following possibilities, each satisfying conditions (ϕ_1)–(ϕ_2).

Case 1. Let $\phi(t) = |t|^{p-2}t$ for $t \neq 0$, $\phi(0) = 0$ with $1 < p < \frac{N}{s}$. In this case, simple computations show that $l = m = p$.

Case 2. Let $\phi(t) = |t|^{p-2}t + |t|^{q-2}t$ for $t \neq 0$, $\phi(0) = 0$ with $1 < p < q < \frac{N}{s} < \frac{pq}{q-p}$. In this case, simple computations show that $l = p, m = q$.

Case 3. Let $\phi(t) = \frac{|t|^{q-2}t}{\log(1+|t|^p)}$ for $t \neq 0$, $\phi(0) = 0$ with $1 < p+1 < q < \frac{N}{s} < \frac{q(q-p)}{p}$. In this case, simple computations show that $l = q - p, m = q$.

Moreover, we provide an additional case that satisfies condition (ϕ_1) but fails to satisfy condition (ϕ_2).

Case 4. Let $\phi(t) = |t|^{q-2}t \log(1 + |t|^p)$ for $t \neq 0$, $\phi(0) = 0$ with $1 < q < p + q < \frac{N}{s} < \frac{q(p+q)}{p}$. In this case, simple computations show that $l = q, m = p + q$.

For example, regarding Case 2, the operator in non-local problem (1) defined by (3) reduces to the following fractional (p,q)-Laplacian operator:

$$\begin{aligned}(-\Delta_p-\Delta_q)^s u(x) &= P.V.\int_{\mathbb{R}^N}\frac{|u(x)-u(y)|^{p-2}(u(x)-u(y))}{|x-y|^{N+ps}}dy\\ &\quad +P.V.\int_{\mathbb{R}^N}\frac{|u(x)-u(y)|^{q-2}(u(x)-u(y))}{|x-y|^{N+qs}}dy.\end{aligned}$$

Let $f(x,t)=qh(x)|t|^{q-2}t\log(1+|t|)+\frac{h(x)|t|^{q-1}t}{1+|t|}$, where $h\in C(\mathbb{R}^N,(0,+\infty))$ is 1-periodic in x. Then, $F(x,t)=h(x)|t|^q\log(1+|t|)$ and $\widehat{F}(x,t)=\frac{h(x)|t|^{q+1}}{1+|t|}$. It is easy to check that f satisfies (f_1)-(f_2), but does not satisfy the (AR) type condition (AR)*. However, we can see that it satisfies (f_3). Indeed, since $\frac{N}{s}<\frac{pq}{q-p}$, then there exists constant $k\in(\frac{N}{sp},\frac{q}{q-p})$ such that:

$$\limsup_{|t|\to\infty}\left(\frac{|F(x,t)|}{|t|^l}\right)^k\frac{1}{\widehat{F}(x,t)}=\limsup_{|t|\to\infty}\frac{h^{k-1}(x)(1+|t|)(\log(1+|t|))^k}{|t|^{(p-q)k+q+1}}=0,$$

which implies that condition (f_3) holds. Therefore, by using Theorem 1, we obtain that Equation (1) has at least one ground state solution when potential V satisfies condition (V).

In addition, let $f(x,t)=h(x)\gamma(t)$, where $h\in C(\mathbb{R}^N,(0,+\infty))$ is 1-periodic in x and:

$$\gamma(t)=\begin{cases}0, & |t|\le 1,\\ \left(|t|^{\frac{q+p^*-4}{2}}-\frac{1}{|t|}\right)t, & |t|>1.\end{cases}$$

Then, $F(x,t)=h(x)\Gamma(t)$, where:

$$\Gamma(t)=\begin{cases}0, & |t|\le 1,\\ \frac{2}{q+p^*}|t|^{\frac{q+p^*}{2}}-|t|+\frac{q+p^*-2}{q+p^*}, & |t|>1.\end{cases}$$

It is easy to check that f satisfies (f_1) and (f_4), but does not satisfy (f_3) and the (Ne) type condition (Ne)*. However, we can see that it satisfies (f_5). Indeed, since:

$$\frac{1-\theta^l}{m}tf(x,t)=\frac{1-\theta^p}{q}h(x)t\gamma(t)\quad\text{and}\quad F(x,t)-F(x,\theta t)\le F(x,t)=h(x)\Gamma(t), \tag{72}$$

for all $\theta\in\mathbb{R}$, $(x,t)\in\mathbb{R}^N\times\mathbb{R}$. Then, it is obvious that:

$$\frac{1-\theta^l}{m}tf(x,t)\ge F(x,t)-F(x,\theta t),\ \text{for all}\ \theta\in\mathbb{R},(x,t)\in\mathbb{R}^N\times[-1,1]. \tag{73}$$

Moreover:

$$\inf_{|t|>1}\frac{t\gamma(t)-q\Gamma(t)}{t\gamma(t)}=\inf_{|t|>1}\frac{\frac{p^*-q}{q+p^*}|t|^{\frac{q+p^*}{2}}+(q-1)|t|-\frac{q^2+qp^*-2q}{q+p^*}}{|t|^{\frac{q+p^*}{2}}-|t|}>0,$$

which implies that there exists a $\theta_0\in(0,1)$ such that:

$$\frac{1-\theta^p}{q}h(x)t\gamma(t)\ge h(x)\Gamma(t),\ \text{for all}\ \theta\in[0,\theta_0],x\in\mathbb{R}^N,|t|>1. \tag{74}$$

Then, combining (73) and (74) with (72), we can conclude that (f_5) holds. Therefore, by using Theorem 2, we obtain that Equation (1) has at least one ground state solution when potential V satisfies condition (V).

5. Conclusions

In this paper, we have explored the existence of ground state solutions for a non-local problem in fractional Orlicz–Sobolev spaces. This problem involves the fractional Φ-Laplacian, a non-local, and a non-homogeneous operator. Our analysis did not rely on traditional assumptions such as the Ambrosetti–Rabinowitz type or Nehari type conditions on the non-linearity. Instead, we utilized a modified version of the mountain pass theorem and a Lions' type result tailored for fractional Orlicz–Sobolev spaces. These techniques allowed us to demonstrate the existence of ground state solutions in the periodic case. This work extends and improves the existing results in the literature. Looking ahead, it is intriguing to consider the potential extension of our work to systems in fractional Orlicz–Sobolev spaces, presenting exciting prospects for future exploration and research.

Author Contributions: Methodology, L.W., X.Z. and C.L.; Validation, L.W. and C.L.; Writing—original draft, L.W.; Writing—review & editing, L.W. and C.L.; Supervision, X.Z. All authors have read and agreed to the published version of the manuscript.

Funding: This project is partially supported by the Guangdong Basic and Applied Basic Research Foundation (No: 2020A1515110706), Research Startup Funds of DGUT (No: GC300501-100), Yunnan Fundamental Research Projects (No: 202301AT070465), and Xingdian Talent Support Program for Young Talents of Yunnan Province.

Data Availability Statement: Data are contained within the article.

Conflicts of Interest: The authors declare no conflicts of interest.

References

1. Laskin, N. Fractional quantum mechanics and Lévy path integrals. *Phys. Lett. A* **2000**, *268*, 298–305. [CrossRef]
2. Alberti, G.; Bouchitté, G.; Seppecher, P. Phase transition with the line-tension effect. *Arch. Ration. Mech. Anal.* **1998**, *144*, 1–46. [CrossRef]
3. Metzler, R.; Klafter, J. The restaurant at the end of the random walk: Recent developments in the description of anomalous transport by fractional dynamics. *J. Phys. A* **2004**, *37*, 161–208. [CrossRef]
4. Mosconi, S.; Squassina, M. Recent progresses in the theory of nonlinear nonlocal problems. *Bruno Pini Math. Anal. Semin.* **2016**, *7*, 147–164.
5. Bonder, J.F.; Salort, A.M. Fractional order Orlicz-Sobolev spaces. *J. Funct. Anal.* **2019**, *277*, 333–367. [CrossRef]
6. Bonder, J.F.; Salort, A.; Vivas, H. Global Hölder regularity for eigenfunctions of the fractional g-Laplacian. *J. Math. Anal. Appl.* **2023**, *526*, 127332. [CrossRef]
7. Salort, A.; Vivas, H. Fractional eigenvalues in Orlicz spaces with no Δ_2 condition. *J. Differ. Equ.* **2022**, *327*, 166–188. [CrossRef]
8. Salort, A. Eigenvalues and minimizers for a non-standard growth non-local operator. *J. Differ. Equ.* **2020**, *268*, 5413–5439. [CrossRef]
9. Alberico, A.; Cianchi, A.; Pick, L.; Slavíková, L. Fractional Orlicz-Sobolev embeddings. *J. Math. Pures Appl.* **2021**, *149*, 216–253. [CrossRef]
10. Azroul, E.; Benkirane, A.; Srati, M. Existence of solutions for a nonlocal type problem in fractional Orlicz Sobolev spaces. *Adv. Oper. Theory* **2020**, *5*, 1350–1375. [CrossRef]
11. Bahrouni, S.; Ounaies, H.; Tavares, L.S. Basic results of fractional Orlicz-Sobolev space and applications to non-local problems. *Topol. Methods Nonlinear Anal.* **2020**, *55*, 681–695. [CrossRef]
12. Chaker, J.; Kim, M.; Weidner, M. Regularity for nonlocal problems with non-standard growth. *Calc. Var.* **2022**, *61*, 227. [CrossRef]
13. Silva, E.D.; Carvalho, M.L.; de Albuquerque, J.C.; Bahrouni, S. Compact embedding theorems and a Lions' type lemma for fractional Orlicz-Sobolev spaces. *J. Differ. Equ.* **2021**, *300*, 487–512. [CrossRef]
14. Dipierro, S.; Palatucci, G.; Valdinoci, E. Existence and symmetry results for a Schrödinger type problem involving the fractional Laplacian. *Matematiche* **2013**, *68*, 201–216.
15. Chang, X.J.; Wang, Z.Q. Ground state of scalar field equations involving a fractional Laplacian with general nonlinearity. *Nonlinearity* **2013**, *26*, 479–494. [CrossRef]
16. Secchi, S. On fractional Schrödinger equations in $\mathbb{R}^N$ without the Ambrosetti-Rabinowitz condition. *Topol. Methods Nonlinear Anal.* **2016**, *47*, 19–41.
17. Nezza, E.D.; Palatucci, G.; Valdinoci, E. Hitchhiker's guide to the fractional Sobolev spaces. *Bull. Sci. Math.* **2012**, *136*, 521–573. [CrossRef]
18. Ambrosio, V.; Isernia, T. Multiplicity and concentration results for some nonlinear Schrödinger equations with the fractional p-Laplacian. *Discrete Contin. Dyn. Syst.* **2018**, *38*, 5835–5881. [CrossRef]

19. Perera, K.; Squassina, M.; Yang, Y. Critical fractional p-Laplacian problems with possibly vanishing potentials. *J. Math. Anal. Appl.* **2016**, *433*, 818–831. [CrossRef]
20. Xu, J.; Wei, Z.; Dong, W. Weak solutions for a fractional p-Laplacian equation with sign-changing potencial. *Complex Var. Elliptic Equ.* **2015**, *61*, 284–296. [CrossRef]
21. Ambrosetti, A.; Rabinowitz, P.H. Dual variational methods in critical point theory and applications. *J. Funct. Anal.* **1973**, *14*, 349–381. [CrossRef]
22. Liu, Z.L.; Wang, Z.Q. On the Ambrosetti-Rabinowitz superlinear condition. *Adv. Nonlinear Stud.* **2004**, *4*, 561–572. [CrossRef]
23. Li, Y.Q.; Wang, Z.Q.; Zeng, J. Ground states of nonlinear Schrödinger equations with potentials. In *Annales de l'Institut Henri Poincaré C, Analyse Non Linéaire*; Elsevier: Amsterdam, The Netherlands, 2006; Volume 23, pp. 829–837.
24. Ding, Y.; Szulkin, A. Bound states for semilinear Schrödinger equations with sign-changing potential. *Calc. Var.* **2007**, *29*, 397–419. [CrossRef]
25. Lin, X.Y.; Tang, X.H. Existence of infinitely many solutions for p-Laplacian equations in $\mathbb{R}^N$. *J. Math. Anal. Appl.* **2013**, *92*, 72–81.
26. Cheng, B.T.; Tang, X.H. New existence of solutions for the fractional p-Laplacian equations with sign-changing potential and nonlinearity. *Mediterr. J. Math.* **2016**, *13*, 3373–3387. [CrossRef]
27. Tang, X.H. New super-quadratic conditions on ground state solutions for superlinear Schrödinger equation. *Adv. Nonlinear Stud.* **2014**, *14*, 349–361. [CrossRef]
28. Mi, H.L.; Deng, X.Q.; Zhang, W. Ground state solution for asymptotically periodic fractional p-Laplacian equation. *Appl. Math. Lett.* **2021**, *120*, 107280. [CrossRef]
29. Sabri, B.; Ounaies, H.; Elfalah, O. Problems involving the fractional g-Laplacian with lack of compactness. *J. Math. Phys.* **2023**, *64*, 011512.
30. Silva, E.A.; Vieira, G.F. Quasilinear asymptotically periodic Schrödinger equations with critical growth. *Calc. Var.* **2010**, *39*, 109. [CrossRef]
31. Jeanjean, L.; Tanaka, K. A positive solution for asymptotically linear elliptic problem on $\mathbb{R}^N$ autonomous at infinity. *ESAIM Control Optim. Calc. Var.* **2002**, *7*, 597–614. [CrossRef]
32. Zhang, W.; Zhang, J.; Mi, H.L. On fractional Schrödinger equation with periodic and asymptotically periodic conditions. *Comput. Math. Appl.* **2017**, *74*, 1321–1332. [CrossRef]
33. Adams, R.A.; Fournier, J.J.F. *Sobolev Spaces*, 2nd ed.; Pure and Applied Mathematics (Amsterdam); Academic Press: Amsterdam, The Netherlands, 2003; p. 140.
34. Rao, M.M.; Ren, Z.D. *Applications of Orlicz Spaces, Monographs and Textbooks in Pure and Applied Mathematics*; Marcel Dekker: New York, NY, USA, 2002; p. 250.
35. Fukagai, N.; Ito, M.; Narukawa, K. Positive solutions of quasilinear elliptic equations with critical Orlicz-Sobolev nonlinearity on $\mathbb{R}^N$. *Funkcial. Ekcac.* **2006**, *49*, 235–267. [CrossRef]
36. Bahrouni, A.; Missaoui, H.; Ounaies, H. On the fractional Musielak-Sobolev spaces in $\mathbb{R}^d$: Embedding results & applications. *J. Math. Anal. Appl.* **2024**, *537*, 128284.
37. Alves, C.O.; Figueiredo, G.M.; Santos, J.A. Strauss and Lions type results for a class of Orlicz-Sobolev spaces and applications. *Topol. Methods Nonlinear Anal.* **2014**, *44*, 435–456. [CrossRef]

Disclaimer/Publisher's Note: The statements, opinions and data contained in all publications are solely those of the individual author(s) and contributor(s) and not of MDPI and/or the editor(s). MDPI and/or the editor(s) disclaim responsibility for any injury to people or property resulting from any ideas, methods, instructions or products referred to in the content.

axioms

MDPI

Article

More Effective Conditions for Testing the Oscillatory Behavior of Solutions to a Class of Fourth-Order Functional Differential Equations

Hail S. Alrashdi [1], Osama Moaaz [1,2,*], Sameh S. Askar [3], Ahmad M. Alshamrani [3] and Elmetwally M. Elabbasy [1]

1 Department of Mathematics, Faculty of Science, Mansoura University, Mansoura 35516, Egypt; hailaldyabai@std.mans.edu.eg (H.S.A.); emelabbasy@mans.edu.eg (E.M.E.)
2 Section of Mathematics, International Telematic University Uninettuno, CorsoVittorio Emanuele II, 39, 00186 Roma, Italy
3 Department of Statistics and Operations Research, College of Science, King Saud University, P.O. Box 2455, Riyadh 11451, Saudi Arabia; saskar@ksu.edu.sa (S.S.A.); ahmadm@ksu.edu.sa (A.M.A.)
* Correspondence: o_moaaz@mans.edu.eg

Abstract: This paper presents an investigation into the qualitative behavior of solutions for a specific class of fourth-order half-linear neutral differential equations. The main objective of this study is to improve the relationship between the solution and its corresponding function. By developing improved relationships, a novel criterion is proposed to determine the oscillatory behavior of the studied equation. The exclusion of positive solutions is achieved through a comparative approach in which the examined equation is compared to second-order equations. Additionally, the significance of the obtained results is demonstrated by applying them to various illustrative examples.

Keywords: oscillatory; non-oscillatory; neutral differential equation; fourth-order

MSC: 34C10; 34K11

Citation: Alrashdi, H.S.; Moaaz, O.; Askar, S.S.; Alshamrani, A.M.; Elabbasy, E.M. More Effective Conditions for Testing the Oscillatory Behavior of Solutions to a Class of Fourth-Order Functional Differential Equations. *Axioms* **2023**, *12*, 1005. https://doi.org/10.3390/axioms12111005

Academic Editors: Hatıra Günerhan, Francisco Martínez González and Mohammed K. A. Kaabar

Received: 28 August 2023
Revised: 13 October 2023
Accepted: 23 October 2023
Published: 25 October 2023

Copyright: © 2023 by the authors. Licensee MDPI, Basel, Switzerland. This article is an open access article distributed under the terms and conditions of the Creative Commons Attribution (CC BY) license (https://creativecommons.org/licenses/by/4.0/).

1. Introduction

Differential equations are fundamental mathematical tools that find extensive applications in numerous scientific disciplines. Among the various types of differential equations, neutral differential equations hold a special place due to their ability to capture dynamic systems influenced by past behaviors. This paper focuses on a specific class of neutral differential equations, namely, fourth-order half-linear equations, which exhibit a combination of linearity and nonlinearity. Understanding the oscillatory nature of solutions to these equations is of paramount importance in light of their practical relevance in modeling complex dynamic systems encountered in engineering, physics, biology, and economics. The analysis of oscillations in such equations offers invaluable insights into system stability and dynamics, ultimately guiding the design and control of real-world systems, including mechanical structures, electrical circuits, biological processes, and economic models. Thus, a comprehensive grasp of oscillatory behavior in these equations serves as a cornerstone for optimizing system performance and ensuring reliability in practical applications; see [1–3].

The qualitative behavior of solutions to differential equations plays a crucial role in understanding the dynamics and stability properties of the underlying systems. Oscillation is an essential aspect that characterizes the periodic and repetitive nature of solutions. The investigation of oscillation criteria has received significant attention in the field of differential equations, aiming to establish the conditions under which solutions exhibit oscillatory behavior. Such criteria are valuable in predicting the presence or absence of oscillations in real-world phenomena, see [4–7].

The practical importance of understanding the oscillatory behavior of solutions to fourth-order functional differential equations lies in its applicability to various real-world phenomena. These equations often model complex dynamic systems encountered in engineering, physics, biology, and economics. Analyzing their oscillatory behavior provides crucial insights into the stability and dynamics of these systems. This knowledge, in turn, guides the design and control of practical systems, such as mechanical structures, electrical circuits, biological processes, and economic models. Therefore, a comprehensive understanding of oscillations in such equations is fundamental for optimizing system performance and ensuring their reliability in practical applications.

In recent years, there has been growing interest in the study of neutral differential equations due to their oscillatory behavior. This literature review aims to highlight notable research studies that have contributed to understanding the oscillatory properties of these types of equations.

One area of focus has been the investigation of oscillation in second-order neutral differential equations. Several studies have explored this topic, including [8–10]. Additionally, the oscillatory behavior of fourth-order neutral differential equations has been examined in studies such as [11–13]. Furthermore, the oscillation properties of even-order neutral differential equations have been investigated in [14–16].

Baculíková [17] focused on the oscillatory and asymptotic properties of the differential equation, as follows:

$$\left(\zeta(\ell)v'(\ell)\right)' + q(\ell)f(v(\mu(\ell))) = 0, \tag{1}$$

which, in the noncanonical case, is

$$\int_{\ell_0}^{\infty} \frac{1}{\zeta^{1/\varrho}(\varsigma)} \mathrm{d}\varsigma < \infty. \tag{2}$$

The function f in Equation (1) is defined as follows: $f \in C(\mathbb{R})$, $vf(v) > 0$ for $v \neq 0$, $f(v_1 v_2) \geq f(v_1)f(v_2)$ for $v_1 v_2 > 0$, and f is non-decreasing.

El-Nabulsi et al. [18] conducted a study on the oscillation properties of solutions to a nonlinear fourth-order differential equation. The equation is represented as follows:

$$\left(\zeta(\ell)\left(v'''(\ell)\right)^{\varrho}\right)' + q(\ell)f(v(\mu(\ell))) = 0. \tag{3}$$

In this equation, the function $f(\theta)/\theta^{\varrho} \geq k > 0$ for $\theta \neq 0$ and condition (5) is satisfied. Zhang et al. [19] conducted an investigation into the oscillatory patterns of (3) while taking into account condition (2).

Karpuz et al. [20] investigated higher-order neutral differential equations of the following form:

$$\kappa^{(n)}(\ell) + q(\ell)v(\mu(\ell)) - 0.$$

They conducted a comparison between the oscillatory and asymptotic characteristics of the solutions for higher-order neutral differential equations and first-order delay differential equations.

Li and Rogovchenko [21] and Zhang et al. [22,23] discussed oscillation results for higher-order half-linear delay differential equations. These equations were of the following form:

$$\left(\zeta(\ell)\left(\kappa^{(n-1)}(\ell)\right)^{\varrho}\right)' + q(\ell)v^{\beta}(\mu(\ell)) = 0.$$

Their results were obtained under condition (2), and they employed the Riccati technique in their analysis.

Alnafisah et al. [24] introduced augmented inequalities in order to enhance the characteristics of solutions to neutral differential equations of even order. These equations can be represented as follows:

$$\left(\zeta(\ell)\left(\kappa^{(n-1)}(\ell)\right)^{\varrho}\right)' + q(\ell)v^{\varrho}(\mu(\ell)) = 0.$$

These improved inequalities were established under condition (2).

This study focuses on investigating the oscillatory behavior exhibited by the solutions of a fourth-order quasi-linear neutral differential equation, provided by

$$\left(\zeta(\ell)(\kappa'''(\ell))^{\varrho}\right)' + q(\ell)v^{\varrho}(\mu(\ell)) = 0,\ \ell \geq \ell_0, \tag{4}$$

where $\kappa(\ell) = v(\ell) + \mathrm{p}(\ell)v(\tau(\ell))$. Note that throughout this paper we consistently make the following assumptions:

(H_1) $\varrho \geq 1$ is expressed as the ratio of two positive odd integers.
(H_2) $\tau, \mu, \zeta \in C^1([\ell_0, \infty))$ and $q(\ell) \in C([\ell_0, \infty))$.
(H_3) $\tau(\ell) \leq \ell$, $\mu(\ell) \leq \ell$, $\mu'(\ell) > 0$, and $\lim_{\ell\to\infty} \tau(\ell) = \lim_{\ell\to\infty} \mu(\ell) = \infty$.
(H_4) $\zeta(\ell) > 0$, $\zeta'(\ell) \geq 0$, $0 \leq \mathrm{p}(\ell) < \mathrm{p}_0$, $q(\ell) \geq 0$, and

$$\int_{\ell_0}^{\ell} \frac{1}{\zeta^{1/\varrho}(\varsigma)} \mathrm{d}\varsigma \to \infty \text{ as } \ell \to \infty. \tag{5}$$

A function $v \in C^3([\mathrm{L}_v, \infty), \mathbb{R})$, $\mathrm{L}_v \geqslant \ell_0$ is said to be a solution of (4) which has the property $\zeta(\kappa''')^{\varrho} \in C^1[\mathrm{L}_v, \infty)$ and satisfies Equation (4) for all $v \in [\ell_v, \infty)$. We consider only those solutions v of (4) which exist on some half-line $[\mathrm{L}_v, \infty)$ and satisfy the condition

$$\sup\{|v(\ell)| : \ell \geqslant \mathrm{L}\} > 0, \text{ for all } \mathrm{L} \geq \mathrm{L}_v.$$

A solution of (4) is called oscillatory if it is neither eventually positive nor eventually negative. Otherwise, it is said to be non-oscillatory. Equation (4) is said to be oscillatory if all of its solutions are oscillatory.

In this paper, we present an investigation of fourth-order half-linear neutral differential equations, with a focus on enhancing the relationship between variables and introducing an improved oscillation criterion. This study contributes to the existing body of knowledge in the field of differential equations and offers valuable insights into the qualitative behavior of solutions for this specific class of equations.

2. Preliminary Considerations

We start by introducing several helpful lemmas that pertain to the monotonic characteristics of the non-oscillatory solutions of the examined equations. In order to make our notation more concise, we define the following expressions:

$$\varphi_0(\ell, \ell_0) := \int_{\ell_0}^{\ell} \frac{1}{\zeta^{1/\varrho}(\varsigma)} \mathrm{d}\varsigma,\ \varphi_i(\ell, \ell_0) := \int_{\ell_0}^{\ell} \varphi_{i-1}(\varsigma, \ell_0) \mathrm{d}\varsigma,\ i = 1, 2,$$

$$\mathrm{G}^{[0]}(\ell) := \mathrm{G}(\ell) \text{ and } \mathrm{G}^{[j]}(\ell) := \mathrm{G}\left(\mathrm{G}^{[j-1]}(\ell)\right), \text{ for } j = 1, 2, \ldots, n,$$

$$\mathrm{p}_1(\ell; n) := \sum_{k=0}^{n} \left(\prod_{i=0}^{2k} \mathrm{p}\left(\tau^{[i]}(\ell)\right)\right) \left[\frac{1}{\mathrm{p}(\tau^{[2k]}(\ell))} - 1\right] \frac{\varphi_2\left(\tau^{[2k]}(\ell), \ell_1\right)}{\varphi_2(\ell, \ell_1)},$$

$$\widehat{\mathrm{p}}_1(\ell, n) := \sum_{k=1}^{n} \left(\prod_{i=1}^{2k-1} \frac{1}{\mathrm{p}(\tau^{[-i]}(\ell))}\right) \left[\frac{\varphi_2\left(\tau^{[-2k+1]}(\ell), \ell_1\right)}{\varphi_2(\tau^{[-2k]}(\ell), \ell_1)} - \frac{1}{\mathrm{p}(\tau^{[-2k]}(\ell))}\right],$$

$$\mathrm{B}_0(\ell,n) := \begin{cases} p_1(\ell;n) & \text{for } p_0 < 1, \\ \hat{p}_1(\ell;n) & \text{for } p_0 > \varphi_2(\ell,\ell_1)/\varphi_2(\tau(\ell),\ell_1), \end{cases}$$

and

$$\mathrm{L} := \max\left\{m(1-m)^{\varrho}\lambda^{-\varrho m} : m \in (0,1)\right\}.$$

In studying the asymptotic properties of the positive solutions of Equation (4), it is easy to verify, as demonstrated in [25] (Lemma 2.2.1), that the function κ exhibits the following two distinct possible cases.

Lemma 1 ([25]). *Assume that v is an eventually positive solution of (4); then, κ eventually satisfies the following cases:*

$$\begin{aligned} C_1 &: \quad \kappa > 0,\ \kappa' > 0,\ \kappa'' > 0,\ \kappa''' > 0,\ \left(\zeta \cdot (\kappa''')^{\varrho}\right)' < 0, \\ C_2 &: \quad \kappa > 0,\ \kappa' > 0,\ \kappa'' < 0,\ \kappa''' > 0, \end{aligned}$$

for $\ell \geqslant \ell_1 \geqslant \ell_0$.

Notation 1. *The symbol Ψ_i (Category Ψ_i) represents the collection of all solutions that eventually become positive for which the corresponding function fulfills condition (C_i) for $i = 1,2$.*

In the oscillation theory of neutral differential equations, the relationship between the solution and its corresponding function holds significant importance. Therefore, our work focuses on improving these relationships through the utilization of the following lemma.

Lemma 2 (see [26], Lemma 1). *Suppose that v represents an eventually positive solution to Equation (4). If $p < 1$, then eventually*

$$v(\ell) > \sum_{k=0}^{n}\left(\prod_{i=0}^{2k}\mathrm{p}\left(\tau^{[i]}(\ell)\right)\right)\left[\frac{\kappa\left(\tau^{[2k]}(\ell)\right)}{\mathrm{p}\left(\tau^{[2k]}(\ell)\right)} - \kappa\left(\tau^{[2k+1]}(\ell)\right)\right]$$

for any integer $n \geq 0$.

Lemma 3. *Suppose that v represents an eventually positive solution to Equation (4). If $p_0 > 1$, then*

$$v(\ell) > \sum_{k=1}^{n}\left(\prod_{i=1}^{2k-1}\frac{1}{\mathrm{p}\left(\tau^{[-k]}(\ell)\right)}\right)\left[\kappa\left(\tau^{[-2k+1]}(\ell)\right) - \frac{1}{\mathrm{p}\left(\tau^{[-2k]}(\ell)\right)}\kappa\left(\tau^{[-2k]}(\ell)\right)\right].$$

Proof. From

$$\kappa(\ell) = v(\ell) + \mathrm{p}(\ell)v(\tau(\ell)),$$

we can deduce that

$$\begin{aligned} v(\ell) &= \frac{1}{\mathrm{p}(\tau^{-1}(\ell))}\left[\kappa\left(\tau^{-1}(\ell)\right) - v\left(\tau^{-1}(\ell)\right)\right] \\ &= \frac{1}{\mathrm{p}(\tau^{[-1]}(\ell))}\kappa\left(\tau^{[-1]}(\ell)\right) \\ &\quad - \frac{1}{\mathrm{p}(\tau^{[-1]}(\ell))}\frac{1}{\mathrm{p}(\tau^{[-2]}(\ell))}\left[\kappa\left(\tau^{[-2]}(\ell)\right) - v\left(\tau^{[-2]}(\ell)\right)\right]. \end{aligned}$$

Therefore,

$$\begin{aligned} v(\ell) &= \frac{1}{\mathrm{p}(\tau^{[-1]}(\ell))}\kappa\left(\tau^{[-1]}(\ell)\right) - \prod_{i=1}^{2}\frac{1}{\mathrm{p}(\tau^{[-i]}(\ell))}\kappa\left(\tau^{[-2]}(\ell)\right) \\ &\quad + \prod_{i=1}^{3}\frac{1}{\mathrm{p}(\tau^{[-i]}(\ell))}\left[\kappa\left(\tau^{[-3]}(\ell)\right) - v\left(\tau^{[-3]}(\ell)\right)\right]. \end{aligned}$$

By employing the same method repeatedly, we achieve

$$v(\ell) > \sum_{k=1}^{n}\left(\prod_{i=1}^{2k-1}\frac{1}{\mathrm{p}(\tau^{[i]}(\ell))}\right)\left[\kappa\left(\tau^{[-2k+1]}(\ell)\right) - \frac{1}{\mathrm{p}(\tau^{[-2k]}(\ell))}\kappa\left(\tau^{[-2k]}(\ell)\right)\right].$$

Hence, we have successfully demonstrated the proof of the lemma. □

3. Asymptotic and Monotonic Properties

This section discusses the characteristics of positive solutions of the studied equation in terms of their asymptotic behavior and monotonic properties. It is further categorized into two distinct subtopics, outlined below.

3.1. Category Ψ_1

Lemma 4. *Suppose that $v \in \Psi_1$. Then, for sufficiently large $\ell \geqslant \ell_1$:*

$(\mathrm{A}_{1,1})$ $\kappa(\ell) \geqslant \zeta^{1/\varrho}(\ell)\kappa'''(\ell)\varphi_2(\ell,\ell_1)$.

$(\mathrm{A}_{1,2})$ $\kappa''(\ell,\ell_1)/\varphi_0(\ell,\ell_1)$, $\kappa'(\ell)/\varphi_1(\ell,\ell_1)$ *and* $\kappa(\ell)/\varphi_2(\ell,\ell_1)$ *are decreasing.*

$(\mathrm{A}_{1,3})$ $\varphi_0(\ell,\ell_1)\kappa(\ell) \geqslant \varphi_2(\ell,\ell_1)\kappa''(\ell)$.

Proof. $(\mathrm{A}_{1,1})$ The monotonicity of $\zeta^{1/\varrho}(\ell)\kappa'''(\ell)$ implies that

$$\begin{aligned} \kappa''(\ell) &\geq \int_{\ell_1}^{\ell}\zeta^{1/\varrho}(\varsigma)\kappa'''(\varsigma)\frac{1}{\zeta^{1/\varrho}(\varsigma)}\mathrm{d}\varsigma \\ &\geq \zeta^{1/\varrho}(\ell)\kappa'''(\ell)\int_{\ell_1}^{\ell}\frac{1}{\zeta^{1/\varrho}(\varsigma)}\mathrm{d}\varsigma \\ &\geq \zeta^{1/\varrho}(\ell)\kappa'''(\ell)\varphi_0(\ell,\ell_1). \end{aligned} \tag{6}$$

Integrating twice more from ℓ_1 to ℓ, we obtain

$$\kappa'(\ell) \geq \zeta^{1/\varrho}(\ell)\kappa'''(\ell)\varphi_1(\ell,\ell_1) \tag{7}$$

and

$$\kappa(\ell) \geq \zeta^{1/\varrho}(\ell)\kappa'''(\ell)\varphi_2(\ell,\ell_1).$$

$(\mathrm{A}_{1,2})$ From (7), we obtain

$$\left(\frac{\kappa''(\ell)}{\varphi_0(\ell,\ell_1)}\right)' = \frac{\zeta^{1/\varrho}(\ell)\kappa'''(\ell)\varphi_0(\ell,\ell_1) - \kappa''(\ell)}{\zeta^{1/\varrho}(\ell)\varphi_0^2(\ell,\ell_1)} \leq 0.$$

Because $\kappa''(\ell)/\varphi_0(\ell,\ell_1)$ is decreasing,

$$\kappa'(\ell) \geq \int_{\ell_1}^{\ell}\frac{\kappa''(\varsigma)}{\varphi_0(\varsigma,\ell_1)}\varphi_0(\varsigma,\ell_1)\mathrm{d}\varsigma \geq \frac{\kappa''(\ell)}{\varphi_0(\ell,\ell_1)}\varphi_1(\ell,\ell_1). \tag{8}$$

From this, we can deduce that

$$\left(\frac{\kappa'(\ell)}{\varphi_1(\ell,\ell_1)}\right)' = \frac{\kappa''(\ell)\varphi_1(\ell,\ell_1) - \varphi_0(\ell,\ell_1)\kappa'(\ell)}{\varphi_1^2(\ell,\ell_1)} \leq 0.$$

Because $\kappa'(\ell)/\varphi_1(\ell,\ell_1)$ is decreasing,

$$\kappa(\ell) \geq \int_{\ell_1}^{\ell} \frac{\kappa'(\varsigma)}{\varphi_1(\varsigma,\ell_1)} \varphi_1(\varsigma,\ell_1) \mathrm{d}\varsigma \geq \frac{\kappa'(\ell)}{\varphi_1(\ell,\ell_1)} \varphi_2(\ell,\ell_1). \tag{9}$$

Consequently,

$$\left(\frac{\kappa(\ell)}{\varphi_2(\ell,\ell_1)}\right)' = \frac{\kappa'(\ell)\varphi_2(\ell,\ell_1) - \varphi_1(\ell,\ell_1)\kappa(\ell)}{\varphi_2^2(\ell,\ell_1)} \leq 0.$$

$(\mathrm{A}_{1,3})$ From (8) and (9), we find that

$$\kappa(\ell) \geq \frac{\varphi_2(\ell,\ell_1)}{\varphi_0(\ell,\ell_1)} \kappa''(\ell).$$

Therefore, we have successfully illustrated the lemma's validity. □

Lemma 5. *Assume that $v \in \Psi_1$. Then,*

$(\mathrm{A}_{2,1})$ $v(\ell) > \mathrm{B}_0(\ell,n)\kappa(\ell)$.
$(\mathrm{A}_{2,2})$ $\left(\zeta(\ell)(\kappa'''(\ell))^{\varrho}\right)' \leq -q(\ell)\mathrm{B}_0^{\varrho}(\mu(\ell),n)\kappa^{\varrho}(\mu(\ell)).$

Proof. $(\mathrm{A}_{2,1})$ If $p_0 < 1$, due to the fact that $\kappa(\ell)$ is increasing and $\tau^{[2k]}(\ell) \geq \tau^{[2k+1]}(\ell)$, we have

$$\kappa(\tau^{[2k]}(\ell)) \geq \kappa(\tau^{[2k+1]}(\ell)),$$

which, along with Lemma 2, implies that

$$\begin{aligned} v(\ell) &> \sum_{k=0}^{n} \left(\prod_{i=0}^{2k} \mathrm{p}\left(\tau^{[i]}(\ell)\right)\right) \left[\frac{\kappa(\tau^{[2k]}(\ell))}{\mathrm{p}(\tau^{[2k]}(\ell))} - \kappa(\tau^{[2k+1]}(\ell))\right] \\ &\geq \sum_{k=0}^{n} \left(\prod_{i=0}^{2k} \mathrm{p}\left(\tau^{[i]}(\ell)\right)\right) \left[\frac{1}{\mathrm{p}(\tau^{[2k]}(\ell))} - 1\right] \kappa(\tau^{[2k]}(\ell)). \end{aligned} \tag{10}$$

Moreover, as $\kappa(\ell)/\varphi_2(\ell,\ell_1)$ is decreasing and $\tau^{[2k]}(\ell) \leq \ell$, we have

$$\frac{\kappa(\tau^{[2k]}(\ell))}{\varphi_2(\tau^{[2k]}(\ell),\ell_1)} \geq \frac{\kappa(\ell)}{\varphi_2(\ell,\ell_1)}$$

and

$$\kappa(\tau^{[2k]}(\ell)) \geq \frac{\varphi_2(\tau^{[2k]}(\ell),\ell_1)}{\varphi_2(\ell,\ell_1)} \kappa(\ell).$$

Thus, using the above inequality and substituting in (10), we obtain

$$\begin{aligned} v(\ell) &> \sum_{k=0}^{n} \left(\prod_{i=0}^{2k} \mathrm{p}\left(\tau^{[i]}(\ell)\right)\right) \left[\frac{1}{\mathrm{p}(\tau^{[2k]}(\ell))} - 1\right] \frac{\varphi_2(\tau^{[2k]}(\ell),\ell_1)}{\varphi_2(\ell,\ell_1)} \kappa(\ell) \\ &= \mathrm{p}_1(\ell;n)\kappa(\ell). \end{aligned}$$

On the other hand, if $p_0 > 1$, then $\kappa(\ell)/\varphi_2(\ell,\ell_1)$ is decreasing and $\tau^{[-2k]}(\ell) \geq \tau^{[-2k+1]}(\ell)$, implying that

$$\frac{\kappa\left(\tau^{[-2k+1]}(\ell)\right)}{\varphi_2(\tau^{[-2k+1]}(\ell),\ell_1)} \geq \frac{\kappa\left(\tau^{[-2k]}(\ell)\right)}{\varphi_2(\tau^{[-2k]}(\ell),\ell_1)}$$

and

$$\kappa\left(\tau^{[-2k+1]}(\ell)\right) \geq \frac{\varphi_2\left(\tau^{[-2k+1]}(\ell),\ell_1\right)}{\varphi_2\left(\tau^{[-2k]}(\ell),\ell_1\right)}\kappa\left(\tau^{[-2k]}(\ell)\right).$$

Using Lemma 3, we can conclude that

$$v(\ell) > \sum_{k=1}^{n}\left(\prod_{i=1}^{2k-1}\frac{1}{\mathrm{p}\left(\tau^{[-i]}(\ell)\right)}\right)\left[\frac{\varphi_2\left(\tau^{[-2k+1]}(\ell),\ell_1\right)}{\varphi_2\left(\tau^{[-2k]}(\ell),\ell_1\right)} - \frac{1}{\mathrm{p}\left(\tau^{[-2k]}(\ell)\right)}\right]\kappa\left(\tau^{[-2k]}(\ell)\right).$$

As $\kappa(\ell)$ is increasing and $\tau^{[-2k]}(\ell) \geq \ell$, we have

$$\begin{aligned} v(\ell) &> \sum_{k=1}^{n}\left(\prod_{i=1}^{2k-1}\frac{1}{\mathrm{p}\left(\tau^{[-i]}(\ell)\right)}\right)\left[\frac{\varphi_2\left(\tau^{[-2k+1]}(\ell),\ell_1\right)}{\varphi_2\left(\tau^{[-2k]}(\ell),\ell_1\right)} - \frac{1}{\mathrm{p}\left(\tau^{[-2k]}(\ell)\right)}\right]\kappa(\ell) \\ &= \widehat{\mathrm{p}}_1(\ell,n)\kappa(\ell). \end{aligned}$$

$(\mathrm{A}_{2,2})$ From (4), we have

$$\left(\zeta(\ell)\left(\kappa'''(\ell)\right)^{\varrho}\right)' = -q(\ell)v^{\varrho}(\mu(\ell)).$$

Using $(\mathrm{A}_{2,1})$, we obtain

$$\left(\zeta(\ell)\left(\kappa'''(\ell)\right)^{\varrho}\right)' \leq -q(\ell)\mathrm{B}_0^{\varrho}(\mu(\ell),n)\kappa^{\varrho}(\mu(\ell)).$$

Therefore, we have successfully illustrated the lemma's validity. □

Lemma 6. *Assume that $v \in \Psi_1$. Then,*

$$\left(\zeta^{1/\varrho}(\ell)\kappa'''(\ell)\right)' + \frac{1}{\varrho}q(\ell)\mathrm{B}_0^{\varrho}(\mu(\ell),n)\varphi_2^{\varrho-1}(\mu(\ell),\ell_1)\kappa(\mu(\ell)) \leq 0.$$

Proof. Assume that $v \in \Psi_1$ for $\ell \geq \ell_1 \geq \ell_0$. Therefore, we obtain

$$\left(\zeta^{1/\varrho}(\ell)\kappa'''(\ell)\right)' = \frac{1}{\varrho}\left(\zeta^{1/\varrho}(\ell)\kappa'''(\ell)\right)^{1-\varrho}\left(\zeta(\ell)\left(\kappa'''(\ell)\right)^{\varrho}\right)'.$$

From $(\mathrm{A}_{2,2})$, we obtain

$$\left(\zeta^{1/\varrho}(\ell)\kappa'''(\ell)\right)' \leq -\frac{1}{\varrho}\left(\zeta^{1/\varrho}(\ell)\kappa'''(\ell)\right)^{1-\varrho}q(\ell)\mathrm{B}_0^{\varrho}(\mu(\ell),n)\kappa^{\varrho}(\mu(\ell)). \tag{11}$$

From Lemma 4, we can deduce that

$$\zeta^{1/\varrho}(\ell)\kappa'''(\ell) \leq \frac{\kappa(\ell)}{\varphi_2(\ell,\ell_1)} \leq \frac{\kappa(\mu(\ell))}{\varphi_2(\mu(\ell),\ell_1)}.$$

Because $\varrho \geq 1$,

$$\left(\zeta^{1/\varrho}(\ell)\kappa'''(\ell)\right)^{1-\varrho} \geq \left(\frac{\kappa(\mu(\ell))}{\varphi_2(\mu(\ell),\ell_1)}\right)^{1-\varrho},$$

which, with (11) provides

$$\begin{aligned}\left(\zeta^{1/\varrho}(\ell)\kappa'''(\ell)\right)' &\leq -\frac{1}{\varrho}\left(\frac{\kappa(\mu(\ell))}{\varphi_2(\mu(\ell),\ell_1)}\right)^{1-\varrho} q(\ell)\mathrm{B}_0^{\varrho}(\mu(\ell),n)\kappa^{\varrho}(\mu(\ell)) \\ &= -\frac{1}{\varrho}q(\ell)\mathrm{B}_0^{\varrho}(\mu(\ell),n)\varphi_2^{\varrho-1}(\mu(\ell),\ell_1)\kappa(\mu(\ell)).\end{aligned}$$

□

Theorem 1. *Assume that $v \in \Psi_1$. Then, the DE*

$$\left(\zeta^{1/\varrho}(\ell)\omega'(\ell)\right)' + \frac{1}{\varrho}q(\ell)\mathrm{B}_0^{\varrho}(\mu(\ell),n)\frac{\varphi_2^{\varrho}(\mu(\ell),\ell_1)}{\varphi_0(\mu(\ell),\ell_1)}\omega(\mu(\ell)) = 0 \tag{12}$$

has a positive solution.

Proof. Assume that $v \in \Psi_1$ for $\ell \geq \ell_1 \geq \ell_0$. From Lemma 4, $(\mathrm{A}_{1,3})$ holds. Hence, it follows that from Lemma 6 we can obtain

$$\begin{aligned}0 &\geq \left(\zeta^{1/\varrho}(\ell)\kappa'''(\ell)\right)' + \frac{1}{\varrho}q(\ell)\mathrm{B}_0^{\varrho}(\mu(\ell),n)\varphi_2^{\varrho-1}(\mu(\ell),\ell_1)\kappa(\mu(\ell)) \\ &\geq \left(\zeta^{1/\varrho}(\ell)\kappa'''(\ell)\right)' + \frac{1}{\varrho}q(\ell)\mathrm{B}_0^{\varrho}(\mu(\ell),n)\varphi_2^{\varrho-1}(\mu(\ell),\ell_1)\frac{\varphi_2(\mu(\ell),\ell_1)}{\varphi_0(\mu(\ell),\ell_1)}\kappa''(\mu(\ell)) \\ &= \left(\zeta^{1/\varrho}(\ell)\kappa'''(\ell)\right)' + \frac{1}{\varrho}q(\ell)\mathrm{B}_0^{\varrho}(\mu(\ell),n)\frac{\varphi_2^{\varrho}(\mu(\ell),\ell_1)}{\varphi_0(\mu(\ell),\ell_1)}\kappa''(\mu(\ell)).\end{aligned} \tag{13}$$

Now, let $\omega(\ell) = \kappa''(\ell) > 0$; then, (14) reduces to

$$\left(\zeta^{1/\varrho}(\ell)\omega'(\ell)\right)' + \frac{1}{\varrho}q(\ell)\mathrm{B}_0^{\varrho}(\mu(\ell),n)\frac{\varphi_2^{\varrho}(\mu(\ell),\ell_1)}{\varphi_0(\mu(\ell),\ell_1)}\omega(\mu(\ell)) \leq 0.$$

Using Corollary 1 in [27], the corresponding DE (12) has a positive solution as well. Therefore, we have completed the proof of the Lemma. □

3.2. Category Ψ_2

Because

$$\kappa(\ell) = v(\ell) + \mathrm{p}(\ell)v(\tau(\ell)),$$

$\kappa(\ell) \geq v(\ell)$ and

$$v(\ell) = \kappa(\ell) - \mathrm{p}(\ell)v(\tau(\ell)) \geq \kappa(\ell) - \mathrm{p}(\ell)\kappa(\tau(\ell)).$$

Because $\kappa(\ell)$ is increasing, $\kappa(\ell) \geq \kappa(\tau(\ell))$ and

$$v(\ell) \geq (1 - \mathrm{p}(\ell))\kappa(\ell). \tag{14}$$

Theorem 2. *Assume that $v \in \Psi_2$; then, the DE*

$$\kappa''(\ell) + \kappa(\mu(\ell))\int_{\ell}^{\infty}\left(\frac{1}{\zeta(u)}\int_{u}^{\infty}q(\varsigma)(1 - \mathrm{p}(\mu(\varsigma)))^{\varrho}\mathrm{d}\varsigma\right)^{1/\varrho}\mathrm{d}u = 0 \tag{15}$$

has a positive solution.

Proof. Assume that $v \in \Psi_2$ for $\ell \geq \ell_1 \geq \ell_0$. Integrating (4) from ℓ to ∞, we have

$$\begin{aligned} \zeta(\ell)(\kappa'''(\ell))^{\varrho} &\geq \int_{\ell}^{\infty} q(\varsigma)v^{\varrho}(\mu(\varsigma))d\varsigma \\ &\geq \int_{\ell}^{\infty} q(\varsigma)(1-\mathrm{p}(\mu(\varsigma)))^{\varrho}\kappa^{\varrho}(\mu(\varsigma))d\varsigma \\ &\geq \kappa^{\varrho}(\mu(\ell))\int_{\ell}^{\infty} q(\varsigma)(1-\mathrm{p}(\mu(\varsigma)))^{\varrho}d\varsigma, \end{aligned}$$

or

$$\kappa'''(\ell) \geq \kappa(\mu(\ell))\left(\frac{1}{\zeta(\ell)}\int_{\ell}^{\infty} q(\varsigma)(1-\mathrm{p}(\mu(\varsigma)))^{\varrho}d\varsigma\right)^{1/\varrho}.$$

Integrating once again from ℓ to ∞, we obtain

$$\kappa''(\ell) \leq -\kappa(\mu(\ell))\int_{\ell}^{\infty}\left(\frac{1}{\zeta(u)}\int_{u}^{\infty} q(\varsigma)(1-\mathrm{p}(\mu(\varsigma)))^{\varrho}d\varsigma\right)^{1/\varrho}du. \tag{16}$$

Therefore, κ is a positive solution of differential inequality (16). Using Corollary 1 in [27], the corresponding DE (15) has a positive solution as well. This ends the proof. □

4. Oscillation Theorem and Examples

In this section, we establish a condition that ensures the occurrence of oscillation in the differential Equation (4). Furthermore, we investigate specific instances of the studied equation by employing this novel criterion.

Theorem 3. *Assume that*

$$\lambda := \liminf_{\ell\to\infty}\frac{\varphi_0(\ell,\ell_0)}{\varphi_0(\mu(\ell),\ell_0)} < \infty. \tag{17}$$

If

$$\liminf_{\ell\to\infty} \zeta^{1/\varrho}(\ell)\varphi_0(\ell,\ell_0)\varphi_2^{\varrho}(\mu(\ell),\ell_0)q(\ell)\mathrm{B}_0^{\varrho}(\mu(\ell),n) > \varrho\mathrm{L} \tag{18}$$

and

$$\liminf_{\ell\to\infty} \ell\mu(\ell)\int_{\ell}^{\infty}\left(\frac{1}{\zeta(u)}\int_{u}^{\infty} q(\varsigma)(1-\mathrm{p}(\mu(\varsigma)))^{\varrho}d\varsigma\right)^{1/\varrho}du > \mathrm{L}, \tag{19}$$

then (4) is oscillatory.

Proof. Let us consider the opposite scenario, where v is assumed to be a positive solution of (4). Then, v satisfies one of the two cases (C_1) and (C_2) for $\varsigma \geq \varsigma_1 \geq \varsigma_0$. From Theorems 1 and 2, we know that the two DEs

$$\left(\zeta^{1/\varrho}(\ell)\omega'(\ell)\right)' + \frac{1}{\varrho}q(\ell)\mathrm{B}_0^{\varrho}(\mu(\ell),n)\frac{\varphi_2^{\varrho}(\mu(\ell),\ell_1)}{\varphi_0(\mu(\ell),\ell_1)}\omega(\mu(\ell)) = 0$$

and

$$\kappa''(\ell) + \left(\int_{\ell}^{\infty}\left(\frac{1}{\zeta(u)}\int_{u}^{\infty} q(\varsigma)(1-\mathrm{p}(\mu(\varsigma)))^{\varrho}d\varsigma\right)^{1/\varrho}du\right)\kappa(\mu(\ell)) = 0$$

have positive solutions. However, according to Theorem 2 in [28], conditions (18) and (19) confirm the oscillation of all solutions of these equations. □

Corollary 1. *Assume that (17) holds. If*

$$\liminf_{\ell\to\infty} \ell\mu^3(\ell)q(\ell)\mathrm{B}_0(\mu(\ell),n) > 6\mathrm{L}$$

and

$$\liminf_{\ell\to\infty} \ell\mu(\ell) \int_{\ell}^{\infty} \int_{u}^{\infty} q(\varsigma)(1-\mathrm{p}(\mu(\varsigma)))\mathrm{d}\varsigma\mathrm{d}u > \mathrm{L},$$

then the linear NDE

$$(v(\ell)+\mathrm{p}(\ell)v(\tau(\ell)))^{(4)} + q(\ell)v(\mu(\ell)) = 0$$

is oscillatory.

Example 1. *Consider the neutral differential equation*

$$\left(\ell^{\varrho-1}\left((v(\ell)+\mathrm{p}_0 v(\tau_0\ell))'''\right)^{\varrho}\right)' + \frac{q_0}{\ell^{2\varrho+2}} v(\mu_0\ell) = 0,\ \ell > 0. \tag{20}$$

Here, $\tau_0, \mu_0 \in (0,1)$ *and* $q_0 > 0$*. We can verify that* $\zeta(\ell) = \ell^{\varrho-1}$*,* $\tau(\ell) = \tau_0\ell$*,* $\mu_0(\ell) = \mu_0\ell$*,* $q(\ell) = q_0/\ell^{2\varrho+2}$*,*

$$\varphi_0(\ell) = \varrho\ell^{1/\varrho},\ \varphi_1(\ell) = \frac{\varrho^2}{\varrho+1}\ell^{1+1/\varrho},\ \varphi_2(\ell) = \frac{\varrho^3}{(\varrho+1)(2\varrho+1)}\ell^{2+1/\varrho},$$

$$\lambda = \frac{1}{\mu_0^{1/\varrho}},$$

$$\mathrm{p}_1(\ell;n) = [1-\mathrm{p}_0]\sum_{k=0}^{n} \mathrm{p}_0^{2k}\tau_0^{2k(2+1/\varrho)},$$

$$\widehat{\mathrm{p}}_1(\ell,n) = \left[\mathrm{p}_0\tau_0^{2+1/\varrho}-1\right]\sum_{k=1}^{n}\frac{1}{\mathrm{p}_0^{2k+1}},$$

and

$$\mathrm{B}_0(\ell,n) = \begin{cases} \mathrm{p}_1(\ell;n) & \text{for } \mathrm{p}_0 < 1, \\ \widehat{\mathrm{p}}_1(\ell;n) & \text{for } \mathrm{p}_0 > 1/\tau^{2+1/\varrho}. \end{cases}$$

Using Theorem 3, we can establish the conditions for the oscillation of all solutions of Equation (20). These conditions are provided by

$$\frac{\varrho^{3\varrho}}{(2\varrho^2+3\varrho+1)^{\varrho}}\mu_0^{2\varrho+1} q_0 \mathrm{B}_0^{\varrho} > \mathrm{L}$$

and

$$\mu_0\frac{(1-\mathrm{p}_0)q_0^{1/\varrho}}{2(1+2\varrho)^{1/\varrho}} > \mathrm{L},$$

where

$$\mathrm{L} = \max\left\{m(1-m)^{\varrho}\mu_0^{m} : m \in (0,1)\right\}.$$

By satisfying these conditions, the oscillation of all solutions of Equation (20) is confirmed.

Example 2. *Consider the neutral differential equation*

$$\left(\ell^2\left((v(\ell)+0.5v(0.8\ell))'''\right)^3\right)' + \frac{q_0}{\ell^8}v(0.5\ell) = 0,\ \ell > 0. \tag{21}$$

We can verify that $\zeta(\ell) = \ell^2$*,* $\tau(\ell) = 0.8\ell$*,* $\mu_0(\ell) = 0.5\ell$*,* $q(\ell) = q_0/\ell^8$*,*

$$\varphi_0(\ell) = 3\ell^{1/3},\ \varphi_1(\ell) = \frac{9}{4}\ell^{4/3},\ \varphi_2(\ell) = \frac{27}{28}\ell^{7/3},$$

$$\lambda = 2^{1/3},$$

$$p_1(\ell;10) = \sum_{k=0}^{10} (0.5)^{2k+1}(0.8)^{14k/3} = 0.54839,$$

and

$$B_0(\ell,10) = p_1(\ell;10) = 0.54839.$$

Using Theorem 3, we can establish the conditions for the oscillation of all solutions of Equation (21). We find that

$$L = 0.08964 \text{ at } m = 0.22024.$$

Therefore, conditions (18) and (19) respectively reduce to

$$q_0 > 34.081L = 3.05469,$$

and

$$q_0 > 3584L^3 = 2.5815.$$

For $q_0 > 3.05469$, the oscillation of all solutions of Equation (21) is confirmed.

Example 3. *Consider the neutral differential equation*

$$(v(\ell) + p_0 v(\tau_0 \ell))^{(4)} + \frac{q_0}{\ell^4} v(\mu_0 \ell) = 0,\ \ell > 0, \tag{22}$$

where $\tau_0, \mu_0 \in (0,1)$ and $q_0 > 0$. We can easily verify that $\zeta(\ell) = 1$, $\tau(\ell) = \tau_0\ell$, $\mu_0(\ell) = \mu_0\ell$, $q(\ell) = q_0/\ell^4$,

$$\varphi_0(\ell) = \ell,\ \varphi_1(\ell) = \frac{1}{2}\ell^2,\ \varphi_2(\ell) = \frac{1}{6}\ell^3,$$

$$\lambda = \frac{1}{\mu_0}$$

$$p_1(\ell;n) = [1 - p_0] \sum_{k=0}^{n} p_0^{2k} \tau_0^{6k},$$

$$\widehat{p}_1(\ell,n) = \left[p_0\tau_0^3 - 1\right] \sum_{k=1}^{n} \frac{1}{p_0^{2k+1}},$$

and

$$B_0(\ell,n) = \begin{cases} p_1(\ell;n) & \text{for } p_0 < 1, \\ \widehat{p}_1(\ell;n) & \text{for } p_0 > 1/\tau^3. \end{cases}$$

Using Corollary 1, the conditions

$$q_0 > \frac{6L}{\mu_0^3 B_0}$$

and

$$q_0 > \frac{6L}{\mu_0(1 - p_0)}$$

confirm the oscillation of all solutions of (22), where

$$L = \max\{m(1-m)\mu_0^m : m \in (0,1)\}.$$

Example 4. *Consider Equation (22) with $\tau(\ell) = 0.8\ell$, $\mu_0(\ell) = 0.5\ell$, and $q(\ell) = 16/\ell^4$. It is straightforward to observe that*

$$\varphi_0(\ell) = \ell,\ \varphi_1(\ell) = \frac{1}{2}\ell^2,\ \varphi_2(\ell) = \frac{1}{6}\ell^3,$$

$$\lambda = 2,$$

$$p_1(\ell;10) = \sum_{k=0}^{10} (0.5)^{2k+1}(0.9)^{6k} = 0.57661,$$

and

$$B_0(\ell,10) = p_1(\ell;10) = 0.57661.$$

Using Corollary 1, we can deduce that

$$L = 0.18209 \text{ at } m = 0.41581,$$

and that conditions

$$q_0 = 16 > \frac{6L}{\mu_0^3 B_0} = 15.158$$

and

$$q_0 = 16 > \frac{6L}{\mu_0(1-p_0)} = 4.3702$$

are satisfied. Therefore, every solution of (22) is oscillatory.

5. Conclusions

In this paper, we have made significant contributions to the study of fourth-order half-linear neutral differential equations by improving the link between the solution and its corresponding function. The identification of these improved links leads to the development of a novel criterion for assessing the oscillatory characteristics of the examined equation. Positive solutions are efficiently excluded using the comparison approach with second-order equations, yielding useful insights into the nature of the solutions. We demonstrate the practical significance and use of the suggested oscillatory standard by applying our findings to several cases.

Overall, our research represents an advance in this field and improves previous findings regarding the qualitative behavior of solutions of fourth-order half-linear neutral differential equations. To further expand the scope of this study, it would be interesting to extend the research to higher-order nonlinear neutral differential equations with $n \geq 4$. Such an extension could deepen our understanding of these equations and contribute to the development of more comprehensive analytical tools.

Author Contributions: Conceptualization, H.S.A., O.M., S.S.A., A.M.A. and E.M.E.; methodology, H.S.A., O.M., S.S.A., A.M.A. and E.M.E.; investigation, H.S.A., O.M., S.S.A., A.M.A. and E.M.E.; writing—original draft preparation, H.S.A., S.S.A. and A.M.A.; writing—review and editing, O.M. and E.M.E. All authors have read and agreed to the published version of the manuscript.

Funding: This project is funded by King Saud University, Riyadh, Saudi Arabia.

Acknowledgments: The authors present their appreciation to King Saud University for funding the publication of this research through the Researchers Supporting Program (RSPD2023R533), King Saud University, Riyadh, Saudi Arabia.

Conflicts of Interest: The authors declare no conflict of interest.

References

1. Myshkis, A.D. On solutions of linear homogeneous differential equations of the first order of stable type with a retarded argument. *Mat. Sb.* **1951**, *70*, 641–658.
2. Hale, J.K. *Theory of Functional Differential Equations*; Springer: New York, NY, USA, 1977.
3. Cooke, K.L. *Differential Difference Equations*; Academic Press: New York, NY, USA, 1963.
4. Gyori, I.; Ladas, G. *Oscillation Theory of Delay Differential Equations with Applications*; Clarendon Press: Oxford, UK, 1991.
5. Ladde, G.S.; Lakshmikantham, V.; Zhang, B.G. *Oscillation Theory of Differential Equations with Deviating Arguments*; Marcel Dekker: New York, NY, USA, 1987.
6. Zafer, A. *Oscillatory and Nonoscillatory Properties of Solutions of Functional Differential Equations and Difference Equations*; Iowa State University: Ames, IA, USA, 1992.
7. Erbe, L.H.; Kong, Q.; Zhong, B.G. *Oscillation Theory for Functional Differential Equations*; Marcel Dekker: New York, NY, USA, 1995.

8. Agarwal, R.P.; Zhang, C.; Li, T. Some remarks on oscillation of second order neutral differential equations. *Appl. Math. Comput.* **2016**, *274*, 178–181. [CrossRef]
9. Baculikova, B. Oscillatory criteria for second order differential equations with several sublinear neutral terms. *Opusc. Math.* **2019**, *39*, 753–763. [CrossRef]
10. Moaaz, O.; Masood, F.; Cesarano, C.; Alsallami, S.A.M.; Khalil, E.M.; Bouazizi, M.L. Neutral Differential Equations of Second-Order: Iterative Monotonic Properties. *Mathematics* **2022**, *10*, 1356. [CrossRef]
11. Li, T.; Baculikova, B.; Dzurina, J.; Zhang, C. Oscillation of fourth-order neutral differential equations with p-Laplacian like operators. *Bound. Value Probl.* **2014**, *2014*, 1–9. [CrossRef]
12. Purushothaman, G.; Suresh, K.; Tunc, E.; Thandapani, E. Oscillation criteria of fourth-order nonlinear semi-noncanonical neutral differential equations via a canonical transform. *Electron. J. Differ. Equ.* **2023**, *2023*, 1–12. [CrossRef]
13. Muhib, A.; Moaaz, O.; Cesarano, C.; Askar, S.; Elabbasy, E.M. Neutral Differential Equations of Fourth-Order: New Asymptotic Properties of Solutions. *Axioms* **2022**, *11*, 52. [CrossRef]
14. Xing, G.; Li, T.; Zhang, C. Oscillation of higher-order quasi-linear neutral differential equations. *Adv. Differ. Equ.* **2011**, *2011*, 1–10. [CrossRef]
15. Zafer, A. Oscillation criteria for even order neutral differential equations. *Appl. Math. Lett.* **1998**, *11*, 21–25. [CrossRef]
16. Agarwal, R.P.; Bohner, M.; Li, T.; Zhang, C. A new approach in the study of oscillatory behavior of even-order neutral delay differential equations. *Appl. Math. Comput.* **2013**, *225*, 787–794. [CrossRef]
17. Baculikova, B. Oscillation of second-order nonlinear noncanonical differential equations with deviating argument. *Appl. Math. Lett.* **2019**, *91*, 68–75. [CrossRef]
18. El-Nabulsi, R.A.; Moaaz, O.; Bazighifan, O. New Results for Oscillatory Behavior of Fourth-Order Differential Equations. *Symmetry* **2020**, *12*, 136. [CrossRef]
19. Zhang, C.; Li, T.; Saker, S. Oscillation of fourth-order delay differential equations. *J. Math. Sci.* **2014**, *201*, 296–308. [CrossRef]
20. Karpuz, B.; Ocalan, O.; Ozturk, S. Comparison theorems on the oscillation and asymptotic behaviour of higher-order neutral differential equations. *Glasgow Math. J.* **2010**, *52*, 107–114. [CrossRef]
21. Li, T.; Rogovchenko, Y.V. On asymptotic behavior of solutions to higher-order sublinear Emden–Fowler delay differential equations. *Appl. Math. Lett.* **2017**, *67*, 53–59. [CrossRef]
22. Zhang, C.; Li, T.; Sun, B.; Thandapani, E. On the oscillation of higher-order half-linear delay differential equations. *Appl. Math. Lett.* **2011**, *24*, 1618–1621. [CrossRef]
23. Zhang, C.; Agarwal, R.P.; Bohner, M.; Li, T. New results for oscillatory behavior of even-order half-linear delay differential equations. *Appl. Math. Lett.* **2013**, *26*, 179–183. [CrossRef]
24. Alnafisah, Y.; Masood, F.; Muhib, A.; Moaaz, O. Improved Oscillation Theorems for Even-Order Quasi-Linear Neutral Differential Equations. *Symmetry* **2023**, *15*, 1128. [CrossRef]
25. Agarwal, R.P.; Grace, S.R.; O'Regan, D. *Oscillation Theory for Difference and Functional Differential Equations*; Kluwer Academic: Dordrecht, The Netherlands, 2000.
26. Moaaz, O.; Cesarano, C.; Almarri, B. An Improved Relationship between the Solution and Its Corresponding Function in Fourth-Order Neutral Differential Equations and Its Applications. *Mathematics* **2023**, *11*, 1708. [CrossRef]
27. Kusano, T.; Naito, M. Comparison theorems for functional-differential equations with deviating arguments. *J. Math. Soc. Japan* **1981**, *33*, 509–532. [CrossRef]
28. Jadlovská, J.; Dzurina, J. Kneser-type oscillation criteria for second-order half-linear delay differential equations. *Appl. Math. Comput.* **2020**, *380*, 125289. [CrossRef]

Disclaimer/Publisher's Note: The statements, opinions and data contained in all publications are solely those of the individual author(s) and contributor(s) and not of MDPI and/or the editor(s). MDPI and/or the editor(s) disclaim responsibility for any injury to people or property resulting from any ideas, methods, instructions or products referred to in the content.

axioms

MDPI

Article

The Regional Enlarged Observability for Hilfer Fractional Differential Equations

Abu Bakr Elbukhari [1,2,*,†], Zhenbin Fan [1,†] and Gang Li [1,†]

1 School of Mathematical Sciences, Yangzhou University, Yangzhou 225002, China; zbfan@yzu.edu.cn (Z.F.); gli@yzu.edu.cn (G.L.)
2 Department of Mathematics, Faculty of Education, University of Khartoum, Khartoum, Omdurman 406, Sudan
* Correspondence: mrbakri123@hotmail.com; Tel.: +86-13270-5513-72
† These authors contributed equally to this work.

Abstract: In this paper, we investigate the concept of regional enlarged observability (ReEnOb) for fractional differential equations (FDEs) with the Hilfer derivative. To proceed this, we develop an approach based on the Hilbert uniqueness method (HUM). We mainly reconstruct the initial state ν_0^1 on an internal subregion ω from the whole domain Ω with knowledge of the initial information of the system and some given measurements. This approach shows that it is possible to obtain the desired state between two profiles in some selective internal subregions. Our findings develop and generalize some known results. Finally, we give two examples to support our theoretical results.

Keywords: Hilfer fractional derivatives; fractional diffusion systems; regional enlarged observability; Hilbert uniqueness method

MSC: 35R11; 33B07; 93C20; 44A10

Citation: Elbukhari, A.B.; Fan, Z.; Li, G. The Regional Enlarged Observability for Hilfer Fractional Differential Equations. *Axioms* **2023**, *12*, 648. https://doi.org/10.3390/axioms12070648

Academic Editors: Hatıra Günerhan, Francisco Martínez González and Mohammed K. A. Kaabar

Received: 30 May 2023
Revised: 20 June 2023
Accepted: 22 June 2023
Published: 29 June 2023

Copyright: © 2023 by the authors. Licensee MDPI, Basel, Switzerland. This article is an open access article distributed under the terms and conditions of the Creative Commons Attribution (CC BY) license (https://creativecommons.org/licenses/by/4.0/).

1. Introduction

In recent decades, fractional calculus theory has proven to be a significant tool for the formulation of several problems in science and engineering, where fractional derivatives and integrals can be utilized to describe the characteristics of various real materials in various scientific disciplines; see, e.g., [1–5]. This theory has recently received a large amount of consideration by many academics; we mention Euler, Laplace, Riemann, Liouville, Marchaud, Riesz, and Hilfer; see, e.g., [6–8]. Distributed parameter systems can be analysed in terms of controllability, observability, and stability, which lead to numerous applications. However, one of the most basic concerns in system analysis and control is observability, which is concerned with the reconstruction of a system's initial state that is taken from measurements on a system by means of so-called sensors; see, [9]. Amouroux et al. [10] developed two approaches to investigate regional observability (ReOb) for distributed systems. The first is state-space-based, and the second allows for estimating the state on the considered subregion. El Jai et al. [11] introduced the concept of regional strategic sensors for a class of distributed systems and presented the sensor characterization for various geometrical situations. In [12], Al-Saphory et al. considered and analysed the notion of regional gradient strategic sensors, and the results applied to a two-dimensional linear infinite distributed system in Hilbert space.

In a problem governed by a diffusion system, it is commonly known that the positioning of sensors is restricted by severe practical restrictions. In fact, observation processes are generally restricted to subsets, boundaries, or points [13,14]. This indicates that the operators of the observation can be unbounded in their state spaces.

Recently, the study of ReOb for partial differential equations (PDEs) has received considerable attention in the literature. Zerrik et al. [15] reviewed regional boundary observability for a two-dimensional diffusion system. In [16], Chen investigated infinite time exact observability for the Volterra system in Hilbert spaces. Chen and Yi [17] studied the observability and admissibility of Volterra systems in Hilbert spaces. Zouiten et al. [18] studied the following ReEnOb for a linear parabolic system.

$$\begin{cases} \frac{\partial}{\partial t} v(y,t) = Av(y,t) & \text{in } \Omega \times [0,T], \\ v(\xi,t) = 0 & \text{on } \Sigma_T, \\ v(y,0) = v_0(y) & \text{in } \Omega, \\ \mathfrak{M}(t) = Cv(t), & t \in [0,T], \end{cases} \tag{1}$$

where A is an infinitesimal operator and generates a strongly continuous semigroup $\{Q(t)\}_{t\geq 0}$ on the state space $L^2(\Omega)$, Ω is an open bound of $L^2(\Omega)$, and $\mathfrak{M}$ is the output function (OuPuFu), which represents the measurements. The authors used the HUM approach to reconstruct the initial state between two profiles in an internal subregion.

More recently, many researchers have investigated the ReOb for fractional differential equations (FDEs). In [19], Zguaid and El Alaoui investigated the notion of the regional boundary observability of Caputo fractional systems. Zguaid et al. [20] studied ReOb for a class of linear time-fractional systems using the HUM approach and proved that the considered approach allows to transform the ReOb problem into a solvability one. Regional gradient observability for Caputo fractional diffusion systems is considered in [21]. In [22], Ge et al. presented the notion of the regional gradient observability for Riemann–Liouville (R-L) diffusion systems for the first time. Cai et al. [23] investigated the concept of exact and approximate ReOb of Hadamard–Caputo diffusion systems using the HUM approach. Zguaid and El Alaoui [24] investigated the notion of regional boundary observability of R-L linear diffusion systems by using an extension of HUM.

On the other hand, some works concerning the concept of ReEnOb-FDEs have recently been conducted. In [25], Zouiten et al. studied the ReEnOb for R-L fractional evolution equations with R-L derivatives:

$$\begin{cases} {}^{RL}_{0}\mathrm{D}^{\eta}_{t} v(y,t) = Av(y,t) & \text{in } \Omega \times [0,T], \\ v(\xi,t) = 0 & \text{on } \Sigma_T, \\ \lim\limits_{t\to 0^+} {}_0I_t^{1-\eta} v(y,t) = v_0(y) & \text{in } \Omega, \\ \mathfrak{M}(t) = Cv(t), & t \in [0,T], \end{cases} \tag{2}$$

where Ω is an open bound of $\mathbb{R}^n (n = 1,2,3)$, with the regular boundary $\partial\Omega$ and ${}^{RL}_{0}\mathrm{D}^{\eta}_{t}$ and ${}_0I_t^{1-\eta}$ are R-L fractional derivatives and R-L fractional integrals of orders $0 < \eta \leq 1$ and $1-\eta$, respectively. The authors developed an approach based on HUM allowing them to reconstruct the initial state between two given functions in an internal subregion of the whole domain. In [26], Zouiten and Boutoulout investigated the ReEnOb for the following Caputo fractional diffusion system in a Hilbert space

$$\begin{cases} {}^{C}_{0}\mathrm{D}^{\eta}_{t} v(y,t) = Av(y,t) & \text{in } \Omega \times [0,T], \\ v(\xi,t) = 0 & \text{on } \Sigma_T, \\ v(y,t) = v_0(y) & \text{in } \Omega, \\ \mathfrak{M}(t) = Cv(t), & t \in [0,T]. \end{cases} \tag{3}$$

The HUM approach for fractional differential systems is used for the process of reconstructing the initial state between two profiles in a considered subregion of the whole domain.

Inspired and motivated by the above discussion, in this manuscript we extend the investigation of the notion of the ReEnOb for sub-diffusion systems with fractional derivatives, augmented and restricted by some measurements given by the so-called OuPuFu.

We note that FDEs have been widely used for modelling in various science and engineering fields due to their well-described systems and high accuracy, as well as yielding better results compared with systems with integer differentiation. Therefore, the results obtained from Systems (2) and (3) are better than those of System (1). Moreover, use the Hilfer fractional derivative as we know it has two parameters and contains Caputo and R-L derivatives in its definition. Thus, our findings can be seen as a generalization of the mentioned results.

This paper is interested in the concept of ReEnOb for the following sub-diffusion system via Hilfer FDs of order η, type κ and augmented with the OuPuFu (5). We first characterize the ReEnOb of a diffusion system augmented with the OuPuFu in an internal subregion ω of Ω. Moreover, we recognize two types of sensors based on the boundness issue of the observation operator C. Then, we reconstruct the initial state ν_0^1 of the addressed system using an approach that relies on the HUM approach introduced by Lions [27]. The investigation of the addressed problem shows that it is possible to obtain the desired state between two profiles in some selective internal subregions. Let Ω be an open bound of $\mathbb{R}^n (n = 1, 2, 3)$ with the regular boundary $\partial\Omega$, and let $\mathfrak{J} = [0, T]$. The space $\mathfrak{S}_T = \Omega \times \mathfrak{J}$ and $\Sigma_T = \partial\Omega \times \mathfrak{J}$. We consider the following diffusion sub-system:

$$\begin{cases} {}^{H}_{0}\mathrm{D}^{\eta,\kappa}_{t}\nu(y,t) = A\nu(y,t) & \text{in } \mathfrak{S}_T, \\ \nu(\xi,t) = 0 & \text{on } \Sigma_T, \\ \lim\limits_{t\to 0^+} {}_0I_t^{1-\zeta}\nu(y,t) = \nu_0(y) & \text{in } \Omega, \end{cases} \tag{4}$$

where ${}^{H}_{0}\mathrm{D}^{\eta,\kappa}_{t}$ stands for the Hilfer fractional derivative (left-sided) of order $0 < \eta < 1$, type $0 \le \kappa \le 1$ with respect to time t, the integral ${}_0I_t^{1-\zeta}$, $\zeta = \eta + \kappa - \eta\kappa$, $0 < \zeta \le 1$ is the left-sided R-L fractional integral operator (1), and the operator A is linear and has a dense domain, so the coefficients are independent of time t. Moreover, operator A is infinitesimal and generates a strongly continuous semigroup $\{Q(t)\}_{t\ge 0}$ on the state space $L^2(\Omega)$, which is a Hilbert space. Here, the initial state $\nu_0 \in L^2(\Omega)$ is assumed to be unknown. The measurements and information of System (4) are obtained by the OuPuFu below:

$$\mathfrak{M}(t) = C\nu(t), \qquad t \in \mathfrak{J}, \tag{5}$$

where C is the observation operator, and it is a linear, not necessary a bounded, operator determined by the number of sensors or their structure, with a dense domain $\mathcal{D}(C) \subseteq L^2(\Omega)$ with range in the observation space $\mathcal{O} = L^2(\mathfrak{J}; \mathbb{R}^q)$ ($q \in \mathbb{N}$ is the number of considered sensors), and $\mathcal{O}$ is a Hilbert space.

This paper is arranged as follows: In Section 2, we review the definitions, basic concepts, and lemmas utilized throughout this paper. In Section 3, we characterize the ReEnOb. Moreover, we present some remarks, then introduce and prove the main theorem of the ReOb of the Hilfer diffusion System (4). In Section 4, the HUM approach is introduced and applied in the reconstruction process of the initial state of System (4). In addition, two theoretical illustrative examples are given to support our results. In Section 5, we give some conclusions.

2. Preliminaries

In this section, we review the essential definitions, notations, and basic facts utilized throughout this paper.

Definition 1. *(See [7]) The R-L fractional integral (left-sided) of order η for a function $f : \mathfrak{J} \to \mathbb{R}$ is defined as*

$${}_0I_t^{\eta} f(t) = \frac{1}{\Gamma(\eta)} \int_0^t (t-s)^{\eta-1} f(s)\mathrm{d}s, \quad 0 < \eta < 1.$$

Definition 2. *(See [7]) The R-L fractional integral (right-sided) of order η for a function $f : \mathfrak{J} \to \mathbb{R}$ is defined as*

$$ {}_tI_T^{\eta} f(t) = \frac{1}{\Gamma(\eta)} \int_t^T (s-t)^{\eta-1} f(s) \mathrm{d}s, \qquad 0 < \eta < 1. $$

Definition 3. *(See [1,28]) The R-L fractional derivative (left-sided) and R-L fractional derivative (right-sided) of order $0 < \eta < 1$ with respect to t for a function f are defined as*

$$ {}^{RL}_{0}\mathrm{D}_t^{\eta} f(t) = \left({}_0I_t^{1-\eta} f(t)\right)' = \frac{1}{\Gamma(1-\eta)} \left(\int_0^t (t-s)^{-\eta} f(s) \mathrm{d}s \right)' \quad \text{for a.e. } t \in \mathfrak{J}, $$

and

$$ {}^{RL}_{t}\mathrm{D}_T^{\eta} f(t) = -\left({}_tI_T^{1-\eta} f(t)\right)' = -\frac{1}{\Gamma(1-\eta)} \left(\int_t^T (s-t)^{-\eta} f(s) \mathrm{d}s \right)' \quad \text{for a.e. } t \in \mathfrak{J}, $$

respectively, where the notation $'$ stands for differentiation.

Definition 4. *(See [1,28]) The Hilfer fractional derivative (left-sided) and the Hilfer fractional derivative (right-sided) of order $0 < \eta < 1$, type $0 \le \kappa \le 1$ with respect to t for a function f are respectively defined by*

$$ \begin{aligned} {}^{H}_{0}\mathrm{D}_t^{\eta,\kappa} f(t) &= \left({}_0I_t^{\kappa(1-\eta)} \left({}_0I_t^{1-\zeta} f\right)'\right)(t) \\ &= {}_0I_t^{\zeta-\eta}\, {}^{RL}_{0}\mathrm{D}_t^{\zeta} f(t) \\ &= \frac{1}{\Gamma(\zeta-\eta)\Gamma(1-\zeta)} \int_0^t (t-s)^{(\zeta-\eta)-1} \left(\int_0^s (s-\tau)^{-\zeta} f(\tau) \mathrm{d}\tau \right)' \mathrm{d}s, \end{aligned} $$

for almost everywhere $t \in \mathfrak{J}$, where $\zeta = \eta + \kappa - \eta\kappa$, $0 < \zeta \le 1$, $\zeta \le \eta$, and $\zeta > \kappa$.

$$ \begin{aligned} {}^{H}_{t}\mathrm{D}_T^{\eta,\kappa} f(t) &= -\left({}_tI_T^{\kappa(1-\eta)} \left({}_tI_T^{1-\zeta} f\right)'\right)(t) \\ &= -\, {}_tI_T^{\zeta-\eta}\, {}^{RL}_{t}\mathrm{D}_T^{\zeta} f(t) \\ &= -\frac{1}{\Gamma(\zeta-\eta)\Gamma(1-\zeta)} \int_t^T (s-t)^{(\zeta-\eta)-1} \left(\int_s^T (\tau-s)^{-\zeta} f(\tau) \mathrm{d}\tau \right)' \mathrm{d}s, \end{aligned} $$

for a.e. $t \in \mathfrak{J}$.

Next, we recall a mild solution for the following Hilfer fractional evolution equation; see [29].

Lemma 1. *Let $\mathcal{X} = L^2(\Omega)$ be a Hilbert space, for any $u_0 \in \mathcal{X}$, $0 < \eta < 1$, $0 \le \kappa \le 1$ and $f \in \mathfrak{J} \times \mathcal{X} \longrightarrow \mathcal{X}$, the function $u \in L^2(\mathfrak{J}; \mathcal{X})$ is said to be a mild solution of the following system*

$$ \begin{cases} {}^{H}_{0}\mathrm{D}_t^{\eta,\kappa} u(t) = Au(t) + f(t,u), & t \in \mathfrak{J}, \\ \lim\limits_{t \to 0^+} {}_0I_t^{1-\zeta} u(t) = u_0, \end{cases} \tag{6} $$

if u fulfils

$$u(t) = \frac{1}{\Gamma(\zeta-\eta)}\int_0^t (t-s)^{(\zeta-\eta)-1}s^{\eta-1}\int_0^\infty \eta\theta M_\eta(\theta)Q(s^\eta\theta))u_0 d\theta ds + \int_0^t\int_0^\infty \eta\theta M_\eta(\theta)Q((t-s)^\eta\theta)(t-s)^{\eta-1}f(s,u(s))d\theta ds, \tag{7}$$

where $P_\eta(t) = \int_0^\infty \eta\theta M_\eta(\theta)Q(t^\eta\theta)d\theta$, *and the function* $M_\eta(\theta) = \sum_{n=1}^\infty \frac{(-\theta)^{n-1}}{(n-1)\Gamma(1-\rho n)}$, *where* $0<\rho<1$, $\theta\in\mathbb{C}$ *is the Wright function, which fulfils the following equality:*

$$\int_0^\infty \theta^\iota M_\eta(\theta)d\theta = \frac{\Gamma(1+\iota)}{\Gamma(1+\eta\iota)} \quad for \quad \iota\geq 0, \quad \theta\geq 0.$$

Remark 1. *(See Remark 2.14 in [29]) Let* $0<\eta<1$, $0\leq\kappa\leq 1$, $0<\zeta\leq 1$ *and* $t\in\mathfrak{J}$*; thus, we have*

$${}^{RL}_{0}\mathrm{D}_t^{\zeta-\eta}\mathcal{S}_{\eta,\kappa}(t) = \mathcal{R}_\eta(t), \quad t\in(0,T], \tag{8}$$

where

$$\mathcal{R}_\eta(t) = t^{\eta-1}P_\eta(t), \tag{9}$$

and

$$\mathcal{S}_{\eta,\kappa}(t) = {}_0I_t^{\zeta-\eta}\mathcal{R}_\eta(t). \tag{10}$$

We can rewrite the equality in (7) as follows:

$$u(t) = \mathcal{S}_{\eta,\kappa}(t)u_0 + \int_0^t \mathcal{R}_\eta(t-s)f(s,u(s))ds. \tag{11}$$

Note that if the non-linear term of System (6) is zero, then the mild solution (11) becomes $u(\cdot) = \mathcal{S}_{\eta,\kappa}(\cdot)u_0$. Consequently, the mild solution of (4) may alternatively be expressed as

$$v(t) = \mathcal{S}_{\eta,\kappa}(t)v_0, \quad t\in\mathfrak{J}. \tag{12}$$

We give the following lemma, which will be utilized afterwards to prove our results.

Lemma 2. *(See [30]) Let a function g be defined on interval* $[S,T]$, $(S<T)$ *and* $S,T\in\mathbb{R}$, *then the reflection operator* $\mathfrak{Q}$ *acting on g is*

$$\mathfrak{Q}[g(t)] = g(S+T-t).$$

Lemma 3. *Let f be a function defined on the interval* $\mathfrak{J}$ *and let f be differentiable and integrable in the Hilfer derivative sense. We now introduce the reflection operator* $\mathfrak{Q}$ *when acting on f as follows:*

$$\mathfrak{Q}[f(t)] = f(T-t), \tag{13}$$

Moreover, the following assertions hold,

(i) ${}_0I_t^\eta\mathfrak{Q}[f(t)] = \mathfrak{Q}\left[{}_tI_T^\eta f(t)\right]$.

(ii) $\mathfrak{Q}\left[{}_0I_t^\eta f(t)\right] = {}_tI_T^\eta\mathfrak{Q}[f(t)]$.

(iii) $-{}^H_0\mathrm{D}_t^{\eta,\kappa}\mathfrak{Q}[f(t)] = \mathfrak{Q}\left[{}^H_t\mathrm{D}_T^{\eta,\kappa}f(t)\right]$.

(iv) $\mathfrak{Q}\left[{}^H_0\mathrm{D}_t^{\eta,\kappa}f(t)\right] = -{}^H_t\mathrm{D}_T^{\eta,\kappa}\mathfrak{Q}[f(t)]$.

Note that, assertions (i) and (ii) are given in [25,26]. Here, we state their proof due to the demonstration of assertions (iii) and (iv).

Proof. Our proof is obtained by virtue of Equation (13) and by utilizing changes in the variables, specifically, changes in the role of time.
(i): We show that ${}_0I_t^{\eta}\mathfrak{Q}[f(t)] = \mathfrak{Q}\left[{}_tI_T^{\eta}f(t)\right]$. Since

$$\begin{aligned} {}_0I_t^{\eta}\mathfrak{Q}[f(t)] &= \frac{1}{\Gamma(\eta)}\int_0^t (t-s)^{\eta-1}\mathfrak{Q}f(s)ds \\ &= \frac{1}{\Gamma(\eta)}\int_0^t (t-s)^{\eta-1}f(T-s)ds. \end{aligned} \tag{14}$$

Using the change in the variables, let $\tilde{s} = T - s$, then $-d\tilde{s} = ds$. Now, for $s = 0$ and $s = t$, we obtain $\tilde{s} = T$ and $\tilde{s} = T - t$, respectively. Let us fix $\mathcal{M} = \frac{1}{\Gamma(\eta)}$. Substituting these values into (14), we obtain

$${}_0I_t^{\eta}\mathfrak{Q}[f(t)] = -\mathcal{M}\int_T^{T-t} (t-T+\tilde{s})^{\eta-1}f(\tilde{s})d\tilde{s},$$

Let $\tilde{s} := s$, we obtain

$${}_0I_t^{\eta}\mathfrak{Q}[f(t)] = \mathcal{M}\int_{T-t}^{T} (s-T+t)^{\eta-1}f(s)ds. \tag{15}$$

We now consider the right-hand side:

$$\begin{aligned} \mathfrak{Q}\left[{}_tI_T^{\eta}f(t)\right] &= \mathfrak{Q}\left[\mathcal{M}\int_t^T (s-t)^{\eta-1}f(s)ds\right] \\ &= \mathcal{M}\int_{T-t}^{T} (s-T+t)^{\eta-1}f(s)ds. \end{aligned} \tag{16}$$

Consequently, from (15) and (16), we can see that ${}_0I_t^{\eta}\mathfrak{Q}[f(t)] = \mathfrak{Q}\left[{}_tI_T^{\eta}f(t)\right]$.
(ii): The proof follows the same way as (i). Considering the left-hand side:

$$\begin{aligned} \mathfrak{Q}\left[{}_0I_t^{\eta}f(t)\right] &= \mathfrak{Q}\left[\mathcal{M}\int_0^t (t-s)^{\eta-1}f(s)ds\right] \\ &= \mathcal{M}\int_0^{T-t} (T-t-s)^{\eta-1}f(s)ds, \end{aligned}$$

and the right-hand side:

$$\begin{aligned} {}_tI_T^{\eta}\mathfrak{Q}[f(t)] &= \mathcal{M}\int_t^T (s-t)^{\eta-1}\mathfrak{Q}f(s)ds \\ &= -\mathcal{M}\int_{T-t}^{0} (T-s-t)^{\eta-1}f(s)ds \\ &= \mathcal{M}\int_0^{T-t} (T-t-s)^{\eta-1}f(s)ds. \end{aligned}$$

(iii): We demonstrate $-{}_{0}^{H}\mathrm{D}_{t}^{\eta,\kappa}\mathfrak{Q}[f(t)] = \mathfrak{Q}\left[{}_{t}^{H}\mathrm{D}_{T}^{\eta,\kappa}f(t)\right]$. Let us fix $\tilde{\mathcal{M}} = \frac{1}{\Gamma(\zeta-\eta)\Gamma(1-\zeta)}$, which will be used in the remainder of the proof of this lemma. We first consider the left-hand side:

$$\begin{aligned} -{}_{0}^{H}\mathrm{D}_{t}^{\eta,\kappa}\mathfrak{Q}[f(t)] &= -\frac{1}{\Gamma(\zeta-\eta)\Gamma(1-\zeta)}\int_{0}^{t}(t-s)^{(\zeta-\eta)-1}\mathfrak{Q}\left(\int_{0}^{s}(s-\tau)^{-\zeta}f(\tau)\mathrm{d}\tau\right)'\mathrm{d}s \\ &= -\tilde{\mathcal{M}}\int_{0}^{t}(t-s)^{(\zeta-\eta)-1}\left(\int_{0}^{s}(s-\tau)^{-\zeta}f(T-\tau)\mathrm{d}\tau\right)'\mathrm{d}s, \end{aligned} \tag{17}$$

Let $\tilde{\tau} = T-\tau$, then $-\mathrm{d}\tilde{\tau} = \mathrm{d}\tau$. Now, for $\tau = 0$ and $\tau = s$, we obtain $\tilde{\tau} = T$ and $\tilde{\tau} = T-s$, respectively. Substituting these values into (17), we obtain

$$-{}_{0}^{H}\mathrm{D}_{t}^{\eta,\kappa}\mathfrak{Q}[f(t)] = -\tilde{\mathcal{M}}\int_{0}^{t}(t-s)^{(\zeta-\eta)-1}\left(-\int_{T}^{T-s}(s-T+\tilde{\tau})^{-\zeta}f(\tilde{\tau})\mathrm{d}\tilde{\tau}\right)'\mathrm{d}s, \tag{18}$$

Let $s = T-\tilde{s}$, then $-\mathrm{d}\tilde{s} = \mathrm{d}s$. Now for $s = 0$ and $\tau = s$, we obtain $\tilde{s} = T$ and $\tilde{s} = T-t$, respectively. Substituting these values into (18), we obtain

$$-{}_{0}^{H}\mathrm{D}_{t}^{\eta,\kappa}\mathfrak{Q}[f(t)] = \tilde{\mathcal{M}}\int_{T}^{T-t}(t-T+\tilde{s})^{(\zeta-\eta)-1}\left(\int_{\tilde{s}}^{T}(\tilde{\tau}-\tilde{s})^{-\zeta}f(\tilde{\tau})\mathrm{d}\tilde{\tau}\right)'\mathrm{d}\tilde{s},$$

Let $\tau := \tilde{\tau}$ and $s := \tilde{s}$, we obtain

$$-{}_{0}^{H}\mathrm{D}_{t}^{\eta,\kappa}\mathfrak{Q}[f(t)] = \tilde{\mathcal{M}}\int_{T}^{T-t}(t-T+s)^{(\zeta-\eta)-1}\left(\int_{s}^{T}(\tau-s)^{-\zeta}f(\tau)\mathrm{d}\tau\right)'\mathrm{d}s.$$

On the other hand, we proceed with the right-hand side as follows:

$$\begin{aligned} \mathfrak{Q}\left[{}_{t}\mathrm{D}_{T}^{\eta,\kappa}f(t)\right] &= \mathfrak{Q}\left[-\tilde{\mathcal{M}}\int_{t}^{T}(s-t)^{(\zeta-\eta)-1}\left(\int_{s}^{T}(\tau-s)^{-\zeta}f(\tau)\mathrm{d}\tau\right)'\mathrm{d}s\right] \\ &= -\tilde{\mathcal{M}}\int_{T-t}^{T}(s-T+t)^{(\zeta-\eta)-1}\left(\int_{s}^{T}(\tau-s)^{-\zeta}f(\tau)\mathrm{d}\tau\right)'\mathrm{d}s \\ &= \tilde{\mathcal{M}}\int_{T}^{T-t}(s-T+t)^{(\zeta-\eta)-1}\left(\int_{s}^{T}(\tau-s)^{-\zeta}f(\tau)\mathrm{d}\tau\right)'\mathrm{d}s, \end{aligned}$$

Hence, $-{}_{0}^{H}\mathrm{D}_{t}^{\eta,\kappa}\mathfrak{Q}[f(t)] = \mathfrak{Q}\left[{}_{t}\mathrm{D}_{T}^{\eta,\kappa}f(t)\right]$.

(iv): The proof follows the same way as (iii). We first consider the left-hand side:

$$\begin{aligned} \mathfrak{Q}\left[{}_{0}^{H}\mathrm{D}_{t}^{\eta,\kappa}f(t)\right] &= \mathfrak{Q}\left[\tilde{\mathcal{M}}\int_{0}^{t}(t-s)^{(\zeta-\eta)-1}\left(\int_{0}^{s}(s-\tau)^{-\zeta}f(\tau)\mathrm{d}\tau\right)'\mathrm{d}s\right] \\ &= \tilde{\mathcal{M}}\int_{0}^{T-t}(T-t-s)^{(\zeta-\eta)-1}\left(\int_{0}^{s}(s-\tau)^{-\zeta}f(\tau)\mathrm{d}\tau\right)'\mathrm{d}s, \end{aligned}$$

then the right-hand side:

$$
\begin{aligned}
-{}^{H}_{t}\mathrm{D}^{\eta,\kappa}_{T}\mathfrak{Q}[f(t)] &= -\left[-\tilde{\mathcal{M}}\int_t^T (s-t)^{(\zeta-\eta)-1}\mathfrak{Q}\left(\int_s^T (\tau-s)^{-\zeta} f(\tau)\mathrm{d}\tau\right)' \mathrm{d}s\right] \\
&= \tilde{\mathcal{M}}\int_t^T (s-t)^{(\zeta-\eta)-1}\left(\int_0^s (\tau-s)^{-\zeta} f(T-\tau)\mathrm{d}\tau\right)' \mathrm{d}s \\
&= \tilde{\mathcal{M}}\int_t^T (s-t)^{(\zeta-\eta)-1}\left(-\int_{T-s}^0 (T-\tilde{\tau}-s)^{-\zeta} f(\tilde{\tau})\mathrm{d}\tilde{\tau}\right)' \mathrm{d}s \\
&= -\tilde{\mathcal{M}}\int_{T-t}^0 (T-\tilde{s}-t)^{(\zeta-\eta)-1}\left(\int_0^{T-s} (\tilde{s}-\tilde{\tau})^{-\zeta} f(\tilde{\tau})\mathrm{d}\tilde{\tau}\right)' \mathrm{d}\tilde{s} \\
&= \tilde{\mathcal{M}}\int_0^{T-t} (T-s-t)^{(\zeta-\eta)-1}\left(\int_0^s (s-\tau)^{-\zeta} f(\tau)\mathrm{d}\tau\right)' \mathrm{d}s.
\end{aligned}
$$

Consequently, $\mathfrak{Q}\left[{}^{H}_{0}\mathrm{D}^{\eta,\kappa}_{t} f(t)\right] = -{}^{H}_{t}\mathrm{D}^{\eta,\kappa}_{T}\mathfrak{Q}[f(t)]$.
Thus, this completes the proof of the lemma. □

Since C is an admissible operator, as we will see later, then the OuPuFu of System (4) is given by

$$
\mathfrak{M}(t) = C\mathcal{S}_{\eta,\kappa}(t)v_0 = \mathcal{K}_{\eta,\kappa}(t)v_0, \quad t \in \mathfrak{J}, \tag{19}
$$

where $\mathcal{K}_{\eta,\kappa} : L^2(\Omega) \longrightarrow \mathcal{O}$ is a fractional linear operator. Let us recall the observation space $\mathcal{O} = L^2(\mathfrak{J}; \mathbb{R}^q)(q \in \mathbb{N})$. Two cases arise for obtaining the adjoint operator of $\mathcal{K}_{\eta,\kappa}$.

- Case 1. C is bounded. In this case, we can define zonal sensors. Let operator C be from $L^2(\Omega)$ to $\mathcal{O}$. Then, if C^* is adjoint on the other hand, the adjoint of operator $\mathcal{K}_{\eta,\kappa}$ can be obtained by

$$
\begin{aligned}
\mathcal{K}^*_{\eta,\kappa} &: \mathcal{O} \longrightarrow L^2(\Omega) \\
\mathfrak{M}^* &\longmapsto \int_0^T \mathcal{S}^*_{\eta,\kappa}(s)C^*\mathfrak{M}^*(s)\mathrm{d}s.
\end{aligned}
$$

- Case 2. C is unbounded. We can define pointwise sensors. However, in this case, the operator C can be introduced from $\mathcal{D}(C) \subseteq L^2(\Omega)$ to the observation space $\mathcal{O}$. Then, C^* is adjoint. However, in order to give this case a sense of (5), we make an assumption on C in the following definition, namely, C is an admissible observation operator, as we will see in Definition 5 below.

Definition 5. *(See [18]) The observation operator C is an admissible of* (4) *and* (5), *if for any* $v_0 \in \mathcal{D}(C)$ *there is a constant* $\mathcal{L} > 0$, *such that*

$$
\int_0^T \|C\mathcal{S}_{\eta,\kappa}(t)v_0\|^2 \mathrm{d}s \le \mathcal{L} \parallel v_0 \parallel .
$$

Note that operator C being admissible assures that the map

$$
v_0 \longmapsto C\mathcal{S}_{\eta,\kappa}(t)v_0 = \mathcal{K}_{\eta,\kappa}(t)v_0
$$

can be extended to a bounded linear operator from $L^2(\Omega)$ to the space $\mathcal{O}$. Thus, we can introduce $\mathcal{K}^*_{\eta,\kappa}$ as the adjoint of operator $\mathcal{K}_{\eta,\kappa}$ as follows:

$$\begin{aligned} \mathcal{K}^*_{\eta,\kappa} : \mathcal{D}(\mathcal{K}^*_{\eta,\kappa}) \subseteq \mathcal{O} &\longrightarrow L^2(\Omega) \\ \mathfrak{M}^* &\longmapsto \int_0^T \mathcal{S}^*_{\eta,\kappa}(s) C^* \mathfrak{M}^*(s) ds \end{aligned}$$

3. Characterization of Enlarged Observability

In this section, we will characterize the ReEnOb of System (4) with the output function (5) in the subregion ω of Ω. Let ω be a positive Lebesgue measure, and let us define the restriction mapping (projection mapping) p_ω, as follows:

$$\begin{aligned} p_\omega : L^2(\Omega) &\longrightarrow L^2(\omega) \\ \nu &\longmapsto p_\omega \nu = \nu_{|\omega}. \end{aligned}$$

We can now define the adjoint p^*_ω of p_ω as follows: $(p^*_\omega \nu)(y) := \nu(y, \cdot)$ when $y \in \omega$, and $(p^*_\omega \nu)(y) := 0$ when $y \in \Omega \backslash \omega$. In addition, we note that the regional exact observability of System (4) with (5) can be achieved at time t in the subregion ω, if $\mathrm{Im}(p_\omega \mathcal{K}^*_{\eta,\kappa}) = L^2(\omega)$, see, e.g., [25,26,31–33]. Now, let $\gamma_1(\cdot)$ and $\gamma_2(\cdot)$, $\gamma_1(\cdot) \leq \gamma_2(\cdot)$ almost everywhere in the subregion ω, be two functions defined in $L^2(\Omega)$. We thus define the following set

$$\mathfrak{Z} = \{\nu \in L^2(\omega) | \gamma_1(\cdot) \leq \nu(\cdot) \leq \gamma_2(\cdot) \text{ almost everywhere in the subregion } \omega\},$$

where $\gamma_1(\cdot)$ and $\gamma_2(\cdot)$ are given functions in ω. We assume that the initial state is given by

$$\nu_0 = \begin{cases} \nu_0^1 & \text{in } \mathfrak{Z}, \\ \nu_0^2 & \text{in } L^2(\Omega) \backslash \mathfrak{Z}. \end{cases}$$

The main objective of the investigation proposed in this paper is to demonstrate ReEnOb for Hilfer time fractional-order diffusion systems, that is, we will answer the following question: Given the Hilfer fractional diffusion System (4) with (5) in the subregion ω at time $t \in \mathfrak{J}$, can we reconstruct ν_0^1 between $\gamma_1(\cdot)$ and $\gamma_2(\cdot)$?

The following definition will be used in the following.

Definition 6. *If* $\mathrm{Ker}(\mathcal{K}_{\eta,\kappa} p^*_\omega) \cap \mathfrak{Z} = \{0\}$, *then System* (4) *with* (5) *is exactly* $\mathcal{E}$*-observable in the subregion* ω.

Definition 7. *A sensor is exactly* $\mathfrak{Z}$*-strategic in the subregion* ω *if the observed system is exactly* $\mathfrak{Z}$*-observable in subregion* ω.

The following three remarks show that the results obtained in [18,25,26] are particular cases of our results.

Remark 2. *If* $\kappa = 0$ *and* $\eta = 1$, *then the Hilfer fractional diffusion* (4) *corresponds to the normal diffusion process, which is investigated in [18].*

Remark 3. *If* $\kappa = 0$ *and* $0 < \eta < 1$, *then the Hilfer fractional diffusion System* (4) *corresponds to the R-L fractional diffusion process, which is investigated in [25].*

Remark 4. *If* $\kappa = 1$ *and* $0 < \eta < 1$, *then the Hilfer fractional diffusion* (4) *corresponds to the Caputo fractional diffusion process, which is considered in [26].*

The following result can be obtained directly from Definition 7.

Remark 5. *If System* (4) *with the OuPuFu* (5) *is exactly $\mathfrak{Z}$-observable in ω_1, then for any subregion ω_2 of ω_1 it is also exactly $\mathfrak{Z}$-observable in ω_2.*

The following remark will be used in the proof of the theorem presented below.

Remark 6. *Let X be a Hilbert space and F a linear subspace of X, then $F \cap F^{\perp} = \{0\}$, where $F^{\perp}$ is the orthogonal complement of F.*

Theorem 1. *The following assertions are equivalent:*

1. *System* (4) *with the OuPuFu* (5) *is exactly $\mathfrak{Z}$-observable in the subregion ω.*
2. $\mathrm{Im}(p_\omega \mathcal{K}^*_{\eta,\kappa}) \cap \mathfrak{Z} \neq \emptyset$.

Proof. We show that Statement 1 implies Statement 2, and Statement 2 implies Statement 1. The following two facts play a key role in the proof.

$$\mathrm{Ker}(\mathcal{K}_{\eta,\kappa} p^*_\omega) = \mathrm{Im}(p_\omega \mathcal{K}^*_{\eta,\kappa})^{\perp}, \tag{20}$$

it follows from Remark 6 that

$$\mathrm{Im}(p_\omega \mathcal{K}^*_{\eta,\kappa}) \cap \mathrm{Im}(p_\omega \mathcal{K}^*_{\eta,\kappa})^{\perp} = \{0\}. \tag{21}$$

We demonstrate that the left-hand side implies the right-hand side, and vice versa:

$$\mathrm{Ker}(\mathcal{K}_{\eta,\kappa} p^*_\omega) \cap \mathfrak{Z} = \{0\} \Longleftrightarrow \mathrm{Im}(p_\omega \mathcal{K}^*_{\eta,\kappa}) \cap \mathfrak{Z} \neq \emptyset.$$

We first show that

$$\mathrm{Ker}(\mathcal{K}_{\eta,\kappa} p^*_\omega) \cap \mathfrak{Z} = \{0\} \Longrightarrow \mathrm{Im}(p_\omega \mathcal{K}^*_{\eta,\kappa}) \cap \mathfrak{Z} \neq \emptyset.$$

Let $y \in \mathrm{Ker}(\mathcal{K}_{\eta,\kappa} p^*_\omega) \cap \mathfrak{Z}$, then $y = 0$. From (20), one can see that $y \in \mathrm{Im}(p_\omega \mathcal{K}^*_{\eta,\kappa})^{\perp} \cap \mathfrak{Z}$. Therefore, it follows from (21) that, $\mathrm{Im}(p_\omega \mathcal{K}^*_{\eta,\kappa})$ has at least one element, which is zero. Thus, $\mathrm{Im}(p_\omega \mathcal{K}^*_{\eta,\kappa}) \cap \mathfrak{Z} \neq \emptyset$.

We now prove that statement 2 implies statement 1, that is,

$$\mathrm{Im}(p_\omega \mathcal{K}^*_{\eta,\kappa}) \cap \mathfrak{Z} \neq \emptyset \Longrightarrow \mathrm{Ker}(\mathcal{K}_{\eta,\kappa} p^*_\omega) \cap \mathfrak{Z} = \{0\}.$$

Suppose

$$\mathrm{Im}(p_\omega \mathcal{K}^*_{\eta,\kappa}) \cap \mathfrak{Z} \neq \emptyset, \tag{22}$$

and

$$\mathrm{Ker}(\mathcal{K}_{\eta,\kappa} p^*_\omega) \cap \mathfrak{Z} \neq \{0\}. \tag{23}$$

Now, let $y \in \mathrm{Ker}(\mathcal{K}_{\eta,\kappa} p^*_\omega) \cap \mathfrak{Z}$, then $y \neq 0$, $y \in \mathfrak{Z}$ and $y \in \mathrm{Ker}(\mathcal{K}_{\eta,\kappa} p^*_\omega)$. From (20) and (21), we have $y \in \mathrm{Im}(p_\omega \mathcal{K}^*_{\eta,\kappa})^{\perp}$ and $y \notin \mathrm{Im}(p_\omega \mathcal{K}^*_{\eta,\kappa})$, respectively. Consequently, one can see that

$$\mathrm{Im}(p_\omega \mathcal{K}^*_{\eta,\kappa}) \cap \left(\mathrm{Ker}(\mathcal{K}_{\eta,\kappa} p^*_\omega) \cap \mathfrak{Z}\right) = \emptyset;$$

therefore,

$$\mathrm{Im}(p_\omega \mathcal{K}^*_{\eta,\kappa}) \cap \mathfrak{Z} = \emptyset,$$

which contradicts (22). Thus, (23) is not true. Consequently,

$$\mathrm{Ker}(\mathcal{K}_{\eta,\kappa} p^*_\omega) \cap \mathfrak{Z} = \{0\}.$$

Therefore, System (4) with (5) is exactly $\mathfrak{Z}$-observable in the subregion ω. This completes the proof. □

4. The Hilbert Uniqueness Method

In this section, we provide an approach for reconstructing the initial state of the system between $\gamma_1(\cdot)$ and $\gamma_2(\cdot)$ in subregion ω. Let $\mathfrak{P}$ be a space defined as

$$\mathfrak{P} = \{g \in L^2(\Omega) | g = 0 \text{ in } L^2(\Omega) \backslash \mathfrak{Z}\}. \tag{24}$$

4.1. Pointwise Sensors

Let System (4) be observed by a pointwise sensor $(l, \delta(l - \cdot))$, where $l \in \overline{\Omega}$ is the location of a sensor and δ is the Dirac mass (delta function), which is concentrated in l. Here, the OuPuFu is introduced as

$$\mathfrak{M}(t) = \psi(b, T - t), \quad t \in \mathfrak{J}. \tag{25}$$

Let ψ_0 be in $\mathfrak{P}$; thus, we examine the following system:

$$\begin{cases} {}^H_0\mathrm{D}^{\eta,\kappa}_t \psi(y,t) = A\psi(y,t) & \text{in } \mathfrak{S}_T, \\ \psi(\xi,t) = 0 & \text{on } \Sigma_T, \\ \lim\limits_{t\to 0^+} {}_0I^{1-\zeta}_t \psi(y,t) = \psi_0(y) & \text{in } \Omega. \end{cases} \tag{26}$$

For simplicity of notation, we denote $\psi(y,t) := \psi(t)$. We note that System (26) admits a unique solution $\psi \in L^2(\mathfrak{J}; \mathcal{D}(A)) \cap C(\Omega \times \mathfrak{J})$ given by $\psi(t) = \mathcal{S}_{\eta,\kappa}(t)\varphi_0$, if $\psi_0(x) \in \mathcal{D}(A)$. Let us denote a semi-norm on $\mathfrak{P}$ by

$$\psi_0 \longmapsto \|\psi_0\|^2_{\mathfrak{P}} = \int_0^T \|C\psi(T-t)\|^2 \mathrm{d}t. \tag{27}$$

In the following lemma, we will see that a norm can be defined.

Lemma 4. *If System* (4) *with OuPuFu* (25) *is exactly $\mathfrak{Z}$-observable in the subregion ω; consequently, Equation* (27) *defines a norm in the space $\mathfrak{P}$.*

Proof. Firstly, in light of Theorem 1 and Definition 6, we suppose that System (4) with the OuPuFu (25) is exactly $\mathfrak{Z}$-observable in the space $\mathfrak{P}$. Now, for $\psi_0 \in \mathfrak{P}$ and a semi-norm in $\mathfrak{P}$, we have

$$\|\psi_0\|_{\mathfrak{P}} = 0 \Longrightarrow C\psi(T-t) = 0 \text{ for all } t \in \mathfrak{J}.$$

Let

$$\psi_0 \in L^2(\Omega) \Longrightarrow p_\omega \psi_0 \in L^2(\omega),$$

then,

$$\mathcal{K}_{\eta,\kappa} p^*_\omega p_\omega \psi_0 = C\mathcal{S}_{\eta,\kappa}(t) p^*_\omega p_\omega \psi_0 = 0.$$

Hence,

$$p_\omega \psi_0 \in \mathrm{Ker}(\mathcal{K}_{\eta,\kappa} p^*_\omega).$$

and for $p_\omega\psi_0 \in \mathfrak{Z}$, one has $p_\omega\psi_0 \in \mathrm{Ker}(\mathcal{K}_{\eta,\kappa} p^*_\omega) \cap \mathfrak{Z}$ and $p_\omega\psi_0 = 0$, since the system is exactly $\mathfrak{Z}$-observable in the subregion ω. Consequently, $\psi_0 = 0$ and (27) is a norm. □

We now consider the following system, which is controlled by the solution to System (26), that is,

$$\begin{cases} \mathfrak{Q}\left[- {}^H_t\mathrm{D}^{\eta,\kappa}_T \mathrm{Y}(y,t)\right] = A^*\mathfrak{Q}[\mathrm{Y}(y,t)] + C^*C\mathfrak{Q}[\psi(y,t)] & \text{in } \mathfrak{S}_T, \\ \mathrm{Y}(\xi,t) = 0 & \text{on } \Sigma_T, \\ \lim\limits_{t\to T^-} \mathfrak{Q}\left[{}_tI^{1-\zeta}_T \mathrm{Y}(y,t)\right] = 0 & \text{in } \Omega. \end{cases} \tag{28}$$

Next, for $\psi_0 \in \mathfrak{P}$, we define the operator $\Lambda : \mathfrak{P} \longrightarrow \mathfrak{P}^*$ by

$$\Lambda\psi_0 = \mathcal{P}\left({}_0I_T^{\zeta-\eta}\Upsilon(0)\right), \tag{29}$$

where $\mathcal{P} = p_\omega^* p_\omega$ and $\Upsilon(0) = \Upsilon(y, 0)$.

Next, let us consider the following system:

$$\begin{cases} \mathfrak{Q}\left[-{}_t^H\mathrm{D}_T^{\eta,\kappa}\Phi(y,t)\right] = A^*\mathfrak{Q}[\Phi(y,t)] + C^*\mathfrak{Q}[\mathfrak{M}(t)] & \text{in } \mathfrak{S}_T, \\ \Phi(\xi, t) = 0 & \text{on } \Sigma_T, \\ \lim\limits_{t\to T^-} \mathfrak{Q}\left[{}_tI_T^{1-\zeta}\Phi(y,t)\right] = 0 & \text{in } \Omega. \end{cases} \tag{30}$$

If we choose the initial state ψ_0 of System (26) such that $\Phi(0) = \Upsilon(0)$ in the subregion ω, then one can see that System (30) stands for the adjoint of System (4). Thus, our problem of ReEnOb can be simplified solved in Equation (29), since following Equation (31) is equivalent to Equation (29).

$$\Lambda\psi_0 = \mathcal{P}\left({}_0I_T^{\zeta-\eta}\Phi(0)\right). \tag{31}$$

Theorem 2. *System* (4) *augmented by* (25) *is exactly* $\mathfrak{Z}$*-observable in* ω*, if Equation* (29) *has a unique solution* $\psi_0 \in \mathfrak{P}$*, that coincides with the state* v_0^1 *observed between functions* $\gamma_1(\cdot)$ *and* $\gamma_2(\cdot)$ *in the subregion* ω*. In addition,* $v_0^1 = p_\omega\varphi_0$.

Proof. We note that, System (4) with (25) is exactly $\mathfrak{Z}$-observable in ω, then the norm $\|\cdot\|_{\mathfrak{P}}$ can be defined on $\mathfrak{P}$ by Lemma 4. Next, we prove that, if Λ is an isomorphism (see [18]), then (29) admits a unique solution in the set $\mathfrak{P}$. For this, we have

$$\begin{aligned} \langle \Lambda\psi_0, \psi_0\rangle_{L^2(\Omega)} &= \left\langle \mathcal{P}\left({}_0I_T^{\zeta-\eta}\Upsilon(0)\right), \psi_0\right\rangle_{L^2(\Omega)} \\ &= \left\langle p_\omega^* p_\omega\left({}_0I_T^{\zeta-\eta}\Upsilon(0)\right), \psi_0\right\rangle_{L^2(\Omega)} \\ &= \left\langle {}_0I_T^{\zeta-\eta}\Upsilon(0), \psi_0\right\rangle_{L^2(\omega)} \end{aligned}$$

We note that the following propositions are important in the following proof.

Proposition 1. *Let* $0 < \eta < 1$, $0 \le \kappa \le 1$, $0 < \zeta \le 1$ *and* $t \in \mathfrak{J}$*. Since System* (30) *is adjoint of* (4)*, then from* (9) *and* (10)*, we have*

$$\mathcal{R}_\eta^*(t) = t^{\eta-1}P_\eta^*(t),$$

and

$$\mathcal{S}_{\eta,\kappa}^*(t) = {}_0I_t^{\zeta-\eta}\mathcal{R}_\eta^*(t).$$

Therefore, the solution to System (28) is given by

$$\Upsilon(t) = \int_0^{T-t} \mathcal{R}_\eta^*(T-t-s)C^*C\psi(T-s)\mathrm{d}s. \tag{32}$$

Proposition 2. *Let* $0 < \eta < 1$, $0 \le \kappa \le 1$, $0 < \zeta \le 1$ *and* $t \in \mathfrak{J}$*, we have*

$${}_0I_T^{\zeta-\eta}\Upsilon(0) = \int_0^T \mathcal{S}_{\eta,\kappa}^*(T-s)C^*C\psi(T-s)\mathrm{d}s. \tag{33}$$

Proof. In view of Fubini's theorem and Equation (32), and for any $\tau \in \mathfrak{J}$, we have

$$\begin{aligned}
{}_{\tau}I_T^{\zeta-\eta}\Upsilon(\tau) =& \frac{1}{\Gamma(\zeta-\eta)}\int_{\tau}^{T}(t-\tau)^{\zeta-\eta-1}\Upsilon(t)\mathrm{d}t \\
=& \frac{1}{\Gamma(\zeta-\eta)}\int_{\tau}^{T}(t-\tau)^{\zeta-\eta-1}\int_0^{T-t}\mathcal{R}_{\eta}^{*}(T-t-s)C^{*}C\psi(T-s)\mathrm{d}s\mathrm{d}t \\
=& \frac{1}{\Gamma(\zeta-\eta)}\int_0^{T}\left(\int_{\tau}^{T-s}(t-\tau)^{\zeta-\eta-1}\mathcal{R}_{\eta}^{*}(T-t-s)\mathrm{d}t\right)C^{*}C\psi(T-s)\mathrm{d}s
\end{aligned}$$

Let $u = T-t-s$, then $\mathrm{d}u = -\mathrm{d}t$. Now, for $t = \tau$ and $t = T-s$, we obtain $u = T-\tau-s$ and $u = 0$, respectively. Thus, we obtain

$$\begin{aligned}
{}_{\tau}I_T^{\zeta-\eta}\Upsilon(\tau) =& \frac{1}{\Gamma(\zeta-\eta)}\int_0^{T}\left(\int_0^{T-\tau-s}(T-s-\tau-u)^{\zeta-\eta-1}\mathcal{R}_{\eta}^{*}(u)\mathrm{d}u\right)C^{*}C\psi(T-s)\mathrm{d}s \\
=& \int_0^{T}\mathcal{S}_{\eta,\kappa}^{*}(T-s-\tau)C^{*}C\psi(T-s)\mathrm{d}s.
\end{aligned}$$

We now let $\tau = 0$, we obtain

$${}_{0}I_T^{\zeta-\eta}\Upsilon(0) = \int_0^{T}\mathcal{S}_{\eta,\kappa}^{*}(T-s)C^{*}C\psi(T-s)\mathrm{d}s.$$

□

Now, we continue the proof of our theorem

$$\begin{aligned}
\langle\Lambda\psi_0,\psi_0\rangle_{L^2(\Omega)} &= \left\langle {}_{0}I_T^{\zeta-\eta}\Upsilon(0),\psi_0\right\rangle_{L^2(\omega)} \\
&= \left\langle \int_0^{T}\mathcal{S}_{\eta,\kappa}^{*}(T-s)C^{*}C\psi(T-s)\mathrm{d}s,\psi_0\right\rangle \\
&= \int_0^{T}\langle C\psi(T-s), C\mathcal{S}_{\eta,\kappa}(T-s)\psi_0\rangle\mathrm{d}s \\
&= \int_0^{T}\langle C\psi(T-s), C\psi(T-s)\rangle\mathrm{d}s \\
&= \int_0^{T}\|C\psi(T-s)\|^2\mathrm{d}s \\
&= \|\psi_0\|_{\mathcal{G}}^2.
\end{aligned}$$

Thus, the operator Λ is an isomorphism. Therefore, we establish that Equation (29) has a unique solution, which corresponds to the desired initial state $v_0^1 = p_{\omega}\psi_0$. This completes the proof. □

4.2. Zone Sensors

Here we suppose the measurements of System (4) are given by an internal zone sensor defined by $(\mathcal{A}, h)$ with $\mathcal{A} \subset \Omega$ and $h \in L^2(\mathcal{A})$. The system is augmented with the OuPuFu

$$\mathfrak{M}(t) = \int_{\mathcal{A}} v(y, T-t)h(y)\mathrm{d}y. \tag{34}$$

In this case, we consider System (26), and we assume $\mathfrak{P}$ is given by Equation (24). Then, a semi-norm can be introduced by

$$\|\varphi_0\|_{\mathfrak{P}}^2 = \int_0^{T}\langle\, \psi(T-t), h\rangle_{L^2(\mathcal{A})}^2\mathrm{d}t, \tag{35}$$

and if System (26) with (25) is exactly $\mathfrak{Z}$-observable in a subregion ω of Ω, then a norm can be defined.

In this case, we can introduce the adjoint System of (26) as follows:

$$\begin{cases} \mathfrak{Q}\Big[-\,{}^{H}_{t}\mathrm{D}^{\eta,\kappa}_{T}\Upsilon(y,t)\Big] = A^{*}\mathfrak{Q}[\Upsilon(y,t)] + \langle\, \mathfrak{Q}[\psi(t)], h\rangle_{L^2(\mathcal{A})} h(y) & \text{in } \mathfrak{S}_T, \\ \Upsilon(\xi,t) = 0 & \text{on } \Sigma_T, \\ \lim\limits_{t\to T^-} \mathfrak{Q}\Big[{}_{t}I^{1-\zeta}_{T}\Upsilon(y,t)\Big] = 0 & \text{in } \Omega. \end{cases} \tag{36}$$

Thus, the operator Λ can be defined by

$$\begin{aligned} \Lambda : \mathfrak{P} &\longrightarrow \mathfrak{P}^{*} \\ \psi_0 &\longmapsto \Lambda\psi_0 = \mathcal{P}\Big({}_{0}I^{\zeta-\eta}_{T}\Upsilon(0)\Big), \end{aligned} \tag{37}$$

where $\mathcal{P} = p^{*}_{\omega}p_{\omega}$ is a projection operator. For simplicity, let us write $\Upsilon(0) = \Upsilon(y,0)$.

We introduce the following system

$$\begin{cases} \mathfrak{Q}\Big[-\,{}^{H}_{t}\mathrm{D}^{\eta,\kappa}_{T}\Phi(y,t)\Big] = A^{*}\mathfrak{Q}[\Phi(y,t)] + \langle\, \mathfrak{Q}[\mathfrak{M}(t)], h\rangle_{L^2(\mathcal{A})} p_{\mathcal{A}} h(y) & \text{in } \mathfrak{S}_T, \\ \Phi(\xi,t) = 0 & \text{on } \Sigma_T, \\ \lim\limits_{t\to T^-} \mathfrak{Q}\Big[{}_{t}I^{1-\zeta}_{T}\Phi(y,t)\Big] = 0 & \text{in } \Omega. \end{cases} \tag{38}$$

If the initial state ψ_0 of System (26) is chosen such that $\Phi(0) = \Upsilon(0)$ in the subregion ω, then one can see that System (38) is the adjoint of System (4); thus, our ReEnOb problem can be simplified and solved by the following equation

$$\Lambda\psi_0 = \mathcal{P}\Big({}_{0}I^{\zeta-\eta}_{T}\Phi(0)\Big), \tag{39}$$

Theorem 3. *If System (4) with OuPuFu (34) is exactly $\mathfrak{Z}$-observable in the subregion ω, then Equation (39) has a unique solution $\psi_0 \in \mathfrak{P}$ that corresponds with the observed initial state v^1_0 between functions $\gamma_1(\cdot)$ and $\gamma_2(\cdot)$ in the subregion ω.*

Proof. The procedures of the proof are remarkably similar to those of Theorem 2. □

4.3. Examples

Example 1. *In this subsection, we will consider the case where C is unbounded (pointwise sensors). The following time fractional diffusion system can be use to describe a chemical reaction or a heat conduction.*

Let $\Omega_1 = [0,l]$ and $\bar{\mathfrak{S}}_T = \Omega_1 \times \mathfrak{J}$, we thus consider

$$\begin{cases} {}^{H}_{0}\mathrm{D}^{\eta,\kappa}_{t} v(y,t) = \aleph_{\eta,\kappa}\frac{\partial^2}{\partial y^2}v(y,t) + f(y,t) & \text{in } \bar{\mathfrak{S}}_T, \\ v(0,t) = h_1(y), \quad v(l,t) = h_2(y) & \text{in } \mathfrak{J}, \\ \lim\limits_{t\to 0^+} {}_{0}I^{1-\zeta}_{t} v(y,t) = v_0(y) & \text{in } \Omega_1, \end{cases} \tag{40}$$

where $f(y,t)$ is the density of the sources that transmits the substance in/out the system, $A = \aleph_{\eta,\kappa}\frac{\partial^2}{\partial x^2}$ and $\aleph_{\eta,\kappa}$ represents a constant of physical dimension $[\aleph_{\eta,\kappa}] = cm^2 s^{\eta}$, which only depends on η and is independent of κ.

For simplicity, we assume $\aleph_{\eta,\kappa} = 1$, $f(y,t) = 0$, $h_1(y) = h_2(y) = 0$, *and* $l = 1$, *obtaining* $\Omega_1 = [0,1]$ *and* $\bar{\bar{\mathfrak{S}}}_T = \Omega_1 \times \mathfrak{J}$. *Hence, System* (40) *can be written as follows*

$$\begin{cases} {}_0^H\mathrm{D}_t^{\eta,\kappa} v(y,t) = \frac{\partial^2}{\partial y^2} v(y,t) & \text{in } \bar{\bar{\mathfrak{S}}}_T, \\ v(\xi,t) = 0 & \text{in } [0,T], \\ \lim_{t\to 0^+} {}_0I_t^{1-\zeta} v(y,t) = v_0(y) & \text{in } [0,1], \end{cases} \tag{41}$$

augmented with the OuPuFu

$$\mathfrak{M}(t) = Cv(y,t) = v(b,t), \tag{42}$$

where $\frac{1}{4} = b \in [0,1]$, *and System* (44) *has a mild solution* $v(y,t)$, $t \in \mathfrak{J}$ *given by*

$$\begin{aligned} v(y,t) =& 2\sum_{n=1}^{\infty} t^{\eta+\kappa(1-\eta)-1} E_{\eta,\kappa(\eta-1)-\eta}(-n^2\pi^2 t^\eta)\sin(n\pi y) \\ & \times \int_0^1 v_0(y)\sin(n\pi y)\mathrm{d}x, \end{aligned} \tag{43}$$

where $E_{\eta,\kappa}(\cdot)$ *stands for the two-parameter Mittag–Leffler function [4], and one can easily see that the operator* $\frac{\partial^2}{\partial y^2}$ *has a complete set of eigenfunctions* $\phi_n = \sin(n\pi y)$ *in the Hilbert space* $L^2(\Omega_1)$ *associated with the eigenvalues* $\lambda_n = -n^2\pi$. *Let us assume the initial state that needs to be observed in System* (44) *is given by* $v_0(y) = \sin(2\pi y)$, $\eta = 0.2$, *and* $\kappa = 0.4$. *Now, for the subregion* $\omega_1 = \left[\frac{1}{2}, \frac{2}{3}\right] \subset [0,1]$, *the following results hold.*

Proposition 3. *There exists a state for which System* (44) *with the OuPuFu* (42) *is not weakly observable in* Ω_1, *but is* $\mathfrak{z}_1$*-observable in the subregion* ω_1.

Proof. To show that System (44) with the OuPuFu (42) is not weakly observable in Ω_1, it sufficient to verify that $v_0 \in \mathrm{Ker}(\mathcal{K}_{\eta,\kappa})$. From Equation (43) and the assumptions above we can now calculate

$$\begin{aligned} \mathcal{K}_{0.2,0.4} v_0 =& 2\sum_{n=1}^{\infty} t^{-0.48} E_{0.2,-0.52}(-n^2\pi^2 t^{0.2})\sin\left(\frac{n\pi}{4}\right) \\ & \times \int_0^1 \sin(2\pi y)\sin(n\pi y)\mathrm{d}y \\ =& 0. \end{aligned}$$

Hence, $v_0 \in \mathrm{Ker}(\mathcal{K}_{\eta,\kappa})$. As a result, System (44) and (42) is not weakly observable in Ω_1,

$$\begin{aligned}\mathcal{K}_{0.2,0.4}p^*_{\omega_1}p_{\omega_1}v_0 =&2\sum_{n=1}^{\infty} t^{-0.48}E_{0.2,-0.52}(-n^2\pi^2t^{0.2})\sin(0.25n\pi)\\ &\times\int_0^1 p^*_{\omega_1}p_{\omega_1}\sin(2\pi y)\sin(n\pi y)dy\\ =&2\sum_{n=1}^{\infty} t^{-0.48}E_{0.2,-0.52}(-n^2\pi^2t^{0.2})\sin\left(\frac{n\pi}{4}\right)\\ &\times\int_{\frac{1}{2}}^{\frac{2}{3}}\sin(2\pi y)\sin(n\pi y)dy\\ =&2t^{-0.48}E_{0.2,-0.52}(-\pi^2t^{0.2})\sin\left(\frac{\pi}{4}\right)\\ &\times\int_{\frac{1}{2}}^{\frac{2}{3}}\sin(2\pi y)\sin(\pi y)dy\\ =&\frac{(3\sqrt{3}-8)t^{-0.48}}{6\sqrt{2}\pi}E_{0.2,-0.52}(-\pi^2t^{0.2})\\ \neq&0.\end{aligned}$$

While on the other hand, this leads us to observe that the initial state v_0 is weakly observable in the subregion ω_1. In addition, for all $y \in \omega_1$, we have

$$\tilde{\gamma_1} = |v^0_{|\omega_1}(y)| - \frac{2}{3} < v^0_{|\omega_1}$$

and

$$\tilde{\gamma_2} = |v^0_{|\omega_1}(y)| + \frac{2}{3} > v^0_{|\omega_1}.$$

Thus, $p_{\omega_1}v_0 \in \mathfrak{Z}_1$ and (44) together with (42) is $\mathfrak{Z}_1$-observable in ω_1. This completes the proof. □

Let the space $\mathfrak{P}_1$ be given by

$$\mathfrak{P}_1 = \{g \in L^2(\Omega_1)|g = 0 \text{ in } L^2(\Omega_1)\backslash\mathfrak{Z}_1\}.$$

From Lemma 4, we have

$$\psi_0 \longmapsto \|\psi_0\|^2_{\mathfrak{P}_1} = \int_0^T \|C\psi(T-t)\|^2 dt.$$

which defines a norm on $\mathfrak{P}_1$, and thus we can introduce the adjoint System of (44) *as follows:*

$$\begin{cases}\mathfrak{Q}\left[-{}^H_tD^{\eta,\kappa}_T\Phi(y,t)\right] = A^*\mathfrak{Q}[\Phi(y,t)] + \mathfrak{M}(b,T-t) & \text{in } \mathfrak{S}_T,\\ \Phi(\xi,t) = 0 & \text{on } \partial\Omega_1\times[0,T],\\ \lim\limits_{t\to T^-}\mathfrak{Q}\left[{}_tI^{1-\zeta}_T\Phi(y,t)\right] = 0 & \text{in } \Omega_1,\end{cases}$$

then, in view of Theorem 2, we can now conclude that $\Lambda\psi_0 = \mathcal{P}\left({}_0I^{\zeta-\eta}_T\Phi(0)\right)$ *has a unique solution in $\mathfrak{P}_1$, and the initial state v_0 is observed between functions $\tilde{\gamma_1}$ and $\tilde{\gamma_2}$ in the subregion ω_1.*

Example 2. *In this example, we consider C as bounded (zone sensors). Considering the following diffusion system*

$$\begin{cases} {}^{H}_{0}\mathrm{D}^{\eta,\kappa}_{t} \nu(y,t) = \frac{\partial^2}{\partial y^2}\nu(y,t) & \text{in } [0,1]\times[0,T], \\ \nu(\xi,t) = 0 & \text{in } [0,T], \\ \lim\limits_{t\to 0^+} {}_0 I_t^{1-\zeta}\nu(y,t) = \nu_0(y) & \text{is unknown in } [0,1], \end{cases} \tag{44}$$

augmented with the OuPuFu

$$\mathfrak{M}(t) = \int_0^1 \nu(y, T-t)h(y)\mathrm{d}y = \nu(b,t), \tag{45}$$

where $A = \frac{\partial^2}{\partial y^2}$ *with eigenvalues* $\lambda_n = -n^2\pi^2$ *and the corresponding eigenfunctions* $\phi_n(y) = \sin(n\pi y)$. *Let us fix* $\frac{1}{3} = b \in [0,1] = \Omega_2$ *and take any internal subregion* $\omega_2 = [\frac{1}{6}, \frac{1}{2}]$ *of the whole domain. We note that System (44) has a unique mild solution* $\nu(y,t)$ *in* $L^2([0,T];\mathcal{D}(A)) \cap C([0,1]\times[0,T])$.

Proposition 4. *There exists a state for which System (44) with the OuPuFu (45) is not weakly observable in* Ω_2*, but is* $\mathfrak{Z}_2$*-observable in the subregion* ω_2.

Proof. To show that System (44) with the OuPuFu (45) is not weakly observable in Ω_2, it is sufficient to verify that $\nu_0 \in \mathrm{Ker}(\mathcal{K}_{\eta,\kappa})$. Thus, we can now derive

$$C\mathcal{S}_{\eta,\kappa}(t)\nu_0 = \mathcal{K}_{\eta,\kappa}(t)\nu_0 = 2\sum_{n=1}^{\infty} t^{\eta+\kappa(1-\eta)-1}E_{\eta,\kappa(\eta-1)-\eta}(-n^2\pi^2 t^\eta)\langle \nu_0, \phi_n\rangle \phi_n\left(\frac{1}{3}\right),$$

where $E_{\eta,\kappa}(\cdot)$ stands for the two-parameter Mittag–Leffler function. Now, for all $y \in [0,1]$, $|\phi_n| \le \sqrt{2}$, the Mittag-Leffler function $E_{\eta,\kappa(\eta-1)-\eta}(-n^2\pi^2 t^\eta)$ is continuous with $|E_{\eta,\kappa(\eta-1)-\eta}(-n^2\pi^2t^\eta)| \le \frac{K}{1+|-n^2\pi^2|t^\eta}$ for $t \ge 0$ with $K > 0$. Hence,

$$|C\mathcal{S}_{\eta,\kappa}(t)\nu_0| = 2\sum_{n=1}^{\infty} \frac{K\sqrt{2}\|\nu_0\| t^{\eta+\kappa(1-\eta)-1}}{1+|-n^2\pi^2|t^\eta}$$

and

$$\begin{aligned} \mathcal{K}^*_{\eta,\kappa}\mathfrak{M}(t) &= 2\sum_{n=1}^{\infty}\phi_n(y)\int_0^{\frac{1}{3}} \sigma^{\eta+\kappa(1-\eta)-1}E_{\eta,\kappa(\eta-1)-\eta}(-n^2\pi^2\sigma^\eta)\langle C^*\mathfrak{M}(\sigma), \phi_n\rangle \mathrm{d}\sigma \\ &= \mathcal{S}^*_{\eta,\kappa}(t)C^*\mathfrak{M}(t). \end{aligned}$$

Thus, the observation operator C is admissible. From the above, we can see that $Ker\mathcal{K}_{\eta,\kappa}(t) \neq 0$, which means System (44) is not observable in the whole domain $[0,1]$. Next, we investigate the observability of the addressed system in the internal subregion ω_2.

$$\mathcal{K}_{\eta,\kappa}p^*_\omega p_\omega \nu_0 = 2\sum_{n=1}^{\infty}\phi_n(y)t^{\eta+\kappa(1-\eta)-1}E_{\eta,\kappa(\eta-1)-\eta}(-n^2\pi^2t^\eta)\langle p^*_\omega p_\omega \nu_0, \phi_n\rangle_{L^2(\omega_2)} \neq 0$$

Thus, the initial state ν_0 is weakly observable in the subregion ω_2. In addition, for all $y \in \omega_2$, we have

$$\bar{\bar{\gamma}}_1 = |\nu^0_{|\omega_2}(y)| - \frac{2}{3} < \nu^0_{|\omega_2}$$

and

$$\bar{\bar{\gamma}}_2 = |\nu^0_{|\omega_2}(y)| + \frac{2}{3} > \nu^0_{|\omega_2}.$$

Thus, $p_{\omega_2} v_0 \in \mathfrak{Z}_2$ and (44) together with (42) is $\mathfrak{Z}_2$-observable in ω_2. This completes the proof. □

Let the space $\mathfrak{P}_2$ *be given by*

$$\mathfrak{P}_2 = \{g \in L^2(\Omega_2) | g = 0 \text{ in } L^2(\Omega_2) \backslash \mathfrak{Z}_2\}.$$

From Lemma 4, we have

$$\psi_0 \longmapsto \|\psi_0\|^2_{\mathfrak{P}_2} = \int_0^T \|C\psi(T-t)\|^2 dt,$$

which defines a norm on $\mathfrak{P}_2$*, and we can introduce the adjoint system of* (44) *as follows:*

$$\begin{cases} \mathfrak{Q}\Big[-{}^H_t D^{\eta,\kappa}_T \Phi(y,t)\Big] = A^* \mathfrak{Q}\big[\Phi(y,t)\big] + \langle C^* \mathfrak{M}(t), h\rangle_{L^2(\omega_2)} h(y) & \text{in } \Omega_2 \times [0,T], \\ \Phi(\xi,t) = 0 & \text{on } \partial\Omega_2 \times [0,T], \\ \lim\limits_{t \to T^-} \mathfrak{Q}\Big[{}_t I^{1-\zeta}_T \Phi(y,t)\Big] = 0 & \text{in } \Omega_2, \end{cases}$$

Then, in view of Theorem 3, we can now conclude that $\Lambda\psi_0 = \mathcal{P}\Big({}_0 I^{\zeta-\eta}_T \Phi(0)\Big)$ *has a unique solution in* $\mathfrak{P}_2$*, and the initial state* v_0 *can be observed between functions* $\bar{\bar{\gamma}}_1$ *and* $\bar{\bar{\gamma}}_2$ *in the subregion* ω_2.

5. Conclusions

In this manuscript we studied the concept of regional enlarged observability (ReEnOb) for fractional differential equations (FDEs) with Hilfer derivatives. We developed an approach based on the Hilbert uniqueness method (HUM). Based on this approach and with the knowledge of the initial information of the system and some given measurements, we reconstructed the initial state v_0^1 on an internal subregion ω from the whole domain Ω. Our findings show that it is possible to obtain the desired state between two profiles in some selective internal subregions. Finally, we gave two illustrative examples to support our theoretical results. It is of great interest for future works to investigate the ReOb of sub-diffusion systems with the Hilfer derivative in cases where the reconstructed initial state is in a subregion on the boundary of the whole domain. Furthermore, our paper motivates the study of the ReEnOb of sub-diffusion systems via ψ-Hilfer or (k,ψ)-Hilfer fractional derivatives.

Author Contributions: All authors contributed equally in this paper. All authors read and approved the final manuscript.

Funding: This work was supported by the National Natural Science Foundation of China (grant numbers: 11871064; 11571300).

Data Availability Statement: No data were used to support this study.

Acknowledgments: The authors are deeply grateful to the two anonymous referees for their great comments and suggestions that improved the quality of this manuscript. This work was supported by the National Natural Science Foundation of China [grant numbers 11871064, 11571300].

Conflicts of Interest: The authors declare no conflict of interest.

References

1. Petráš, I. *Handbook of Fractional Calculus with Applications*; Walter de Gruyter GmbH & Co. KG: Berlin, Germany, 2019.
2. Yang, X.-J. *General Fractional Derivatives: Theory, Methods and Applications*; CRC Press/Taylor and Francis Group: New York, NY, USA, 2019.
3. Baleanu, D.; Lopes, A.M. *Handbook of Fractional Calculus with Applications in Engineering, Life and Social Sciences, Part B*; Walter de Gruyter GmbH & Co. KG: Berlin/Boston, Germany, 2019.
4. Rosa, S.; Torres, D.F. Fractional Modelling and Optimal Control of COVID-19 Transmission in Portugal. *Axioms* **2022**, *11*, 170. [CrossRef]

5. Elbukhari, A.B.; Fan, Z.; Li, G. Existence of Mild Solutions for Nonlocal Evolution Equations with the Hilfer Derivatives. *J. Funct. Spaces* **2023**, *2023*. [CrossRef]
6. Hilfer, R. *Applications of Fractional Calculus in Physics*; World Scientific Pub. Co.: Singapore, 2000.
7. Podlubny, I. *Fractional Differential Equations, Mathematics in Science and Engineering*; Academic Press: New York, NY, USA, 1999.
8. Kilbas, A.A.; Srivastava, H.M.; Trujillo, J.J. Theory and Applications of Fractional Differential Equations. In *North-Holland Mathematics Studies*; van Mill, J., Ed.; Elsevier: Amsterdam, The Netherland, 2006.
9. Curtain, R.F.; Zwart, H. *An Introduction to Infinite-Dimensional Linear Systems Theory*; Springer Science and Business Media: New York, NY, USA, 2012.
10. Amouroux, M.; El Jai, A.; Zerrik, E. Regional observability of distributed systems. *Int. J. Syst. Sci.* **1994**, *25*, 301–313. [CrossRef]
11. El Jai, A.; Simon, M.C.; Zerrik, E. Regional observability and sensor structures. *Sens. Actuators Phys.* **1993**, *39*, 95–102. [CrossRef]
12. Al-Saphory, R.A.; Al-Jawari, N.J.; Al-Janabi, A.N. Regional gradient strategic sensors characterizations. *arXiv* **2005**, arXiv:2005.07497v1.
13. Courant, R.; Hilbert, D. *Methods of Mathematical Physics: Partial Differential Equations*; J. Wily & Sons Inc.: Singapore, 2008.
14. Curtain, R.F. On semigroup formulations of unbounded observations and control action for distributed systems. In *Mathematical Theory of Networks and Systems: Proceedings of the MTNS-83 International Symposium, Beer Sheva, Israel, 20–24 June 1983*; Springer: Berlin/Heidelberg, Germany, 1984.
15. Zerrik, E.H.; Bourray, H.; Boutoulout, A. Regional boundary observability: A numerical approach. *Int. J. Appl. Math. Comput. Sci.* **2002**, *12*, 143–151.
16. Chen, J.H. Infinite-time exact observability of Volterra systems in Hilbert space. *Syst. Control Lett.* **2019**, *126*, 28–32. [CrossRef]
17. Chen, J.H.; Yi, N.Y. Infinite-time Admissibility and Exact Observability of Volterra Systems. *SIAM J. Control Optim.* **2021**, *59*, 1275–1292. [CrossRef]
18. Zouiten, H.; Boutoulout, A.; El Alaoui, F.Z. On the regional enlarged observability for linear parabolic Systems. *J. Math. Syst. Sci.* **2017**, *7*, 79–87.
19. Zguaid, K.; El Alaoui, F.Z. Regional boundary observability for linear time-fractional systems. *Partial Differ. Equations Appl. Math.* **2022**, *6*, 100432. [CrossRef]
20. Zguaid, K.; El Alaoui, F.Z.; Boutoulout, A. Regional observability for linear time fractional systems. *Math. Comput. Simul.* **2021**, *185*, 77–87. [CrossRef]
21. Zguaid, K.; El Alaoui, F.Z.; Torres, D.F.M. Regional gradient observability for fractional differential equations with Caputo time-fractional derivatives. *Int. J. Dynam. Control* **2023**. [CrossRef]
22. Ge, F.; Chen, Y.; Kou, C. On the regional gradient observability of time fractional diffusion processes. *Automatica* **2016**, *74*, 1–9. [CrossRef]
23. Cai, R.; Ge, F.; Chen, Y.; Kou, C. Regional observability for Hadamard-Caputo time fractional distributed parameter systems. *Appl. Math. Comput.* **2019**, *360*, 190–202. [CrossRef]
24. Zguaid, K.; El Alaoui, F.Z. Regional boundary observability for Riemann-Liouville linear fractional evolution systems. *Math Comput. Simul.* **2022**, *199*, 272–286. [CrossRef]
25. Zouiten, H.; Boutoulout, A.; Torres, D.F. Regional Enlarged Observability of Fractional Differential Equations with Riemann-Liouville Time Derivatives. *Axioms* **2018**, *7*, 92. [CrossRef]
26. Zouiten, H.; Boutoulout, A.; Torres, D.F. Regional enlarged observability of Caputo fractional differential equations. *Discret. Contin. Dynam. Syst.-S* **2020**, *13*, 1017–1029. [CrossRef]
27. Lions, J.L. Sur la Controlabilite Exacte Elargie. In *Partial Differential Equations and the Calculus of Variations. Progress in Nonlinear Differential Equations and their Applications*; Colombini, F., Marino, A., Modica, L., Spagnolo, S., Eds.; Birkhauser: Boston, MA, USA, 1989, pp. 703–727.
28. Kamochi, R. A new representation formula for the Hilfer fractional derivative and its application. *J. Comput. Appl. Math.* **2016**, *308*, 39–45. [CrossRef]
29. Gu, H.; Trujillo, J.J. Existence of mild solution for evolution equation with Hilfer fractional derivative. *Appl. Math. Comput.* **2015**, *257*, 344–354. [CrossRef]
30. Abdeljawad, T.; Atangana, A.; Gómez-Aguilar, J.F.; Jarad, F. On a more general fractional integration by parts formulae and applications. *Stat. Mech. Appl.* **2019**, *536*, 122494. [CrossRef]
31. Dolecki, S.; Russell, D.L. A general theory of observation and control. *SIAM J. Control Optim.* **1977**, *15*, 185–220. [CrossRef]
32. Pritchard, A.J.; Wirth, A. Unbound control and observation systems and their duality. *SIAM J. Control Optim.* **1978**, *16*, 535–545. [CrossRef]
33. Ge, F.; Chen, Y.; Kou, C. *Regional Analysis of Time Fractional Diffusion Processes*; Springer International Publishing: Berlin, Germany, 2018.

Disclaimer/Publisher's Note: The statements, opinions and data contained in all publications are solely those of the individual author(s) and contributor(s) and not of MDPI and/or the editor(s). MDPI and/or the editor(s) disclaim responsibility for any injury to people or property resulting from any ideas, methods, instructions or products referred to in the content.

axioms

MDPI

Article

The Investigation of Dynamical Behavior of Benjamin–Bona–Mahony–Burger Equation with Different Differential Operators Using Two Analytical Approaches

Xiaoming Wang [1], Rimsha Ansar [2], Muhammad Abbas [2,*], Farah Aini Abdullah [3] and Khadijah M. Abualnaja [4]

[1] School of Mathematics & Computer Science, Shangrao Normal University, Shangrao 334001, China
[2] Department of Mathematics, University of Sargodha, Sargodha 40100, Pakistan
[3] School of Mathematical Sciences, Universiti Sains Malaysia, Penang 11800, Malaysia
[4] Department of Mathematics and Statistics, College of Science, Taif University, P.O. Box 11099, Taif 21944, Saudi Arabia
* Correspondence: muhammad.abbas@uos.edu.pk

Abstract: The dynamic behavior variation of the Benjamin–Bona–Mahony–Burger (BBM-Burger) equation has been investigated in this paper. The modified auxiliary equation method (MAEM) and Ricatti–Bernoulli (RB) sub-ODE method, two of the most reliable and useful analytical approaches, are used to construct soliton solutions for the proposed model. We demonstrate some of the extracted solutions using definitions of the β-derivative, conformable derivative (CD), and M-truncated derivatives (M-TD) to understand their dynamic behavior. The hyperbolic and trigonometric functions are used to derive the analytical solutions for the given model. As a consequence, dark, bell-shaped, anti-bell, M-shaped, W-shaped, kink soliton, and solitary wave soliton solutions are obtained. We observe the fractional parameter impact of the derivatives on physical phenomena. The BBM-Burger equation is functional in describing the propagation of long unidirectional waves in many nonlinear diffusive systems. The 2D and 3D graphs have been presented to confirm the behavior of analytical wave solutions.

Keywords: BBM-Burger equation; modified auxiliary equation method (MAEM); Ricatti–Bernoulli (RB) sub-ODE method; β-derivative; M-truncated derivative (M-TD); conformable derivative (CD); soliton solutions

MSC: 39A12; 39B62; 33B10; 26A48; 26A51

Citation: Wang, X.; Ansar, R.; Abbas, M.; Abdullah, F.A.; Abualnaja, K.M. The Investigation of Dynamical Behavior of Benjamin–Bona–Mahony–Burger Equation with Different Differential Operators Using Two Analytical Approaches. *Axioms* **2023**, *12*, 599. https://doi.org/10.3390/axioms12060599

Academic Editors: Hatıra Günerhan, Francisco Martínez González and Mohammed K. A. Kaabar

Received: 14 May 2023
Revised: 11 June 2023
Accepted: 14 June 2023
Published: 16 June 2023

Copyright: © 2023 by the authors. Licensee MDPI, Basel, Switzerland. This article is an open access article distributed under the terms and conditions of the Creative Commons Attribution (CC BY) license (https://creativecommons.org/licenses/by/4.0/).

1. Introduction

Nonlinear partial differential equations (NLPDEs) are frequently used in science and engineering to model a variety of nonlinear problems that can occur in real-life applications [1]. These equations, for instance, can be applied to the modeling of fluid dynamical issues, wave propagation in corrugated media, the study of earthquakes and seismic waves, and the modeling of optical fibers, among other things. The field of fluid dynamics is still important even if it is an older one that received a lot of attention. As an extension of differential equations (DEs) [2] of integer order, there are fractional order differential equations. Models of NLPDEs from physics and mathematics serve as essentials in theoretical sciences. Numerous practical fields, including meteorology, oceanography, and the aerospace industry, depend on a grasp of these NLPDEs.

Fractional differential equations (FDEs) [3] are becoming more and more prevalent today in a variety of disciplines, including dynamic systems and mathematics. Leibniz and L'Hôpital introduced the first idea for FDEs in 1695. In mathematical models incorporating FDEs, the nonlocal behavior of the fractional order derivatives provides the memory feature. Several researchers have been attracted to the flexibility of fractional theory and the numerous interesting features of fractional calculus (FC) [4–9]. New definitions of fractional derivatives were introduced by Caputo–Hadamard [10], Katugampola [11], Weyl [12], Riemann–Liouville [13], and Erdélyi–Kober [14], which enabled fractional calculus to deal with challenging natural phenomena. Throughout the past few decades, Caputo derivative [15] has been one of the most frequently employed fractional derivatives (FDs) in numerous research.

The mathematical model for small-amplitude long wave propagation in nonlinear dispersive media is described by the Benjamin–Bona–Mahony–Burger (BBM-Burger) equation [16]. The BBM equation has been proven to be preferable to the Korteweg–De Vries (KdV) [17] equation. The wave-breaking models are essential to the BBM-Burger equation and the KdV equation. The KdV equation was driven by water waves, and it was utilized in many other physical systems as a model for long waves. Solitary wave solutions of the BBM-Burger equation [18] reflect the dynamics of waves in the medium and are essential to many fields such as physics and dispersive systems [19]. In this study, the BBM-Burger equation is considered for analytical solutions in the sense of β-derivative, CD, and M-TD. In β-derivative, the proposed model has the following form

$$D^{\sigma}_{\beta,t}w - D^{\sigma}_{\beta,t}w_{zz} + w_z + \left(\frac{w^2}{2}\right)_z = 0, \tag{1}$$

where $D^{\sigma}_{\beta,t}$ is β-derivative and σ is fractional parameter.

In M-TD, the proposed model has the following form

$$D^{\sigma,\beta}_{j,t}w - D^{\sigma,\beta}_{j,t}w_{zz} + w_z + \left(\frac{w^2}{2}\right)_z = 0, \tag{2}$$

where $D^{\sigma,\beta}_{j,t}$ is M-TD and σ and β are fractional parameters.

In CD, the proposed model has the following form

$$D^{\sigma}_{c,t}w - D^{\sigma}_{c,t}w_{zz} + w_z + \left(\frac{w^2}{2}\right)_z = 0, \tag{3}$$

where $D^{\sigma}_{c,t}$ is CD and σ is fractional parameter.

The following is the BBM-Burger equation when $\beta = 0$ and $\sigma = 1$ are used.

$$w_t - w_{zzt} + w_z + \left(\frac{w^2}{2}\right)_z = 0. \tag{4}$$

Atangana was the one who first introduced the fractional "β-derivative" [20,21]. The recently introduced derivatives, which are used to depict various medical situations, meet a number of requirements that were previously thought to be limits for the fractional derivatives. Basic and satisfying most of the criteria for the classical integral derivative, the conformable fractional derivative definition includes linearity, Rolle's theorem, mean value theorem [22], product rule, quotient rule, power rule, and chain rule. The M-TD [23,24], which uses a Mittag–Leffler function with one parameter that satisfies several properties of integer-order calculus, was introduced in 2017 by Sousa and Oliveira. M-TD also satisfies the fundamental differential calculus mathematical principles, which stimulates additional research utilizing these newly formed notions. On conformable and M-TD models in the field of ocean engineering, there are some recent studies in the literature. The goal of these investigations is to find soliton solutions for the models with local derivatives. A novel solution for various FDEs is provided by the conformable fractional derivative, which aims to expand the ordinary derivative while satisfying some natural properties.

Numerous methods, including the extended $(\frac{G'}{G^2})$ expansion method [25], the multiple exp-function method [26], the M-lump solution [27], Sardar-subequation technique [28], the Jacobi elliptic function method (JEFM) [29], Painleve analysis, and many others, can be used to find the solitary wave solutions of NLPDEs. However, in this work, the MAEM and RB sub-ODE method [30] have been utilized for finding efficient and effective traveling wave solutions. The RB sub-ODE technique is originally created to produce precise traveling wave solutions, solitary wave solutions, and peaked wave solutions for NLPDEs. Backlund transformation is applied to the RB equation [31]. NLPDE [32,33] may be converted into a set of algebraic equations using the RB equation and a traveling wave transformation.

An approach for creating precise differential equation solutions is the MAEM [34]. The auxiliary equation approach has been expanded in this way. It offers a simple method for handling the solutions of nonlinear evolution equations. This effective method has been used to achieve findings that are pleasing and aid in the investigation of answers to numerous issues that are appearing in applied mathematics and physics. Although there are many different types of traveling wave solutions that may be built using exact solution techniques, approximation solution approaches are also useful when studying evolution equations. This study was inspired by recent developments in fractional nonlinear evolution equations' traveling wave solutions. Recently, it has been discovered that a variety of exact solution techniques are useful in creating potential wave behaviors that correspond to the physical system defined by a specific evolution equation. Reading the published research papers [21,24,35–38] also inspired the authors. In this paper, we use two effective analytical approaches to derive the precise soliton solutions of the BBM-Burger equation while taking into account three natural extensions of the classical derivative, namely the *beta*-derivative, M-TD, and CD. Additionally, using the Wolfram Mathematica 12 software, we provide several 2D and 3D graphical representations of the analytical soliton solutions of the BBM-Burger equation and investigate the impact of the fractional parameters employed in *beta*-derivative, M-TD, and CD.

This paper is organized as follows: Basic definitions and their properties are explained in Section 2. Section 3 represents the mathematical interpretation of the BBM-Burger equation. Sections 4 and 5 conduct the algorithmic steps of the RB-sub ODE method and MAEM and apply them to the proposed model. In addition to computing, graphs are used to show how the result can be physically explained in Section 6. In Section 7, there are some concluding remarks to wrap up the work.

2. Preliminaries

The definitions of derivatives along with their fundamental properties are discussed in this section.

2.1. *β*-Derivative and Its Properties

Definition 1. *The β-derivative is another kind of conformable derivative that can be defined, as [20]*

$$D^{\sigma}_{\beta,t}w(t) = \lim_{\varepsilon\to 0}\frac{w(t+\varepsilon(t+\frac{1}{\Gamma(\sigma)})^{1-\sigma}) - w(t)}{\varepsilon},\quad 0<\sigma\leq 1.$$

The β-derivative has the following properties.

- The β-derivative is a linear operator; $D^{\sigma}_{\beta,t}(cd(z)+rq(z)) = c\,D^{\sigma}_{\beta,t}d(z) + rD^{\sigma}_{\beta,t}q(z)$, $\forall c, r \in \Re$.
- It satisfies the product rule; $D^{\sigma}_{\beta,t}(d(z)*q(z)) = q(z)D^{\sigma}_{\beta,t}d(z) + d(z)D^{\sigma}_{\beta,t}q(z)$.
- It satisfies the quotient rule; $D^{\sigma}_{\beta,t}\left\{\frac{d(z)}{q(z)}\right\} = \frac{q(z)D^{\sigma}_{\beta,t}d(z)-d(z)D^{\sigma}_{\beta,t}q(z)}{q^2(z)}$.
- The β-derivative of a constant is zero; $D^{\sigma}_{\beta,t}(c) = 0$, for any constant c.

2.2. M-Truncated Derivative and Its Properties

This section defines an M-TD and presents several results that are surprisingly similar to those of classical calculus. Sousa et al. [39] recently presented the M-TD, which is a natural extension of the ordinary derivative. This derivative does not have the shortcomings of the preceding ones. The M-TD is also known as a conformable fractional derivative [23,40].

The M-TD can readily satisfy some features of classical calculus, including the quotient rule, product rule, linearity, chain rule, and function composition rule. The M-TD, which makes use of a one-parameter Mittag–Leffler function, also satisfies the requirements of integer-order calculus.

Definition 2. *The M-TD for the function $w : [0,\infty) \to R$ of order $\sigma \in (0,1)$ is defined, as [35]*

$$D^{\sigma,\beta}_{j,t} w(t) = \frac{\lim_{\varepsilon\to 0} w(tE^{\beta}_{j}(\varepsilon t^{-\sigma})) - w(t),}{\varepsilon}$$

for $t > 0$. Where $E^{\beta}_{j}(.), \beta > 0$ is a truncated Mittag–Leffler function of one parameter defined, as:

$$E^{\beta}_{j}(t) = \sum_{k=0}^{j} \frac{t^k}{\Gamma(\beta k+1)}.$$

The M-TD has the following properties.

- The M-TD is a linear operator; $D^{\sigma,\beta}_{j,z}(cd(z) + rq(z)) = cD^{\sigma,\beta}_{j,z} d(z) + rD^{\sigma,\beta}_{j,z} q(z)$, $\forall\, c, r \in \Re$.
- It satisfies the product rule; $D^{\sigma,\beta}_{j,z}(d(z) * q(z)) = q(z)D^{\sigma,\beta}_{j,z} d(z) + d(z)D^{\sigma,\beta}_{j,z} q(z)$.
- It satisfies the quotient rule; $D^{\sigma,\beta}_{j,z}\left\{\frac{d(z)}{q(z)}\right\} = \frac{q(z)D^{\sigma,\beta}_{j,z} d(z) - d(z)D^{\sigma,\beta}_{j,z} q(z)}{q^2(z)}$.
- The M-TD for a differentiable function $q(z)$ is defined, as:

$$D^{\sigma,\beta}_{j,z} q(z) = \frac{z^{1-\sigma}}{\Gamma(\beta+1)} \frac{dq}{dz}.$$

2.3. *Conformable Derivative*

Definition 3. *The conformable derivative of order σ for a function $w : [0,\infty) \to \Re$ is written as:*

$$D^{\sigma}_{c,t} w(t) = \lim_{\varepsilon\to 0} \frac{w(t + \varepsilon(t)^{1-\sigma}) - w(t)}{\varepsilon}, \quad \forall t > 0.$$

If w has σ-differentiability in any interval $(0, a)$ with $a > 0$, then

$$D^{\sigma}_{c}(w(0)) = \lim_{t\to 0^+} D^{\sigma}_{c}(w(t)),$$

whenever the limit of the right-hand side exists.

Further, properties and theorems related to CD are discussed in [37].

3. Mathematical Interpretation of the Proposed Model

To obtain soliton solutions for Equation (4), the following transformations have been employed.

$$W(z,t) = w(\eta). \tag{5}$$

Three definitions are provided for the traveling wave parameter η.
For β-derivative, η has the following form

$$\eta = Kz + \frac{R}{\sigma}\left(t + \frac{1}{\Gamma(\sigma)}\right)^{\sigma}. \tag{6}$$

For M-TD, η has the following form

$$\eta = Kz + \frac{R\Gamma(\beta+1)}{\sigma} t^{\sigma}. \tag{7}$$

For CD, η has the following form

$$\eta = Kz + \frac{R}{\sigma}t^{\sigma}, \tag{8}$$

where K, R are arbitrary constants with $K, R \neq 0$. Utilizing the transformation Equation (5) together with Equations (6)–(8), the obtained ordinary differential equation is

$$(K + R)w' - K^2Rw''' + ww'K = 0.$$

This, when integrated with the integration constant set to zero, yields

$$(K + R)w - K^2Rw'' + \frac{w^2}{2}K = 0, \tag{9}$$

where $w' = \frac{dw}{d\eta}$.

4. Application of RB Sub-ODE Method

According to RB sub-ODE method [30], the solution for Equation (9) is

$$w' = H_1w^{2-L} + F_1w + G_1w^L, \tag{10}$$

where the constants H_1, F_1, G_1, and L will be found later.

Substituting Equation (10) into Equation (9), we have

$$\begin{aligned} -3K^2RF_1H_1w(\eta)^2 + K^2LRF_1H_1w(\eta)^2 - 2K^2RH_1^2w(\eta)^{3-L} + K^2LRH_1^2w(\eta)^{3-L} \\ -K^2RF_1G_1w(\eta)^{2L} - K^2LRF_1G_1w(\eta)^{2L} + Kw(\eta)^{1+L} + Rw(\eta)^{1+L} - K^2RF_1^2w(\eta)^{1+L} \\ -2K^2RG_1H_1w(\eta)^{1+L} + \frac{1}{2}Kw(\eta)^{2+L} - K^2LRG_1^2w(\eta)^{-1+3L} = 0. \end{aligned} \tag{11}$$

Setting $L = 0$ in the above equation, we obtain

$$\begin{aligned} -K^2RF_1G_1 + Kw(\eta) + Rw(\eta) - K^2RF_1^2w(\eta) - 2K^2RG_1H_1w(\eta) + \frac{1}{2}Kw(\eta)^2 \\ -3K^2RF_1H_1w(\eta)^2 - 2K^2RH_1^2w(\eta)^3. \end{aligned} \tag{12}$$

Adjusting each coefficient of $w^i (i = 0, 1, 2, 3)$ to zero, we have

$$\begin{aligned} -K^2RF_1G_1 &= 0, \\ K + R - K^2RF_1^2 - 2K^2RG_1H_1 &= 0, \\ \frac{K}{2} - 3K^2RF_1H_1 &= 0, \\ -2K^2RH_1^2 &= 0. \end{aligned} \tag{13}$$

Equation (13) produces the following results when it is solved.

$$H_1 = \mp\frac{1}{6\sqrt{R}\sqrt{K+R}}, F_1 = \mp\frac{\sqrt{K+R}}{K\sqrt{R}}, G_1 = 0.$$

Case 1.

when $L \neq 1, F_1 \neq 0$ and $G_1 = 0$, the algebraic solution can be obtained.

$$w(\eta) = \left(-\frac{H_1}{F_1} + Pe^{F_1(L-1)\eta}\right)^{\frac{1}{L-1}}, \tag{14}$$

$$W_{1,1}(z,t) = \frac{1}{\left(e^{\frac{3\sqrt{K+R}\eta}{K\sqrt{R}}} P - \frac{K}{6(K+R)}\right)^{1/3}}.$$

Case 2.
when $L \neq 1, H_1 \neq 0$ and $F_1{}^2 - 4H_1G_1 < 0$, the solitary periodic solutions can be obtained.

$$w(\eta) = \left(-\frac{F_1}{2H_1} + \frac{\sqrt{4H_1G_1 - (F_1)^2}}{2H_1}\tan(\frac{(1-L)\sqrt{4H_1G_1 - (F_1)^2}}{2}(\eta + P))\right)^{\frac{1}{1-L}}, \tag{15}$$

$$W_{1,2}(z,t) = \left(-\frac{3(K+R)}{K} - 3\sqrt{R}\sqrt{K+R}\sqrt{-\frac{K+R}{K^2R}}\tan\left(\frac{3}{2}\sqrt{-\frac{K+R}{K^2R}}(P+\eta)\right)\right)^{1/3}.$$

and

$$w(\eta) = \left(-\frac{F_1}{2H_1} - \frac{\sqrt{4H_1G_1 - (F_1)^2}}{2H_1}\cot(\frac{(1-L)\sqrt{4H_1G_1 - (F_1)^2}}{2}(\eta + P))\right)^{\frac{1}{1-L}}, \tag{16}$$

$$W_{1,3}(z,t) = \left(-\frac{3(K+R)}{K} - 3\sqrt{R}\sqrt{K+R}\sqrt{-\frac{K+R}{K^2R}}\cot\left(\frac{3}{2}\sqrt{-\frac{K+R}{K^2R}}(P+\eta)\right)\right)^{1/3}.$$

Case 3.
when $L \neq 1, H_1 \neq 0$ and $F_1{}^2 - 4H_1G_1 > 0$, these dark optical and solitary optical soliton solutions are found, respectively.

$$w(\eta) = \left(-\frac{F_1}{2H_1} - \frac{\sqrt{-4H_1G_1 + (F_1)^2}}{2H_1}\coth(\frac{(1-L)\sqrt{-4H_1G_1 + (F_1)^2}}{2}(\eta + P))\right)^{\frac{1}{1-L}}, \tag{17}$$

$$W_{1,4}(z,t) = \left(-\frac{3(K+R)}{K} - 3\sqrt{R}\sqrt{K+R}\sqrt{\frac{K+R}{K^2R}}\coth\left(\frac{3}{2}\sqrt{\frac{K+R}{K^2R}}(P+\eta)\right)\right)^{1/3}.$$

and

$$w(\eta) = \left(-\frac{F_1}{2H_1} + \frac{\sqrt{-4H_1G_1 + (F_1)^2}}{2H_1}\tanh(\frac{(1-L)\sqrt{-4H_1G_1 + (F_1)^2}}{2}(\eta + P))\right)^{\frac{1}{1-L}}, \tag{18}$$

$$W_{1,5}(z,t) = \left(-\frac{3(K+R)}{K} - 3\sqrt{R}\sqrt{K+R}\sqrt{\frac{K+R}{K^2R}}\tanh\left(\frac{3}{2}\sqrt{\frac{K+R}{K^2R}}(P+\eta)\right)\right)^{1/3}.$$

Case 4.
when $L \neq 1, H_1 \neq 0$ and $F_1{}^2 - 4H_1G_1 = 0$, the following algebraic solution is found.

$$w(\eta) = \left(-\frac{F_1}{2H_1} + \frac{1}{H_1(L-1)(\eta + P)}\right)^{\frac{1}{1-L}}, \tag{19}$$

$$W_{1,6}(z,t) = \left(-\frac{3(K+R)}{K} + \frac{2\sqrt{R}\sqrt{K+R}}{P+\eta}\right)^{1/3}.$$

Case 5.
when $L \neq 1, H_1 \neq 0$ and $G_1 = 0$, the following solution is obtained.

$$w(\eta) = (H_1(L-1)(\eta + P))^{\frac{1}{L-1}}, \tag{20}$$

$$W_{1,7}(z,t) = \frac{\left(\frac{3}{2}\right)^{1/4}}{\left(\frac{P+\eta}{\sqrt{R}\sqrt{K+R}}\right)^{1/4}}.$$

where P is an arbitrary constant.

5. Utilizing the MAEM

For obtaining the solutions, the MAEM [34] provides the general solution in the form

$$w(\eta) = H_0 + \sum_{k=1}^{m} \left[H_K(\phi^h)^k + F_k(\phi^h)^{-k} \right], \tag{21}$$

where H_0, H_k's and F_k's are unknown constants. The auxiliary equation defines the function $h(\eta)$.

$$h'(\eta) = \frac{s + m\phi^{-h} + n\phi^h}{\ln \phi}, \tag{22}$$

for arbitrary constant values of s, m and n ($\phi > 0, \phi \neq 1$).
Cases for the Equation (22) are discussed below.

1. If $s^2 - 4mn < 0$ and $n \neq 0$, then, $\phi^{h(\eta)} = \frac{-s+\sqrt{4mn-s^2}\tan\left(\frac{\sqrt{4mn-s^2}\eta}{2}\right)}{2n}$, or $\phi^{h(\eta)} = -\frac{s+\sqrt{4mn-s^2}cot\left(\frac{\sqrt{4mn-s^2}\eta}{2}\right)}{2n}$.
2. If $s^2 - 4mn > 0$ and $n \neq 0$, then, $\phi^{h(\eta)} = -\frac{s+\sqrt{s^2-4mn}\tanh\left(\frac{\sqrt{s^2-4mn}\eta}{2}\right)}{2n}$, or $\phi^{h(\eta)} = -\frac{s+\sqrt{s^2-4mn}\coth\left(\frac{\sqrt{s^2-4mn}\eta}{2}\right)}{2n}$.
3. If $s^2 - 4mn = 0$ and $n \neq 0$, then, $\phi^{h(\eta)} = -\frac{2+s\eta}{2n\eta}$.

The highest order derivative w'' and the highest order nonlinear term w^2 in Equation (9) are balanced according to the homogeneous balance principle, yields that $m = 2$, gives

$$w(\eta) = H_0 + H_1\phi^h + F_1\phi^{-h} + H_2\phi^{2h} + F_2\phi^{-2h}. \tag{23}$$

The following set of algebraic equations is obtained by equating each coefficient of $\phi^{h(\eta)}$ to zero:

$$\phi^{h(\eta)^{-4}} : \tfrac{1}{2}KF_2(-12Km^2R + F_2) = 0,$$
$$\phi^{h(\eta)^{-3}} : K(-10KmRsF_2 + F_1(-2Km^2R + F_2)) = 0,$$
$$\phi^{h(\eta)^{-2}} : -3K^2mRsF_1 + \tfrac{KF_1^2}{2} + F_2(K + R - 4K^2R(2mn + s^2) + KH_0) = 0,$$
$$\phi^{h(\eta)^{-1}} : F_1(K + R - K^2R(2mn + s^2) + KH_0) + KF_2(-6KnRs + H_1) = 0,$$
$$\phi^{h(\eta)^{0}} : -K^2nRsF_1 - 2K^2n^2RF_2 + KH_0 + RH_0 + \tfrac{KH_0^2}{2} - K^2mRsH_1 + KF_1H_1 - 2K^2m^2RH_2 + KF_2H_2 = 0,$$
$$\phi^{h(\eta)^{1}} : (K + R - K^2R(2mn + s^2) + KH_0)H_1 + K(-6KmRs + F_1)H_2 = 0,$$
$$\phi^{h(\eta)^{2}} : -3K^2nRsH_1 + \tfrac{KH_1^2}{2} + (K + R - 4K^2R(2mn + s^2) + KH_0)H_2 = 0,$$
$$\phi^{h(\eta)^{3}} : K(-10KnRsH_2 + H_1(-2Kn^2R + H_2)) = 0,$$
$$\phi^{h(\eta)^{4}} : K(-10KnRsH_2 + H_1(-2Kn^2R + H_2)) = 0.$$

Solving the above equations, yields, the following families.

Family 1:

when $H_0 = \frac{-K-R+8K^2mnR+K^2Rs^2}{K}, H_1 = 12KnRs, H_2 = 12Kn^2R, F_1 = 0, F_2 = 0.$
The following cases have occurred.

- For $s^2 - 4mn < 0$ and $n \neq 0$, the trigonometric solutions are found.

$$W_{1,1}(z,t) = -1 - \frac{R}{K} + 8KmnR - 2KRs^2 + 3KR\left(4mn - s^2\right)\tan\left(\frac{1}{2}\sqrt{4mn - s^2}\eta\right)^2,$$

or

$$W_{1,2}(z,t) = -1 - \frac{R}{K} + KR\left(4mn - s^2\right)\left(-1 + 3\csc\left(\frac{1}{2}\sqrt{4mn - s^2}\eta\right)^2\right).$$

- For $s^2 - 4mn > 0$ and $n \neq 0$, the hyperbolic solutions are obtained.

$$W_{1,3}(z,t) = -1 - \frac{R}{K} + 8KmnR - 2KRs^2 + 3KR\left(-4mn + s^2\right)\tanh\left(\frac{1}{2}\sqrt{-4mn + s^2}\eta\right)^2,$$

or

$$W_{1,4}(z,t) = -1 - \frac{R}{K} + 8KmnR - 2KRs^2 + 3KR\left(-4mn + s^2\right)\coth\left(\frac{1}{2}\sqrt{-4mn + s^2}\eta\right)^2.$$

Family 2:

When $H_0 = \frac{-K-R+8K^2mnR+K^2Rs^2}{K}, H_1 = 0, H_2 = 0, F_1 = 12KmRs, F_2 = 12Km^2R.$
The following cases are obtained.

- For $s^2 - 4mn < 0$ and $n \neq 0$, the following trigonometric solutions resulted.

$$W_{2,1}(z,t) = -1 - \frac{R}{K} + KR\left(s^2 + 8mn\left(1 + \frac{3\left(2mn - s^2 + s\sqrt{4mn - s^2}\tan\left(\frac{1}{2}\sqrt{4mn - s^2}\eta\right)\right)}{\left(s - \sqrt{4mn - s^2}\tan\left(\frac{1}{2}\sqrt{4mn - s^2}\eta\right)\right)^2}\right)\right),$$

or

$$W_{2,2}(z,t) = -1 - \frac{R}{K} + KR\left(s^2 + 8mn\left(1 + \frac{6mn}{\left(s+\sqrt{4mn-s^2}\cot\left(\frac{1}{2}\sqrt{4mn-s^2}\eta\right)\right)^2} - \frac{3s}{s+\sqrt{4mn-s^2}\cot\left(\frac{1}{2}\sqrt{4mn-s^2}\eta\right)}\right)\right).$$

- For $s^2 - 4mn > 0$ and $n \neq 0$, the following hyperbolic solutions are found.

$$W_{2,3}(z,t) = -1 - \frac{R}{K} + KR\left(s^2 + 8mn\left(1 + \frac{6mn}{\left(s+\sqrt{-4mn+s^2}\tanh\left(\frac{1}{2}\sqrt{-4mn+s^2}\eta\right)\right)^2} - \frac{3s}{s+\sqrt{-4mn+s^2}\tanh\left(\frac{1}{2}\sqrt{-4mn+s^2}\eta\right)}\right)\right),$$

or

$$W_{2,4}(z,t) = -1 - \frac{R}{K} + KR\left(s^2 + 8mn\left(1 + \frac{6mn}{\left(s+\sqrt{-4mn+s^2}\coth\left(\frac{1}{2}\sqrt{-4mn+s^2}\eta\right)\right)^2} - \frac{3s}{s+\sqrt{-4mn+s^2}\coth\left(\frac{1}{2}\sqrt{-4mn+s^2}\eta\right)}\right)\right).$$

Family 3:

When $H_0 = \frac{-K-R+8K^2mnR+K^2Rs^2}{K}, H_1 = 12KnRs, H_2 = 12Kn^2R, F_1 = 12KmRs, F_2 = 12Km^2R.$

The cases listed below have occurred.

- For $s^2 - 4mn < 0$ and $n \neq 0$, the trigonometric solutions are found.

$$W_{3,1}(z,t) = -1 - \frac{R}{K} - 2KRs^2 + 3KR\left(4mn - s^2\right)\tan\left(\frac{1}{2}\sqrt{4mn - s^2}\eta\right)^2 + 8KmnR\left(1 + \frac{3\left(2mn - s^2 + s\sqrt{4mn - s^2}\tan\left(\frac{1}{2}\sqrt{4mn - s^2}\eta\right)\right)}{\left(s - \sqrt{4mn - s^2}\tan\left(\frac{1}{2}\sqrt{4mn - s^2}\eta\right)\right)^2}\right),$$

or

$$W_{3,2}(z,t) = -1 - \frac{R}{K} - 2KRs^2 + 3KR\left(4mn - s^2\right)\cot\left(\frac{1}{2}\sqrt{4mn - s^2}\eta\right)^2 + 8KmnR\left(1 + \frac{6mn}{\left(s + \sqrt{4mn - s^2}\cot\left(\frac{1}{2}\sqrt{4mn - s^2}\eta\right)\right)^2} - \frac{3s}{s + \sqrt{4mn - s^2}\cot\left(\frac{1}{2}\sqrt{4mn - s^2}\eta\right)}\right).$$

- For $s^2 - 4mn > 0$ and $n \neq 0$, the following hyperbolic solutions are obtained.

$$W_{3,3}(z,t) = -1 - \frac{R}{K} - 2KRs^2 + 3KR\left(-4mn + s^2\right)\tanh\left(\frac{1}{2}\sqrt{-4mn + s^2}\eta\right)^2 + 8KmnR\left(1 + \frac{6mn}{\left(s + \sqrt{-4mn + s^2}\tanh\left(\frac{1}{2}\sqrt{-4mn + s^2}\eta\right)\right)^2} - \frac{3s}{s + \sqrt{-4mn + s^2}\tanh\left(\frac{1}{2}\sqrt{-4mn + s^2}\eta\right)}\right),$$

or

$$W_{3,4}(z,t) = -1 - \frac{R}{K} - 2KRs^2 + 3KR\left(-4mn + s^2\right)\coth\left(\frac{1}{2}\sqrt{-4mn + s^2}\eta\right)^2 + 8KmnR\left(1 + \frac{6mn}{\left(s + \sqrt{-4mn + s^2}\coth\left(\frac{1}{2}\sqrt{-4mn + s^2}\eta\right)\right)^2} - \frac{3s}{s + \sqrt{-4mn + s^2}\coth\left(\frac{1}{2}\sqrt{-4mn + s^2}\eta\right)}\right).$$

6. Graphical Illustration

This section provides a graphical representation of the BBM-Burger equation solutions that have been found. Concerning the 2D and 3D graphs of $W_{1,1}(z,t)$, $W_{1,3}(z,t)$, $W_{1,4}(z,t)$, respectively, provided the periodic and single wave solutions for the values $\sigma = 0.5, 1$, P = 1.7, 5.5, K = 14.5, 15.5, R = −0.5, $\beta = 0.35$, within the interval $-5 \leq z \leq 5, 0 \leq t \leq 2$ for 3D graph and t = 1 for 2D plots, as shown in Figures 1–3 by RB sub-ODE method. Figures 4 and 5 represent the Kink and Pulse shape soliton 3D solutions of $W_{1,5}(z,t)$ and $W_{1,6}(z,t)$ for the values $\sigma = 0.5$, P = −1.7, 5.5, K = 14.5, 10.5, R = 14.5, 0.5, $\beta = 0.35$ and 2D plots at t = 1 for the same values in the interval $-5 \leq z \leq 5, 0 \leq t \leq 2$ by RB sub-ODE method.

The solutions for the trigonometric and hyperbolic functions in $W_{1,1}(z,t)$ and $W_{1,3}(z,t)$ are that we obtain the anti-bell-shaped solitons and dark soliton solutions, respectively, by choosing the values $\sigma = 0.5$, m = 1, K = 2, R = 1, $\beta = 0.35$, s = 0.1, n = 1, within the range $-10 \leq z \leq 10, -10 \leq t \leq 10$, and t = 1 for 2D surfaces in Figures 6 and 7 by MAEM. The dark soliton solution, in which the intensity profile of the soliton displays a dip in a uniform backdrop, this hole-soliton, often referred to as a dark soliton, causes a transient reduction in wave amplitude. Solutions for the Family 2 in $W_{2,1}(z,t)$ and $W_{2,3}(z,t)$, by MAEM provides the bright and bell-shaped soliton solutions by taking the values $\sigma = 0.5$, m = 1, K = −2.5, R = 1, $\beta = 0.35$, s = 0.1, n = 1, within the range $-10 \leq z \leq 10, -10 \leq t \leq 10$, and t = 1 for 2D surfaces in Figures 8 and 9.

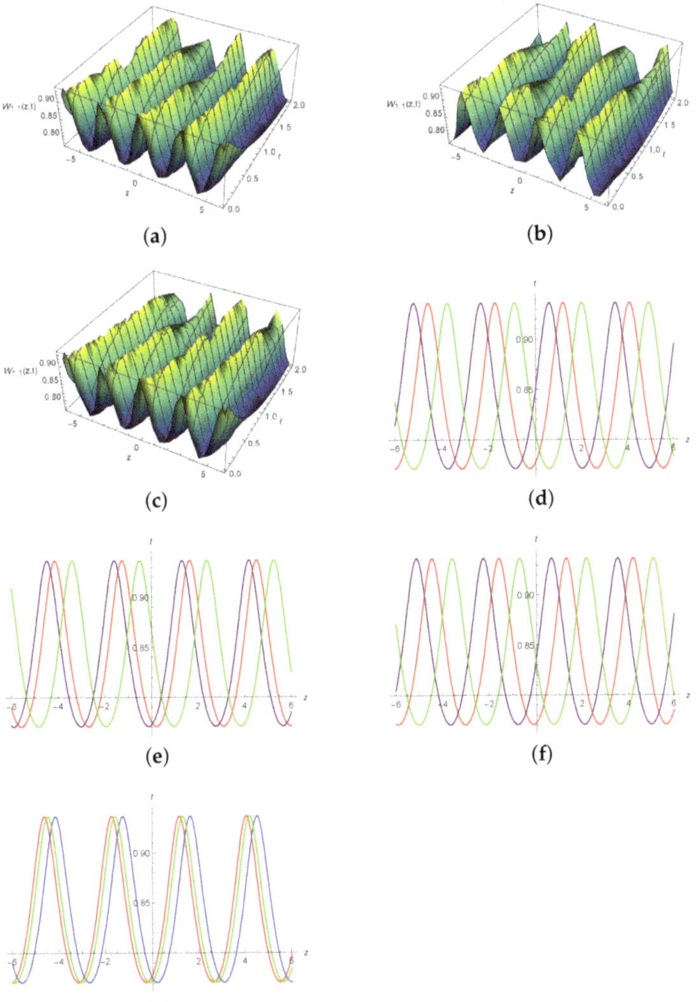

Figure 1. Graphical representation of analytical solution $W_{1,1}(z,t)$ by RB sub-ODE method, when $\sigma = 0.5, P = 1.7, K = 14.5, R = -9.5, \beta = 0.35$. (**a**) M-TD 3D graph at σ = 0.5; (**b**) β-derivative 3D graph at σ = 0.5; (**c**) CD 3D graph at σ = 0.5; (**d**) 2D plot of M-TD at different values of σ = 0.5, β = 0.25 (red), σ = 1, β = 0.5 (purple), σ = 0.3, β = 0.75 (green); (**e**) 2D plot of β-derivative at different values of σ = 0.5 (red), 1 (purple), 0.3 (green); (**f**) 2D plot of CD at different values of σ = 0.5 (red), 1 (purple), 0.3 (green); (**g**) A comparison between M-TD (red), β-derivative (blue) and CD (green) at $\sigma = 0.5$. (**d–g**) 2D comparison plots at $t = 1$.

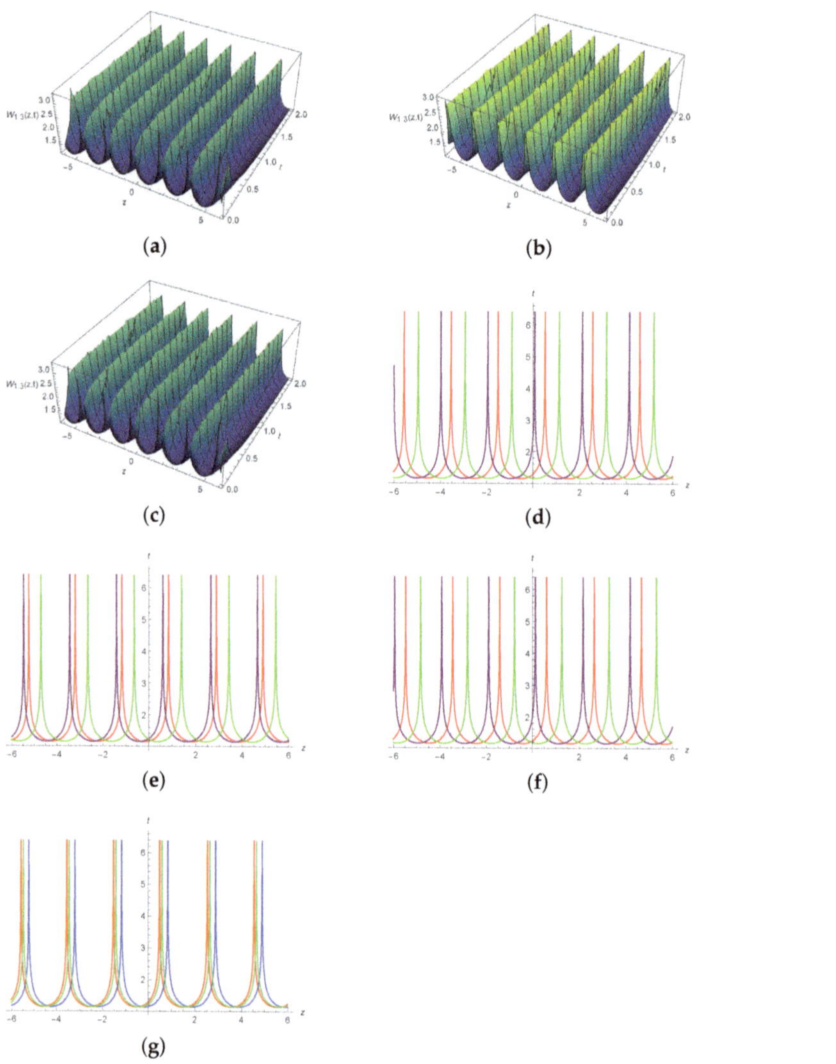

Figure 2. Graphical representation of analytical solution $W_{1,3}(z,t)$ by RB sub-ODE method, when $\sigma = 0.5, P = 5.5, K = 15.5, R = -7.5, \beta = 0.35$. (**a**) M-TD 3D graph at $\sigma = 0.5$; (**b**) β-derivative 3D graph at $\sigma = 0.5$; (**c**) CD 3D graph at $\sigma = 0.5$; (**d**) 2D plot of M-TD at different values of $\sigma = 0.5$, $\beta = 0.25$ (red), $\sigma = 1$, $\beta = 0.5$ (purple), $\sigma = 0.3$, $\beta = 0.75$ (green); (**e**) 2D plot of β-derivative at different values of $\sigma = 0.5$ (red), 1 (purple), 0.3 (green); (**f**) 2D plot of CD at different values of $\sigma = 0.5$ (red), 1 (purple), 0.3 (green); (**g**) A comparison between M-TD (red), β-derivative (blue) and CD (green) at $\sigma = 0.5$. (**d–g**) 2D comparison plots at $t = 1$.

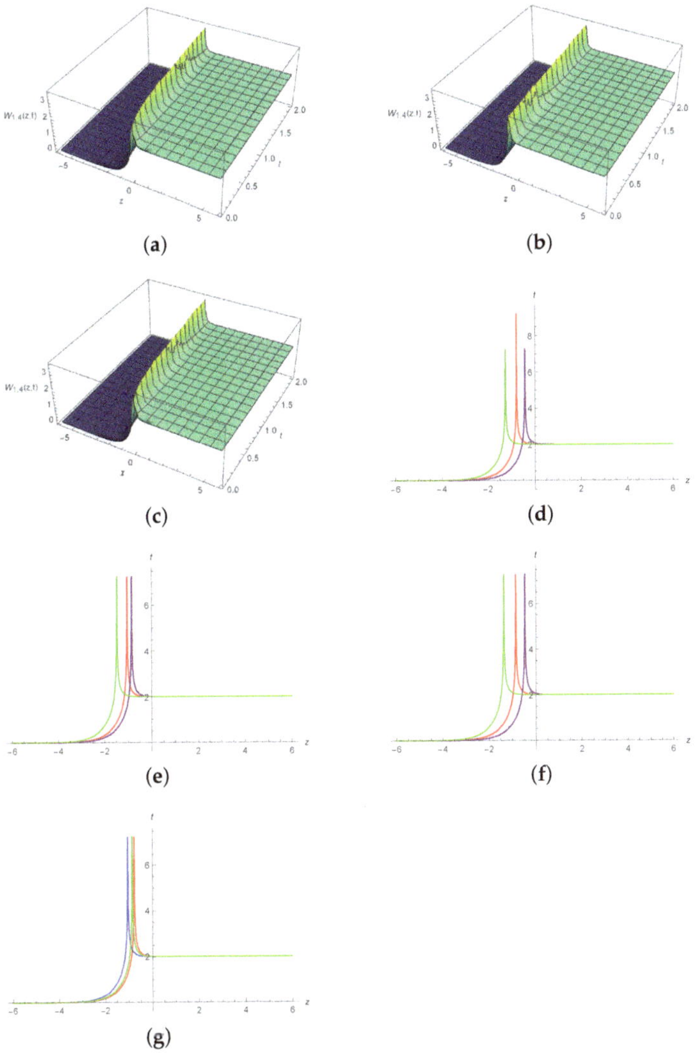

Figure 3. Graphical representation of analytical solution $W_{1,4}(z,t)$ by RB sub-ODE method, when $\sigma = 0.5, P = 1.5, K = 18.5, R = 7, \beta = 0.35$. (**a**) M-TD 3D graph at σ = 0.5; (**b**) β-derivative 3D graph at σ = 0.5; (**c**) CD 3D graph at σ = 0.5; (**d**) 2D plot of M-TD at different values of σ = 0.5, β = 0.25 (red), σ = 1, β = 0.5 (purple), σ = 0.3, β = 0.75 (green); (**e**) 2D plot of β-derivative at different values of σ = 0.5 (red), 1 (purple), 0.3 (green); (**f**) 2D plot of CD at different values of σ = 0.5 (red), 1 (purple), 0.3 (green); (**g**) A comparison between M-TD (red), β-derivative (blue) and CD (green) at $\upsilon = 0.5$. (**d–g**) 2D comparison plots at $t = 1$.

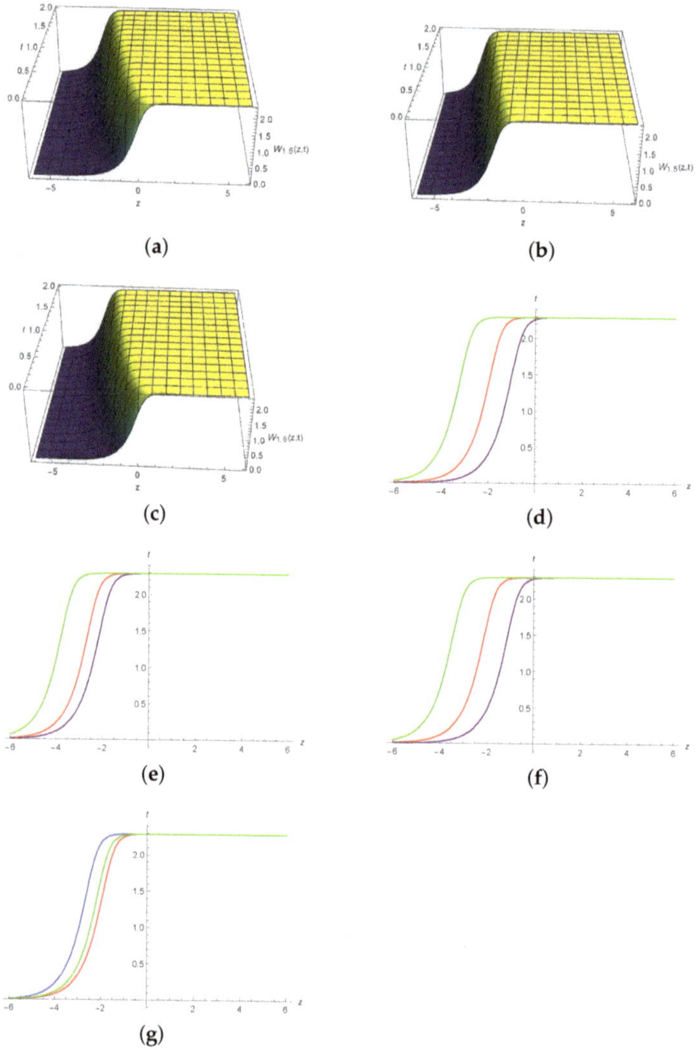

Figure 4. Graphical representation of analytical solution $W_{1,5}(z,t)$ by RB sub-ODE method, when $\sigma = 0.5, P = -1.7, K = 14.5, R = 14.5, \beta = 0.35$. (**a**) M-TD 3D graph at $\sigma = 0.5$; (**b**) β-derivative 3D graph at $\sigma = 0.5$; (**c**) CD 3D graph at $\sigma = 0.5$; (**d**) 2D plot of M-TD at different values of $\sigma = 0.5$, $\beta = 0.25$ (red), $\sigma = 1$, $\beta = 0.5$ (purple), $\sigma = 0.3$, $\beta = 0.75$ (green); (**e**) 2D plot of β-derivative at different values of $\sigma = 0.5$ (red), 1 (purple), 0.3 (green); (**f**) 2D plot of CD at different values of $\sigma = 0.5$ (red), 1 (purple), 0.3 (green); (**g**) A comparison between M-TD (red), β-derivative (blue) and CD (green) at $\sigma = 0.5$. (**d–g**) 2D comparison plots at $t = 1$.

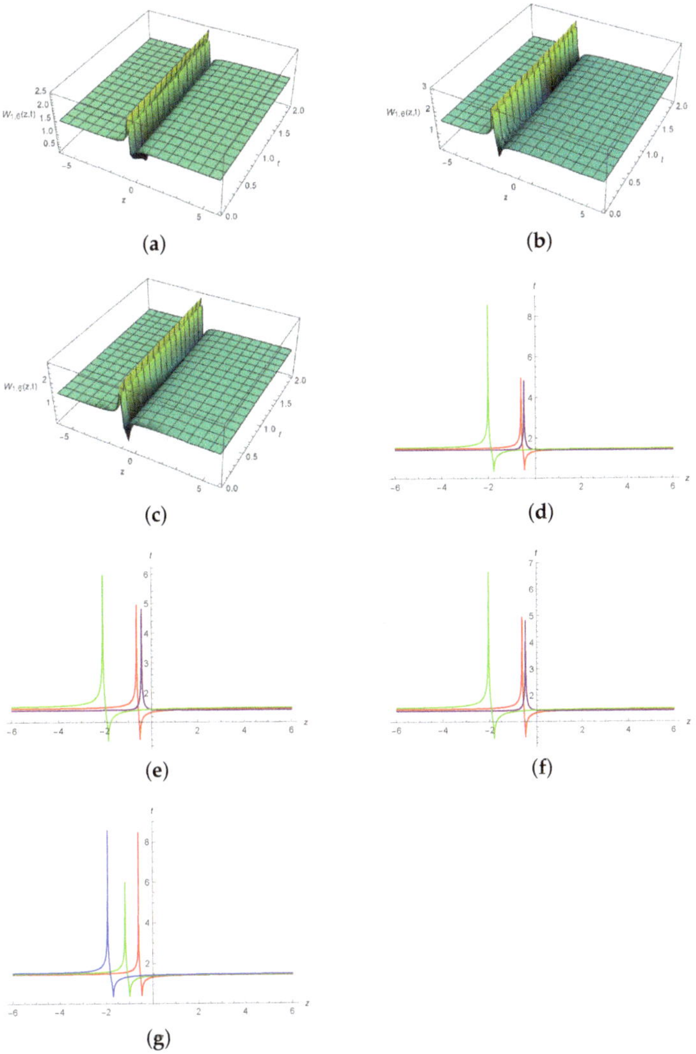

Figure 5. Graphical representation of analytical solution $W_{1,6}(z,t)$ by RB sub-ODE method, when $\sigma = 0.5, P = 5.5, K = 10.5, R = 0.5, \beta = 0.35$. (**a**) M-TD 3D graph at σ = 0.5; (**b**) β-derivative 3D graph at σ = 0.5; (**c**) CD 3D graph at σ = 0.5; (**d**) 2D plot of M-TD at different values of σ = 0.5, β = 0.25 (red), σ = 1, β = 0.5 (purple), σ = 0.3, β = 0.75 (green); (**e**) 2D plot of β-derivative at different values of σ = 0.5 (red), 1 (purple), 0.3 (green); (**f**) 2D plot of CD at different values of σ = 0.5 (red), 1 (purple), 0.3 (green); (**g**) A comparison between M-TD (red), β-derivative (blue) and CD (green) at $\sigma = 0.5$. (**d**–**g**) 2D comparison plots at $t = 1$.

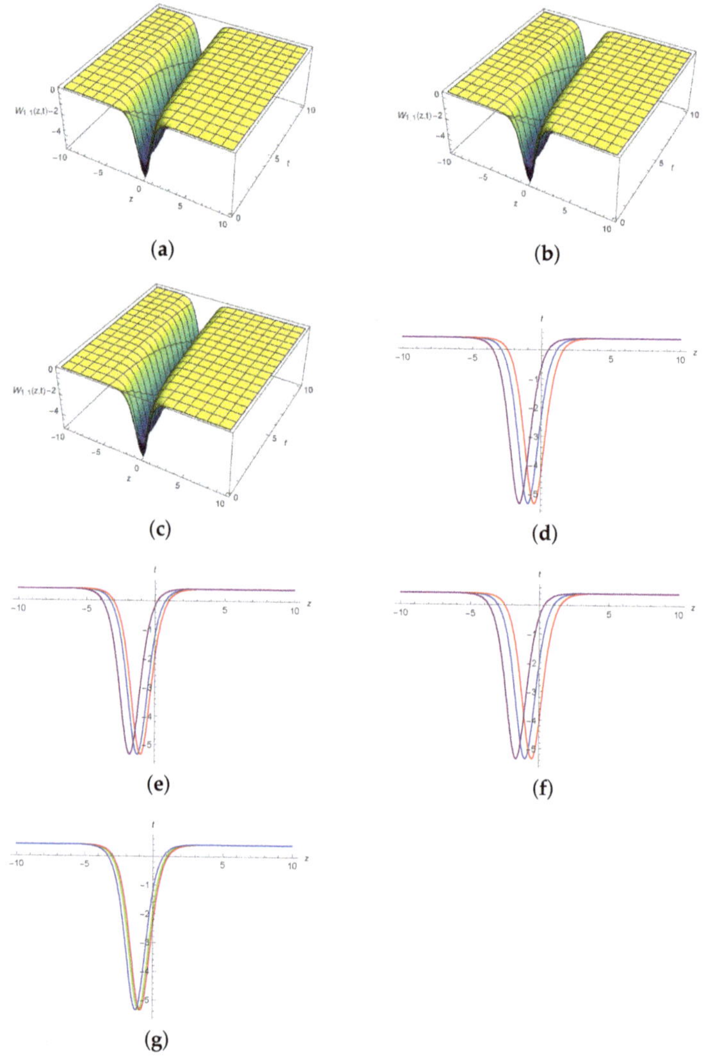

Figure 6. Graphical representation of analytical solution $W_{1,1}(z,t)$ by MAEM, when $K = 2$, $m = 0.1, s = 1, n = 0.1, R = 1, \sigma = 0.5, \beta = 0.35$. (**a**) M-TD 3D graph at σ = 0.5; (**b**) β-derivative 3D graph at σ = 0.5; (**c**) CD 3D graph at σ = 0.5; (**d**) 2D plot of M-TD at different values of σ = 0.5, β = 0.25 (blue), σ = 1, β = 0.5 (red), σ = 0.3, β = 0.75 (purple); (**e**) 2D plot of β-derivative at different values of σ = 0.5 (blue), 1 (red), 0.3 (purple); (**f**) 2D plot of CD at different values of σ = 0.5 (blue), 1 (red), 0.3 (purple); (**g**) A comparison between M-TD (red), β-derivative (blue) and CD (green) at $\sigma = 0.5$. (**d–g**) 2D comparison plots at $t = 1$.

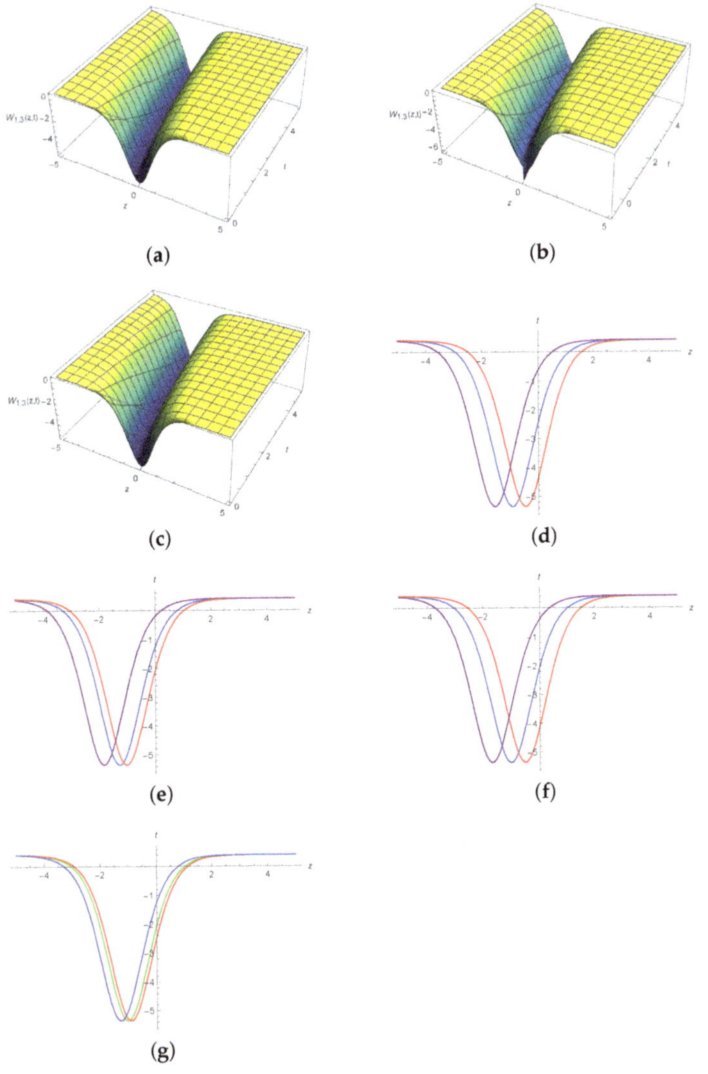

Figure 7. Graphical representation of analytical solution $W_{1,3}(z,t)$ by MAEM, when $K = 2$, $m = 0.1, s = 1, n = 0.1, R = 1, \sigma = 0.5, \beta = 0.35$. (**a**) M-TD 3D graph at $\sigma = 0.5$; (**b**) β-derivative 3D graph at $\sigma = 0.5$; (**c**) CD 3D graph at $\sigma = 0.5$; (**d**) 2D plot of M-TD at different values of $\sigma = 0.5$, $\beta = 0.25$ (blue), $\sigma = 1$, $\beta = 0.5$ (red), $\sigma = 0.3$, $\beta = 0.75$ (purple); (**e**) 2D plot of β-derivative at different values of $\sigma = 0.5$ (blue),1 (red), 0.3 (purple); (**f**) 2D plot of CD at different values of $\sigma = 0.5$ (blue), 1 (red), 0.3 (purple); (**g**) A comparison between M-TD(red), β-derivative (blue) and CD (green) at $\sigma = 0.5$. (**d**–**g**) 2D comparison plots at $t = 1$.

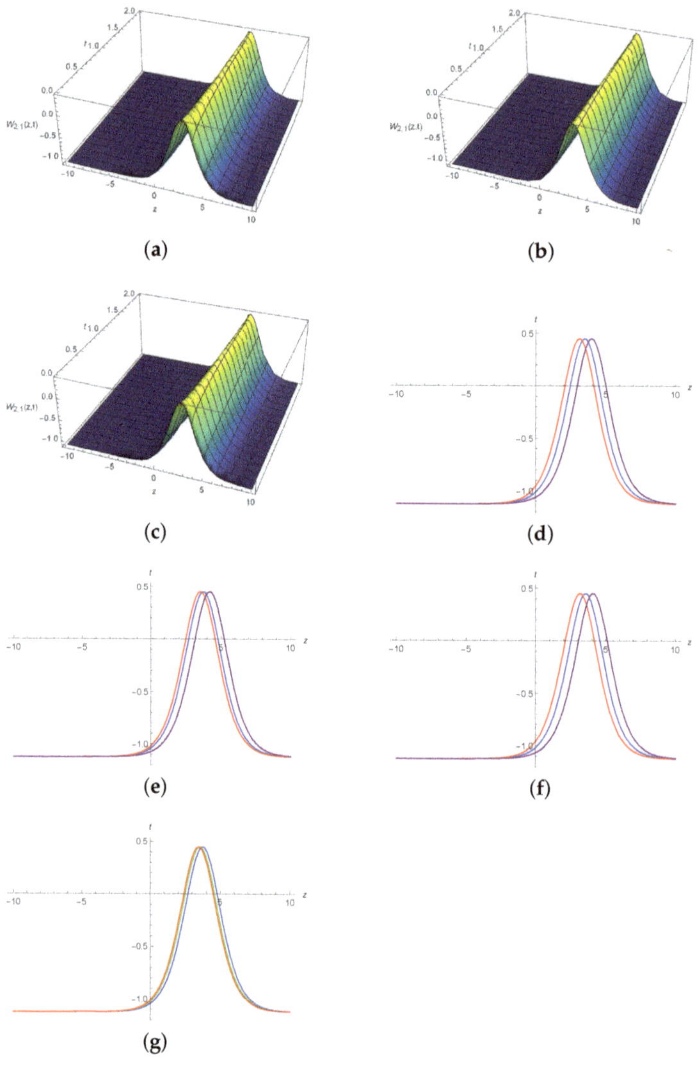

Figure 8. Graphical representation of analytical solution $W_{2,1}(z,t)$ by MAEM, when $K = -2.5$, $m = 0.1, s = 0.5, n = 0.1, R = 1, \sigma = 0.5, \beta = 0.35$. (a) M-TD 3D graph at $\sigma = 0.5$; (b) β-derivative 3D graph at $\sigma = 0.5$; (c) CD 3D graph at $\sigma = 0.5$; (d) 2D plot of M-TD at different values of $\sigma = 0.5$, $\beta = 0.25$ (blue), $\sigma = 1$, $\beta = 0.5$ (red), $\sigma = 0.3$, $\beta = 0.75$ (purple); (e) 2D plot of β-derivative at different values of $\sigma = 0.5$ (blue), 1 (red), 0.3 (purple); (f) 2D plot of CD at different values of $\sigma = 0.5$ (blue), 1 (red), 0.3 (purple); (g) A comparison between M-TD (red), β-derivative (blue) and CD (green) at $\sigma = 0.5$. (d–g) 2D comparison plots at $t = 1$.

In Figures 10 and 11, the trigonometric and hyperbolic solutions of $W_{3,1}(z,t)$ and $W_{3,3}(z,t)$, we receive the M-shape and W-shape soliton solutions, respectively, by choosing the values $\sigma = 0.5$, m $= 1$, K $= -1$, R $= 0.5$, $\beta = 0.35$, s $= 0.1$, n $= 1$, within the domain $-10 \leq y \leq 10, 0 \leq t \leq 5$, and t $= 1$ for 2D surfaces by MAEM. In applied sciences, particularly in dispersive systems, the retrieved solutions are important for describing a variety of natural phenomena.

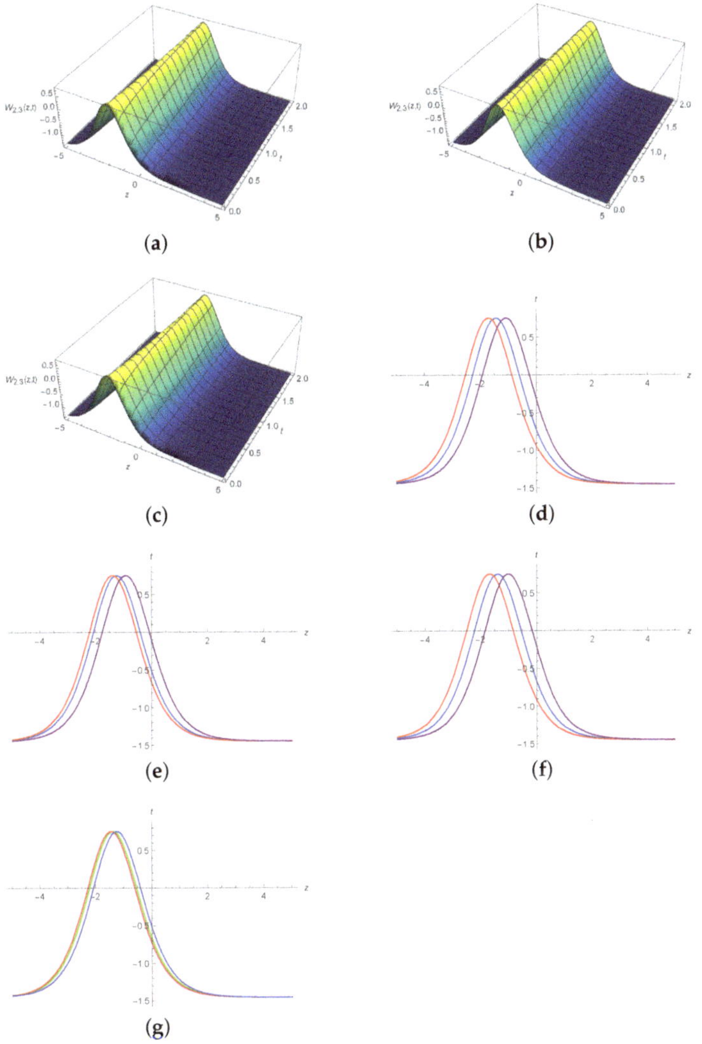

Figure 9. Graphical representation of analytical solution $W_{2,3}(z,t)$ by MAEM, when $K = 3.5$, $m = 0.1, s = 0.5, n = 0.1, R = -1, \sigma = 0.5, \beta = 0.35$. (a) M-TD 3D graph at σ = 0.5; (b) β-derivative 3D graph at σ = 0.5; (c) CD 3D graph at σ = 0.5; (d) 2D plot of M-TD at different values of σ = 0.5, β = 0.25 (blue), σ =1, β = 0.5 (red) , σ = 0.3, β = 0.75(purple); (e) 2D plot of β-derivative at different values of σ = 0.5 (blue),1 (red), 0.3 (purple); (f) 2D plot of CD at different values of σ = 0.5 (blue), 1 (red), 0.3 (purple); (g) A comparison between M-TD (red), β-derivative (blue) and CD (green) at $\sigma = 0.5$. (d–g) 2D comparison plots at $t = 1$.

The construction of dark and bright solitons can be seen in Figure 1. The RB sub-ODE technique provides solutions in the algebraic form in Figure 1, the periodic form in Figure 2, and the hyperbolic form in Figure 3. The MAEM also gives trigonometric in Figures 6, 8 and 10 and hyperbolic in Figures 7, 9 and 11 solutions. The bell-shaped soliton in Figure 9, W-shaped soliton in Figure 10 and M-shaped soliton in Figure 11 are also achieved in this work. These graphs demonstrate the dynamical and dispersive behavior of the solitary wave solutions with a suitable choice of parameters. It can be noticed that the wave profile slightly varies when the fractional parameter's value is changed without changing the form of the curve. A very useful comparison among the different fractional derivatives, including β, conformable, and M-TD's, is shown in two-dimensional line graphs.

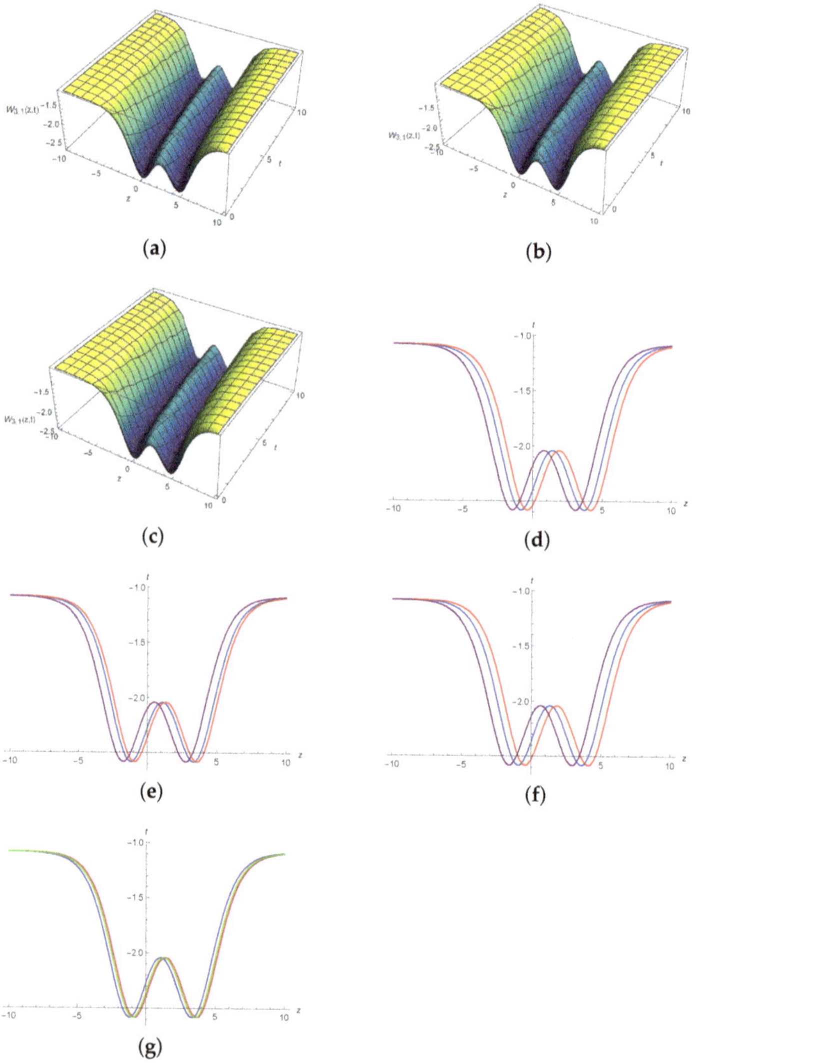

Figure 10. Graphical representation of analytical solution $W_{3,1}(z,t)$ by MAEM, when $K = -1$, $m = 0.1, s = 1, n = 0.1, R = -0.5, \sigma = 0.5, \beta = 0.35$. (**a**) M-TD 3D graph at σ = 0.5; (**b**) β-derivative 3D graph at σ = 0.5; (**c**) CD 3D graph at σ = 0.5; (**d**) 2D plot of M-TD at different values of σ = 0.5, β = 0.25 (blue), σ =1, β = 0.5 (red) , σ = 0.3, β = 0.75 (purple); (**e**) 2D plot of β-derivative at different values of σ = 0.5 (blue),1 (red), 0.3 (purple); (**f**) 2D plot of CD at different values of σ = 0.5 (blue), 1 (red), 0.3 (purple); (**g**) A comparison between M-TD (red), β-derivative (blue) and CD (green) at $\sigma = 0.5$. (**d–g**) 2D comparison plots at $t = 1$.

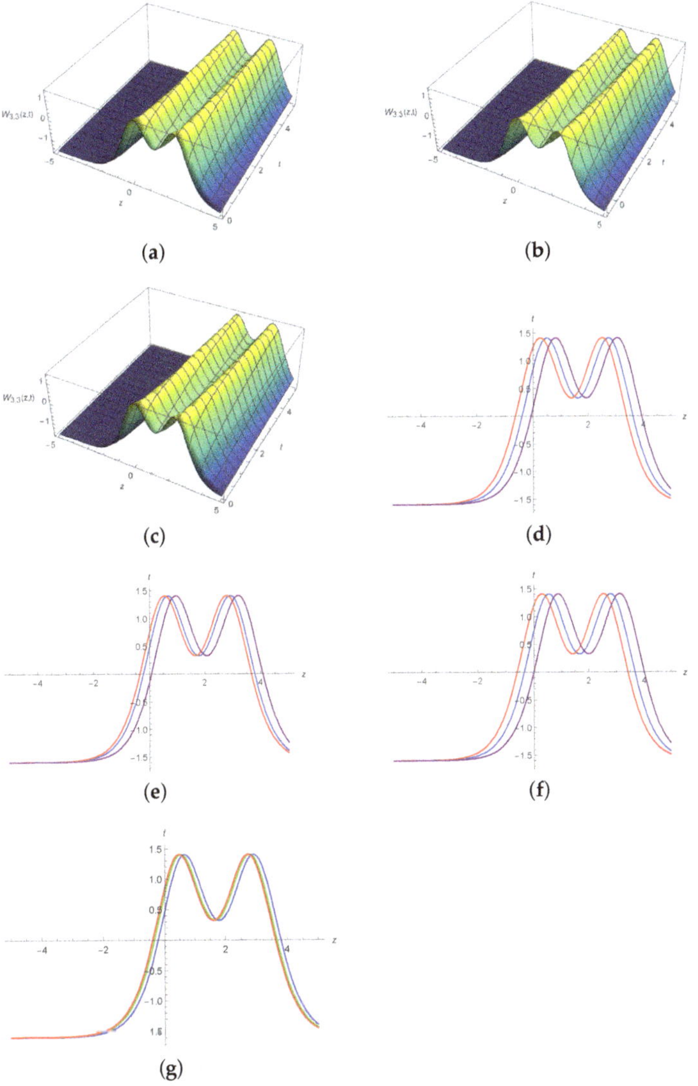

Figure 11. Graphical representation of analytical solution $W_{3,3}(z,t)$ by MAEM, when $K = -2$, $m = 0.1, s = 1, n = 0.1, R = 0.5, \sigma = 0.5, \beta = 0.35$. (**a**) M-TD 3D graph at $\sigma = 0.5$; (**b**) β-derivative 3D graph at $\sigma = 0.5$; (**c**) CD 3D graph at $\sigma = 0.5$; (**d**) 2D plot of M-TD at different values of $\sigma = 0.5$, $\beta = 0.25$ (blue), $\sigma = 1$, $\beta = 0.5$ (red) , $\sigma = 0.3$, $\beta = 0.75$ (purple); (**e**) 2D plot of β-derivative at different values of $\sigma = 0.5$ (blue),1 (red), 0.3 (purple); (**f**) 2D plot of CD at different values of $\sigma = 0.5$ (blue), 1 (red), 0.3 (purple); (**g**) A comparison between M-TD (red), β-derivative (blue) and CD (green) at $\sigma = 0.5$. (**d–g**) 2D comparison plots at $t = 1$.

7. Conclusions

In this study, the RB sub-ODE approach and the MAEM were used to solve the nonlinear BBM-Burger problem, yielding novel, accurate, and analytical solitary wave solutions. These methods provided remarkable solutions that can be operated consistently and simply. Using these conventional and computerized techniques, we could comprehend difficult nonlinear differential equations in a range of scientific domains. The solitons and other traveling wave solutions of the governing model could be found by applying the definitions of derivatives with fractional parameters, i.e., β-derivative, CD, and M-TD, to each function. Trigonometric and hyperbolic function solutions could be found in the extracted solutions. The outcomes indicated that the MAEM and RB sub-ODE approaches might be used as helpful mathematical tools for extracting the various solitary wave solutions with different differential operators. The current work can be modified in the future to include more evolution equation kinds with various nonlinearities. This paper has studied the comparison of three derivatives. The analysis says that by changing the values of fractional parameters, an effect on wave solutions is observed but M-TD is considered more valuable because, by changing its parameter values, a smooth wave has been observed. This transitive is very effective and useful. The reason for smooth waves is the Mittag–Leffler function of one parameter, which is why better results are obtained in comparison with other derivatives. They can be used by the researcher in the next phases as well. Future research on the BBM-Burger equation may explore the fractional impacts on the solutions of the governing system using, the fractional local derivative, the Atangana–Baleanu derivative, and other recently proposed definitions of fractional derivatives. We can also consider the BBM-Burger equation with stochastic terms. This study confirms that the RB sub-ODE approach and MAEM are effective and useful mathematical methods and are applicable to investigating other fractional NLEEs in science and engineering.

Author Contributions: Conceptualization, R.A. and M.A.; Formal analysis, R.A., M.A. and F.A.A.; Funding acquisition, X.W. and K.M.A.; Investigation, X.W., R.A., M.A., F.A.A. and K.M.A.; Methodology, X.W., R.A., M.A., F.A.A. and K.M.A.; Project administration, X.W., M.A. and K.M.A.; Software, R.A. and M.A.; Supervision, M.A.; Validation, X.W., R.A. and M.A.; Writing—original draft, X.W., R.A., M.A., F.A.A. and K.M.A.; Writing—review & editing, X.W., R.A., M.A. and K.M.A. All authors have read and agreed to the published version of the manuscript.

Funding: This research received no external funding.

Institutional Review Board Statement: Not applicable.

Informed Consent Statement: Not applicable.

Data Availability Statement: Not applicable.

Acknowledgments: The research of X. Wang is supported by the Science and Technology Foundation of Jiangxi Provincial Department of Education (Grant No. GJJ2201802) and the National Natural Science Foundation of China (Grant No. 11861053). The researchers would like to acknowledge Deanship of Scientific Research, Taif university for funding this work.

Conflicts of Interest: The authors declare no conflict of interest.

Abbreviations

The following abbreviations are used in this manuscript:

BBM-Burger	Benjamin–Bona–Mahony–Burger
MAEM	Modified auxiliary equation method
RB	Ricatti–Bernoulli
CD	Conformable derivative
M-TD	M-truncated derivatives
DEs	Differential equations
NLPDEs	Nonlinear partial differential equations
FDEs	Fractional differential equations
FC	Fractional calculus
FDs	Fractional derivatives
β-derivative	Beta-derivative
JEFM	Jacobi elliptic function method

References

1. Ablowitz, M.J.; Ramani, A.; Segur, H. Nonlinear evolution equations and ordinary differential equations of Painleve'type. *Lett. Nuovo Cim.* **1978**, *23*, 333–338. [CrossRef]
2. Renardy, M.; Rogers, R.C. *An Introduction to Partial Differential Equations*; Springer Science & Business Media: Berlin/Heidelberg, Germany, 2006; Volume 13.
3. Podlubny, I. *Fractional Differential Equations: An Introduction to Fractional Derivatives, Fractional Differential Equations, to Methods of Their Solution and Some of Their Applications*; Academic Press: New York, NY, USA, 1998; p. 198.
4. Oldham, K.B.; Spanier, J. *The Fractional Calculus*; Academic Press: New York, NY, USA, 1974.
5. Singh, J.; Kumar, D.; Al Qurashi, M.; Baleanu, D. A new fractional model for giving up smoking dynamics. *Adv. Differ. Equ.* **2017**, *2017*, 88. [CrossRef]
6. Caputo, M.; Mainardi, F. A new dissipation model based on memory mechanism. *Pure Appl. Geophys.* **1971**, *91*, 134–147. [CrossRef]
7. Caputo, M.; Fabricio, M. A new definition of fractional derivative without singular kernel. *Prog. Fract. Differ. Appl.* **2019**, *1*, 73–85.
8. Atangana, A.; Baleanu, D. New fractional derivatives with nonlocal and non-singular kernel. Theory and application to heat transfer model. *Therm. Sci.* **2016**, *20*, 763–769. [CrossRef]
9. Khalil, R.; Al Horani, M.; Yousef, A.; Sababheh, M. A new definition of fractional derivative. *J. Comput. Appl. Math.* **2014**, *264*, 65–70. [CrossRef]
10. Almeida, R. Caputo–Hadamard fractional derivatives of variable order. *Numer. Funct. Anal. Optim.* **2017**, *38*, 1–19. [CrossRef]
11. Anderson, D.R.; Ulness, D.J. Properties of the Katugampola fractional derivative with potential application in quantum mechanics. *J. Math. Phys.* **2015**, *56*, 063502. [CrossRef]
12. Amado Mendez Cruz, G.; Torres Ledesma, C.E. Multiplicity of solutions for fractional Hamiltonian systems with Liouville-Weyl fractional derivatives. *Fract. Calc. Appl. Anal.* **2015**, *18*, 875–890. [CrossRef]
13. Jumarie, G. Modified Riemann-Liouville derivative and fractional Taylor series of nondifferentiable functions further results. *Comput. Math. Appl.* **2006**, *51*, 1367–1376. [CrossRef]
14. Hanna, L.M.; Luchko, Y.F. Operational calculus for the Caputo-type fractional Erdélyi–Kober derivative and its applications. *Integral Transform. Spec. Funct.* **2014**, *25*, 359–373. [CrossRef]
15. Huang, F.; Liu, F. The space-time fractional diffusion equation with Caputo derivatives. *J. Appl. Math. Comput.* **2005**, *19*, 179–190. [CrossRef]
16. Kumar, V.; Gupta, R.K.; Jiwari, R. Painlevé analysis, Lie symmetries and exact solutions for variable coefficients Benjamin-Bona-Mahony-Burger (BBMB) equation. *Commun. Theor. Phys.* **2013**, *60*, 175. [CrossRef]
17. Hirota, R. Exact solution of the Korteweg—de Vries equation for multiple collisions of solitons. *Phys. Rev. Lett.* **1971**, *27*, 1192. [CrossRef]
18. Jena, S.R.; Senapati, A. On numerical soliton and convergence analysis of Benjamin-Bona-Mahony-Burger equation via octic B-spline collocation. *Arab. J. Basic Appl. Sci.* **2023**, *30*, 146–163. [CrossRef]
19. Alharbi, F.M.; Baleanu, D.; Ebaid, A. Physical properties of the projectile motion using the conformable derivative. *Chin. J. Phys.* **2019**, *58*, 18–28. [CrossRef]
20. Wang, X.; Ehsan, H.; Abbas, M.; Akram, G.; Sadaf, M.; Abdeljawad, T. Analytical solitary wave solutions of a time-fractional thin-film ferroelectric material equation involving beta-derivative using modified auxiliary equation method. *Results Phys.* **2023**, *48*, 106411. [CrossRef]
21. Mohammed, W.W.; Al-Askar, F.M.; Cesarano, C.; Aly, E.S. The Soliton Solutions of the Stochastic Shallow Water Wave Equations in the Sense of Beta-Derivative. *Mathematics* **2023**, *11*, 1338. [CrossRef]
22. Martínez, F.; Martínez, I.; Kaabar, M.K.; Paredes, S. Generalized conformable mean value theorems with applications to multivariable calculus. *J. Math.* **2021**, *2021*, 5528537. [CrossRef]
23. Hussain, A.; Jhangeer, A.; Abbas, N.; Khan, I.; Sherif, E.S.M. Optical solitons of fractional complex Ginzburg-Landau equation with conformable, beta, and M-truncated derivatives: A comparative study. *Adv. Differ. Equ.* **2020**, *2020*, 612. [CrossRef]
24. Mohammed, W.W.; Cesarano, C.; Al-Askar, F.M. Solutions to the (4+1)-Dimensional Time-Fractional Fokas Equation with M-Truncated Derivative. *Mathematics* **2022**, *11*, 194. [CrossRef]
25. Akram, G.; Gillani, S.R. Sub pico-second Soliton with Triki–Biswas equation by the extended $(\frac{G'}{G^2})$-expansion method and the modified auxiliary equation method. *Optik* **2021**, *229*, 166227. [CrossRef]
26. Wan, P.; Manafian, J.; Ismael, H.F.; Mohammed, S.A. Investigating one-, two-, and triple-wave solutions via multiple exp-function method arising in engineering sciences. *Adv. Math. Phys.* **2020**, *2020*, 8018064. [CrossRef]
27. He, X.J.; Lü, X. M-lump solution, soliton solution and rational solution to a (3+1)-dimensional nonlinear model. *Math. Comput. Simul.* **2022**, *197*, 327–340. [CrossRef]
28. Rehman, H.U.; Iqbal, I.; Subhi Aiadi, S.; Mlaiki, N.; Saleem, M.S. Soliton solutions of Klein–Fock–Gordon equation using Sardar subequation method. *Mathematics* **2022**, *10*, 3377. [CrossRef]
29. Parkes, E.J.; Duffy, B.R.; Abbott, P.C. The Jacobi elliptic-function method for finding periodic-wave solutions to nonlinear evolution equations. *Phys. Lett. A* **2002**, *295*, 280–286. [CrossRef]
30. Yusuf, A.; Inc, M.; Aliyu, A.I.; Baleanu, D. Optical solitons possessing beta derivative of the Chen-Lee-Liu equation in optical fibers. *Front. Phys.* **2019**, *7*, 34. [CrossRef]

31. Hassan, S.Z.; Abdelrahman, M.A. A Riccati–Bernoulli sub-ODE method for some nonlinear evolution equations. *Int. J. Nonlinear Sci. Numer. Simul.* **2019**, *20*, 303–313. [CrossRef]
32. Arife, A.S. The modified variational iteration transform method (MVITM) for solve non linear partial differential equation (NLPDE). *World Appl. Sci. J.* **2011**, *12*, 2274–2278. [CrossRef]
33. Jiong, S. Auxiliary equation method for solving nonlinear partial differential equations. *Phys. Lett. A* **2003**, *309*, 387–396. [CrossRef]
34. Akram, G.; Sadaf, M.; Abbas, M.; Zainab, I.; Gillani, S.R. Efficient techniques for traveling wave solutions of time-fractional Zakharov–Kuznetsov equation. *Math. Comput. Simul.* **2022**, *193*, 607–622. [CrossRef]
35. Al-Askar, F.M.; Cesarano, C.; Mohammed, W.W. Abundant Solitary Wave Solutions for the Boiti–Leon–Manna–Pempinelli Equation with M-Truncated Derivative. *Axioms* **2023**, *12*, 466. [CrossRef]
36. Al-Askar, F.M.; Cesarano, C.; Mohammed, W.W. The Influence of White Noise and the Beta Derivative on the Solutions of the BBM Equation. *Axioms* **2023**, *12*, 447. [CrossRef]
37. Ghanbari, B.; Baleanu, D. New optical solutions of the fractional Gerdjikov-Ivanov equation with conformable derivative. *Front. Phys.* **2020**, *8*, 167. [CrossRef]
38. Mohammed, W.W.; Al-Askar, F.M.; Cesarano, C.; El-Morshedy, M. Solitary Wave Solutions of the Fractional-Stochastic Quantum Zakharov–Kuznetsov Equation Arises in Quantum Magneto Plasma. *Mathematics* **2023**, *11*, 488. [CrossRef]
39. Sousa, J.V.D.C.; de Oliveira, E.C. A new truncated M-fractional derivative type unifying some fractional derivative types with classical properties. *Int. J. Anal. Appl.* **2018**, *16*, 83–96. [CrossRef]
40. Ozdemir, N.; Esen, H.; Secer, A.; Bayram, M.; Yusuf, A.; Sulaiman, T.A. Optical solitons and other solutions to the Hirota–Maccari system with conformable, M-truncated and beta derivatives. *Mod. Phys. Lett. B* **2022**, *36*, 2150625. [CrossRef]

Disclaimer/Publisher's Note: The statements, opinions and data contained in all publications are solely those of the individual author(s) and contributor(s) and not of MDPI and/or the editor(s). MDPI and/or the editor(s) disclaim responsibility for any injury to people or property resulting from any ideas, methods, instructions or products referred to in the content.

axioms

MDPI

Article

Stability Results for the Darboux Problem of Conformable Partial Differential Equations

Rebiai Ghania [1], Lassaad Mchiri [2], Mohamed Rhaima [3], Mohamed Hannabou [4] and Abdellatif Ben Makhlouf [5,*]

1 Department of Mathematics, University of 8 May 1945 Guelma, P.O. Box 401, Guelma 2400, Algeria; rebiai.ghania@univ-guelma.dz
2 ENSIIE, University of Evry-Val-d'Essonne, 1 Square de la Résistance, 91025 Évry-Courcouronnes, France
3 Department of Statistics and Operations Research, College of Science, King Saud University, P.O. Box 2455, Riyadh 11451, Saudi Arabia
4 Department of Mathematics, Faculty of Sciences and Technics, Sultan Moulay Slimane University, BP 523, Beni Mellal 23000, Morocco
5 Department of Mathematics, Faculty of Sciences of Sfax, University of Sfax, Route Soukra, BP 1171, Sfax 3000, Tunisia
* Correspondence: abdellatif.benmakhlouf@fss.usf.tn

Abstract: In this paper, we investigate the Darboux problem of conformable partial differential equations (DPCDEs) using fixed point theory. We focus on the existence and Ulam–Hyers–Rassias stability (UHRS) of the solutions to the problem, which requires finding solutions to nonlinear partial differential equations that satisfy certain boundary conditions. Using fixed point theory, we establish the existence and uniqueness of solutions to the DPCDEs. We then explore the UHRS of the solutions, which measures the sensitivity of the solutions to small perturbations in the equations. We provide three illustrative examples to demonstrate the effectiveness of our approach.

Keywords: generalized conformable derivative; Darboux problem; Ulam–Hyers–Rassias stability

MSC: 34A08; 26A33; 47H10

Citation: Ghania, R.; Mchiri, L.; Rhaima, M.; Hannabou, M.; Ben Makhlouf, A. Stability Results for the Darboux Problem of Conformable Partial Differential Equations. *Axioms* **2023**, *12*, 640. https://doi.org/10.3390/axioms12070640

Academic Editors: Feliz Manuel Minhós, Francisco Martínez González, Mohammed K. A. Kaabar and Hatıra Günerhan

Received: 17 May 2023
Revised: 19 June 2023
Accepted: 26 June 2023
Published: 28 June 2023

Copyright: © 2023 by the authors. Licensee MDPI, Basel, Switzerland. This article is an open access article distributed under the terms and conditions of the Creative Commons Attribution (CC BY) license (https://creativecommons.org/licenses/by/4.0/).

1. Introduction

Fractional calculus (FC) is a fascinating and dynamic branch of mathematical analysis that focuses on studying the properties and applications of fractional derivatives and integrals. These noninteger order operators offer a powerful way to model complex physical, chemical, and engineering systems that cannot be easily described using traditional calculus techniques. In particular, FC has found applications in fields ranging from fluid mechanics, electromagnetism, and signal processing to finance, biology, and medicine. One of the key advantages of FC is its ability to describe nonlocal and memory-dependent phenomena, making it a powerful tool for modeling and analyzing complex systems in both time and space domains. As research in this field continues to grow, we can expect to see even more exciting applications and innovations in the years to come (see [1–3]).

In the past decade, a groundbreaking concept known as the fractional conformable derivative (FCD) has emerged as a transformative tool in the realm of FC, revolutionizing the investigation of nonregular solutions. The introduction of the FCD by Khalil et al. (see [4]) has brought about a profound shift in the understanding and application of fractional derivatives. By possessing properties akin to their integer-order counterparts, the FCD has opened up new avenues for modeling and analyzing intricate systems across diverse disciplines. The study of conformable derivatives has attracted considerable attention, with numerous researchers exploring their definitions, properties, and applications. The work of Khalil et al. has laid the foundation for the understanding of the FCD, highlighting its efficacy in capturing the behavior of complex systems that elude traditional calculus approaches. This novel approach has found application in a wide range of fields, including physics, engineering, biology, and finance. Further advancements in conformable calculus have been documented in a series of seminal publications. For instance, ref. [5] delved into the exploration of controllability in a class of conformable differential systems, shedding light on the efficient manipulation of these systems. Meanwhile, ref. [6] focused on the investigation of nonlinear evolution equations within a Wick-type stochastic environment, incorporating conformable derivatives to account for the inherent uncertainties. In [7], the researchers successfully established the existence of solutions to the conformable diffusion equation, enriching our understanding of diffusion processes influenced by conformable calculus. Furthermore, ref. [8] explored the notion of stability in the Ulam sense for conformable differential equations, presenting crucial insights into the behavior and predictability of such equations. These noteworthy contributions underscore the growing significance of the FCD and conformable calculus, as researchers strive to unravel its full potential and push the boundaries of its applications. As the scientific community continues to delve into the intricacies of conformable derivatives, we anticipate further groundbreaking developments and novel insights in the coming years, propelling us towards a deeper understanding of complex systems through the lens of fractional calculus.

In 1940, Ulam posed the question of stability for functional equations at Wisconsin University (see [9]). The Ulam–Hyers stability was first established by Hyers in 1941 in the context of Banach spaces (see [10]). This type of stability is now referred to as Ulam–Hyers stability. In 1978, Rassias [11] extended the Ulam–Hyers stability (UHS) to include functions of multiple variables. The monographs [12,13] present a comprehensive overview of the UHS and UHRS of various functional equations. Recently, the study of Ulam's problem has been extended to include a wide range of functional equations, such as symmetrical differential equations, integral equations, integro-differential equations, partial differential equations, and other types of equations (see [8,14–22]). For example, in [15], the authors studied the UHRS of pseudoparabolic partial differential equations, while in [19], the UHS of pantograph fractional stochastic differential equations was investigated. However, to the best of our knowledge, there is no existing work on the HHRS of the DPCDEs. Building upon the research conducted by [8], our article aims to generalize the UHRS for PCDEs. The main contributions of our work can be summarized as follows:

1. Existence and uniqueness of the solution: We provide a rigorous proof of the existence and uniqueness of the solution for the DPCDEs.
2. UHRS of the DPCDEs: Our study delves into the UHRS of the DPCDEs. We explore the behavior and stability characteristics of solutions to the DPCDEs under perturbations, taking into account the principles and methodologies established in the UHRS framework.

The organization of our paper is as follows: Section 2 provides the necessary preliminaries, setting the foundation for the subsequent analyses. In Section 3, we delve into the investigation of the existence, uniqueness, and UHRS of the DPCDEs. To illustrate the practical relevance and applicability of the obtained results, Section 4 showcases three carefully selected examples. Finally, in Section 5, we summarize our contributions and discuss directions for future research.

2. Basic Definitions and Tools

In this section, we introduce and define some key terms and concepts that are essential for understanding the subsequent discussions and analyses presented in this paper [4,5,7,23,24].

Definition 1. *Let $\phi : [w, d) \longrightarrow \mathbb{R}$. The generalized conformable derivative of ϕ is defined by*

$$T_w^{\delta,\psi_w}\phi(y) = \lim_{\sigma\to 0}\frac{\phi(y+\sigma\psi_w(y,\delta)) - \phi(y)}{\sigma}, \tag{1}$$

for every $y > w$, where $\delta \in (0,1)$, and $\psi_w(y,\delta)$ is continuous and nonnegative with

$$\psi_w(y,1) = 1,$$

$$\psi_w(.,\delta_1) \neq \psi_w(.,\delta_2), \text{ where } \delta_1 \neq \delta_2, \text{ and } \delta_1, \delta_2 \in (0,1].$$

If $T_w^{\delta,\psi_w}\phi(y)$ exists, for every $y \in (w,a)$, for some $a > w$, $\lim_{y \longrightarrow w^+} T_w^{\delta,\psi_w}\phi(y)$ exists; therefore,

$$T_w^{\delta,\psi_w}\phi(w) := \lim_{y \longrightarrow w^+} T_w^{\delta,\psi_w}\phi(y).$$

Remark 1. *We assume that $\psi_w(y,\delta) > 0$, for all $y > w$, and $\frac{1}{\psi_w}(.,\delta)$ is locally integrable.*

Definition 2. *For $\delta \in (0,1)$, the conformable fractional integral of ϕ is defined by*

$$I_w^{\delta,\psi_w}\phi(y) = \int_w^y \frac{\phi(l)}{\psi_w(l,\delta)}dl. \quad (2)$$

Remark 2. *Let $l \in \mathbb{R}^*$. If*

$$h(z) := \mathbb{E}_\delta^{\psi_w}(l,z,w) = e^{l\int_w^z \frac{1}{\psi_w(x,\delta)}dx},$$

then

$$T_w^{\delta,\psi_w}h(z) = lh(z), \quad \text{and} \quad I_w^{\delta,\psi_w}h(z) = \frac{1}{l}(h(z)-1).$$

The objective of this investigation is to explore and assess the stability properties of the system described by the following set of equations

$$T_{c_1}^{\theta_1,\psi_{c_1}} T_{c_2}^{\theta_2,\psi_{c_2}} u(\lambda_1,\lambda_2) = f(\lambda_1,\lambda_2,u(\lambda_1,\lambda_2)), \quad (3)$$

for all $(\lambda_1,\lambda_2) \in J = [c_1,d_1] \times [c_2,d_2]$, with

$$\begin{cases} u(\lambda_1,c_2) = \varphi(\lambda_1), & \text{if } \lambda_1 \in [c_1,d_1] \\ u(c_1,\lambda_2) = \tilde{\varphi}(\lambda_2), & \text{if } \lambda_2 \in [c_2,d_2] \\ \varphi(c_1) = \tilde{\varphi}(c_2), \end{cases}$$

where $f \in C(J \times \mathbb{R},\mathbb{R})$ and $\varphi : [c_1,d_1] \to \mathbb{R}$, $\tilde{\varphi} : [c_2,d_2] \to \mathbb{R}$ are given absolutely continuous functions. Equation (3) is equivalent to the following equation

$$u(\lambda_1,\lambda_2) = \Phi(\lambda_1,\lambda_2) + \int_{c_1}^{\lambda_1}\int_{c_2}^{\lambda_2} \frac{f(t,s,u(t,s))}{\psi_{c_1}(t,\theta_1)\psi_{c_2}(s,\theta_2)}dsdt,$$

with

$$\Phi(\lambda_1,\lambda_2) = \varphi(\lambda_1) + \tilde{\varphi}(\lambda_2) - \varphi(c_1).$$

In this study, we proceed by considering a crucial assumption that plays a fundamental role in our analysis.
$\mathcal{H}_1$: There exists $\bar{K} > 0$, such that

$$|f(\lambda_1,\lambda_2,u_1) - f(\lambda_1,\lambda_2,u_2)| \leq \bar{K}|u_1 - u_2|, \quad (4)$$

for all $(\lambda_1,\lambda_2) \in J$, $u_1,u_2 \in \mathbb{R}$.

3. Stability Results

In this part, we present the definitions of the UHR and proceed to showcase our main results.

Definition 3. *Equation (3) is UHR stable with respect to* (ϵ, π), *with* $\epsilon > 0$ *and* $\psi \in C(J, \mathbb{R})$ *if there is* $r > 0$, *such that for each solution* V *of*

$$\left| T_{c_1}^{\theta_1,\psi_{c_1}} T_{c_2}^{\theta_2,\psi_{c_2}} V(\lambda_1, \lambda_2) - f(\lambda_1, \lambda_2, V(\lambda_1, \lambda_2)) \right| \leq \epsilon\pi(\lambda_1, \lambda_2), \tag{5}$$

$\forall\, (\lambda_1, \lambda_2) \in J$, *there is a solution* $U^*(\lambda_1, \lambda_2)$ *to (3):*

$$|V(\lambda_1, \lambda_2) - U^*(\lambda_1, \lambda_2)| \leq r\epsilon\pi(\lambda_1, \lambda_2),\ \forall(\lambda_1, \lambda_2) \in J.$$

Theorem 1. *Suppose that* $\mathcal{H}_1$ *holds. If* $V \in AC(J, \mathbb{R})$ *satisfies*

$$\left| T_{c_1}^{\theta_1,\psi_{c_1}} T_{c_2}^{\theta_2,\psi_{c_2}} V(\lambda_1, \lambda_2) - f(\lambda_1, \lambda_2, V(\lambda_1, \lambda_2)) \right| \leq \epsilon\pi(\lambda_1, \lambda_2), \tag{6}$$

$\forall\, (\lambda_1, \lambda_2) \in J$, *where* $\epsilon > 0$, *and* $\pi \in C(J, \mathbb{R})$ *is nondecreasing with respect to* λ_1 *and* λ_2*; then, there is a unique solution* U^* *to* (3), *such that*

$$|V(\lambda_1, \lambda_2) - U^*(\lambda_1, \lambda_2)| \leq \epsilon\frac{\bar{K} + \varrho}{\varrho} \int_{c_1}^{d_1} \frac{ds_1}{\psi_{c_1}(s_1, \theta_1)} \int_{c_2}^{d_2} \frac{ds_2}{\psi_{c_2}(s_2, \theta_2)} \beta(d_1, d_2)\pi(\lambda_1, \lambda_2), \forall(\lambda_1, \lambda_2) \in J,$$

for any positive constant ϱ, *where*

$$\beta(\lambda_1, \lambda_2) = \mathbb{E}_{\theta_1}^{\psi_{c_1}}\left(\sqrt{\bar{K} + \varrho}, \lambda_1, c_1\right) \times \mathbb{E}_{\theta_2}^{\psi_{c_2}}\left(\sqrt{\bar{K} + \varrho}, \lambda_2, c_2\right).$$

Proof. Let us consider the metric d on $C(J, \mathbb{R})$, given by:

$$d(\vartheta_1, \vartheta_2) = \sup_{(\lambda_1, \lambda_2) \in J} \frac{|\vartheta_1(\lambda_1, \lambda_2) - \vartheta_2(\lambda_1, \lambda_2)|}{\beta(\lambda_1, \lambda_2)\pi(\lambda_1, \lambda_2)}. \tag{7}$$

We have $(C(J, \mathbb{R}), d)$, which is a complete metric space. Let $\mathcal{A} : C(J, \mathbb{R}) \to C(J, \mathbb{R})$, such that

$$(\mathcal{A}u)(\lambda_1, \lambda_2) := V(c_1, \lambda_2) + V(\lambda_1, c_2) - V(c_1, c_2) + \int_{c_1}^{\lambda_1} \int_{c_2}^{\lambda_2} \frac{f(t, s, u(t, s))}{\psi_{c_1}(t, \theta_1)\psi_{c_2}(s, \theta_2)} dsdt,\ \forall(\lambda_1, \lambda_2) \in J.$$

Let $u_1, u_2 \in C(J, \mathbb{R})$. By using $\mathcal{H}_1$, we obtain

$$\begin{aligned}
&|(\mathcal{A}u_1)(\lambda_1, \lambda_2) - (\mathcal{A}u_2)(\lambda_1, \lambda_2)| \\
&\leq \left| \int_{c_1}^{\lambda_1} \int_{c_2}^{\lambda_2} \frac{f(s_1, s_2, u_1(s_1, s_2)) - f(s_1, s_2, u_2(s_1, s_2))}{\psi_{c_1}(s_1, \theta_1)\psi_{c_2}(s_2, \theta_2)} ds_2 ds_1 \right| \\
&\leq \int_{c_1}^{\lambda_1} \int_{c_2}^{\lambda_2} \left| \frac{f(s_1, s_2, u_1(s_1, s_2)) - f(s_1, s_2, u_2(s_1, s_2))}{\psi_{c_1}(s_1, \theta_1)\psi_{c_2}(s_2, \theta_2)} \right| ds_2 ds_1 \\
&\leq \bar{K} \int_{c_1}^{\lambda_1} \int_{c_2}^{\lambda_2} \frac{|u_1(s_1, s_2) - u_2(s_1, s_2)|}{\psi_{c_1}(s_1, \theta_1)\psi_{c_2}(s_2, \theta_2)} ds_2 ds_1 \\
&\leq \bar{K} \int_{c_1}^{\lambda_1} \int_{c_2}^{\lambda_2} \frac{|u_1(s_1, s_2) - u_2(s_1, s_2)|}{\beta(s_1, s_2)\pi(s_1, s_2)} \frac{\beta(s_1, s_2)\pi(s_1, s_2)}{\psi_{c_1}(s_1, \theta_1)\psi_{c_2}(s_2, \theta_2)} ds_2 ds_1 \\
&\leq \bar{K} d(u_1, u_2) \int_{c_1}^{\lambda_1} \int_{c_2}^{\lambda_2} \frac{\beta(s_1, s_2)\pi(s_1, s_2)}{\psi_{c_1}(s_1, \theta_1)\psi_{c_2}(s_2, \theta_2)} ds_2 ds_1 \\
&\leq \bar{K} d(u_1, u_2)\pi(\lambda_1, \lambda_2) \int_{c_1}^{\lambda_1} \int_{c_2}^{\lambda_2} \frac{\beta(s_1, s_2)}{\psi_{c_1}(s_1, \theta_1)\psi_{c_2}(s_2, \theta_2)} ds_2 ds_1 \\
&\leq \bar{K} d(u_1, u_2)\pi(\lambda_1, \lambda_2) \int_{c_1}^{\lambda_1} \frac{\mathbb{E}_{\theta_1}^{\psi_{c_1}}\left(\sqrt{\bar{K} + \varrho}, s_1, c_1\right)}{\psi_{c_1}(s_1, \theta_1)} ds_1 \int_{c_2}^{\lambda_2} \frac{\mathbb{E}_{\theta_2}^{\psi_{c_2}}\left(\sqrt{\bar{K} + \varrho}, s_2, c_2\right)}{\psi_{c_2}(s_2, \theta_2)} ds_2.
\end{aligned} \tag{8}$$

By using Remark 2, we obtain

$$|(\mathcal{A}u_1)(\lambda_1,\lambda_2)-(\mathcal{A}u_2)(\lambda_1,\lambda_2)|\leq\frac{\bar{K}}{\bar{K}+\varrho}d(u_1,u_2)\pi(\lambda_1,\lambda_2)\mathbb{E}_{\theta_1}^{\psi_{c_1}}\left(\sqrt{\bar{K}+\varrho},\lambda_1,c_1\right)\mathbb{E}_{\theta_2}^{\psi_{c_2}}\left(\sqrt{\bar{K}+\varrho},\lambda_2,c_2\right). \tag{9}$$

Then,

$$|(\mathcal{A}u_1)(\lambda_1,\lambda_2)-(\mathcal{A}u_2)(\lambda_1,\lambda_2)|\leq\frac{\bar{K}}{\bar{K}+\varrho}d(u_1,u_2)\pi(\lambda_1,\lambda_2)\beta(\lambda_1,\lambda_2).$$

Therefore,

$$\frac{|(\mathcal{A}u_1)(\lambda_1,\lambda_2)-(\mathcal{A}u_2)(\lambda_1,\lambda_2)|}{\pi(\lambda_1,\lambda_2)\beta(\lambda_1,\lambda_2)}\leq\frac{\bar{K}}{\bar{K}+\varrho}d(u_1,u_2). \tag{10}$$

It follows from (7) and (10) that

$$d(\mathcal{A}u_1,\mathcal{A}u_2)\leq\frac{\bar{K}}{\bar{K}+\varrho}d(u_1,u_2).$$

Consequently, by establishing the contractiveness of $\mathcal{A}$, we can derive from (6) that

$$\begin{aligned}|V(\lambda_1,\lambda_2)-\mathcal{A}V(\lambda_1,\lambda_2)| &\leq \epsilon\int_{c_1}^{\lambda_1}\int_{c_2}^{\lambda_2}\frac{\pi(s_1,s_2)}{\psi_{c_1}(s_1,\theta_1)\psi_{c_2}(s_2,\theta_2)}ds_2ds_1\\ &\leq \epsilon\pi(\lambda_1,\lambda_2)\int_{c_1}^{d_1}\frac{ds_1}{\psi_{c_1}(s_1,\theta_1)}\int_{c_2}^{d_2}\frac{ds_2}{\psi_{c_2}(s_2,\theta_2)},\ \forall(\lambda_1,\lambda_2)\in J;\end{aligned}$$

then,

$$\frac{|V(\lambda_1,\lambda_2)-\mathcal{A}V(\lambda_1,\lambda_2)|}{\beta(\lambda_1,\lambda_2)}\leq\epsilon\pi(\lambda_1,\lambda_2)\int_{c_1}^{d_1}\frac{ds_1}{\psi_{c_1}(s_1,\theta_1)}\int_{c_2}^{d_2}\frac{ds_2}{\psi_{c_2}(s_2,\theta_2)},\ \forall(\lambda_1,\lambda_2)\in J,$$

so that

$$d(V,\mathcal{A}V)\leq\epsilon\int_{c_1}^{d_1}\frac{ds_1}{\psi_{c_1}(s_1,\theta_1)}\int_{c_2}^{d_2}\frac{ds_2}{\psi_{c_2}(s_2,\theta_2)}.$$

It follows from Theorem 2 in [18] that there is a solution U^* to (3) such that

$$d(V,U^*)\leq\epsilon\frac{\bar{K}+\varrho}{\varrho}\int_{c_1}^{d_1}\frac{ds_1}{\psi_{c_1}(s_1,\theta_1)}\int_{c_2}^{d_2}\frac{ds_2}{\psi_{c_2}(s_2,\theta_2)},$$

so that

$$|V(\lambda_1,\lambda_2)-U^*(\lambda_1,\lambda_2)|\leq\epsilon\frac{\bar{K}+\varrho}{\varrho}\int_{c_1}^{d_1}\frac{ds_1}{\psi_{c_1}(s_1,\theta_1)}\int_{c_2}^{d_2}\frac{ds_2}{\psi_{c_2}(s_2,\theta_2)}\beta(d_1,d_2)\pi(\lambda_1,\lambda_2),$$

for all $(\lambda_1,\lambda_2)\subset J$. □

In order to investigate the Ulam stability of Equation (3), we present the following notable results.

Theorem 2. *Suppose that $\mathcal{H}_1$ holds. If $V\in AC(J,\mathbb{R})$ satisfies*

$$\left|T_{c_1}^{\theta_1,\psi_{c_1}}T_{c_2}^{\theta_2,\psi_{c_2}}V(\lambda_1,\lambda_2)-f(\lambda_1,\lambda_2,V(\lambda_1,\lambda_2))\right|\leq\epsilon, \tag{11}$$

$\forall\,(\lambda_1,\lambda_2)\in J$, where $\epsilon>0$; then, there is a unique solution U^* to (3)*, such that*

$$|V(\lambda_1,\lambda_2)-U^*(\lambda_1,\lambda_2)|\leq\epsilon\frac{\bar{K}+\varrho}{\varrho}\int_{c_1}^{d_1}\frac{ds_1}{\psi_{c_1}(s_1,\theta_1)}\int_{c_2}^{d_2}\frac{ds_2}{\psi_{c_2}(s_2,\theta_2)}\beta(d_1,d_2),\forall(\lambda_1,\lambda_2)\in J,$$

for any positive constant ϱ*, where*

$$\beta(\lambda_1,\lambda_2) = \mathbb{E}_{\theta_1}^{\psi_{c_1}}\left(\sqrt{\bar{K}+\varrho},\lambda_1,c_1\right) \times \mathbb{E}_{\theta_2}^{\psi_{c_2}}\left(\sqrt{\bar{K}+\varrho},\lambda_2,c_2\right).$$

Proof. The proof is similar to Theorem 1. □

Remark 3. *An important observation to highlight is that the outcomes presented in [18] align with our findings when* $\theta_1 = \theta_2 = 1$ *within the current context.*

4. Illustrative Examples

In this section, we provide three illustrative examples to corroborate the major results outlined in Section 3.

Example 1. *We consider Equation* (3) *for* $c_1 = c_2 = 0$, $d_1 = d_2 = 1$, $\theta_1 = 1$, $\theta_2 = 0.5$, $\psi_{c_2}(s,\theta_2) = s^{1-\theta_2}$*, and* $f(v_1,v_2,r) = {v_1}^3 v_2 \sin(r)$*.*
We have

$$\left|{v_1}^3 v_2 \sin(r_1) - {v_1}^3 v_2 \sin(r_2)\right| \leq |r_1 - r_2|,\ \forall\ (v_1,v_2) \in [0,1]\times[0,1],\ r_1,r_2 \in \mathbb{R}.$$

Then, $\bar{K} = 1$*. Suppose that* V *satisfies*

$$\left|T_{c_1}^{\theta_1,\psi_{c_1}} T_{c_2}^{\theta_2,\psi_{c_2}} V(\lambda_1,\lambda_2) - f(\lambda_1,\lambda_2,V(\lambda_1,\lambda_2))\right| \leq 0.1(\lambda_1+\lambda_2+2), \quad (12)$$

for all $(\lambda_1,\lambda_2) \in [0,1]\times[0,1]$*. Here,* $\epsilon = 0.1$*, and* $\pi(\lambda_1,\lambda_2) = \lambda_1+\lambda_2+2$*. It follows from Theorem 1 that there is a solution* U^* *to the equation, and* $L > 0$*, such that*

$$|V(\lambda_1,\lambda_2) - U^*(\lambda_1,\lambda_2)| \leq 0.1L(\lambda_1+\lambda_2+2),\ \forall\ (\lambda_1,\lambda_2) \in [0,1]\times[0,1].$$

The exact solution U^* *and the approximate solution* V *are plotted in Figure 1.*

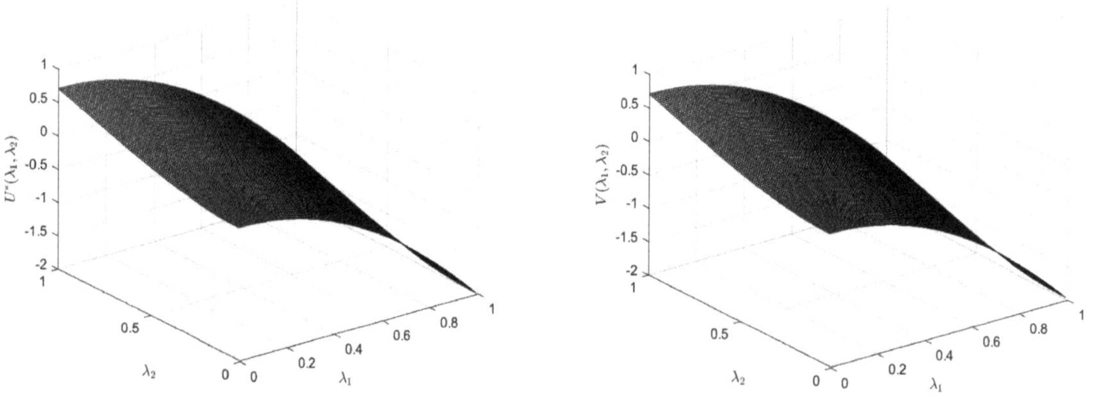

Figure 1. Side-by-side comparison of the exact solution (**left**) and the approximate solution (**right**) for Example 1, with $\theta_1 = 1, \theta_2 = 0.5$, $\varphi(\lambda) = -2\lambda^2$, and $\bar{\varphi}(\lambda) = \sin^2(\lambda)$, on the domain $[0,1]\times[0,1]$.

Example 2. *We consider Equation* (3) *for* $c_1 = c_2 = 0$, $d_1 = d_2 = 2$, $\theta_1 = 0.8$, $\theta_2 = 0.6$, $\psi_{c_1}(s,\theta_1) = s^{1-\theta_1}$, $\psi_{c_2}(s,\theta_2) = s^{1-\theta_2}$ *and* $f(v_1,v_2,r) = v_1{v_2}^2\cos(r)$*.*
We have

$$\left|v_1{v_2}^2\cos(r_1) - v_1{v_2}^2\cos(r_2)\right| \leq 8|r_1 - r_2|,\ \forall\ (v_1,v_2) \in [0,2]\times[0,2],\ r_1,r_2 \in \mathbb{R}.$$

Then, $\bar{K} = 8$. *Suppose that* V *satisfies*

$$\left| T_{c_1}^{\theta_1,\psi_{c_1}} T_{c_2}^{\theta_2,\psi_{c_2}} V(\lambda_1,\lambda_2) - f(\lambda_1,\lambda_2,V(\lambda_1,\lambda_2)) \right| \le 0.01(\lambda_1^2+\lambda_2^2+5), \tag{13}$$

for all $(\lambda_1,\lambda_2) \in [0,2]\times[0,2]$. *Here,* $\epsilon = 0.01$, *and* $\pi(\lambda_1,\lambda_2) = (\lambda_1^2+\lambda_2^2+5)$. *It follows from Theorem 1 that there is a solution* U^* *to the equation, and* $L > 0$, *such that*

$$|V(\lambda_1,\lambda_2) - U^*(\lambda_1,\lambda_2)| \le 0.01L(\lambda_1^2+\lambda_2^2+5),\ \forall\ (\lambda_1,\lambda_2) \in [0,2]\times[0,2].$$

The exact solution U^* *and the approximate solution* V *are plotted in Figure 2.*

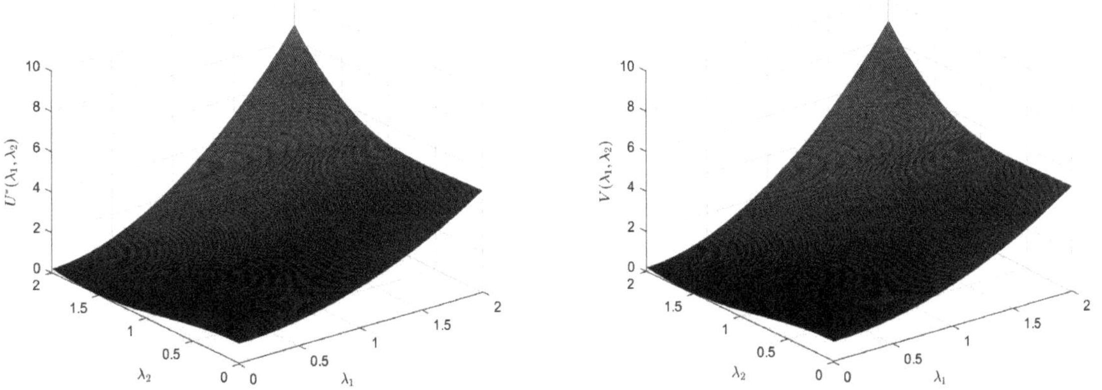

Figure 2. Comparison of the precise solution (on the **left**) and the approximated solution (on the **right**) for Example 2, considering $\theta_1 = 0.8$, $\theta_2 = 0.6$, $\varphi(\lambda) = 1+\lambda^2$, and $\tilde{\varphi}(\lambda) = \cos^2(\lambda)$ on the interval $[0,2]\times[0,2]$.

Example 3. *We consider Equation* (3) *for* $c_1 = c_2 = 0$, $d_1 = d_2 = 3$, $\theta_1 = 0.4$, $\theta_2 = 0.6$, $\psi_{c_1}(s,\theta_1) = s^{1-\theta_1}$, $\psi_{c_2}(s,\theta_2) = s^{1-\theta_2}$, *and* $f(v_1,v_2,r) = \cos(v_1)v_2 r$.
We have

$$|\cos(v_1)v_2r_1 - \cos(v_1)v_2r_2| \le 3|r_1-r_2|,\ \forall\ (v_1,v_2) \in [0,3]\times[0,3],\ r_1,r_2 \in \mathbb{R}.$$

Then, $\bar{K} = 3$. *Suppose that* V *satisfies*

$$\left| T_{c_1}^{\theta_1,\psi_{c_1}} T_{c_2}^{\theta_2,\psi_{c_2}} V(\lambda_1,\lambda_2) - f(\lambda_1,\lambda_2,V(\lambda_1,\lambda_2)) \right| \le 0.01, \tag{14}$$

for all $(\lambda_1,\lambda_2) \in [0,3]\times[0,3]$. *Here,* $\epsilon = 0.01$. *It follows from Theorem 2 that there is a solution* U^* *to the equation, and* $L > 0$, *such that*

$$|V(\lambda_1,\lambda_2) - U^*(\lambda_1,\lambda_2)| \le 0.01L,\ \forall\ (\lambda_1,\lambda_2) \in [0,3]\times[0,3].$$

The exact solution U^* *and the approximate solution* V *are plotted in Figure 3.*

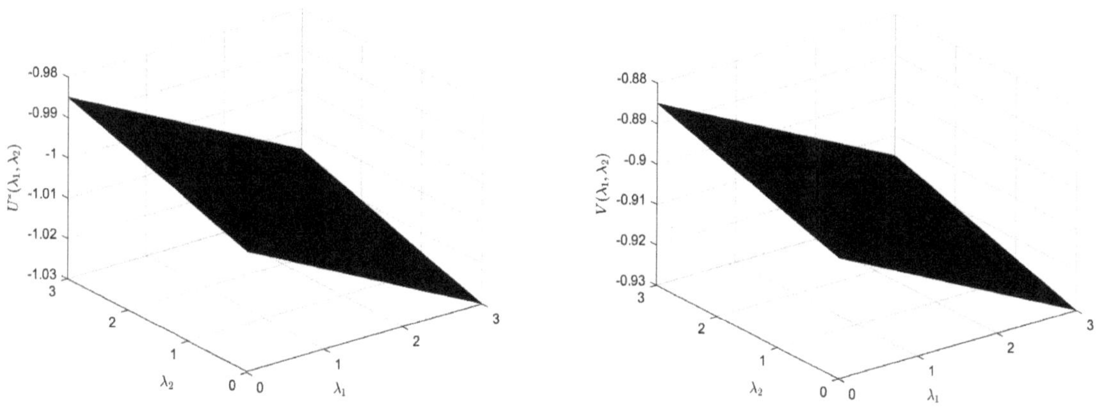

Figure 3. The exact solution (**left**) and the approximate solution (**right**) for Example 3, with $\theta_1 = 0.4$, $\theta_2 = 0.6$, $\varphi(\lambda) = -1 + \frac{1}{200}\lambda$, and $\tilde{\varphi}(\lambda) = -1 - \frac{1}{100}\lambda$, on the interval $[0,3] \times [0,3]$, displayed side by side for easy comparison.

5. Conclusions

In conclusion, this paper delved into a comprehensive investigation of the existence, uniqueness, and UHRS for the DPCDEs. Using the Banach fixed-point theorem, we established the existence and uniqueness of solutions to the DPCDEs that satisfy the prescribed boundary conditions. Furthermore, our exploration of the UHRS for the DPCDEs shed light on the robustness and resilience of the solutions under perturbations. By considering the appropriate stability concepts and utilizing analytical tools, we quantified the stability properties of the solutions. The inclusion of three illustrative examples in this paper serves to solidify and showcase the main obtained results. We can generalize our work by using the operators given in [25–34].

Author Contributions: Conceptualization, L.M. and R.G.; methodology, M.R. and M.H.; writing-original draft, A.B.M. All authors have read and agreed to the published version of the manuscript.

Funding: This research is funded by "Researchers Supporting Project number (RSPD2023R683), King Saud University, Riyadh, Saudi Arabia".

Data Availability Statement: Not applicable.

Acknowledgments: The authors extend their appreciation to King Saud University in Riyadh, Saudi Arabia for funding this research work through Researchers Supporting Project number (RSPD2023R683).

Conflicts of Interest: The authors declare no conflict of interest.

References

1. Atanackovic, T.M.; Pilipovic, S.; Stankovic, B.; Zorica, D. *Fractional Calculus with Applications in Mechanics*; Wiley-ISTE: London, UK; Hoboken, NJ, USA, 2014.
2. Baleanu, D.; Machado, J.A.; Luo, A.C. *Fractional Dynamics and Control*; Springer Science and Business Media: New York, NY, USA, 2011.
3. Podlubny, I. *Fractional Differential Equations*; Academic Press: Cambridge, MA, USA, 1999
4. Khalil, R.; Al Horani, M.; Yousef, A.; Sababheh, M. A new definition of fractional derivative. *J. Comput. Appl. Math.* **2014**, *264*, 65–70. [CrossRef]
5. Azouz, F.; Boucenna, D.; Ben Makhlouf, A.; Mchiri, L.; Benchaabane, A. Controllability of Differential Systems with the General Conformable Derivative. *Complexity* **2021**, *2021*, 2817092. [CrossRef]
6. Hyder, A.A.; Soliman, A.H. An extended Kudryashov technique for solving stochastic nonlinear models with generalized conformable derivatives. *Commun. Nonlinear Sci. Numer. Simul.* **2021**, *97*, 105730. [CrossRef]
7. Li, S.; Zhang, S.; Liu, R. The Existence of Solution of Diffusion Equation with the General Conformable Derivative. *J. Funct. Spaces* **2020**, *2020*, 3965269. [CrossRef]

8. Ben Makhlouf, A.; El-Hady, E.; Boulaaras, S.; Hammami, M.A. Stability analysis for differential equations of the general conformable type. *Complexity* **2022**, *2022*, 7283252 [CrossRef]
9. Ulam, S.M. *A Collection of Mathematical Problems, Interscience Tracts in Pure and Applied Mathematics*; No. 8 Interscience Publishers: New Yor, NY, USA; London, UK, 1960.
10. Hyers, D.H. On the stability of the linear functional equation. *Proc. Nat. Acad. Sci. USA* **1941**, *27*, 222–224. [CrossRef]
11. Rassias, T.M. On the stability of linear mappings in Banach spaces. *Proc. Am. Math. Soc.* **1978**, *72*, 297–300. [CrossRef]
12. Hyers, D.H.; Isac, G.; Rassias Th, M. *Stability of Functional Equations in Several Variables*; Birkhauser: Boston, MA, USA, 1998.
13. Jung, S.M. *Hyers-Ulam-Rassias Stability of Functional Equations in Mathematical Analysis*; Hadronic Press: Palm Harbor, FL, USA, 2001.
14. Jung, S.-M. Hyers-Ulam stability of linear differential equations of first order. *Appl. Math. Lett.* **2004**, *17*, 1135–1140. [CrossRef]
15. Lungu, N.; Ciplea, S.A. Ulam-Hyers-Rassias stability of pseudoparabolic partial differential equations. *Carpathian J. Math.* **2015**, *31*, 233–240 [CrossRef]
16. Shikhare, P.U.; Kucche, K.D. Existence, Uniqueness and Ulam Stabilities for Nonlinear Hyperbolic Partial Integrodifferential Equations. *Int. J. Appl. Comput. Math.* **2019**, *5*, 156. [CrossRef]
17. Wang, S.; Jiang, W.; Sheng, J.; Li, R. Ulam's stability for some linear conformable fractional differential equations. *Adv. Differ. Equations* **2020**, *2020*, 251. [CrossRef]
18. El-hady, E.; Ben Makhlouf, A. A novel stability analysis for the Darboux problem of partial differential equations via fixed point theory. *AIMS Math.* **2021**, *6*, 12894–12901. [CrossRef]
19. Mchiri, L.; Ben Makhlouf, A.; Rguigui, H. Ulam–Hyers stability of pantograph fractional stochastic differential equations. *Math. Methods Appl. Sci.* **2023**, *46*, 4134–4144. [CrossRef]
20. Kahouli, O.; Ben Makhlouf, A.; Mchiri, L.; Rguigui, H. Hyers–Ulam stability for a class of Hadamard fractional Itô–Doob stochastic integral equations. *Chaos Solitons Fractals* **2023**, *166*, 112918. [CrossRef]
21. Houas, M.; Martinez, F.; Samei, M.E.; Kaabar, M.K.A. Uniqueness and Ulam-Hyers–Rassias stability results for sequential fractional pantograph q-differential equations. *J. Inequalities Appl.* **2022**, *2022*, 93. [CrossRef]
22. Alzabut, J.; Selvam, A.G.M.; Dhineshbabu, R.; Kaabar, M.K.A. The existence, uniqueness, and stability analysis of the discrete fractional three-point boundary value problem for the elastic beam equation. *Symmetry* **2021**, *13*, 789. [CrossRef]
23. Abdeljawad, T. On conformable fractional calculus. *J. Comput. Appl. Math.* **2015**, *279*, 57–66. [CrossRef]
24. Zhao, D.; Luo, M. General conformable fractional derivative and its physical interpretation. *Calcolo* **2015**, *54*, 903–917. [CrossRef]
25. Guzman, P.M.; Langton, G.; Bittencurt, L.M.L.M.; Medina, J.; Valdes, J.E.N. A New Definition of a fractional derivative of local type. *J. Math. Anal.* **2018**, *9*, 88–98.
26. Valdes, J.E.N.; GuzmÁNPM, L.L.M. Some New Results on Nonconformable Fractional Calculus. *Adv. Dyn. Syst. Appl.* **2018**, *13*, 167–175.
27. Guzmán, P.M.; Lugo, L.M.; Valdes, J.E.N.; Vivas Cortez, M. On a New Generalized Integral Operator and Certain Operating Properties. *Axioms* **2020**, *9*, 69. [CrossRef]
28. Martínez, F.; Valdes, J.E.N. Towards a Non-conformable Fractional Calculus of n-Variables. *J. Math. Appl.* **2020**, *43*, 87–98. [CrossRef]
29. Fleitas, A.; Valdes, J.E.N.; Rodríguez, J.M.; Sigarreta, J.M. Note on the generalized conformable derivative. *Revista UMA* **2021**, *62*, 443–457. [CrossRef]
30. Vivas-Cortez, M.; Lugo, L.M.; Valdes, J.E.N.; Samei, M.E. A Multi-Index Generalized Derivative Some Introductory Notes. *Appl. Math. Inf. Sci.* **2022**, *16*, 883–890.
31. Inc, M.; Yusuf, A.; Aliyu, A.I.; Baleanu, D. Soliton solutions and stability analysis for some conformable nonlinear partial differential equations in mathematical physics. *Opt. Quantum Electron.* **2018**, *50*, 190. [CrossRef]
32. Martinez, F.; Martinez, I.; Kaabar, M.K.A.; Paredes, S. Solving systems of conformable linear differential equations via the conformable exponential matrix. *Ain Shams Eng. J.* **2021**, *12*, 4075–4080. [CrossRef]
33. Martinez, F.; Martinez, I.; Kaabar, M.K.A.; Paredes, S. Novel results on conformable Bessel functions. *Nonlinear Eng.* **2022**, *11*, 6–12. [CrossRef]
34. Awadalla, M.; Subramanian, M.; Abuasbeh, K.; Manigandan, M. On the Generalized Liouville–Caputo Type Fractional Differential Equations Supplemented with Katugampola Integral Boundary Conditions. *Symmetry* **2022**, *14*, 2273. [CrossRef]

Disclaimer/Publisher's Note: The statements, opinions and data contained in all publications are solely those of the individual author(s) and contributor(s) and not of MDPI and/or the editor(s). MDPI and/or the editor(s) disclaim responsibility for any injury to people or property resulting from any ideas, methods, instructions or products referred to in the content.

axiom s

MDPI

Article

The Influence of White Noise and the Beta Derivative on the Solutions of the BBM Equation

Farah M. Al-Askar [1], Clemente Cesarano [2] and Wael W. Mohammed [3,4,*]

[1] Department of Mathematical Science, Collage of Science, Princess Nourah Bint Abdulrahman University, P.O. Box 84428, Riyadh 11671, Saudi Arabia; famalaskar@pnu.edu.sa
[2] Section of Mathematics, International Telematic University Uninettuno, Corso Vittorio Emanuele II, 39, 00186 Roma, Italy; c.cesarano@uninettuno.it
[3] Department of Mathematics, Collage of Science, University of Ha'il, Ha'il 2440, Saudi Arabia
[4] Department of Mathematics, Faculty of Science, Mansoura University, Mansoura 35516, Egypt
* Correspondence: wael.mohammed@mans.edu.eg

Abstract: In the current study, we investigate the stochastic Benjamin–Bona–Mahony equation with beta derivative (SBBME-BD). The considered stochastic term is the multiplicative noise in the Itô sense. By combining the $\mathcal{F}$-expansion approach with two separate equations, such as the Riccati and elliptic equations, new hyperbolic, trigonometric, rational, and Jacobi elliptic solutions for SBBME-BD can be generated. The solutions to the Benjamin–Bona–Mahony equation are useful in understanding various scientific phenomena, including Rossby waves in spinning fluids and drift waves in plasma. Our results are presented using MATLAB, with numerous 3D and 2D figures illustrating the impacts of white noise and the beta derivative on the obtained solutions of SBBME-BD.

Keywords: stability by noise; exact solutions; $\mathcal{F}$-expansion method; beta-derivative; stochastic BBM

MSC: 35C08; 35C07; 35C05; 83C15; 35A20

Citation: Al-Askar, F.M.; Cesarano, C.; Mohammed, W.W. The Influence of White Noise and the Beta Derivative on the Solutions of the BBM Equation. *Axioms* **2023**, *12*, 447. https://doi.org/10.3390/axioms12050447

Academic Editors: Hatıra Günerhan, Francisco Martínez González and Mohammed K. A. Kaabar

Received: 10 April 2023
Revised: 26 April 2023
Accepted: 28 April 2023
Published: 30 April 2023

Copyright: © 2023 by the authors. Licensee MDPI, Basel, Switzerland. This article is an open access article distributed under the terms and conditions of the Creative Commons Attribution (CC BY) license (https://creativecommons.org/licenses/by/4.0/).

1. Introduction

Nonlinear evolution equations (NEEs) are utilized to explain complex phenomena in many disciplines, including optical fiber communication, chemical kinetics, population dynamics, chaotic systems, photonic, plasma physics, electromagnetism, ocean wave, wave propagation, nuclear physics, fluid mechanics, and solid-state physics. Obtaining traveling wave solutions for NEEs is the most significant physical challenge. There are several effective methods for solving NEEs, including the generalized Kudryashov approach [1], modified decomposition approach [2], Riccati equation expansion [3], sine-Gordon expansion [4], sine-cosine method [5], Exp-function [6], improved $\tan(\varphi/2)$-expansion [7], Lie symmetry [8], Jacobi elliptic function [9], and the tanh–sech method [10].

Recently, numerous mathematicians have introduced several fractional derivatives. Some of the most well-known are those presented by Caputo, Riemann-Liouville, Grunwald-Letnikov, Kober, Erdelyi, Marchaud, Hadamard, and Riesz [11–14]. Most kinds of fractional derivatives do not follow the chain rule, quotient rule, or product rule. In recent years, Atangana et al. [15] produced a new operator derivative called the beta-derivative (BD), which extends the classical derivative. If $f:(0,\infty)\to\mathbb{R}$ then its beta derivative [15] is defined as:

$$\mathcal{D}_x^{\beta}\phi(x)=\frac{d^{\beta}\phi}{dx^{\beta}}=\lim_{h\to 0}\frac{\phi(x+h(x+\frac{1}{\Gamma(\beta)})^{1-\beta})-\phi(x)}{h},\ 0<\beta\leq 1.$$

Moreover, the BD possesses the following properties [15] for all real numbers a and b:
(1) $\mathcal{D}_x^{\beta}f(y)=(x+\frac{1}{\Gamma(\beta)})^{1-\beta}\frac{df}{dx}$,

(2) $\mathcal{D}_x^{\beta}(af+bg)=a\mathcal{D}_x^{\beta}(f)+b\mathcal{D}_x^{\beta}(g)$,
(3) $\mathcal{D}_x^{\beta}(f\circ g(x))=(x+\frac{1}{\Gamma(\beta)})^{1-\beta}g'(x)f'(g(x))$,
(4) $\mathcal{D}_x^{\beta}(a)=0$.

Moreover, stochastic partial differential equations (SDEs) have a wide range of applications in physics, including molecular dynamics, neurodynamics, climate dynamics, geophysics, biology, physics, chemistry, and other scientific disciplines [16–18]. More precisely, SDEs characterize all dynamical equations in which quantum influences are either insignificant or can be accounted for as perturbations. SDEs are an extension of the theory of dynamical systems to models with noise. This is a significant generalization because actual systems cannot be entirely isolated from their surroundings and, as a result, are always subject to external stochastic influence.

As a consequence, obtaining exact solutions to fractional or stochastic differential equations is critical. Many analytical and numerical methods, including the (G'/G)-expansion method [19], the mapping method [20], the Jacobi elliptic function technique [21], the extended tanh-coth method [22], bifurcation analysis [23,24], and more.

Therefore, it is critical here to look at the stochastic Benjamin–Bona–Mahony equation with beta derivative (SBBME-BD) as follows:

$$\mathcal{Q}_t+6\mathcal{Q}\mathcal{D}_x^{\beta}\mathcal{Q}+\mathcal{D}_{xxx}^{\beta}\mathcal{Q}-\alpha\mathcal{D}_{xx}^{\beta}\mathcal{Q}_t=\sigma(\mathcal{Q}-\alpha\mathcal{D}_{xx}^{\beta}\mathcal{Q})\mathcal{B}_t, \tag{1}$$

where the function $\mathcal{Q}=\mathcal{Q}(x,t)$ is real, σ is the strength of the noise, $\mathcal{B}=\mathcal{B}(t)$ is a white noise that satisfies the following properties: (i) $\mathcal{B}$ has continuous trajectories, (ii) $\mathcal{B}(0)=0$, and (iii) $\mathcal{B}(t_{i+1})-\mathcal{B}(t_i)$ has standard normal distribution. If we put $\sigma=0$, and $\beta=1$, then we obtain the Benjamin–Bona–Mahony equation as follows:

$$\mathcal{Q}_t+6\mathcal{Q}\mathcal{Q}_x+\mathcal{Q}_{xxx}-\alpha\mathcal{Q}_{xxt}=0. \tag{2}$$

Benjamin, Bona, and Mahony [25] investigated Equation (2) as a modification of the KdV equation. The modified equation was proposed to simulate long surface gravity waves with small amplitudes propagating in a 1 + 1 dimension. Many researchers have acquired the exact solutions of Equation (2) by applying many various methods, such as the generalized (G'/G)-expansion method [26], (G'/G)-expansion method [27], Hirota's bilinear method [28], the Lie group method [29], the exp-function method [30], the tanh–coth method, and the sn–ns method [31]. The stochastic Benjamin–Bona–Mahony equation with beta derivative has not been considered until now.

The motivation behind this study is to obtain exact stochastic solutions of SBBME-BD (1) using the $\mathcal{F}$-expansion approach combined with two distinct equations, namely the Riccati and elliptic equations. The presence of a stochastic term in the equation makes these solutions particularly useful for physicists in understanding important physical phenomena. Moreover, we present various 2D and 3D graphical representations using the MATLAB program to explore the impact of the Beta derivative and noise on the exact solution of SBBME-BD (1).

The sequence of the paper is as follows: In Section 2, we derive the wave equation for the SBBME-BD (1). In Section 3, the solution of the SBBME-BD (1) may be obtained by using $\mathcal{F}$ white noise and the BD on the obtained solutions of SBBME-BD (1). In the end, the conclusions of this paper are introduced.

2. Traveling Wave Equation for SBBME-BD

The wave equation for SBBME-BD (1) is achieved by applying:

$$\mathcal{Q}(x,t)=\mathcal{G}(\zeta)e^{[\sigma\mathcal{B}(t)-\frac{1}{2}\sigma^2 t]},\quad \zeta=\frac{\zeta_1}{\beta}(x+\frac{1}{\Gamma(\beta)})^{\beta}+\zeta_2 t, \tag{3}$$

where $\mathcal{G}$ is a deterministic function, and ζ_1, ζ_2 are unknown constants. We note that

$$\begin{aligned}\mathcal{Q}_t &= [\zeta_2\mathcal{G}' + \sigma\mathcal{G}\mathcal{B}_t + \frac{1}{2}\sigma^2\mathcal{G} - \frac{1}{2}\sigma^2\mathcal{G}]e^{[\sigma\mathcal{B}(t)-\frac{1}{2}\sigma^2 t]} \\ &= [\zeta_2\mathcal{G}' + \sigma\mathcal{G}\mathcal{B}_t]e^{[\sigma\mathcal{B}(t)-\frac{1}{2}\sigma^2 t]},\end{aligned} \tag{4}$$

and

$$\mathcal{D}^{\beta}_{xx}\mathcal{Q}_t = [\zeta_1^2\zeta_2\mathcal{G}''' + \sigma\zeta_1^2\mathcal{G}''\mathcal{B}_t]e^{[\sigma\mathcal{B}(t)-\frac{1}{2}\sigma^2 t]} \tag{5}$$

$$\mathcal{D}^{\beta}_{x}\mathcal{Q} = \zeta_1\mathcal{G}'e^{[\sigma\mathcal{B}(t)-\frac{1}{2}\sigma^2 t]}, \mathcal{D}^{\beta}_{xxx}\mathcal{Q} = \zeta_1^3\mathcal{G}'''e^{[\sigma\mathcal{B}(t)-\frac{1}{2}\sigma^2 t]}. \tag{6}$$

Inserting Equation (3) into Equation (1) and utilizing (4)–(6), we obtain

$$\zeta_2\mathcal{G}' + (\zeta_1^3 - \alpha\zeta_1^2\zeta_2)\mathcal{G}''' + 6\zeta_1\mathcal{G}\mathcal{G}'e^{[\sigma\mathcal{B}(t)-\frac{1}{2}\sigma^2 t]} = 0. \tag{7}$$

Taking the expectations on both sides, we have

$$\zeta_2\mathcal{G}' + (\zeta_1^3 - \alpha\zeta_1^2\zeta_2)\mathcal{G}''' + 6\zeta_1\mathcal{G}\mathcal{G}'e^{-\frac{1}{2}\sigma^2 t}\mathbb{E}e^{[\sigma\mathcal{B}(t)]} = 0. \tag{8}$$

Since $\mathcal{B}(t)$ is a Gaussian process, then $\mathbb{E}(e^{\sigma\mathcal{B}(t)}) = e^{\frac{1}{2}\sigma^2 t}$. Thus, Equation (8) becomes

$$\zeta_2\mathcal{G}' + (\zeta_1^3 - \alpha\zeta_1^2\zeta_2)\mathcal{G}''' + 6\zeta_1\mathcal{G}\mathcal{G}' = 0. \tag{9}$$

Integrating Equation (9) once with a zero integration constant yields

$$\mathcal{G}'' + \gamma_1\mathcal{G} + \gamma_2\mathcal{G}^2 = 0, \tag{10}$$

where

$$\gamma_1 = \frac{\zeta_2}{(\zeta_1^3 - \alpha\zeta_1^2\zeta_2)} \text{ and } \gamma_2 = \frac{3}{(\zeta_1^2 - \alpha\zeta_1\zeta_2)}.$$

3. Exact Solutions of SBBME-BD

Utilizing the $\mathcal{F}$-expansion method ($\mathcal{F}$-EM) with two different equations, such as the Riccati equation and elliptic equation, the solutions to Equation (10) are discovered. Afterward, the SBBME-BD solutions (1) can be obtained.

3.1. $\mathcal{F}$-EM with Riccati Equation

Assuming that the solution $\mathcal{G}$ of Equation (10) has the form:

$$\mathcal{G}(\zeta) = \hbar_0 + \sum_{k=1}^{J}\hbar_k\mathcal{F}^k, \tag{11}$$

where $\mathcal{F}$ is the solution of the Riccati equation:

$$\mathcal{F}' = \mathcal{F}^2 + \phi, \tag{12}$$

Determining J needs balancing $\mathcal{G}''$ with $\mathcal{G}^2$ in Equation (10) as

$$J + 2 = 2J \Rightarrow J = 2.$$

Equation (11) becomes

$$\mathcal{G}(\zeta) = \hbar_0 + \hbar_1\mathcal{F} + \hbar_2\mathcal{F}^2. \tag{13}$$

Equation (12) has the following solution:

$$\mathcal{F}(\zeta) = \sqrt{\phi}\tan(\sqrt{\phi}\zeta) \text{ or } \mathcal{F}(\zeta) = -\sqrt{\phi}\cot(\sqrt{\phi}\zeta), \tag{14}$$

If $\phi > 0$, or

$$\mathcal{F}(\zeta) = -\sqrt{-\phi}\tanh(\sqrt{-\phi}\zeta) \text{ or } \mathcal{F}(\zeta) = -\sqrt{-\phi}\coth(\sqrt{-\phi}\zeta), \tag{15}$$

If $\phi < 0$, or

$$\varphi(\zeta) = \frac{-1}{\zeta}, \tag{16}$$

If $\phi = 0$.

Now, putting Equation (13) into Equation (10), we have

$$(6\hbar_2 + \gamma_2\hbar_2^2)\mathcal{F}^4 + (2\hbar_1 + 2\gamma_2\hbar_1\hbar_2)\mathcal{F}^3 + (8\phi\hbar_2 + 2\hbar_0\hbar_2\gamma_2 + \hbar_1^2\gamma_2 + \gamma_1\hbar_2)\mathcal{F}^2$$
$$(2\phi\hbar_1 + \gamma_1\hbar_1 + 2\gamma_2\hbar_0\hbar_1)\mathcal{F} + (2\phi^2\hbar_2 + \gamma_1\hbar_0 + \gamma_2\hbar_0^2) = 0$$

Putting the coefficients of $\mathcal{F}$ to zero:

$$6\hbar_2 + \gamma_2\hbar_2^2 = 0,$$

$$2\hbar_1 + 2\gamma_2\hbar_1\hbar_2 = 0,$$

$$8\phi\hbar_2 + 2\hbar_0\hbar_2\gamma_2 + \hbar_1^2\gamma_2 + \gamma_1\hbar_2 = 0,$$

$$2\phi\hbar_1 + \gamma_1\hbar_1 + 2\gamma_2\hbar_0\hbar_1 = 0,$$

and

$$2\phi^2\hbar_2 + \gamma_1\hbar_0 + \gamma_2\hbar_0^2 = 0.$$

By solving these equations, we obtain the two families of solutions:

First family:

$$\hbar_0 = \frac{-6\phi}{\gamma_2},\ \hbar_1 = 0,\ \hbar_2 = \frac{-6}{\gamma_2},\ \zeta_2 = \frac{4\phi\zeta_1^3}{1 + 4\alpha\phi\zeta_1^2}, \tag{17}$$

Second family:

$$\hbar_0 = \frac{-2\phi}{\gamma_2},\ \hbar_1 = 0,\ \hbar_2 = \frac{-6}{\gamma_2},\ \zeta_2 = \frac{-4\phi\zeta_1^3}{1 - 4\alpha\phi\zeta_1^2}, \tag{18}$$

First family: The solution to Equation (10) is as follows:

$$\mathcal{G}(\zeta) = \frac{-6\phi}{\gamma_2} - \frac{6}{\gamma_2}\mathcal{F}^2(\zeta).$$

There are three distinct cases for $\mathcal{F}(\zeta)$:

Case 1: If $\phi > 0$, then with (14), we have

$$\mathcal{G}(\zeta) = \frac{-6\phi}{\gamma_2} - \frac{6\phi}{\gamma_2}\tan^2(\sqrt{\phi}\zeta) = -\frac{6\phi}{\gamma_2}\sec^2(\sqrt{\phi}\zeta),$$

and

$$\mathcal{G}(\zeta) = \frac{-6\phi}{\gamma_2} - \frac{6\phi}{\gamma_2}\cot^2(\sqrt{\phi}\zeta) = \frac{-6\phi}{\gamma_2}\csc^2(\sqrt{\phi}\zeta).$$

Consequently, the solution of SBBME-BD (1) is

$$\mathcal{Q}(x,t) = -\frac{6\phi}{\gamma_2}\sec^2(\sqrt{\phi}\zeta)e^{(\sigma\mathcal{B}(t)-\frac{1}{2}\sigma^2 t)}, \tag{19}$$

and

$$\mathcal{Q}(x,t) = \frac{-6\phi}{\gamma_2}\csc^2(\sqrt{\phi}\zeta)e^{(\sigma\mathcal{B}(t)-\frac{1}{2}\sigma^2 t)}, \tag{20}$$

where $\zeta = \frac{\zeta_1}{\beta}(x+\frac{1}{\Gamma(\beta)})^{\beta} + \frac{4\phi\zeta_1^3}{1+4\alpha\phi\zeta_1^2}t$.

Case 2: If $\phi < 0$, then by using (15), we have

$$\mathcal{G}(\zeta) = \frac{-6\phi}{\gamma_2} + \frac{6\phi}{\gamma_2}\tanh^2(\sqrt{-\phi}\zeta) = \frac{-6\phi}{\gamma_2}\mathrm{sech}^2(\sqrt{-\phi}\zeta),$$

and

$$\mathcal{G}(\zeta) = \frac{-6\phi}{\gamma_2} + \frac{6\phi}{\gamma_2}\coth^2(\sqrt{-\phi}\zeta) = \frac{6\phi}{\gamma_2}\mathrm{csch}^2(\sqrt{-\phi}\zeta).$$

Consequently, the solution of SBBME-BD (1) is

$$\mathcal{Q}(x,t) = \frac{-6\phi}{\gamma_2}\mathrm{sech}^2(\sqrt{-\phi}\zeta)e^{(\sigma\mathcal{B}(t)-\frac{1}{2}\sigma^2 t)}, \tag{21}$$

and

$$\mathcal{Q}(x,t) = \frac{6\phi}{\gamma_2}\mathrm{csch}^2(\sqrt{-\phi}\zeta)e^{(\sigma\mathcal{B}(t)-\frac{1}{2}\sigma^2 t)}. \tag{22}$$

Case 3: If $\phi = 0$, then by using (16), we have

$$\mathcal{G}(\zeta) = \frac{6}{\gamma_2}\frac{1}{\zeta^2}.$$

Consequently, the solution of SBBME-BD (1) is

$$\mathcal{Q}(x,t) = [-\frac{6}{\gamma_2}\frac{1}{\zeta^2}]e^{(\sigma\mathcal{B}(t)-\frac{1}{2}\sigma^2 t)}, \tag{23}$$

where $\zeta = \frac{\zeta_1}{\beta}(x+\frac{1}{\Gamma(\beta)})^{\beta} + \frac{4\phi\zeta_1^3}{1+4\alpha\phi\zeta_1^2}t$.

Second family: Equation (10) has the solution

$$\mathcal{G}(\zeta) = \frac{-2\phi}{\gamma_2} - \frac{6}{\gamma_2}\mathcal{F}^2(\zeta)$$

There are three distinct cases for $\mathcal{F}(\zeta)$:

Case 1: If $\phi > 0$, then by using (14), we have

$$\mathcal{G}(\zeta) = \frac{-2\phi}{\gamma_2} - \frac{6\phi}{\gamma_2}\tan^2(\sqrt{\phi}\zeta),$$

and

$$\mathcal{G}(\zeta) = \frac{-2\phi}{\gamma_2} - \frac{6\phi}{\gamma_2}\cot^2(\sqrt{\phi}\zeta).$$

Consequently, the solution of SBBME-BD (1) is

$$\mathcal{Q}(x,t) = [\frac{-2\phi}{\gamma_2} - \frac{6\phi}{\gamma_2}\tan^2(\sqrt{\phi}\zeta)]e^{(\sigma\mathcal{B}(t)-\frac{1}{2}\sigma^2 t)}, \tag{24}$$

and

$$\mathcal{Q}(x,t) = [\frac{-2\phi}{\gamma_2} - \frac{6\phi}{\gamma_2}\cot^2(\sqrt{\phi}\zeta)]e^{(\sigma\mathcal{B}(t)-\frac{1}{2}\sigma^2 t)}, \tag{25}$$

where $\zeta = \frac{\zeta_1}{\beta}(x + \frac{1}{\Gamma(\beta)})^\beta - \frac{4\phi\zeta_1^3}{1-4\alpha\phi\zeta_1^2}t$.

Case 2: If $\phi < 0$, then by using (15), we have

$$\mathcal{G}(\zeta) = \frac{-2\phi}{\gamma_2} + \frac{6\phi}{\gamma_2}\tanh^2(\sqrt{-\phi}\zeta),$$

and

$$\mathcal{G}(\zeta) = \frac{-2\phi}{\gamma_2} + \frac{6\phi}{\gamma_2}\coth^2(\sqrt{-\phi}\zeta).$$

Consequently, the solution of SBBME-BD (1) is

$$\mathcal{Q}(x,t) = [\frac{-2\phi}{\gamma_2} + \frac{6\phi}{\gamma_2}\tanh^2(\sqrt{-\phi}\zeta)]e^{(\sigma\mathcal{B}(t)-\frac{1}{2}\sigma^2 t)}, \tag{26}$$

and

$$\mathcal{Q}(x,t) = [\frac{-2\phi}{\gamma_2} + \frac{6\phi}{\gamma_2}\coth^2(\sqrt{-\phi}\zeta)]e^{(\sigma\mathcal{B}(t)-\frac{1}{2}\sigma^2 t)}, \tag{27}$$

where $\zeta = \frac{\zeta_1}{\beta}(x + \frac{1}{\Gamma(\beta)})^\beta - \frac{4\phi\zeta_1^3}{1-4\alpha\phi\zeta_1^2}t$.

Case 3: If $\phi = 0$, then by using (16), we have

$$\mathcal{G}(\zeta) = \frac{6}{\gamma_2}\frac{1}{\zeta^2}.$$

Consequently, the solution of SBBME-BD (1) is

$$\mathcal{Q}(x,t) = \frac{6}{\gamma_2}\frac{1}{\zeta^2}e^{(\sigma\mathcal{B}(t)-\frac{1}{2}\sigma^2 t)}, \tag{28}$$

where $\zeta = \frac{\zeta_1}{\beta}(x + \frac{1}{\Gamma(\beta)})^\beta - \frac{4\phi\zeta_1^3}{1-4\alpha\phi\zeta_1^2}t$.

3.2. *$\mathcal{F}$-EM with Elliptic Equation*

Suppose that the solution of Equation (10) has the form (13). However, at this time, $\mathcal{F}$ solves the following elliptic equation:

$$\mathcal{F}' = \sqrt{R + K\mathcal{F}^2 + P\mathcal{F}^4}, \tag{29}$$

where R, K, and P are constants. Differentiating Equation (13) twice and using (29), we have

$$\mathcal{G}'' = \hbar_1(K\mathcal{F} + 2P\mathcal{F}^3) + 2\hbar_2(R + 2K\mathcal{F}^2 + 3P\mathcal{F}^4). \tag{30}$$

Setting Equations (13) and (30) into Equation (10), we have

$$(6\hbar_2 P + \gamma_2\hbar_2^2)\mathcal{F}^4 + (2P\hbar_1 + 2\hbar_1\hbar_2\gamma_2)\mathcal{F}^3 + (4\hbar_2 K + 2\gamma_2\hbar_0\hbar_2 + \hbar_1^2$$
$$+\hbar_2\gamma_1)\mathcal{F}^2 + (\hbar_1 K + 2\gamma_2\hbar_0\hbar_1 + \gamma_1\hbar_1)\mathcal{F} + (2R\hbar_2 + \gamma_1\hbar_0 + \gamma_2\hbar_0^2) = 0.$$

If we assign each coefficient of $\mathcal{F}^k$ to 0, we will have a system of equations. Here are the two families we obtain when we solve this system for $K^2 - 3RP > 0$:

First family:

$$\hbar_0 = -2(\frac{K+\sqrt{(K^2-3RP)}}{\gamma_2}),\ \hbar_1 = 0,\ \hbar_2 = \frac{-6P}{\gamma_2},\ \zeta_2 = \frac{4\sqrt{(K^2-3RP)}\zeta_1^3}{1+4\alpha\sqrt{(K^2-3RP)}\zeta_1^2}.$$

Second family:

$$\hbar_0 = -2(\frac{K-\sqrt{(K^2-3RP)}}{\gamma_2}),\ \hbar_1 = 0,\ \hbar_2 = \frac{-6P}{\gamma_2},\ \zeta_2 = \frac{-4\sqrt{(K^2-3RP)}\zeta_1^3}{1-4\alpha\sqrt{(K^2-3RP)}\zeta_1^2}.$$

In both families, the solution of Equation (10) takes the form:

$$\mathcal{G}(\zeta) = \hbar_0 + \hbar_2\mathcal{F}^2(\zeta). \tag{31}$$

There are many cases for $\mathcal{F}$ depending on P, K and R such that $K^2 - 3RP > 0$ as follows:

Case	P	K	R	$F(\zeta)$
1	ρ^2	$-(1+\rho^2)$	1	$sn(\zeta)$
2	1	$2\rho^2-1$	$-\rho^2(1-\rho^2)$	$ds(\zeta)$
3	1	$2-\rho^2$	$(1-\rho^2)$	$cs(\zeta)$
4	$-\rho^2$	$2\rho^2-1$	$(1-\rho^2)$	$cn(\zeta)$
5	-1	$2-\rho^2$	(ρ^2-1)	$dn(\zeta)$
6	$\frac{\rho^2}{4}$	$\frac{(\rho^2-2)}{2}$	$\frac{1}{4}(\text{or } \frac{\rho^2}{4})$	$\frac{sn(\zeta)}{1\pm dn(\zeta)}$
7	$\frac{-1}{4}$	$\frac{(\rho^2+1)}{2}$	$\frac{-(1-\rho^2)^2}{4}$	$\rho cn(\zeta) \pm dn(\zeta)$
8	$\frac{\rho^2-1}{4}$	$\frac{(\rho^2+1)}{2}$	$\frac{(\rho^2-1)}{4}$	$\frac{dn(\zeta)}{1\pm sn(\zeta)}$
9	$\frac{1-\rho^2}{4}$	$\frac{(1-\rho^2)}{2}$	$\frac{(1-\rho^2)}{4}$	$\frac{cn(\zeta)}{1\pm sn(\zeta)}$

For the first family: the solutions of SBBME-BD (1) are

$$\mathcal{Q}_1(x,t) = [\frac{2(1+\rho^2) - 2\sqrt{\rho^4-\rho^2+1}}{\gamma_2} - \frac{6\rho^2}{\gamma_2}sn^2(\zeta)]e^{[\sigma\mathcal{B}(t)-\frac{1}{2}\sigma^2 t]}, \tag{32}$$

$$\mathcal{Q}_2(x,t) = [\frac{(2-4\rho^2) - 2\sqrt{\rho^4-\rho^2+1}}{\gamma_2} - \frac{6}{\gamma_2}ds^2(\zeta)]e^{[\sigma\mathcal{B}(t)-\frac{1}{2}\sigma^2 t]}, \tag{33}$$

$$\mathcal{Q}_3(x,t) = [\frac{(2\rho^2-4) - 2\sqrt{\rho^4+\rho^2+1}}{\gamma_2} - \frac{6}{\gamma_2}cs^2(\zeta)]e^{[\sigma\mathcal{B}(t)-\frac{1}{2}\sigma^2 t]}, \tag{34}$$

$$\mathcal{Q}_4(x,t) = [\frac{(2-4\rho^2) - 2\sqrt{\rho^4-\rho^2+1}}{\gamma_2} + \frac{6\rho^2}{\gamma_2}ds^2(\zeta)]e^{[\sigma\mathcal{B}(t)-\frac{1}{2}\sigma^2 t]}. \tag{35}$$

$$\mathcal{Q}_5(x,t) = [\frac{(2\rho^2-4) - 2\sqrt{\rho^4-\rho^2+1}}{\gamma_2} + \frac{6}{\gamma_2}dn^2(\zeta)]e^{[\sigma\mathcal{B}(t)-\frac{1}{2}\sigma^2 t]}. \tag{36}$$

$$\mathcal{Q}_6(x,t) = [\frac{(4-2\rho^2) - \sqrt{4\rho^4-19\rho^2+16}}{2\gamma_2} - \frac{3\rho^2}{2\gamma_2}\frac{sn^2(\zeta)}{(1\pm dn(\zeta))^2}]e^{[\sigma\mathcal{B}(t)-\frac{1}{2}\sigma^2 t]}. \tag{37}$$

$$\mathcal{Q}_7(x,t) = [\frac{-(2\rho^2+2) - \sqrt{\rho^4+14\rho^2+1}}{2\gamma_2} + \frac{3}{2\gamma_2}(\rho cn(\zeta) \pm dn(\zeta))^2]e^{[\sigma\mathcal{B}(t)-\frac{1}{2}\sigma^2 t]}. \tag{38}$$

$$\mathcal{Q}_8(x,t) = [\frac{-(2\rho^2+2) - \sqrt{\rho^4+14\rho^2+1}}{2\gamma_2} - \frac{3(\rho^2-1)}{2\gamma_2}\frac{dn^2(\zeta)}{[1\pm sn(\zeta)]^2}]e^{[\sigma\mathcal{B}(t)-\frac{1}{2}\sigma^2 t]}. \tag{39}$$

$$\mathcal{Q}_9(x,t) = [\frac{(2\rho^2-2)-\sqrt{\rho^4-2\rho^2+1}}{2\gamma_2} - \frac{3(1-\rho^2)}{2\gamma_2}\frac{cn^2(\zeta)}{[1\pm sn(\zeta)]^2}]e^{[\sigma\mathcal{B}(t)-\frac{1}{2}\sigma^2 t]}. \quad (40)$$

If $\rho \to 1$ in Equations (32)–(40), then we attain the soliton solutions for SBBME-BD (1) as:

$$\mathcal{Q}(x,t) = [\frac{2}{\gamma_2} - \frac{6}{\gamma_2}\tanh^2(\zeta)]e^{[\sigma\mathcal{B}(t)-\frac{1}{2}\sigma^2 t]}. \quad (41)$$

$$\mathcal{Q}(x,t) = [\frac{-4}{\gamma_2} - \frac{6}{\gamma_2}\text{csch}^2(\zeta)]e^{[\sigma\mathcal{B}(t)-\frac{1}{2}\sigma^2 t]}. \quad (42)$$

$$\mathcal{Q}(x,t) = [\frac{-4}{\gamma_2} + \frac{6}{\gamma_2}\text{sech}^2(\zeta)]e^{[\sigma\mathcal{B}(t)-\frac{1}{2}\sigma^2 t]}. \quad (43)$$

$$\mathcal{Q}(x,t) = [\frac{1}{2\gamma_2} - \frac{3}{2\gamma_2}\frac{\tanh^2(\zeta)}{(1\pm\text{sech}(\zeta))^2}]e^{[\sigma\mathcal{B}(t)-\frac{1}{2}\sigma^2 t]}. \quad (44)$$

$$\mathcal{Q}(x,t) = [\frac{1}{2\gamma_2} - \frac{3}{2\gamma_2}(\coth(\zeta)\mp\text{csch}(\zeta))^2]e^{[\sigma\mathcal{B}(t)-\frac{1}{2}\sigma^2 t]}. \quad (45)$$

If $\rho \to 0$ in Equations (32)–(40), then we acquire the triangular periodic solutions for SBBME-BD (1) as:

$$\mathcal{Q}(x,t) = -\frac{6}{\gamma_2}\csc^2(\zeta)]e^{[\sigma\mathcal{B}(t)-\frac{1}{2}\sigma^2 t]}. \quad (46)$$

$$\mathcal{Q}(x,t) = [\frac{-6}{\gamma_2} - \frac{6}{\gamma_2}\cot^2(\zeta)]e^{[\sigma\mathcal{B}(t)-\frac{1}{2}\sigma^2 t]} = -\frac{6}{\gamma_2}\csc^2(\zeta)e^{[\sigma\mathcal{B}(t)-\frac{1}{2}\sigma^2 t]}. \quad (47)$$

$$\mathcal{Q}(x,t) = \frac{-3}{2\gamma_2}[1 - \frac{1}{[1\pm\sin(\zeta)]^2}]e^{[\sigma\mathcal{B}(t)-\frac{1}{2}\sigma^2 t]}. \quad (48)$$

$$\mathcal{Q}(x,t) = \frac{-3}{2\gamma_2}[1 + \frac{\cos^2(\zeta)}{[1\pm\sin(\zeta)]^2}]e^{[\sigma\mathcal{B}(t)-\frac{1}{2}\sigma^2 t]}. \quad (49)$$

Second Family: By following the same steps as the first family, the same solutions may be found with various coefficients.

4. Impacts of the Beta Derivative and Noise on SBBME-BD Solutions

We discuss the impact of the BD and white noise on the exact solutions of the SBBME-BD (1). To demonstrate the behavior of these solutions, we provide various graphs. For a different σ (noise intensity), we run some simulations for acquired solutions, including Equations (26) and (32). Let us first fix the parameters $\zeta_1 = 1$, $\phi = -1$, $\alpha = \frac{1}{2}$ and $\rho = 0.5$. Moreover, let $x \in [0,6]$ and $t \in [0,3]$.

Effects of the beta derivative: When β decreases, we can observe in Figures 1 and 2 that the form of the graph is compressed:

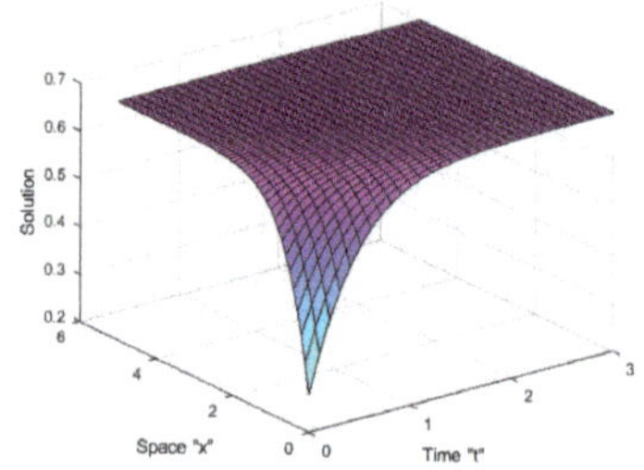

(**a**) $\sigma = 0$, and $\beta = 1$

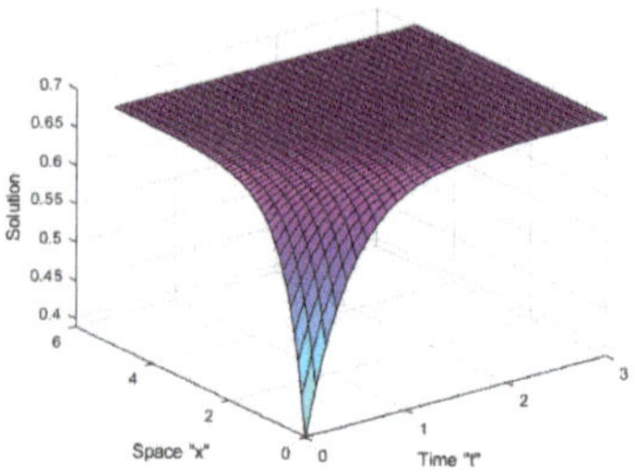

(**b**) $\sigma = 0$, and $\beta = 0.7$

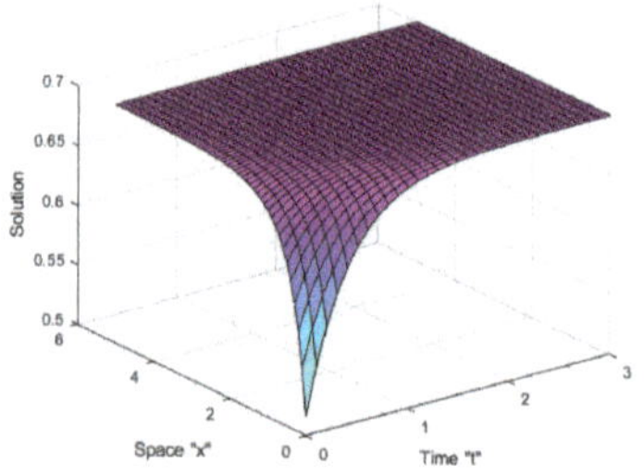

(**c**) $\sigma = 0$, and $\beta = 0.5$

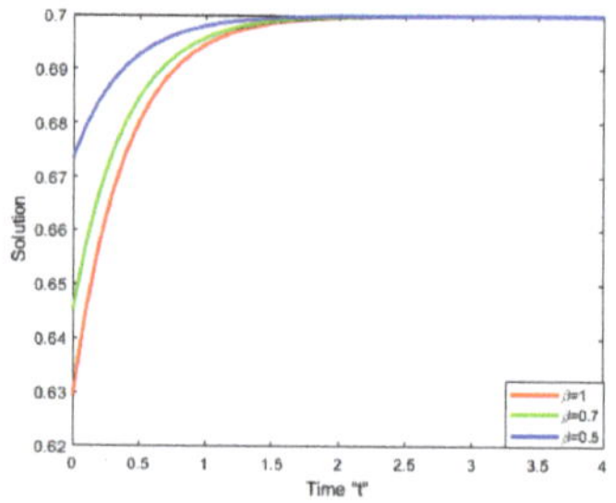

(**d**) $\sigma = 0$, and $\beta = 1,\ 0.7,\ 0.5$

Figure 1. (**a**–**c**) show the 3D shapes of Equation (26) with $\sigma = 0$ and different values of $\beta = 1,\ 0.7,\ 0.5$ (**d**) Depicts a graph in two dimensions for these values of β.

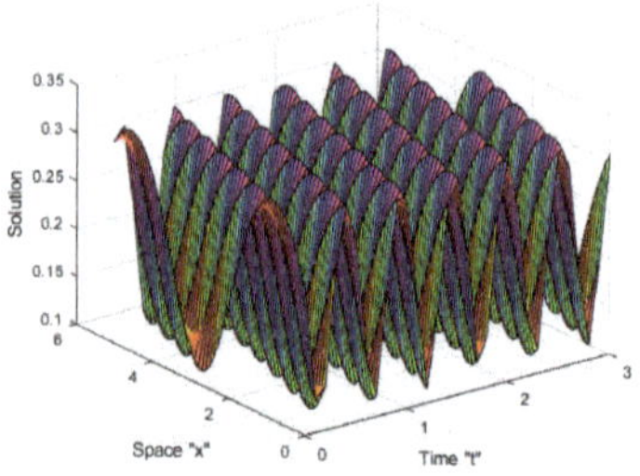

(**a**) $\sigma = 0$, and $\beta = 1$

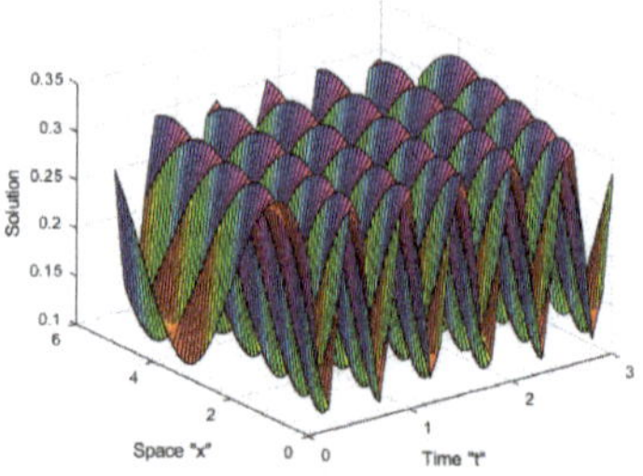

(**b**) $\sigma = 0$, and $\beta = 0.7$

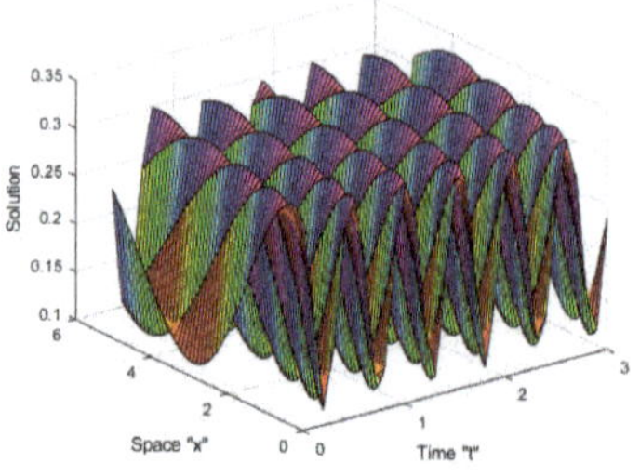

(**c**) $\sigma = 0$, and $\beta = 0.5$

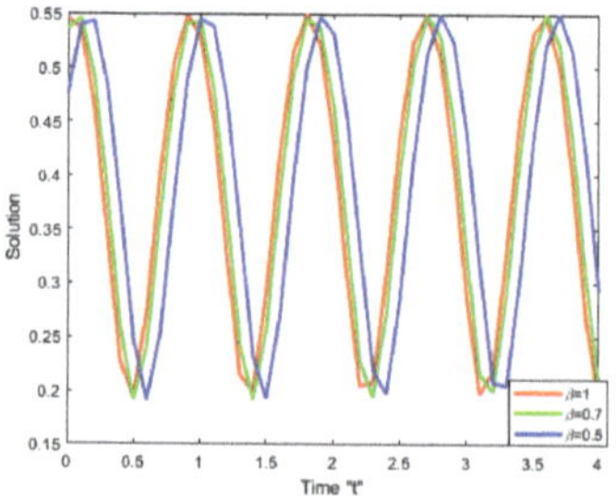

(**d**) $\sigma = 0$, and $\beta = 1,\ 0.7,\ 0.5$

Figure 2. (**a**–**c**) show the 3D shapes of Equation (32) with $\sigma = 0$ and various values of $\beta = 1,\ 0.7,\ 0.5$ (**d**) Depicts a graph in two dimensions for these values of β.

As we can see in Figures 1 and 2, the solution curves do not intersect. Additionally, the curves shift to the right when the order of the beta derivative increases.

Impacts of white noise: The impact of noise on the solutions is seen in Figures 3 and 4 as follows:

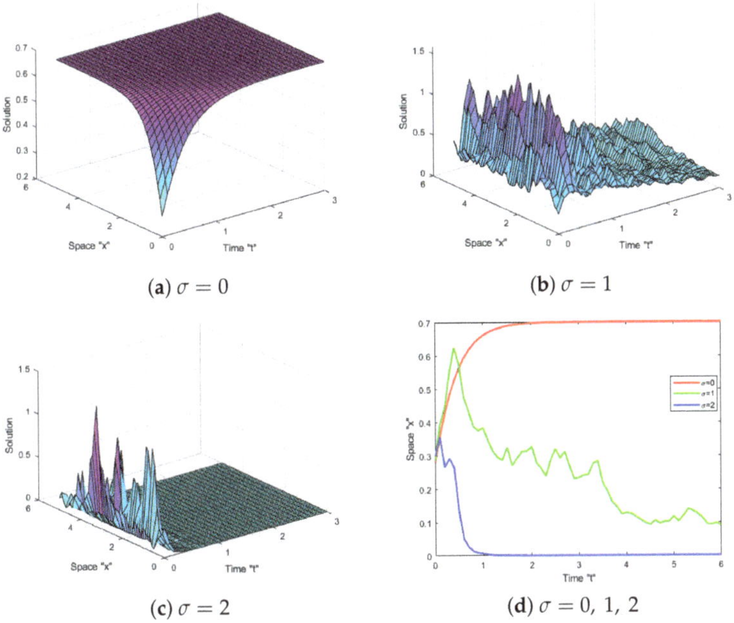

(**a**) $\sigma = 0$ (**b**) $\sigma = 1$ (**c**) $\sigma = 2$ (**d**) $\sigma = 0,\ 1,\ 2$

Figure 3. (**a–c**) show the 3D shapes of the solution $\mathcal{Q}(x,t)$ to Equation (26) for various values of $\sigma = 0,\ 1,\ 2$ (**d**) Depicts a graph in two dimensions for these values of σ.

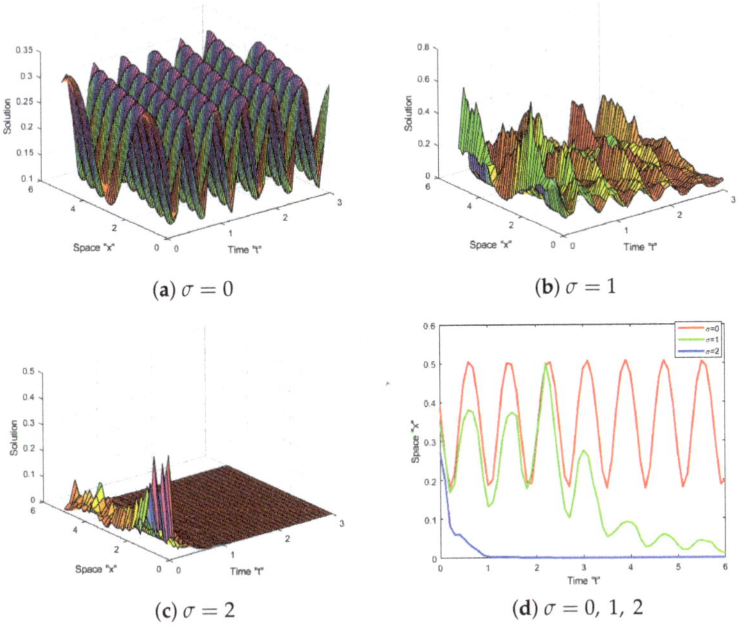

(**a**) $\sigma = 0$ (**b**) $\sigma = 1$ (**c**) $\sigma = 2$ (**d**) $\sigma = 0,\ 1,\ 2$

Figure 4. (**a–c**) show the 3D shapes of the solution $\mathcal{Q}(x,t)$ to Equation (32) for various values of $\sigma = 0,\ 1,\ 2$ (**d**) Depicts a graph in two dimensions for these values of σ.

From Figures 3 and 4, we can conclude that there are distinct types of solutions, such as hyperbolic, trigonometric, rational, and Jacobi elliptic solutions, when the noise is ignored (i.e., at $\sigma = 0$). Adding noise with a strength of $\sigma = 1, 2$ causes the surface to become much flatter following tiny transit patterns, as verified by the 2D graph. This demonstrates that the solutions of SBBME-BD (1) tend to converge around zero when white noise is present.

5. Conclusions

We looked at the stochastic Benjamin–Bona–Mahony Equation (1) with beta derivative (SBBME-BD). The solutions to the Benjamin–Bona–Mahony equation are helpful in understanding several exciting scientific phenomena, such as Rossby waves in rotating fluids and drift waves in plasma. New hyperbolic, trigonometric, rational, and Jacobi elliptic solutions for SBBME-BD were obtained by combining the $\mathcal{F}$-expansion approach with two separate equations, namely the Riccati and elliptic equations. Numerous fascinating and difficult physical occurrences may only be understood with these solutions. The MATLAB program was utilized to investigate the impact of the Gaussian process and beta derivative on the solutions of SBBME-BD (1). It was observed that the white noise component kept the solutions centered around zero. It was concluded that reducing the derivative order resulted in an enlargement of the surface. In future work, we can address Equation (1) with additive noise.

Author Contributions: Data curation, F.M.A.-A. and W.W.M.; formal analysis, W.W.M., F.M.A.-A. and C.C.; funding acquisition, F.M.A.-A.; methodology, C.C.; project administration, W.W.M.; software, W.W.M.; supervision, C.C.; visualization, F.M.A.-A.; writing—original draft, F.M.A.-A.; writing—review and editing, W.W.M. and C.C. All authors have read and agreed to the published version of the manuscript.

Funding: This research received no external funding.

Data Availability Statement: Not applicable.

Acknowledgments: Princess Nourah bint Abdulrahman University Researcher Supporting Project number (PNURSP2023R 273), Princess Nourah bint Abdulrahman University, Riyadh, Saudi Arabia.

Conflicts of Interest: The authors declare no conflict of interest.

References

1. Zhou, Q.; Ekici, M.; Sonmezoglu, A.; Manafian, J.; Khaleghizadeh, S.; Mirzazadeh, M. Exact solitary wave solutions to the generalized Fisher equation. *Optik* **2016**, *127*, 12085–12092. [CrossRef]
2. Alshammari, M.; Iqbal, N.; Mohammed, W.W.; Botmart, T. The solution of fractional-order system of KdV equations with exponential-decay kernel. *Results Phys.* **2022**, *38*, 105615. [CrossRef]
3. Zhou, Q.; Zhu, Q. Optical solitons in medium with parabolic law nonlinearity and higher order dispersion. *Waves Random Complex Media* **2015**, *25*, 52–59. [CrossRef]
4. Baskonus, H.M.; Bulut, H. New wave behaviors of the system of equations for the ion sound and Langmuir. *Waves Waves Random Complex Media* **2016**, *26*, 613–625. [CrossRef]
5. Al-Askar, F.M.; Mohammed, W.W.; Albalahi, A.M.; El-Morshedy, M. The influence of noise on the solutions of fractional stochastic bogoyavlenskii equation. *Fractal Fract.* **2022**, *6*, 156. [CrossRef]
6. Manafian, J.; Lakestani, M. Optical solitons with Biswas-Milovic equation for Kerr law nonlinearity. *Eur. Phys. J. Plus* **2015**, *130*, 61. [CrossRef]
7. Manafian, J. Optical soliton solutions for Schrodinger type nonlinear evolution equations by the $\tan(\varphi/2)$-expansion method. *Optik* **2016**, *127*, 4222–4245. [CrossRef]
8. Tchier, F.; Yusuf, A.; Aliyu, A.I.; Inc, M. Soliton solutions and conservation laws for lossy nonlinear transmission line equation. *Superlattices Microstruct.* **2017**, *107*, 320–336. [CrossRef]
9. Yan, Z.L. Abunbant families of Jacobi elliptic function solutions of the dimensional integrable Davey-Stewartson-type equation via a new method. *Chaos Solitons Fractals* **2003**, *18*, 299–309. [CrossRef]
10. Malfliet, W.; Hereman, W. The tanh method. I. Exact solutions of nonlinear evolution and wave equations. *Phys. Scr.* **1996**, *54*, 563–568. [CrossRef]
11. Katugampola, U.N. New approach to a generalized fractional integral. *Appl. Math. Comput.* **2011**, *218*, 860–865. [CrossRef]
12. Katugampola, U.N. New approach to generalized fractional derivatives. *Bull. Math. Anal. Appl.* **2014**, *6*, 1–15.

13. Kilbas, A.A.; Srivastava, H.M.; Trujillo, J.J. *Theory and Applications of Fractional Differential Equations*; Elsevier: Amsterdam, The Netherlands, 2016.
14. Samko, S.G.; Kilbas, A.A.; Marichev, O.I. *Fractional Integrals and Derivatives, Theory and Applications*; Gordon and Breach: Yverdon, Switzerland, 1993.
15. Atangana, A.; Baleanu, D.; Alsaedi, A. Analysis of time-fractional Hunter-Saxton equation: A model of neumatic liquid crystal. *Open Phys.* **2016**, *14*, 145–149. [CrossRef]
16. Mohammed, W.W. Stochastic amplitude equation for the stochastic generalized Swift–Hohenberg equation. *J. Egypt. Math. Soc.* **2015**, *23*, 482–489. [CrossRef]
17. Imkeller, P.; Monahan, A.H. Conceptual stochastic climate models. *Stoch. Dynam.* **2002**, *2*, 311–326. [CrossRef]
18. Mohammed, W.W.; Blömker, D. Fast-diffusion limit for reaction-diffusion equations with multiplicative noise. *Stoch. Anal. Appl.* **2016**, *34*, 961–978. [CrossRef]
19. Al-Askar, F.M.; Cesarano, C.; Mohammed, W.W. The analytical solutions of stochastic-fractional Drinfel'd-Sokolov-Wilson equations via (G′/G)-expansion method. *Symmetry* **2022**, *14*, 2105. [CrossRef]
20. Mohammed, W.W.; Al-Askar, F.M.; Cesarano, C. The analytical solutions of the stochastic mKdV equation via the mapping method. *Mathematics* **2022**, *10*, 4212. [CrossRef]
21. Al-Askar, F.M.; Mohammed, W.W. The Analytical Solutions of the Stochastic Fractional RKL Equation via Jacobi Elliptic Function Method. *Adv. Math. Phys.* **2022**, *2022*, 1534067. [CrossRef]
22. Mohammed, W.W.; Cesarano, C. The soliton solutions for the (4+1)-dimensional stochastic Fokas equation. *Math. Methods Appl. Sci.* **2023**, *46*, 7589–7597. [CrossRef]
23. Alhamud, M.; M Elbrolosy, M.; Elmandouh, A. New Analytical Solutions for Time-Fractional Stochastic (3+ 1)-Dimensional Equations for Fluids with Gas Bubbles and Hydrodynamics. *Fractal Fract.* **2023**, *7*, 16. [CrossRef]
24. Elmandouh, A.; Fadhal, E. Bifurcation of Exact Solutions for the Space-Fractional Stochastic Modified Benjamin–Bona–Mahony Equation. *Fractal Fract.* **2022**, *6*, 718. [CrossRef]
25. Benjamin, T.B.; Bona, J.L.; Mahony, J.J. Model Equations for Long Waves in Nonlinear Dispersive Systems. *Philos. Trans. R. Soc. Lond. Ser. Math. Phys. Sci.* **1972**, *272*, 47–78.
26. Manafianheris, J. Exact solutions of the BBM and MBBM equations by the generalized (G'/G)-expansion method equations. *Int. J. Genet. Eng.* **2012**, *2*, 28–32. [CrossRef]
27. Das, A.; Ganguly, A. A variation of (G'/G)-expansion method: Travelling wave solutions to nonlinear equations. *Int. J. Nonlinear Sci.* **2014**, *17*, 268–280.
28. Alsayyed, O.; Jaradat, H.M.; Jaradatd, M.M.; Mustafad, Z.; Shatate, F. Multi-soliton solutions of the BBM equation arisen in shallow water. *J. Nonlinear Sci. Appl.* **2016**, *9*, 1807–1814. [CrossRef]
29. Singh, K.; Gupta, R.K.; Kumar, S. Benjamin–Bona–Mahony (BBM) equation with variable coefficients: Similarity reductions and Painlev é analysis. *Appl. Math. Comput.* **2011**, *217*, 7021–7027. [CrossRef]
30. Jahania, M.; Manafian, J. Improvement of the exp-function method for solving the BBM equation with time-dependent coefficients. *Eur. Phys. J. Plus* **2016**, *131*, 54. [CrossRef]
31. Gündogdu, H.; Gözükizil, O.F. Solving Benjamin-Bona-Mahony equation by using the sn–ns method and the tanh-coth method. *Math. Moravica* **2017**, *21*, 95–103. [CrossRef]

Disclaimer/Publisher's Note: The statements, opinions and data contained in all publications are solely those of the individual author(s) and contributor(s) and not of MDPI and/or the editor(s). MDPI and/or the editor(s) disclaim responsibility for any injury to people or property resulting from any ideas, methods, instructions or products referred to in the content.

axioms

Article

Study on the Nonlinear Dynamics of the (3+1)-Dimensional Jimbo-Miwa Equation in Plasma Physics

Peng Xu [1], Bing-Qi Zhang [1], Huan Huang [1] and Kang-Jia Wang [2,*]

[1] School of Electronics and Information, Guangdong Polytechnic Normal University, Guangzhou 510665, China
[2] School of Physics and Electronic Information Engineering, Henan Polytechnic University, Jiaozuo 454003, China
* Correspondence: konka05@163.com

Abstract: The Jimbo-Miwa equation (JME) that describes certain interesting (3+1)-dimensional waves in plasma physics is studied in this work. The Hirota bilinear equation is developed via the Cole-Hopf transform. Then, the symbolic computation, together with the ansatz function schemes, are utilized to seek exact solutions. Some new solutions, such as the multi-wave complexiton solution (MWCS), multi-wave solution (MWS) and periodic lump solution (PLS), are successfully constructed. Additionally, different types of travelling wave solutions (TWS), including the dark, bright-dark and singular periodic wave solutions, are disclosed by employing the sub-equation method. Finally, the physical characteristics and interaction behaviors of the extracted solutions are depicted graphically by assigning appropriate parameters. The obtained outcomes in this paper are more general and newer. Additionally, they reveal that the used methods are concise, direct, and can be employed to study other partial differential equations (PDEs) in physics.

Keywords: Hirota bilinear equation; Cole-Hopf transform; multi-wave complexiton solution; multi-wave solution; periodic lump solution; sub-equation method

MSC: 35C07; 35A22

Citation: Xu, P.; Zhang, B.-Q.; Huang, H.; Wang, K.-J. Study on the Nonlinear Dynamics of the (3+1)-Dimensional Jimbo-Miwa Equation in Plasma Physics. *Axioms* **2023**, *12*, 592. https://doi.org/10.3390/axioms12060592

Academic Editors: Francisco Martínez González, Mohammed K. A. Kaabar and Hatıra Günerhan

Received: 24 May 2023
Revised: 8 June 2023
Accepted: 13 June 2023
Published: 15 June 2023

Copyright: © 2023 by the authors. Licensee MDPI, Basel, Switzerland. This article is an open access article distributed under the terms and conditions of the Creative Commons Attribution (CC BY) license (https://creativecommons.org/licenses/by/4.0/).

1. Introduction

Complex phenomena in engineering and physics can usually be reduced to PDEs [1–6]. The study on the properties of these equations such as the explicit analytical solutions, especially the soliton solutions, is of great significance since they can help us to better understand complex phenomena and their inner nature. Up to now, a series of different effective methods have been developed to construct the exact solutions of PDEs such as the Hirota bilinear method [7–10], Wang's Bäcklund transformation-based method [11,12], trial equation method [13,14], Sardar subequation method [15–17], exp-function method [18,19], Riccati equation mapping method [20] and so on [21–28]. In this work, we aim to examine the (3+1)-dimensional JME given by [29]:

$$\Pi_{xxxy} + 3\Pi_x\Pi_{xy} + 3\Pi_y\Pi_{xx} + 2\Pi_{yt} - 3\Pi_{xz} = 0, \quad (1)$$

Equation (1) is derived from the second equation in the well-known KP hierarchy of integrable systems and used widely to describe some interesting (3+1)-dimensional waves in plasma and optics. Up to now, some important research achievements have been developed to deal with Equation (1). In [29], the Kudryashov method is used with the symbolic computation and different solutions are obtained. In [30], four kinds of different wave forms are constructed via the Hirota bilinear method. In [31], the authors employ the direct algebraic method to handle Equation (1) and some different wave forms are constructed. In [32], several closed-form solutions are developed by using the singular manifold method. In [33], the Riccati equation mapping method is adopted. The exp-function method is utilized in [34] and some generalized solutions with parameters are constructed. In [35], the authors carry out the linear superposition principle to seek for multi-resonant solutions of Equation (1). In [36], the authors make use of the generalized Bernoulli equation method to inquire into Equation (1). In this study, we will present th results of a detailed investigation of Equation (1). The rest of the content of this work is given as follows. In Section 2, the Cole-Hopf transform is adopted to establish the Hirota bilinear form, and symbolic computation, combined with the ansatz function schemes, is utilized to search for the MWCS, MWS and PLS. In Section 3, the sub-equation method is used to seek for the TWSs. In Section 4, the physical characteristics and interaction behaviors are presented. Finally, we reach a conclusion in Section 5.

2. The Hirota Bilinear Equation and the Exact Solutions

To obtain the Hirota bilinear form of Equation (1), we adopt the Cole-Hopf transform as:

$$\Pi = 2\ln(\Xi)_x, \tag{2}$$

Taking it into Equation (1), we can obtain the bilinear form as:

$$\left(D_x^3D_y + 2D_yD_t - 3D_xD_z\right)\Xi\cdot\Xi = 0. \tag{3}$$

Here, the definition of the operators $D_x^mD_\tau^n$ is [37,38]:

$$D_x^mD_t^n f\cdot g = \left(\frac{\partial}{\partial x} - \frac{\partial}{\partial x'}\right)^m\left(\frac{\partial}{\partial t} - \frac{\partial}{\partial t'}\right)^n f(x,t)g(x',t')|_{x=x',t=t'}. \tag{4}$$

Additionally, there are

$$D_x(f\cdot g) = f_xg - fg_x,$$

$$D_x^2(f\cdot g) = f_{xx}g - 2f_xg_x + fg_{xx},$$

$$D_x^2(f\cdot f) = 2\left(f_{xx}f - f_x^2\right),$$

$$D_tD_x(f\cdot g) = f_{tx}g - f_tg_x - f_xg_t + g_{tx}f.$$

2.1. The MWCS

In order to find the MWCS, it is assumed that the solution of Equation (3) is:

$$\Xi = u_1e^p + u_2e^{-p} + u_3\sin(q) + u_4\sinh(\rho), \tag{5}$$

with

$$\begin{cases} p = x + k_1y + k_2z + k_3t \\ q = x + k_4y + k_5z + k_6t \\ \rho = x + k_7y + k_8z + k_9t \end{cases},$$

where $u_i(i = 1,2,3,4.)$ and $k_i(i = 1,2,3,4,5,6,7,8,9.)$ are constants that can be determined later. Substituting Equation (5) into Equation (3) and setting the coefficients of different terms to zero, an algebraic equation system is attained. Solving it, we derive:

Case 1:

$$k_1 = \frac{3k_2}{2(k_9+2)},\ k_2 = k_2,\ k_3 = k_9,\ k_4 = -\frac{3k_2}{2(k_9+2)},\ k_5 = \frac{k_2 - k_2k_9}{2+k_9},\ k_6 = k_9 + 1,\ k_7 = \frac{3k_2}{2(2+k_9)},$$
$$k_8 = k_2,\ k_9 = k_9,\ u_1 = u_1,\ u_2 = u_2,\ u_3 = u_3,\ u_4 = u_4.$$

The MWCS is obtained as:

$$\Pi(x,y,z,t)=\frac{2\left[\begin{array}{l} u_1 e^{x+\frac{3k_2}{2(k_9+2)}y+k_2z+k_9t}-u_2e^{-(x+\frac{3k_2}{2(k_9+2)}y+k_2z+k_9t)}+u_3\cos\left(x-\frac{3k_2}{2(k_9+2)}y+\frac{k_2-k_2k_9}{2+k_9}z+(k_9+1)t\right)\\ +u_4\cosh\left(x+\frac{3k_2}{2(2+k_9)}y+k_2z+k_9t\right)\end{array}\right]}{\begin{array}{l} u_1e^{x+\frac{3k_2}{2(k_9+2)}y+k_2z+k_9t}+u_2e^{-(x+\frac{3k_2}{2(k_9+2)}y+k_2z+k_9t)}+u_3\sin\left(x-\frac{3k_2}{2(k_9+2)}y+\frac{k_2-k_2k_9}{2+k_9}z+(k_9+1)t\right)\\ +u_4\sinh\left(x+\frac{3k_2}{2(2+k_9)}y+k_2z+k_9t\right)\end{array}}. \quad (6)$$

For the special case $u_1=-u_2=2u_4$, Equation (6) becomes:
Case 2:

$$k_1=k_1,\ k_2=k_2,\ k_3=-2+\tfrac{3k_2}{2k_1},\ k_4=-k_1,\ k_5=2k_1-k_2,\ k_6=-1+\tfrac{3k_2}{2k_1},\ k_7=k_1,\ k_8=k_2,$$
$$k_9=-2+\tfrac{3k_2}{2k_1},\ u_1=u_1,\ u_2=u_2,\ u_3=u_3,\ u_4=u_4.$$

Thus, we can obtain the MWCS as:

$$\Pi(x,y,z,t)=\frac{2\left[\begin{array}{l} u_1e^{x+k_1y+k_2z+(-2+\frac{3k_2}{2k_1})t}-u_2e^{-(x+k_1y+k_2z+(-2+\frac{3k_2}{2k_1})t)}+u_3\cos\left(x-k_1y+(2k_1-k_2)z+\left(-1+\frac{3k_2}{2k_1}\right)t\right)\\ +u_4\cosh\left(x+k_1y+k_2z+\left(-2+\frac{3k_2}{2k_1}\right)t\right)\end{array}\right]}{\begin{array}{l} u_1e^{x+k_1y+k_2z+(-2+\frac{3k_2}{2k_1})t}+u_2e^{-(x+k_1y+k_2z+(-2+\frac{3k_2}{2k_1})t)}+u_3\sin\left(x-k_1y+(2k_1-k_2)z+\left(-1+\frac{3k_2}{2k_1}\right)t\right)\\ +u_4\sinh\left(x+k_1y+k_2z+\left(-2+\frac{3k_2}{2k_1}\right)t\right)\end{array}}. \quad (7)$$

Case 3:

$$k_1=k_1,\ k_2=\tfrac{2}{3}(2k_1+k_1k_9),\ k_3=k_9,\ k_4=-k_1,\ k_5=-\tfrac{2}{3}(-k_1+k_1k_9),\ k_6=-1+k_9,\ k_7=k_1,$$
$$k_8=\tfrac{2}{3}(2k_1+k_1k_9),\ k_9=k_9,\ u_1=u_1,\ u_2=u_2,\ u_3=u_3,\ u_4=u_4.$$

Thus, we obtain the MWCS solution as:

$$\Pi(x,y,z,t)=\frac{2\left[\begin{array}{l} u_1e^{x+k_1y+\frac{2}{3}(2k_1+k_1k_9)z+k_3t}-u_2e^{-(x+k_1y+\frac{2}{3}(2k_1+k_1k_9)z+k_3t)}+u_3\cos(x+k_4y+k_5z+(k_9-1)t)\\ +u_4\cosh\left(x+k_1y+\frac{2}{3}(2k_1+k_1k_9)z+k_9t\right)\end{array}\right]}{\begin{array}{l} u_1e^{x+k_1y+\frac{2}{3}(2k_1+k_1k_9)z+k_3t}+u_2e^{-(x+k_1y+\frac{2}{3}(2k_1+k_1k_9)z+k_3t)}+u_3\sin(x+k_4y+k_5z+(k_9-1)t)\\ +u_4\sinh\left(x+k_1y+\frac{2}{3}(2k_1+k_1k_9)z+k_9t\right)\end{array}}. \quad (8)$$

Case 4:

$$k_1=-\frac{3k_5}{2(k_9-1)},\ k_2=-\frac{2k_5(1+k_9)}{k_9-1},\ k_3=k_9,\ k_4=\frac{3k_5}{2(k_9-1)},\ k_5=k_5,\ k_6=k_9-1,$$
$$k_7=-\frac{3k_5}{2(k_9-1)},\ k_8=-\frac{2k_5(1+k_9)}{k_9-1},\ k_9=k_9,\ u_1=u_1,\ u_2=u_2,\ u_3=u_3,\ u_4=u_4.$$

Accordingly, the MWCS is:

$$\Pi(x,y,z,t)=\frac{2\left[\begin{array}{l} u_1e^{x-\frac{3k_5}{2(k_9-1)}y-\frac{2k_5(1+k_9)}{k_9-1}z+k_9t}-u_2e^{-(x-\frac{3k_5}{2(k_9-1)}y-\frac{2k_5(1+k_9)}{k_9-1}z+k_9t)}+u_3\cos\left(x+\frac{3k_5}{2(k_9-1)}y+k_5z+(k_9-1)t\right)\\ +u_4\cosh\left(x-\frac{3k_5}{2(k_9-1)}y-\frac{2k_5(1+k_9)}{k_9-1}z+k_9t\right)\end{array}\right]}{\begin{array}{l} u_1e^{x-\frac{3k_5}{2(k_9-1)}y-\frac{2k_5(1+k_9)}{k_9-1}z+k_9t}+u_2e^{-(x-\frac{3k_5}{2(k_9-1)}y-\frac{2k_5(1+k_9)}{k_9-1}z+k_9t)}+u_3\sin\left(x+\frac{3k_5}{2(k_9-1)}y+k_5z+(k_9-1)t\right)\\ +u_4\sinh\left(x-\frac{3k_5}{2(k_9-1)}y-\frac{2k_5(1+k_9)}{k_9-1}z+k_9t\right)\end{array}}. \quad (9)$$

Case 5:

$$k_1 = -k_4,\ k_2 = k_8,\ k_3 = -\left(2 + \tfrac{3k_8}{2k_4}\right),\ k_4 = k_4,\ k_5 = -(2k_4 + k_8),\ k_6 = -\left(1 + \tfrac{3k_8}{2k_4}\right),\ k_7 = -k_4,$$
$$k_8 = k_8,\ k_9 = -\left(2 + \tfrac{3k_8}{2k_4}\right),\ u_1 = u_1,\ u_2 = u_2,\ u_3 = u_3,\ u_4 = u_4.$$

where $k_4 \neq 0$. Thus, we can obtain the MWCS as:

$$\Pi(x,y,z,t) = \frac{2\left[\begin{array}{l} u_1 e^{x - k_4 y + k_8 z - (2 + \frac{3k_8}{2k_4})t} - u_2 e^{-(x - k_4 y + k_8 z - (2 + \frac{3k_8}{2k_4})t)} + u_3 \cos\left(x + k_4 y - (2k_4 + k_8)z - \left(1 + \frac{3k_8}{2k_4}\right)t\right) \\ + u_4 \cos\mathrm{h}\left(x - k_4 y + k_8 z - \left(2 + \frac{3k_8}{2k_4}\right)t\right) \end{array}\right]}{\begin{array}{l} u_1 e^{x - k_4 y + k_8 z - (2 + \frac{3k_8}{2k_4})t} + u_2 e^{-(x - k_4 y + k_8 z - (2 + \frac{3k_8}{2k_4})t)} + u_3 \sin\left(x + k_4 y - (2k_4 + k_8)z - \left(1 + \frac{3k_8}{2k_4}\right)t\right) \\ + u_4 \sin\mathrm{h}\left(x - k_4 y + k_8 z - \left(2 + \frac{3k_8}{2k_4}\right)t\right) \end{array}}. \quad (10)$$

For the special case $u_1 = -u_2 = 2u_4$, Equations (6)–(10) become:

$$\Pi(x,y,z,t) = 2\cot\left(x - \frac{3k_2}{2(k_9 + 2)}y + \frac{k_2 - k_2 k_9}{2 + k_9}z + (k_9 + 1)t\right).$$

$$\Pi(x,y,z,t) = 2\cot\left(x - k_1 y + (2k_1 - k_2)z + \left(-1 + \frac{3k_2}{2k_1}\right)t\right).$$

$$\Pi(x,y,z,t) = 2\cot(x + k_4 y + k_5 z + (k_9 - 1)t).$$

$$\Pi(x,y,z,t) = 2\cot\left(x + \frac{3k_5}{2(k_9 - 1)}y + k_5 z + (k_9 - 1)t\right).$$

$$\Pi(x,y,z,t) = 2\cot\left(x + k_4 y - (2k_4 + k_8)z - \left(1 + \frac{3k_8}{2k_4}\right)t\right).$$

2.2. *The MWS*

Here, we can use the following ansatz function:

$$\Xi = u_1 \cos(p) + u_2 \cos\mathrm{h}(q) + u_3 \cos\mathrm{h}(\rho), \quad (11)$$

with

$$\begin{cases} p = x + k_1 y + k_2 z + k_3 t \\ q = x + k_4 y + k_5 z + k_6 t \\ \rho = x + k_7 y + k_8 z + k_9 t \end{cases},$$

where $u_i (i = 1,2,3.)$ and $k_i (i = 1,2,3,4,5,6,7,8,9.)$ are constants that can be determined later. In the same manner, substituting Equation (11) into Equation (3) and making the corresponding adjustments, we derive:

Case 1:

$$k_1 = k_1,\ k_2 = k_2,\ k_3 = 2 + \frac{3k_2}{2k_1},\ k_7 = -k_1,\ k_8 = -2k_1 - k_2,\ k_9 = 1 + \frac{3k_2}{2k_1},\ u_1 = u_1,\ u_2 = 0,\ u_3 = u_3.$$

Then, we obtain the MWS as:

$$\Pi(x,y,z,t) = \frac{2\left[-u_1 \sin\left(x + k_1 y + k_2 z + \left(2 + \frac{3k_2}{2k_1}\right)t\right) + u_3 \sin\mathrm{h}\left(x - k_1 y - (2k_1 + k_2)z + \left(1 + \frac{3k_2}{2k_1}\right)t\right)\right]}{u_1 \cos\left(x + k_1 y + k_2 z + \left(2 + \frac{3k_2}{2k_1}\right)t\right) + u_3 \cos\mathrm{h}\left(x - k_1 y - (2k_1 + k_2)z + \left(1 + \frac{3k_2}{2k_1}\right)t\right)}. \quad (12)$$

Case 2:

$$k_1 = k_1,\ k_2 = -2k_1 - k_5,\ k_3 = -1 - \frac{3k_5}{2k_1},\ k_4 = -k_1,\ k_5 = k_5,\ k_6 = -2 - \frac{3k_5}{2k_1},\ u_1 = u_1,\ u_2 = u_2,\ u_3 = 0.$$

Thus, we obtain the MWS as:

$$\Pi(x,y,z,t) = \frac{2\left[-u_1\sin\left(x+k_1y-(2k_1+k_5)z-\left(1+\frac{3k_5}{2k_1}\right)t\right)+u_2\sin\mathrm{h}\left(x-k_1y+k_5z-\left(2+\frac{3k_5}{2k_1}\right)t\right)\right]}{u_1\cos\left(x+k_1y-(2k_1+k_5)z-\left(1+\frac{3k_5}{2k_1}\right)t\right)+u_2\cos\mathrm{h}\left(x-k_1y+k_5z-\left(2+\frac{3k_5}{2k_1}\right)t\right)}. \quad (13)$$

2.3. The PLS

The solution of Equation (3) is assumed as:

$$\Xi = u_1\sin(p)+u_2\cos\mathrm{h}(q)+k_7, \quad (14)$$

with

$$\begin{cases} p = x+k_1y+k_2z+k_3t \\ q = x+k_4y+k_5z+k_6t \end{cases},$$

where $u_i(i=1,2.)$ and $k_i(i=1,2,3,4,5,6,7.)$ are constants to be determined later. In the same manner, substituting Equation (14) into Equation (3) and making the corresponding adjustments, we derive:

Case 1:

$k_1=k_1$, $k_2=\frac{2}{3}k_1(k_6-1)$, $k_3=k_6+1$, $k_4=-k_1$, $k_5=-\frac{2}{3}k_1(2+k_6)$, $k_6=k_6$, $k_7=0$, $u_1=u_1$, $u_2=u_2$.

The PLS to Equation (1) is:

$$\Pi(x,y,z,t) = \frac{2\left[u_1\cos\left(x+k_1y+\frac{2}{3}k_1(k_6-1)z+(k_6+1)t\right)+u_2\sin\mathrm{h}\left(x-k_1y-\frac{2}{3}k_1(2+k_6)z+k_6t\right)\right]}{u_1\sin\left(x+k_1y+\frac{2}{3}k_1(k_6-1)z+(k_6+1)t\right)+u_2\cos\mathrm{h}\left(x-k_1y-\frac{2}{3}k_1(2+k_6)z+k_6t\right)}. \quad (15)$$

Case 2:

$k_1=\frac{3k_2}{2(k_6-1)}$, $k_2=k_2$, $k_3=k_6+1$, $k_4=-\frac{3k_2}{2(k_6-1)}$, $k_5=-\frac{2k_2(k_6+1)}{k_6-1}$, $k_6=k_6$, $k_7=0$, $u_1=u_1$, $u_2=u_2$.

Thus, we obtain the PLS of Equation (1) as:

$$\Pi(x,y,z,t) = \frac{2\left[u_1\cos\left(x+\frac{3k_2}{2(k_6-1)}y+k_2z+(k_6+1)t\right)+u_2\sin\mathrm{h}\left(x-\frac{3k_2}{2(k_6-1)}y-\frac{2k_2(k_6+1)}{k_6-1}z+k_6t\right)\right]}{u_1\sin\left(x+\frac{3k_2}{2(k_6-1)}y+k_2z+(k_6+1)t\right)+u_2\cos\mathrm{h}\left(x-\frac{3k_2}{2(k_6-1)}y-\frac{2k_2(k_6+1)}{k_6-1}z+k_6t\right)}. \quad (16)$$

Case 3:

$k_1=-\frac{3k_5}{2(k_3+1)}$, $k_2=\frac{k_5(2-k_3)}{k_3+1}$, $k_3=k_3$, $k_4=\frac{3k_5}{2(k_3+1)}$, $k_5=k_5$, $k_6=k_3-1$, $k_7=0$, $u_1=u_1$, $u_2=u_2$

The PLS of Equation (1) is obtained as:

$$\Pi(x,y,z,t) = \frac{2\left[u_1\cos\left(x-\frac{3k_5}{2(k_3+1)}y+\frac{k_5(2-k_3)}{k_3+1}z+k_3t\right)+u_2\sin\mathrm{h}\left(x+\frac{3k_5}{2(k_3+1)}y+k_5z+(k_3-1)t\right)\right]}{u_1\sin\left(x-\frac{3k_5}{2(k_3+1)}y+\frac{k_5(2-k_3)}{k_3+1}z+k_3t\right)+u_2\cos\mathrm{h}\left(x+\frac{3k_5}{2(k_3+1)}y+k_5z+(k_3-1)t\right)}. \quad (17)$$

Case 4:

$k_1=-k_4$, $k_2=-\frac{2}{3}k_4(k_3-2)$, $k_3=k_3$, $k_4=k_4$, $k_5=\frac{2}{3}k_4(k_3+1)$, $k_6=k_3-1$, $k_7=0$, $u_1=u_1$, $u_2=u_2$.

Thus, the PLS of Equation (1) is attained as:

$$\Pi(x,y,z,t) = \frac{2\left[u_1\cos(x - k_4y - \frac{2}{3}k_4(k_3-2)z + k_3t) + u_2\sin\text{h}(x + k_4y + \frac{2}{3}k_4(k_3+1)z + (k_3-1)t)\right]}{u_1\sin(x - k_4y - \frac{2}{3}k_4(k_3-2)z + k_3t) + u_2\cos\text{h}(x + k_4y + \frac{2}{3}k_4(k_3+1)z + (k_3-1)t)}. \quad (18)$$

Case 5:

$$k_1 = k_1,\ k_2 = k_2,\ k_3 = 2 + \frac{3k_2}{2k_1},\ k_4 = -k_1,\ k_5 = -2k_1 - k_2,\ k_6 = 1 + \frac{3k_2}{2k_1},\ k_7 = 0,\ u_1 = u_1,\ u_2 = u_2.$$

We obtain the PLS of Equation (1) as:

$$\Pi(x,y,z,t) = \frac{2\left[u_1\cos\left(x + k_1y + k_2z + \left(2 + \frac{3k_2}{2k_1}\right)t\right) + u_2\sin\text{h}\left(x - k_1y - (2k_1+k_2)z + \left(1 + \frac{3k_2}{2k_1}\right)t\right)\right]}{u_1\sin\left(x + k_1y + k_2z + \left(2 + \frac{3k_2}{2k_1}\right)t\right) + u_2\cos\text{h}\left(x - k_1y - (2k_1+k_2)z + \left(1 + \frac{3k_2}{2k_1}\right)t\right)}. \quad (19)$$

3. The TWS

This section aims to study the TWS using the sub-equation method [39,40]. For this end, we apply the following variable transformation to Equation (1):

$$\Pi(x,y,z,t) = \Im(\chi),\ \chi = mx + ny + kz + st, \quad (20)$$

where m, n, k, and s are non-zero constants. Equation (1) can be converted as:

$$m^3n\Im^{(4)} + 6m^2n\Im'\Im'' + (2ns - 3mk)\Im'' = 0, \quad (21)$$

where $\Im^{(4)} = \frac{d^4\Im}{d\chi^4}$, $\Im'' = \frac{d^2\Im}{d\chi^2}$, $\Im' = \frac{d\Im}{d\chi}$. Integrating Equation (21) with respect to χ once and setting the integral constant to zero, we derive:

$$m^3n\Im''' + 3m^2n(\Im')^2 + (2ns - 3mk)\Im' = 0. \quad (22)$$

Based on the sub-equation method, the solution of Equation (22) can be assumed as:

$$\Im(\chi) = \sum_{i=0}^{c} \varepsilon_i \aleph^i(\chi). \quad (23)$$

where $\varepsilon_i (i = 0,1,2,\ldots,c.)$ are constants that can be determined later. Additionally, there is:

$$\aleph'(\chi) = \sigma + \aleph^2(\chi). \quad (24)$$

Here, σ is a constant. Equation (24) has the following different solutions:

$$\aleph(\chi) = \begin{cases} -\sqrt{-\sigma}\tan\text{h}(\sqrt{-\sigma}\chi), & \sigma < 0 \\ -\sqrt{-\sigma}\cot\text{h}(\sqrt{-\sigma}\chi), & \sigma < 0 \\ \sqrt{\sigma}\tan(\sqrt{\sigma}\chi), & \sigma > 0 \\ -\sqrt{\sigma}\cot(\sqrt{\sigma}\chi), & \sigma > 0 \\ -\frac{1}{\zeta+\Lambda},\ \Lambda \text{ is a constant}, & \sigma = 0 \end{cases}. \quad (25)$$

We can determine the value of c in Equation (23) via balancing $\Im'''$ and $(\Im')^2$ in Equation (22) as:

$$c = 1. \quad (26)$$

Then, Equation (23) becomes:

$$\Im(\chi) = \varepsilon_0 + \varepsilon_1\Im(\chi). \quad (27)$$

Substituting Equation (27) with Equation (24) into Equation (22) and setting their coefficients of the different powers of $\Im(\chi)$ to zero, it yields:
Solving them, we derive:

$$\Im^0(\chi): -3km\sigma\varepsilon_1 + 2ns\sigma\varepsilon_1 + 2m^3n\sigma^2\varepsilon_1 + 3m^2n\sigma^2\varepsilon_1^2 = 0,$$
$$\Im^2(\chi): -3km\varepsilon_1 - ns\varepsilon_1 + 8m^3n\sigma\varepsilon_1 + 6m^2n\sigma\varepsilon_1^2 = 0,$$
$$\Im^4(\chi): 6m^3n\varepsilon_1 + 3m^2n\varepsilon_1^2 = 0.$$

Case 1:

$$\varepsilon_0 = \varepsilon_0,\ \varepsilon_1 = \varepsilon_1,\ m = -\frac{\varepsilon_1}{2},\ n = n,\ k = k,\ s = -\frac{\varepsilon_1(3k + n\sigma\varepsilon_1^2)}{4n},\ \sigma = \sigma.$$

Thus, the TWS of Equation (1) can be obtained as:

$$\Pi(x,y,z,t) = \varepsilon_0 - \varepsilon_1\sqrt{-\sigma}\tanh\left[\sqrt{-\sigma}\left(-\frac{\varepsilon_1}{2}x + ny + kz - \frac{\varepsilon_1(3k + n\sigma\varepsilon_1^2)}{4n}t\right)\right], \sigma < 0. \tag{28}$$

$$\Pi(x,y,z,t) = \varepsilon_0 - \varepsilon_1\sqrt{-\sigma}\coth\left[\sqrt{-\sigma}\left(-\frac{\varepsilon_1}{2}x + ny + kz - \frac{\varepsilon_1(3k + n\sigma\varepsilon_1^2)}{4n}t\right)\right], \sigma < 0. \tag{29}$$

$$\Pi(x,y,z,t) = \varepsilon_0 + \varepsilon_1\sqrt{\sigma}\tan\left[\sqrt{\sigma}\left(-\frac{\varepsilon_1}{2}x + ny + kz - \frac{\varepsilon_1(3k + n\sigma\varepsilon_1^2)}{4n}t\right)\right], \sigma > 0. \tag{30}$$

$$\Pi(x,y,z,t) = \varepsilon_0 - \varepsilon_1\sqrt{\sigma}\cot\left[\sqrt{\sigma}\left(-\frac{\alpha_1}{2}x + ny + kz - \frac{\varepsilon_1(3k + n\sigma\varepsilon_1^2)}{4n}t\right)\right], \sigma > 0. \tag{31}$$

Case 2:

$$\varepsilon_0 = \varepsilon_0,\ \varepsilon_1 = -2m,\ m = m,\ n = n,\ k = -\frac{2(2m^3n\sigma - ns)}{3m},\ s = s,\ \sigma = \sigma.$$

Thus, the TWS of Equation (1) can be obtained as:

$$\Pi(x,y,z,t) = \varepsilon_0 + 2m\sqrt{-\sigma}\tanh\left[\sqrt{-\sigma}\left(mx + ny - \frac{2(2m^3n\sigma - ns)}{3m}z + st\right)\right], \sigma < 0. \tag{32}$$

$$\Pi(x,y,z,t) = \alpha_0 + 2m\sqrt{-\sigma}\coth\left[\sqrt{-\sigma}\left(mx + ny - \frac{2(2m^3n\sigma - ns)}{3m}z + st\right)\right], \sigma < 0. \tag{33}$$

$$\Pi(x,y,z,t) = \varepsilon_0 - 2m\sqrt{\sigma}\tan\left[\sqrt{\sigma}\left(mx + ny - \frac{2(2m^3n\sigma - ns)}{3m}z + st\right)\right], \sigma > 0. \tag{34}$$

$$\Pi(x,y,z,t) = \varepsilon_0 + 2m\sqrt{\sigma}\cot\left[\sqrt{\sigma}\left(mx + ny - \frac{2(2m^3n\sigma - ns)}{3m}z + st\right)\right], \sigma > 0. \tag{35}$$

4. The Physical Interpretations

The obtained solutions will be presented by the 3D plot and 2D contour in this section by taking the reasonable parameters.

By assigning the parameters as $k_2 = 1$, $k_9 = 2$, $u_1 = 1$, $u_2 = 1$, $u_3 = 1$, the multi-wave complexiton solution given by Equation (6) for the different time is illustrated in Figure 1 in the form of the 3D plot and 2D contour. Obviously, we can find there is a collision phenomenon between the singular periodic wave and the lump in the outline. As t increases, the waveform propagates in the negative direction of the x axis and y axis.

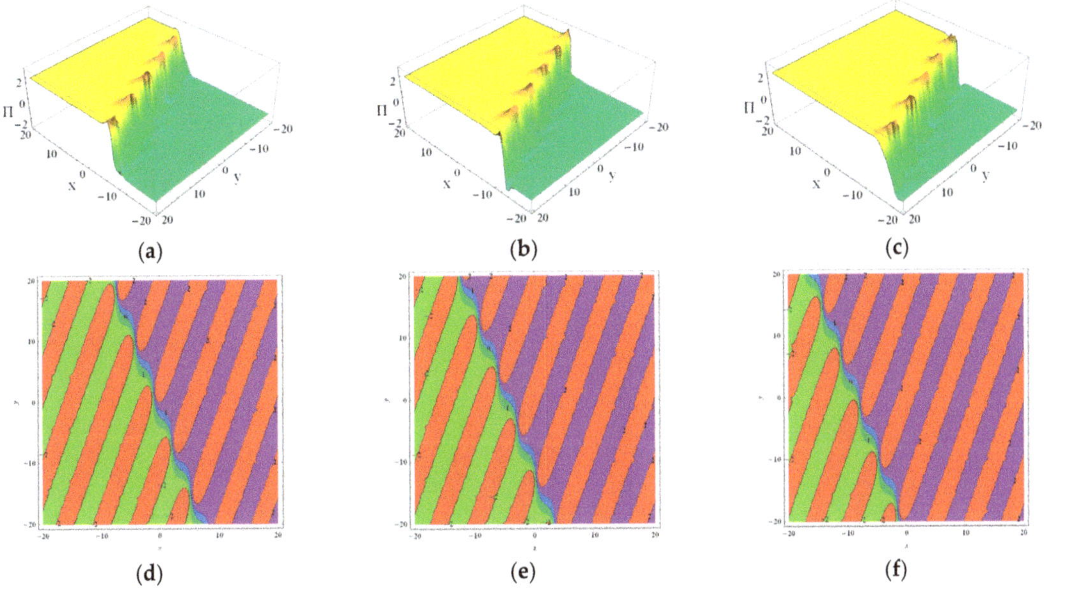

Figure 1. The graphical description of Equation (6) with $k_2 = 1$, $k_9 = 2$, $u_1 = 1$, $u_2 = 1$, $u_3 = 1$ at $z = 0$, (**a**,**d**) for $t = 0$, (**b**,**e**) for $t = 2$, (**c**,**f**) for $t = 4$.

We illustrate the dynamic behavior of Equation (12) by selecting $k_1 = 1$, $k_2 = 1$, $u_1 = 0.6$, $u_2 = 0.4$ in Figure 2. From this, collision phenomena between the breather waves and singular periodic waves are revealed. We can observe that the waveform travels along the negative direction of the x axis and positive direction of y axis.

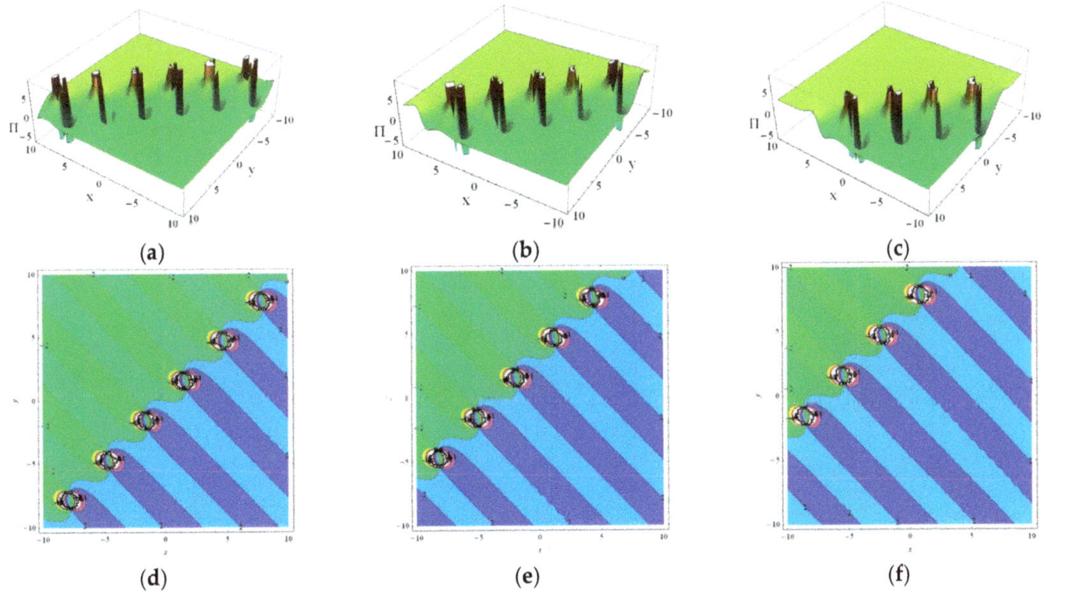

Figure 2. The graphical description of Equation (12) with $k_1 = 1$, $k_2 = 1$,$u_1 = 0.6$, $u_2 = 0.4$ at $z = 0$. (**a**,**d**) for $t = 0$, (**b**,**e**) for $t = 1$, (**c**,**f**) for $t = 2$.

Selecting $k_1 = 1, k_2 = 2, u_1 = 1, u_2 = 1, u_3 = 1, u_4 = 1$, we present the performance of Equation (15) in Figure 3. Here, it can be found the waveform propagates along the negative direction of the x axis and positive direction of y axis. Additionally, the outline of the wave can be explained as the interaction between lump solution and trigonometric function solution.

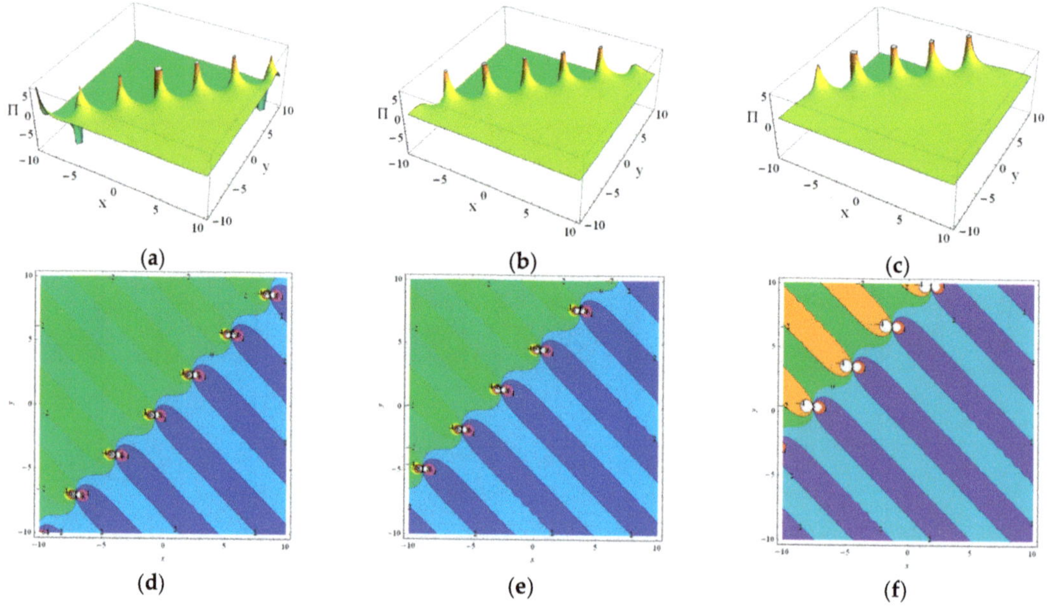

Figure 3. The graphical description of Equation (15) with $k_1 = 1, k_2 = 2, u_1 = 1, u_2 = 1, u_3 = 1$ at $z = 0$. (**a**,**d**) for $t = 0$, (**b**,**e**) for $t = 2$, (**c**,**f**) for $t = 4$.

By using the parameters as $\varepsilon_0 = 1, \varepsilon_1 = 1, n = 1, k = 1, \sigma = -1$, the dynamic characteristics of Equation (28) are revealed in Figure 4, where Figure 4a is the 3D plot, Figure 4b is the 2D contour and Figure 4c represents the 2D curve. In our observation, it is a dark wave. With the same parameters, Figure 5 illustrates the behaviors of Equations (3) and (10), which is a bright-dark wave.

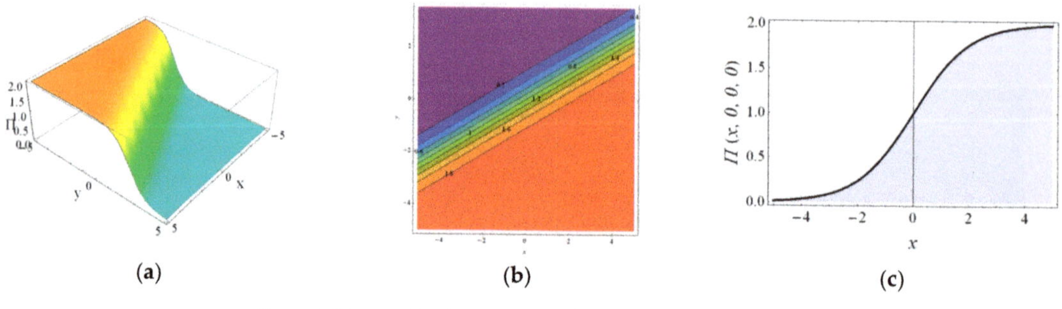

Figure 4. The graphical description of Equation (28) with the parameters as $\varepsilon_0 = 1, \varepsilon_1 = 1, n = 1, k = 1, \sigma = -1$. (**a**) for $z = 0, t = 0$, (**b**) for $z = 0, t = 0$, (**c**) for $y = 0, z = 0, t = 0$.

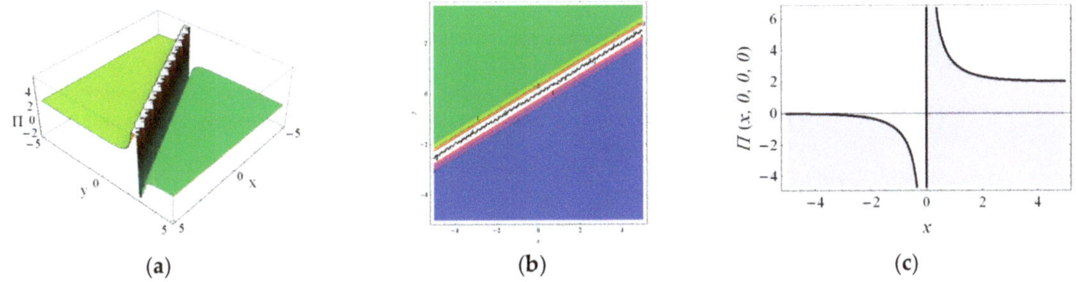

Figure 5. The graphical description of Equation (29) with the parameters as $\varepsilon_0 = 1$, $\varepsilon_1 = 1$, $n = 1$, $k = 1$, $\sigma = -1$. (**a**) for $z = 0$, $t = 0$, (**b**) for $z = 0$, $t = 0$, (**c**) for $y = 0$, $z = 0$, $t = 0$.

The performances of Equations (29) and (30) are presented in Figures 6 and 7, respectively with $\varepsilon_0 = 1$, $\varepsilon_1 = 1$, $n = 1$, $k = 1$, $\sigma = 1$. We find that the profiles are both singular periodic waves.

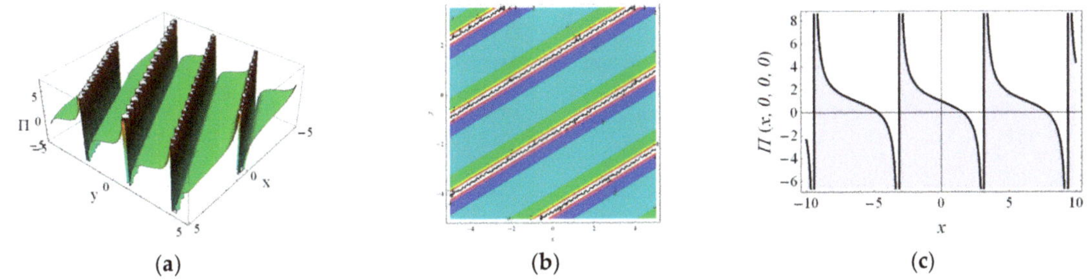

Figure 6. The graphical description of Equation (29) with the parameters as $\varepsilon_0 = 1$, $\varepsilon_1 = 1$, $n = 1$, $k = 1$, $\sigma = 1$. (**a**) for $z = 0$, $t = 0$, (**b**) for $z = 0$, $t = 0$, (**c**) for $y = 0$, $z = 0$, $t = 0$.

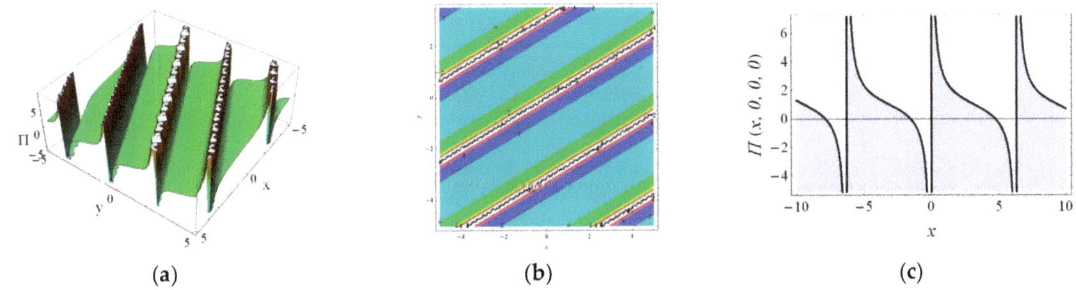

Figure 7. The graphical description of Equation (30) with the parameters as $\varepsilon_0 = 1$, $\varepsilon_1 = 1$, $n = 1$, $k = 1$, $\sigma = 1$. (**a**) for $z = 0$, $t = 0$, (**b**) for $z = 0$, $t = 0$, (**c**) for $y = 0$, $z = 0$, $t = 0$.

5. Conclusions and Future Recommendation

In this article, we obtained multi-wave complexiton solutions, multi-wave solutions and periodic lump solutions of the (3+1)-dimensional Jimbo-Miwa equation with the help of the Hirota bilinear method. Besides, we also construct its diverse travelling wave solutions like the dark, bright-dark and singular periodic wave solutions by applying the sub-equation method. The evolution phenomenon of these different solutions are described graphically. From these descriptions, the physical behavior and the interaction are presented. The obtained results in this work are all new and have not been reported elsewhere. Additionally, they show that the methods adopted are effective and direct, and can moreover be used to study the other PDEs arising in physics.

In recent years, the interest in fractal and fractional calculus [41–49] has intensified in different fields due to their strong ability to describe complex phenomena. Applying the fractal and fractional calculus to Equation (1) and obtaining the exact solutions will animate our future research.

Author Contributions: Conceptualization, K.-J.W.; methodology, K.-J.W.; writing—original draft preparation, B.-Q.Z.; supervision, K.-J.W.; writing—review and editing, P.X.; data curation, H.H. All authors have read and agreed to the published version of the manuscript.

Funding: This work was supported by Guangzhou Basic Research Program (Grant No. 202201011286), Scientific Research Startup Project of Guangdong Polytechnic Normal University (Grant No. 2021SD-KYA032).

Data Availability Statement: The data that support the findings of this study are available from the corresponding author upon reasonable request.

Conflicts of Interest: This research does not have any conflicts of interest.

Nomenclature

Multi-wave complexiton solutions	MWCS
Multi-wave solutions	MWS
Periodic lump solutions	PLS
Travelling wave solutions	TWS
The Jimbo-Miwa equation	JME
Travelling wave solutions	TWS

References

1. Sohail, M.; Nazir, U.; Bazighifan, O.; El-Nabulsi, R.A.; Selim, M.M.; Alrabaiah, H.; Thounthong, P. Significant involvement of double diffusion theories on viscoelastic fluid comprising variable thermophysical properties. *Micromachines* **2021**, *12*, 951. [CrossRef]
2. Nazir, U.; Saleem, S.; Al-Zubaidi, A.; Shahzadi, I.; Feroz, N. Thermal and mass species transportation in tri-hybridized Sisko martial with heat source over vertical heated cylinder. *Int. Commun. Heat Mass Transf.* **2022**, *134*, 106003. [CrossRef]
3. Wang, K.J.; Si, J. Dynamic properties of the attachment oscillator arising in the nanophysics. *Open Phys.* **2023**, *21*, 20220214. [CrossRef]
4. Lü, X.; Chen, S.-J. New general interaction solutions to the KPI equation via an optional decoupling condition approach. *Commun. Nonlinear Sci. Numer. Simul.* **2021**, *103*, 105939. [CrossRef]
5. Liu, J.-G.; Yang, X.-J.; Wang, J.-J. A new perspective to discuss Korteweg-de Vries-like equation. *Phys. Lett. A* **2022**, *451*, 128429. [CrossRef]
6. Seadawy, A.R.; Rizvi, S.T.; Mustafa, B.; Ali, K.; Althubiti, S. Chirped periodic waves for an cubic-quintic nonlinear Schrödinger equation with self steepening and higher order nonlinearities. *Chaos Solitons Fractals* **2022**, *156*, 111804. [CrossRef]
7. Ma, W.X. Lump solutions to the Kadomtsev-Petviashvili equation. *Phys. Lett. A* **2015**, *379*, 1975–1978. [CrossRef]
8. Liu, J.G.; Ye, Q. Stripe solitons and lump solutions for a generalized Kadomtsev-Petviashvili equation with variable coefficients in fluid mechanics. *Nonlinear Dyn.* **2019**, *96*, 23–29. [CrossRef]
9. Liu, J.G.; Eslami, M.; Rezazadeh, H.; Mirzazadeh, M. Rational solutions and lump solutions to a non-isospectral and generalized variable-coefficient Kadomtsev–Petviashvili equation. *Nonlinear Dyn.* **2019**, *95*, 1027–1033. [CrossRef]
10. Zhang, Z.; Li, B.; Chen, J.; Guo, Q. Construction of higher-order smooth positons and breather positons via Hirota's bilinear method. *Nonlinear Dyn.* **2021**, *105*, 2611–2618. [CrossRef]
11. Wang, K.J.; Liu, J.H. Diverse optical solitons to the nonlinear Schrödinger equation via two novel techniques. *Eur. Phys. J. Plus* **2023**, *138*, 74. [CrossRef]
12. Wang, K.J.; Si Jing Wang, G.D.; Shi, F. A new fractal modified Benjamin-Bona-Mahony equation: Its generalized variational principle and abundant exact solutions. *Fractals* **2023**, *31*, 2350047. [CrossRef]
13. Afzal, U.; Raza, N.; Murtaza, I.G. On soliton solutions of time fractional form of Sawada-Kotera equation. *Nonlinear Dyn.* **2019**, *95*, 391–405. [CrossRef]
14. Raza, N.; Javid, A. Optical dark and dark-singular soliton solutions of (1+2)-dimensional chiral nonlinear Schrodinger's equation. *Waves Random Complex Media* **2019**, *29*, 496–508. [CrossRef]

15. Wang, K.J.; Si, J. Diverse optical solitons to the complex Ginzburg-Landau equation with Kerr law nonlinearity in the nonlinear optical fiber. *Eur. Phys. J. Plus* **2023**, *138*, 187. [CrossRef]
16. Rezazadeh, H.; Inc, M.; Baleanu, D. New solitary wave solutions for variants of (3+1)-dimensional Wazwaz-Benjamin-Bona-Mahony equations. *Front. Phys.* **2020**, *8*, 332. [CrossRef]
17. Wang, K.J.; Liu, J.H. On abundant wave structures of the unsteady korteweg-de vries equation arising in shallow water. *J. Ocean. Eng. Sci.* 2022, *in press*. [CrossRef]
18. He, J.H.; Wu, X.H. Exp-function method for nonlinear wave equations. *Chaos Solitons Fractals* **2006**, *30*, 700–708. [CrossRef]
19. Mohyud-Din, S.T.; Khan, Y.; Faraz, N.; Yıldırım, A. Exp-function method for solitary and periodic solutions of Fitzhugh-Nagumo equation. *Int. J. Numer. Methods Heat Fluid Flow* **2012**, *22*, 335–341. [CrossRef]
20. Al-Askar, F.M.; Cesarano, C.; Mohammed, W.W. The Solitary Solutions for the Stochastic Jimbo-Miwa Equation Perturbed by White Noise. *Symmetry* **2023**, *15*, 1153. [CrossRef]
21. Alharbi, A.R.; Almatrafi, M.B.; Seadawy, A.R. Construction of the numerical and analytical wave solutions of the Joseph-Egri dynamical equation for the long waves in nonlinear dispersive systems. *Int. J. Mod. Phys. B* **2020**, *34*, 2050289. [CrossRef]
22. Wang, K.J. Diverse wave structures to the modified Benjamin-Bona-Mahony equation in the optical illusions field. *Mod. Phys. Lett. B* **2023**, *37*, 2350012. [CrossRef]
23. Seadawy, A.R.; Kumar, D.; Chakrabarty, A.K. Dispersive optical soliton solutions for the hyperbolic and cubic-quintic nonlinear Schrödinger equations via the extended sinh-Gordon equation expansion method. *Eur. Phys. J. Plus* **2018**, *133*, 182. [CrossRef]
24. Raza, N.; Arshed, S.; Sial, S. Optical solitons for coupled Fokas-Lenells equation in birefringence fibers. *Mod. Phys. Lett. B* **2019**, *33*, 1950317. [CrossRef]
25. Wang, K.-J.; Shi, F.; Wang, G.-D. Abundant soliton structures to the (2+1)-dimensional Heisenberg ferromagnetic spin chain dynamical model. *Adv. Math. Phys.* **2023**, *2023*, 4348758. [CrossRef]
26. Sağlam Özkan, Y.; Seadawy, A.R.; Yaşar, E. Multi-wave, breather and interaction solutions to (3+1) dimensional Vakhnenko-Parkes equation arising at propagation of high-frequency waves in a relaxing medium. *J. Taibah Univ. Sci.* **2021**, *15*, 666–678. [CrossRef]
27. Seadawy, A.R.; Bilal, M.; Younis, M.; Rizvi, S.; Althobaiti, S.; Makhlouf, M. Analytical mathematical approaches for the double-chain model of DNA by a novel computational technique. *Chaos Solitons Fractals* **2021**, *144*, 110669. [CrossRef]
28. Rizvi, S.T.; Seadawy, A.R.; Ali, I.; Bibi, I.; Younis, M. Chirp-free optical dromions for the presence of higher order spatio-temporal dispersions and absence of self-phase modulation in birefringent fibers. *Mod. Phys. Lett. B* **2020**, *34*, 2050399. [CrossRef]
29. Ali, K.K.; Nuruddeen, R.I.; Hadhoud, A.R. New exact solitary wave solutions for the extended (3+1)-dimensional Jimbo-Miwa equations. *Results Phys.* **2018**, *9*, 12–16. [CrossRef]
30. Yue, Y.; Huang, L.; Chen, Y. Localized waves and interaction solutions to an extended (3+1)-dimensional Jimbo-Miwa equation. *Appl. Math. Lett.* **2019**, *89*, 70–77. [CrossRef]
31. Duran, S. Exact solutions for time-fractional Ramani and Jimbo-Miwa equations by direct algebraic method. Advanced Science. *Eng. Med.* **2020**, *12*, 982–988.
32. Rashed, A.S.; Mabrouk, S.M.; Wazwaz, A.M. Forward scattering for non-linear wave propagation in (3+1)-dimensional Jimbo-Miwa equation using singular manifold and group transformation methods. *Waves Random Complex Media* **2022**, *32*, 663–675. [CrossRef]
33. Dai, Z. Abundant new exact solutions for the (3+1) -dimensional Jimbo-Miwa equation. *J. Math. Anal. Appl.* **2010**, *361*, 587–590.
34. Öziş, T.; Aslan, I. Exact and explicit solutions to the (3+1)-dimensional Jimbo-Miwa equation via the Exp-function method. *Phys. Lett. A* **2008**, *372*, 7011–7015. [CrossRef]
35. Kuo, C.K.; Ghanbari, B. Resonant multi-soliton solutions to new (3+1)-dimensional Jimbo-Miwa equations by applying the linear superposition principle. *Nonlinear Dyn.* **2019**, *96*, 459–464. [CrossRef]
36. Kolebaje, O.T.; Popoola, O.O. Exact solution of fractional STO and Jimbo-Miwa equations with the generalized Bernoulli equation method. *Afr. Rev. Phys.* **2014**, *9*, 26.
37. Liu, J.G.; Zhu, W.H.; Osman, M.S.; Ma, W.X. An explicit plethora of different classes of interactive lump solutions for an extension form of 3D-Jimbo-Miwa model. *Eur. Phys. J. Plus* **2020**, *135*, 412. [CrossRef]
38. Ma, W.X. N-soliton solution and the Hirota condition of a (2+1)-dimensional combined equation. *Math. Comput. Simul.* **2021**, *190*, 270–279. [CrossRef]
39. Akinyemi, L.; Şenol, M.; Iyiola, O.S. Exact solutions of the generalized multidimensional mathematical physics models via sub-equation method. *Math. Comput. Simul.* **2021**, *182*, 211–233. [CrossRef]
40. Bekir, A.; Aksoy, E.; Cevikel, A.C. Exact solutions of nonlinear time fractional partial differential equations by sub-equation method. *Math. Methods Appl. Sci.* **2015**, *38*, 2779–2784. [CrossRef]
41. Wang, K.-J.; Shi, F.; Si, J.; Liu, J.-H.; Wang, G.-D. Non-differentiable exact solutions of the local fractional Zakharov-Kuznetsov equation on the Cantor sets. *Fractals* **2023**, *31*, 2350028. [CrossRef]
42. İlhan, E.; Kıymaz İ, O. A generalization of truncated M-fractional derivative and applications to fractional differential equations. *Appl. Math. Nonlinear Sci.* **2020**, *5*, 171–188. [CrossRef]
43. Wang, K.L. Exact travelling wave solution for the fractal Riemann wave model arising in ocean science. *Fractals* **2022**, *30*, 2250143. [CrossRef]
44. Singh, J. Analysis of fractional blood alcohol model with composite fractional derivative. *Chaos Solitons Fractals* **2020**, *140*, 110127. [CrossRef]

45. He, J.H.; Ji, F.Y. Two-scale mathematics and fractional calculus for thermodynamics. *Therm. Sci.* **2019**, *23*, 2131–2133. [CrossRef]
46. Wang, K.-J.; Liu, J.-H.; Si, J.; Shi, F.; Wang, G.-D. N-soliton, breather, lump solutions and diverse travelling wave solutions of the fractional (2+1)-dimensional Boussinesq equation. *Fractals* **2023**, *31*, 2350023. [CrossRef]
47. Wang, K.J.; Shi, F. The pulse narrowing nonlinear transmission lines model within the local fractional calculus on the Cantor sets. *COMPEL Int. J. Comput. Math. Electr. Electron. Eng.* **2023**. [CrossRef]
48. He, C.H.; Liu, C.; He, J.H.; Gepreel, K.A. Low frequency property of a fractal vibration model for a concrete beam. *Fractals* **2021**, *29*, 2150117. [CrossRef]
49. Asjad, M.I.; Ullah, N.; Rehman, H.U.; Baleanu, D. Optical solitons for conformable space-time fractional nonlinear model. *J. Math. Comput. Sci.* **2022**, *27*, 28. [CrossRef]

Disclaimer/Publisher's Note: The statements, opinions and data contained in all publications are solely those of the individual author(s) and contributor(s) and not of MDPI and/or the editor(s). MDPI and/or the editor(s) disclaim responsibility for any injury to people or property resulting from any ideas, methods, instructions or products referred to in the content.

MDPI AG
Grosspeteranlage 5
4052 Basel
Switzerland
Tel.: +41 61 683 77 34
www.mdpi.com

Axioms Editorial Office
E-mail: axioms@mdpi.com
www.mdpi.com/journal/axioms

Disclaimer/Publisher's Note: The statements, opinions and data contained in all publications are solely those of the individual author(s) and contributor(s) and not of MDPI and/or the editor(s). MDPI and/or the editor(s) disclaim responsibility for any injury to people or property resulting from any ideas, methods, instructions or products referred to in the content.

www.ingramcontent.com/pod-product-compliance
Lightning Source LLC
LaVergne TN
LVHW070201100526
838202LV00015B/1976
* 9 7 8 3 7 2 5 8 1 6 4 8 4 *